STUDIES AND TEXTS

48

DATE DUE FOR RETURN

A

B

C

A. *Archbishop Walter Reynolds' great seal of episcopal office*: the archbishop in full pontificals with primatial cross, symbols of the four evangelists, and shields bearing the arms of England. From BL. Add. Charter 17353 (obverse). For discussion see below, p. 259 n. 83.

B. *Small counterseal of Archbishop Reynolds*: the martyrdom of St. Thomas Becket. From BL. Add. Charter 17353 (reverse). For discussion see below, p. 271 and n. 177.

C. *Small private round seal of Archbishop Simon Sudbury, 1376, of which the earliest description and evidence for use is found in the register of Archbishop Reynolds*: the Trinity and eighteen mitred bishops with the primate in top center. From PRO E327/479. For discussion see below, p. 266 n. 137.

A and B are reproduced by permission of the British Library Board, and C by permission of the Public Record Office in whose custody it remains.

THE CHURCH
AND THE ENGLISH CROWN
1305-1334

A Study based on the Register
of Archbishop Walter Reynolds

by

J. ROBERT WRIGHT

St. Mark's Professor of Ecclesiastical History
in the General Theological Seminary, New York City

PONTIFICAL INSTITUTE OF MEDIAEVAL STUDIES
TORONTO, 1980

ACKNOWLEDGMENT

This book has been published with the help of a grant from the Canadian Federation for the Humanities, using funds provided by the Social Sciences and Humanities Research Council of Canada.

CANADIAN CATALOGUING IN PUBLICATION DATA

Wright, John Robert, 1936-
    The Church and the English crown, 1305-1334

(Studies and texts — Pontifical Institute of Mediaeval Studies ; 48 ISSN 0082-5328)

Bibliography: p.
Includes index.
ISBN 0-88844-048-0

1. Church and state in England — History.   2. Papacy — History — 1309-1378.   3. Reynolds, Walter, Abp. of Canterbury, d. 1327.   Register.   I. Title.   II. Series: Pontifical Institute of Mediaeval Studies.   Studies and texts — Pontifical Institute of Mediaeval Studies ; 48.

BR750.W75   274.2   C79-094271-2

PONTIFICAL INSTITUTE OF MEDIAEVAL STUDIES
59 Queen's Park Crescent East
Toronto, Ontario, Canada M5S 2C4

PRINTED BY UNIVERSA, WETTEREN, BELGIUM

to my Mother

Contents

Preface

Anglo-papal and church-state relations in the early fourteenth century are subjects that have not hitherto been examined collectively in the scope undertaken here. This was the formative period of the Avignon papacy and also a time when the relations of England with France were not yet clouded by the full impact of the Hundred Years War. In England, this era coincided with the primacy at Canterbury of Walter Reynolds, a man in whom the interest of historians thus far has been relatively negative and minor but for whom a certain shift of perspective is now suggested. In addition to Reynolds, the principal figures here are the first two popes of Avignon, Clement v and John xxii, whose pontificates span the years 1305-1334, and the English king, Edward ii (1307-1327). The first part of this book studies 'papal provisions', the single issue of Anglo-papal relations that looms largest in the contemporary sources and over which the papacy exercised the greatest control at this time. The second part is a consideration of Anglo-papal diplomacy primarily from the viewpoint of the crown's essays to safeguard the royal prerogative. The objective of the third part is to assess the domestic issues of conflict and cooperation between church and state and the part in them that Walter Reynolds played as archbishop of Canterbury in the years 1314-1327. In all three parts, the focus of this book is more upon the church, in its relations with the state, than vice versa.

Nearly every attempt at serious scholarship is descended from a long line of progenitors, and is able to make some contribution to knowledge only by exploring, initially at least, paths charted by previous studies, and it will be my pleasant obligation to acknowledge this inheritance frequently in the pages that follow. I have in no way tried to duplicate the definitive work of Professor Lunt on the financial relations between England and the papacy at this time, although references are made to it and a few supplementary observations are offered. Conclusions, however, from the important relevant monographs by Miss Kathleen Edwards on the episcopate, Miss Ann Deeley on provisions, W. E. L. Smith on episcopal appointments, and from many other works are assessed and modified.

The principal source on which this study is based is the register of Archbishop Walter Reynolds, the major unpublished ecclesiastical source of the fourteenth century in England, at least for the southern province. Whatever his personal qualities (and they seldom appear in the records of ecclesiastical administration), Reynolds as primate of all England could not avoid, even if he had wished to do so, a position as titular head of the church in England and this at a time when the secular government itself was subject to frequent change. Considerable work has been done by others on the registers and careers of Reynolds' two immediate predecessors Pecham and Winchelsey, and the publication of *Councils and Synods* II (eds. F. M. Powicke and C. R. Cheney) has provided a superb collection of printed documents for the thirteenth century ending in the year of Reynolds' translation to Canterbury. The registers of his two immediate successors Mepham and Stratford have disappeared, and the registers of most later fourteenth-century archbishops have been examined exhaustively by scholars. Dr. J. R. L. Highfield has used the latter registers in his Oxford doctoral thesis for a study of Anglo-papal and church-state relations from the death of Archbishop Stratford to the outbreak of the Great Schism, thus covering the last thirty years of the Avignon period and implicitly raising questions of comparison with the earlier part of the century. The first thirty years, however, are a period comparatively unexplored and one for which Reynolds' register, still at Lambeth Palace, is of central importance. Its detailed memoranda about the use of apostolic provisory faculties and about the results of the bull *Execrabilis* are especially significant, and its quire of royal writs is unusually fine. The material in its 314 folios permits Reynolds' attitudes and administrative action to be appraised with respect to most of the major themes under consideration.

Further research in many other places, however, has been stimulated and indeed necessitated by the themes raised in Reynolds' register. Another important source for this study is the register of Andreas Sapiti, principal contemporary proctor for the English crown at the Roman court, which I have consulted both in the transcript by W. H. Bliss and (by microfilm) in its Vatican original. Numerous other manuscripts have also been used. Among printed sources, the register of John xxii, already filling more than sixteen volumes in calendar form, is certainly one of the largest and perhaps the most outstanding papal register of the whole medieval series. It and the register of Clement v have been examined in their Latin and English calendars, and a number of comparisons have been made with the original papal registers in the Vatican Archives. Contemporary episcopal registers (including those in manuscript at Lincoln and York) as well as many other published documents have also been investigated.

*
* *

Work on this study has been spread over several years and many places, and it is a pleasure to acknowledge my gratitude to the many individuals and institutions who have helped it along the way. My thanks are due, first of all, to His Grace the Archbishop of Canterbury for access and permission to quote from the register of his predecessor Walter Reynolds, and for the hospitality not only of his archiepiscopal library and archives but also of Lambeth Palace itself, where I was privileged to live one summer. Thanks are especially due to the Lambeth Librarian, Mr. E. G. W. Bill, who did so much to facilitate my work in Reynolds' register and other manuscripts.

The officers and staffs of several other libraries and archival depositories have greatly assisted my investigations, in particular the Public Record Office and the British Library in London, the Dean and Chapter Library of Canterbury Cathedral, the Bodleian Library at Oxford, the Cambridge University Library, the Borthwick Institute at York, the Society of Antiquaries in London, the Lincolnshire Archives Office, the Vatican Library, and the Vatican Archives. To the authorities of these institutions and of the others listed in my Bibliography of Manuscript Sources, I wish to acknowledge my thanks for access and permission to include citations and quotations from documents in their custody. The transcripts and translations of Crown copyright records in the Public Record Office appear by permission of the Controller of H.M. Stationery Office. I also wish to thank the authors of those university theses to which I have had access and which are listed under Secondary Works in the Bibliography, as well as the editors of *Studies in Church History* for leave to use portions of my previously published work.

This book has gradually developed, by revision and expansion, out of a thesis originally accepted for the degree of D.Phil. by the University of Oxford. Portions of the work in manuscript have been read at one time or another by the late W. A. Pantin and by Professors C. R. Cheney, Giles Constable, Colin Morris, M. M. Sheehan, Bertie Wilkinson, and Norman Zacour, whose perceptive criticisms have saved it from many errors. To them, to Professors Rosalind Hill and E. B. Graves, and to the numerous scholars whose help is acknowledged in footnotes, I am indebted for generous advice on many particular matters.

Appreciation for encouragement and assistance of a more remote but no less tangible sort is also due: to the late Dr. James M. Grimes, who led me to love the study of history, to Professor G. P. Cuttino, who first introduced me to the ways of medievalists, and to the Revd. Canon Powel Mills Dawley, successively at the General Theological Seminary my professor, then my patron, and now my predecessor, for stimulation and enthusiasm in the study of church history. Without the generosity of a Fulbright Scholarship from the United States government and of a fellowship from the Episcopal Church Foundation, my original work on this study would not have been financially possible. Special thanks are also due to the Trustees of the General Theological Seminary, who granted me an extended sabbatical leave so that work on this book might finally be completed. This period was spent as a research associate of the Pontifical Institute of Mediaeval Studies in Toronto, and I gladly record my gratitude to its faculty and staff for encouragement and for the freedom of its convenient library and extensive microfilm collection, as well as to the Basilian fathers of St. Michael's College for their friendly hospitality.

There remain two others whose assistance has been invaluable, upon whose time I have often prevailed, whose generosity I can never repay, and to whose examples of scholarly dedication I stand much in debt. Dr. J. R. L. Highfield of Merton College, Oxford, as the supervisor of my thesis, guided my work at every stage for four years, gave unselfishly of his knowledge to my often elementary questions, and by patient and constructive criticism gradually led me to resolve a mass of data into a coherent study. Professor Leonard E. Boyle, O.P., gave my entire manu-script in its later stages the benefit of his broad erudition and mature judgment, and without his constant encouragement I would never have brought this work in its present form to completion and publication. Whatever merits this book may have derive largely from their guidance, although the errors which remain are entirely my own.

*
**

A preface seldom indicates what the reader may expect to find, but in view of the nature of this book I have thought it may be helpful to add the following preview.

This work opens with a reconsideration of the often-discussed topic of papal provisions. The first few pages, the least original part of the entire book, have been thought necessary in order to lay the ground for that which follows. After an introductory chapter summarizing the canon law and theory of provisions, tabulations of provisions for the period here under review are compiled from the evidence surviving in the calendared papal registers. Graces to poor clerks and university graduates are then discussed. Next, the differences between canon law and the practice of the period are measured. It is shown in these same pages that the percentage of direct provisions not entered in the papal registers at this time was very small, and that the success of provisors in obtaining their provided benefices varied from about fifty to seventy-five percent. The great increase in raw numbers of provisions under John XXII was accompanied by a decrease in their effectiveness. There was considerable manipulation and extension of papal power by provisory faculties at this time, a fact that points to the existence of a secondary but rather extensive network of 'provisions' only one step removed from the pope himself. That these faculties could take real effect is proved by evidence from Reynolds' register, which shows that he made thirty provisions of canonries and prebends under such a faculty largely to clerks in his own service. There was a fair balance, therefore, between the diminution of his ordinary rights of collation under papal provisions and the increase of powers that he enjoyed from the same system. Both Reynolds and the crown knew well how to utilize the provisions system for their own interests.

As regards the papal interest in provisions, revised interpretations of the papal constitutions *Ex debito* and *Execrabilis* are presented. Recent work has suggested that the former bull may be dated after 1325, or at least not in 1316 as commonly supposed, and this is supported by indications that some of its principles were already in practice under Clement V, that the bulk of John XXII's English provisions were not made with particular reference to its principles, and that in itself it was not responsible for any significant increase of papal provisions in John's first pontifical year or later. In the scramble for patronage appointments released by Pope John's constitution *Execrabilis* against pluralities, it is shown that the real gain was made by the English diocesan bishops – acting together as a group, to the exclusion of the crown, some times with consent of the apostolic see and other times in contravention of it. They in effect determined the way in which the bull was received in England. In the long run, moreover, *Execrabilis* did not really create any permanent or significant new source of papal provisions, although it did place some check on pluralism.

The second part of this book shows that the English crown at this time, in spite of domestic crises and the personal weakness of Edward II, seems to have had a very definite policy in papal relations, consistent in many of its particulars, that met with a degree of success in many areas: influence upon provisions, influence in the audience of causes of the apostolic palace, proctorial representation, frequent diplomatic embassies, cardinals' pensions and benefices, litigation in the Roman court, royal control of episcopal temporalities, and nonresidence for king's clerks. The role of Andreas Sapiti in this business is set forth. Tabulations indicate that the holding by cardinals of English benefices – at least twenty-nine cardinals held some 103 of them at this time – was much greater in proportion to the total number of papal provisions during the first thirty years of the

Avignon period than in the last thirty. This was largely due to a policy of John xxii to provide English benefices – often parish churches vacated at the apostolic see by *Execrabilis* or by consecrations or by deaths of litigants – to the cardinals, and this policy was encouraged by the crown's own policy to exempt cardinals from payment of the tenth.

A brief study is next offered of the origins, development, and significance of the 'privilege of England' as the theoretical basis upon which the crown by this time had come to restrict litigation from going to the Roman curia. Granted by the pope in 1231 by virtue of his plentitude of power and enjoying some considerable significance throughout the rest of the thirteenth century, this privilege had, by the period under review, become one more element merged into the great mass of custom or tradition known as the 'royal prerogative'. The strongest resistance that the English crown offered to papal claims in this period, however, may well have been its enforcement of oaths by episcopal provisors to the effect that they would receive their temporalities at the king's pleasure and not by the pope's grant. By these oaths the crown's theoretical position was secure, no matter how it chose to negotiate with the pope about which man should have which see. Nonresidence for king's clerks in their ecclesiastical benefices was also a policy the crown had established firmly by the period under review, and it is interesting to find that it had done this largely by claiming possession of another papal privilege that had an evolution in usage quite similar to that of the privilege of England. A certain continuity of papal policy in this period is also indicated by the striking parallels between complaints about the English situation made by Clement v in 1309 and by John xxii in 1317; this point is established by the transcription of a bull of Pope John in Appendix 7.

With a few exceptions, these studies in royal policy confirm the trend of interpretation set by Professor Lunt's studies in Anglo-papal finances – that the crown must be seen in a somewhat stronger position vis-à-vis the papacy at this time, and that it achieved no small measure of success in safeguarding its prerogative. Later in the century, with the Hundred Years War under way and with stronger elements of the commons in parliament, the crown may have been more inclined to allow its policy to be directed by parliamentary pressures. But in the present period, even at the Carlisle and Stamford parliaments, there is a definite impression that these pressures were not so strong nor the protests nearly so effective. For the pontificates of Clement v and John xxii, therefore, it is not possible to say, as Dr. Highfield has done for the years 1342-1378, that each peak period of papal provisions was followed by a violent reaction in England. It is probable that the pontificate of John xxii marked not only the zenith of cardinals' provisions in the entire Avignon period but also the minimum of resentment against them by king or parliament.

The final part of this book is directed to English internal matters, and consideration is given to Reynolds' administration of several ecclesiastical institutions in which the crown also exercised or claimed jurisdiction. The quire of royal writs in his register permits a reconstruction of the borderline between the church and state courts on the basis of writs of prohibition and consultation. As in the late thirteenth century, the boundaries of the state seem to be advancing at the expense of the church's territory. The complex question of clerical grievances is discussed, and an estimate made of the importance of the *Articuli cleri* of 1316. A comparison with papal grievance-letters suggests that the English concerns were, perhaps understandably, somewhat insular. There are indications that the *Articuli* did achieve a certain measure of success during Reynolds' archiepiscopate, one of these indications being the increased availability of writs of consultation. In ecclesiastical discipline, the period under review saw a growth of secular assistance in the handling of excommunicates, criminous clerks, and rebellious monks, but this assistance also meant a greater dependence of the church upon the power of the state. The English church and the papacy, in return, were often willing to use excommunication in support of the crown against its criminal and political enemies. Other topics selected for brief treatment include the question of the transfer of Templars' properties to the Hospitallers, royal requests for favours from religious houses, the affection of both Edward II and Reynolds for the Dominicans, and the confiscation of alien priories. On the first of these, it is suggested that Reynolds' decision to follow the papal mandate about the Templars after the crisis in the October parliament of 1320 may have turned the tide in the Hospitallers' favour.

An evaluation of the man whom Edward II chose for primate of all England concludes the last chapter of the third part of this book. On many questions, of course, the evidence is simply insufficient for generalization, and the available materials do not lend themselves to a biographical approach. Nor is it the purpose of this book to do equal justice to all aspects of Reynolds' career. Yet there are important points in Reynolds' archiepiscopate at which the impersonal office and the individual person do merge, and a study of these leads me to draw him with the following contours: practical, modest, somewhat withdrawn, certainly literate but not a scholar, a moderate patron of academic learning, of at least average competence as an administrator, helpful friend of the monks of Canterbury, a leader of the prelates mediating between the king and the magnates, a moderate leader also of the hierarchy in several ways but definitely unpopular with the lower clergy and a number of the chroniclers, attempting to steer a middle course between king and pope, clearly breaking with the tradition of Winchelsey, scrupulously deliberative even to the point of indecision at times.

Indecision is perhaps the strongest charge we can lay to Reynolds, but indecision – or, rather, exceedingly cautious deliberation – may not be a vice in a primate whose king is foolish and whose pope is clever. The reassessment offered here does not demand a complete reversal of traditional views, but it does enter a plea for considerable modification of conventional notions, more along the lines of the chronicler Trokelowe, who praised Reynolds as a man who could moderate the tribulations of the English church and realm. Reynolds was more effective in doing this than has been previously acknowledged, and an edition of his archiepiscopal register should provide even further confirmation of this estimate.

Feast of St. Thomas Becket,   JRW
29 December 1976

Select List of Abbreviations

abp.	= archbishop.
AHP	= *Archivum Historiae Pontificiae.*
AHR	= *American Historical Review.*
A.S.	= apostolic see.
BEFAR	= *Bibliothèque des Écoles françaises d'Athènes et de Rome.*
BIHR	= *Bulletin of the Institute of Historical Research.*
BJRL	= *Bulletin of the John Rylands Library.*
BL	= British Library, London.
biog.	= biography.
Bod.	= Bodleian Library, Oxford.
bp.	= bishop.
Cant. Cath.	= Canterbury Cathedral Library.
card.	= cardinal.
CCR	= *Calendar of the Close Rolls.*
CCW	= *Calendar of Chancery Warrants.* Vol. i, Privy Seals 1244-1326.
CFR	= *Calendar of the Fine Rolls.*
Chron.	= Chronica, Chronicle, Chronicon.
CIC	= *Corpus Iuris Canonici,* ed. E. A. Friedberg. 2 vols., Leipzig, 1879-81. Citations are from this edition.
Close Rolls	= *Close Rolls of the Reign of Henry III.*
CMH	= *Cambridge Medieval History.*
cons.	= consecration.
CPL	= *Calendar of Entries in the Papal Registers Relating to Great Britain and Ireland: Papal Letters. 1198-1484.*
CPR	= *Calendar of the Patent Rolls.*
CQR	= *The Church Quarterly Review.*
CUL	= Cambridge University Library.
CYS	= Canterbury and York Society.
D.Cn.L.	= Doctor of Canon Law.
D.C.L.	= Doctor of Civil Law.
D.Cn.&C.L.	= Doctor of Canon and Civil Law.
D.M.	= Doctor of Medicine.
D.Th.	= Doctor of Divinity or Theology.
dioc.	= diocese.
DNB	= *Dictionary of National Biography.*
Edw.	= King Edward.

EHR	= *English Historical Review.*
HMC	= Historical Manuscripts Commission.
HMSO	= Her (His) Majesty's Stationery Office.
John XXII, Secret Letters	= *Lettres secrètes et curiales du pape Jean XXII, 1316-1334, relatives à la France,* eds. A. Coulon and S. Clémencet.
JEH	= *Journal of Ecclesiastical History.*
Lambeth	= Lambeth Palace Library, London.
LAO	= Lincolnshire Archives Office.
Le Neve	= *Fasti Ecclesiae Anglicanae,* new editions, London, 1962 *seq.* Each volume is cited by its modern title or an abbreviation thereof. The '1066-1300' series is cited by those dates following 'Le Neve'. Citations of any volume without dates always refer to the '1300-1541' series.
M.	= magister, master.
m.	= membrane.
O.Cist.	= Cistercian Order.
OFM	= Order of Friars Minor (Franciscans or Grey Friars).
OP	= Order of Friars Preachers (Dominicans or Black Friars).
O.Praem.	= Premonstratensians.
OSA	= Order of St. Augustine (Austin Friars).
OSB	= Order of St. Benedict.
OU	= Oxford University.
P&C	= *Councils and Synods with Other Documents Relating to the English Church,* vol. ii, 1205-1313, eds. F. M. Powicke and C. R. Cheney, 2 parts. 'P&C ii' indicates part ii of vol. ii.
PRO	= Public Record Office, London.
prov.	= provision, provided.
Rec. Com.	= Record Commission.
Reg. John XXII	= *Jean XXII: Lettres communes analysées d'après les registres dits d'Avignon et du Vatican,* ed. G. Mollat.
Reg.	= Register, Regesta, Registrum, etc.
Reg. London	= *Registrum Radulphi Baldock, Gilberti Segrave, Ricardi Newport, et Stephani Gravesend, Episcoporum Londoniensium,* A.D. *1304-1338,* ed. R. C. Fowler.
RR	= Register of Walter Reynolds, archbishop of Canterbury. Lambeth Palace Library, manuscript.
RS	= Rolls Series, i.e. *Rerum Britannicarum medii aevi scriptores, or, Chronicles and Memorials of Great Britain and Ireland during the Middle Ages,* published under the direction of the Master of the Rolls, 1858-1911.
RWR	= *The Register of Walter Reynolds, Bishop of Worcester, 1308-1313,* ed. R. A. Wilson.

Rymer = *Foedera, Conventiones, Litterae....* London, Rec. Com., 1816-69. All citations are from this edition unless otherwise noted. Method: Rymer II:i, 348 = Rymer, vol. ii, part i, page 348.

sede vac. = *sede vacante.*

TRHS = *Transactions of the Royal Historical Society.*

VCH = *The Victoria History of the Counties of England.*

WAM = Westminster Abbey Muniments.

Notes on Style

The rendering of English proper names has followed the principles of Dr. Emden's *Biographical Registers*, with some modifications. The names of cardinals and most other non-Englishmen have been rendered in vernacular forms unless other usage seems to dictate. The names of cardinals' titular churches have been retained in Latin.

The dioceses of Bath and Wells and of Coventry and Lichfield have been designated by their double names in order to facilitate reference to such works as the revised Le Neve's *Fasti* and Powicke and Fryde's *Handbook of British Chronology*, although in contemporary sources single names were employed.

Double indication of year dates is given for the period between 1 January and 24 March, the first date being *secundum consuetudinem ecclesiae Anglicanae* as it appears in contemporary manuscripts and the second being the historical year beginning January 1 as it is now commonly reckoned. (For this, see Cheney, *Handbook of Dates*, 4-5.)

In quotations from manuscripts generally 'e' has been preferred to 'ae' and 'c' preferred to 't' before 'i' when followed by another vowel. Capitalization and punctuation have been modernized. Latin quotations from manuscripts have been standardized, but those from printed sources have not been changed. Occasionally this has resulted in slight incongruities when quotations from manuscript and printed sources are juxtaposed, but on the whole I have felt that the interests of scholarship are better served by leaving the printed quotations as they were rather than altering them to fit my own principles of transcription.

In order to lighten the apparatus of the footnotes, full titles and particulars of all works cited are given in the Bibliography and not in the footnotes. Secondary works are generally designated in the footnotes by short titles only. Printed calendars or editions of papal and episcopal registers are generally indicated by the word 'Reg.' followed by a modern name of the pope or bishop and may be further identified by reference to the section of Printed Sources in the Bibliography.

Part I

Papal Provisions

The relations between the papacy and the English crown during the first thirty years of the Avignon period were on the whole fairly smooth and harmonious. Clement v was, as a Gascon, the subject of the English crown; and John XXII maintained a paternal interest in Edward II at the same time that he was utilizing his legal abilities to strengthen the administrative efficiency of the Roman curia. Politically, it may be thought, the papal power at this time was at a low ebb; but administratively and juridically this was in fact the great age of ecclesiastical centralization, characterized by widespread activity, careful planning, and intelligent organization.

Finances and provisions were probably the two most significant aspects of this centralization. The former has already been so well narrated by Professor Lunt in his numerous works as to necessitate no further detailed study here. His most striking conclusion for this period is the fact that Edward II managed to retain for his own uses some ninety-two percent of the tenths collected from English clergy under papal authority even though the pope was blamed for imposing the taxes.[1] The controversial question of papal provisions in England, on the other hand, has not been sufficiently investigated for the early years of the Avignon period even though it was probably the most far-reaching aspect of the papal centralization of church government – centralization as applied to ecclesiastical appointments and related litigation. Although one cannot assess the significance of documents by their sheer numbers, it is the issue of provisions that looms largest in the surviving papal registers.

The present study of relations between the church and the English crown,[2] therefore, begins with an investigation of provisions in England under Clement v and John XXII, and the question must first be described in

[1] Lunt, 'Clerical tenths levied in England by papal authority during the reign of Edward II', 157-82.

[2] From time to time in the present study I shall employ the terms 'church' and 'state' to refer to these two powers. I am aware of the objections that some have raised to the use of these terms with medieval reference, but I tend to agree with the refutation of such objections set forth in Cheney, *Hubert Walter*, 10. On the applicability of the term 'state' to medieval England, see also Ehler, 'On applying the modern term "state" to the Middle Ages', 492-501.

the context of the canon law. Canonical legislation itself was one aspect of papal centralization, and a summary of the relevant canon law, even at the risk of repeating some of what other writers have noted, is necessary here for a proper explanation of the thousands of provisions that were issued under its authority and of the way in which these provisions were handled in England in the early fourteenth century. In the summary that follows, moreover, an attempt will be made to elucidate the canons in the light of the early fourteenth-century practice.

1

Canon Law and Theory of Provisions

In his bull of 1 October 1313 providing Walter Reynolds to the see of
Canterbury, Clement v chose words that explained well the power he was
using. He said that, because the care of all the churches was incumbent
upon him and because he did not wish the church of Canterbury to
'remain exposed to the detriments of dangerous vacancy', he therefore
desired 'to provide a suitable person by the providence of the apostolic
see'.[1] This was the basis upon which the papacy for some 150 years
previous had been developing its theoretical powers of provision, or
appointment, to ecclesiastical benefices,[2] and this basis of power was
already well established in the church's canon law when the papal see
moved to Avignon.

The succession of bulls by which the papacy developed and
consolidated its powers of provision has been discussed by numerous
writers,[3] but it seems helpful now to tabulate them in chronological order
before reviewing them here:

---

[1] 'Personam utilem per apostolice sedis providenciam providere' (RR f. 2v; Cant. Cath.
MS Reg. Q, ff. 90-90v). The verb 'providere' was not a precise term in medieval usage and
was not limited to actions of the papacy. The Canterbury monks, for example, used the
same verb to describe their own preparations for the election of Thomas Cobham in 1313:
'ecclesie nostre supradicte vacanti pastore idoneo providere' (Cant. Cath. MS Reg. Q, ff. 75-
75v); and Edward II in selecting a successor for the same Canterbury vacancy was told by
Clement v to 'provide' with care: 'caute provideas' (Richardson, EHR lvi (1941), 102; cf.
below, p. 60 n. 33; also p. 224). In modern writers the direct object of the verb 'to provide'
is sometimes the church in question and sometimes the person in question, and in this
book both usages have been employed.

[2] Barraclough, *Papal Provisions*, 5, 154, 156.

[3] Barraclough, *Papal Provisions*; Highfield, 'The Relations between the Church and
the English Crown 1349-1378' i, 13-16; Hinschius, *System des katholischen Kirchenrechts*
iii, 113-64; Lunt, *Papal Revenues* ii, 217-33; Lux, *Constitutionum Apostolicorum*, 11-46;
Mollat, *La Collation*, 24-40; Reg. Chichele, vol. i, p. lxxxix; Powicke, *Henry III and the
Lord Edward* i, 259-89; Cheney, *From Becket to Langton*, 75-82; Caillet, *La papauté
d'Avignon et l'église de France*, 23, 25, 189-90.

PAPAL PROVISORY LEGISLATION

1265	Clement IV	*Licet ecclesiarum*
1274	Gregory X	*Statutum*
1294-1303	Boniface VIII	*Praesenti declaramus*
1295	Boniface VIII	*Piae sollicitudinis*
1298	Boniface VIII	*Si apostolica*
1305	Clement V	*Etsi in temporalium*
1307	Clement V	*Ex supernae providentia*
1316, *or* 1320-1321, *or* post-1325	John XXII	*Ex debito*
1317	John XXII	*Execrabilis*
1335	Benedict XII	*Ad regimen*

By *Licet ecclesiarum*[4] of 1265, Clement IV had reserved the right to provide to all benefices falling vacant 'apud sedem apostolicam', and under Clement V, 1305-1314, the papacy drew upon this power to provide at least nine English benefices that fell vacant by the deaths of their incumbents at the apostolic see.[5] But *Licet ecclesiarum* was not only the first general reservation of one whole class of benefices as distinct from special reservations of individual benefices;[6] its preamble also set forth for the first time in canon law the classical theory that the Roman pontiff has the right to full disposal (*plenaria dispositio*) by provision or reservation of all churches, parsonages,[7] dignities, and other ecclesiastical benefices.

It was this preamble to *Licet ecclesiarum* that furnished the theoretical background for all subsequent papal legislation on provisions, and this preamble was no doubt the rationale implicit in Clement V's translation of

[4] 27 Aug. 1265. CIC, Sext., lib. III, tit. iv, cap. 2 (Friedberg, vol. ii, col. 1021); transl. Lunt, *Papal Revenues* ii, 220; cf. Highfield, 'The Relations between the Church and the English Crown 1349-1378' i, 13; Lux, *Constitutionum Apostolicorum*, 11-12; Mollat, *La Collation*, 24.

[5] Reg. Clem. v, nos. 2562, 2830, 4424, 4871, 5464, 6412, 7212, 7228, 7455.

[6] Churchill, *Canterbury Administration*, vol. i, p. 254 n. 3. Barraclough regards *Licet ecclesiarum* as expressing in law what had already become established in practice without direct papal intervention during the preceding century, and he suggests that it caused no evident increase in the number of provisions immediately after its issue. Its real historical significance, he quite rightly suggests, was in relation to the future (*Papal Provisions*, 127, 155-6, 164).

[7] This word is 'personatuum'. Lunt, *Papal Revenues* ii, 220, translates it as 'benefices giving stalls in churches'. Deeley, EHR xliii (1928), p. 503 n. 2, says that the word means 'the chief offices in cathedral and collegiate churches'. Schroeder, *Disciplinary Decrees*, 305, defines it as 'an ecclesiastical dignity without jurisdiction', as contrasted with 'dignitas' which did imply jurisdictional administration.

Reynolds. But for the time being the next advance in canon law of the papal claim – *Praesenti declaramus*[8] of Boniface viii – was merely a cautious widening of the interpretation of vacancies 'apud sedem apostolicam' to include the benefices of papal legates and nuncios and anyone travelling to or from the Roman curia who happened to die within a radius of a journey of two legal days from the place where it was officially residing at the time. This bull also reserved the benefices of curial officials[9] who died either within or without the limit of two days. Clement v used the terms of *Praesenti declaramus* to make provisions to some nine English benefices vacated by papal chaplains or litigants or others who died at or near the Roman curia.[10]

There were also two limitations upon the papal provisory power written into the canon law by the time of Clement v. In *Statutum*[11] of 1274 Gregory x at the second council of Lyons, perhaps influenced by the strong English complaints against *Licet ecclesiarum* there,[12] had decreed that any benefice vacant 'apud sedem apostolicam' and therefore reserved could be collated by the normal patron if the pope failed to provide after a vacancy of one month. In 1295 the essential terms of *Licet ecclesiarum* and *Statutum* were confirmed by Boniface viii in *Piae sollicitudinis*,[13] which specifically reserved to the pope the provision of all benefices falling vacant 'apud sedem apostolicam' within one month from its date of issue or thereafter. The second limitation came in *Si apostolica*[14] of 1298, whereby Boniface viii decreed that in the case of a parish church having cure of souls and falling vacant 'apud sedem apostolicam' under the terms of *Licet ecclesiarum* or *Praesenti declaramus*, if the vacancy was not filled

[8] 1294-1303. cic, Sext., lib. III, tit. iv, cap. 34 (Friedberg, vol. ii, col. 1031); transl. Lunt, *Papal Revenues* ii, 220-1; cf. Boase, *Boniface viii*, 102; Highfield, 'The Relations between the Church and the English Crown' i, 15; Hinschius, *System des katholischen Kirchenrechts* iii, 125; Lux, *Constitutionum Apostolicorum*, 13; Mollat, *La Collation*, 25; Reg. Chichele, vol. i, p. lxxxix.

[9] The word is 'curialis'. Mollat, *La Collation*, 25, says it means anyone attached to the service of pope, cardinals, or papal court or anyone else who happens to be residing there. Guillemain (*La Cour pontificale*, 2, 39) and Lunt (*Financial Relations* ii, 321) have similar definitions.

[10] Reg. Clem. v, nos. 1407, 1492 (cf. Emden, *Oxford* i, 672), 2331, 3962, 7229, 7382, 7454, 8703, 9841.

[11] 1 Nov. 1274, cic, Sext., lib. III, tit. iv, cap. 3 (Friedberg, vol. ii, col. 1021); text and transl. Schroeder, *Disciplinary Decreees*, 348-9; cf. Highfield, 'The Relations' i, 14; Lux, *Constitutionum Apostolicorum*, 12; Mollat, *La Collation*, 24.

[12] p&c ii, 811-14, nos. 4, 15, 18.

[13] 5 May 1295. cic, Extravag. comm., lib. III, tit. ii, cap. 1 (Friedberg, vol. ii, col. 1257); cf. Lux, *Constitutionum Apostolicorum*, 13; Mollat, *La Collation*, 25.

[14] cic, Sext., lib. III, tit. iv, cap. 35 (Friedberg, vol. ii, col. 1031); cf. Boase, *Boniface viii*, 102; Highfield, 'The Relations' i, 14; Lux, *Constitutionum Apostolicorum*, 14.

before the pope's death or if the vacancy should occur during the time when the apostolic see itself was vacant, then the church could be collated immediately by the ordinary patron in spite of the papal reservation.

Such was the state of the canon law at the time of the accession of Clement v: on the one hand, *Licet ecclesiarum* had been extended to *Praesenti declaramus* probably as a result of pressure to secure and expand the income of benefices for the papal administrative staff; and on the other hand there had been some attempt to limit abuses, such as lengthy vacancies particularly in parish churches, by the terms of *Statutum* and *Si apostolica*. The plenary powers implied in the preamble to *Licet ecclesiarum* were always present, and there is some evidence to suggest that Boniface viii had made use of these powers in his reservation of French sees early in the fourteenth century.[15] His reservations were quashed, however, in the general revocation of expectative grants during the nine month pontificate of Benedict xi.[16]

The main addition of Clement v to the canons on provisions was *Etsi in temporalium*[17] of 1305, in which he defined the types of benefices vacated 'apud sedem apostolicam' and coming under papal reservation to include 'generally patriarchates, archbishoprics, bishoprics, monasteries, priories, parsonages, dignities, offices, canonries, prebends, churches with cure or without cure, and any other ecclesiastical benefices'. Although in *Licet ecclesiarum* the word 'benefices' as used for the reservation of vacancies 'apud sedem apostolicam' had probably been meant to include archbishoprics and bishoprics,[18] this interpretation was now written into canon law. The terms of *Etsi in temporalium* also suggest that Clement may have intended thereby to abolish the time limitations of *Statutum* and *Si apostolica* as well as the qualification 'apud sedem apostolicam';[19] the wording, however, is perhaps intentionally unclear, for Clement himself observed in the same passage that 'what is enjoined specially is accustomed to be feared more than what is commanded generally'. But

---

[15] Boase, *Boniface viii*, 101.

[16] Lux, *Constitutionum Apostolicorum*, 19-20.

[17] 31 July 1305. CIC, Extravag. comm., lib. III, tit. ii, cap. 3 (Friedberg, vol. ii, cols. 1258-9); transl. Lunt, *Papal Revenues* ii, 221-2. Friedberg in CIC dates it 1300, which is obviously wrong. Mollat, *La Collation*, 26, dates it 20 Feb. 1307, which is in fact the date of cap. 2 of the same section of the CIC. Lux, *Constitutionum Apostolicorum*, 15, notes the error in Friedberg.

[18] Churchill, *Canterbury Administration*, vol. i, p. 254 n. 3; Mollat, *La Collation*, 27.

[19] After enumerating the types of vacant benefices, *Etsi* continues: 'quae apud sedem apostolicam vacare noscuntur ad praesens, et quae toto nostri pontificatus tempore vacare contigerit in futurum, ... constitutione Clementis iv. et Bonifacii viii. Romanorum Pontificum praedecessorum nostrorum et alia qualibet, in contrarium edita non obstante'.

whatever Clement intended in theory by *Etsi in temporalium*, it is certain that in practice he did regard the benefices of certain classes of persons as already reserved even if not vacated 'apud sedem apostolicam', and these classes included cardinals, papal chaplains, apostolic nuncios, recipients of episcopal consecration at the curia, and those whose benefices fell vacant at the curia by resignation, transfer, or exchange. An exact date or specific inclusion in the canon law of this extension is difficult to determine.[20]

One additional modification in the canons by Clement v was *Ex supernae providentia*[21] of 1307 by which he revoked provisions of all major benefices made *in commendam* on the ground that their cures were thereby being neglected. This action seems to have affected a few minor benefices in England, which the pope then provided *de novo*.[22] In 1312 Clement reserved all benefices in certain lands that were in the gift of the Templars, but this reservation did not extend to England.[23]

Clement's successor, the lawyer-pope John xxii, issued at some time during his pontificate the bull *Ex debito*,[24] which followed closely but

[20] Lux, *Constitutionum Apostolicorum*, 20-3, and Mollat, *La Collation*, 11-12, cite examples from the registers of Clement v and John xxii; cf. Highfield, 'The Relations' i, 14, and Lunt, *Papal Revenues*, vol. i, p. 85 and n. 228, and vol. ii, p. 222. Additional evidence of this extended reservation is found in Reg. Clem. v, no. 2248; Cardinal Peter of Spain, sent to England, Scotland, Ireland, and Wales by Clement v in 1306 with authority to provide to any benefices, including dignities, vacated by death or resignation of any of his or of the pope's chaplains who were absent from the papal curia in his own company. Several references suggest an even more general reservation by Clement: Reg. Clem. v, no. 9781: (26 Sept. 1313) 'reservatione a predicto pontifice facta de quibuscunque beneficiis per obitum cardinalium, capellanorum et aliorum suorum officialium ubicunque cedentium vel decedentium aut apud eandem sedem quoquomodo vacantibus'. John xxii's very first individual reservation of a specific benefice, issued even before his coronation, used similar language and cited Clement v's general reservation as his authority (Lux, *Constitutionum Apostolicorum*, 24); cf. also Reg. John xxii, no. 6113: 'reservatis autem a Clemente v omnibus beneficiis capellanorum et officialium suorum decedentium'. John xxii himself, in a provisory bull, stated 'Clemens, Papa v, predecessor noster, ... canonicatus et prebendas, ceteraque beneficia ecclesiastica quorumcumque Capellanorum ejusdem Sedis ubicumque decedencium, tunc vacancia et in antea vacatura, sue et Sedis predicte disposicioni et ordinacioni reservans' (as printed in Reg. Asserio, 590); and in a letter to Archbishop Reynolds, dated 1323, he used very similar words (Cant. Cath. ms Reg. I, f. 393; hmc Ninth Rep., I, app., 72). For another instance of similar phraseology see Reg. Orleton Hereford, 187-8.

[21] 20 Feb. 1306/1307. cic, Extravag. comm., lib. III, tit. ii, cap. 2 (Friedberg, vol. ii, cols. 1257-8); Reg. Clem. v, no. 2263.

[22] E.g., Reg. Clem. v, nos. 1670, 2513. Cf. Reg. Clem. v, no. 1694: provision of a parish church in Lincoln dioc. that had been wrongfully received *in commendam* (9 June 1307).

[23] Lux, *Constitutionum Apostolicorum*, 22.

[24] cic, Extravag. comm., lib. I, tit. iii, cap. 4 (Friedberg, vol. ii, cols. 1240-1); better text in Lux, *Constitutionum Apostolicorum*, 51-4; transl. Lunt, *Papal Revenues* ii, 222-4; cf.

enlarged upon the specific terms of *Etsi in temporalium*. *Ex debito* began by enumerating once more, with only slight variation, the types of benefices reserved: episcopal sees and higher,[25] monasteries and regular churches of which the heads are ordinarily elected, priories, offices and administrative posts in the same, dignities, parsonages, prebends, and other ecclesiastical benefices with cure or without cure. This list in *Ex debito* differed little from the list already written in *Etsi*,[26] but *Ex debito* marked an advance over the former by clarifying the ambiguities of vacancy 'apud sedem apostolicam' and by definitely abolishing the limitations of *Statutum* and *Si apostolica*. The term 'apud sedem apostolicam' was clarified in *Ex debito* by two clauses. (1) The ways in which a vacancy might occur 'apud sedem apostolicam' were specified as death, deposition, privation, quashing of elections, rejection of postulations, renunciation, provision, translation, consecration, and benediction. (2) Vacancies 'apud sedem apostolicam' were extended in a general way to include vacancies anywhere[27] resulting from the deaths of cardinals, the vice-chancellor, the 'camerarius', the notaries, the auditors of contradicted letters, correctors, writers of letters, penitentiaries, abbreviators, commensal chaplains, legates, and nuncios. And *Ex debito* also finally did away with the limitations of *Statutum* and *Si apostolica* by stating that the papal reservation was to include all such benefices vacant 'apud sedem apostolicam' which had not been filled at the time of the death of Clement v or that had become thus vacant since Clement's death (which was more than twenty-eight months before John's coronation) 'notwithstanding the constitutions of Gregory x and Boniface viii'. Pensions and benefices held *in commendam* were excepted from the reservation.

In short, the terms of *Ex debito* moved the papal position in canon law closer to that of *plenaria dispositio* already implied by the preamble of *Licet ecclesiarum*. Pope John himself expressed this position in a long curial letter to his nuncios in England, Cardinals Gaucelme de Jean and

---

Highfield, 'The Relations' i, 15-17; Hinschius, *System des katholischen Kirchenrechts* iii, 130 (esp. note 3), 131; Lux, *Constitutionum Apostolicorum*, 25-6; Mollat, *La Collation*, 28-9. For the date of this bull see below, pp. 11-12, 67-71.

[25] The phrase is 'et earum superiores'. These were defined in the bull *Ad regimen* of Benedict xii as including archiepiscopal and patriarchal sees (Lunt, *Financial Relations*, vol. ii, p. 321 n. 101).

[26] The words of *Ex debito*, after enumerating the types of vacant benefices, followed closely the words of *Etsi*. For the words of *Etsi*, see above, p. 8 n. 19. The words of *Ex debito* were: 'quae apud predictam sedem vacant ad praesens, et exnunc in antea, (donec Christi dignatio nos dignebitur universalis ecclesiae sponsae suae regimini praesidere), vacare contigerit apud eam'.

[27] The phrase is 'sive inibi sive alibi ubicunque'.

Luca Fieschi, written in March of 1316/1317. The full text of the pope's letter,[28] which was entered in the register of Archbishop Reynolds but has apparently not yet been printed anywhere, is strikingly parallel to the contents of an earlier letter from Clement v to Archbishop Winchelsey in 1309, which has long been accessible to historians in Rymer's *Foedera*. The expression of papal power used by both pontiffs is identical. After a strong complaint against various inhibitions of papal mandates in England, Pope John maintained that the apostolic see, as had been the custom in time past, had the right to make provisions to ecclesiastical benefices in the realm 'divino et humano iure' – one of many phrases lifted verbatim out of the bull of his predecessor.[29] This classical position was held, moreover, by the theorists of papal power in John xxii's time. The Italian Augustinus Triumphus of Ancona wrote that the pope possessed immediate jurisdiction over every diocese because all episcopal jurisdiction was derived immediately from him, and in 1330-1332 the Spanish Franciscan Alvarus Pelagius was writing – in a treatise composed for John xxii at his own request – that the Roman pontiff was 'the distributor of all ecclesiastical dignities, offices, and benefices'.[30] One should not overestimate the effects of *Ex debito*, however, for neither the theory nor the practice of *plenaria dispositio* originated with John xxii, and later in this book it will be shown that *Ex debito* by itself was probably not responsible for any significant increase in the numbers of papal provisions to England.

The case for a reassessment of *Ex debito* is strengthened by the uncertainty of its date, which must be discussed now. Professor Stephan Kuttner has questioned the widespread assumption that *Ex debito* was issued on 15 September 1316 during John xxii's first pontifical year, and he has presented tentative evidence – in a footnote to an article on another topic[31] – that argues for a date subsequent to 1325. His case against the earlier date rests upon the fact that the canonists Guillaume de Mont-

[28] Printed below, Appendix 7.

[29] Clement also employed the same phrase in a letter to Edward ii written a year earlier than this bull to Winchelsey (Rymer II:i, 41-2; 9 April 1308). Lunt, AHR xviii (1912), 62, has noticed close parallels in the wording of bulls of these two popes concerning annates. See also P&C ii, 1285.

[30] Guillemain, *La politique bénéficiale*, 21-2; Wilks, *The Problem of Sovereignty*, part iv, pp. 331-411. For further discussion of Pope John's own high views of papal power, see Weakland, *Catholic Historical Review* liv (1968), 40-3.

[31] *Studi e Testi*, vol. 234 (1964), p. 440 n. 48. In a personal communication dated 29 March 1976, Professor Kuttner informed me that he had gathered nothing further on the date of *Ex debito*.

lauzun and Jesselin de Cassagnes, writing on papal powers over the reservation of benefices in 1319 and 1325, respectively, do not mention *Ex
debito*. Of course this is an argument from silence, and perhaps it does not
take sufficient account of the reference in the bull itself to the death of
Clement v, but it does cast doubt upon the traditional dating of 1316.
Professor Lunt,[32] earlier than Kuttner, had refused to date it any more
specifically than '1316-1324', and still another possibility is opened by a
mid-fourteenth-century glossed collection of papal *extravagantes* in
which *Ex debito* is found 'datum anno quinto' (month and day are not
given) which would define its issue between 5 September 1320 and 5
September 1321.[33] At all events, for the present its date must remain
uncertain, and the significance of this uncertainty will appear when we
come to discuss what effect if any it had in England.

On 19 November 1317 John xxii added another chapter to the canons
on provisions by issue of the constitution *Execrabilis*,[34] which revoked all
dispensations of previous popes for plurality and reserved the plural
benefices for papal provision. It required every holder of two or more
incompatible benefices with cure of souls – excepting only cardinals[35] and
sons of kings – to resign all but one such benefice before the ecclesiastical
ordinary under public testimony within one month of local publication of
the constitution, even if the incompatible benefices were held by papal
dispensation. If the incompatible benefices had previously been held by
any canonical dispensation, the holder could choose which one to retain;
if they had been held without dispensation, the holder could retain only
the last one received by canonical collation. Exchange of incompatible
benefices for compatible ones was forbidden except at the apostolic see.
Failure to comply with the decree would deprive the pluralist *ipso iure* of

[32] *Papal Revenues* ii, 222.

[33] Vatican Library MS Vat. Lat. 1404, f. 15v. That this MS dates from the mid-
fourteenth century is established from a note on the flyleaf, which records that it was
purchased by Bernard de la Tour, cardinal deacon of S. Eustachius 1342-1361. *Ex debito*
was certainly issued by 1331, when a papal collector carried a copy of it with him to
Hungary: Vatican Archives, Collectoriae 184, ff. 13v-14. For both these references I am
indebted to J. Tarrant.

[34] 19 Nov. 1317. CIC, Extravag. Joan. XXII, tit. iii, cap. 1 (Friedberg, vol. ii, col. 1207)
and repeated in Extravag. comm., lib. III, tit. ii, cap. 4 (Friedberg, vol. ii, col. 1259); Reg.
John XXII, no. 8137 (curial letter); transl. Lunt, *Papal Revenues* ii, 225-8, and cf. 374-5; cf.
also Kuttner, *Studi e Testi*, vol. 234 (1964), 434; Lux, *Constitutionum Apostolicorum*, 26-7;
Mollat, *La Collation*, 30, 56-64, 67; Thompson, *Associated Architectural Societies' Reports
and Papers* xxxiii (1915), 61-8.

[35] The constitution described the cardinals as persons 'who, serving the universal
church about us, devote themselves to the advantages of individual churches'. Cf. BL MS
Cott. Cleopatra E.i, f. 262 (top foliation).

all his benefices and of the right to hold any benefices in the future. The decree in reserving all the resigned benefices to papal provision also directed each bishop to inform the pope of the benefices thus resigned or deprived. The law was both retroactive and also valid for the future.

At a subsequent date in correspondence with the archbishop of Braga and the king of Portugal, Pope John clarified the terms of *Execrabilis* by asserting that it had not been his intention to include benefices of lay patronage within his general reservation of benefices vacated by force of the new constitution [36] (although the bull itself had made no such exception). As will be shown later,[37] this exception of benefices in lay patronage is also confirmed by his treatment of such benefices in England. In other respects, however, papal policy as to the disposal of benefices vacated by *Execrabilis* varied at different times in different places the world over. In parts of Spain, for example, apostolic nuncios were granted authority to confer such benefices themselves, with the advice of the local ordinaries (August 1326)[38] or if the benefices came below a certain value (December 1327).[39] The rector of Campania was given authority in May of 1327 to confer the benefices vacated by *Execrabilis* if they did not exceed a certain sum.[40] In March of 1330/1331, provision of benefices in Hungary vacated by the new constitution was to be made by 'those to whom it pertains',[41] and this policy, as I shall show later,[42] is the closest to the situation that came to prevail in England.

An immediate effect of *Execrabilis* in England was to enable the pope to provide to a large number of parish churches hitherto unaffected by provision; but its immediate effects redounded less to the power of the pope than to that of the local ordinaries as true patrons of the benefices vacated. Consequently, its long-term effects were not so great as some writers have imagined. What it brought to the pope in annates was probably more significant than the added number of provisions he gained from it. Its ultimate significance for Anglo-papal relations, moreover, lies

---

[36] Vatican Archives, Reg. Vat. 110A, ff. 76v-77 (nos. 177-8): 'Quia igitur intencionis nostre non extitit nec existit quod per reservacionem collacionis beneficiorum dimittendorum seu vaccaturorum ex ipsius constitucionis edicto nobis et apostolice sedi factam laycis veris patronis illorum aliquod preiudicium fieret, quin eis ad illa sicut prius libere presentare liceret'. I am indebted to J. Tarrant for initially suggesting this and some of the following references to me.

[37] Below, pp. 78-79.

[38] Vatican Archives, Reg. Vat. 113, f. 230v.

[39] Vatican Archives, Reg. Vat. 114, f. 354v (no. 229).

[40] Vatican Archives, Reg. Vat. 114, ff. 25-25v (no. 99).

[41] Vatican Archives, Reg. Vat. 116, ff. 112v-113 (no. 86).

[42] Below, pp. 90-91.

in the way its rules were modified in actual practice by the English episcopal hierarchy under Archbishop Reynolds.

The constitution *Ad regimen*,[43] which came in 1335 at the outset of the pontificate of Benedict XII and which marks the end of the thirty years under review in the present study, reaffirmed the essential terms of *Ex debito*, making frequent reference to the provisory legislation of John XXII and to the two-days clause of Boniface VIII's *Praesenti declaramus*. It also made quite clear one particular stipulation found in *Ex debito* and already common in practice, viz., the reservation to the apostolic see of all benefices vacated anywhere by anyone who was provided to a higher benefice by the pope or by apostolic authority.

No further canonical legislation on provisions after *Ad regimen* need concern us here, but we must note that such bulls did not cease then and that every pope of the Avignon succession made his own further contribution to the canons on this subject.[44]

[43] 11 Jan. 1334/1335. CIC, Extravag. comm., lib. III, tit. ii, cap. 13 (Friedberg, vol. ii, cols. 1266-7); better text in Lux, *Constitutionum Apostolicorum*, 54-6; transl. Lunt, *Papal Revenues* ii, 228-30; cf. Guillemain, *La politique bénéficiale*, 30-1; Highfield, 'The Relations' i, 16; Lux, *Constitutionum Apostolicorum*, 32; Mollat, *La Collation*, 30; Reg. Chichele, vol. i, p. lxxxix.

[44] Barraclough, *Papal Provisions*, 9; Highfield, 'The Relations' i, 16, 125-31; Lunt, *Papal Revenues* ii, 230-3; Lux, *Constitutionum Apostolicorum*, 33-46; Mollat, *La Collation*, 31-40; Reg. Chichele, vol. i, p. lxxxix. Benedict XII himself added further legislation (Guillemain, *La politique bénéficiale*, 30-1).

2

The Papal Registers

Such was the canon law that had developed on the subject of provisions by the pontificates of Clement v and John xxii. But what was the actual practice of papal provisions to English benefices at this time, and to what extent was it affected by factors other than the canons? We must examine the texture of our sources – what the papal registers say and what they do not say – before we can proceed (in chapter four) to tabulate and assess the actual numbers of provisions at this time.

The registers of both these popes are in the Vatican Archives.[1] Those of Clement survive only in the so-called Vatican series, which are the final registrations before the bulls were actually delivered, and these have been calendared in eight volumes in Latin by the Benedictines of Monte Cassino. Under John a much greater degree of systematization is apparent in the registers, and from his pontificate there survive not only the Vatican registers (on parchment) but also the Avignon series of registers (on paper).[2] The latter series, so called because it remained at Avignon until 1783, consists of copies of the minutes or drafts of the letters that were made soon after the petitions were granted and prior to the Vatican registers. The *litterae communes*, together with the *litterae de curia* and some related documents, of John xxii have been calendared in sixteen volumes in Latin by Msgr. Mollat, and the *litterae de curia* and the *litterae secretae* of that pope pertaining to France have been calendared in Latin by the French Schools of Athens and Rome. A convenient, but in some ways unsatisfactory, English calendar of documents pertaining to England from the Vatican series of registers (only) of both these popes was edited by W. H. Bliss for the English government's record publications in 1895. It was the intention of Bliss and his colleagues to

---

[1] Cf. MacFarlane, *Archives* iv (1959), 29-44, 84-101. Full references to the various calendars of these papal registers will be found in the Bibliography.

[2] Further see Boyle, *Survey of the Vatican Archives*, 114-24.

print a further volume containing certain supplementary material extracted from the Avignon series,[3] but this has never appeared. The Latin calendar of John XXII's *litterae communes* by Mollat, in addition to its greater degree of accuracy and the fact that Mollat has also consulted the Avignon series that began under the same pope, has the great merit of rearranging all the entries from both series in a strict chronological order.[4]

Some additional information is found in the Latin calendars of the registers of Popes Clement and John that is not found in the English calendars, and vice versa.[5] In this book the term 'papal registers' will be used to designate information found in either the Latin calendar or the English calendar or both. Provisions to Welsh benefices will always be included in the discussions of English provisions unless a specific distinction is made.

That there were many technical varieties of papal provisions is amply attested by the thirty-two diverse rules in John XXII's chancery ordinances for drawing up different bulls of provision,[6] by the 134 entries of 'processus in causis beneficialibus' in a contemporary formulary of the Roman curia to enable executors of papal mandates to inform the ordinary collators that provisions had been made,[7] and by the entries in the papal registers themselves. Here we shall be concerned primarily with the most direct kinds of provisions made by the popes and entered in their registers, although it will be shown that the popes did often empower lesser ecclesiastics to provide by apostolic authority and that a few direct provisions, as well as an indeterminable number of papal graces to poor

[3] CPL., vol. iii, p. viii.

[4] On the inadequacies of the calendar by Bliss, see Watt, *Scottish Historical Review* xxxii (1953), 104-7, 109-10, who draws attention to criticisms of Bliss's work in the House of Commons when it appeared. There are two major errors that I have encountered in Mollat's Latin calendar of John XXII's *litterae communes*. The first of these is the fact that his numbering (in vol. vii, p. 130) skips from number 30999 to number 40000. No entries from the MS registers seem to be omitted, but his mistake does mean that the total number of documents in the sixteen vols. of Reg. John XXII is really 9000 less than the final entry number 64421 would suggest. The second important error I have encountered is in the printing of vol. ix: the *recto* of p. 201 is followed by the *verso* of p. 206 and the next few pages are transposed, thus breaking the order of document numbers 48441-78.

[5] We also know from manuscript sources that the papal camera for financial purposes began at least by 1330 to keep separate registers of benefices filled by provision in order to inform its collectors who were charged with the collection of annates (Boyle, *Vatican Archives*, 167-8; Lunt, *Accounts rendered by Papal Collectors in England*, xlix).

[6] Ottenthal, *Regulae Cancellariae Apostolicae*, 1-9; cf. Fayen, *Lettres de Jean XXII* (Analecta Vaticano-Belgica ii), vol. i, pp. xlviii-xlix; Guillemain, *La politique bénéficiale*, 21; and see generally Tangl, *Die päpstlichen Kanzlei-Ordnungen*.

[7] Barraclough, *Public Notaries and the Papal Curia*, nos. 1-134.

clerks, did escape the listings in the papal registers. Indirect papal grants such as special reservations, expectations unaccompanied by actual provisions, commends, surrogations, renewals of provisions, mentions of former provisions, mandates to provide,[8] confirmations of elections, or provisions cancelled at the apostolic see will not be considered or tabulated. An actual, direct provision by the pope himself, whereby the provisor could immediately attempt to obtain the provided benefice, was generally the most valuable type of grant and had the greatest chance of fulfilment, but even it required a complicated process and – as will be shown – was not at all certain of consummation.

Miss Ann Deeley has distinguished[9] between direct collations (a provision to a specific named benefice already vacant) and expectations (a promise of an unspecified benefice when it should fall vacant in the future), the two principal ways in which the Avignonese popes intervened in the collation of benefices. Although this distinction is useful, it must nevertheless be emphasized and will be shown that the most frequent major intervention in the collation of English benefices recorded in the papal registers was the 'provisio canonicatus sub expectatione prae-bendae', a form that combined both provision and expectation.[10] All direct provisions, including this combination form but not including expectations alone, will be tabulated and considered in the present study in order to present a comprehensive and statistical view of the English provisions of the first two popes of Avignon.

[8] There is some evidence, however, to suggest that such mandates were regarded as being of an authority equal to that of direct provisions (CPL. ii. 324; BL MS Royal 12.D.xi. f. 39v). I have used such mandates for the purpose of establishing vacancies forced by the constitution *Execrabilis* in Appendix 1, table D, below, but I have not counted them as provisions.

[9] EHR xliii (1928), 497-527.

[10] Guillemain, *La politique bénéficiale*, 26-7; below, pp. 31-32; and cf. Caillet, *La papauté d'Avignon et l'église de France*, 23, 54, 124, 243.

3

Graces to Poor Clerks and Other
Provisions outside the Registers

An expectation unaccompanied by a direct provision normally took the form of a promise of an unnamed benefice (usually a church, or, less frequently, a canonry and prebend) of designated value in a specified diocese or in the gift of a specific bishop or abbey or priory when such a benefice should become vacant in the future.[1] Of such expectative graces there were two types: those *in forma speciali* were generally entered in the papal registers in the early fourteenth century and those *in forma communi* were generally not. Both types were comparatively vague in their wording, were less certain of fulfilment than a direct provision, and will not be included in the tabulation of actual provisions that follows in the next chapter.[2] Some comment must be made here, however, upon the latter type as well as upon the extent of other provisions made at this time but not entered in the papal registers.

Expectative graces *in forma communi* were grants of benefices usually worth (in England) not more than twenty marks with cure of souls or fifteen without[3] to poor clerks having no benefice or one of little or

---

[1] Barraclough, *Acta Congressus Iuridici Internationalis Romae 1934*, iii, 128; Guillemain, *La Cour pontificale*, 525-6; Tihon, *Bulletin de l'Institut historique belge de Rome*, v, 57.

[2] There are, however, eight grants *in forma speciali* by Clement v and one by John xxii of English benefices in gift of specified ecclesiastical patrons that are classified in the Latin calendars of the papal registers as definite provisions, and these have therefore been included in the tabulation (Reg. Clem. v, nos. 1486, 1488-91, 4133-4, 9535; CPL. ii, 21-2, 56, 114; Reg. John xxii, no. 55145; CPL. ii, 351). On the other hand, there are at least ten grants by John xxii to English benefices in gift of specified ecclesiastical patrons that are called provisions in the English calendar of Bliss but are classified in Mollat's Latin calendar of the register as expectative graces, and these have not been tabulated (Reg. John xxii, nos. 2293, 4368-9, 4374, 10314, 11662, 12324, 23413, 30271-2; CPL. ii, 143, 154, 164, 200, 203, 216, 249, 280). For further distinctions between *in forma speciali* and *in forma communi*, see Tihon, *Bulletin de l'Institut historique belge de Rome* v, 59, 79-80, 95.

[3] These figures were often exceeded in practice (Guillemain, *La politique bénéficiale*, 25-6; Mollat, *La Collation*, 75; Tihon, *Bulletin de l'Institut historique belge de Rome* v, 85).

insufficient value. Hence they were also known as expectatives *in forma pauperum*, or 'poor clerks' provisions'. They often stipulated that the recipient be given a suitable pension in the event that no benefice was vacant. Their recipients were exempt from the payment of annates on them.[4] They were generally contingent upon two examinations: (1) usually at Avignon, but sometimes locally,[5] as to the clerk's capacity and learning, and (2) within the local diocese, as to the clerk's manner of life.[6] They were usually issued without the personal knowledge or fiat of the pope himself,[7] and during the period between Urban IV (1261-1264) and Clement VI (1342-1352) they were generally not entered in the papal registers.[8] Under Clement VI the custom began of registering not only the graces themselves but also the antecedent petitions, both *in forma pauperum*.[9] Although no volumes of papal petitions survive before 1342,[10] yet the fragments of the drafts or minutes (*notae*) of forty-nine

---

The difference in the higher value was probably intended to allow payment for a clerk to exercise cure of souls on behalf of the incumbent who would be nonresident (Flanagan, 'Papal Provisions in Ireland', 95).

[4] Lunt, *Financial Relations* ii, 325.

[5] Barraclough, *Public Notaries and the Papal Curia*, 269, shows that a petition for a grant *in forma pauperum* could be presented at the curia for one absent as well as for one present, and the formulary itself (p. 157, no. 34) shows that such a grant could be accepted by proxy. Cf. Tihon, *Bulletin de l'Institut historique belge de Rome* v, 71-3.

[6] PRO SC7/44/1, 19, is a case in which the 'poor clerk' was examined first at the curia by three chaplains of Clement v, where he was found diligent, suitable, and unbeneficed, and then he was examined in the diocese to which he was provided (Coventry and Lichfield) as to manner of life by two commissaries of the bishop, who was the principal executor (cf. below, p. 22 n. 26). For another case of such double examination, see Cant. Cath. MS Reg. I, ff. 383v-384v. Forms showing local examinations by the executors of poor clerks' provisions survive in the formulary of John of Bologna dedicated to Archbishop Pecham (Rockinger, *Briefsteller und Formelbücher*, 709).

[7] Barraclough, *Studi e Testi*, vol. 165 (1952), 113 n. 18.

[8] Barraclough, *Papal Provisions*, 27-8, 31 (cf. n. 2), 105, 107; Guillemain, *La Cour pontificale*, 105, 525-6; Guillemain, *La politique bénéficiale*, 14 (cf. n. 2), 25-6; Tihon, *Bulletin de l'Institut historique belge de Rome* v, 58.

[9] Guillemain, *La politique bénéficiale*, p. 14 n. 2.

[10] It would still seem an open question whether any such registers of petitions did exist before 1342 (Barraclough, *Public Notaries*, 123). A few original petitions do survive from John XXII's pontificate (Moé, *Bibliothèque de l'École des Chartes* xcii (1931), 267; Barraclough, *Public Notaries*, 270-1; Bartoloni, *Bullettino dell'Istituto storico italiano per il medio evo e Archivio muratoriano*, no. 67 (1955), pp. 1-187; Reg. London, 196-7). A large number of English petitions during the last years of John XXII's pontificate and the first half of that of Benedict XII are recorded in the register of Andreas Sapiti, principal contemporary proctor for English business at the curia (Kirsch, *Historisches Jahrbuch* xiv (1893), 582-601; Giblin, *Archivium Hibernicum* xviii (1955), 67-144). None of the petitions recorded in Sapiti's register seems to be *in forma pauperum*. Information from Sapiti's register in this study is generally cited from the transcript by W. H. Bliss in PRO

graces *in forma pauperum* discovered at Cambridge and dating from 1316-1317 do reveal the basic formula used for such grants.[11] Lack of registration prohibits any certain assessment of their frequency, but the term *in forma communi* itself suggests that they were made quite often[12] and the chronicle sources indicate that they were most frequent at the beginning of a new pontificate.[13] Both Clement v and John XXII are known to have made liberal grants to poor clerks in the first years of their pontificates,[14] and John again at Pentecost of 1322.[15] The practice of Benedict XII is thought to have been restrained,[16] but Clement VI began his pontificate in May of 1342 by promising these grants to all poor clerks who would come to Avignon for them within two months of his coronation, and Barraclough is seriously convinced that the number of those who came in even less than two months was between 80,000 and 100,000.[17]

31/9/17a, although comparison (by microfilm) with the original (Vatican Library MS Barb. Lat. 2126) indicates that Bliss's transcript is quite thorough and reliable.

[11] Barraclough, *Studi e Testi*, vol. 165 (1952), 112. These drafts all begin 'Constitutus in presencia nostra .. pauper clericus .. diocesis, nobis humiliter supplicavit, ut, cum ipse, sicut asserit, nullum ecclesiasticum beneficium assecutus, ...' and all make specific mention of the examination prescribed. The original records of a poor clerk's grace from Clement v, preserved in PRO SC7/44/1, 19, follow this same form. The procedure at the time of Clement v and John XXII whereby the executors notified the bishop or abbot in whose gift the grant was made, and whereby the executor himself could collate and invest the recipient, is set forth in Barraclough, *Public Notaries*, pp. 157, 166, nos. 32-3, 60.

[12] Barraclough, *Acta Congressus Iuridici Internationalis Romae 1934*, iii. p. 137 n. 102.

[13] Barraclough, *Studi e Testi*, vol. 165 (1952), pp. 113-14; Tihon, *Bulletin de l'Institut historique belge de Rome* v, 63-4.

[14] Murimuth, *Con. Chron.*, 25; Barraclough, *Studi e Testi*, vol. 165 (1952), 114, 123; Tihon, *Bulletin de l'Institut historique belge de Rome* v, 63-4. Clement v also apparently legislated a procedure for the granting of benefices *in forma pauperum* at the council of Vienne in his constitution *Quum ei quem* (CIC, Clem., lib. III. tit. iii, cap. 1; Friedberg, vol. ii, cols. 1159-60). Although this constitution does not mention poor clerks' graces by name, Reg. Martival (i, 142-6) records a poor clerk's provision that was made according to the form of this constitution.

[15] Murimuth, *Con. Chron.*, 37.

[16] Tihon, *Bulletin de l'Institut historique belge de Rome* v, 91. On 10 Jan. 1334/1335, in his first consistory just two days after his coronation, Benedict XII commanded all clerks who did not have serious reasons for remaining to leave the curia by the following 2 Feb. (Guillemain, *La Cour pontificale*, 522-3; Guillemain, *La politique bénéficiale*, 14, 31; Mollat, *La Collation*, 75). In spite of what has been said by these writers about Benedict XII's restraint, however, Dr. David Robinson has informed me, from his research in the register of Archbishop Melton, of no less than twenty-three provisions *in forma pauperum* by Benedict XII in the archdeaconries of Cleveland and the East Riding in York diocese alone. Some of his research is summarized in Robinson, *Beneficed Clergy*, 24-5.

[17] Barraclough, *Acta Congressus Iuridici Internationalis Romae 1934*, iii, pp. 109, 111 (cf. n. 2), 128 (cf. n. 4); Barraclough, *Papal Provisions*, viii, 31 (cf. n. 2), 105-6;

The evidence of expectative graces *in forma pauperum* under Clement v and John xxii must needs come from many sources. There is one indirect mention of such a grant to an English benefice in Clement's register,[18] and seven in the register of John.[19] A search by the present writer for these papal grants to poor clerks over the years 1305-1334 in the indexes of all contemporary English episcopal registers published so far (1976) reveals a total of fifty-two in eleven registers.[20] There are fifteen other printed registers whose indexes record no such grants, but some editors may have chosen not to index them.[21] The manuscript register of Archbishop Reynolds contains one of these expectative grants,[22] there are at least five from the pontificate of John xxii in Archbishop Melton's register,[23] and the priory archives at Canterbury reveal at least two more.[24] Examination of all poor clerks' graces in these various sources confirms that such grants were generally not entered in the corresponding papal registers and suggests that they could be used as sufficient titles for

---

Barraclough, *Studi e Testi*, vol. 165 (1952), p. 113 n. 23; Tihon, *Bulletin de l'Institut historique belge de Rome* v, 63-4. Clement vi's coronation was on 19 May and the figures are for the period 19 May – 25 June. Barraclough points out that these figures are further supported by the fact that 6000 clerks of the dioceses of Mainz and Cologne alone, who had petitioned for benefices *in communi forma pauperum*, were at this time examined in the curia.

[18] Reg. Clem. v, no. 5943; CPL. ii, 74.

[19] Reg. John xxii, nos. 7071-2, 25139-40, 44182, 50500, 60941, 64333; CPL. ii, 171-2, 251, 286, 375.

[20] Cal. Reg. Droxford – 1; Reg. Cobham – 17; Reg. Gandavo – 1; Reg. London – 2; Reg. Martival – 4; Reg. Northburgh – 7; Reg. Orleton Hereford – 3; RWR – 3; Reg. Sandale – 6; Reg. Winchelsey – 1; Reg. Woodlock – 7. For a tabulation of such grants from 1328 throughout much of the fourteenth century, see Lunt, *Financial Relations* ii, 324-5.

[21] For example, there is at least one (not indexed) in Reg. Greenfield (vol. v, p. 168, no. 2631), and others could possibly be found even in Greenfield's register by tracing all the references listed in the indexes under Pope Clement v.

[22] Peter Scot, poor priest of Canterbury diocese, provided by John xxii and Archbishop Reynolds to a collegiate prebend or other benefice without cure valued at eighteen marks, or to a parish church or other benefice with cure valued at twenty-five marks, in Canterbury diocese and in the gift of the prior and convent of St. Martin's, Dover (no date given). Reynolds by papal authority caused inquiry to be made into the candidate's life and conversation, and he was found satisfactory (RR ff. 39v-40; Wilkins ii, 466).

[23] Brown, *Yorkshire Archaeological Society, Record Series* lxi (1920), 143, records one (I owe this reference to Dr. David Robinson). Four others can be found in Reg. Melton, f. 529v (664v), according to notes transcribed by Miss Ann Deeley and supplied to me with her permission by Prof. E. B. Graves.

[24] Roger Digge, 1321-1323 (Cant. Cath. MS Reg. I, ff. 383v-384v; Reg. L, ff. 122v, 123, 126), and John of Cirencester, 1328-1329 (Cant. Cath. MS Reg. L, ff. 164v, 165, 165v). The case of Digge is extensively recorded, and Digge's bull of provision (dated 12 June 1311 and not in Clement's register) is fully copied in Reg. I, ff. 383v-384v. Further information on Digge may be found in Woodruff, *Archaeologia Cantiana* xl (1928), 58.

ordination,[25] that they were commonly called 'provisions' by the scribes of episcopal chanceries, and that usually the local inquiry about the clerk's life and conversation was made among both clergy and laity by a commissary at the direction of the bishop who was himself often the executor of the grace. In the surviving records the original dates of the papal grants are not usually given, but the information that does remain suggests that in the period under review most of these grants were made in 1305-1306 or 1316-1317. These instances combine with the literary evidence and the forty-nine graces discovered at Cambridge to confirm that such grants to benefices in England were frequent in the first pontifical years of Clement v and John xxii.

In the class of papal bulls and elsewhere in the Public Record Office there are several documents connected with one particular poor clerk's provision, dating from the first year of Clement v, which affords considerable insight into the execution of such a grace.[26] The evidence of a pair of notarial instruments and a royal writ of prohibition among these documents, as well as the number of parties involved and the sheer length of the documents themselves, show that – even for a clerk who was supposedly 'poor' – the process to obtain a benefice *in forma pauperum* could be complicated and expensive.

[25] Thus on 12 March 1322/1323, Bishop Cobham of Worcester ordained a man to the diaconate 'ad titulum provisionis sue in forma communi super domo majoris Malvernie' (Reg. Cobham, 148). For other instances, see Reg. Cobham, 67, 69, 82, 118, 123, 141-2, 158, 195; RWR, 119.

[26] PRO SC7/44/1, 19: Elias Joneston, poor clerk of Coventry and Lichfield dioc., provided by Clement v to a benefice in the city or diocese of Coventry and in the gift of the archbishop of Dublin, valued at at least twenty-five marks if a cathedral or collegiate prebend or forty marks if a parish church or other benefice with cure, unless he will accept one of less value; 12 Jan. 1305/1306. For examinations of the candidate and execution of the bull, see above, p. 19 and n. 6. Joneston was provided to the prebend of Dunstan in the royal free chapel of Penkridge, and a writ of prohibition was issued (PRO C47/19/2/34). Although the king's council could describe Joneston as 'poor' as late as the year 1321 (Davies, *Baronial Opposition*, 264), Joneston was really a rather important clerk and in fact a technical expert to whom was entrusted – just a few months after his provision – a significant aspect of the diplomatic relations between England and France: in October of 1321 he was appointed keeper of processes for Aquitaine, in which office he succeeded a M. Philip Martel who had in fact been one of the commissaries charged with the execution of Joneston's provision (Cuttino, *English Diplomatic Administration*, 35-9; Cuttino, *Speculum* xvii (1942), 74-85). Joneston was soon to assist in compiling the Gascon Calendar of 1322 (Davies, *Baronial Opposition*, 531), and for a total of some thirty years he was intimately concerned with diplomatic documents relating to France and Gascony (Galbraith, 'The Tower as an Exchequer record office in the reign of Edward ii', 242). Although Joneston obtained at least three other English benefices in the years to come, he was still seeking to secure his poor clerk's provision circa 1336, when he was granted leave to go to the court of Rome for that purpose (Cuttino, *English Diplomatic Administration*, p. 38 n. 3).

The printed calendars of episcopal registers, therefore, as well as a few other sources, prove that at least fifty expectative graces *in forma communi* or *in forma pauperum* were made to English benefices by Clement v and John xxii and were not entered in the papal registers that have survived. The evidence also indicates that the numbers of these grants were the largest in the first years of their pontificates, but it does not suggest that the volume approached anything like the bulk of the first year of Clement vi's pontificate or the numbers under later Avignonese popes. Moreover, this evidence leads us to the conclusion that such graces were not so extensive and widespread in England in the early fourteenth century as Barraclough would seem to suggest by his statement that the expectative grant *in forma pauperum* was the normal means of access to a benefice.[27] Because of their vague wording, their uncertainty of fulfilment, their comparatively small value, and – above all – because they were not registered, no further major consideration will be accorded them here.

In view of the above conclusions, and in spite of what Barraclough and some other writers[28] have suggested, it would not seem true (for the first thirty years of the Avignon period) to say that vast numbers of provisions of any sort, perhaps even in the thousands, were being made by the popes to benefices in England and not being entered in the papal registers. Undoubtedly some regular provisions did miss registration, but these were not many. A check made by the present writer in the registers of Reynolds (Worcester and Canterbury), Sandale (Winchester), and Winchelsey (Canterbury) shows that all but one of the direct provisions that happen to be mentioned in them can in fact be found recorded in the printed calendars of papal registers.

A more comprehensive check upon the registration of English cathedral provisions can be made by comparing the evidence in the papal registers with that assembled in the revised volumes of Le Neve's *Fasti*. Even this method, however, has its limits, for these volumes do not pretend to be complete and they show little or no evidence that their editors have consulted the Latin calendars of the papal registers. To make this comparison I have selected Lincoln and Salisbury, the two cathedrals that saw the greatest numbers of provisions in this period, for examination. Over the years 1305-1334 the papal registers record provisions to

---

[27] *Acta Congressus Iuridici Internationalis Romae 1934*, iii, p. 128; Barraclough, *Papal Provisions*, 28, 30, 73-4, 105.

[28] Haines, *Administration of the Diocese of Worcester*, 213; Jacob, TRHS, 4th series, vol. xxvii (1945), pp. 42-3; Tihon, *Bulletin de l'Institut historique belge de Rome* v, 52, 58, 63.

seventy-nine dignities,[29] canonries, and prebends in Lincoln cathedral, and the revised volume of Le Neve's *Fasti* for Lincoln reveals eight further grants of dignities and prebends[30] that are said to have been secured by papal provisions[31] during these years of which as provisions no trace can be found in the papal registers. Thus, of a total of eighty-seven fairly definite provisions to dignities, canonries, and prebends in Lincoln between 1305 and 1334, only eight – just over nine percent – are not found in the papal registers. At Salisbury, the papal registers record provisions to eighty-one dignities, canonries, and prebends in the same period, whereas the revised volume of Le Neve for Salisbury reveals five further grants of dignities and prebends that are said to have been secured by papal provisions[32] during these years of which as provisions no trace can be found in the papal registers. Thus, of a total of eighty-six fairly definite provisions to dignities, canonries, and prebends in Salisbury between 1305 and 1334, apparently only five[33] – just under six percent – are not found in the papal registers.

[29] In the tabulations that follow, the term 'dignities' is used to include archdeaconries, although techncally an archdeaconry was not a cathedral dignity. The term 'dignities' is not used to include bishoprics.

[30] Canonries as such are not listed in many of the new volumes of Le Neve; cf. Le Neve, *Introduction* (vol. xii), 9-10.

[31] Still three more such grants are described as provisions in the revised Le Neve for Lincoln, but in the Latin calendars of papal registers they are identified as only mandates to assign or as reservations, and therefore I have not included them in this calculation.

[32] Still four more such grants are described as provisions in the revised Le Neve for Salisbury, but in the Latin calendars of papal registers they are identified as only mandates to assign or as reservations, and therefore I have not included them in this calculation.

[33] The picture at Salisbury is complicated by a fascinating but confusing piece of evidence recorded in Bishop Martival's register, now completely in print, of which the Le Neve revisers made very little use. Whereas in all the rest of his register there is clear evidence of a total of only four provisions, of which only one can be found in the calendared papal registers, there also survives a letter of Martival to Pope John XXII complaining that the large number of papal provisions to benefices in his patronage prevents the preferment of his own clerks and asking that a small number of them may be provided in preference to other clerks already expecting by way of provision (Reg. Martival ii, 549-52). The bishop employs language that is quite flattering to the pope, describing Salisbury cathedral itself several times as 'ecclesia vestra cathedralis' and asking that the pope exercise moderation for the sake of 'Jhesu Christi cuius locum in terris eo disponente tenetis'. Dated 21 March 1326/1327, this letter goes on to specify a total of thirty-seven benefices in the bishop's collation to which papal provisions are said to have been made, twenty-one by John himself, eight by his predecessors, and eight further by John by way of expectation. Most of these are to canonries and prebends in the cathedral, and in every case the name of the person as well as the benefice is given. Of this list, I have been able to trace about fifty-five percent in the printed calendars of papal registers, and thus it would seem that a greater number of provisions were being made, at least to Salisbury, than the evidence in the papal registers and Le Neve serves to indicate.

Therefore, even though a moderate number of poor clerks' provisions to minor unspecified benefices were not being registered at this time, it would seem that the great majority of papal provisions from 1305-1334 to English sees, abbeys, priories, dignities, canonries, and prebends in cathedral and collegiate churches, and parish churches can in fact be found in the printed papal registers. For this reason, but without exaggerating the importance of figures alone, it will be possible for us here to draw a fairly accurate picture of the provisory policies of Clement v and John xxii in England from their registers – as Guillemain found he could do on the same basis from the registers of John's successor Benedict xii,[34] and as Gaignard has done generally for the last three years of the

---

However, the information from this letter is seldom quoted in the revised Le Neve volume for Salisbury, even though the revisers state that they consulted Martival's register in manuscript (Le Neve, *Salisbury*, viii), and even though there are several appointments to Salisbury prebends concerning which the Le Neve's revisers' avowed aim to show 'how and when the man secured and left the office' (Le Neve, *Introduction* (vol. xii), 9) could have been assisted if they had chosen to regard each of these thirty-seven men as in fact provided to the named benefices at least by the time of the date of Martival's letter. The revised Le Neve does not explain why this evidence has not been cited, but it seems possible that the bishop in this letter has chosen to exaggerate some of his assertions. His claim that 'hardly three' of all these persons reside in their benefices and his statement about the importance of canonical residence at Salisbury are not cited in the study that Miss Edwards has made on this subject (*English Secular Cathedrals*, 76-84). Further, at least one of the alleged provisors whose appointment does not appear in the calendared papal registers, Francesco Gaetani, seems in fact to have been collated to his prebend of Netherbury by Bishop Gandavo rather than to have received it by papal provision as Martival's letter asserts (Reg. Martival iii, 236-7). Another, Vitalis de Testa, received his prebend of Torleton under a papal faculty for exchange of benefices rather than by direct papal provision (Chew, *Hemingby's Register*, 235). For three more of the alleged provisors whose appointments do not appear in the registers, I have in fact been able to locate sources outside the registers indicating that they were provided, but for a great many others my preliminary investigation has produced no record of any papal provision at all. It is possible, also, that some of the appointments Martival here describes as papal provisions were in fact made under the provisory faculties customarily given to the numerous papal nuncios sent to England in this period, and that the bishop here is engaging in a form of special pleading to describe such appointments, frequently indeed of foreigners, in this way (below, pp. 47-49; I owe this suggestion to Fr. L. E. Boyle). Martival was in general an extremely conscientious bishop, however, and any final estimate of this particular letter's significance must await a more thorough study of the methods by which all the alleged provisors here obtained their benefices, as well as the full study of his episcopal career which Miss Edwards, the general editor of his register, proposed before her death in 1976 (Reg. Martival iv, pp. xxvii, xxxvii; I am grateful to Miss Edwards for her comments upon this note).

[34] *La politique bénéficiale*, 15. Some interesting figures are available for comparison from the later fourteenth century: a doctoral thesis in 1933 by Miss Candace Carstens, under the direction of Professor Helen M. Cam, established total figures for English provisions between 1342 and 1378 using a number of sources in addition to the papal

pontificate of Clement v.[35] The picture which follows, then, is based upon tabulations from the papal registers as they have now been explained. Later in the course of this book, evidence will be drawn from a wide variety of other sources in order to deepen our knowledge of the ways in which this system worked in actual practice. It will also be shown that a secondary but rather extensive network of 'provisions' was created just beneath the surface of these registers by the granting of numerous 'apostolic provisory faculties'.

---

registers. When these figures are compared with the totals established by Dr. Highfield in his thesis for the same period, using only the papal registers, it appears that nearly eighty percent of all provisions granted in that period were being entered in the papal registers (below, Appendix 1, table A).

[35] *Annales du Midi* lxxii (1960), 169 seq. His statement (p. 173) that he has found no letter of Clement v destined for England in the years 1311-1314 apart from those in Clement's register can be amended, to cite only one way, by the evidence of some poor clerks' provisions whose bulls survive in English episcopal registers and elsewhere.

4

A Statistical Analysis of the Provisions

When Reynolds of Canterbury took his oath of obedience to the apostolic see upon receipt of the pallium in 1314, he was not then required – as would be demanded in some papal appointments of bishops at least by the time of Martin v in the fifteenth century – to enumerate reservations and provisions among the papal acts that he swore to defend,[1] and indeed such acts were not nearly so frequent in the time of Reynolds as they would become later in his own century. The raw numbers of direct provisions to English benefices recorded in the registers of Clement v and John xxii, which can be compared with the calculations already established by Professor Guillemain for Benedict xii and by Drs. Carstens and Highfield for the later Avignon popes, reveal that the provisions system was very much in its infancy under Clement v, saw a considerable expansion under John xxii, dropped sharply under Benedict xii, but then jumped to its peak under Clement vi and remained at a consistent high throughout the rest of the period until 1378.[2] The numbers

---

[1] RR f. 211. The oaths of Archbishops Stratford (1334), Langham (1366), Courtenay (1381), and Arundel (1396) also contain no promise to defend papal acts of provision (Stratford's is in Reg. Hethe, 550-1; cf. Reg. Langham, 115; Lambeth MS Reg. Courtenay, f. 1v; Lambeth MS Reg. Arundel I, f. 3). These may be compared with the oath, including a promise to defend such acts, which was administered to the bishop-elect of Salisbury in 1427, printed in Reg. Chichele, vol. i, p. xc. The archbishop of Salzburg made a similar promise in the same year (text in Gottlob, *Der kirchliche Amtseid*, 180-1). For the earlier history of the archiepiscopal oath of obedience, see Kantorowicz, *Speculum* xxix (1954), 488-502, and Gottlob, *Der kirchliche Amtseid*, 42 seq. Also see Hall, *Henry viii*, ed. Whibley, ii, 211.

[2] The tables of provisions that I have compiled are to be found in Appendix 1. I am particularly indebted to J. R. L. Highfield for permission to use the figures in his Oxford D.Phil. thesis, 'The Relations between the Church and the English Crown 1349-1378', for the purpose of making these comparisons with the later fourteenth century. For a summary view of English provisions throughout the Avignon period see below, Appendix 1, table A. For comparisons with the provisions of John xxii to French benefices see L. Caillet, *La papauté d'Avignon et l'église de France*, which appeared in

in the last thirty years of the Avignon period were over five times as great as those in the first thirty years: Clement v made provisions to some sixty-nine English benefices during his pontificate from 1305 to 1314 and John xxii to some 782 English benefices in the years 1316-1334 (a total of 851 during the first thirty years of the period), whereas by comparison the total recorded number of provisions to English benefices by Clement vi, Innocent vi, Urban v, and Gregory xi in the years 1348-1377 was some 4658.[3] The recorded Avignon provisions dropped to their lowest figures under the austere Cistercian Benedict xii, 1334-1342, who provided to only seventy-eight English benefices;[4] but following his death they leaped to the highest point of the entire Avignon period in the very first year of Clement vi, who that year issued at least 441 direct provisions to England.[5]

By far the greatest number of all the provisions between 1305 and 1334 (as well as under Benedict xii) was to dignities, canonries, and prebends of cathedral and collegiate churches. These types of benefices accounted for thirty-three of Clement v's sixty-nine provisions and for 647 of John xxii's 782 provisions (and for sixty-three of Benedict xii's seventy-eight).[6] The collegiate churches[7] were subject to considerably fewer provisions than the cathedrals, there being five collegiate but twenty-eight cathedral provisions under Clement and 177 collegiate but 470 cathedral provisions under John. Cathedral and collegiate prebends were the major sort of ecclesiastical benefice without cure of souls, thus not requiring special papal dispensation for nonresidence, and examination will show that the vast majority of these provisions went to important officers of church and state – often to cardinals or king's clerks – whose work elsewhere was generally regarded as valuable to society and hence justifying their

---

print just as this book was going to press. Overall, if commends and expectative graces are excluded so that correlation with my own figures can be made, his study (pp. 54, 124) shows that John xxii's provisions to both major and minor benefices totaled 11,327 in France alone and 10,864 elsewhere in the world. Of the latter, my own study shows that a total of 782, or nearly one in every fourteen, were to benefices in England (below, Appendix 1, table D).

[3] Highfield, 'The Relations' i, 409; Clement vi's pontificate began in 1342 but this figure has been calculated only for the years following 1348. The total for all of his pontificate (1342-1352), which apparently marked the zenith of Avignonese provisions to English benefices, was between 1396 and 1610 (ibid., 406; below, Appendix 1, table A).

[4] Cf. above, p. 20 n. 16.

[5] Highfield, *History*, n.s. vol. xxxix (1954), 332.

[6] Guillemain, *La politique bénéficiale*, 129; below, Appendix 1, tables C and E.

[7] In this book I generally use the term 'collegiate churches' to include, for example, royal free chapels and nunneries with attached secular prebends.

payment in this way.[8] The residence of important canons either at the curia or with the king, moreover, could be a source of pride and indeed usefulness to an ecclesiastical chapter.[9]

The cathedrals receiving the largest numbers of provisions under both Clement v and John xxii were Salisbury, Lincoln, and York (as was true also under Benedict xii).[10] The secular cathedral receiving the smallest number of provisions under both popes was Exeter. The monastic cathedrals, of course, received no provisions to prebends as such, and the four Welsh cathedrals had no provisions under Clement and only eighteen total under John.[11] The comparative values of the various dignities and prebends in the English secular cathedrals undoubtedly influenced the frequency of provisions (York, Salisbury, and Lincoln being the most valuable and Hereford and Exeter the least),[12] but there was also definitely some correlation between the numbers of prebends in each and the numbers of provisions to each.[13] Clement made provisions in only four different collegiate churches and John in some thirty of them, the largest numbers under the latter pope going to Southwell, Beverley, Bosham, Ripon, and Howden, respectively. In the cathedrals, the largest number of provisions was of course made to canonries and prebends: of Clement's twenty-eight cathedral provisions only five were to archdeaconries and two to other dignities, and of John's 470 cathedral provisions only twenty-seven were to archdeaconries and eleven to other dignities.

Some provisions, also, were made to benefices other than dignities, canonries, and prebends of cathedral and collegiate churches.[14] Of Clement's sixty-nine provisions, some twenty were to parish churches, three to bishoprics, two to abbeys, three to priories, and eight to unspecified benefices in particular dioceses or in the gifts of particular bishops. Of John's 782 provisions, some 105 were to parish churches,[15]

[8] Edwards, *English Secular Cathedrals*, 83-96, 321-30; below, pp. 36-37, 94 seq., 164 seq.

[9] Davies, *Baronial Opposition*, 234-5; Reg. Halton, pp. xxxv-xxxvi; *Chapter Act Book of Beverley*, ed. Leach, i, 301, 338-9.

[10] Guillemain, *La politique bénéficiale*, 80.

[11] For further analysis of all Welsh provisions by John xxii, see Williams, *The Welsh Church*, 62, 76-7.

[12] Pantin, *The English Church in the Fourteenth Century*, 60, 62; Barraclough, *Papal Provisions*, 47; Driver, cQR cxlv (1947), 35; Greenaway, cQR clxii (1961), 34; Edwards, *English Secular Cathedrals*, 39-49, 74.

[13] Below, Appendix 1, table G.

[14] Below, Appendix 1, tables B, D.

[15] By comparison, the same pope made a total of 1303 provisions to parish churches in France (Caillet, *La papauté d'Avignon et l'église de France*, 172).

twenty to bishoprics, three to abbeys, five to priories, one to an unspecified benefice in gift of a bishop, and one to a hospital. (Of Benedict xii's seventy-eight, three went to bishoprics, three to abbeys, none to priories, and nine to minor benefices.)[16] Lincoln was the diocese to receive the largest number of provisions to parish churches under both popes, and York and Norwich dioceses received the next largest numbers under John xxii. By way of comparison it may be observed that in Ireland throughout the entire Avignon period from 1305 to 1378 there were no provisions to parish churches and only twenty-five to dignities, canonries, and prebends.[17]

[16] Guillemain, *La politique bénéficiale*, 79, 129.
[17] Flanagan, 'Papal provisions in Ireland', 100-1.

5

The Degree of Success of the
Provisors in Obtaining Their Benefices

If such were the raw numbers of provisions recorded in the papal registers between 1305 and 1334, one may wonder to what extent the provisors were successful in obtaining their provided benefices. Barraclough and others have gathered much evidence to show that if the ordinary collator refused to accept the papal provisor, the only certain right conveyed by even a direct provision was the privilege of the provisor to request one of the executors named in the bull – perhaps the one resident at the curia – to initiate the judicial process that could eventually lead to possession of the benefice. In this process the executors acted very much as judges delegate empowered to hear and decide the case between the ordinary collator and the provisor. They verified the terms of the bull, examined the personal qualities of the provisor, and heard any opposition. If the provisor could prove that the statements of fact in his provision, which were usually taken from the original petition, were complete and accurate, he then became the defendant and it next lay with the ordinary collator to adduce every lawful objection. If any of the objections carried the provision failed, although recourse could always be had to appeal and to another trial either locally or at the curia.[1]

There was, however, one sense in which most provisions at this time can be said to have taken effect more or less automatically – in that they conveyed a title if not a benefice. Of the 851 direct provisions between 1305 and 1334, there were 680 to dignities and canonries and prebends of cathedral and collegiate churches; and it must be noted that – at least in

---

[1] Barraclough, *Acta Congressus Iuridici Internationalis Romae 1934*, iii, 126-34, 151; Barraclough, *Papal Provisions*, 88, 93-4, 97-9, 137-8; Barraclough, *Public Notaries*, 29; Barraclough, *Zeitschrift der Savigny-Stiftung für Rechtsgeschichte* lviii (1938), 100-1; Flanagan, 'Papal provisions in Ireland', 93; Guillemain, *La politique bénéficiale*, 13; Tihon, *Bulletin de l'Institut historique belge de Rome* v, 81-3.

the style of the apostolic chancery – a person receiving provision of a
canonry of any given cathedral or collegiate church (whether he was at
the same time provided a vacant prebend or granted an expectation of a
prebend) became in title a canon of that place by the very fact of his
provision.[2] He was in effect an 'expectant' canon, and even though he
might be assigned a stall in choir he received no prebendal income and
had no right to attend chapter meetings. Such a canonry was in practice
not much more than an honorary title, whereas a prebend carried with it
the exclusive right to the income of a manor or landed estate customarily
having a name of its own.[3] Effective possession of a prebend in a certain
cathedral or collegiate church (whether provided when vacant or granted
by expectation when a canonry was provided) was often difficult to
obtain, and it might involve the provisor and the principal executor in
years of litigation in secular and ecclesiastical courts between the
nominees of pope, king, bishop, and any other principal who claimed the
right to collate.

Some further attention will be given to such disputes later, but it is
possible now to give an overall picture of the effectiveness of the papal
provisions. To consider first the total of sixty-nine registered provisions

[2] Boase, *Boniface VIII*, p. 101 n. 3; Edwards, *English Secular Cathedrals*, 34; Emden,
review of new volumes of Le Neve in *Medium Aevum* xxxii (1963), 97; Jenkins, 'Lichfield
Cathedral in the Fourteenth Century' i, 187. The customary form of provision of a
canonry with expectation of a prebend included the statement 'canonicatus ecclesie . .
cum plenitudine juris canonice apostolica tibi auctoritate conferimus et de illo eciam
providemus' (Fayen, *Lettres de Jean xxii* (Analecta Vaticano-Belgica ii), vol. i, p. xlv;
Guillemain, *La politique bénéficiale*, 26). In the petitions submitted to the pope for such
grants it was customary to request that he 'providere' the canonry and 'reservare' the
prebend (e.g., PRO 31/9/17a, f. 11v). In some local practice, however, it would seem that a
person provided to a canonry with expectation of a prebend might not be regarded as even
a canon by the local chapter until he had been formally admitted as such (*Chapter Act
Book of Beverley*, ed. Leach, i, 14; Bradshaw and Wordsworth, *Statutes of Lincoln
Cathedral* i, 281).

[3] For the varieties of prebendal income, see Thompson, *Associated Architectural
Societies' Reports and Papers* xxxiii (1915), 64-6. At Lincoln in the early fourteenth
century there seems to have been a waiting period of one month for canons expecting
prebends under papal provision after the time that a prebend was officially announced as
vacant, and Bishop Dalderby in 1317 found it necessary to ask that the dean and chapter
make such announcements openly in the presence of notaries: 'Cum nonnulli in dicta
ecclesia nostra sint recepti in canonicos, et in fratres et prebendas in eadem ecclesia sub
acceptacione facienda infra mensem a tempore noticie vacacionis earum auctoritate
apostolica expectantes, ne ipsi ignoranciam decetero pretendere valeant in hac parte vobis
iniungimus suadendo quatinus, in loco sollempni ecclesie nostre prefate in notariorum
presencia, vacaciones prebendarum in dicta nostra ecclesia cum contigerint ac
vacacionum earum tempora quamcito vobis constiterit de eisdem publicare et palam
proscribere non tardetis' (LAO, MS Reg. Dalderby III, f. 376).

made in England by Clement v, my research has found varied evidence about the fulfilment of forty-four of them and this evidence suggests that some thirty-three of the forty-four did or probably did receive their provided benefices while some eleven of the forty-four did not or probably did not.

A representative view of provisions under John xxii, moreover, can be obtained by using again the revised volumes of Le Neve as a check upon recorded[4] provisions to dignities and prebends in English cathedral churches alone – which account for 470 – just over 60 percent – of the total of 782 English provisions under that pope. But a caveat must first be entered as regards the value of the new volumes of Le Neve for this purpose, because their best use is a negative one. If a provisor is not listed at all in the new Le Neve, it will be assumed in this study that he did not receive his prebend. But if his name is printed in Le Neve under one particular prebend, such a listing may still indicate that he never obtained effective possession or that he was probably unsuccessful in litigation; or, on the other hand, it may indicate that he did obtain possession or that he was probably successful but with some question. Often the only available evidence in Le Neve is the provision and the bishop's mandate to admit; for our purposes this will be taken as indicating that the provisor did receive his prebend, although there is some evidence to suggest that under some types of episcopal mandates to admit less than fifty percent of the provisors even then were successful in finally obtaining possession.[5] But with these cautions we shall proceed to select the two cathedrals that received the greatest numbers of provisions under John xxii and to assess their effectiveness.[6]

At Lincoln,[7] of the seventy-three provisions to dignities (short of the episcopal), canonries, and prebends under Pope John that I have tabulated

---

[4] As has been suggested above, pp. 23-26, a small percentage of major provisions was not being recorded in the registers that have survived.

[5] Thompson, *Archaeological Journal* lxxiv (1917), p. 150 n. 1. Reg. Orleton Hereford, p. v, shows that even an episcopal mandate to install might not mean that the provisor was definitely installed in consequence. Edwards, *English Secular Cathedrals*, 34, says that even when such an 'expectant' canon was assigned a stall in choir, he might still receive no prebendal income and be excluded from chapter meetings. The revised volumes of Le Neve, however, often list, under specific named prebends, provisors about whom no further information is given than that episcopal mandates to admit were issued in their favour. Such entries certainly imply acceptance of the provisors' claims by the ordinary collators, who were normally the bishops who had issued the mandates to admit.

[6] Below, Appendix 1, table F.

[7] Cf. Cole, *Associated Architectural Societies' Reports and Papers* xxxiv (1918), 219-58.

from the papal registers, the names of twenty-one provisors do not appear at all in the revised volume of Le Neve, four more are shown by that volume never to have obtained effective possession, and another four probably to have been unsuccessful. But there is evidence in Le Neve to suggest that thirty-seven of the provisors did obtain possession and that a further seven were successful but with some question. Thus, at Lincoln, the effectiveness of the seventy-three provisions under John xxii was some forty-four affirmative and twenty-nine negative; that is, approximately, out of every five provisions three were successful and two were not.

At Salisbury, on the other hand, there was less success. Of the seventy-seven provisions there to dignities (short of the episcopal), canonries, and prebends under John, the names of forty provisors do not appear at all in the revised Le Neve,[8] two more never obtained effective possession, and another two were probably unsuccessful. But Le Neve's evidence suggests that thirty-one of the provisors did obtain possession, and that a further two were successful but with some question. At Salisbury, therefore, the effectiveness of the seventy-seven provisions under John xxii was some thirty-three affirmative and forty-four negative; that is, out of every seven provisions three were successful and four were not. It is interesting to note, moreover, a striking change of balance at Salisbury in the fifteenth year of John's pontificate: before that time the ratio of successful provisions was slightly weighted to the affirmative, but in 1330-1331 only one of eleven provisions was successful, the next year one of four, the next year one of nine, and the next three of nine.[9]

To summarize the effect at both Lincoln and Salisbury, therefore, it may be said that slightly over fifty percent of John's provisors were successful, or at least obtained episcopal mandates to admit. This may be compared with the success of the seventy-five percent of Clement's forty-four provisions for which evidence has been found. At Lincoln, five of

---

[8] An interesting case of failure to obtain a provided benefice is that of Johannes de Tarenta, 'iurisperitus', who was provided by John xxii to the canonry and prebend of Salisbury vacated at the apostolic see by the consecration of John de Ros to the see of Carlisle. Even though this provision was made by John xxii at the request of the Salisbury chapter itself, there is no mention at all of Tarenta in the new Le Neve volume for Salisbury, and the same volume (p. 68) states that Ros's prebend in fact went to someone else (cf. Reg. John xxii, no. 47915).

[9] The year 1330 marks the accession of the king's clerk Robert Wyvil to the see of Salisbury, which may account for some change of policy, although Bishop Martival had already made a strong complaint against papal provisions to Salisbury in 1327 (Pantin, *The English Church*, 70; above, p. 24 n. 33).

Clement's provisions succeeded and one failed; at Salisbury, it was two affirmative and two negative. Just as there was an increase in the raw numbers of provisions under Pope John, therefore, there was also a decrease in the measure of success attained by the provisors themselves.[10]

[10] *The Accounts rendered by Papal Collectors in England,* transcribed by Lunt and edited by Graves, record the payments of annates by holders of benefices that changed hands during a few years of the period under review, but they are not of much help in determining whether provisors obtained their provided benefices because they reveal only the benefice, and not the incumbent, that paid the annates, and in some cases the annates may have been paid in anticipation of obtaining a benefice that was never in fact obtained.

6

Who Were the Provisors and Their Sponsors?

What sort of persons were the recipients of direct provisions under Popes Clement and John? An estimate of the proportion of alien provisors to Englishmen at this time has been made by Dr. W. A. Pantin, which suggests that the number of aliens provided to English bishoprics and parish churches was minimal and that to cathedral and collegiate churches not excessive.[1] Moreover, an analysis of the cathedral chapter at Salisbury over the years 1329-1348 shows that the alien provisors there were frequently the king's clerks – a type of provisor that the crown encouraged when it suited its purpose.[2]

Often the papal registers give no description of the provisor beyond his name; and the rules of the apostolic chancery under John XXII excluded from papal bulls all mention of the person at whose instance the petition was granted, except in the cases of kings, queens, cardinals, and – under certain circumstances – bishops and abbots.[3] The supplications that produced these various papal documents did not begin to be registered until the pontificate of John's successor, and no trace of such registers of pleas survives until the pontificate of Clement VI, 1342-1352. But we can still make some observations for our period about the sponsors of

---

[1] *The English Church*, 56, 59-62. Under Benedict XII there were not more than twelve foreign provisors, and all of these were provided to canonries and prebends (Guillemain, *La politique bénéficiale*, 80). The number of foreign provisors at Salisbury 1329-1348 was very small (Chew, *Hemingby's Register*, 11-13). Later in the fourteenth century, at Lichfield cathedral, the number of foreign provisors decreased sharply (Jenkins, 'Lichfield Cathedral in the Fourteenth Century' i, 185-6, 190). For other estimates see Edwards, *English Secular Cathedrals*, 83-5. A tabulation of fifty-one admissions to canonries and prebends of York recorded in the register of Archbishop Melton shows twenty-six foreigners, but not all of these succeeded in gaining installation (VCH *Yorks*. iii, 378). An estimate of the number of foreign provisors holding French benefices in the time of John XXII suggests that there too the figure was relatively negligible (Caillet, *La papauté d'Avignon et l'église de France*, 305).

[2] Chew, *Hemingby's Register*, 12-13; Edwards, *English Secular Cathedrals*, 84-5.

[3] Ottenthal, *Regulae Cancellariae Apostolicae*, p. 1, rule 2.

provisions from the evidence that does survive. The papal registers of Clement and John do reveal that a very large proportion, much larger than in the final thirty years of the Avignon period, of their English provisions went to cardinals and to various agents of the pope and curia; and such provisors will be discussed more fully in a later chapter. Another class of persons who benefited from these provisions was royal officials, and the papal registers show that at least 176 of John's 782 provisions to English benefices were made at the request of the king (Edward II or III) or queen (Isabella or Philippa) to their own clerks, 'familiares', chaplains, secretaries, treasurers, confessors, almoners, and other ministers and servants. On the other hand, only five of Clement's sixty-nine provisions are described as made at the request of the king (Edward I or II) or queen (Isabella). And the crown made such requests not only on behalf of its own officials, for from sources outside the papal registers, for example, we can find Edward III asking Pope John to provide an English benefice for a foreign notary on the staff of the papal collector in England, on account of his extensive labours in the collection of the tenth and annates.[4]

Nor did the crown's influence over papal provisions stop at the English coast or even at the boundaries of its Gascon territories. Although continental provisions are not the subject of this study, it is nevertheless interesting to find in the Latin calendars of the papal registers, but seldom in the English calendar of Bliss, a number of provisions to benefices outside England, chiefly in France but not all in Gascony, made at the request of the English king or queen to their clerks.[5]

But there were other sponsors, and the papal registers disclose that some 105 provisions were granted by Clement and John to English benefices at the request of persons other than the king or queen of England. These included at least twenty-five provisions at the requests of seventeen various cardinals, twenty-nine provisions at the requests of twelve English diocesan bishops, twenty-seven at the requests of fourteen members of the lay nobility,[6] and thirteen at the requests of six foreign

---

[4] Lunt, *Accounts*, xxvi.

[5] E.g., Reg. John XXII, nos. 53938, 53998, 54000, 54961, 57036 (all at king's request); 10887, 18039, 20637, 22648, 24338, 29309, 30275 (all at queen's request). Also see Rymer II:i, 112, 213; II:ii, 796. For the extent of the crown's attempted ecclesiastical influence in Gascon dioceses and religious houses in 1315 and 1322-1323, see Brown, *Studies in Medieval and Renaissance History* viii (1971), 137, 154, 159-63. Caillet (*La papauté d'Avignon et l'église de France*, 297, 299) found a total of twenty-four Englishmen provided to French benefices under John XXII.

[6] In some cases John XXII's chancery rules had excluded the mention of lay nobility at whose requests the bulls were granted, but apparently not in these cases (Moé, *Bibliothèque de l'École des Chartes* xcii (1931), 269-70, 274-6).

kings and queens; and many of these provisors were probably in the service of the persons making the requests. The register of Andreas Sapiti, for example, a proctor who handled much English business at the curia at this time, reveals that late in the pontificate of John xxii and in that of Benedict xii, the king and queen, the earl of Lancaster, Bishop John Stratford of Winchester and later archbishop of Canterbury, Bishop Richard de Bury of Durham, and Bishop Roger Northburgh of Coventry and Lichfield all sent the pope rolls or lists petitioning provisions for their various ministers, clerks, and relatives.[7]

Yet there are still some 565 provisions, of the total 851 issued by Clement and John to English benefices, for which the names of the persons making the requests do not survive in the English calendars. Nor is there any evidence to suggest that the popes made any of these interventions upon their own initiative, apart from the instance of the parties. It would seem reasonable to conclude, then, that many – if not most – of these 565 provisors were in the service of persons who did in fact petition the pope for them, rather than to assume that these provisors were all of a status sufficiently high to enable them to tender the requests by themselves.[8] This assumption is strengthened by the fact that petitions for provisions at the request of influential persons survive with their names recorded in Sapiti's register which were subsequently granted and are found in the printed calendars of papal registers with no mention of the original petitioners.[9] Moreover, it must be pointed out that not all the recorded provisions went to different men. Clement's sixty-nine provisions went to fifty-five different men, twenty-three of the sixty-nine provisions being distributed (by two's and three's and four's) among nine different provisors.[10]

---

[7] PRO 31/9/17a. Northburgh once even petitioned the pope to provide a benefice in his own patronage to his own nephew (ibid., ff. 86v-87). The provision was granted and duly entered in the register of Benedict xii (CPL ii, 531). The influence of the crown, diocesan bishops, and lay magnates in the granting of provisions at Salisbury in the period 1329-1348 has been set forth in Chew, *Hemingby's Register*, 14.

[8] Jacob, TRHS, 4th series, vol. xxvii (1945), p. 43, underlines the greater probability of obtaining a provision if the potential provisor's name was submitted to the pope on the roll of some influential person or group. See also Barraclough, *Public Notaries*, 272-4; Watt, *Speculum* xxxiv (1959), 213. Gaignard, *Annales du Midi* lxxii (1960), 174, found that sixty-eight percent of all of Clement's bulls in the years 1311-1314 were issued in response to petitions.

[9] E.g., PRO 31/9/17a, ff. 6, 40v-41: the provision of the priory of Bath to Thomas Christi was at request of the bishop of Winchester, a fact not entered in Reg. John xxii, no. 57788 or CPL ii, 357. Similarly, f. 11v of PRO 31/9/17a (Sapiti's register) records further information not found in Reg. John xxii, no. 59762 and CPL ii, 373.

[10] For the sponsors of John xxii's provisors in France, see Caillet, *La papauté d'Avignon et l'église de France*, 351-65.

7

Provisions for University Graduates

What was the academic status of the persons receiving provisions to English benefices from Clement and John? The papacy, in using its influence for over a century to encourage the study of theology and the growth of schools, had become the friend of the university-trained clerk.[1] The practice under Clement is uncertain, although the desire of university clerks at this time for support from a plurality of benefices is underscored by the title of an Oxford *Quodlibet* dated about 1312: 'Utrum sit magis licitum magistro in theologia tenere plura beneficia quam alteri'.[2] John xxii in the first year of his pontificate was exceptionally generous in the granting of provisions to graduates of Oxford and Paris,[3] and by the same year Oxford definitely and Paris probably had begun the practice of sending the pope lists of graduates and scholars whom they recommended for provisions and reservations of benefices.[4]

The earliest suggestion in the papal registers of such a list from Oxford would seem to be the records of some fifty provisions and reservations to fellows of Merton and other Oxford graduates on 9 and 10 July 1317.[5] There is also specific evidence outside the papal registers that the pope

[1] Barraclough, *Papal Provisions*, 161; Pantin, *The English Church*, 16-17, 64-5; Watt, *Speculum* xxxiv (1959), 214.

[2] Boyle, *The Thomist* xxxviii (1974), 241.

[3] Murimuth, *Con. Chron.*, 26, records under the year 1317 that the pope 'multis magistris nominatis per universitatem Parisiensem et Oxoniensem gratias multas fecit'. On 13 Nov. 1316 John xxii wrote to all major ecclesiastics of the world urging them to provide masters and scholars of Paris to ecclesiastical benefices (Denifle and Chatelain, *Chartularium Universitatis Parisiensis*, vol. ii, pp. 184-5, no. 729). And again on 1 March 1316/1317, the same pope sent a secret letter to all major ecclesiastics 'ut ... in conferendis beneficiis ecclesiasticis magistros et studentes Parisienses commendatos habeant' (John xxii, Secret Letters, no. 131).

[4] For Paris, see Watt, *Speculum* xxxiv (1959), 214, 225.

[5] Reg. John xxii, no. 4326 seq.; cpl ii, 137, 143, 153-4, 157-60, 162-5; Emden, *Oxford*, vol. i, p. xxxvi; Pantin, *The English Church*, 50.

granted a number of provisions to Oxford men in response to a petition from the University as early as 1317-1318.[6] Information about four of these men is known, at least three of whom received papal reservations of benefices and at least one of whom definitely got the benefice reserved.[7]

A letter survives from the University of Oxford to John XXII circa 1322 urging that Oxford doctors in philosophy and theology receive papal promotion to ecclesiastical benefices as was already being done at Paris.[8] Seven further provisions to Oxford men on 23 November 1329 would suggest another list in that year; and a roll of Oxford masters submitted to the pope with royal support is suggested by a series of nineteen such reservations on 26 September 1331,[9] probably the last major occurrence of such grants under John XXII. The earliest discernible list from Cambridge would seem to have produced thirteen provisions and reservations on 7 October 1331,[10] although there is clear indication of papal provision to a group of Cambridge men with some sort of assistance from the English Dominican friar Nicholas Wisbech, at the pope's own initiative but without the crown's foreknowledge, as early as 1317.[11]

---

[6] Reg. Cobham, 36; Reg. Halton ii, 165-7.

[7] (1) *M. John de Braybrok, D.C.L.*, was granted papal reservation of a benefice valued at 50 marks in the gift of the abbot of Ramsey on 8 July 1317 (CPL ii, 154; Emden, *Oxford* i, 253), and the University commended him to the abbot for promotion circa 1317-1318 as having received the papal grace 'ad nostri instanciam'. The University asked the abbot to promote Braybrok out of reverence for the apostolic mandate and 'in augmentum profectus studii', but it is not certain that he received the benefice (cf. Salter, Pantin, and Richardson, *Formularies*, vol. i, pp. 32-3, no. 23).

(2) *M. John de Greyville, B.Th.*, was granted papal reservation of a benefice valued at 30 marks in the gift of the bishop of Carlisle on 10 July 1317 (CPL ii, 158; Emden, *Oxford* ii, 825), and the University commended him to the bishop for a benefice on 7 May 1318 as one who had been unanimously recommended by the University to John XXII for provision. He was admitted by the bishop as rector of Ousby (Cumb.) on 27 June 1318 (Reg. Halton ii, 165-7, 169; Emden, *Oxford* ii, 825).

(3) *M. Thomas de Cherminstre, B.C.L.*, was granted papal reservation of a benefice valued at 20 marks in the gift of the bishop of Worcester on 10 July 1317 (CPL ii, 143; Emden, *Oxford* i, 404-5), and the University commended him to the bishop on 21 Dec. 1319 as one who had been unanimously recommended to John XXII for provision. He was rector of Naunton (Glos.) by 19 May 1326 (Reg. Cobham, 36, 263).

(4) The fourth graduate recommended to the pope by the University was one 'Master I de K', about whom nothing further seems known (Salter, Pantin, and Richardson, *Formularies*, vol. i, p. 34, no. 24).

[8] BL MS Cott. Faustina A.v, ff. 2-2v; printed in Denifle and Chatelain, *Chartularium* ii, 269. The date is uncertain.

[9] Reg. John XXII, nos. 55116-34; CPL ii, 364-5; BL MS Cott. Vespasian E.xxi, ff. 94v-95; Emden, *Oxford* ii, 1002.

[10] CPL ii, 352-3; Emden, *Cambridge*, p. xxiv; cf. Cobban, BJRL xlvii (1964), 49-78.

[11] Vatican Archives, Reg. Vat. 109, f. 233v, John XXII to Edward II: 'Carissimo in Christo filio Eduardo regi Anglie illustri. Ut animi tui pacem adversus dilectum filium

But whatever may have been the success of these early petitions to John xxii for the promotion of university graduates, it would be a mistake to conclude that university men did not fare well in the years before the time that such petitions became customary. For the pontificate of Clement v, a check of names in Dr. Emden's biographical registers shows that at least twelve of Clement's sixty-nine provisions to English benefices went to five university masters – all of whom were Oxford men and one of whom was a doctor of civil law.[12]

The printed papal registers afford no evidence for the custom of university petitions under Clement v, perhaps only because apostolic chancery practice then – as under John xxii – may have excluded the mention of universities at whose requests petitions were granted. Nevertheless, the submission of such lists to the pope was undoubtedly an effective way to secure promotion for graduates that would commend itself to the universities and soon would become very much the way of the future. By 1335, shortly after the accession of Benedict xii, Oxford University was requesting that the pope would – after the usual custom – mark his election by a liberal grant of provisions 'sicuti solent in summorum pontificum novis creationibus emanare', and there seems no doubt that the University sent him a list of suitable names at that time which resulted in twenty-one more such grants.[13] The Oxford lists, which have been traced well by Dr. Emden in his biographical register, continued at frequent intervals throughout the fourteenth century.[14]

The crown's encouragement of university provisions, which has already been seen in 1331 and possibly earlier, had a further development under Benedict xii when the king and queen themselves petitioned the

---

fratrem Nicolaum Guischech' de ordine predicatorum per te pridem ad presenciam nostram missum assercione minus veridica fortasse turbatam placatam serenatamque reddat patefaccio veritatis, excellenciam regiam cupimus pro certo tenere quod idem frater Nicolaus beneficia illa que a nobis pro certis personis obtinuit non regio peciit nomine nec tanquam pro clericis regis impetravit. Set nos aliquibus bene meritis in studio Cantabrigiensis de gentibus providere volentes eidem fratri Nicolao suasimus ut nobis aliquas personas idoneas de ipso studio nominaret, ad cuius equidem nominacionem utique sinceram et fidelem ut credimus nonnullis considerata illorum sufficiencia certa duximus beneficia conferenda'. Cf. cpl. ii, 423; *Liber Epistolaris* of Richard de Bury, ed. Denholm-Young, nos. 182, 216, 240, 245-6, 258; Rymer II:i, 399, 424; below, p. 102.

[12] The five were: M. Walter de Chilton, M. Richard de Haverings, M. Thomas of Lugoure, D.C.L., M. Walter de Maidstone, and M. Thomas de Southwerke. None of Clement's provisors can be found in Emden, *Cambridge*.

[13] Salter, Pantin, and Richardson, *Formularies* i, 85-9; Emden, *Oxford*, vol. i, p. xxxvi n. 4; Jacob, trhs, 4th series, vol. xxvi (1945), 43-4; Fletcher, *OHS Collectanea, First Series*, 26-8.

[14] *Oxford*, vol. i, p. xxxvi.

pope through their proctor Andreas Sapiti for canonries and prebends in five English collegiate churches for five of their clerks 'studying at that time at Oxford'.[15]

By way of comparison, we may note that in Ireland throughout the entire Avignon period there were only two provisions of canonries and prebends (and none of parish churches) to university graduates.[16]

---

[15] PRO 31/9/17a, ff. 92v-93.
[16] Flanagan, 'Papal provisions in Ireland', 101.

8

The Large Numbers at the Outset
of Each Pontificate

It was a characteristic of the Avignonese popes that their first pontifical years generally saw the greatest total numbers of provisions. John XXII, for example, granted just under 3000 in his first.[1] In England too this practice prevailed under Popes Clement and John, the former providing to twenty-six English benefices in 1305-1306 and the latter to 121 in 1316-1317. By way of comparison, their successor Benedict XII made twenty-four of his seventy-eight English provisions during his first pontifical year.[2] The chronicler of St. Mary's abbey in York even remarked about the year 1306, 'Anno eodem Clemens papa concessit provisiones plurimas inscienter omnibus fere petentibus ... et omne quod vendi potuit per pecuniam; ideo inconstans semper fuit et erit in eternum'.[3]

The requests from Oxford may account for some slight increase on the registers in the first year of John XXII, and together with the graces *in forma pauperum* they may perhaps be considered as part of a policy of John at the outset of his pontificate to treat both poor clerks and scholars as a category deserving of special favour.[4] There are at least ten English provisors (as distinct from those receiving reservations) during John's first pontifical year whose academic titles recorded in the papal registers suggest that they may have been on a list of candidates from Oxford. But these university graces do not in themselves account for the larger numbers on the registers in the first pontifical years, and the graces *in forma pauperum* were not being entered on the registers at this time anyway, so we must look elsewhere for an explanation.

[1] Guillemain, *La Cour pontificale*, 105; cf. Caillet, *La papauté d'Avignon et l'église de France*, 54, 124.

[2] Below, Appendix 1, table A.

[3] *Chronicle of St. Mary's Abbey, York*, eds. Craster and Thornton, 40.

[4] Watt, *Speculum* xxxiv (1959), 216; Tihon, *Bulletin de l'Institut historique belge de Rome* v, 59-60, 63-5.

At least by the time of John XXII and Benedict XII there was a tradition that the Roman pontiff should celebrate his coronation by the granting of unusually large numbers of various graces then.[5] Moreover, during a vacancy of the holy see the granting of papal provisions and indeed of all papal documents *ad perpetuam rei memoriam* stopped; there are no papal *sede vacante* registers such as survive for many medieval bishoprics.[6] The papal throne had been vacant over sixteen months when Clement v was crowned on 14 November 1305 and over twenty-eight months when John XXII was crowned on 5 September 1316, and large numbers of vacant benefices under the wide definition of 'apud sedem apostolicam' were certain to have accumulated during the vacancies. Both Clement and (if *Ex debito* be assigned its traditional date of 1316) John followed the example of Boniface VIII's *Piae sollicitudinis* by issuing canonical legislation in their first pontifical years to state their own policies about the reservation and provision of benefices – a practice that came to be characteristic of most Avignon pontiffs.[7] Clement v's *Etsi in temporalium* possibly, and John XXII's *Ex debito* definitely, did away with the one month and immediate limitations of *Statutum* and *Si apostolica*, thus technically forbidding time to run against a new pope. Nevertheless, not all ordinary collators might agree that time was on the pope's side, and Clement and John would quite understandably have desired to fill as soon as possible the benefices vacated 'apud sedem apostolicam' since the deaths of their predecessors.[8] This motive probably accounts in large part for the greater numbers of provisions during the first years of their pontificates.[9]

Pope John, in fact, even made a large number of special reservations to particular benefices immediately after his election on 7 August 1316 and before his coronation on 5 September, fifteen of which were made to English benefices on 12 and 13 August. He had refused to attach his seal to any such documents before his coronation,[10] but shortly after it he

[5] An English petition presented by Andreas Sapiti to Benedict XII at the time of his coronation describes this as already a custom: 'Et quia sicut vosmetipse melius noscis Romani pontifices in nova creacione sua gracias petentes consueverunt prompte et favorabiliter exaudire, quorum mores et actus laudabilis iste dominus novus papa imitabitur ut speratur' (PRO 31/9/17a, f. 52; Vatican Library MS Barb. Lat. 2126, f. 178).

[6] Guillemain, *La Cour pontificale*, 108.

[7] Highfield, 'The Relations' i, 16; Lunt, *Papal Revenues* ii, 228-31.

[8] Cf. Guillemain, *La politique bénéficiale*, 141; Mollat, *La Collation*, p. 26 n. 15.

[9] The limitation of *Si apostolica* had probably caused an eagerness at the papal court to provide to all vacant benefices as a pope seemed to be approaching death (above, pp. 7-8).

[10] Baumgarten, *Von der apostolischen Kanzlei*, 483; Reg. John XXII, vol. i, p. v.

issued these grants officially as provisions and they were duly entered in his register.[11]

Furthermore, quite often petitions for many benefices for the household members of cardinals were presented to a pope at the beginning of his pontificate,[12] and he would also need to provide at this time for his own ministers and servants and 'familiares'. There is evidence in the names of those receiving provisions to English benefices during the initial years of Clement and John to suggest that such pressure to provide for curial officials of all sorts may also account for the unusually large numbers in their first years. Thus, of the twenty-six English provisions in Clement's first year, six went to papal chaplains, four to chaplains or nephews of the English cardinal Thomas Jorz, four to provisors having French names and four more to provisors having Italian names. Of the fifteen English provisions that had been reserved before John's coronation, two went to papal chaplains or nuncios, nine to clerks or relatives of Cardinal Napoleone Orsini, and four to clerks or relatives of three other cardinals. And of the remaining 106 English provisions during John's first year, twelve went to six different cardinals, three to papal chaplains, five to chaplains of four different cardinals, and eighteen more to provisors having Italian names and four more to those with French names.

Many of the remaining provisions are entered in the calendars of papal registers with no description of the provisor or indication of the person at whose request the provision was granted. Where such information is printed, it indicates that only three of the English provisions during Clement's first year were granted to clerks of Edward I at his request (and two more at the request of the prince of Wales), and that only two during John's first year went to clerks of Edward II at his request. We can not conclude, however, that the crown had no influence upon the larger numbers of provisions in the first pontifical years. The chronicler Adam Murimuth, who was at the curia during much of this time, seems to suggest a causal connection between the large numbers and the royal mission sent to Avignon in 1316-1317 to treat of various matters between the new pope and Edward II.[13] It is interesting to note that ten of the

---

[11] Reg. John XXII, nos. 37, 82, 134, 306, 427, 487, 560, 713, 744, 809, 811, 812, 814.

[12] Guillemain, *La Cour pontificale*, 267. John XXII granted thirty-seven provisions to various canonries and prebends on one day in his first pontifical year that were all made at the request of Cardinal Luca Fieschi of S. Maria in Via Lata for the cardinal's clerks, 'nepotes', 'familiares', kinsmen, chaplains, and physicians (Reg. John XXII, nos. 2139-77, all on 4 Dec. 1316). Of these provisions, two went to English benefices (nos. 2170-1).

[13] *Con. Chron.*, 26.

provisions during John's first year were granted at the request of a member of this mission, Aymer de Valence, earl of Pembroke, one of the lords ordainers and loyal ally of the king.[14] The ten were all issued in March of 1316/1317, nine of them on the same day.[15] The strongest influence of the crown upon papal provisions, however, as will be shown in a later chapter, did not come until the accession of Edward III.

[14] For refutation of the traditional view that there was a 'middle party' of which Valence was the leader, see Phillips, *Aymer de Valence*, viii, 135, 155, 270; but see also Maddicott, *Thomas of Lancaster*, 199, 208.

[15] Reg. John XXII, nos. 3209-10, 3213-14, 3217, 3219-20, 3224, 3233 (all on 19 March 1316/1317), no. 3147 (16 March).

9

Manipulation and Extension
of the Papal Provisory Power

Another way in which influential persons could manipulate the papal provisory power, in addition to tendering lists of petitions to the pope for their clerks and 'familiares', was by obtaining papal faculties to make provisions themselves or by securing faculties for others to make provisions on their behalf. A method probably surviving from the practice of earlier days when direct provisions were hardly known,[1] such faculties really served to extend the papal power by applying papal sanction to numerous areas of ecclesiastical appointment which the pope himself was less able to control from Avignon. Later in the fourteenth century the English crown gained such powers,[2] and the crown in France had already enjoyed them since the late thirteenth century.[3] In the first thirty years of the Avignon period, however, the papacy generally only delegated its provisory power in England to higher ecclesiastics – to nuncios and cardinals and bishops – although at times these provisory powers were delegated at the request of the king or queen and were certainly used to secure benefices for royal clerks. The provisions by apostolic authority that were made by virtue of these faculties were not, of course, entered in the papal registers because they were not direct papal grants themselves, but their papal origin and their frequency in the early fourteenth century and the fact that at least some of them did take effect all point to the existence of a secondary, rather extensive network of provisions only one step removed from the pope himself. One such faculty, to Archbishop Reynolds, will be examined in greater detail in the next chapter.

The power to provide to certain benefices was a customary clause in the commissions of cardinal legates and nuncios, although Boniface VIII had

---

[1] Mollat, *La Collation*, 48 seq.
[2] Pantin, *The English Church*, 51.
[3] Boase, *Boniface VIII*, 101; Caillet, *La papauté d'Avignon et l'église de France*, 401.

decreed that a legatine provision was to lapse if the benefice was not filled
before the legateship terminated.[4] When Cardinal Peter of Spain was sent
to England, Scotland, Ireland, and Wales by Clement v in 1306, he had
apostolic authority to provide to any vacant benefices with or without
cure, including dignities, that had devolved to the collation of the apostolic
see.[5] He also had power from Clement to provide to benefices vacated by
death or resignation of any of his or the pope's chaplains who were absent
from the curia in his company. The grant of this power tends to
substantiate the impression, mentioned earlier, that Clement in practice, if
not in his own canonical legislation, regarded the benefices of curial
officers as reserved even if not vacated 'apud sedem apostolicam'.[6]
Cardinal Peter also had a papal faculty to receive resignations and
facilitate permutations of benefices.[7]

The provisory powers of a later papal mission to England, that of
Cardinal Arnaud Nouvel of S. Prisca and Bishop (later Cardinal) Arnaud
d'Aux of Poitiers in 1312-1313, were more limited. Nouvel had a vague
faculty to bestow benefices and dignities on his clerks[8] and a faculty to
provide three English parish churches vacant at the apostolic see to clerks
nominated by Queen Isabella;[9] and they both had powers to effect
permutation of benefices.[10]

When John xxii sent Cardinals Gaucelme[11] de Jean and Luca Fieschi as
nuncios to England in 1317-1318, he gave them faculties to effect

---

[4] cic, Sext., lib. I, tit. xv, cap. 3 (Friedberg, vol. ii, col. 984); Boase, *Boniface VIII*, 103.
Innocent IV had decreed that legates who were not cardinals could not confer benefices
without special papal mandate (cic, Sext., lib. I, tit. xv, cap. 1; Friedberg, vol. ii, cols. 983-
4). With such authority, however, legates could definitely provide to benefices even by
way of expectation (Barraclough, *Public Notaries*, p. 168, no. 67). For a provisory faculty
granted to the legate Ottobon in England in 1265, see Lux, *Constitutionum Apostolicorum*,
16-17. On the fluidity of terminology in the use of the words 'legate' and 'nuncio' at this
time, see Mollat, *Revue d'histoire ecclésiastique* xlvi (1951), 566-74.
[5] Reg. Clem. v, no. 2246; cpi. ii, 31; Lux, *Constitutionum Apostolicorum*, 22.
[6] Reg. Clem. v, no. 2248; cpi. ii, 31; above, pp. 8-9.
[7] Reg. Clem. v, no. 2247.
[8] Reg. Clem. v, no. 8796; cpi. ii, 105.
[9] Reg. Clem. v, no. 8177; cpi. ii, 96; for the cardinal's use of this faculty, see Reg.
Clem. v, no. 9568. Much later, under John xxii in 1317, Cardinal Arnaud Nouvel again
had a faculty to exercise provisory powers in favour of Isabella's clerks (Reg. John xxii,
no. 3226; cpi. ii, 150).
[10] Reg. Clem. v, nos. 8817, 8825; cpi. ii, 106-7. By this time Clement (in the council of
Vienne) had regularized permutations by declaring the practice valid only as between
clerks who had resigned their benefices for the express purpose of exchanging them
reciprocally (cic, Clem., lib. III, tit. v, cap. 1; Friedberg, vol. ii, col. 1161).
[11] I accept the arguments for this spelling of the cardinal's name set forth by Bresslau,
Handbuch der Urkundenlehre, p. 256 n. 7.

permutations,[12] to provide benefices resigned into their hands,[13] and to provide benefices vacant by the deaths or resignations of their chaplains and clerks.[14] He also gave them power to provide to single benefices or canonries and prebends in Durham, Carlisle, the four Welsh dioceses, and several other dioceses in Scotland and Ireland.[15] They also had special faculties to provide clerks nominated by Queen Isabella to canonries and prebends in the cathedrals of Lichfield, Wells, Salisbury, Lincoln, Exeter, York, Hereford, and London, and in the collegiate churches of Beverley, Darlington, Crediton, Ripon, Bosham, Southwell, and Howden,[16] and also in certain benefices outside England.[17]

All these powers granted to nuncios strengthened the pope's own *plenitudo potestatis* in the field of reservations and provisions, increased the prestige and patronage of the nuncios and enabled them to provide for their own households, assured that benefices technically vacant 'apud sedem apostolicam' would be provided at least by the authority of apostolic representatives, enabled Queen Isabella to exercise influence and to provide for her clerks, and offered a method of exchanging benefices by apostolic authority without the necessity of a trip to the curia itself.

In a limited way, moreover, many other cardinals shared in the papal provisory powers. More than fifteen additional cardinals were granted papal faculties during the years 1305-1334 to provide specific English benefices, sometimes vacant by resignation into their hands, sometimes vacant at the apostolic see, and sometimes vacant in other ways, to persons of their choice or to persons named by the pope.[18] Some of these

---

[12] Reg. John xxii, nos. 5164, 10138; cpl. ii, 130. An example of the use of this faculty is in cul. ms Ee.v.31, f. 192: consent of prior and chapter of Christ Church Canterbury to permutation of benefices (one of which, St. Dunstan by the Tower, London, was in their patronage) effected by resignation into hands of Cardinal Luca and provision by him under authority of a papal grace: 27 June 1318.

[13] Reg. John xxii, nos. 5208, 10139, 10140; cpl. ii, 129.

[14] Reg. John xxii, nos. 5158, 10137; cpl. ii, 128. Cardinal Luca, for example, provided by apostolic faculty the canonry of Salisbury and prebend of Grimston vacant by death of his chaplain, 'commensalis', and 'consanguineus' Gabriel de Canville, to his 'nepos' Innocenzo Fieschi (Reg. John xxii, nos. 9383, 9398, 16820; cpl. ii, 186). It does not seem that Innocenzo ever got possession of the prebend (Le Neve, *Salisbury*, 57).

[15] Reg. John xxii, no. 5152; cpl. ii, 128.

[16] Reg. John xxii, nos. 3137, 8453; cpl. ii, 146, 183.

[17] Reg. John xxii, nos. 3133, 8085; cpl. ii, 145, 172.

[18] For such faculties from Clement, see cpl. ii, 33-4, 49, 58, 61, 67-8, 73-4, 80, 82, 87, 95, 98; from Pope John: Reg. John xxii, nos. 2262, 3680, 3858, 9328, 10899, 42235, 43350, 45367, 48664, 62781, and cpl. ii, 150, 188, 197, 279, 295, 316, 406. See also Barraclough, *Public Notaries*, 158-60. Sometimes, the pope himself would provide a benefice resigned into a cardinal's hands – as he did for the priory of Bath in 1332 (Reg. John xxii, no. 57788; cpl. ii, 357; pro 31/9/17a, ff. 6, 40v-41).

faculties were issued to facilitate permutations of benefices, some to
terminate cases at the Roman court involving benefices, and still others
were papal mandates to provide. Thus Clement in 1309 empowered his
'nepos' Cardinal Raymond de Got to provide anyone of his choice to the
canonry and prebend of Southwell vacant by resignation of the papal
chaplain M. John of Ferrara, who was also a chamberlain of that cardinal.[19] And John XXII in 1328 empowered Cardinal Giovanni Gaetani
Orsini to receive from Francesco Gaetani – who was about to get married
– his resignation of the treasurership of York and prebends of Lincoln and
Salisbury and of other benefices on the continent, and to confer them
upon persons of his choice.[20] William Testa, as papal representative in
England even before his promotion to the cardinalate, held and used a
provisory faculty from Clement V to effect permutations of the benefices
of his clerks.[21]

Individual English bishops also were delegated various provisory
powers by apostolic authority. They included the more common kinds,
such as permutations,[22] mandates to assign,[23] and provisions of benefices
resigned into their hands.[24] And there were also less usual faculties, such
as to appoint any suitable person as prior of Winchester[25] or as prior of
Durham,[26] to provide persons nominated by Queen Isabella as canons in
certain cathedrals of Canterbury province,[27] to receive the resignations of
Queen Isabella's clerks and to provide their benefices to other persons

---

[19] Reg. Clem. V, no. 3749; CPL. ii, 49.

[20] Reg. John XXII, no. 43350; Le Neve, *Salisbury*, 73.

[21] Reg. Gandavo, 439-44.

[22] E.g., Reg. John XXII, no. 16298; CPL. ii, 225.

[23] E.g., Reg. John XXII, no. 47260; CPL. ii, 152, 172, 178, 310. The mandate to assign
was a power often also delegated to ecclesiastics below episcopal rank, but it probably had
less legal status than a direct provision. Cf. Barraclough, *Acta Congressus Iuridici
Internationalis Romae 1934*, iii, 135 seq.; Barraclough, *Papal Provisions*, p. 104 n. 2; CPL.
ii, 152; above, pp. 16-17.

[24] E.g., Reg. Clem. V, nos. 10089, 10150; CPL. ii, 119, 121.

[25] Reg. John XXII, no. 41156; CPL. ii, 274; addressed to the bishop of Winchester.

[26] Reg. John XXII, no. 9422; CPL. ii, 187; addressed to the bishop of Durham. A similar
faculty had been held by the previous bishop from Clement V.

[27] Reg. Clem. V, no. 3069; CPL. ii, 45; Reg. London, 108; addressed to the archbishop of
Canterbury and the bishop of London. For the use of this faculty, see CCW, 356. For
another similar faculty in favour of Queen Isabella, and its use, see CCW, 347-8, 353, 383.
Clement V had also granted a faculty (not found in Bliss's English calendar) to the bishop
of Evreux and two English abbots to provide clerks nominated by Queen Margaret in
canonries and prebends of York, London, Chichester, Salisbury, Hereford, Lichfield, and
Rouen, and this faculty was still operative in 1307 (CCW, 263; Deputy Keeper, *Seventh
Report*, app. ii, p. 249; Browne, *Maidstone*, 66).

named by her,[28] to provide persons named by Prince Edward to single benefices in the gifts of six religious houses,[29] and to provide benefices in gift of the abbot of St. Mary's, York, to two clerks named by the earl of Richmond.[30] A continental parallel to these faculties was the powers given by Clement v to bishops of France and Sicily to provide to canonries and other benefices there at the nomination of their respective rulers.[31]

But by far the most common provisory power delegated to English diocesan bishops in these years was the faculty to provide persons of their own choice to benefices normally of their own patronage, some of which had become technically vacant at the apostolic see and others of which were expected to become vacant elsewhere in the normal course of things. Such grants can be found in the papal registers over the years 1305-1334 to the bishops of Ely, Exeter, Hereford, Lincoln, London, Norwich, Worcester, and to the archbishops of Canterbury and York.[32] These faculties probably reflect the desire of diocesan bishops to retain at least some of their patronage even at the expense of first surrendering it to the pope, as well as a willingness of the pope to delegate some of his *plenaria dispositio* once his theoretical position was secure. This same desire and this same willingness will be shown in a later chapter on the attitudes of English bishops and of the pope towards English benefices vacated by the constitution *Execrabilis*.

A few instances of these faculties to English bishops to provide to benefices of their own patronage are worthy of special mention. Bishop John Ketton of Ely in 1313 received from Clement v the reversion of the collation of the archdeaconry of Ely, which was normally in his collation but which had been reserved to the pope and was currently held by Cardinal William Testa. The right to provide the archdeaconry was to go to the bishop upon the death or resignation of the cardinal even if such occurred 'apud sedem apostolicam'.[33] Archbishop Melton of York in 1328 received a faculty from John xxii that enabled him, among other things, to provide persons of his choice to canonries and prebends of York,

[28] Reg. John xxii, no. 3141; cpi. ii, 44, 54, 97, 149.

[29] pro SC7/10/28; Cant. Cath. ms S.V. i, 144; Rymer I:ii, 980; addressed to the bishop of London and the abbots of Westminster and St. Albans. The bull is not in the Latin calendar of Clement's register.

[30] Reg. Clem. v, no. 4138; cpi. ii, 56; rwr, 31; addressed to Walter Reynolds as bishop of Worcester.

[31] Lux, *Constitutionum Apostolicorum*, 21.

[32] cpi. ii, 17, 29, 30, 53, 116, 166-7, 219, 262, 268, 326; Reg. John xxii, nos. 5822, 5825, 29284-6, 29305, 30990, 53199, 55156, 55961-2.

[33] Reg. Clem. v, no. 9781; cpi. ii, 116.

Southwell, Beverley, and Ripon, which were in his gift; he had received similar faculties in 1317, and his predecessor Greenfield had had two similar faculties from Clement v in 1306 and 1307.[34] Another interesting case can be seen at Exeter, the English secular cathedral with the smallest number of prebends. In 1331 Bishop Grandisson of Exeter complained to the pope that the numerous provisions in his cathedral, which was comparatively small in its complement of canonries and prebends, were keeping him from making provisions there in his own right;[35] and in the same year 'in consideration of the small number of canonries and prebends of his church' Grandisson received from John xxii a faculty to provide two canonries and prebends in his own cathedral to persons of his choice notwithstanding any papal or legatine provisions of them. About that time he received two more similar faculties.[36] When John Stratford was translated to Canterbury in 1333-1334, he petitioned the pope for an indult to provide all benefices in his diocese that had become vacant 'apud sedem apostolicam' before his translation, but it is doubtful whether his request was granted.[37]

A parallel to these faculties to English bishops to provide to benefices of their own patronage was the indult of Clement v that the deaneries of York and Lincoln, held by Cardinal Raymond de Got, should (at the cardinal's own request) revert to the disposal of their respective chapters when vacated by the cardinal's death or resignation even at the apostolic see.[38] Likewise Clement decreed that the benefices in England, Wales, Scotland, and Ireland of the English cardinal Thomas Jorz held by him *in commendam* up to the value of 1000 marks, should revert to their normal collators upon his death or resignation and not be subject to papal provision.[39]

---

[34] Reg. John xxii, nos. 5822, 5825, 30990; cpl. ii, 17, 29, 166-7, 268.

[35] Pantin, *The English Church*, 116, 151. Grandisson may have been overstating his case, however, for in the four years since his consecration (1327-1331) he had in fact already made at least seven appointments in his own right to prebends of Exeter (Le Neve, *Exeter*, 27-8).

[36] Reg. John xxii, nos. 55156, 55961-2; cpl. ii, 354-5.

[37] pro 31/9/17a, ff. 82-82v. I cannot locate any such grant in cpl. Richard de Haverings, papal chaplain and archbishop-elect of Dublin, did secure a faculty like it from Clement v in 1308 (Reg. Clem. v, no. 3190; cpl. ii, 46).

[38] Reg. Clem. v, nos. 2630-1, 6329-30; cpl. ii, 38, 78. The cardinal did in fact die at the apostolic see.

[39] Reg. Clem. v, no. 3558; cpl. ii, 48; Reg. Gandavo, 263-7. This is the closest similarity I have found in the registers of Popes Clement and John to the type of 'block' provision that was later used by Clement vi to grant one person an indefinite number of unspecified benefices within a definite geographical area up to a designated value (e.g., cpl. iii, 74).

The studies of Gaignard[40] have shown the wide range in which Clement granted such various provisory faculties throughout the world in the years 1311-1314 – he granted 149 to bishops, 103 to cardinals, fourteen to abbots, twelve to papal chaplains – and it is a fact that such powers mark a widespread extension of the apostolic authority in provisions.

[40] *Annales du Midi* lxxii (1960), 175.

10

Archbishop Reynolds and Provisions

The share enjoyed by local ordinaries of the early fourteenth century in the pope's *plenaria dispositio* can be analyzed at considerable depth by an examination of the total effect of papal provisions upon the primate of all England, Walter Reynolds. For the truth is, at least in the case of Reynolds, that there was a fair balance between the diminution of his rights of collation under papal provisions and the increase of powers that he enjoyed from the same system.

First, we must ask, how did provisions intrude upon Reynolds' ordinary rights of collation? There are only two indirect provisions to Reynolds' patronage recorded in his Lambeth register: one expectative grace *in forma pauperum* [1] and one expectative *in forma speciali*, both of which he accepted and acted upon. The outcome of the former grant is not known, but in the case of the latter the collation reverted to Reynolds after the death of the provisor. [2]

There are only five direct provisions to Reynolds' patronage noted in his Lambeth register. Two of these are benefices vacated by the provision at the curia on 13 February 1324/1325 of M. John de Ros, D.C.L., papal chaplain and auditor of causes of the apostolic palace, to the see of Carlisle, and in both of these Reynolds' rights of patronage were challenged by Pope John because Ros had been provided at the Roman court. These benefices were the parish church of Bishopsbourne (Kent), which Reynolds collated to M. Robert de Redeswell, his chancellor, and a

---

[1] Above, p. 21 n. 22.

[2] Grace of a benefice valued at £20 with or without cure in Canterbury diocese and in the gift of the archbishop, granted by John xxii on 7 Sept. 1316 to Andrew Foel of Teignmouth (Devon.), clerk of Exeter diocese and clerk of Cardinal Bernard de Garves of S. Agatha (Reg. John xxii, no. 298; cpl ii, 123). The benefice was granted at the request of the cardinal, who had been seeking promotion for Foel from Reynolds as early as 1314 (rr f. 34v). Reynolds in obedience collated Foel to the church of Wittersham (Kent) on 12 March 1316/1317 (rr f. 19), but there was no further provision after Foel's death (rr f. 27v).

canonry and prebend of Wingham, which Reynolds collated to M. Robert de Norton, dean of the arches. They were not collated by Reynolds until 23 January 1325/1326, nearly a year after they were vacated by Ros, but they were also both provided by John xxii, also by reason of the promotion of Ros, on dates contemporary with or subsequent to the date of Reynolds' collations.[3] The scribal notations 'salvo iure domini pape' beside each of the collations of these benefices in the margin of Reynolds' register suggest that the archbishop accepted the pope's right to provide.[4]

The next two direct papal provisions to Reynolds' patronage mentioned in his Lambeth register were both made to the archdeaconry of Canterbury in a rather complex case. M. John de Bruyton, the nominee in 1323 of both Reynolds and the crown (he was Reynolds' chancellor and a king's clerk), lost the archdeaconry in litigation during the same year to the papal provisor Raymond de Roux, cardinal of S. Maria in Cosmedin.[5] The previous archdeacon, a papal chaplain, had died in Paris, and Pope John claimed the right to provide by virtue of the general reservation by Clement v of all benefices of papal chaplains dying anywhere.[6] There is no evidence that Reynolds resisted the papal provision, even though there was a royal prohibition that he should not disturb Bruyton. After Cardinal Raymond died in 1325, the pope again provided the archdeaconry, this time to M. Hugh of Angoulême, and Reynolds again acquiesced.[7]

Only one papal provision resulting from *Execrabilis* is mentioned in Reynolds' register, and it is the fifth and final instance recorded therein of a direct provision that challenged his patronage. On 22 January 1317/1318 John xxii provided to Cardinal William Testa the church of Shoreham (Kent) in Reynolds' immediate jurisdiction and patronage, vacant by resignation at the curia of Vitalis de Testa, the cardinal's 'nepos', under force of the pope's new constitution. Reynolds accepted the provision and admitted the cardinal by proctor on 10 July 1318.[8] After the

[3] The former was provided to M. John Lutterel, the latter to Queen Isabella's clerk Arnold of Vernolio (Reg. John xxii, nos. 24248, 26604; cpl. ii, 248, 254).

[4] rr f. 257v; cf. Cant. Cath. ms Reg. L, f. 145v. Lutterel was described as rector of Bishopsbourne in 1327 (rr f. 200), and the pope provided it again in 1335 when it was vacated by Lutterel's death (cpl ii, 524).

[5] Smith, *Episcopal Appointments and Patronage in the Reign of Edward ii*, 76, 78; Le Neve, *Mon. So. Prov.*, 7; Churchill, *Canterbury Administration* i, 46-7; rr ff. 130v, 250, 254v, 307v; ccr 1323-7, 129; cpl ii, 229, 452, 456, 459, 461; pro SC7/56/14; hmc Ninth Rep., I, app., 72; Reg. John xxii, no. 17222; below, p. 90.

[6] Above, pp. 8-9.

[7] rr f. 147v. The date of Reynolds' mandate to admit Hugh is 14 March 1325/1326 and not 13 March as stated in Le Neve, *Mon. So. Prov.*, 7.

[8] Reg. John xxii, no. 6214; cpl ii, 169; rr f. 23v; below, Appendix 3, no. 41.

cardinal's death, however, Pope John once again provided Shoreham, now vacant at the apostolic see, back to Vitalis. This provision, which was on 19 January 1326/1327 and in the last year of Reynolds' life, was entered in the papal register but cannot be traced in Reynolds' Lambeth register.[9] Shoreham, valued at £53.6s.8d. in the *Taxatio* of 1291,[10] was a desirable benefice, and it is interesting to find that Vitalis himself had earlier been collated to this church by William Testa sometime in the period 20 April 1306 – 15 February 1307/1308 while the future cardinal was papal administrator of the see of Canterbury during the suspension of Archbishop Winchelsey.[11]

Of both direct and indirect provisions to benefices of Reynolds' patronage specifically mentioned in his Lambeth register, therefore, the total is only seven instances. In the calendars of papal registers there are only eight further instances (including the provision of Shoreham back to Vitalis) of direct provisions to benefices in his patronage, all by John XXII.

One of these eight was, again, the archdeaconry of Canterbury, vacated earlier by resignation at the apostolic see and provided in 1319.[12] Although it was technically in his patronage, Reynolds never successfully named an archdeacon of Canterbury. The post was held in his time by four provisors, who were often nonresident and each of whom had – apparently in addition to his official[13] – a 'proctor and vicar-general'[14] to make presentations to benefices in the archdeacon's gift and to handle

---

[9] Reg. John XXII, no. 27599; CPL ii, 255.

[10] *Taxatio Eccl.*, 7; this value is the same as that reported by the papal collector d'Assier (Lunt, *Accounts*, 10).

[11] CPL ii, 69; below, Appendix 3, no. 41.

[12] Reg. John XXII, no. 9363; CPL ii, 186.

[13] Churchill, *Canterbury Administration* i, 30, and ii, 229, gives a list of the archdeacons' officials at this time. The list of archdeacons is found in Le Neve, *Mon. So. Prov.*, 6-7.

[14] The following served the archdeacons in the office of proctor and vicar-general during Reynolds' archiepiscopate:

Name:	Dates acting:	RR ff.:
M. Peter de Talar'	20 March 1316/1317, 15 May 1317	19v, 20.
Adamar de Faya (or Feya)	5 March 1319/1320; 22 May, 10 July, 8 Oct., 24 Dec. 1320	25v, 26, 27, 96, 96v.
M. William Arnaldi	28 May, 11 Aug. 1322	30, 31.
Peter Laurencii	19 Nov. 1324	254v.
Aycius de Clarencio	14 March 1325/1326	147v.

M. Peter Arnaldi de Talar' was appointed on 7 July 1315, according to a notarial instrument certifying his appointment and specifying the limits of his authority as printed in Reg. Martival ii, 42-5. He was still serving as proctor of the archdeacon on 4 Dec. 1318 (CCW, 494-5; M. Pieres de Taler).

other matters including custody of the seal, register, rolls, and other muniments.[15]

In addition to the provision to Wingham mentioned above which is indicated in Reynolds' register, the papal registers record only two more direct provisions in Reynolds' time to the two collegiate foundations under the archbishop's patronage, Wingham and South Malling. Both of these were made in John XXII's first pontifical year; the calendared papal registers do not record the grounds upon which they were made, and there is no satisfactory information as to their outcome.[16] Reynolds himself, on the other hand, was able to exercise his patronage at Wingham and South Malling on certain occasions, at times by collations to members of his own household.[17] Even in John XXII's first pontifical year when provisions of the early fourteenth century were at their zenith in England, Reynolds successfully collated the provostship of Wingham to his crucifer and attorney, Walter de Kemeseye.[18]

Another provision to a benefice of Reynolds' immediate jurisdiction vacated by force of *Execrabilis*, in addition to the curious case of Shoreham, was the rectory of St. Vedast, London. The papal registers show that this was provided in 1322, but the provision is not mentioned in Reynolds' register.[19]

The final three of the eight benefices provided in Reynolds' patronage and recorded in the calendars of papal registers but not in his Lambeth register were all parish churches in Canterbury diocese vacated at the apostolic see by episcopal consecrations and provided by John XXII. Hollingbourne (Kent) and Boxley (Kent) were both vacated by the provision and consecration at Avignon of M. Thomas Cobham, D.Th., to the see of Worcester; the former was provided to the pope's 'nepos' Cardinal Gaucelme de Jean, who was at the time a nuncio in England, and the latter to Cardinal Vidal du Four.[20] And the very valuable parish church of Maidstone (Kent), taxed at £106.13s.4d. in 1291,[21] vacant in 1326 by the consecration of Guy de la Valle to the see of Le Mans, was

---

[15] Reynolds did make at least one presentation to a benefice in the archdeacon's gift during a vacancy of the archdeaconry (RR f. 258v).

[16] Reg. John XXII, nos. 3236, 3266; CPL ii, 146, 153.

[17] E.g., his chancellor M. John de Bruyton to Wingham (RR f. 26v), his 'consanguineus' Ralph de Windsor to South Malling (RR ff. 30, 200v, 250). For other collations at Wingham and South Malling see RR f. 259v.

[18] RR f. 19; VCH *Kent* ii, 235; for payment of annates see Lunt, *Accounts*, 1.

[19] Reg. John XXII, no. 15260; CPL ii, 222; Reg. Cobham, 107.

[20] Reg. John XXII, nos. 3614, 4492; CPL ii, 147, 156; below, Appendix 3, nos. 12, 17.

[21] *Taxatio Eccl.*, 3.

successfully provided to Theobald de la Valle.[22] There is no evidence in Reynolds' register or in the calendared papal registers to suggest that Reynolds resisted any of these three provisions, although his successor Archbishop Melton was later suspended from office by John XXII for refusing to admit the provisor Cardinal Annibaldo Gaetani da Ceccano to the rectory of Maidstone after it had been vacated by the death of Theobald.[23]

The total number of papal provisions intruding upon Reynolds' patronage as archbishop of Canterbury, therefore, was probably not much greater than the fifteen cases mentioned above. Only the Canterbury archdeaconry was permanently lost to his collation. He retained effective control of the vacancies at Wingham and South Malling. *Execrabilis* resulted in only two provisions to benefices of his patronage and in fact, as will be shown below,[24] netted him several fresh vacancies for his own collation. Moreover, the vast majority of the parish churches of his patronage still remained open to his own nominations. His Lambeth register records over the years of his archiepiscopate, 1314-1327, no less than 198 collations by him, of benefices in his own gift for various reasons, that were entirely free of papal provisions. The evidence from Canterbury in the time of Reynolds, therefore, does not allow us to concur with Barraclough that 'in the fourteenth century, papal provision was the normal means of access to a benefice'.[25]

Innocent IV in 1246 had granted a privilege to the archbishop of Canterbury, at his own request, that no provision would be made to any benefice in archiepiscopal patronage unless the apostolic letters made express mention of the privilege itself.[26] There is no evidence that Reynolds ever reminded Clement V or John XXII of this privilege, nor do the calendars of their registers make any note of it when recording their provisions to benefices of his patronage. Indeed, there is no information as to whether he or they were even aware of it, but it is a fact that provisions by the pope caused very little diminution of Archbishop Reynolds'

---

[22] Reg. John XXII, no. 24828; CPL ii, 250; below, pp. 238-9; below, Appendix 3, no. 5.

[23] Emden *Oxford* ii, 1261; Reg. John XXII, nos. 42873, 46697; CPL ii, 282, 299.

[24] Below, Part I, chapter 12.

[25] Barraclough, *Papal Provisions*, 106.

[26] Lambeth MS 1212, pp. 270-1 (ff. 139-139v): 'tuis precibus inclinati, quod nulli possit de ecclesiis vel beneficiis ad collacionem tuam spectantibus auctoritate litterarum sedis apostolice provideri expressam non faciencium de hac indulgencia mencionem' (10 Sept. 1246); not in Potthast but cf. CPL i, 226. The bishop of Coventry and Lichfield had obtained a similar privilege on 5 March 1245/1246 (*Magnum Registrum Album*, ed. Savage, no. 449).

ordinary rights of patronage. The system probably disturbed him only slightly more than the fact that Edward II was using the doctrine that time does not run against the king to present royal nominees to benefices in Reynolds' collation, such as the Canterbury archdeaconry, months and even years after Reynolds had assumed the temporalities of the see.[27]

On the other hand, Reynolds gained much from the system of provisions. Although he was not the pope's original candidate for the vacancy at Worcester,[28] yet his technical appointment to that see in February of 1307/1308 was by provision of Clement v.[29] Again, in the only English (as apart from Welsh) episcopal translation during the reign of Edward II, he was provided to Canterbury by Clement in October of 1313 at the request of Edward II in spite of the election of Cobham by the monks of Christ Church. He was the king's candidate for both these vacancies, yet he owed both appointments to papal provision. Canterbury would not have been his without the pope's exercise of *plenaria dispositio*, even though Clement himself may have favoured Cobham or even the infamous former royal treasurer Walter Langton, bishop of Coventry and Lichfield.[30]

Reynolds while at Canterbury also influenced the pope to grant at least two direct provisions to English benefices not in his own patronage, both of which were entered in the papal registers as being made at his request.[31] One of these was a canonry and prebend of Hereford to M. Adam Murimuth, D.C.L., his clerk and 'familiaris' and proctor at the Roman curia. In addition, as archbishop he was often named among the executors of papal provisions.

Reynolds also enjoyed a rather extensive increase of his own power from the same system as a result of the papacy's frequent delegation of provisory faculties in the early fourteenth century. On 13 January 1313/1314, not long after his translation to Canterbury, Clement v granted Reynolds a bull – probably at his own request[32] – empowering him to

---

[27] CPR 1313-17, 168; CPR 1321-4, 280.

[28] Smith, *Episcopal Appointments*, 11-12.

[29] Reg. Clem. v, no. 2464; CPL ii, 34; Richardson, *Speculum* xxiii (1948), 631-2; Ullmann, JEH vi (1955), 36.

[30] Richardson, EHR lvi (1941), 97-103; Denton, *Journal of Medieval History* i (1975), 323.

[31] Reg. John XXII, nos. 1207, 7970; CPL ii, 123, 181.

[32] There is no definite evidence that the bull was granted at his request, but this is probable because: (1) at least seven other papal faculties were granted to Reynolds at his own request at the outset of his archiepiscopate (RR ff. 50v, 196, 211, 211v, 212, 212v); and (2) the popes at this time did not generally grant such faculties except at the request of

'provide'[33] one suitable person to a canonry and prebend of every cathedral and collegiate church of Canterbury province, even if this resulted in plurality of benefices with cure. Faculties of a similar magnitude were held during the period 1305-1334 by Cardinals Gaucelme and Luca,[34] by Archbishop Winchelsey,[35] in the northern province by Archbishops Greenfield and Melton,[36] and in the province of Dublin by Archbishop-elect Haverings.[37] There is some evidence in Greenfield's register of his use of one such provisory faculty,[38] and a few such instances survive for the pontificate of Winchelsey.[39] The evidence of Reynolds' register, however, affords an exceptionally good opportunity, probably better than any other English source of this period, to observe the scope and application of such a faculty. It records exactly thirty provisions that he made by virtue of this bull, twelve to secular cathedrals and eighteen to collegiate churches. These provisions formed the principal source of his patronage at the outset of his archiepiscopate, and it is interesting to discover that at least twenty-two of the thirty were made to clerks who in various ways can be said to have been members of his own household. No less than twelve of the twenty-two had recently moved together with the new primate to Canterbury from his service at Worcester. Only one of the twenty-two, the notary who drew up the very documents of provision for Reynolds, had previously been in the service of Winchelsey.[40] Let us now follow the course of these provisions.

The earliest recorded attempt of Reynolds to use the bull, his provision of his clerk Ralph de Stokes to a canonry and prebend of St. Paul's London on 7 May 1314, seems to have been unsuccessful[41] – even though

the would-be recipient, and it was probably a custom for the Canterbury archbishops to request such faculties at the outset of their archiepiscopates. Abp. Stratford, for example, in 1333-1334 requested just such a provisory faculty from John xxii (PRO 31/9/17a, ff. 81v-82; for Archbishop Mepham, see HMC Ninth Rep., I, app., 74).

[33] RR f. 47v; Reg. Clem. v, no. 10157; CPL ii, 121; Reg. Swinfield, 519-20; Wilkins ii, 440; 'providendi ... concedimus facultatem'. On the uses of the verb 'providere', see above, p. 5 n. 1.

[34] Above, p. 49 nn. 15 and 16.

[35] Reg. Winchelsey, 22, 31-2, 38; RR f. 108v; above, p. 50 n. 27.

[36] Above, p. 52 n. 34.

[37] Reg. Clem. v, no. 3187; CPL ii, 46.

[38] Reg. Greenfield i, 112-14, 131; iv, 46. Greenfield, being extra diocesim, commissioned his vicar-general to make the provisions for him.

[39] Above, n. 35.

[40] Geoffrey de Brampton. RR ff. 47v, 49; Charles and Emanuel, Cal. Hereford Muniments, vol. ii, pp. 748-9, no. 3155; Reg. Winchelsey, index.

[41] RR f. 47v. Stokes is not found in Le Neve, St. Paul's London, nor in the printed contemporary London episcopal register, nor in the related contemporary MS WD1 (Liber

Reynolds proclaimed a reservation if no prebend was vacant and even though he threatened the dean and canons with major excommunication, the chapter with suspension, the church of St. Paul's with interdict, and the bishop of London with suspension from entry of the church and from pontifical office and, after thirty-six more days, with major excommunication. A feature of Reynolds' provision that paralleled the provisions of the pope himself was the appointment of certain executors to direct the course of the provision; we do not know their names but we do know that Reynolds counted upon them, because he threatened them also with major excommunication if they did not comply.

But Reynolds' failure to secure a place at St. Paul's for Stokes did not dissuade him from further use of the bull, for on 12 May and 11 June of 1314 his register records that he made twenty-nine further provisions to canonries and prebends of cathedral and collegiate churches throughout the province.[42] Most of these provisors can be shown to have been in his service in one way or another. In the English cathedrals, M. Adam Murimuth, D.C.L., Reynolds' proctor at the curia, was appointed to a canonry and prebend of Bath and Wells, M. Richard de Stanhoe, a member of Reynolds' council, to the same at Chichester, M. Thomas Charlton at Coventry and Lichfield, M. Benedict de Paston, an auditor of the archbishop's court, at Exeter, M. William de Knapton, D.Cn.&C.L., one of the archbishop's important clerks, at Hereford, M. William de Birston, Reynolds' chancellor, at Lincoln, and M. Gilbert Middleton, Reynolds' official and a member of his council, at Salisbury.

There were protests over these provisions from some quarters, notably from the bishops of Lincoln[43] and Salisbury,[44] but Reynolds eventually subdued these by various threats and notarial instruments and private letters a latere. He reminded Bishops Dalderby and Gandavo of the benefits to their churches that Birston and Middleton could bring, because each of them was a clerk who 'ipsam ecclesiam in suis indigenciis noverit relevare'. Alongside most of the names of the provisors to English cathedrals in Reynolds' register it is recorded that the clerks were admitted, and the revised volumes of Le Neve confirm that every one of

---

A) in St. Paul's Cathedral Library. On 15 June 1315 Reynolds again wrote the bishop of London on behalf of Stokes (RR f. 65).

[42] RR ff. 48-9.

[43] RR ff. 48, 123v, 125v.

[44] Reg. Gandavo, 501-7; Reg. Martival i, 4-5. Middleton was persuaded to renounce his provision to Salisbury, but then on the same day he accepted collation to the prebend of Netheravon there by Bishop Gandavo himself.

these seven clerks did in time come to hold positions in these respective cathedrals.[45]

In Wales, Reynolds provided M. Stephen de Haslingfield at Llandaff, M. Richard de Staynton at St. Asaph, and Roger Northburgh at St. David's. At Bangor too a provisor was appointed, but he died soon after nomination and his name is not given in Reynolds' register. The revised Le Neve volume for Wales suggests that the provision of Northburgh was successful. Le Neve gives no information as to the outcome of the provisions at Llandaff and St. Asaph, although in both cases Reynolds' register records that they were admitted.

Of the eighteen collegiate provisions,[46] Reynolds named no less than fifteen of his household:

> John de Windsor, his clerk, at Bosham (Sussex)
> Walter de Kemeseye, his crucifer and attorney, at Bromyard (Heref.)
> William Drax, his treasurer, at Chulmleigh (Devon.)
> M. Roland de Acre, his physician, at Crediton (Devon.)
> Richard of Newcastle, his clerk, at Gnosall (Staffs.)
> M. Robert de Norton, a member of Reynolds' council and an auditor of his court, at Llanddewibrefi (Cards.)
> William Airmyn, his clerk, at Romsey (Hants)
> M. Simon Moene, D.M., another of his physicians, at St. Crantock (Corn.)
> Geoffrey de Brampton, his notary and 'commensalis', at St. Endellion (Corn.)
> William de Notley, his 'commensalis' and crucifer, at St. Probus (Corn.)
> Ralph de Windsor, his 'consanguineus', at Shaftesbury (Dorset)
> M. Thomas de Teffont, a member of the archbishop's council and proctor general of his court, at Westbury-on-Trym (Glos.)
> M. Geoffrey de Eyton, his clerk, at Wherwell (Hants)
> John de Ringwood, another treasurer of Reynolds, at Wilton (Wilts.)
> Robert Ambroys, his clerk, at St. Mary's, Winchester (Hants)

[45] For a straightforward process of admission of one of Reynolds' provisors, see Reg. Swinfield, 513-14.

[46] My information about collegiate churches in general comes from Thompson, *Archaeological Journal* lxxiv (1917), 139-239; Cook, *English Collegiate Churches in the Middle Ages*, and Denton, *English Royal Free Chapels 1100-1300*.

He also made provisions at Derby (Derby.), Penkridge (Staffs.), and St. Teath (Corn.). It is significant that Reynolds apparently did not use the papal faculty to provide men at either of the two collegiate churches that were already in his own patronage, Wingham and South Malling.

The success of the collegiate provisions is not so easy to establish because of the absence, in most cases, of lists comparable to those for cathedrals in the new volumes of Le Neve. Reynolds' register, however, suggests that his collegiate provisions raised a number of interesting questions in the face of episcopal, royal, lay, and monastic patronage.

One clash with episcopal patronage, in the collegiate church of Bosham, which was a royal free chapel in the peculiar jurisdiction of the bishop of Exeter, revealed Reynolds' own attitude towards provisions and his enthusiasm for the mutual advantages that the papal faculty afforded. On 12 May 1314 he provided John de Windsor at Bosham, and Reynolds' register records that Windsor was admitted on condition that a provision in the said church came within the limits of Reynolds' apostolic indult.[47] The background to this conditional admission was undoubtedly a letter from Bishop Walter Stapledon of Exeter telling Reynolds that he was perplexed at the provision and requesting a delay.[48] Reynolds in his reply rebuked Stapledon sternly and pointed out that the other suffragans of the province had not rebelled in that way. Stapledon's perplexity and complaint, it seems, came from the fact that Reynolds had provided men in not one but several churches of Stapledon's patronage. Reynolds, however, went on to stress that his intention was not to limit Stapledon's own grace from the apostolic see, but rather 'to esteem the more that same grace which is itself limiting, and which – if you rightly regard it – can be changed with a joyful mind into a large and grand opportunity and advantage'.[49] Stapledon may have been persuaded by this reasoning, for his register shows him admitting another of Reynold's provisors, the physician Simon Moene, to a canonry and prebend of the collegiate

[47] RR f. 48v.

[48] RR f. 108v. This letter does not survive in the printed calendar of Stapledon's register, although there is a letter, written in April probably of 1315, in which Stapledon explains that he is unable to confer a certain vacant prebend of Bosham upon a certain clerk because 'nostre Piere Esperital, le ArceEvesque de Cantelburie, permy privilege q'il ad de la Curt de Rome, ad fet une reservacion de la precheyne Provende vacante en la dite Esglise de Boseham pour un de ses clierks' (Reg. Stapledon, 101).

[49] RR f. 108v. In addition to canonries of Exeter and Bosham (the latter was situated in Chichester diocese), Reynolds had named provisors to six collegiate churches within the boundaries of Exeter diocese. For Stapledon's acceptance of Reynolds' provision of Benedict de Paston to Exeter cathedral itself, see Reg. Stapledon, 213.

church of St. Crantock in May of 1316.[50] In another collegiate church, that of Westbury, a possible clash with episcopal patronage was probably avoided by Reynolds' clever decision to name a man who was not only his clerk but at the same time a clerk of the church's patron, Bishop Maidstone of Worcester, and Maidstone proceeded to send this name to the dean of Westbury for the next vacant prebend.[51]

The notes that accompany these provisions in Reynolds' register also suggest possible conflicts with royal and lay patronage in some cases. The collegiate church of All Saints, Derby, the registrar noted, was a royal free chapel with nominations to its canonries made by the dean of Lincoln, and this may have posed a difficulty.[52] At the royal free chapel of Penkridge, although the archbishop of Dublin was the normal patron, the king had the right to provide to the prebends during vacancies in the see of Dublin – and that see was vacant from 10 August 1313 to 20 August 1317.[53] The collegiate churches of Chulmleigh and St. Endellion were portionary and largely in the gift of lay patrons, the families of Courtenay and Bodrigan, respectively.[54] The churches of St. Probus and St. Teath were also portionary.

In monastic patronage, in the prebends attached to the Benedictine nunneries of Shaftesbury and Wilton, Reynolds' provisors were admitted but with some reservations.[55] In still another case, the nunnery of Wherwell, Reynolds eventually decided to write to the king for secular aid against certain persons who were occupying by lay force the prebend of Middleton that he had provided.[56] In two more nunneries, Romsey and St. Mary's, Winchester, Reynolds' provisions are known to have been successful.[57]

---

[50] Reg. Stapledon, 250.

[51] Haines, *Administration*, pp. 92 (cf. n. 1), 213 (cf. n. 2); Wilkins, *Westbury College*, 64.

[52] RR f. 49.

[53] Powicke and Fryde, *Handbook of British Chronology*, 336; VCH *Staffs*. iii, 298-303.

[54] One of the three portions of St. Endellion was in the gift of the prior and convent of Bodmin.

[55] The final outcome of the provision to Shaftesbury is not certain. It was made originally to Ralph de Windsor on 12 May 1314 (RR f. 48). Reynolds again wrote Windsor on 10 March 1314/1315 collating and providing him to the prebend of Gillingham in the church of Shaftesbury vacant by death of Henry de Bluntesdon (RR f. 61v), and on the same day he issued a mandate to the prior of Bath to assign, admit, and induct Windsor (RR f. 15). But by 8 Nov. 1316 Windsor had resigned the prebend, on 17 Dec. 1316 Reynolds revoked the 'process and censure' about the matter, and by 7 Jan. 1316/1317 Reynolds had withdrawn his claim to provide it under apostolic authority (Reg. Martival i, 65-72).

[56] RR f. 272v.

[57] RR ff. 48v, 225; Reg. Martival i, 74, 229.

Nevertheless, in spite of the difficulties encountered in some individual cases, Reynolds' provisions under the apostolic faculty on the whole had a large measure of success – certainly in all of the cathedral provisions and in a majority of the collegiate ones. In three bold strokes on 7 May, 12 May, and 11 June of 1314, just a few months after his translation to Canterbury, Reynolds had used the papal prerogative to provide positions of prestige and solid financial remuneration throughout the province for thirty clerks, at least twenty-two of whom were members of his own household in various capacities. By contrast, there is evidence of only one provision made by Winchelsey under the similar faculty that he had received from Celestine v in 1294.[58] Under Reynolds the papal provisory faculty was employed positively to give a new strength to archiepiscopal patronage. Reynolds showed that he was not afraid to back up his provisions by covering letters, stern rebukes, ecclesiastical censures, and invocation of the secular arm, when necessary; and, like the pope, he used the services of executors to bring about the success of his own provisions.[59]

Moreover, the 'archbishop's option', a long-standing custom whereby the archbishop of Canterbury after confirming the election of each of his provincial suffragans could nominate one suitable clerk for promotion to a canonry and prebend in that bishop's cathedral,[60] was all but superseded under Reynolds by the stronger and wider basis of the provisory faculty. Neither Winchelsey nor Reynolds had been able to use the 'option' with

[58] Reg. Winchelsey, 31. The Celestinian faculty may, however, have been among those cancelled by Boniface viii (Boase, *Boniface viii*, 55-6). I can find no other mention of its use in Winchelsey's register.

[59] RR f. 47v; Reg. Martival i, 74.

[60] If there was no vacancy in the cathedral at the time, or if the cathedral was monastic rather than secular, the clerk was to be provided with a competent benefice in the bishop's patronage and/or a pension until a vacancy occurred. Churchill, *Canterbury Administration* i, 350, explains the 'option' and quotes from Lambeth MS *Registrum Album* to show that this privilege came to the archbishop immediately after confirming an episcopal election. Cant. Cath. MS Reg. G (a mid-fourteenth-century treatise on the powers of the archbishop), f. 1v, also explains the option in the same way, but on f. 12v it indicates that this right came to the archbishop immediately after he had performed the actual consecration of the new bishop. Cf. Bradshaw and Wordsworth, *Statutes of Lincoln Cathedral*, vol. ii, pp. cxlii-cxliii; Haines, *Administration*, p. 95 n. 3. That the right devolved to the archbishop only after he had consecrated the new bishop seems perhaps less likely in our time, as Archbishop Reynolds once attempted by this privilege to nominate a clerk to a new bishop whom he had not consecrated (Reg. Orleton Hereford, 14-15). Compliance with the archbishop's option was not stipulated as an obligation in contemporary episcopal profession oaths at Canterbury (Cant. Cath. MS Reg. A, circa f. 245; Cant. Cath. MS Reg. B, ff. 420-421; BL MS Cott. Galba E.iv, f. 25).

much success – there is record of only two attempts, probably unsuccessful, by Reynolds to use it;[61] and the 'option' at best applied only to cathedrals (not collegiate churches), was often resisted, and could be used only when there was a change in the episcopate. Reynolds undoubtedly saw that the provisory faculty could extend the number of major positions in his patronage far beyond the number of episcopal vacancies that might happen to occur during his time, and he also perhaps realized in 1314 that the age of provisions was at hand – an age in which almost any appointment he made would carry additional weight if he could say that he did it by the pope's authority.

Clearly, therefore, Archbishop Reynolds gained as much patronage – gained more in fact – from the papal system of provisions than any diminution of his ordinary rights of collation. He did not fight the system, but rather he regarded it – as he said to Stapledon – as something which could be changed by a joyful mind into a large and grand opportunity and advantage. The possibilities of papal provisory faculties were such in the early fourteenth century that no bishop or archbishop could afford to overlook them. Hitherto they have received little detailed attention from historians, but the total effect of the system of papal provisions can not be adequately assessed apart from them.

---

[61] (1) Shortly after he moved to Canterbury, Reynolds, describing the option as a 'pious and laudable custom from time immemorial', nominated his clerk Hugh Bordel to David ap Blethyn, whom he had consecrated bishop of St. Asaph on 12 Jan. 1314/1315. Blethyn refused to comply, and on 22 Feb. 1314/1315 Reynolds commanded the official of the bishop of London to warn Blethyn to promote Bordel within eight days or be suspended from entry of church (RR f. 53).

(2) On 6 Aug. 1317 Reynolds nominated Thomas de Eytone, a king's clerk, for a benefice or pension from Adam Orleton because he had recently been made bishop of Hereford (Reg. Orleton Hereford, 14-15). There is no other evidence about Eytone in Orleton's register.

For the attempts of Abp. Winchelsey to use the option, see Cant. Cath. MS Cart. Ant. A193a; Cant. Cath. MS Reg. G, f. 12v; HMC Fifth Rep., app., 446; Literae Cantuarienses no. 40; Wilkins ii, 406; Reg. Winchelsey, pp. xxii and 1185-6.

11

The Constitution *Ex debito*

Five of the fifteen papal provisions mentioned in the last chapter as affecting Archbishop Reynolds' patronage were made during John XXII's first pontifical year, but none of them needs to be attributed to the bull *Ex debito* even if it was issued in that year. One of the five was an expectative grace *in forma speciali*, an indirect provision granted to a cardinal's clerk at the request of the same cardinal, and is merely indicative of the habit of cardinals to seek papal promotion for men in their service at the outset of a new pontificate.[1] Two more of the five were direct provisions to parish churches vacated by episcopal consecration at the apostolic see, and it has been shown that this type of provision was already being made under Clement V.[2] The other two, provisions of canonries with expectations of prebends, have no designation in the printed papal registers to reveal upon what grounds they were provided.[3]

These facts about the provisions of benefices in Reynolds' patronage during the year 1316-1317 now lead us to question whether *Ex debito* itself was really responsible for any significant increase in the numbers of papal provisions to English benefices. John XXII was crowned on 5 September 1316, and *Ex debito* may have been issued on 15 September of that year, some time between 5 September 1320 and 5 September 1321, or at some date after 1325. The tentative evidence advanced by Professor Kuttner to question the date of this bull, as well as its dating 'anno quinto' in another manuscript, has already been set forth. The largest number of English provisions during John's pontificate came within his first pontifical year, but it has already been shown that this number can and probably should be attributed to a variety of factors other than *Ex debito* – to the requests from Oxford, the tradition of large numbers in the

---

[1] Above, pp. 45 and 54 n. 2.
[2] Above, pp. 8-9, 57-58.
[3] Above, pp. 56-57.

first year, the long twenty-eight-month vacancy of the throne of Peter, and the petitions from cardinals and from Aymer de Valence.[4] Moreover, the numbers of provisions throughout John xxii's pontificate never again reached the peak of the first year, and it is not as though great new categories of benefices were opened in 1316 that would enable provisions to remain at a constant high level throughout the pontificate. Indeed, the number of John's provisions to England in his last full pontifical year, forty-nine, was only forty percent of the record 121 in his first year. Furthermore, if it be true that 'a host of petitioners seeking ecclesiastical preferment' went to the papal court during John xxii's first pontifical year, they were certainly not attracted there by the opportunities afforded by *Ex debito*, as has been suggested,[5] but rather probably by the prospects of benefices *in forma pauperum*.[6]

It is true that *Ex debito* codified and clarified the papal provisory legislation, but it is doubtful whether *Ex debito* introduced any new principle into English provisions that was not already being followed in practice. It has already been shown that much of the papal provisory legislation was couched in terminology that left unanswered many questions of interpretation, and that all of it fell under the sweeping general preamble of *Licet ecclesiarum*. Most of the terms clearly specified in *Ex debito* could have been read into *Etsi in temporalium* of 1305 and many of them can be found in practice under Clement v.[7]

Moreover, the printed calendars of papal registers more often than not are silent as to why the pope is making a particular provision.[8] Of the 851 direct provisions over the years 1305-1334, 521 of the 680 provisions to dignities or canonries with expectations of prebends are undesignated, i.e., the reasons for provision are not given and no previous incumbent or particular prebend is specified. Only 159 of the 680 are designated. On the other hand, all but thirteen of the remaining 171 provisions out of the total of 851 are designated, and it is probable that in these the popes had particular vacancies in mind that fell clearly within the canons already established. But in a majority of the provisions to cathedral and collegiate positions the popes seem to have made provisions, usually in response to requests, yet without any reference to actual vacancies reserved to them for particular reasons. Indeed, when the crown petitioned John xxii for cathedral provisions through Andreas Sapiti it often listed as many as

---

[4] Above, p. 43 seq.
[5] Greenaway, cqr clxii (1961), 39.
[6] Above, pp. 20-22.
[7] Above, pp. 8-10; cf. Caillet, *La papauté d'Avignon et l'église de France*, 59, 109.
[8] Below, Appendix 1, tables B, D.

three different cathedrals to any one of which a provision of canonry with expectation of a prebend would be acceptable.[9] Clearly the pope was expected to, and did in fact, operate under no canon more specific than the preamble of *Licet ecclesiarum* for the vast majority of his provisions. For example, ninety-seven of John's 109 cathedral and collegiate provisions during his first pontifical year have no designation at all in the papal registers that would indicate a particular vacancy or explain the specific basis of provision. *Ex debito* – whenever it was issued – undoubtedly clarified the special reservation of a number of categories of benefices, but the bulk of John xxii's provisions in England were made outside its categories.

Let us turn, however, to provisions that did fall within these categories. In a valuable pioneer article Miss Ann Deeley has already discussed some interesting examples of English provisions under some of the categories of reservations clarified in *Ex debito*,[10] but her procedure and conclusions must be questioned. She has noted some of the specific categories of reservations clarified in *Ex debito* and then has proceeded to look for provisions of John xxii that would fit these categories and allow her to conclude that he was working within them. Interesting as such cases may be, her method does not prove any causal relationship between the two, and further examination of the evidence indicates that (1) examples of the same principles of reservation can at times be found already among the provisions of Clement v several years before the publication of *Ex debito*, and (2) the primary innovation that she ascribes to *Ex debito* – dispensation with the qualification 'apud sedem apostolicam' for the provision of benefices vacated by bishops – was in fact a principle already used on occasion by Clement v and yet, on the other hand, not always used by John xxii.

The two main principles of reservation clarified in *Ex debito* for which Miss Deeley cites examples among the provisions of John xxii are that lapse of time could not run against the pope and that the pope could provide benefices vacated by bishops not consecrated at the apostolic see. Let us consider the first principle, lapse of time. It has already been shown that *Etsi in temporalium* of 1305 may have been intended to abolish the time limitations of *Statutum* and *Si apostolica*,[11] and there is some evidence that even Benedict xi held the principle that time could not run against him – in a provision to Lincoln cathedral in 1304 which was

[9] PRO 31/9/17a, e.g. ff. 59v, 72.
[10] EHR xliii (1928), 245-6.
[11] Above, pp. 8-9.

accepted by Bishop Dalderby.[12] There is another case – the chancellorship of Salisbury – in which Clement v continued to support his candidate over a vacancy of at least two years in spite of the bishop's collation to someone else apparently on the grounds that Clement had failed to provide within the one month limit.[13] There is evidence, moreover, to show that John XXII himself – even before the possible issue date of 15 September 1316 for *Ex debito* – was conferring vacant benefices as though lapse of time could not run against him.[14]

The second principle of reservation clarified in *Ex debito* for which Miss Deeley cites examples among the provisions of John XXII, dispensation with the qualification 'apud sedem apostolicam' for the provision of benefices vacated by bishops, was also probably not an innovation with, nor an invariable principle after, the possible issue date of 15 September 1316. In the calendars of Clement v's registers there is only one case of any English benefice directly provided by the pope after being vacated by consecration of an English bishop either at the apostolic see or elsewhere,[15] and this one case is insufficient evidence from which to draw a conclusion as to what Clement's practice really was. John XXII indeed provided some benefices of some bishops consecrated at Avignon and of some consecrated elsewhere; but the papal registers do not allow us to conclude that he provided all of the benefices vacated in either of such instances, and there is positive evidence in some cases that he did not.[16] Moreover, if the pope after the possible issue date of 15 September 1316 had an automatic right (understood by him as an innovation upon or clarification of the general authority he had always had since the preamble of *Licet ecclesiarum* in 1265) to provide all benefices vacated by provided

[12] Cole, *Associated Architectural Societies' Reports and Papers* xxxiv (1918), 245-6.

[13] The pope's candidate was his kinsman, a boy of thirteen, Pontius de Varesio, who carried the case to the Roman court but died before a decision was given. Papal surrogation was then made to Tydo de Varesio, probably the brother of Pontius. Bishop Gandavo collated the chancellorship to William de Bosco. It seems that Tydo was not successful. For the documents see Reg. Clem. v, nos. 91, 7443-4; Le Neve, *Salisbury*, 17. For the family of Varesio, see Reg. Clem. v, year 1, p. 12 n. 3; Chew, *Hemingby's Register*, 242-3; Jenkins, 'Lichfield Cathedral' ii, app. F.

[14] Lux, *Constitutionum Apostolicorum*, 24.

[15] The case is a benefice vacated by the promotion of Greenfield to York (Reg. Clem. v, no. 268; CPL. ii, 4). Miss Deeley (EHR xliii (1928), 500) says there were six such papal grants, but she gives no evidence for them and she probably means to include reservations.

[16] For benefices of Cobham (who was consecrated at Avignon) vacated upon his promotion but not provided, see e.g. Le Neve, *Hereford*, 39; Le Neve, *Nor. Prov.*, 10, 48. For the same of Newport (consecrated at Canterbury), see Le Neve, *St. Paul's London*, 11. For the same of Gravesend, see ibid., 68. Other examples could be added.

bishops no matter where they were consecrated, there would have been no need for him to make additional special reservations of such benefices, which he often did.[17] Furthermore, there is no trace in the papal registers of provision of the benefices, for example, of Bishops Hotham of Ely, Newport of London, Beaumont of Durham,[18] and Gravesend of London, to name a few, who were all consecrated 'extra curiam' after *Ex debito*'s possible issue date of 15 September 1316.

The great increase in the number of bishops' benefices provided by John XXII over the number provided by Clement V, which Miss Deeley has ascribed to *Ex debito*'s omission of the qualification 'apud sedem apostolicam' for such vacancies,[19] therefore, seems really due to a number of other factors that characterized John XXII's pontificate as a whole. These include the systematization of provisions under a lawyer who was perhaps the cleverest pope of the Avignon period, the greater total numbers of episcopal consecrations and provisions during John's time, the increase of consecrations at the papal court, and the greater length of John's pontificate − it was more than twice as long as Clement's.

These are the factors that must account for the increase, in the face of proof that the most outstanding principles of reservation clarified by *Ex debito* were already practiced by Clement V and that the principles of *Ex debito* itself were only variably followed by John XXII, and in view of the uncertainties about the date of the bull itself. *Ex debito*, whenever it was issued, was a skilful codification of provisory canons and practice and it forms part of the total picture of John XXII's policies on ecclesiastical appointments, but in itself it probably introduced nothing that Clement V could not or did not do. In itself it was not responsible for any significant increase in the numbers of papal provisions to England, and in this respect historians[20] are hardly justified in describing it as 'epoch-making'.

---

[17] E.g., Reg. John XXII, nos. 14936, 19380, 50190, 61468. It would seem that English bishops of the early fourteenth century generally did vacate their benefices upon consecration, although certainly some Irish and continental bishops at this time were permitted to retain benefices. E.g., CPL. ii, 26; Reg. Clem. V, no. 1764; Reg. Woodlock, 332-4; Reg. John XXII, no. 58660. Reynolds himself was permitted to retain his benefices for two years after his provision to Worcester (Reg. Clem. V, nos. 4014-15; CPL. ii, 52).

[18] CPL. ii, 401, the only evidence cited by Miss Deeley (EHR xliii (1928), p. 501 n. 1) of a benefice vacated by Beaumont upon consecration and provided by the pope, is not actually a provision but rather a papal judicial decision made some fifteen years after the benefice had been vacated. Beaumont in fact resigned all his benefices by proxy into the pope's hands ten days after he was provided in February of 1316/1317 (Burns, AHP ix (1971), no. 93).

[19] EHR xliii (1928), 500. Her figures seem to include reservations as well as direct provisions.

[20] Chew, *Hemingby's Register*, 9; Mollat, *Revue d'histoire ecclésiastique* lix (1964), 167.

12

The Constitution *Execrabilis*

Execrabilis (19 November 1317),[1] on the other hand, brought an immediate increase in the numbers of provisions to English benefices, although in the long run it too did not really create any extensive new source of provisions. It did, however, provide an opportunity for collective action by the English episcopal hierarchy, and the rather brief treatment accorded to *Execrabilis* by Miss Deeley[2] will be revised and considerably expanded along these lines in the pages that follow.

The thirteenth century had seen manifold legislation against pluralism.[3] Clement v in his constitution *Si plures*[4] had made a gesture towards the curbing of pluralists who held no dispensations, but this seems to have had little effect in England and the papal registers of the early fourteenth century abound with numerous dispensations for plurality granted at the request of such influential persons as cardinals or the crown or individual

---

[1] The text of *Execrabilis* has survived in at least five English MSS of the early fourteenth century: Lambeth MS 171, f. 127v; Cambridge, Corpus Christi College MS 450, pp. 301-6; Reg. Halton ii, 156; *Liber Epistolaris* of Richard de Bury, ed. Denholm-Young, no. 178; and Durham, Dean and Chapter Muniments, Locellus I, 38, as reported by Lunt, *Financial Relations* i, 495 n. 8. The last three instances are noted from printed sources, and in none of them is the text of the bull given. In Reg. Halton the bull is dated '13 Kal. Nov.' (= 20 Oct.) 1317, whereas the other four have the common date of 13 Kal. Dec. (= 19 Nov.) 1317. The date of '13 Kal. Nov.' in Reg. Halton, noted as different by the editor, may be a scribal error for 13 Kal. Dec. *Execrabilis* was also entered in one quire that is now missing from the register of Bishop Martival of Salisbury, together with a certificate of benefices vacated by it and a letter entitled 'Supplicatoria domino pape pro ecclesia Anglicana' (Reg. Martival ii, 11).

[2] EHR xliii (1928), 503-4.

[3] For canon law on pluralism and discussion of the developments prior to *Execrabilis*, see Churchill, *Canterbury Administration* i, 113-16; Haines, *Administration*, 193; P&C ii, 1435 (index); Douie, *Archbishop Pecham*, 98-111; Powicke, *Thirteenth Century*, p. 474 n. 1; Thompson, *Associated Architectural Societies' Reports and Papers* xxxiii (1915), 35-93; Waugh, EHR xxviii (1913), 625-35; Pennington, *Speculum* li (1976), 35-48; Reg. Winchelsey, 1289 seq.

[4] CIC, Clem., lib. III, tit. ii, cap. 3 (Friedberg, vol. ii, col. 1159).

bishops.[5] The cardinal nuncios in England, Gaucelme and Luca, had a dispensatory faculty granted by John xxii on 24 April 1317 to enable ten pluralists not dispensed by the apostolic see to retain their last benefice received by canonical collation once they had resigned all other incompatible benefices, which the cardinals themselves could then provide.[6] And the papal bulls of provision themselves were often accompanied by dispensations for plurality.

Archbishop Reynolds, for one, probably had no papal authority to grant dispensations for plurality, and this probability is strengthened by the fact that none survive in his register.[7] Yet in his first year at Canterbury he tried to do something about pluralism as a problem, investigating pluralism on at least three diocesan visitations,[8] acting in two cases to deprive pluralists,[9] clearing five other incumbents of the charge of plurality (at least two of whom had papal dispensation).[10] But Reynolds himself by the provisory faculty granted him in the same year was specifically allowed by Clement v to create pluralities of benefices with cure among his own provisors,[11] and after his first year as archbishop – apart from his dealings with *Execrabilis* soon to be discussed and his proposed investigation of pluralism in his Lincoln visitation of 1319[12] – no surviving record suggests that he did anything more about pluralism during his entire archiepiscopate. He could and did dispense for nonresidence,[13] but plurality – perhaps more than other irregularities for

[5] On occasions, instead of single dispensations to individual clerks at the crown's request, the pope might grant a broad indult dispensing a given number of clerks whom the king or prince of Wales or some bishop or noble might choose. E.g., cpi. ii, 6, 7, 26, 30, 40, 55; Reg. Clem. v, no. 2854.

[6] Reg. John xxii, no. 5220 (curial letter).

[7] Abp. Winchelsey also, if we may judge from the entries under 'pluralism' in the index to his register, had no such authority. At Worcester, Reynolds had had a papal faculty to dispense six of his clerks for plurality, and one such dispensation survives (cpi. ii, 52; rwr, 84).

[8] rr ff. 52, 53.

[9] rr ff. 33v, 34v.

[10] rr ff. 52, 59v, 105, 111v.

[11] rr f. 47v.

[12] rr f. 97v. There is evidence that Reynolds deprived one pluralist, M. Robert of Gloucester, rector of Wraysbury (Bucks.), by authority of *Execrabilis* as a result of his visitation of Lincoln diocese (lao, ms Dvj/23/3; cf. Emden, *Oxford* ii, 773-4).

[13] E.g., rr ff. 7 seq., 166 seq., 200 seq., 287 seq.; cf. Haines, *Administration*, pp. 91 (cf. n. 4), 205. In 1322 Reynolds announced a general investigation of nonresidence in Canterbury diocese with citation and canonical punishment of offenders (rr f. 287v; Cant. Cath. ms Reg. L, f. 122v; *Lit. Cant.* no. 87; Cant. Cath. ms Reg. Q, ff. 103, 119v). He had taken a similar step at Worcester in 1309 (Haines, *Administration*, 204).

which dispensatory faculties might be obtained – was in the hands of the sovereign pontiff.[14]

What was perhaps new about *Execrabilis*, as the chronicler Murimuth emphasized [15] and as dispossessed incumbents came to realize,[16] was that it began by revoking all dispensations of previous popes for plurality.[17] The studies of Gaignard have demonstrated that Clement v's dispensatory policy in England was extremely lax during the final three years of his pontificate – out of a total of 191 dispensations for plurality granted by that pope in the years 1311-1314, there were seventy-six that pertained to England alone.[18] The revocation of all these and of even more dispensations by John xxii could have made some lasting reduction of pluralism, and it probably did curtail the numbers of benefices held by pluralists. But it did not stop the pope from making further grants that created pluralities, and the papal registers show that he continued to do so in the years after *Execrabilis* was issued.[19]

As well as the probability of some serious desire to limit great excesses of plurality, the pope's motives for issuing *Execrabilis* undoubtedly embraced the financial possibilities. Many of the contemporary chroniclers described it largely in financial terms.[20] Murimuth suggests the possibility of some connection with John xxii's bull *Si gratanter advertitis* (8 December 1316) which had reserved to the apostolic see the first fruits of all benefices falling vacant within three years from that date,[21] and there is no question that it substantially augmented the number of benefices

---

[14] For the development of papal monopoly in the centralization of dispensations for plurality at this time, see Gray, *Studies in Church History* iii (1966), 58.

[15] *Con. Chron.*, 28. There is no evidence for Smith's statement (*Episcopal Appointments*, p. 110 n. 8) that Murimuth himself was deprived of a benefice by force of *Execrabilis*; cf. Reg. Orleton Hereford, 186-8.

[16] Below, p. 78 n. 38.

[17] On *Execrabilis* itself see above, pp. 12-14. A note by the copy of *Execrabilis* in Reg. Halton ii, 156, remarks that the new constitution did not quash dispensations for plurality in the case of anyone holding two churches with cure if one or both of them were served by a perpetual vicar. Later, the canonist Ayton was to imply that the bull did not apply to churches held *in commendam* (Haines, *Administration*, 194).

[18] *Annales du Midi* lxxii (1960), 176, 197. Only sixty-nine of the dispensations pertained to France.

[19] E.g., Reg. John xxii, no. 8423, 16 Sept. 1318, dispensation for plurality to Rigaud d'Assier, papal chaplain, collector, and nuncio. Also, see Reg. John xxii, nos. 7239, 7254, 7914; cpl ii, 172-4, 178, 193-4, 197-8; Driver, cqr cxlv (1947), 44; Lunt, *Financial Relations* ii, p. 322 n. 105; Mollat, *La Collation*, 63.

[20] Mollat, *La Collation*, 58.

[21] *Con. Chron.*, 29; for the text see Lunt, *Papal Revenues* ii, 324-8.

subject to this recent levy of annates.[22] Clearly *Execrabilis* was of great immediate financial significance, no matter who secured the disposal of the benefices thus vacated. A third motive of the pope, certainly, was his desire to provide these benefices himself, but for this he had to contend with the crown and with other patrons, and the ensuing contest called forth clever litigation and diplomacy on all sides.

If *Execrabilis* did not put an end to dispensations for plurality, at least it did threaten to deprive a large number of pluralists of their benefices, and the authorities in England were quick to realize that this would happen when the new constitution was enforced.[23] Of prime interest is the apparent fact that, nearly a month before it was promulgated, Pope John sent the English king a secret letter enclosing an advance copy of this constitution together with a list of his reasons for issuing it. The pope's words about it come at the end of a letter (entered in the Vatican register) to Edward II concerning another matter, and mention of them was omitted entirely by Bliss when he compiled his English calendar: 'Sed ut contra illos qui dispensative vel alias plures dignitates aut personatus vel beneficia ecclesiastica detinent, certam ordinacionem ex causis Deo et mundo placidis et gratis, ut credimus, duximus faciendam, quam equidem ordinacionem, et causas illius constitucionis inde facte series cuius copiam presentibus inclusam tibi transmittimus'. This letter is dated 21 or 22 October 1317, nearly a month in advance of the publication of *Execrabilis* on 19 November.[24] John at the same time sent the same information to Cardinals Gaucelme and Luca as the papal nuncios in England then, and I have found no evidence in the Vatican registers or elsewhere that such advance notice of *Execrabilis* was sent to any other rulers or nuncios in other places. The earliest clear evidence that *Execrabilis* had reached the attention of Edward II, a letter of the king to the pope dated 10 January

[22] Lunt, *Financial Relations* i, 494-6. In the accounts of d'Assier, the papal collector in England 1317-1323, *Si granter* was described as having reserved the benefices themselves falling vacant for three years, and not just the first fruits thereof: 'Hec sunt beneficia vacantia in provinciis Cantuariensi et Eboracensi in primo anno reservationis omnium beneficiorum ecclesiasticorum in ipsis provinciis vacantium per dominum nostrum Dominum Johannem divina providentia papam XXII ad triennium facte', and the initial date given is 8 December 1316 (Lunt, *Accounts*, 1). I have found no other evidence that *Si granter* was described in this way.

[23] For the reaction in other parts of Europe, see Mollat, *La Collation*, 60-2; Barraclough, *Zeitschrift der Savigny-Stiftung für Rechtsgeschichte* lviii (1938), 112.

[24] Vatican Archives, Reg. Vat. 109, f. 96, and 110, ff. 123-123v (top foliation); John XXII, Secret Letters, nos. 422-3 (which establishes the year date convincingly); cf. CPL ii, 419, 432. For the date of *Execrabilis* itself see Kuttner, *Studi e Testi*, vol. 234 (1964), 434, and John XXII, Secret Letters, no. 732, note 1.

1317/1318, may in fact be referring to receipt of John's secret letter when the king describes the new constitution as 'quod etiam, transmissae nobis, vestrae beatitudinis litterae plenius exprimebant'.[25] If we may judge from the king's letter, the bull produced a commotion especially among the magnates and 'proceres' of the realm, who – together with the king himself – were disturbed that the clerks in their own services, as well as other learned persons already dispensed for plurality by the pope's predecessors, would stand to lose their benefices. The king asked the pope not to apply the law in England, and he sent similar letters – charging that patronage rights would be violated and suggesting that no more faith could be placed in the indults of the Roman church[26] – to thirteen cardinals (at least eleven of whom are known to have had strong English connections)[27] and to his proctor Andreas Sapiti at the curia. He also directed the English clergy to hold their benefices until the papal reply should be received, and informed the pope that he was doing this.

Nevertheless, the royal protest did not prevent the execution of the decree and apparently did not even delay it. Resignations of English benefices forced by the new constitution began as early as 16 December 1317 at the Roman court and 22 January 1317/1318 in England, and they continued throughout the following year.[28] The diocesan bishops began to prepare the lists of benefices thus resigned – which lists the constitution required that they send the pope – as early as 31 March 1318.[29] The bishops of Canterbury province, however, seem to have withheld these lists from the pope until the end of May in 1318, perhaps in the hope that the king's protest might have its desired effect. The problem of *Execrabilis* had been raised in an ecclesiastical assembly[30] of the southern province, perhaps in February of 1317/1318, and the

[25] Rymer II:i, 354-5, printed from PRO C70; Lambeth MS 171, ff. 128-31; HMC Fourth Rep., app., 382; BL MS Cott. Cleopatra E.i, f. 264 (top foliation); cf. *Reg. Pal. Dunelm.*, vol. iv, p. xlix, and *Liber Epistolaris* of Richard de Bury, nos. 165, 169 (calendared letter of Edward II to Andreas Sapiti).

[26] 'Modicaque, vel nulla, ut dicunt, privilegiis et indulgentiis Romanae Ecclesiae adhibebitur exnunc fides', written in the letters to the cardinals but not in the one to the pope.

[27] Below, Appendix 3, nos. 2, 6, 12, 20, 22, 28, 29, 33, 34, 41, 42.

[28] CCW, 498-9; Emden, *Cambridge*, 376. Lunt, *Financial Relations* i, 496, says they began early in February, and the earliest in RR (f. 23v) is dated 22 Jan.

[29] Reg. Sandale, 88-9.

[30] I use this term here in order to leave open the question still under discussion of differences between a provincial council, convocation, and congregation. (For terminology, see Kemp, *Counsel and Consent*, 97; Powicke and Fryde, *Handbook*, 545; Churchill, *Canterbury Administration* i, 360.)

bishops had decided to send the pope a joint letter under the care of their trusted messenger M. Andrew de Bruges (Bregges, Brigges), D.C.L.[31] This letter,[32] dated 30 May 1318 under the seals of Reynolds and most of the bishops of the province, asked the pope either (1) to allow all benefices in Canterbury province vacated by force of *Execrabilis* to be conferred by the diocesan bishops and other clerical patrons, or (2) to provide them himself to approved clerks named in separate schedules to be presented to him by Master Andrew. Apparently not all the lists were ready for Andrew by the time he departed from England, for on 7 June of the same year Bishop Dalderby of Lincoln sent his own messenger from Stow Park to the Roman curia carrying just such a schedule addressed to Master Andrew as well as a letter directed to Dalderby's proctor at the curia M. William de Otringham, which contained copies of this list and of a certain letter from Dalderby to the pope about the whole matter.[33]

Master Andrew, however, had to represent many interests. The king's letters of protection for him, dated 4 June,[34] state that he was sent 'in obsequium regis, per preceptum regis', and the truth is that the king also sent the pope at this time another letter[35] about *Execrabilis* by the hand of the same messenger. This letter is worthy of note. After complaining that papal provisions restricted the benefices available for learned and prudent men to serve as chancery clerks, the king asked either (1) that Bishop John Sandale, the chancellor, be empowered to confer benefices not of episcopal patronage, resigned before Sandale by force of *Execrabilis*, upon the king's clerks both in his own diocese and elsewhere, or (2) that the pope himself provide such benefices upon certain chancery clerks named in a list to be presented by Master Andrew, who was himself both a king's clerk and also the official of Sandale.

The list of benefices resigned before Sandale, dated 29 May 1318 and

---

[31] Emden, *Oxford* iii, 2156.

[32] Printed in Reg. Sandale, 90-3; transl. ibid., pp. xli-xliv; also printed in Reg. London, 182-4; summarized in Cal. Reg. Droxford, 15. The letter implies that the bishops had considered the matter in a provincial assembly. The meeting possibly held on 23 Feb. 1317/1318 was probably the only such assembly held before the date of the episcopal letter but after the date of *Execrabilis* (Powicke and Fryde, *Handbook*, 554).

[33] LAO, MS Reg. Dalderby III, f. 389v. Otringham's stay in the curia about this time is noted in Vatican Archives, Collectoriae 52, ff. 27-8, according to information supplied me by the kindness of Prof. B. Guillemain.

[34] CPR 1317-21, 152; transcribed from the patent roll in Reg. Sandale, p. 93 n. 3.

[35] 7 June 1318; transcribed from PRO C70 in Reg. Sandale, p. 93 n. 4; also printed in Rymer II:i, 364. The king's letter to Cardinal Vidal du Four, relative to the events in consequence of the pope's new constitution, may date from this point (calendared in *Reg. Pal. Dunelm.*, vol. iv, p. 1).

addressed to the pope and presumably one that Master Andrew took with him, is printed in Sandale's register[36] and contains twenty-nine names. They are divided twice over: (1) benefices in Sandale's own diocese of (a) clerical (both monastic and episcopal) patronage (seven of these), and (b) lay patronage (six); and (2) benefices outside the Winchester diocese of (a) clerical (both monastic and episcopal) patronage (eight), and (b) lay patronage (eight). At least some of the incumbents who resigned these benefices are known to have been chancery clerks,[37] and some of the incumbents had previously been dispensed for plurality by Clement v to hold these very benefices now resigned.[38] The taxation values of the twenty-nine benefices range from five pounds to sixty marks, and their average value is twenty-nine marks each.[39]

Analysis of the collations and institutions in Sandale's register indicates that the pope did not choose the first alternative proposed by the king, for there is no record that Sandale himself conferred any of these twenty-nine benefices that had been thus resigned. If the pope had elected the first alternative, the crown's own patronage not only would have been strengthened but also would have been consolidated even more in the power of Sandale, who as chancellor already had the customary right to nominate to all benefices of the king's gift valued at twenty marks a year or less.[40] As for the second alternative, the list of chancery clerks nominated for these benefices by the king apparently does not survive, but the papal registers reveal that the pope himself did provide at least thirteen of the twenty-nine benefices that had been resigned.

Fourteen of the twenty-nine resigned benefices were in lay patronage, and none of these were affected by provision. The six benefices in lay gift resigned in Winchester diocese at this time were all presented again by their own patrons, and Sandale had even admitted all the patrons' nominees before the end of May when he sent the list of vacated benefices to the pope.[41] For example, the church of Farley Chamberlayne (Hants) in his diocese, valued at eighteen marks, was resigned by Walter de Bertone under force of *Execrabilis* on 12 February 1317/1318 and then on 18

---

[36] Reg. Sandale, 94-100; cf. pp. 77-9.

[37] The most notable among these was William de Thorntoft, chancery clerk and keeper of the hanaper until 16 Nov. 1318, who alone resigned four of these twenty-nine benefices by force of *Execrabilis* (Reg. Sandale, 99-100).

[38] CPL. ii, 5, 11, 67, 90, 95, 113.

[39] See below, p. 86.

[40] Pantin, *The English Church*, 30. For Reynolds' use of this right when he was chancellor, see ccw, 395 seq., 401.

[41] Reg. Sandale, 147-8, 153.

March Sandale admitted John de Bertone to it, who was presented by the patron Nicholas de Bertone.[42] On 2 June of the same year Sandale gave the same John de Bertone, who was still an acolyte, letters dimissory for the subdiaconate, and on 10 October he granted him licence to study for one year.[43] Another of the benefices in lay gift was in royal patronage, and the king presented to it in due course.[44]

Clearly, the benefices in lay patronage resigned by force of the new constitution before Sandale, about half of the twenty-nine, were not disturbed by provision – a policy that Pope John himself enunciated in his letters clarifying the terms of *Execrabilis* to the archbishop of Braga and the king of Portugal.[45] The one benefice of lay patronage vacated by *Execrabilis* to be mentioned in Reynolds' archiepiscopal register, moreover, the church of Charlton by Dover (Kent), was also again presented by its true patron, the lord Bartholomew Badlesmere, and there is no hint of attempted papal provision to it.[46] All this evidence, then, confirms the general consensus of historical evidence that English benefices in lay gift were customarily immune from papal provisions, at least during the early fourteenth century.[47]

[42] Reg. Sandale, 95, 97, 148.
[43] Reg. Sandale, 201-2.
[44] Reg. Sandale, 95, 147.
[45] Above, p. 13.
[46] RR f. 24.
[47] Reg. Orleton Hereford, 88-9; Murimuth, *Con. Chron.*, 28; P&C i, 97; Leadam and Baldwin, *Select Cases before the King's Council*, p. lvii; *Yearbooks of Edward II*, Selden Soc. vol. 22, p. 171; Deeley, EHR xliii (1928), 505-6; Driver, CQR cxlv (1947), 46; Lunt, *Financial Relations* i, 496; Lunt, *Papal Revenues* ii, 217 seq.; Pantin, *The English Church*, 58, 66, 69; Powicke, *King Henry III and the Lord Edward*, vol. i, p. 279 n. 3; Smith, *Episcopal Appointments*, 111-12. Occasionally, however, there were exceptions. In 1317 the earl of Gloucester was contesting the patronage of the church of Rotherfield (Sussex), when the pope provided it to a cardinal (below, Appendix 3, no. 12). In 1318 the pope made provision to a canonry and prebend of St. Martin's, London; the vacancy was caused by death at the apostolic see, but St. Martin's was a royal free chapel and may have been considered as of lay patronage (Reg. John XXII, no. 7465; CPL ii, 173). In 1320-1321 the pope provided the parish church of Catton (Yorks., E. Riding) to a cardinal, but as this church was in lay patronage the provision probably did not take effect (below, Appendix 3, no. 32). In June of 1318 the pope at royal request provided to the rectory of Long Newton (co. Durham), which had been vacated by force of *Execrabilis*, but the lay patron of the benefice vindicated his right against the provision in the king's court (CPL ii, 177, 200; Reg. John XXII, no. 7420). Another dispute between a papal provisor and a lay patron is found in Reg. Martival i, 44-7. Still another apparent exception was the priory of Lewes, in lay patronage but provided (by papal mandate to assign) in 1330; the king's writ of prohibition was apparently unsuccessful (Cant. Cath. MS Reg. L, f. 174; *Lit. Cant.* nos. 310-11; HMC Ninth Rep., I, app., 99; Reg. John XXII, no. 43649; CPL ii, 293, 346). Professor Lunt has shown that annates were paid on benefices in lay patronage in the time of

All thirteen provisions that the pope did make from Sandale's list[48] fell upon the benefices in clerical patronage, and the final two benefices of clerical patronage for which no provisions can be found in the papal registers were already litigious before the time that *Execrabilis* was published.[49] Most of these thirteen were provided in July and August of 1318, but three of them, although resigned in February of 1317/1318, were not provided until much later – in 1319, 1323, and 1327. The benefice not provided until 1327 was granted at the request of three cardinals to a clerk who was their 'familiaris' and proctor. In one other case of the thirteen, the pluralist tried to impede the constitution by resigning his benefice before the papal nuncio Cardinal Luca Fieschi, who then collated it in ignorance that the pluralist had been compelled to give it up.

It is possible to trace a very few of the thirteen provisors' names as king's clerks in the various calendars of record publications, but it seems probable that the pope did not in fact make these thirteen provisions from any list of names sent by the king as the second alternative. This probability is corroborated by the fact that in nine of the thirteen, provided in July and August of 1318, the pope specifically stated that he was providing at the requests of various diocesan bishops – almost certainly from the schedule of names that the bishops too, as a result of their provincial assembly, had sent along with Master Andrew.

In two of the thirteen cases, the churches of Beddington (Surrey) and Itchen Stoke (Hants) both of which were in monastic patronage, the king himself made presentations on the grounds that the temporalities of these monastic patrons had been in royal hands during former vacancies.[50] In both cases the king informed Sandale that he had recovered the advowsons in the royal court, and Sandale saw that the king's nominees were admitted to these in advance of the time that the list of benefices vacated by *Execrabilis* was forwarded to the apostolic see. The pope's subsequent attempt to provide these two benefices was probably unsuccessful. Both churches were resigned in February 1317/1318, the king claimed in the middle of May 1318 that he had recovered both

---

Clement v and John xxii, although such benefices were exempt from annates later in the century (AHR xviii (1912), p. 54 n. 52).

[48] Reg. John xxii, nos. 7072, 7883, 7895-6, 7970, 7994, 8001-4, 10384, 17151, 29988; CPL. ii, 171-2, 180-1, 191, 230, 264.

[49] The two were Ewell (Surrey), to which Sandale admitted a clerk presented by the true patron, and a benefice in the diocese of Florence, over which a case was pending in the curia (Reg. Sandale, 94, 96, 147).

[50] Reg. Sandale, 95, 98, 151-4.

advowsons, the list of benefices vacated was sent to the pope on 29 May, and the pope named provisors (at the requests of diocesan bishops) to both churches on 9 August 1318.[51] There is no record of either of these provisors in Sandale's register, and it is probable that these two benefices – together with the one royal living already mentioned – mark the totality of patronage that the crown secured from Sandale's list of twenty-nine benefices sent with Master Andrew. Miss Deeley has suggested that the crown tried to counter the pope's provisions of benefices vacated under *Execrabilis* by the principle that time could not run against the king's rights of presentation, but these same two benefices are the only examples that she cites in which the crown successfully did counter the pope in this way.[52] The king did present to at least one other benefice on Sandale's list, of alien monastic patronage,[53] before the time that Master Andrew went to Avignon, but by 1324 his nominee had lost it to the papal provisor. Over still another benefice on the list there was a contest between king and pope in 1327, but here too the crown eventually abandoned its claim.[54]

If the king, therefore, gained very little from Sandale's list, to which he had specifically called the pope's attention, it seems probable that he gained even less from the other lists that were sent in accord with the decision of the provincial assembly. Only three more such lists survive in contemporary printed episcopal registers – twenty-three names sent by Bishop Newport of London, six names sent by Bishop Droxford of Bath and Wells, and five names listed in the register of Bishop Stapledon of Exeter – although none of these gives so much detailed information as is found in Sandale's register.[55] From Newport's list, dated 30 May 1318 and

[51] Reg. John XXII, nos. 8001-2; CPL. ii, 182.

[52] Deeley, EHR xliii (1928), 518.

[53] The church of Arreton (I.O.W.), in gift of the Norman abbey of Lire (Eure); Smith, *Episcopal Appointments*, 95.

[54] The rectory of Fishlake (Yorks.), Reg. John XXII, no. 29988; CPL. ii, 11, 264; *Rot. Parl.* ii, 45; Reg. Sandale, 96, 100; Leadam and Baldwin, *Select Cases*, pp. lxiii-lxiv; Deeley, EHR xliii (1928), 525-6; Thompson and Clay, *Fasti Parochiales* i, 115-18; Wilkinson, *Chancery under Edward III*, 32-3; Brown, *Yorkshire Archaeological Society, Record Series* lxi (1920), 140. See also PRO K.B. 27/272, rex m. 3, and 27/275, rex m. 16 (ex inf. E. B. Graves).

[55] Some interesting lists of vacated benefices at this time sent to the papal collector d'Assier for taxation purposes survive in Reg. Martival ii, 221-31, but benefices vacated by *Execrabilis* are not specified, at least in the abbreviated form in which they are printed. Stapledon's register notes the appointment of an 'yconomus super beneficiis vacantibus per constitucionem Johannis Pape XXII' on 26 Feb. 1317/1318. It is not clear that the list in Stapledon's register was actually intended to be sent to the papal court (Reg. Stapledon, 43, 265, 411).

broken into categories similar to those in Sandale's, we know that the king presented to one benefice of monastic patronage by reason of the temporalities in his hands during vacancy of the patron. Eight of the twenty-three benefices were in Newport's diocese, of which four were in clerical patronage and four in lay. Fifteen were in other dioceses but were resigned before Newport 'racione more in mea diocesi', and their patronage was described as unknown.[56] The six benefices in Droxford's list (dated 25 May 1318) range in value from ten to thirty marks and average nineteen each. Five of the benefices were in his diocese and one outside. On his own authority Droxford permitted one pluralist to retain two benefices without dispensation, both of which were in lay patronage and one of which was not worth enough to be taxed.[57]

Apart from the printed episcopal registers, there are two other instances in which the crown is known to have made successful presentations to benefices vacated by *Execrabilis*, but at least one of these was probably in the king's own patronage.[58] In still another case, involving at least nine royal writs of various kinds and litigation in both secular and ecclesiastical courts, the crown was unsuccessful in an attempt to secure its candidate in such a benefice.[59]

In sum, the mission of Master Andrew had been a success, at least from the viewpoint of the English episcopate. To top it all the pope on 23 September 1318 provided Master Andrew himself to a canonry of St. Paul's London with expectation of a prebend, probably in recognition of his diplomacy.[60] In the provincial assembly at London on or after 16 April 1319 one of the articles proposed for business by Archbishop Reynolds was 'provisio beneficiorum ecclesiasticorum per dimissionem vacancium personis ex parte prelatorum nominatis per sedem apostolicam facienda', and there must have been a general satisfaction among the bishops as Master Andrew related there this part of the business for which he had been sent to the Roman curia.[61] It may be too much to say that Edward II's bishops had acted in opposition to the crown on this matter, but they had certainly acted independently of it.

---

[56] Reg. London, 185-6, 196-7 (cf. Vatican Archives, R.A. 160, f. 28v), 237.

[57] Cal. Reg. Droxford, 15.

[58] Smith, *Episcopal Appointments*, 100, 102; Deeley, EHR xliii (1928), 509-10.

[59] CCW, 498-9; Reg. John XXII, no. 6968; CPL ii, 272, 312; CPR 1317-21, 222, 419.

[60] Reg. John XXII, no. 8449; CPL ii, 183.

[61] Reported in similar – but not identical – accounts of this assembly in Lambeth MS 1213, ff. 103v-104 (a register of St. Augustine's, Canterbury) and in Bod. MS Kent Charters 84, o and p (mutilated documents from Tonbridge Priory). These sources are not listed in Weske, *Convocation of the Clergy*, 242, or Powicke and Fryde, *Handbook*, 554.

In the northern province Archbishop Melton had been consecrated slightly less than two months before *Execrabilis* was issued, and a certificate of benefices resigned in consequence of it, beginning as early as 7 February 1317/1318, is one of the first entries in his (as of 1976 still unpublished) register.[62] Dated 27 May 1318, about the same time that the certificates went out to the pope from the southern province, this list shows that twenty persons had resigned some twenty-nine benefices by force of the new constitution, most of them in the month of February. One resignation, of the rectory of Kirk Ella (Yorks.) by the pluralist Peter de Dene, was made with the protest that Peter had consulted skilled persons including the papal nuncio Cardinal Gaucelme who had informed him that his benefices did not fall within the scope of the pope's decree.[63] Fourteen of the twenty-nine were in lay patronage, and the archbishop stated that he had admitted presentees to them saving however the pope's right if such benefices were included in the reservation which the bull levied. As for the others, he begged that the pope would grant him the faculty to make provision of three or four of them to his own clerks, either under papal or his own authority. The pope's response had an interesting sequel.

The papal registers show that Melton on 26 April 1319 was granted a papal faculty to provide persons of his choice to four parish churches of his diocese which had been vacated by *Execrabilis* and provided by the pope already in July of 1318 to clerks of Melton at his own request[64] but which had all been refused as being of too little value and disturbed by conflicts.[65] Then on 4 June 1319 Melton sent the pope another list of benefices vacated by *Execrabilis* in his diocese and asked that he be empowered to provide them to his clerks. He may have been encouraged by the faculty the pope had granted him on 26 April, if it reached him by 4 June, or he may have simply been making a routine repetition of his earlier request. Melton's letter explains that his request is made necessary by the pope's own numerous provisions:

> Although I your devoted creature have need of the counsels and assistance of many experts satisfactorily to support and usefully to direct the weight of the cure incumbent upon my office, the doctors and clerks of this nation and tongue, however, perceiving the numerous multitude of

[62] York, Borthwick Institute MS Reg. Melton, f. 3 (9), transcribed by Miss Ann Deeley and used here with her permission by courtesy of Prof. E. B. Graves.

[63] Cf. below, Appendix 6, nos. 3, 11, 12, 68; Emden, *Oxford* iii, 2168-9.

[64] Robinson, *Beneficed Clergy*, 23.

[65] CPL. ii, 186-7; cf. 179-80.

provisions made by the apostolic see of benefices and prebends of my
patronage, have fallen into such despair of obtaining any promotion from
me for their labours rendered to me that I am able to add none of them to
my company without establishing a monetary payment and an excessive
annual salary for them – which indeed wrenches and pierces my heart with
terrible stings. Especially is this so because first of all my manor of Hexham
in which a third part of my archiepiscopate consists, and thereafter now
recently my other manor of Ripon, have been destroyed by the Scots,
besides other discomforts which I bear these days which J. de Nevile the
bearer of these presents knows to explain to you *viva voce*.... Wherefore I
ask that you revoke these destructions and losses at the court of your mind
and extend your gracious bowels of mercy after the accustomed manner,
conceding from the benefices resigned in my diocese by your vigorous
constitution and listed in the schedule herein enclosed, which [benefices] are
abused in their rights and liberties many times over during their long
vacancies, some grace to me for my clerks moderating the decision of your
liberality, so that with your assistance in the aforesaid my counsel (MS
consilium) can be abundantly supported and strengthened by persons solid
and perfect, by which [action on your part] my affairs can be directed to the
desired good pleasure of the Eternal King. ... Given at Thorpe near York, 4
June 1319.[66]

Whatever the relationship of Melton's letter to the faculty granted on 26
April, it can be said with certainty that Melton's letter produced no further
indult that has made its way into the papal registers in the years
immediately afterwards. Of the total of seven vacancies by *Execrabilis* in
York diocese after the date of Melton's letter that are mentioned in the
registers of John xxii, four were provided by the pope to members of the
college of cardinals.[67] Two others of the seven do bear reflections of
Melton's letter: one a faculty to Melton in 1322 to provide the archdeaconry of the East Riding, vacated by a pluralist, and the other an appropriation in 1323 for Melton's life of a parish church vacated by a
pluralist and valued at forty pounds, because the archbishop has been
'reduced to poverty by the Scottish invasions'.[68]

Melton's letter of 4 June 1319 must also bear some relationship to the
long list in his register of benefices vacated in York diocese over the three
years following 8 December 1316 which he sent to the papal collector

---

[66] York, Borthwick Institute, MS Reg. Melton, f. 504v; transcribed, translated, and
words within brackets supplied, by the present writer. Latin text also printed in *Historical
Papers*, ed. Raine, 289-91.

[67] Reg. John xxii, nos. 11192, 13033, 13706, 29988; CPL ii, 198, 210, 213, 264.

[68] Reg. John xxii, nos. 15044, 18261; CPL ii, 219, 235.

Rigaud d'Assier in response to an enquiry by authority of the papal bull *Si gratanter advertitis*.[69] A summary of this list as edited by W. Brown[70] indicates that only seven of the some 146 vacancies recorded therein were forced by *Execrabilis*, a few of which seven are not mentioned in the papal registers. A great many of the 146 benefices are only described as 'vacant by resignation' in the printed version of the list, although a few of these are known from other sources to have been forced by *Execrabilis*. Further details of this picture in the northern province, and the part that the crown played in it, will undoubtedly come from the editing of Melton's register that is currently in process.[71]

Such was the immediate contest among the crown, bishops, and pope for the benefices vacated by *Execrabilis*. The exact number of benefices vacated by its force is not certain. Miss Deeley estimated 'not less than eighty',[72] but the number was certainly far in excess of this and it must be computed from many sources. The most complete information we have comes from the contemporary accounts of the papal tax collectors in England, which were not available in print to Miss Deeley but are now fully edited.[73] Not all these have survived, and vacancies forced by *Execrabilis* are only recorded for the two-year period from 8 December 1317 to 8 December 1319. Yet this period, corresponding roughly with John xxii's second and third pontifical years and with the first two years following the issue of *Execrabilis* itself, probably represents the high watermark of papal cognizance of such vacancies in England. These accounts, of the papal collector Rigaud d'Assier, which are his complete records of the payment of annates on English benefices during these two years and which specify which benefices were vacated by force of *Execrabilis*, are therefore of considerable significance. They show a total of 772 English (and Welsh) benefices vacated during this two-year

[69] Above, p. 74.

[70] *Yorkshire Archaeological Society, Record Series*, lxi (1920), 136-48, from Reg. Melton, f. 636 seq.

[71] I am informed by Dr. David Robinson that Melton's register gives details of 'the commission of custody of sequestration of benefices vacated by *Execrabilis*, e.g., f. 442'. The excommunication of pluralists proclaimed by Abp. Greenfield in an appendix to his statutes for the York consistory court in 1311 must also form some part of the earlier background to *Execrabilis* in the north (Wilkins ii, 415).

[72] EHR xliii (1928), 503.

[73] Lunt, *Accounts*, 10-26. Professor E. B. Graves, who shouldered the Herculean task of editing Professor Lunt's transcriptions of these for publication, informs me that footnote 31 on page 12, which is missing from the text of the printed edition, properly belongs at the end of the top entry of the left-hand column on this page (i.e., after the word 'totum' concluding the entry for the church of Shenfield), and this establishes the first nine entries on this page as the ones vacated by *Execrabilis* to which this footnote refers.

period,[74] of which 169 – nearly twenty-two percent – are described as having been forced by *Execrabilis*. Payments are listed from vacancies in a total of twenty-one dioceses. The accounts show no vacancies from *Execrabilis* in the four Welsh dioceses or Carlisle, only two each in Canterbury, Chichester, Durham, and Hereford, and only three each in Salisbury and Ely. The largest numbers of vacancies from *Execrabilis* are found in Lincoln diocese with forty, Norwich with thirty-eight, and York with twenty-three. Of the total of 169 there are 161 parish churches,[75] as well as one deanery (Chester), four archdeaconries, and three prebends. The values of these 169 benefices recorded in d'Assier's accounts average out to almost twenty-nine marks each, which is, interestingly, exactly the same as the average value of the benefices in Sandale's list.[76] Five are valued at 100 marks or over, the greatest being Holbeach (Lincs.) at 180 marks.[77] The lowest are valued at six marks each, and there are six of these.

For comparison we may turn to the calendared papal registers, which seem to have been the main source of Miss Deeley's figures. For all of John xxii's pontificate, they reveal a total of only eighty-six English benefices vacated by the new constitution,[78] of which fifty-seven fell during his second and third pontifical years. Many, but not all, of these fifty-seven can be found in d'Assier's list of 169, and of course many of the latter are not found in the former. The list preserved in the registers of Sandale, Newport, Droxford, and Melton show still others that are not to be found in d'Assier's account or in the calendared papal registers, and d'Assier's account shows some such benefices from these dioceses that are not found in the surviving episcopal lists.[79] All told, on the basis of

[74] Returns from both these years are merged in d'Assier's account and it is not possible to ascertain which vacancies pertain to which year. Names of incumbents are not given.

[75] Of these 161, three are moieties, one is a third portion, and one is described as being two parts of a church put to farm.

[76] Above, p. 78.

[77] Same valuation, expressed as £120, in *Taxatio Eccl.*, 62.

[78] Below, Appendix 1, table D. In France likewise, the total of 185 resignations of French benefices forced by *Execrabilis*, as computed by Caillet (*La papauté d'Avignon et l'église de France*, 205) from the calendared papal registers alone, is probably much less than the full picture.

[79] It may also be observed that d'Assier's account (edited by Lunt) of benefices vacated in York diocese during the three years following the issue of *Si grananter advertitis* numbers a total of ninety-six vacated for all reasons, whereas the parallel list (edited by Brown) of such benefices recorded in Melton's register as being reported to d'Assier totaled 146. The numbers of benefices explicitly described in each list as vacated by *Execrabilis*, however, are twenty-three of the ninety-six but only seven of the 146 (Lunt, *Accounts*, 8-9, 24-5; Brown, *Yorkshire Archaeological Society, Record Series*, lxi (1920), 136-48).

d'Assier's account and the other evidence, I think a conservative estimate of the total number of English benefices vacated by force of *Execrabilis* during its first two years of operation must be not less than two hundred, but it should be noted (and will be shown below) that vacancies continued to be forced by it long after its first two years and that not all such vacancies reached the attention of the apostolic see.

Of the eighty-six vacancies found in the papal registers, fifty-seven were again granted by direct papal provisions and most of the rest by mandates to provide. In at least one case, the chancellorship of Lincoln, where an enquiry was made through Bishop Dalderby's proctor at the curia as to whether it was with or without cure and if the former whether dispensation might be had to hold it as well as benefices with cure, the benefice was vacated and then immediately again granted *in commendam* to the person who had just resigned it.[80] The papal registers record in thirty-seven cases out of the eighty-six the names of the persons at whose requests the grants were made, and analysis of these names again suggests that the bishops were the ones who gained in patronage: of the thirty-seven, twenty-five were made at the requests of English diocesan bishops, only seven at the requests of royalty (Edward II, Isabella, Edmund of Woodstock), three at the requests of cardinals, and two at the requests of lay nobility. As is also true of d'Assier's record, the vast majority of the benefices shown here as vacated by the new constitution – seventy-six out of the eighty-six – were parish churches; there were also seven arch-deaconries vacated and three miscellaneous. Eight of the eighty-six were granted to six different cardinals,[81] who of course could hold in plurality under the terms of the bull, and it has been shown that most of the eighty-six were conferred upon English clerks.[82] With perhaps three exceptions, the pope did not start to provide to English benefices vacated by *Execrabilis* until after the time that Master Andrew would have reached the curia with his lists. The evidence from the papal registers, from the lists in the registers of Sandale, Newport, and Stapledon, and from

[80] Reg. John XXII, no. 7914; CPL ii, 178; LAO, MS Reg. Dalderby III, f. 381v; Le Neve, *Lincoln*, 23; Highfield, 'The Relations' i, 18. The enquiry was sent to the Roman court from Lincoln on 25 Feb. 1317/1318, and the papal grant was dated 30 July. There is no evidence in RR to suggest that Reynolds attempted to use commendation as a means to evade the force of *Execrabilis*, although benefices held or granted *in commendam* were apparently not covered by the regulations of the bull (Haines, *Administration*, 194).

[81] Reg. John XXII, nos. 6214, 7338, 11903, 12945, 12993, 13008, 13033, 13706; CPL ii, 169, 204, 210, 213.

[82] Deeley, EHR xliii (1928), 503.

elsewhere,[83] confirms that the gain in patronage from *Execrabilis* was made by the bishops, under papal authority, and at the exclusion of the crown.

Yet some further evidence exists to suggest that additional gains were made by the bishops alone, in circumvention of the apostolic see. The calendared papal registers record (by way of silence) an acute decrease in the numbers of vacancies forced by *Execrabilis* after its initial impact.[84] During John xxii's second pontifical year (5 September 1317 – 5 September 1318) the total number of such vacancies mentioned in his register is fifty-three, of which thirty-four were provided. In his third pontifical year these figures drop to four vacancies of which three were provided, in the fourth twelve and eight, in the fifth eight and eight, in the sixth four and two, in the seventh two and one; and only four more recorded vacancies lie scattered throughout the remainder of his pontificate. The register of Archbishop Reynolds, which preserves nothing of the mission of Master Andrew in 1318-1319 nor the lists that he took then, mentions only three vacancies forced by the new constitution during the first four years of its existence.[85] Yet this same register records some ten further resignations because of *Execrabilis* before Reynolds, beginning no earlier than September 1322 – just as the mention of such vacancies has all but vanished from the papal registers. What are we to make of these resignations?

John xxii in his chancery rules had tried to ensure that even benefices vacated 'extra curiam' by *Execrabilis* would be provided under apostolic authority,[86] but apparently Reynolds and some other diocesans were able to get around this by accepting resignations in their presence and then immediately collating or instituting other clerks to the resigned churches usually on the same day. There is no indication that the pope was informed at all. Reynolds handled some ten benefices in this way over the years 1322-1327, some of them not even in his own patronage; and none of these cases is mentioned in the papal registers.[87] There is also evidence

---

[83] There is further evidence from 1320 and 1321 in the registers of Bishops Halton (ii, 202-3) and Cobham (107) of direct intervention by these bishops with the pope to secure suitable provision of two benefices vacated by the new constitution.

[84] Below, Appendix 1, table D.

[85] Above, pp. 55-57; RR ff. 23v-24.

[86] Ottenthal, *Regulae Cancellariae Apostolicae*, p. 6, no. 21.

[87] The name of each benefice is followed by its major reference in RR. Subsidiary documents in RR, and the references to the values of these benefices in the *Taxatio Eccl.* of 1291, are given in parentheses:

    (1) Brook (Kent); RR f. 31 (ff. 287, 292; *Taxatio*, pp. 2, 19).

    (2) Elmstone (Kent); RR f. 31v (*Taxatio*, p. 3).

that Bishops Droxford, Hethe, and Martival followed a similar practice at times.[88] Another feature of these resignations said to have been forced by *Execrabilis* before Reynolds, Hethe, Droxford, and Martival was that the dispossessed pluralists themselves were generally collated or instituted by the same ordinaries to other benefices with cure at the very same time that they resigned their former benefices. The *Taxatio* of 1291 indicates that the values of the new benefices taken up were generally slightly higher than the values of the ones resigned.[89]

In most of this last group of cases arising from *Execrabilis* an interesting device was also used as a safeguard: the constitution *Si beneficia*[90] of Boniface VIII, which stipulated that anyone resigning one benefice in order to receive another which – unknown to him – had been previously reserved or collated by the pope could return to his former benefice if forced to give up the latter, notwithstanding any subsequent collation made to the former. In the above cases this stipulation was usually repeated under oath before a notary in the form of a protest by the clerk who was resigning, and three complete specimens of the oath survive in Reynolds' register.[91] If the pope then attempted to provide to the benefice newly taken up, there was always recourse by *Si beneficia* to one's former benefice.[92]

---

    (3) West Hythe (Kent); RR f. 31v again (f. 32; *Taxatio*, p. 3).

    (4) Woodchurch (Kent); RR f. 32v (f. 254; *Taxatio*, pp. 2, 3).

    (5) Godmersham (Kent); RR f. 250 (ff. 29v, 130v, 147v, 251, 254v, 307v; *Taxatio*, p. 2).

    (6) Merstham (Surrey); RR f. 250v (ff. 252v, 257, 291; *Taxatio*, pp. 3, 208).

    (7) Hospital of Sts. Peter and Paul, Maidstone (Kent); RR f. 254 (ff. 262v, 263, 264).

    (8) Wittersham (Kent); RR f. 255 (ff. 24, 27v, 264v; *Taxatio*, p. 3).

    (9) Broughton Gifford (Wilts.); RR f. 264v (*Taxatio*, p. 17).

    (10) Framfield (Sussex); RR f. 266.

  [88] Cal. Reg. Droxford, 182-3; Reg. Hethe, 529-30; Reg. Martival i, 164-7.

  [89] It has been suggested that the constitution *Execrabilis* was responsible for a gradual increase in the proportion of exchanged benefices during the first half of the fourteenth century, as dispossessed pluralists each sought to retain and secure their single most valuable rectory (Haines, *Administration of Worcester*, p. 210 n. 1; Robinson, *Beneficed Clergy*, 22). The evidence in Reynolds' register is insufficient to confirm or deny that exactly this was happening in the cases of benefices vacated by *Execrabilis* which it records. Indeed, benefices handled 'causa permutacionis' are carefully distinguished in this register from those vacated 'secundum formam constitucionis novelle'.

  [90] CIC, Sext., lib. III, tit. iv, cap. 20 (Friedberg, vol. ii, cols. 1027-8). For similar use of this constitution before the time of *Execrabilis*, see Reg. Martival i, 32-3; Reg. Gandavo, 804.

  [91] RR ff. 32v, 250, 264v. The last of these is transcribed in Churchill, *Canterbury Administration* ii, 31-2.

  [92] The practice continued throughout the century: Churchill, *Canterbury Administration* ii, 31-4; Reg. Hethe, 529.

The most interesting example of this procedure at work in Reynolds'
register arises as a side issue from the attempt of both Reynolds and the
king to secure the archdeaconry of Canterbury for M. John de Bruyton in
1323-1324, which has already been discussed.[93] Bruyton was collated by
Reynolds to the archdeaconry on 18 April 1323. On 15 May before
Reynolds and a notary and two witnesses he resigned by force of
Execrabilis his parish church of Godmersham (Kent), to which he had
been collated by Reynolds on 11 December 1321, protesting under the
notarial instrument that if the archdeaconry were taken from him by
papal provision or any other way he would return to Godmersham. Godmersham, taxed at £53.5s.8d. in 1291,[94] was well worth having, and on
the same 15 May 1323 Reynolds collated it to M. John de Bruyton, junior,
clerk, 'consanguineus' of the said archdeacon-elect. But on 23 April 1323
the pope had issued a mandate to admit Cardinal Raymond de Roux to the
archdeaconry, which was vacant by the death of a provisor, and on 19
November 1323 Reynolds finally accepted the papal mandate and
admitted the cardinal's claim. Bruyton, therefore, had lost the archdeaconry, but the diocesan records do not tell whether he tried to return to
Godmersham. It may be that he was content to leave it to the possession
of his younger namesake and 'consanguineus', for the senior Bruyton held
numerous other benefices at the time. The pope had secured his provision
to the archdeaconry – not a surprising victory, but there is nothing in the
papal registers to suggest that he touched Godmersham, the parish vacated
by *Execrabilis*, at this time.

That the real gain in privileges of patronage set free by *Execrabilis* was
made by the English diocesan bishops at the exclusion of the crown,
sometimes with the consent of the apostolic see and other times in contravention of it, finds interesting confirmation in the history of the canon law
at this time. It so happens that John xxii, in addition to *Execrabilis*, was
also responsible for another strong constitution against plurality, *Ut quos
virtutis*,[95] which has entered the *Extravagantes communes* with no date
attached to it in the Friedberg edition; and its similarity to the contents of
the final section of *Execrabilis*[96] is so close as to be startling. The only
significant difference in the terms of the two constitutions is that *Ut quos
virtutis* stipulates that the benefices resigned for plurality are to be at the

[93] Above, p. 55; RR ff. 29v, 130v, 147v, 250, 251, 254v, 307v.
[94] *Taxatio Eccl.*, 2.
[95] CIC, Extravag. comm., lib. I, tit. vii, cap. 2 (Friedberg, vol. ii, cols. 1244-5).
[96] Beginning 'Porro, quia quorundam'.

disposal of 'him or them to whom the collation falls', whereas *Execrabilis* states that they are to be reserved to the disposition of the apostolic see. The precise relationship between these two constitutions has not yet been sufficiently determined. Mollat and Haller are of the opinion that *Ut quos* is anterior in date to *Execrabilis*,[97] and in Reynolds' register *Ut quos* is entered without date and with the comment 'Ista constitucio non processit'.[98] In my research I have found no evidence of any benefice the resignation or collation of which is specifically ascribed to *Ut quos*.

Now it is interesting to observe that in a majority of resignations for plurality after 1317 in England it was neither the king nor the pope who secured the patronage but rather 'him or them to whom the collation falls' – as was in fact stipulated in *Ut quos virtutis*. If we may judge from the lists of Sandale, Newport, and Melton, perhaps fifty percent of the benefices vacated were of lay patronage, and they all reverted to their true patrons. Another large proportion of the benefices, as seen in these three registers and in that of Reynolds, was of clerical patronage and was presented again by the bishops or other clerical patrons. And almost half of such benefices mentioned in the papal registers were provided at the requests of the diocesan bishops themselves. Clearly, the situation in England was a pattern such as *Ut quos virtutis* would have produced.

Indeed, the decreasing frequency of papal provisions mentioning *Execrabilis* after the first few years might even suggest that *Ut quos* was issued at a date subsequent to the other and in recognition of existing practice, were it not known that the pope continued to act on the assumption that the provision of such benefices was reserved to himself even when he proceeded to authorize other persons to confer them in his stead.[99] In Ireland, for example, he is known to have written on 1 April 1324 urging the archbishops and bishops there to publish *Execrabilis*,[100] perhaps after some local reluctance. And on 7 March 1325/1326 he ordered his nuncio and collector in England M. Hugh of Angoulême, archdeacon of Canterbury then, to send him a list of the benefices reserved to the apostolic see by *Execrabilis* with particulars of their rents and profits.[101]

---

[97] Mollat, *La Collation*, p. 56 n. 68.

[98] RR f. 39v.

[99] 'Cum de illis nullus preter nos potuerit disponere, generali reservacione per nos facta de talibus beneficiis obsistente': Vatican Archives, Reg. Vat. 113, f. 230v, John XXII to papal nuncios in Spain, 21 Aug. 1326; cf. above, p. 13.

[100] Reg. John XXII, no. 20368; Burns, AHP ix (1971), no. 107.

[101] CPL. ii, 474; Vatican Archives, Reg. Vat. 113, f. 214.

Over a longer range of years, of course, the crown began to experience
the results of *Execrabilis* in various other ways, even though it had been
able to secure very few, if any, of the resigned benefices for its own clerks.
One of these ways was in the difficulties of actual transfer of benefices
from the dispossessed pluralists to their new incumbents. Some of the
former had already sold the grain on their benefices before the new
constitution was promulgated, and when they lost their benefices they had
apparently not yet delivered the grain even though they had already
received the price of it. Explaining their plight to king and council, these
dispossessed pluralists petitioned for remedy; and it was recommended
that they proceed in common law by writs of trespass or replevin.[102]

Another of these ways in which the crown began to experience the
results of *Execrabilis* was expounded by Maitland after a comparison of
the year books and the plea rolls. Under Edward III the crown took the
position that benefices supposed to be vacated by force of *Execrabilis*
were de jure vacant, that it could present to such benefices when it could
establish a claim, and that the royal courts had cognizance of such cases.[103]
About this development we may observe that there were already cases
under Edward II in which the crown had tried to use canon law in this
way;[104] but in at least one of these earlier cases, when the crown in 1313-
1314 had tried to dispossess a pluralist by invoking Archbishop Pecham's
constitution of 1279, the crown had lost its case by decision in the royal
court that under the common law a man might hold as many benefices as
he wished.[105]

In conclusion we may say that *Execrabilis* in England did not put an
end to further papal dispensations for plurality, even though it did force
the resignation of many benefices. The pope presumably made financial
gain from most of these resignations, as d'Assier's accounts show, because
he had previously in *Si gratanter advertitis* reserved the annates of
vacated benefices to himself. He was also able to provide a large number
of the vacated benefices during the first year of the constitution's

---

[102] PRO C49/4/21 (no date). I am indebted to Dr. M. G. A. Vale for assistance in
translation of this document. It was formerly in the PRO obsolete class of 'parliamentary
petitions' (no. 3035), and I have been unable to locate the petition or any resultant writs.

[103] Maitland, '*Execrabilis* in the common pleas', in *Roman Canon Law in the Church of
England*, 148-57, and in *Collected Papers* iii, 54-64; for some modifications of Maitland's
comments see Plucknett, *Cambridge Law Journal* i (1921), 60-3, 74. Another such case is
in PRO C47/15/3/32 (date 1339; misdated 1309 and 1319).

[104] For examples, see Deeley, EHR xliii (1928), p. 509 n. 2.

[105] *Yearbooks of Edward II*, Selden Soc. vol. 39, pp. xxxviii-xli; for similar decisions in
some cases before 1313-1314, see Plucknett, *Cambridge Law Journal* i (1921), 66.

operation. But *Execrabilis* in the long run did not create any permanent or significant new source of papal provisions, and we may conclude this for three reasons that emerge from the previous discussion: (1) after John xxii's second pontifical year (the first of the operation of *Execrabilis*) the papal registers record an acute decrease in the numbers of provisions to benefices vacated under the force of the new constitution; (2) the great majority of benefices vacated by *Execrabilis* were parish churches, and the papal registers after John's second pontifical year record very, very few provisions to parish churches for any reason at all;[106] (3) the vacated benefices in lay gift reverted to their true patrons, the crown secured the presentation of a few such benefices in its own gift by various ways, and the English diocesan bishops were able to influence the appointments to most of the vacated benefices in clerical patronage at first in cooperation with and later in circumvention of the pope. *Execrabilis* did serve to check pluralism, especially the holding of more than one parish church with cure of souls. Yet the degree and extent of its 'actual reception' in England was effectively and ultimately determined by Reynolds and the English episcopate, in much the same way as J. W. Gray has interestingly observed that 'actual reception' was eventually accorded by Archbishop Pecham to the papal legislation of the thirteenth century against pluralism.[107]

The picture presented by W. E. L. Smith and Miss Deeley, and even that implied by Maitland and Plucknett, of the victorious pope after *Execrabilis* reaping 'a rich harvest of benefices for his servants and favourites'[108] in a contest where the king was the only opponent, must be modified by our knowledge of the influence of the bishops. It was the English episcopal hierarchy, largely as a result of its joint action in the provincial assemblies of 1318 and 1319 under the presidency of Archbishop Reynolds, that made the greatest gains in patronage released by Pope John's new constitution.

---

[106] Below, Appendix 1, table D.

[107] *Studies in Church History* iii (1966), 57.

[108] Smith, *Episcopal Appointments*, 99; Deeley, EHR xliii (1928), 504; Maitland, *Collected Papers* iii, 56; Plucknett, *Cambridge Law Journal* i (1921), 61.

13

The Crown and Provisions

Over the years 1305-1334 and particularly during the long pontificate of John xxii the papal registers do reveal a marked increase in the numbers of direct provisions made annually to English benefices.[1] Especially is this noticeable in and after his twelfth pontifical year – 5 September 1327 – 5 September 1328. It has already been shown that no such extensive increase can be ascribed to the effects of *Ex debito* or *Execrabilis* alone, but there is one other factor to be found in the papal registers that does suggest a reason for it. The year in and after which the total number of all English provisions rises sharply is also the same year in and after which there is the greatest increase in the number of provisions that are stated to be granted at the request of the English crown. After the twelfth pontifical year of John xxii and throughout the remainder of his pontificate both these figures continue at a much higher level than in previous years.

This evidence encourages us to conclude with some certainty that the crown itself was under Edward iii at least partly responsible for the sharp increase in the numbers of English provisions over the last seven years of John xxii's pontificate. With the deposition of Edward ii, the restoration of temporalities to Bishops Orleton and Burghersh, and the adjustments of ecclesiastical policy in which the pope's claims were vindicated in several cases,[2] a relationship may well have been established in which the apostolic see was unusually responsive to royal requests for provisions. Indeed, the flood of royal petitions submitted to the pope and recorded in the register of Andreas Sapiti certainly confirms that requests for provisions were frequent during the regency of Mortimer and Isabella as well as in the early years of Edward iii's personal rule, and in the papal

[1] Below, Appendix 1, tables B, D.
[2] Deeley, EHR xliii (1928), 510; Emden, *Oxford* ii, 1403; Reg. Orleton Hereford, pp. xxvii (cf. n. 2), xl seq.

registers several series of provisions and reservations at the crown's request during these years show that the petitions were not without effect.[3] Moreover, the evidence of petitions in Sapiti's register suggests that if anything the crown at this time was requesting more of the provisions than the papal registers indicate.[4] Guillemain's analysis of the English provisions under Benedict XII shows, moreover, that the proportion (although not the raw numbers) of papal provisions granted at royal request during the succeeding years of Edward III continued to rise at least until the death of Benedict XII in 1342.[5]

And yet, if the crown itself encouraged the increase of provisions under Edward III, we must not conclude that there was a lack of cooperation between the popes and Edward II. Extensive analysis of the English episcopal provisions by Clement V and John XXII has already been made,[6]

---

[3] E.g., Reg. John XXII, nos. 60823-40, 60862-3, 61184-8; CPL. ii, 292-3, 376-8, 391.

[4] Above, p. 38 and n. 9.

[5] *La politique bénéficiale*, 83.

[6] Smith, *Episcopal Appointments*, chapter 2, and Pantin, *The English Church*, 9-26, 54-8, both provide convenient summaries. In the same year that Smith's book was published (1938), Miss Kathleen Edwards completed her very fine London M.A. thesis 'The Personnel and Political Activities of the English Episcopate during the Reign of Edward II', which presents much additional information on the same subject. Many (but not all) of her important findings have been published as 'The political importance of the English bishops during the reign of Edward II', EHR lix (1944), 311-47; 'Bishops and learning in the reign of Edward II', CQR cxxxviii (1944), 57-86; and 'The social origins and provenance of the English bishops during the reign of Edward II', TRHS, 5th series, vol. ix (1959), 51-79. Comprehensive biographies are now provided for the graduate bishops in Emden, *Oxford* and *Cambridge*, and for some of the Welsh bishops in the new *Dictionary of Welsh Biography*. For John XXII's episcopal appointments after the death of Edward II see also Highfield, 'The English hierarchy in the reign of Edward III', TRHS, 5th series, vol. vi (1956), 115-38. A summary of some of the information on episcopal appointments in Reynolds' register is given by Miss Churchill, *Canterbury Administration* i, 252-7. Because of the cumulative value of these several works, no further extensive consideration will be given to individual bishops as such in the present study, although three additional points from Reynolds' register are worthy of mention: (1) Reynolds himself seems to have taken an active part in the promotion of Cobham for the see of Worcester in 1317. He may have been encouraged by Cardinal Vidal du Four to influence the king to support Cobham for promotion (RR ff. 38v, 115v, and cf. PRO SC1/32/121). Cobham was a 'familiaris' of this cardinal, and after Cobham's promotion the cardinal was provided to at least three of Cobham's former benefices (below, Appendix 3, no. 12; cf. Reg. Cobham, 97, 169, 174). (2) There seems to have been a prior reservation in the Norwich vacancy of 1325 (RR f. 138; John XXII, Secret Letters, no. 2544; CPL. ii, 466), apparently unknown to Smith (*Episcopal Appointments*, 43) and Grassi (EHR lxx (1955), 556-7). (3) RR ff. 206v-207 does mention delivery of spiritualities to Wulfstan de Bransford on 3 October in the Worcester election of 1327, a point which has not generally been noted: Churchill, *Canterbury Administration* i, 253; Powicke and Fryde, *Handbook*, 261; Haines, JEH xiii (1962), 164, 166; Haines, *University of Birmingham Historical Journal* viii (1962), 104-5.

and this has shown that the reign of Edward II was a major turning point in the development of episcopal provisions. Although the papal provisions of bishops that were against Edward II's wishes all came after 1316, yet a larger proportion of the king's servants was provided to the English episcopate under the more authoritarian and systematic John XXII than under the weaker Clement V who was himself a close friend and former clerk of the English crown. Moreover, in spite of the contests between church and state that most episcopal vacancies occasioned, it will be shown in a later chapter that the crown throughout this period kept the theoretical claims of the papacy firmly under control by the enforcement of an oath from every episcopal provisor acknowledging that he received the temporalities of his see by the grace of the king and not by that of the pope.

The function of ecclesiastical benefices as a method of payment for the servants of pope and king was of fundamental importance in the development of the provisions system. Most of the categories of benefices reserved to the Roman see that were clarified by the terms of *Ex debito* were those of which the incumbents were themselves in the pope's service in one way or another, and analysis in a later chapter of this book will demonstrate the great extent to which such persons – from the cardinals on down – were beneficed in England at this time. Archbishop Reynolds and other high ecclesiastics, as we have seen, made extensive use of this same system to support their own clerks and assistants. The king, too, utilized the provisions system in this way, although in addition he had an extensive patronage of his own that was generally immune from provisions.[7] The need to reward their clerks adequately encouraged both crown and pope to seek the most satisfactory means of providing salaries for them. Both king's clerks and pope's men, on their part, realized that a

---

[7] This patronage is outlined in Pantin, *The English Church*, 30-2. To his summary may be added the customary commissions of the crown to the seneschal of Gascony to present suitable persons in the king's name to all crown livings in the duchy of Aquitaine (*Gascon Rolls*, ed. Renouard, pp. 29, 489, nos. 29, 1675; cf. *Liber Epistolaris* of Richard de Bury, no. 323). The king's use of crown patronage to reward his own clerks has been discussed extensively in Howell, *The King's Government and Episcopal Vacancies*, 381-430, and Hartridge, *Cambridge Historical Journal* ii (1922), 171-7. It appears that the greatest proportion of the king's patronage was not his *pleno iure* but devolved to him in various ways (Howell, *King's Government*, 381). In 1317 Cardinals Gaucelme and Luca made certain petitions to Edward II about royal presentations to benefices (Rymer II:i, 349), but I have been unable to discover what they were. For the ecclesiastical patronage of the French crown at this time, see Caillet, *La papauté d'Avignon et l'église de France*, 399-428.

papal provision was the most efficient way to financial security in their kind of work, so they in turn encouraged the growth of the same system.[8]

No further assessment of the crown's attitude to the provisions system will be made until various safeguards to the royal prerogative have been discussed in the next part of this book. At the moment, however, it may be observed that the crown itself was content to work with the system and to use it for its own interests. Indeed, papal intervention in ecclesiastical appointments at this time was largely at the requests of other parties, and in such a situation the crown was understandably eager to gain the most as one of those parties. The practice of provisions was not arbitrary or capricious, and there were considerable safeguards to respect the claims of all persons seeking any one particular benefice. On the whole the papacy over the period 1305-1334 used the system well, perhaps with even greater justice for the majority of lesser benefices than was true in the case of episcopal provisions. The complaints raised in this period against provisions, at the parliaments of Carlisle and Stamford and at the general council of Vienne, were not the main topics of these assemblies and were decidedly minor when compared with the complaints against provisions that arose later in the century.[9]

The system of provisions did remove the powers of collation from many persons who at an earlier time had been acknowledged as the true patrons of their benefices – a well-founded complaint, and the substance of the objections voiced by the bishop of Angers at the council of Vienne in 1311-1312.[10] But provisions offered a system, comprehensive and equitable, and to men of its day proper and reasonably fair, for the distribution of ecclesiastical appointments. And this system came at a time when the absence of any such system would have undoubtedly meant the domination of those appointments by parties such as royal officials and local magnates, whose interests were even less comprehensive and just than the interests of Clement v and John xxii. The English government knew how to utilize this system, and perhaps even how to get the best of it, in the period under review, and to the crown's strategy we now turn.

---

[8] Howell, *The King's Government and Episcopal Vacancies*, 396-8, 406, points out that the initiative for royal presentations *iure devoluto* had often come from the clerks who were themselves presented. See below, pp. 162-3, 164 seq. For Walter Reynolds as the beneficiary of crown patronage before his consecration, see below, Appendix 12.

[9] Barraclough, *Papal Provisions*, 171; Pantin, *The English Church*, 82 seq.; below, pp. 172-3. Comparatively minor complaints against provisions were also raised by the commons at the York parliament in the fall of 1318 (Richardson and Sayles, *Rot. Parl. Ang. hac. Ined.*, 75), and in the first parliament of Edward iii, Epiphany 1327 (*Rot. Parl.* ii, 76).

[10] Barraclough, *Papal Provisions*, 24-5; Guillemain, *La politique bénéficiale*, 27.

Part II

Safeguarding the Royal Prerogative

1

Unofficial Royal Contacts at the Papal Court

Before considering the major official English contacts at Avignon by way of proctors, diplomatic envoys, and cardinals, it is first necessary to look at the crown's unofficial influence within the residential staff of the curia as well as at the various occasional English visitors to the Roman court. Professor Guillemain in his fine study of the curial personnel at Avignon has concluded on the basis of papal sources that 'Pour les Anglais, Avignon n'était pas un bon lieu'.[1] While this may be true in terms of the small number of English 'curiales' resident there with whom his study is especially concerned, yet evidence will be presented here from English sources to indicate that his numbers are no final indication of the remarkably well-planned strategy of the English crown and episcopal hierarchy in the contemporary Roman curia. This strategy extended beyond the curialists and unofficial visitors to the fields of proctorial representation, frequent diplomatic embassies, and persuasive measures on behalf of the college of cardinals. It is probable that much of the crown's success at this time in manipulating papal measures on finances and provisions as well as in safeguarding its own prerogative in its dealings with the Roman see can be attributed to this strategy as it was worked out in both unofficial and official channels.

Guillemain's analysis of 'curiales' can appropriately be summarized here with respect to English curialists during the pontificates of Clement v and John xxii: he has found a total of 4253 'curialists', or officers performing definite functions in the papal court,[2] during the entire Avignon period from 1309 to 1376 whose names are known. Of these, he has determined the national origins of 2224; there were 1552 French, 521 Italian, sixty-nine from the Empire, fifty Spanish, twenty-four English, and eight others. Of the twenty-four English, one was appointed by

---

[1] *La Cour pontificale*, 614.
[2] Guillemain's definition: *La Cour pontificale*, 2.

Clement v, nine by John xxii. The former was an auditor of causes of the apostolic palace; the other nine comprised three auditors of causes, two minor penitentiaries, two 'capellani commensales', one scribe of apostolic letters, and one scribe of the penitentiary. The largest raw number, as well as the largest percentage, of English curialists under all the Avignonese popes was found under John xxii.[3]

Perhaps the most striking observation about these English curialists is that they were so few. A parallel exists, however, in the comparatively small numbers of papal officials who were beneficed in England at this time. My own research has uncovered, apart from the cardinals and the honorary papal chaplains, eighteen such men: six auditors of causes of the apostolic palace, four papal notaries, one minor penitentiary, one papal 'commensalis', one scribe of apostolic letters, one scribe of the penitentiary, one papal physician, one 'referendarius', and two other members of the papal household who held or claimed English benefices under Clement v and John xxii, and not all of these were Englishmen.[4] Clearly, the English numbers at Avignon were not spectacular, whether we are considering Guillemain's number of Englishmen holding resident positions at the curia (ten), or my own number of papal officials beneficed in England (eighteen). But these numbers do not tell the full story.

English influence in the early years at Avignon was in fact rather strong in two curial departments, one of these being the papal penitentiary. There were three minor penitentiaries under Clement v and John xxii who were English Dominicans and who succeeded one another: John Eclescliff,[5] Nicholas Wisbech,[6] and John Wrotham.[7] Eclescliff was provided to the episcopate in 1318, and Wrotham was a papal chaplain. Wisbech and Wrotham, who were both named as minor penitentiaries by John xxii at the request of Edward ii, also both served at times as crown envoys to the curia and their business was not limited to spiritual matters alone.

It was in the audience of causes of the apostolic palace, however, that Englishmen and English friends were most prominent at this time, and it

---

[3] *La Cour pontificale*, 329, 336, 344, 352, 369, 441, 447, 451, 454.

[4] Below, Appendix 5.

[5] Below, Appendix 5, no. 23. An interesting case of Eclescliff absolving an English layman at the apostolic see from excommunication for laying violent hands upon a clerk, 1310, is preserved in Reg. Greenfield iv, 65.

[6] Clarke, 'Some Secular Activities of the English Dominicans during the Reigns of Edward i, Edward ii, and Edward iii', 144-6, 158, 164-6; above, p. 40 and n. 11.

[7] Emden, *Oxford* iii, 2095-6; Clarke, 'Some Secular Activities', 144-6, 158, 164-6; ccw, 519, 525; Rymer II:i, 424; *Liber Epistolaris* of Richard de Bury, nos. 245-6.

is most of all in this department of the curia that the few English names found by Guillemain in the papal sources do not tell the full story. The total of four English auditors that he has found can be augmented by two non-Englishmen who were beneficed in the realm, and by seven more auditors who had very strong English connections.

Let us begin with the auditors who were beneficed in England during the years 1305-1334, of which there were at least six: M. Rigaud d'Assier, D.C.L., M. William Bateman ('de Norwico'), D.C.L., M. Thomas Fastolf, D.C.L., M. Hugh Geraldi, M. Adam Orleton, D.Cn.L., and M. John de Ros, D.C.L.[8] Geraldi, who had been papal nuncio in England as well as a member of the king's council in Aquitaine, was deposed in 1317 and executed for his attempt to assassinate Pope John xxii.[9] All the other five, papal chaplains and appointees of John xxii, eventually obtained English bishoprics by papal provision. Bateman, Fastolf, Orleton, and Ros were natives of England holding doctorates in law from Oxford or Cambridge.

The audience, known by the end of 1336 as the *rota* either from the round table about which or from the circular hall in which its members sat, was the supreme judicial organ of the curia. In this age of papal centralization, the audience is an example of distribution of power within the curia itself. Clement v in 1309 extended the competence of its auditors to settle all cases involving benefices, and John xxii regulated the work of the audience by his constitution *Ratio iuris* of 16 November 1331.[10] The auditors formed a college having a common liturgical practice for the celebration of mass, they were to wear proper clerical garb in their chambers and to begin hearing cases immediately after the cathedral bells sounded the hour of terce, and each auditor customarily consulted the opinions of the others before giving a final decision in a case.[11] If an

---

[8] Below, Appendix 5, nos. 5, 8, 25, 30, 41, 48.

[9] Below, Appendix 5, no. 30. His register as an auditor, dating from 1311, survives in Vatican Archives, Collectoriae 492A (Barraclough, *Public Notaries*, p. 126 n. 7). The register is partly calendared by Albe, *Autour de Jean xxii. Hugues Géraud*, 139-42. Cf. Göller, *Römische Quartalschrift für christliche Altertumskunde und für Kirchengeschichte* xviii (1904), 101-2. Geraldi was pensioned by Bp. Kellawe of Durham (*Reg. Pal. Dunelm.* iv, 432-3).

[10] Printed in Cerchiari, *Sacra Rota* iii, 69-78, and in Tangl, *Die päpstlichen Kanzlei-Ordnungen*, 83-91. For the audience, see also Boyle, *Vatican Archives*, 90-1; Weakland, *Catholic Historical Review* liv (1968), 53; Sayers, *Papal Judges Delegate*, 14-19; Guillemain, *La Cour pontificale*, 346-8, and Mollat, *The Popes at Avignon*, 299-303. Cerchiari, *Sacra Rota* ii, 22-7, gives an incomplete list of the auditors under Clement v and John xxii.

[11] Fliniaux, *Revue historique de droit français et étranger*, sér. iv, vol. iv (1925), 64-5, underlines the principle of collegiality observed by the auditors. Generally, it would seem

auditor revealed the details of a case or the names of the people involved before the case was closed, or if he accepted any money, he was, under John's constitution, to be suspended from office for a month at the first offense and for life if he offended again. The influence of these auditors in giving final settlement to disputes over English benefices and other matters in the time of Clement v and John xxii was considerable,[12] even though many contemporary English cases were being heard at Avignon by cardinals rather than by auditors.[13]

The biographies of Bateman, Orleton, and Ros compiled by Dr. Emden illustrate the importance attached by the crown and other principals in England to the friendship of these English auditors at Avignon. All three of them, as well as d'Assier, were king's clerks. The career of Ros provides a noteworthy example. He was a papal chaplain, chaplain of the English cardinal Thomas Jorz and of another cardinal, and proctor at the curia for Archbishop Winchelsey, Bishop Swinfield, the episcopal hierarchy of Canterbury province, and Oxford University.[14] He was Archbishop Reynolds' chancellor for some six months in the latter part of 1315.[15] Appointed papal auditor, he took up residence at the Roman curia in 1317 with dispensation for nonresidence in his numerous English benefices, and he was provided to the see of Carlisle in 1325. The influence of Ros as an auditor during his time at Avignon can be seen in his own lengthy dispute at the Roman court over the years 1317-1324 with the Hereford cathedral chapter, where he held a canonry and prebend. This concerned their refusal to make payments of his 'greater commons' because he was not resident. Claiming that he was entitled to such payments by virtue of his service to the apostolic see, Ros at one point managed to procure excommunication of the entire chapter and at

---

that the more important the case under consideration, the more extensive was the consultation among other auditors. When the auditor Oliverus de Cerzeto in 1326 gave definitive sentence in the long and complicated dispute over the prebend of Blewbury in Salisbury, it was said that he did so 'factaque de hiis omnibus cum coauditoribus nostris primi gradus sacri palacii relacione plenaria et fideli, et cum ipsis et nobiscum et eciam cum nonnullis aliis peritis deliberacione super hiis prehabita diligenti, de omnium ipsorum coauditorum nostrorum consilio et assensu' (Reg. Martival i, 222). Cf. below, Appendix 6, no. 50.

[12] Mollat, *Revue d'histoire ecclésiastique* xxxii (1936), 883-7; below, Appendix 6, nos. 4, 17, 18, 20, 24, 29, 39, 40, 42, 50-2, 59, 65, 75.

[13] Below, Appendix 6, nos. 10, 12, 19, 22, 26, 32, 34, 36, 39, 41, 48, 49, 56; Mollat, *Revue d'histoire ecclésiastique* xlvi (1951), 91.

[14] Emden, *Oxford* iii, 1591.

[15] RR f. 16; Churchill, *Canterbury Administration* ii, 244.

another time the chapter's proctors were even refused admission to the papal palace – of which, of course, he was an auditor![16]

In addition to the six auditors beneficed in England, several other members of the audience at this time also had close English connections. Three auditors appointed by Clement v – Hugh Geraldi (already mentioned), Bernard Royardi, and Gaucelme de Jean (created cardinal by John xxii in 1316) – were members of the English king's council in Aquitaine.[17] Hugh and Bernard were both pensioned by the English king in 1311.[18] Gaucelme was working for the interests of Edward ii at the Roman court as early as 1314, for which he was granted a pension and other honours by the crown.[19] Two more auditors came on papal diplomatic missions to England – M. Sicardus de Vauro, as one of the papal inquisitors for the process against the Templars in 1309-1311,[20] and M. Bérenger d'Olargues, who had come to England in the company of Cardinal Arnaud Nouvel in 1312-1313 and was later appointed auditor by John xxii.[21] Another auditor, M. Raymond Subirani, was counted by both Edward ii and Archbishop Reynolds (as well as Philip iv of France) as being among their clerks and good friends at Avignon, and over the years from 1313 to 1320 the English king sought his assistance in various matters at the Roman court.[22] Still another papal auditor, M. Bertrandus de Mediolano, papal chaplain, who had often served as an executor for papal provisions to English benefices and heard some English cases at the Roman court, is known to have been pensioned by the crown and was described as its 'advocate' in the curia.[23]

[16] Below, Appendix 6, no. 39.

[17] *Gascon Rolls*, ed. Renouard, pp. xxiv-xxv; Cerchiari, *Sacra Rota* ii, 23; Guillemain, *La Cour pontificale*, 483.

[18] Vatican Archives, Collectoriae 492A, f. 20v.

[19] Below, Appendix 3, no. 17.

[20] Cerchiari, *Sacra Rota* ii, 23; Reg. John xxii, no. 291; Lunt, *Financial Relations* i, 560-2.

[21] Cerchiari, *Sacra Rota* ii, 24-7; Reg. John xxii, no. 496; Guillemain, *La Cour pontificale*, 354.

[22] RR f. 119; PRO E101/375/8, ff. 10, 12; CCR 1313-18, 92, 144; CCW, 405, 514; CPR 1313-17, 85, 87; CPR 1317-21, 248; *Treaty Rolls*, ed. Chaplais, nos. 522, 523, 527; *Reg. Pal. Dunelm.* i, 359; Reg. Sandale, 330-1; Rymer II:i, 229, 240, 243, 247, 250, 302, 305, 368; Langlois, *Revue historique* lxxxvii (1905), p. 77 n. 2; Roberts, 'Edward ii, the Lords Ordainers, and Piers Gaveston's Jewels and Horses', 21; Davies, *Baronial Opposition*, 281. For identification of Subirani as correspondent of Petrarch, see *Liber Epistolaris* of Richard de Bury, p. xii n. 1; cf. below, p. 111.

[23] PRO E101/309/32; E372/177, m. 40; CPL ii, 141; Reg. John xxii, nos. 2293, 3210, 7431, 7436, 11639; Reg. Martival i, 223; iv, 225-6. The last of these references establishes that he was an auditor.

Such close connections between numerous auditors and the crown suggest that English influence in the apostolic audience under Popes Clement and John was much stronger than is indicated by the four English auditors named by Guillemain or even by the proportion of English auditors during the entire Avignon period (ten out of 140) that he has found in the papal sources. Indeed, in 1337 it was another English auditor and canonist, Thomas Fastolf, who compiled the earliest known collection of the decisions of the *rota*.[24] Just as Professor Jacob has observed that the most important position held by up-and-coming English clerks at the papal curia in the early fifteenth century was that of abbreviator of the papal chancery,[25] so without doubt in the early fourteenth century the corresponding post was that of auditor of causes of the apostolic palace. The audience wielded important powers, the English influence there was very strong, and those members of the audience who served the crown were well rewarded for their efforts.

In addition to the English members of the resident curial staff, numerous other Englishmen also went to Avignon on various occasions. Bishops-elect might go there to persuade the pope to confirm their elections. Ten English bishops received their consecrations from cardinals or from the pope himself at Avignon during the pontificates of Clement and John, and two more did so at Lyons when the papal court was there in January of 1305/1306.[26] The requirement for bishops of trips 'ad limina apostolorum' every three years, however, had by the early fourteenth century been replaced by standard visitation taxes paid through proctors and Italian bankers, and even the verb 'visitare' used in this context no longer necessarily meant a personal visit.[27] But the abbots-elect of English monastic houses exempt from episcopal control and dependent directly upon the apostolic see still at this time usually had to go there for confirmation of their elections and often received their blessing there as

---

[24] Cerchiari, *Sacra Rota* ii, 26; Boyle, *Vatican Archives*, 91; Guillemain, *La Cour pontificale*, 348; Pantin, *The English Church*, p. 21 n. 3; Pantin essay in *The English Church and the Papacy*, ed. Lawrence, 173. The collection attributed to Fastolf is apparently known only from early printed editions. The decisions recorded in it all date from 1336-1337, the earliest being 11 Dec. 1336 (Fliniaux, *Revue historique de droit français et étranger*, sér. iv, vol. iv (1925), 63, 390, 393). For Englishmen in the *rota* at this time and for other fourteenth-century collections of its decisions, see Ullmann, 'A Decision of the Rota Romana on the Benefit of Clergy in England', 464 seq.

[25] 'To and from the court of Rome', 161-2.

[26] Stubbs, *Registrum Sacrum Anglicanum*, 70-4.

[27] Lunt, *Financial Relations* i, 482-6; Göller, *Die Einnahmen der apostolischen Kammer* i, 74; RR f. 211.

well,[28] although late in the fourteenth century it became the custom for this obligation to be commuted for a fixed annual premium.[29]

A number of English scholars and theologians, moreover, were drawn to contemporary Avignon as an intellectual centre – FitzRalph, Lutterel, Ockham, Waleys[30] – and Lutterel was urged to seek ecclesiastical preferment there. It was not until later in the century that English students of law were registered there in the university.[31] In the time of John XXII there was also an English stonemason in Avignon – one Hugh Wilfred, who worked in construction of the chapel of angels and archangels in Avignon cathedral and may also possibly have been responsible for John XXII's funerary monument which in its architecture and sculpture is said to bear analogies to early fourteenth-century monuments in the south of England.[32] Moreover, there was a steady stream of Englishmen going to Avignon to seek absolution in reserved cases and to defend their legal rights in other matters of litigation.[33]

The divers reasons of all these men for going to Avignon ensured that at any given time there was certain to be a number of Englishmen resident there, and by 1331 the proprietor of at least one of the lodging houses in Avignon, Peter Miller by name, was an Englishmen.[34] But the interests of these men were not regularly directed to the major concerns of the English crown and hierarchy, even if the English Dominican Thomas Waleys on one occasion attacked the very provisions system itself. This was during the controversy over the beatific vision in 1333 when he

[28] *William Thorne's Chronicle*, 395, 483; Reg. John XXII, nos. 2827, 5469; Pantin, *The English Church*, 57; Walsingham, *Gesta Abbatum* ii, 113-14, 185-92.

[29] Knowles, *The Religious Orders* i, 278-9; ii, 249; Lunt, *Financial Relations* ii, 233-9.

[30] Emden, *Oxford* ii, 692-4, 1181-2, 1384-7; iii, 1508, 1961-2; Guillemain, *La Cour pontificale*, 614; Knowles, *The Religious Orders* i, 245-52; Leff, *Richard FitzRalph*, 1-2, 6; Lunt, *Financial Relations* ii, 208; Pantin, *The English Church*, 16-17, 20, 64-5, 120-1, 145-6, 151-64; Pantin essay in *The English Church and the Papacy*, ed. Lawrence, 170-3.

[31] Guillemain, *La Cour pontificale*, 613.

[32] Girard, *Évocation du vieil Avignon*, 166; Guillemain, *La Cour pontificale*, 504.

[33] Below, Appendix 6; RR f. 51; Haines, *Administration*, 178; Moorman, *Church Life*, 151; HMC Eighth Rep., I, app., 350; *Historical Papers*, ed. Raine, 317-18, 330; Reg. Cobham, 48-9, 81; Reg. Greenfield ii, 88, 121, 164-5; ibid. iv, 65, 222; Reg. Hethe, 446-7; Reg. London, 69-71, 119, 125; *Reg. Pal. Dunelm.* i, 210-12. At times absolution in reserved cases could be obtained from the papal nuncios in England (RR f. 5v; RWR, 57-8, 71, 80, 84; Reg. Greenfield ii, 28, 39, 40-1, 178-9).

[34] 'Petrus Molinerius': Vatican Archives, Collectoriae 52, f. 239. Guillemain, *La Cour pontificale*, 534, 549, 554, indicates that the names of at least thirty Englishmen who stayed overnight at Avignon in the years 1318-1334 are known from the surviving registers of the assignators and taxators of lodgings there, and he proposes to utilize this and much other information in a future work on daily life at Avignon.

preached that the only scriptural words in support of John xxii's view were those from the conclusion of Psalm 71 (in the Vulgate), which were identical with the formula for conceding a papal grace: 'Fiat, fiat. Your devoted son begs your holiness for such and such a benefice. Granted, granted'.[35]

[35] Knowles, *The Religious Orders* i, 250.

2

English Proctors at Avignon

The crown and hierarchy needed regular and official channels for the transaction of their affairs at Avignon. Already Professors Lunt and Jacob have partly sketched the outlines of English proctorial representation at the Roman curia in the late fourteenth and fifteenth centuries,[1] and Miss Sayers has collected the names of British proctors at the curia endorsed on bulls over the period from 1198 to 1415.[2] It was, then, through the proctors, in addition to the diplomatic envoys, that the major portion of English business at Avignon was handled in the early fourteenth century. The crown, most bishops, Oxford University, and the more important religious houses, all had proctors in the Roman court, and a number of clients might often share the same proctor. These proctors, acting under notarial commission, were of two sorts – men sent there ad hoc from England to represent their principals in specific cases, and men in more-or-less permanent residence there who were usually paid regular salaries to look after any business that might arise. A proctor might facilitate the obtaining of papal bulls and other grants, contract loans, make payments of incidental fees or major expenses, advise his principal about developments in the curia, and represent his client at the audience of contradicted letters[3] or in legal proceedings. It was imperative that the proctor's instrument of procuration state exactly what he was empowered to do.[4] Some further indication of the wide variety of a proctor's business may be had from the fifty-five different proctorial commissions in the

---

[1] Lunt, *Financial Relations* ii, 195-9, 255-63; Jacob, 'To and from the court of Rome', 161-81. Cf. Behrens, EHR xlix (1934), 640-56.

[2] Sayers, 'Proctors representing British Interests at the Papal Court, 1198-1415', 143-63.

[3] See, for example, Sayers, 'Canterbury Proctors at the Court of *Audientia Litterarum Contradictarum'*, *Traditio* xxii (1966), 311-45, and Sayers, *Papal Judges Delegate*, 11-14, 55-8.

[4] Brentano, *York Metropolitan Jurisdiction and Papal Judges Delegate*, 220-5.

contemporary formulary of the Roman curia edited by Barraclough.[5] And a proctor's contacts could be interesting and varied. M. Stephen of St. George, for example, a foreign wardrobe clerk in England who was proctor of Edward I at Rome in 1283-1290, was a scribe of the papal chancery and a clerk of Charles of Salerno king of Sicily. His brother, Peter of St. George, a monk of Monte Cassino, was made king's chaplain by Edward I 'in consideration of the merits of Master Stephen his brother'.[6] There was at least one case in this period, moreover, of an Englishman at the curia, one William of York, who claimed to be a proctor and sold bulls of provision there to another Englishman which were later declared to be false after they had been inspected by officials of the bishop of Salisbury.[7]

The most important resident proctor of the English crown at Avignon in the early fourteenth century was M. Andreas Sapiti, a citizen of Florence who was at work as a 'tabellio' in the curia at least by 1304.[8] At various times he also served as proctor for Archbishops Reynolds and Stratford of Canterbury, for the monks of Westminster and of Christ Church Canterbury, for Bishops Beaumont and Bury of Durham, Northburgh of Coventry and Lichfield, Orleton of Hereford, Burghersh of Lincoln, Airmyn of Norwich, Sandale of Winchester, and Reynolds and Orleton of Worcester, for Bonus abbot of Tavistock, and for numerous Irish, Scottish, and Welsh prelates as well as for some bishops on the continent.[9] Although resident at Avignon he made numerous trips to England, for example in 1313, 1317, 1325, 1334, and 1336.[10] He died before 21 November 1338.[11] Edward II described Sapiti as his 'clericus et

---

[5] *Public Notaries*, 5, 180-92.

[6] Powicke, *Thirteenth Century*, p. 263 n. 1; Tout, *Chapters* ii, p. 24 n. 1; *Treaty Rolls*, ed. Chaplais, nos. 137-8, 146-51. For the crown's proctors at Rome in the thirteenth century, see Brentano, *Two Churches*, 1-61, and *The English Church and the Papacy*, ed. Lawrence, 126-7; for those in the twelfth, see Richardson and Sayles, *Governance*, 298.

[7] Reg. Martival iv, 92-6; for other cases of forged bulls relating to English matters, cf. CPL ii, 101, 246, 254-5, 263, 350; Reg. John XXII, nos. 26395, 29937, 58209.

[8] Kirsch, *Historisches Jahrbuch* xiv (1893), 590.

[9] RR ff. 1, 1v, 84v, 237; PRO C47/15/1/3; Cant. Cath. MS Reg. G, f. xxxv verso; Cant. Cath. MS S.V. i, 53; RWR, 4; Reg. Hethe, 550; Reg. Orleton Hereford, 77; Reg. Sandale, 7; *Chartulary of Winchester Cathedral*, ed. Goodman, nos. 177, 198, 200-2; Boyle, *Vatican Archives*, 123, 149, 170; Göller, *Einnahmen* i, 694 (index). He was pensioned by the monks of Westminster Abbey in 1331 (HMC Fourth Rep., app., 175).

[10] CPR 1313-17, 45; CPR 1317-21, 16; CPR 1324-7, 125; CPR 1330-4, 558; CPR 1334-8, 7, 316. Royal power was issued in 1334 for removal of Sapiti as king's proctor, but as early as 1336 he was again active as king's proctor in the curia (CPR 1334-8, 33, 316, 330; Rymer II:ii, 895; PRO E372/177, m. 40).

[11] Kirsch, *Historisches Jahbruch* xiv (1893), 594.

familiaris',[12] and Sapiti styled himself, even when writing to a foreign king, as 'illustris regis Anglie procurator in Romana curia'.[13] Sapiti was granted a pension of five pounds a year by Walter Reynolds as bishop of Worcester in January of 1308/1309 shortly before Reynolds set out for Avignon as a royal envoy,[14] and as early as 1311 the king was seeking Sapiti's help as his clerk in the curia.[15] On 26 May 1314 he was granted an annual pension of fifty marks from the English crown at the suggestion of Archbishop Reynolds,[16] and this fee, together with an annual issue of two robes, seems to have continued throughout his life.[17] Shortly after this grant he sent a number of confidential letters to Edward II concerning prospects for the election of a new pope.[18] He was working with the papal auditor Raymond Subirani on behalf of Edward II and other English interests at the curia at this time as well as later.[19] One particular assignment of Sapiti and Subirani, during the summer of 1314 when Sapiti was granted the crown's pension, was to arrange easier terms for repayment of a major loan granted to Edward II by the late Clement v.[20] In 1321 Edward II asked Sapiti to secure access at the papal throne for the Dominican John Wrotham, who had recently been made papal penitentiary.[21] Much use has already been made in this book of one of Sapiti's registers, dating from the fourth decade of the fourteenth century, that survives among the Barberini manuscripts at Rome. Its entries indicate that Sapiti handled a far greater volume of English business at the curia than might be guessed from the numbers of references to him in Rymer's *Foedera*, the calendared papal registers, and other printed publications.

[12] PRO E43/528.

[13] Kirsch, *Historisches Jahrbuch* xiv (1893), 590.

[14] RWR, 4.

[15] Rymer II:i, 126, 131; Reg. Sandale, 284, 324.

[16] CPR 1313-17, 95, 117.

[17] He was paid 100 marks on 8 June 1314 (PRO E43/528). Larson, EHR liv (1939), 403, recounts payments of fifty marks in 1333 and 1336, and the late Dr. J. T. Ferguson informed me of the same issue in 1337 (PRO E403/294, m. 4).

[18] Langlois, *Journal des Savants*, n.s., 2nd year (1904), 449-51; PRO SC1/34/176.

[19] Langlois, *Revue historique* lxxxvii (1905), p. 77 n. 2; CCW, 525; Rymer II:i, 302, 305; HMC Fourth Rep., app., 385; *Reg. Pal. Dunelm.* iv, 392; PRO E101/375/8, ff. 7-10; PRO SC1/37/62; PRO SC1/49/38; PRO SC1/49, verso of piece 96 (also called 105); PRO SC1/55/47; Burns, AHP ix (1971), no. 98; Smalley, *English Friars and Antiquity*, 69; *Liber Epistolaris* of Richard de Bury, nos. 172, 218, 251; Brown, *Studies in Medieval and Renaissance History* viii (1971), 147; above, p. 105.

[20] Cf. below, p. 171.

[21] Rymer II:i, 444; CCW, 525.

The interests of Sapiti's family in England demonstrate the influence that a curial proctor could wield in the land of his major clients, as well as the extent to which the crown was willing to go in encouraging Sapiti's loyalty and service. J. P. Kirsch made a few comments about Sapiti's family in his monograph published in 1893, but we can know much more about his relatives now thanks to the printed Latin calendars of the papal registers and the pertinent British calendars of record publications, all of which have appeared since Kirsch was writing. Andreas, who was the son of Filippo Sapiti of Florence,[22] had at least three brothers: Ranuccio, Pietro, and Simone.[23] Ranuccio was a proctor for Edward II in Florence in 1311,[24] and his brother Pietro was resident in England in 1318-1320 while acting as executor of numerous papal bulls.[25] Simone, a papal chaplain, held various prebends and a parish church in England,[26] and both Simone and Pietro were provided to foreign benefices at the request of Edward II.[27] Andreas, Ranuccio, and Pietro, together with their nephew Stephanus Gutii of Florence, had important interests in Ireland and somehow managed to secure for themselves some or all of the profits of the temporalities of the see of Armagh during its vacancies after the successive resignations of the brothers Walter and Roland Jorz.[28] In October of 1323 the king took action against them for this, and issued a prohibition against their attempt to collect further such profits by causing the archbishop-elect Stephen Segrave to be cited outside the realm. However, this incident seems to have done no permanent damage to the standing of the Sapiti family with the crown.[29] The pensions that Reynolds and Edward II had granted Andreas in 1309 and 1314 were to continue until one of his sons received an English benefice in the gift of each, and it is interesting to find that no less than three of his sons − Eduardo, Otto, and Filippo − came to hold several English benefices in the years following.[30] Filippo, a papal chaplain, received a parish church by

[22] Reg. Clem. v, no. 10161.

[23] That Simone was the brother of Andreas is established by Reg. Clem. v, no. 10161.

[24] CPR 1307-13, 306, 320.

[25] CPL ii, 178, 187, 192, 196.

[26] Le Neve, *Chichester*, 43; Le Neve, *Coventry and Lichfield*, 58; CPL ii, 543; 590; CPR 1324-7, 19, 49; CPR 1334-8, 24.

[27] Reg. John XXII, nos. 3167, 3169.

[28] For disputes over the Armagh temporalities in the previous century, see Watt, 'English Law and the Irish Church', 145-53.

[29] CPR 1313-17, 380; CPR 1317-21, 2, 263, 406; CPR 1321-4, 137, 346; CPR 1324-7, 132; CFR 1319-27, 241.

[30] EDUARDO: Le Neve, *Coventry and Lichfield*, 58.

OTTO: Le Neve, *Chichester*, 43; Le Neve, *Nor. Prov.*, 93; Le Neve, *Welsh*, 30; CPL ii, 326.

royal presentation, and Otto later became a king's clerk and the principal heir and executor of his father Andreas.[31] Another son, Berto, was provided to a foreign benefice at the English king's request,[32] and still another – Remigio – became a Cistercian monk.[33]

The distinction between resident and ad hoc proctors at the curia, although convenient today for purposes of discussion, must not however be regarded as a distinction which is clear in the contemporary records. For, whereas Andreas Sapiti was a Florentine who made several trips from the curia to England, there were in fact a number of Englishmen holding numerous types of procurations from the crown or other principals in England, who resided for various periods of time in the curia. One of the most important of these was Adam Murimuth, an English ecclesiastical lawyer and administrator who went to Avignon on numerous occasions as proctor for the king, Archbishops Winchelsey and Reynolds, Christ Church Canterbury, Bishop Orleton of Hereford, and Oxford University.[34] Provisions and elections to English sees, as well as other contemporary events at the papal court, form some of the main themes of his chronicle. And among many other representatives of the English crown there, such as the influential Adam Orleton, or the Dominicans John Wrotham and Nicholas Wisbech, or the royal clerks Thomas of Lugoure, Walter de Maidstone, Robert de Solbury, Thomas de Southwerke, and William de Weston, the distinction is not always clear between proctors, envoys, or messengers, and it is probable that contemporary terminology did not intend it to be so.[35]

FILIPPO: CPL ii, 268, 279; CPR 1313-17, 95; CPR 1324-7, 19, 49; Le Neve, *Mon. So. Prov.*, 50. Filippo was reported as alien and nonresident in his parish church of Merriott (Som.) on 26 Jan. 1324/1325, when his goods in this church were sequestrated on account of the war of St. Sardos (PRO C47/18/1/4).

That Eduardo and Otto were sons of Andreas is established from the above references; that Filippo was, is indicated in Reg. Clem. v, nos. 3098, 5796, and Reg. John XXII, no. 10389.

[31] CCR 1333-7, 708; CPR 1338-40, 384.

[32] Reg. John XXII, no. 3168.

[33] Kirsch, *Historisches Jahrbuch* xiv (1893), 584, 594. Andreas tried to secure a position for his son Remigio teaching theology in the University of Paris.

[34] Emden, *Oxford* ii, 1329-30.

[35] Information on the activities of each of these men at Avignon is found in Emden, *Oxford*, with the exception of Wisbech, for whom see Clarke, 'Some Secular Activities of the English Dominicans', 141, 145; John XXII, Secret Letters, no. 792; and above, p. 40. For Wrotham, in addition to Emden, see Clarke, 'Some Secular Activities', 30-1, 165-6. For other king's clerks in the Roman curia see Rymer II:i, 131, 185, 305, 392.

3

Crown Envoys to the Roman Court

A number of the Englishmen holding procurations for the curia were
sent there by the crown on diplomatic missions, and for the sake of order
we can separate these missions and discuss them as a category in
themselves. For, in addition to its proctors, the crown's major medium for
the transaction of business at the papal court was the frequent dispatch of
diplomatic envoys to Avignon. Each embassy, or mission, consisted of a
number of persons, each usually paid at a per diem rate in accord with his
own status,[1] who travelled to the Roman court in order to transact royal
business there and perhaps elsewhere. Professor Cuttino has described the
sort of persons selected to go on these missions.[2] They would present the
crown's requests in the curia on such standard topics as clerical taxation,
Robert Bruce and Scotland, marriage dispensations, relations with France,
a crusade, canonization of saints, the ordinances, Piers Gaveston, Ireland,
Gascony, papal provisions and other bulls, as well as on less common
matters such as Edward II's request for a papal loan which resulted in the
'tempus obligacionis' of Gascony,[3] papal recognition of the University of
Cambridge, the question of whether Edward II should be anointed with
the holy oil of St. Thomas of Canterbury,[4] and the arrangements for the
Pater sancte signature whereby John XXII would be able to distinguish the

---

[1] Larson, EHR liv (1939), 406, gives a graduated schedule of their wages. Unusually
full records of wages for proctors at the Roman court are recorded in LAO, MS Reg.
Dalderby III, ff. 374, 381v, 399v, 427.

[2] *English Diplomatic Administration*, 134-44.

[3] Below, p. 171.

[4] Renouard, *Annales du Midi* lxvii (1955), 130-2; Cobban, BJRL xlvii (1964), 67-8; Reg.
Orleton Hereford, p. xvii; CPL ii, 436-7; Ullmann, *Journal of Theological Studies*, n.s. vol.
viii (1957), 129-33; Sandquist, 'The Holy Oil of St. Thomas of Canterbury'. To this, the
pope replied, rather ambiguously, that there would be neither superstition nor sin
involved in so doing, but that if it were done it should be kept secret and private. It is not
known whether Edward proceeded with the proposal, but the probability is that he did
not.

genuine requests of the young Edward III.[5] But the crown could not expect to receive unless it also gave, and so it was also customary for the envoys at Avignon to make judicious distribution of annual pensions and gifts to various cardinals and other curial agents, as well as to convey costly gifts at times from the king to the pope himself. Often the crown enhanced its position to receive favours by making such financial payments as the census, tribute, tenth, or cardinals' pensions by the agency of its envoys.

These missions or embassies varied widely in importance,[6] and in some cases their effects extended far beyond the intended results. For example, the nucleus of the household that Walter Reynolds was to have as archbishop of Canterbury can be found in close company with him on the embassy that he led in 1309 less than a year after his consecration to Worcester.[7] In the embassy of 1316-1317 J. C. Davies and T. F. Tout found the origins of the 'middle party' in the struggle between Edward II and Lancaster,[8] but this has more recently been denied by both Phillips and Maddicott.[9] The total number of these embassies is uncertain, but their frequency and magnitude were far greater than the numbers suggested by Professor Guillemain.[10] The present writer has found

[5] Below, p. 169.

[6] For one very helpful attempt to classify the varieties, see Cuttino, *Eng. Dip. Adm.*, 127-44; for another attempt see Queller, *The Office of Ambassador*, and the review of this work by Chaplais in *History*, n.s., vol. liii (1968), 403-4.

[7] CPR 1307-13, 102-7.

[8] Davies, *Baronial Opposition*, 429.

[9] Phillips, *Aymer de Valence*, 107, 145; Maddicott, *Thomas of Lancaster*, 195, 199, 208, 215.

[10] The evidence for these embassies which I have set forth below suggests that the total number of Englishmen who went to Avignon during the entire period when the papal court was there must have been considerably greater than the ninety whose names are known to Guillemain (*La Cour pontificale*, 612), and that the total number of English ecclesiastics sent to the curia by the English king during the entire Avignon period was much greater than the 'good ten' whose names Guillemain has found (ibid., 613: 'une bonne dizaine').

The following is a list of sources that I have collected to use in discussing English royal missions to the papal court during the pontificates of Clement V and John XXII. A complete list of sources for such missions would have to include additional material from the enrolled accounts, wardrobe books, and calendars of patent and close rolls, as well as from other sources. A number and date is assigned here to each group of sources appearing to represent one mission, but this classification must remain highly tentative until a full study of all sources is made.

(1) *1305*: PRO E101/309/9; E101/367/6; E101/369/11, f. 184v; SC7/10/19; Bod. MS Tanner 197, f. 41v; CCR 1302-7, 351; *Liber Epistolaris* of Richard de Bury, p. xxix-xxx; Reg. Gainsborough, 26; Reg. Winchelsey, pp. xxiii, 1036-7; *Ann. London*, 143; *Flores Hist.* iii, 127; P&C ii, 1230; Rymer I:ii, 975; II:i, 98; Clarke, 'Some Secular Activities', 150; Fraser, *Bek*, 164-5, 211; Kingsford, 'John de Benstede and his missions for Edward I',

considerable evidence for some twenty-five such royal embassies to the papal court during the years 1305-1334, and there were undoubtedly a

---

350-9; Lunt, AHR xviii (1912), 52-3; Lunt, 'Clerical tenths levied in England by papal authority during the reign of Edward II', 157; Lunt, *Financial Relations* i, 165, 378, 382, 488; Powicke, *Thirteenth Century*, p. 541 n. 1; Denton, EHR lxxxiii (1968), 312.

(2) *1306*: PRO E101/309/12; Rymer I:ii, 984-5; Emden, *Oxford* i, 451; *Liber Epistolaris* of Richard de Bury, p. 299.

(3) *1307*: PRO 1301-7, 533; Murimuth, *Con. Chron.*, 12; Rymer I:ii, 1017-18; Emden, *Oxford* ii, 751; Ullmann, JEH vi (1955), 31, 36.

(4) *1307-1308*: BL MS Cott. Cleopatra E.i, f. 252 (top foliation); Rymer II:i, 13; Emden, *Oxford* ii, 1402.

(5) *1309*: PRO E159/82, m. 57; E159/83, mm. 10, 11d; E101/372/23; E403/144, m. 5-6; SC7/10/33; CPR 1307-13, 102-7; CCW, 279, 283; RWR, 7-11, 181; Reg. Winchelsey, 1036; *Ann. Paul.*, 267; Rymer II:i, 68-72; *Liber Epistolaris* of Richard de Bury, no. 34; Clarke, 'Some Secular Activities', 155; Baluzius, *Vitae Paparum Avenionensium* ii, 99; Davies, *Baronial Opposition*, 101, 265, 323; Emden, *Oxford* ii, 1402; Lunt, EHR xli (1926), 349; Lunt, *Financial Relations* i, 384.

(6) *1310*: Emden, *Oxford* ii, 1402.

(7) *1311*: PRO C47/27/8/10; C81/1705/3, 79; CCW, 374; Rymer II:i, 128, 145; Davies, *Baronial Opposition*, 260, 262.

(8) *1311-1312 (council of Vienne)*: BL MS Cott. Nero C.viii, ff. 55-8; P&C ii, 1350-6; RWR, v-vi, 23, 182; CCW, 348-9, 363, 366-7, 369-70, 377; Rymer II:i, 101, 135-6, 141-2, 145; CPR 1307-13, 376, 378, 380, 382, 385, 388, 397, 459; CCR 1307-13, 373, 435, 438; HMC Fifth Rep., app., 453; HMC, *Wells* i, 62; Lunt, *Financial Relations* i, 394-5; Müller, *Das Konzil von Vienne*, 37, 65-84, 663-70; Stubbs, *Registrum Sacrum Anglicanum*, 204; Reg. Halton, vol. i, pp. xxvi, xxxv; vol. ii, pp. 1-9, 38-41, 72; Reg. Orleton Hereford, p. v; Reg. Greenfield i, 59; Cal. Reg. Droxford, 44; *Treaty Rolls*, ed. Chaplais, no. 493.

(9) *1312*: PRO E101/375/8; CPL ii, 107; Rymer II:i, 156, 161, 166, 175-6, 178, 190, 191, 194, 208; Davies, *Baronial Opposition*, 173, 190, 280; Renouard, *Annales du Midi* lxvii (1955), 130-1.

(10) *1313*: Rymer II:i, 227; Renouard, *Annales du Midi* lxvii (1955), 132; Roberts, 'Edward II, the Lords Ordainers, and Piers Gaveston's Jewels and Horses (1312-1313)', p. 21.

(11) *1314*: Rymer II:i, 277; Emden, *Oxford* ii, 1402.

· (12) *1315-1316*: PRO E101/309/20, E101/354/11/18; Brown, *Studies in Medieval and Renaissance History* viii (1971), 149.

(13) *1316-1317*: PRO C47/27/8/36; C47/29/9/4-5; C81/1706/2; SC1/45/192; SC7/56/26; Soc. Ant. MS 120, ff. 23v-27, 53v-54, 92v; BL MS Cott. Cleopatra E.i, f. 260v (top foliation); RR ff. 119, 215v; LAO, MS Reg. Dalderby III, f. 361; CPL ii, 240, 417, 442-4; Devon, *Issues of the Exchequer*, 133; *Reg. Pal. Dunelm.*, vol. iv, pp. xlix, lxiii, lxviii, 393; *Liber Epistolaris* of Richard de Bury, nos. 164, 167, 172-3; *Treaty Rolls*, ed. Chaplais, nos. 556, 560, 612; CCW, 444, 450, 455; *Early Registers of Writs*, ed. de Haas and Hall, pp. lvii, 186; Murimuth, *Con. Chron.*, 26; *Vita Edwardi Secundi*, 78-9; Rymer II:i, 302-3, 308, 311-12, 347; Cobban, BJRL xlvii (1964), 67-8; Davies, *Baronial Opposition*, 112, 285, 429; Emden, *Oxford* ii, 1402; Kirsch, *Historisches Jahrbuch* xiv (1893), 591; Lunt, 'Clerical tenths levied in England by papal authority during the reign of Edward II', p. 170 n. 88; Lunt, *Financial Relations* i, 166, 518; Phillips, *Aymer de Valence*, 107-11, 115, 259; BL Cott. Charter II.26.8.

(14) *1319*: Reg. John XXII, no. 11737; CPR 1317-21, 343; Rymer II:i, 383, 387, 399; Emden, *Oxford* ii, 1330; Lunt, *Financial Relations* i, 407.

few others. Separate embassies were also sent from the prince of Wales.[11] It is not possible here to recount the details of all these missions – who went on them, the exact dates, routes travelled, salaries paid, business proposed and accomplished, although in many cases this information is to be found in the documents that survive.

For the purpose of showing the influence that these English embassies brought to bear in the Roman court, however, we may note certain points about them. It has been shown that these missions to the curia often resulted in papal provisions to bishoprics or other promotions for the

---

(15) 1320: PRO E372/170, m. 20v; BL MS Add. 17362, f. 11v; CPL ii, 445; CPR 1317-21, 433; *Treaty Rolls*, ed. Chaplais, no. 610, and p. 234 n. 3; Reg. Cobham, 80-2; Murimuth, *Con. Chron.*, 31; Rymer II:i, 420, 433; *Liber Epistolaris* of Richard de Bury, nos. 29, 32, 37, 249; Salter, Pantin, and Richardson, *Formularies* i, 61; Emden, *Oxford* ii, 1403; Lunt, *Financial Relations* i, 169, 409-10; Maddicott, *Thomas of Lancaster*, 255-6.

(16) 1321: Rymer II:i, 463-64, 466; Emden, *Oxford* iii, 2026.

(17) 1322-1323: PRO C47/27/3-5; C47/27/12/3, 32; C47/29/9/9; E101/309/27; SC7/25/3, 25; Reg. Asserio, 576-81; Rymer II:i, 494, 504, 507, 541-4; *Liber Epistolaris* of Richard de Bury, nos. 146, 148; Sayles, *Select Cases in the Court of King's Bench under Edward II*, pp. 122-32; Clarke, 'Some Secular Activities', 168-70; Deeley, EHR xliii (1928), 521-2; Emden, *Oxford* iii, 1797; Le Neve, *Lincoln*, 79, 91; Lunt, *Financial Relations* i, 410; Lunt, *Accounts*, xxii; Stubbs, *Constitutional History* ii, 355; Fryde, BIHR xliv (1971), 153-61.

(18) 1323: Murimuth, *Con Chron.*, 41; Davies, *Baronial Opposition*, 227; Emden, *Oxford* ii, 1330.

(19) 1325-1326: PRO E101/309/32; E372/175, m. 45; Reg. John XXII, no. 26261; CPL ii, 251; Rymer II:i, 621; Emden, *Oxford* iii, 2026.

(20) 1327: PRO E30/1214; E101/309/37-8; E372/175, m. 46; BL MS Cott. Cleopatra E.ii, f. 4; Reg. Orleton Hereford, pp. xlii-xliii; Rymer II:ii, 698; Emden, *Oxford* i, 65-6; ii, 1403; Mirot and Déprez, *Bibliothèque de l'École des Chartes* lix (1898) (hereafter in this note abbreviated 'Mirot and Déprez'), nos. 3 and 4, p. 556.

(21) 1328-1329: PRO E101/309/32; E352/125/31; E372/177, m. 40; Emden, *Oxford* iii, 2026; Mirot and Déprez, no. 7, p. 556; Larson, EHR lv (1940), 425.

(22) 1329-1330: PRO E101/127/12, 26, 27 (I owe these references to Dr. E. B. Fryde); BL MS Cott. Vespasian E.xxi, f. 77v; CPR 1327-30, 371; Rymer II:ii, 803; Crump, EHR xxvi (1911), 331-2; Fryde, EHR lxx (1955), p. 203 nn. 4-7; Kirsch, *Historisches Jahrbuch* xiv (1893), 591.

(23) 1330: Rymer II:ii, 833; Denholm-Young, TRHS, 4th series, vol. xx (1937), 147; Emden, *Oxford* i, 325; Faucon, *La Librairie des papes d'Avignon* i, 22-3; *Liber Epistolaris* of Richard de Bury, p. xxiv.

(24) 1333: PRO 31/9/17a, f. 62 seq.; E30/1217-18; E30/1418; E43/104; E101/310/40; E101/386/11; CPL ii, 512; Rymer II:ii, 854; Denholm-Young, TRHS, 4th series, vol. xx (1937), 148-50; Emden, *Oxford* i, 325; iii, 1696; Faucon, *La Librairie des papes d'Avignon* i, 22-3; Le Neve, *Nor. Prov.*, 107; Mirot and Déprez, no. 37, p. 560; Larson, EHR lv (1940), 426; Segrè, *Nuova antologia*, 4th series, vol. xciii (1901), 612-22.

(25) 1334: PRO 31/9/17a, ff. 65v-66; E101/311/8; Emden, *Oxford* i, 171; Mirot and Déprez, no. 48, p. 561; Larson, EHR lv (1940), 426.

[11] *Letters of Edward, Prince of Wales*, ed. Johnstone, pp. 1, 74, 80, 94, 142, 145-51; in October of 1305.

envoys themselves as well as for those whose names they carried from the king to the pope.[12] Particularly important missions were sent in the coronation years of Clement v and John xxii, precisely the same years in which papal provisions to English benefices reached their zeniths under each pontiff. The envoys on these missions presented very handsome gifts to the popes, those for John xxii's coronation including gold tableware and altar vessels enamelled with the arms of both pope and king.[13] Presents from Archbishop Reynolds were also conveyed by these same envoys.[14] It is interesting to note that the greatest volume of letters recorded in the Roman rolls from Edward ii to members of the college of cardinals was sent in John xxii's coronation year.[15]

The embassy of 1322-1323 had instructions to treat at the highest level concerning disputes over certain prebends in Lincoln cathedral,[16] and the envoys on that mission made a gift of twenty shillings to Gualtero, clerk of Andreas Sapiti, because he had laboured and written many things.[17] Another important mission was that of 1327, to justify the assumption of the throne by Edward iii.[18] There is specific evidence that the royal embassies in 1316-1317 and 1330 had dealings with Andreas Sapiti as the crown's proctor,[19] and in 1330 or 1333, 1334, 1335, and 1336-1337 they are known to have presented Sapiti with lists of royal candidates for papal provisions which he in turn set in supplicatory form to be forwarded as petitions to the pope.[20] The royal envoys in 1333 paid a gratuity to Roberto della Torre d'Adria, a king's clerk who served as an abbreviator in the papal chancery from 1322 until (at least) 1343 and who formulated the king's petitions at times and set them in writing.[21] Roberto was beneficed in England in the time of Benedict xii.

---

[12] Pantin, *The English Church*, p. 12 n. 3; Le Neve, *Nor. Prov.*, 107.

[13] Below, Appendix 2.

[14] RR ff. 215v, 237; CPL ii, 417.

[15] Total of 306 letters sent in the tenth year of Edward ii (PRO C70/3; cf. below, Appendix 4).

[16] Le Neve, *Lincoln*, 79, 91; Rymer II:i, 541-4; Sayles, *Select Cases in the Court of King's Bench under Edward ii*, pp. 126, 128.

[17] PRO E101/309/27.

[18] Emden, *Oxford* ii, 1403.

[19] Kirsch, *Historisches Jahrbuch* xiv (1893), 591; RR f. 237.

[20] PRO 31/9/17a, ff. 62 seq., 65v, 72, 76, 88v.

[21] PRO E101/386/11; CPL ii, 540, 545; Baumgarten, *Von der apostolischen Kanzlei*, 21, 25; Guillemain, *La Cour pontificale*, 324.

4

Pensions to Cardinals

One particular aspect of the business of royal envoys to the papal court
was the payment of pensions to selected cardinals from the English
crown. This practice went back at least to the reign of King John,[1] and
Cardinal Benedetto Gaetani had received pensions from a number of
English sources before he became Pope Boniface VIII.[2] Our records about
pensions are far from complete, but such information as the present writer
has found suggests that in the early fourteenth century it was quite often
the royal envoys to the curia – probably only the more important envoys
and primarily in the years when political and other conditions were most
appropriate – who took the news of grants of such pensions by the crown
to the cardinals and often made the payments as well. At times the various
cardinals' pensions would be allowed to fall in arrears, only to be paid up
in full by a new mission of royal envoys upon their arrival at the
curia – such as the payments to cardinals for two years' arrears by the
envoys in 1305,[3] four years in 1327,[4] two in 1328-1329,[5] two in 1329-
1330,[6] and two in 1333.[7] At other times the envoys would have royal
powers to grant cardinals pensions at their own discretion – such as the
powers granted to the embassy in John XXII's coronation year of 1316-
1317 which probably resulted in pensions to four cardinals,[8] or the
authority held by the royal envoys of 1319 to grant a pension of twenty-
five marks a year to 'a discreet man staying at the court of Rome for

---

[1] Cheney, *Becket to Langton*, 81.

[2] PRO E36/274 (I owe this reference to Dr. E. B. Fryde); Cant. Cath. MS Misc. Accts. i,
ff. 137v, 191, 191v, 197, 248; Guillemain, *La Cour pontificale*, 68; Sutcliffe, *Speculum* X
(1935), 59.

[3] PRO E101/369/11, f. 184v.

[4] PRO E30/1214; E101/309/27; E372/175, m. 46v.

[5] PRO E372/177, m. 40.

[6] PRO E101/127/26, 27.

[7] PRO E30/1217, 1218; E101/386/11.

[8] Below, Appendix 3, nos. 17, 28, 34, 41.

conducting the king's business there'.[9] Perhaps the largest number of pensions granted at any one time to cardinals during the years 1305-1334 by the English crown was the six granted in 1309 by the mission led by Walter Reynolds.[10] In September of 1308 Edward II had asked the pope to excuse him for not sending messengers since the time that he had received the government of the realm, the reason being unstable political conditions, and the mission led by Reynolds in 1309 seems to have been the first major embassy sent to the Roman court under Edward II.[11]

Some idea of the thought that brought about these pensions is offered by the fact that the decision to grant them in 1316 was made upon the opinion of the chancellor (Sandale) and others of the council.[12] Earlier, in 1311, the king had asked the advice of Henry de Lacy (keeper of the realm), Reynolds (chancellor), and Sandale (treasurer) as to which cardinals were receiving royal pensions, what their amounts were, and whether any more should be retained and at what fees.[13] Sometimes the pensions were paid in florins bought at Avignon, often with the assistance of Italian banking firms.[14] At other times, payments might be made by the constable of Bordeaux from the issues of the king's treasury in Aquitaine.[15] Generally, once a pension was granted, the crown did keep up some attempt at payment. Many cardinals probably received no English pensions at all, but there were certainly more than the three mentioned in the studies of Lizerand and Renouard.[16] The present writer has found evidence of at least eighteen cardinals pensioned by the English crown out of a total of some seventy who lived during the pontificates of Clement V and John XXII.[17]

Lack of evidence makes it unwise to draw any conclusions as to which cardinals were the crown's favourites, although some observations can be made with reference to their pensions. Undoubtedly the royal policy was to award pensions to those cardinals thought to be unusually influential or favourable to the king's interests, and the crown did often pension the following categories of cardinals: 'camerarii' of the apostolic camera (in

---

[9] CPR 1317-21, 343; cf. *Liber Epistolaris* of Richard de Bury, no. 249.

[10] CPR 1307-13, 105; Rymer II:i, 69.

[11] CCW, 279. One of its important results was Gaveston's recall.

[12] CCW, 455.

[13] CCW, 338.

[14] Fryde, EHR lxx (1955), p. 203 nn. 4, 5, 6; Lunt, *Financial Relations* ii, 207-8.

[15] E.g., Rymer II:i, 403; II:ii, 854, 894.

[16] Lizerand, *Clément V et Philippe IV le Bel*, 394; Renouard, *Annales du Midi* lxvii (1955), p. 122 n. 18.

[17] Below, Appendix 3, nos. 2, 3, 5, 7, 11, 17-23, 28, 29, 34, 38, 39, 41.

charge of papal finance),[18] the vice-chancellor of the apostolic chancery (in charge of papal letters),[19] major penitentiaries (in charge of cases reserved to the pope),[20] the 'referendarius' (who read petitions requiring specific papal approval),[21] an Englishman,[22] members of the king's council in Aquitaine,[23] nuncios to England,[24] and the royal 'consanguineus' Cardinal Luca Fieschi.[25] It would seem that the crown generally knew the importance and value of these cardinals and was willing to subsidize their friendship to some extent.

Yet a caveat must be entered even with respect to the cardinals in the above categories. Crown pensions have not been found for all cardinals in all of these categories, and a notable exception is the vice-chancellor of the apostolic chancery. A cardinal in such a position would seem an eminent candidate for a royal pension, in view of the facts that (1) the vice-chancellor wielded great influence in the process of papal provisions,[26] (2) Sapiti's register shows that English petitions to the pope were often referred to him,[27] and (3) there is evidence of English attempts to influence his subordinates. In 1322-1323, for example, a gratuity was given to the 'armiger' and 'nepos' of the cardinal vice-chancellor who led the English envoys into the cardinal's presence,[28] and in 1333 two scutifers of the vice-chancellor were paid forty shillings for bringing the letters granted by the pope to the royal envoys.[29] In spite of diligent search in the several pension lists that do survive from the period under review, however, I have been able to find evidence of an English royal pension to only one of the five cardinals who held the post of vice-chancellor over the years under consideration here.

It is not possible to say more about cardinals' pensions on the basis of the positions they held within the curia, although we may note that the crown at times did seek the favour of certain cardinals because of some ad hoc service they could render. On Christmas eve of 1322, for example, we

[18] Below, Appendix 3, nos. 2, 3; Guillemain, *La Cour pontificale*, 278-9, 294-5.

[19] Below, Appendix 3, no. 17; Guillemain, *La Cour pontificale*, 309, 333.

[20] Below, Appendix 3, nos. 13, 17, 21; Göller, *Einnahmen* i, 90-1; Guillemain, *La Cour pontificale*, 332-4.

[21] Below, Appendix 3, no. 38; Guillemain, *La Cour pontificale*, 307, 311.

[22] Below, Appendix 3, no. 18.

[23] Below, Appendix 3, nos. 3, 17.

[24] Below, Appendix 3, nos. 2, 11, 17, 39, 41.

[25] Below, Appendix 3, no. 11.

[26] Guillemain, *La Cour pontificale*, 305.

[27] E.g., PRO 31/9/17a, f. 11; Kirsch, *Historisches Jahrbuch* xiv (1893), 587-8.

[28] PRO E101/309/27.

[29] PRO E101/386/11.

find the envoys giving presents to two named cardinals who 'have the business of Scotland in their hands'; cash gifts were also made to the auditors of these two cardinals upon the advice of the envoys.[30] In 1324 it was reported to the crown that six named Gascon cardinals had contributed to the cause of the war of Saint-Sardos by making their friends turn to the French king, but a year later pensions were again being paid to at least two of them.[31]

Another possible indication of the relative importance of various cardinals to Edward II can be seen by the frequency of the crown's letters to them as recorded on the Roman rolls.[32] It would be tempting to draw conclusions about the importance of the cardinals by comparing the frequency of their letters with the occurrence of their pensions, but the records of royal letters to cardinals under the privy seal are now lost and if found they might well present a different picture.[33]

The crown's policy vis-à-vis the cardinals undoubtedly varied according to the politics of the moment, although in some cases the crown probably had no advance information as to the moves that would be made in the curia. There seems to be no discernible pattern, for example, in the papal appointments of specific cardinals at the apostolic see to confirm episcopal and abbatial elections, to handle permutations of benefices, or to hear and terminate cases of litigation.[34]

The surviving evidence does, however, enable us to make one comparison between the policy of the crown and that of the English hierarchy on the question of cardinals' pensions. Most of the bishops appear to have followed interests independent of the crown in their own grants of pensions, although Archbishop Reynolds probably did not. In addition to the eighteen cardinals pensioned by the crown between 1305 and 1334, my own studies have found five more cardinals pensioned by members of the English hierarchy for whom no crown pensions could be discovered.[35] Reynolds' pensions, on the other hand, closely paralleled those of the crown. The major grant of pensions recorded in Reynolds' Lambeth register is to four cardinals in 1316-1317;[36] three of these were

---

[30] PRO E101/309/27; below, Appendix 3, nos. 14, 22; Sayles, *Select Cases in the Court of King's Bench under Edward II*, pp. 126-7.

[31] Chaplais, *War of Saint-Sardos*, no. 90, pp. 104-5; below, Appendix 3, nos. 22, 41.

[32] Below, Appendix 4.

[33] Chaplais, EHR lxxiii (1958), 270-3.

[34] Above, pp. 49 (cf. n. 18), 104 (cf. n. 13); Reg. John XXII, no. 5824.

[35] Below, Appendix 3, nos. 1, 10, 26, 31, 40.

[36] Below, Appendix 3, nos. 17, 29, 34, 41; RR ff. 87v-88.

the same cardinals pensioned by Edward II in the same year, and the fourth pension was for a cardinal to whom Reynolds himself had delivered the news of the grant of a royal pension in 1309 at Avignon.[37] Reynolds also duplicated the crown's policy of late 1316 by empowering his proctors to grant pensions at discretion.[38] One of the most popular cardinals with both crown and hierarchy was Arnaud de Pellegrue, pensioned by the crown and four English bishops (including Reynolds)[39] and receiving a very high percentage of the crown letters on the Roman rolls.[40] He was thought by many to be the most important person in the papal curia, and it was at his chamber in Avignon that the English envoys met with Adam Orleton in 1316-1317.[41] Both a messenger of his and a 'nepos' of his were among the persons bringing the news of the election of John XXII to Edward II.[42]

The historian Bernard has spoken of the 'sous-népotisme' which Pope Clement's nepotism engendered,[43] and the crown did not omit also to seek the favour of numerous persons subordinate to the pope and cardinals themselves. Additional gratuities, either money payments or gifts in kind, were often given by the royal envoys to the pope's 'nepotes' and 'consanguinei',[44] as well as to a number of minor officials in the papal palace, such as to the 'armigeri', 'camerarii', 'cubicularii', 'cursores', 'familiares', 'garciones', 'mariscalli', 'secretarii', 'ianitores in prima porta', 'ianitores in secunda porta', 'notarii', 'protonotarii', 'hostiarii', 'hostiarii forinsece', 'milites hostiariorum', 'servientes hostiariorum', 'servientes armorum', and 'servientes officiorum'.[45] There seems to have been a particular custom for such gifts to be more extensive if the envoys were in the papal court before Christmas or Easter.[46] And in 1316-1317 the envoys made a special payment to the pope's notary and secretary in order to hasten the copying and registration of certain bulls.[47]

[37] Below, Appendix 3, no. 29.
[38] RR ff. 87v, 88.
[39] Below, Appendix 3, no. 29.
[40] Below, Appendix 4, no. 8.
[41] Lizerand, *Clément v et Philippe iv le Bel*, 307; CPL. ii, 443-4; Guillemain, *La Cour pontificale*, p. 236 n. 278.
[42] Soc. Ant. MS 120, ff. 48, 52, 92v, 93v; RR f. 76.
[43] *Annales du Midi* lxi (1948-9), 407.
[44] Below, p. 171 and n. 19.
[45] Particularly full records of gratuities to such people will be found in the manuscript sources listed in note 10, pp. 115-17, nos. 13, 17, 20, 24. Cf. Lunt, *Financial Relations* ii, 271-3. For brief summaries of the duties of some of these minor officials, see Mollat, *The Popes at Avignon*, 282 seq., and Guillemain, *La Cour pontificale*, ch. 4.
[46] PRO E101/309/27.
[47] Soc. Ant. MS 120, f. 24v.

The constitution *Excommunicamus*[48] of Boniface VIII, which pronounced excommunication upon anyone who gave or received anything great or small in order to obtain favour at the apostolic see, was apparently not very effective at this time. Clement V, for example, absolved his 'nepos' Bertrand de Got from any sentence of excommunication thus incurred by accepting large grants of Gascon property from Edward II in return for a promise to promote the king's interests at the Roman court.[49]

[48] Dated 1295. CIC, Extravag. Comm., lib. V, tit. x, cap. 1 (Friedberg, vol. ii, cols. 1309-10).

[49] Reg. Clem. v, no. 7584; CPR 1307-13, 83; Guillemain, *La Cour pontificale*, 165-6; PRO E135/25/3.

5

An English Cardinal?

Edward II knew well the importance of the college of cardinals – throughout his reign he sent them an average of nearly eighty
letters yearly that have survived on the Roman rolls alone,[1] and the
English cardinal Thomas Jorz's activities at the Roman curia were of great
value to him and his father.[2] Indeed, Jorz had been named cardinal by
Clement V at royal request during the very time when he was acting as
royal envoy to the papal court.[3] It is not surprising, therefore, to find that
after the death of Jorz on 13 December 1310 the king attempted to secure
the promotion of another Englishman to the sacred college.

Jorz had been the fourth English Dominican cardinal in succession
after Kilwardby, Macclesfield, and Winterbourne, and it might have been
thought that the pope would continue the succession – especially in view
of the satisfaction that Pope Clement had apparently shown in 1305 when
he announced the promotion of one non-French cardinal (i.e., Jorz) in
spite of strong French pressure from Philip the Fair.[4] Moreover, England
had been unfortunate in the lifespans of her recent cardinals – Macclesfield had died just before or just after his promotion, Winterbourne within
two years of his, and Jorz in less than five years. Also, there must have
been strong traces of English prestige remaining in the sacred college, for
in the election of 1304-1305 that eventually chose Clement half the votes
at one time had gone to Winterbourne.[5] But at Clement's second creation

---

[1] Below, Appendix 4.

[2] Rymer I:ii, 998; Clarke, 'Some Secular Activities', 149-57. Part of my information
about the Dominican cardinals and about John Lenham is summarized from this very
helpful thesis.

[3] Clarke, 'Some Secular Activities', 150; Langlois, *Revue historique* lxxxvii (1905), 69-
71.

[4] Langlois, ibid.

[5] According to Ullmann, JEH vi (1955), p. 28 n. 2.

of cardinals, held just some five or six days after Jorz's death, the only men promoted were French.[6]

There had not been time for Edward to nominate anyone to Clement after Jorz's death and before this second creation of cardinals, but about the middle of February 1310/1311 the king did make a nomination, the friar John Lenham.[7] Like Winterbourne and Jorz, Lenham was the king's confessor and a Dominican. It is to be noted that the king's confessor at this time definitely took part in the administrative processes of government,[8] and Lenham was unusually close to the king because he had also been his confessor while prince of Wales.[9] On 20 July of the same year Edward wrote again to Clement in favour of Lenham, but this time not quite so hopefully, as he requested the promotion of some other Englishman in the event of Lenham's unsuitability.[10] Letters were also sent to the influential Cardinal Arnaud de Pellegrue and to six other friendly cardinals, stressing the desirability of an English cardinal before the approaching council of Vienne.[11] But Clement's third creation, 23 or 24 December 1312, again promoted all Frenchmen,[12] although one of them – William Testa – had especially strong English connections. Testa had been papal nuncio and general papal collector in England from August of 1305 to March of 1312/1313 and held numerous English benefices; Edward II's attempts to cultivate Testa's favour are indicated by the crown pension to him [13] and by the very high proportion of crown letters to him that survive on the Roman rolls.[14] There is evidence that, in the absence of an English cardinal, the crown at times relied upon Testa's influence at the Roman court.[15]

Lenham died in 1316,[16] and in 1320 Edward II tried again – this time he was writing to John XXII – to secure an English cardinal. His candidate

---

[6] Eubel, *Hierarchia Catholica* i, 14; Guillemain, *La Cour pontificale*, p. 187 n. 33.

[7] BL MS Cott. Cleopatra E.i. f. 256v (top foliation); Rymer II:i, 127; Clarke, 'Some Secular Activities', 29, 30 (cf. n. 1).

[8] Davies, *Baronial Opposition*, 71, 182, 187, 213, 251; Reg. Winchelsey, 1043; below, pp. 232-233.

[9] BL MS Add. 22923, f. 9v; PRO E101/363/18, ff. 3, 3v; *Letters of Edward, Prince of Wales*, ed. Johnstone, 139.

[10] Rymer II:i, 139.

[11] CCW, 337; Rymer II:i, 140.

[12] Eubel, *Hierarchia Catholica* i, 14.

[13] Below, Appendix 3, no. 41.

[14] Below, Appendix 4, no. 4.

[15] CCW, 528; Rymer II:i, 321, 371, 390; Lunt, AHR xviii (1912), 56; examples could be multiplied.

[16] Soc. Ant. MS 120, f. 8v; Clarke, 'Some Secular Activities', 32.

now was Roger Northburgh, who was his keeper of the wardrobe. Edward entrusted the promotion of Northburgh to his brother Edmund of Woodstock and the other royal envoys to the curia in 1320, and he also commanded that letters about the matter be written to twenty-one cardinals – with special requests to those pensioned by him.[17] But this attempt, another the following year, and a secret verbal communication taken to the pope by Edward II's envoys in 1322,[18] were also unsuccessful. The comment of the author of the *Annales Paulini* upon the pope's creation of cardinals in 1320 was to the point: 'omnes de partibus suis et de Francia'.[19] Still another major creation of cardinals, in 1327, was also predominantly French.

It is conceivable that John XXII entertained the thought of creating an English cardinal, for in September of 1331 he set forth, as a major reason for refusing to promote a French nominee of the French queen to the sacred college, the argument that it already at that time consisted of sixteen Frenchmen, six Italians, one Spaniard, and no others, and that other rulers were pressing for their own candidates. But he also argued that the college was already large enough and that many of its members already were having difficulty achieving the sufficiencies necessary for their status.[20] His pontificate in fact saw only one more cardinal created after the date of this reply to the French queen, but he too was French.

No Englishman was created cardinal by John XXII, Edward III's attempt to secure one in 1350 was not successful, and not until the Benedictine Simon Langham in 1368 would there be another English cardinal.[21] Langham and Jorz comprised the total of only two English cardinals in the entire Avignon period, as contrasted with 112 Frenchmen and fourteen Italians.[22] It is interesting to observe that the titular church of S. Sabina, traditional church of the Dominican order, which had been held successively by Macclesfield, Winterbourne, and Jorz, was left vacant after Jorz's death until the accession of Clement VI in 1342 when it was given to another Dominican but not an Englishman.[23] Cardinals Kilwardby and Langham had both been archbishops of Canterbury as had

---

[17] PRO C47/27/12/25; Rymer II:i, 431-3, 452; *Liber Epistolaris* of Richard de Bury, no. 229.

[18] Sayles, *Select Cases in the Court of King's Bench under Edward II*, pp. 126, 129.

[19] *Ann. Paul.*, 290.

[20] John XXII, Secret Letters, no. 4692; cf. no. 4573.

[21] Highfield, 'The Relations' i, 8-11; Emden, *Oxford* iii, 1799.

[22] Guillemain, *La Cour pontificale*, 187.

[23] Eubel, *Hierarchia Catholica* i, 18, 46.

been Cardinal Stephen Langton[24] earlier in the thirteenth century,[25] and there had been at least a possibility that Archbishop Pecham would be made cardinal.[26] The chronicler 'Birchington' also reports that the pope had wanted to make Robert Winchelsey a cardinal while he was awaiting consecration, but that Winchelsey, considering what this would mean to the church of Canterbury, had refused.[27] It might have been thought that Edward II would nominate his favourite Walter Reynolds to the sacred college at some time, but there is no evidence in Reynolds' register or elsewhere to suggest that this was done.

[24] After his promotion to the cardinalate.
[25] For English cardinals in the thirteenth century see Brentano, *Two Churches*, 48-56.
[26] Cant. Cath. MS Eastry Cor. ii, 17, 19; HMC Rep. Var. Coll., i, 276-7.
[27] Wharton, *Anglia Sacra* i, 12: 'considerans dispendium summum Cantuariensis Ecclesiae'.

6

English Benefices Held by Cardinals
and Other Curial Officials

Another important aspect of the crown's policy toward the college of cardinals was its attitude in respect to the benefices they held in England. As early as 1309 Clement v was complaining, first to Walter Reynolds and the other royal envoys at the papal court and then by letters sent to Archbishop Winchelsey, to Reynolds as bishop of Worcester, and perhaps to other bishops, that certain cardinals were being disturbed in their English benefices by royal officials.[1] The following year, after Edward II and his council had considered Clement's letter, the crown took at least some action to protect them.[2] John XXII made another strong protest of the same sort in the first year of his pontificate, if we may judge from his mandate to his nuncios Cardinals Gaucelme and Luca which repeats many of the passages in Clement's bull.[3]

The crown policy towards cardinals' benefices was in fact a generous one. In 1320 Edward II exempted three of the cardinals holding English benefices – Raymond Guilhem de Farges, Gaucelme de Jean, and Bertrand du Poujet – from the annual tenth of 1319.[4] In 1325 the king, 'at the request of Pope John XXII and out of his own affection to the Roman church', pardoned all of the cardinals anything they owed for any tenth or other quota previously levied during his reign,[5] and shortly afterwards the pope thanked the king for this action.[6] Professor Lunt has shown that the

---

[1] Reg. Winchelsey, 1031-46; Rymer II:i, 97-8; Wilkins ii, 322-5; P&C ii, 1285; Edwards, EHR lix, 319. For the original bull to Reynolds, see BI. MS Cott. Cleopatra E.i, f. 255 (top foliation).

[2] CCR 1307-13, 251.

[3] Below, Appendix 7.

[4] CCR 1318-23, 188; Rymer II:i, 423.

[5] CCR 1323-7, 258, 415; Rymer II:i, 595; Cal. Memoranda Rolls 1326-7, nos. 354, 494.

[6] John XXII, Secret Letters, no. 2462; CPL. ii, 469.

cardinals appear to have paid nothing up to this date anyway, so in effect the cancellation was an exemption from all the tenths of Edward II's reign.[7] Edward III on 23 February 1326/1327, in his first year, announced that this same policy of exemption for the cardinals would continue 'in consideration of their affection to the crown',[8] and he renewed the exemption in 1328, 1329, 1332, and 1333.[9] There is at least a slight suggestion from the early years of Edward III's reign that the cardinals acted collectively to secure their exemption.[10]

It is to be observed that these exemptions were generally made at papal request, and the pope for his part granted similar exemptions to cardinals.[11] With the papacy removed from Rome to Avignon, the income that cardinals received from their titular churches was now apparently negligible,[12] and it was a part of papal policy to assist the cardinals to gain the maximum revenue from their numerous benefices. The proposal of Honorius III in 1225, repeated by Innocent IV in 1244, that one prebend in every cathedral and collegiate church as well as fixed payments from monasteries and bishops should be reserved for papal uses, had been rejected by the English king and clergy, and the request of Gregory IX in 1241 that each English abbey transfer the patronage of one church worth at least 100 marks to the apostolic see had met a similar fate.[13] Nor had the offer of Innocent IV in 1254 to limit papal provisions for aliens in England to an annual total value of 8000 marks been found acceptable, although his bull was transcribed again at Lambeth in 1324 and later found its way into at least one English episcopal register.[14] The suggestion of the canonist Johannes Andreae in 1311-1312 at the council of Vienne that a direct income tax be levied on the whole church to support the pope and cardinals was also unsuccessful.[15] Undoubtedly one of the main papal aims in the canonical legislation on reservations and provisions that has

[7] Lunt, *Financial Relations* i, 413. For this policy applied to cardinals in the parish churches of Pagham and Boxley, see RR f. 312v; below, Appendix 3, nos. 12, 17.

[8] CCR 1327-30, 62.

[9] CCR 1327-30, 282; Rymer II:ii, 772, 845, 872.

[10] PRO C47/18/9/6 (Exchequer report of the papal collector Concoreto, 1329): 'Qui quidem cardinales clamant esse quieti de dicta decima'.

[11] Lunt, *Financial Relations* i, 387; ibid., ii, 80; Reg. Halton i, 253; CPL ii, 509.

[12] Barraclough, *Papal Provisions*, 71-6.

[13] Lunt, *Financial Relations* i, 178-86, 205-19; Kemp, *Counsel and Consent*, 68; Bradshaw and Wordsworth, *Statutes of Lincoln Cathedral*, vol. ii, p. cxliii; Churchill, *Canterbury Administration* i, 361-2; Powicke, *King Henry III and the Lord Edward* i, 348-9; P&C i, 155-6.

[14] Reg. Martival ii, 446-8; cf. Powicke, *Henry III and the Lord Edward* i, 278-81.

[15] Pantin, *The English Church*, 42.

already been discussed in an earlier chapter was the pope's desire to retain the benefices of deceased cardinals and other curial officials within his own court. When the pope revoked the collation of John de Bruyton, candidate of both Edward II and Walter Reynolds for the archdeaconry of Canterbury in 1323, he told Reynolds that the provisor Cardinal Raymond de Roux should receive the benefice, 'as a subsidy for the expenses which his status demands'.[16] Even though such provisions of benefices to cardinals could give the king some ground for complaint when his policy called for it, yet the holding of benefices in plurality by cardinals was clearly a practical necessity for their financial support and was more or less acknowledged as such by both king and pope.

In attempting to gauge the extent of this aspect of the crown's policy during the first thirty years of the Avignon period, we may observe − from the papal registers and many other sources − that at least twenty-nine of the seventy cardinals who lived during these years held or laid claim to some 103 benefices in England during the pontificates of Clement V and John XXII.[17] Perhaps the most spectacular cardinal-pluralist of the period was Gaucelme de Jean, son of one of Pope John XXII's sisters, who held or laid claim at various times during the pontificate of his uncle to no less than twelve English benefices of which eight were parish churches. His accumulation of English benefices was noted, with adverse comment, by the chronicler Murimuth.[18] The cardinal's sale of the tithes from some of these benefices in 1328 raised a dispute about the place of royal prohibitions that will be discussed later in the third part of this book as part of the conflict between the courts within England.

A parallel study has already been made by Dr. Highfield for the last thirty years of the Avignon period, 1349-1378, which shows at least thirty-eight cardinals holding claim to no less than 128 English benefices.[19] In view of the fact that the total numbers of provisions recorded in the papal registers during the last thirty years of the Avignon period are over five times as great as those in the first thirty years,[20] the extent of English benefices held by cardinals during the pontificates of Clement V and John XXII would seem to be very great indeed in

[16] HMC Ninth Rep., I, app., 72; Cant. Cath. MS Reg. I, ff. 393-393v.

[17] Below, Appendix 3; Murimuth, *Con. Chron.*, 27-8. For the French situation during the pontificate of John XXII, see Caillet, *La papauté d'Avignon et l'église de France*, 319 seq.

[18] Below, Appendix 3, no. 17. For his French benefices, see Caillet, *La papauté d'Avignon et l'église de France*, 325.

[19] Highfield, 'The Relations' i, 346-63.

[20] Above, pp. 27-28.

proportion to the total number of provisions at the time. In both periods, the same three cathedrals – Lincoln, York, and Salisbury, respectively – claimed the greatest numbers of cathedral positions held by cardinals,[21] and the collegiate provisions to cardinals were practically nil. No evidence has been found of any cardinals holding cathedral positions during the first thirty years in Hereford, Exeter, or the Welsh dioceses.[22]

One great contrast, however, emerges when comparing the studies for the two periods: only fourteen cases of cardinals holding or claiming English parish churches were found during the last thirty years, whereas some thirty-nine such cases have been found in the first thirty years. All but six of these thirty-nine were held during the pontificate of John XXII, most of them by provision from him. Only three of the thirty-nine were granted by the crown. Of the thirty-three parish churches held under John XXII (thirty-nine minus six held under Clement V), six had been vacated by force of *Execrabilis*, eight by consecration of English bishops at the apostolic see, three more by consecration of English bishops elsewhere, and another three[23] by the deaths of litigants at the apostolic see. We may recall that the cardinals themselves had been exempted by the pope from the requirement to resign pluralities of benefices under *Execrabilis*.[24] Most provisions of John XXII to the cardinals were simultaneously accompanied by explicit dispensations for plurality and were often followed by indults for nonresidence. The papacy, therefore, especially under John XXII, made extensive use of its privileges in canon law to provide numerous English benefices, often parish churches, to cardinals.

Again, if we consider all the benefices granted to cardinals, both parish churches and cathedral positions, John XXII once more emerges as the one who granted the most. Of the total of at least 103 English benefices held or claimed by cardinals in the period 1305-1334, there were some fifty that were clearly granted by John XXII, as contrasted with about fifteen granted by Clement V. These figures may be compared with Guillemain's finding that only six English benefices were granted to cardinals by Benedict XII, all of which were canonries rather than parish churches.[25] Certainly for

---

[21] These three cathedrals, in different order, received the largest numbers of all provisions to English benefices under both John XXII and Benedict XII; above, p. 29.

[22] These three received the smallest numbers of all provisions under John XXII; below, Appendix 1, table E.

[23] Below, Appendix 6, nos. 33, 35, 57; cf. below, Appendix 3, nos. 17, 33, 23, respectively.

[24] Above, pp. 12, 87.

[25] *La politique bénéficiale*, 80-1, 138. It must be remembered that Guillemain is working here only from the papal registers.

the years 1305-1334, and probably for the entire Avignon period, cardinals' benefices in England reached their peak under John XXII.

From all this evidence, therefore, three conclusions are suggested: (1) cardinals' holdings of English benefices were much more extensive in proportion to the total numbers of papal provisions during the first thirty years of the Avignon period than in the last thirty, (2) this was largely due to a policy of John XXII to provide English benefices – often parish churches vacated at the apostolic see by *Execrabilis* or by consecrations or by deaths of litigants – to the cardinals, and (3) this policy was encouraged by the crown's own policy at papal request – under Edward II and the early years of Edward III[26] – to exempt cardinals from payment of the tenth. The crown maintained this policy even though it was often aware of which benefices the cardinals held and even though the holding of such benefices was at times discussed before the king's council.[27] A complaint was registered in 1307 at the parliament of Carlisle against the holding of cathedral deaneries and religious houses by cardinals, but at that date cardinals probably held no more than three such benefices and the king apparently did nothing about the protest.[28] Edward II was certainly willing to cooperate with John XXII's policy over cardinals' benefices – even if he did not go so far as Edward III's move actually to petition the pope for provisions to alien cardinals in the years immediately following the reissue of the statute of Provisors in 1365.[29]

And just as the holding of over 100 English benefices by the cardinals was a fact in which both pope and king could see advantages during the early fourteenth century, so it is interesting to find a considerable number of other contemporary papal officials who were beneficed in England. Many of these were members of the working staff at Avignon, and several were in the service of both pope and king. Of about sixty papal officials other than cardinals beneficed in England in the years 1305-1334, no less than nineteen – nearly one-third – were also king's clerks.[30] The royal exemption of cardinals from the tenth did not extend to these other papal officials, but king's clerks as well as some papal officials did have the

[26] Lunt, *Financial Relations* ii, 88.

[27] CCR 1323-7, 415; Rymer II:ii, 845; PRO C49/5/13.

[28] *Rot. Parl.* i, 207-8, 220-1; *Vita Edwardi Secundi*, 47; below, Appendix 3, nos. 4, 16. The specific protest against cardinals is not repeated in the documents surviving from the Stamford parliament of 1309 (P&C ii, 1236-40).

[29] Highfield, *History*, n.s. vol. xxxix (1954), 332.

[30] Below, Appendix 5, nos. 4, 5, 8, 11, 14, 20, 22, 32, 34, 36, 38, 40, 41, 43, 48, 51, 52, 57, 58.

privilege of nonresidence[31] and when a royal clerk was made papal chaplain the king might well have a man on his side who could also be trusted with matters of ecclesiastical importance in which the king was interested. The papacy, for its part, would have another clerk whose benefices would come more readily under the canon law on reservations when he died or resigned.

There was a specific form for the conferment of a papal chaplaincy,[32] and it – like a provision – was often conferred as the result of a petition from a third party to the pope.[33] This standard type of papal chaplaincy – to be distinguished from the pope's 'capellani commensales', who were very few in number[34] – was primarily an honorary title that entailed no additional cure or change of residence or further income.[35] The king's clerk, therefore, would be free to carry on as before. Well known men who had such double status were, for example, Richard de Bury, John Droxford, William Greenfield, Simon Montacute, Adam Orleton, Walter Stapledon, and Robert Stratford. About fifty papal chaplains were beneficed in England at this time, and it must also be noted that there were a few English religious – such as the Dominicans Thomas Dunheved[36] and John Wrotham – who were papal chaplains but not beneficed. Whereas in the period 1349-1378 there were no less than sixteen religious who were also papal chaplains beneficed in England, in the earlier years of the century members of the religious orders did not generally hold English benefices.[37]

The holding of English benefices by papal chaplains and other curial officials, therefore, was a fact that paralleled in some ways the holding of benefices by cardinals, and the crown was willing to tolerate and indeed encourage these holdings because they could work in its favour and in the early part of the century it undoubtedly saw advantages to be gained

[31] Below, pp. 164 seq.

[32] Fayen, *Lettres de Jean xxii* (Analecta Vaticano-Belgica iii), vol. ii, p. xi, no. 35.

[33] Guillemain, *Mélanges d'archéologie et d'histoire de l'École française de Rome* lxiv (1952), 219.

[34] Guillemain, *La Cour pontificale*, 361-70, 495 (cf. n. 77).

[35] The wording of the form for its conferment suggests its honorary nature: 'Nos te in capellanum nostrum gratiose recipimus et capellanorum nostrorum consortio favorabiliter aggregamus, sperantes in Domino quod per honorem tibi exhibitum de devoto efficieris devotior, sicque mentem et actus tuos ad salubria jugiter diriges, quod nostram et apostolice Sedis gratiam promereberis ampliorem'. Fayen, *Lettres de Jean xxii* (Analecta Vaticano-Belgica iii), vol. ii, p. xi, no. 35.

[36] Tanquerey, EHR xxxi (1916), 119-24; Reg. John xxii, no. 23426; Clarke, 'Some Secular Activities', 190-213, 259-60.

[37] Highfield, 'The Relations' i, 364-7; Knowles, *The Religious Orders* ii, 171-2.

thereby. This policy, which in one sense was the counterpart on English soil of the crown's pensions and letters and envoys and proctors at the curia itself, was all part of the crown's way in which it retained friends and safeguarded its prerogative. The crown could have complained loudly against such things if it wished, but at the moment it preferred to register its protests in other ways.

7

English Litigation at the Roman Court

In spite of a general policy in the early fourteenth century of cooperation between crown and papacy in such fields as finances, provisions, and the interests of cardinals and curial officials, there were nevertheless some areas where the crown showed itself prepared to offer more than token resistance to papal decrees. Two such areas will be considered: litigation, and episcopal temporalities. After considering the former of these and before taking up the latter, a discussion will be made of the 'privilege of England', which had served as the theoretical basis upon which the crown often presumed to prohibit litigation from going to the Roman court. It will be important to remember that an 'appeal to Rome' at this time indicated litigation not at the eternal city but wherever the pope happened to be residing at the time; this followed from the principle emphasized in the contemporary canonists Guillaume de Mont-lauzun and Jesselin de Cassagnes, 'Ubi est papa, ibi est Romana curia'.[1]

Royal opposition to English litigation at the Roman court in the early fourteenth century seems to have been confined for the most part to cases in which the crown itself stood to lose ground, although the theoretical basis of such opposition in past history had been a wider claim that no ecclesiastical person or case of appeal might go to the Roman court, nor might any papal nuncio or bull prejudicial to the crown enter the English realm, without royal permission.[2] In the practice of the early fourteenth century these stipulations were often continued. It was often – if not always – necessary to secure royal letters of protection before one could appeal or travel to the Roman curia,[3] royal prohibitions against appeals to

---

[1] *Histoire littéraire* xxxv, 357 (Fournier).

[2] Davies, *Baronial Opposition*, 13. For the background, see Brooke, *The English Church and the Papacy*, 203; Cheney, *Becket to Langton*, 88-94; Makower, *Constitutional History*, 228, 232-7, 239-40; Mayr-Harting, JEH xvi (1965), 40.

[3] Emden, *Oxford* ii, 1182; Fraser, *Antony Bek*, 151, 157, 164-5, 202.

Rome were issued at times,[4] and offenders were liable to judicial proceedings in the court of king's bench or elsewhere.[5] An appellant might even be stopped and imprisoned at Dover while trying to leave the realm contrary to a royal prohibition.[6] Appeals to Rome were made more difficult by the crown's ban on the export of money, gold, and silver, although – just as persons cited to appear at the curia could often be represented by a proctor who was already there – financial arrangements could often be made with Italian banking firms having offices in both London and Avignon.[7] There is also some evidence to suggest that the crown did not enforce strictly its ban on the export of money.[8]

The crown frequently attempted to check citations to the Roman court even before they were delivered to the defendants, by its claim to the right to examine all bulls brought into the realm and to prohibit the entry of those prejudicial to the royal prerogative. The crown would often command the constable of Dover and other bailiffs and sheriffs to search all persons entering the realm and to inform it of any such bulls; the crown from its own foreknowledge might even specify on occasions the names of the persons or the nature of the bulls that were to be deemed prejudicial.[9] At times such bulls were discussed and rejected in the king's council or parliament,[10] and at times the crown would send warnings to bishops,[11] abbots,[12] provincial councils,[13] or papal collectors[14] not to sanction the execution of such bulls or to attempt anything else that might be prejudicial to the royal prerogative. At the parliament of Carlisle in 1307 certain clerks were tried and fined for enforcing papal mandates

---

[4] Fraser, *Bek*, 194; RR f. 300; Rymer II:i, 196; PRO C47/18/4/2.

[5] Fraser, *Antony Bek*, 193; *Placitorum Abb.*, 258, 335, 336, 343; PRO E159/84, m. 57; Sayles, *Select Cases in the Court of King's Bench under Edward III*, pp. 103-5.

[6] CCR 1307-13, 174, 434-5; Walsingham, *Gesta Abbatum* ii, 136-9 (detailed account of prohibition and arrest of Abbot Hugh de Eversdon of St. Albans in 1319).

[7] Brentano, *York Metropolitan Jurisdiction*, 221; Lunt, *Financial Relations* ii, 203, 207; Powicke, *Thirteenth Century*, p. 712 n. 1; Reg. Winchelsey, p. xxiv; CCR 1296-1302, 370.

[8] Lunt, EHR xli (1926), 346.

[9] CCR 1307-13, 173; ibid. 1323-7, 1; Rymer II:i, 13; ibid. II:ii, 627, 726.

[10] E.g., Fraser, *Antony Bek*, 194; Lunt, EHR xli (1926), 347-8; Davies, *Baronial Opposition*, 272.

[11] BL MS Cott. Cleopatra E.i, f. 287v (top foliation); CCR 1323-7, 533; Reg. Hethe, 289; Reg. Martival iii, 172.

[12] BL MS Cott. Vespasian E.xxi, f. 57v; Powicke, *Thirteenth Century*, 460-1.

[13] Kemp, *Counsel and Consent*, 72-3, 76, 90; Kemp, 'The archbishop in convocation', 27; BL MS Cott. Cleopatra E.i, ff. 261, 268v (top foliation); Wilkins ii, 509; Rymer II:i, 356; CPR 1321-4, 38; examples could be multiplied.

[14] Rymer I:ii, 1014.

without royal consent,[15] and as a result of protests at that parliament the papal collector William Testa was warned to attempt nothing in prejudice of the royal dignity.[16]

The papacy, for its part, seems to have had a definite policy of encouraging litigation in the Roman court at this time. Clement v made a strong protest against the crown's prohibitions upon citations to Rome in 1309, which was repeated by John xxii in 1317,[17] and the latter pope empowered Cardinals Gaucelme and Luca, his nuncios in England, to relax sentences issued against persons appealing to the apostolic see.[18] Clement v by his constitution *Saepe* of 1312-1314 established a special summary procedure for use in beneficial cases and other appeals to the Roman court,[19] and a treatise with forms for appeals survives from the judicial organization under John xxii.[20] The constitution *Cupientes* in the Sext[21] required bishops-elect to proceed to the Roman court in person within one month in the case of disputed elections, and there are instances of the application of this constitution to contemporary episcopal elections in England.[22] The decree *Multorum ad nos* of the council of Vienne in 1311-1312 decreed strong penalties for those who prevented persons cited to the apostolic see from going there,[23] a person cited to Rome could be excommunicated for failing to appear,[24] and John xxii gave new emphasis to a constitution of Boniface viii that pronounced *ipso facto* excommunication upon any who inhibited persons going to or returning from the apostolic see.[25]

---

[15] Fraser, *Antony Bek*, 167-8, 202, 205-6; Lunt, *Financial Relations* i, 504.

[16] Lunt, *Financial Relations* i, 577-8; Lunt, *Accounts*, xxiv-xxv; Lunt, AHR xviii (1912), 55. Cf. PRO E159/84, m. 57: Testa was later cited for attempting to take a plea outside the realm in derogation of the royal dignity (1310).

[17] Below, Appendix 7.

[18] Reg. John xxii, no. 5169; CPL. ii, 131.

[19] CIC, Clem., lib. V, tit. xi, cap. 2 (Friedberg, vol. ii, col. 1200). Kuttner (*Studi e Testi*, vol. 234 (1964), 427-52) proves that this constitution dates not from 19 Nov. 1306 as in Friedberg, but rather within the period 6 May 1312 – 21 March 1313/1314, probably closer to the latter date. The older, incorrect date was assimilated from that of the constitution *Execrabilis* ('.xiii. kal' Dec. (= 19 Nov.), pontificatus nostri anno secundo').

[20] Barraclough, *Public Notaries*, nos. 388-94; cf. p. 33.

[21] CIC, Sext., lib. I, tit. vi, cap. 16 (Friedberg, vol. ii, cols. 954-6).

[22] Reg. Hethe, p. xi; Smith, *Episcopal Appointments*, 32; PRO 31/9/17a, f. 20v; below, Appendix 6, no. 38.

[23] Schroeder, *Disciplinary Decrees*, 404 (transl.), 620 (Latin text); *Conciliorum Oecumenicorum Decreta*, ed. Alberigo, 389-90; CIC, Clem., lib. V, tit. viii, cap. 2 (Friedberg, vol. ii, col. 1188-9).

[24] Smith, *Episcopal Appointments*, 85.

[25] Reg. John xxii, no. 24125. For a general summary of some contemporary legal procedure in the Roman court, see Mollat, *The Popes at Avignon*, 294, 305.

A wide variety of English cases were in fact subjected to consideration at the Roman court in the early fourteenth century, although they were frequently matters of primarily spiritual nature. It is difficult from contemporary sources to ascertain whether any given case was in fact heard at the Roman court at Avignon or not when only the initial citation or appeal is all that survives; even the papal record of the appointment of specific cardinals or auditors for a case is no guarantee that the case was definitely heard before them. With these difficulties in mind, however, I have proceeded to collect information about seventy-six English cases that apparently did go to the court of Rome in the years 1305-1334, and they can be seen to encompass such subjects as disputes over bishoprics and other benefices, visitation rights, first-fruits and tithes, consecration *alibi*, testamentary cases, defect of orders, payments for nonresidence, university teaching rights, excommunication, appropriations of churches, monastic apostasy, heretical doctrine, and matrimonial appeals.[26] The crown was most often involved in cases concerning disputes over bishoprics and other benefices, when it had a candidate or some particular interest in the matter, and W. E. L. Smith has made a detailed study of several beneficial cases of this sort.[27]

As to whether Englishmen of the early fourteenth century preferred their ecclesiastical litigation at home or in Avignon, it is not really possible to say. Barraclough has gone so far as to state that 'in beneficial litigation, appeal [to Rome] was less a remedy than a normal part of proceedings',[28] but the evidence of beneficial disputes from 1305-1334 that I have examined does not suggest that even initial appeals to Rome were so frequent as this. Royal prohibitions, or even the crown's complaint to John XXII in 1318 against superfluous delays and litigation imposed upon Englishmen who had gone to the Roman court for confirmation of their elections,[29] were a standard part of diplomatic interchange and one can not tell from them whether the parties cited to the curia had any personal feelings at all about the transfer of litigation to Avignon. Apart from the crown's words, the few other surviving protests against appeals to Rome – such as those at the parliament of Carlisle in 1307, or the complaint 'causa que curiam semel ingreditur pene immortalis efficitur' of the author of the *Vita Edwardi Secundi*, or the denunciation of 'lites quasi

---

[26] Below, Appendix 6.
[27] *Episcopal Appointments*, 11-49, 61-85.
[28] Barraclough, *Zeitschrift der Savigny-Stiftung für Rechtsgeschichte* lviii (1938), 127.
[29] Lunt, *Financial Relations* i, 521.

immortales in curia Romana' by Prior Henry Eastry in 1330 [30] – do not really permit conclusions to be drawn.

On English soil, some cases were definitely heard by English judges delegated by the pope, although this procedure was probably not so frequent as in the previous century.[31] The crown does not seem to have made any strong protest against citations before English judges delegate, and Edward II recognized their status in a way when he secured a papal privilege that no judge delegate or subdelegate might exercise jurisdiction over royal free chapels and oratories.[32] Still another method of hearing disputes in England under papal authority was before papal nuncios who might happen to be within the realm at any given time; the dispute between York and Canterbury over the carrying of the primatial cross, for example, was at one time to be heard before the cardinal nuncios Gaucelme and Luca.[33]

The technical form known as an 'appeal to the apostolic see and for the protection (tuition) of the court of Canterbury', at this time did not mean that such a case would necessarily go to the Roman court. The tuitorial appeal to Canterbury was, rather, a request that the Canterbury archbishop as *legatus natus* of the apostolic see protect the goods and person of the appellant from the jurisdiction of his diocesan bishop pending litigation.[34] Tuitorial appeal was, for this reason, particularly attractive to

---

[30] *Vita Edwardi*, 46. Cant. Cath. MS Reg. L, ff. 173v, 174v; *Lit. Cant.*, nos. 309, 317.

[31] Pantin essay in *The English Church and the Papacy*, ed. Lawrence, 177; Cheney, JEH xviii (1967), 178-9; Donahue, *Michigan Law Review* 72 (1974), 671. For procedure in cases before judges delegate, see Sayers, *Papal Judges Delegate*, and Brentano, *York Metropolitan Jurisdiction*, 148-64. Examples of contemporary cases before judges delegate: PRO E135/22/51, E135/24/35; BL MS Cott. Vespasian E.xxi, ff. 69v, 70; *Rot. Parl.* i, 298; Reg. Martival i, 300; ii, 46-7, 386-8; Reg. Woodlock, 141, 144-6; *Magnum Registrum Album*, ed. Savage, no. 477; Logan, *Excommunication and the Secular Arm in Medieval England*, 124; below, Appendix 6, nos. 4, 23, 26, 43, 45, 73.

[32] PRO SC7/24/9; BL MS Cott. Cleopatra E.i, f. 259v (top foliation); CPL ii, 135, 433; Reg. John XXII, no. 3357; Rymer II:i, 119.

[33] Reg. John XXII, no. 5824; CPL ii, 166-7.

[34] Churchill, *Canterbury Administration* i, 156-7, 427 seq., 459-67; Haines, *Administration*, 305; Henriques, 'Articles of Grievances of the English Clergy' (Oxford B.Litt. thesis), 116-17; Sayers, *Papal Judges Delegate*, 96-9; Woodcock, *Medieval Ecclesiastical Courts*, 64-7, 126-33; Makower, *Constitutional History and Constitution of the Church of England*, p. 229 n. 10; *Reg. Ep. Pecham*, vol. ii, pp. cvii-cviii. An extremely well documented tuitorial appeal, involving a beneficial dispute and an excommunication, is located in RR f. 60v; PRO C85/8/3; and Reg. Gandavo, 185-6, 324-5, 413-14, 546-8, 667, 766, 776. For some other contemporary tuitorial appeals see Cant. Cath. MS S.V. i, 113, 116; PRO C85/7/28, C85/8/56; Reg. Martival i, 38, 49, 159-60, 187-8, 201-4, 207, 235, 280, 305, 378; HMC, *Wells* i, 178, 193, 233; Pantin, *Chapters of the English Black Monks* i, 197-9, 209-12; Sayles, *Select Cases in the Court of King's Bench under Edward III*, pp. 51-

the parties who already possessed benefices that were in dispute, for such appeal enabled them to continue drawing their income while in possession. Once tuition was granted, the appellant had, theoretically, a year and a day in which to make further appeal to Rome. One of the clerical grievances in the Epiphany parliament of 1327 protested against the crown's use of writs of prohibition to stop tuitorial appeals to Canterbury,[35] and the clergy of Exeter diocese protested against the misuse of such appeals.[36] Tuitorial appeal seems to have been an institution peculiar to the two English provinces of Canterbury and York, but little is known of its working.[37]

2; Walsingham, *Gesta Abbatum* ii, 133; *Magnum Registrum Album*, ed. Savage, pp. 230-7, 272-3.

[35] Richardson and Sayles, *Rot. Parl. Ang. hac. Ined.*, p. 110.

[36] Wilkins ii, 549.

[37] For a summary of evidence, especially as pertains to York, see Donahue, *Michigan Law Review* 72 (1974), 671-4. For some discussion of Canterbury tuitorial appeal in William of Pagula's *Summa Summarum*, see Oxford, Bodleian Library, MS Bodley 293, f. 99.

8

The 'Privilege of England'

The theoretical basis upon which the crown in the early fourteenth century rested its claim to the right to prohibit cases from going for litigation to the Roman court has not received much attention from modern historians nor, indeed, is it at first sight apparent in the original records themselves. Yet there was thought to exist a specific papal privilege to the English king and people 'quod ipse vel Anglici citra mare Anglicanum ad iudicium non trahantur', which was still regarded as legally binding in the early fourteenth century. In 1325 Cardinal Gaillard de la Mothe as archdeacon of Oxford used these words to describe it when requesting John XXII to cite the chancellor and masters of Oxford University to the Roman court for judgement in his dispute with them concerning archidiaconal jurisdiction, notwithstanding this privilege; this citation is entered in Archbishop Reynolds' register and alongside it in a post-medieval hand are written the words *privilegium Angliae*.[1]

Knowledge of this privilege has also come to the attention of the present writer in another way, from instruments of procuration. English proctors to the Roman curia were at times empowered to renounce this English privilege on behalf of their clients, if necessary, in order to contract loans there. In this way the creditor at the curia would be assured that the debtor in England would not use this privilege to avoid legal proceedings if he failed to make repayment. One example can be taken from the instrument that empowered three monks of Christ Church Canterbury to act as its proctors at the Roman curia in 1293:

> Et ad renunciandum excepcioni non numerate non recepte et in nostram et dicti monasterii utilitatem non converse pecunie, et excepcioni doli, et constitucioni de duabus dietis edite in concilio generali, et convencioni iudicum et locorum, iuri revocandi domum, beneficio restitucionis in

---

[1] RR f. 145v; printed in Wilkins ii, 526-8; Reg. Martival ii, 582-6; below, Appendix 6, no. 56. I have found no medieval evidence for use of the term *privilegium Angliae*.

integrum, omnibus apostolicis litteris *et maxime illis per quas ab apostolica sede dicitur Anglicis esse indultum ne ultra mare seu extra regnum Anglie conveniri vel ad iudicium evocari valeant sine speciali mandato dicte sedis faciente mencionem de dicto indulto,* et omnibus aliis excepcionibus et iuribus....[2]

To identify and trace this papal indult to the English has not been easy.[3] Some historians have printed documents that cite the privilege of England, but they have not ventured to identify it. A few cite, but without comment, the page numbers of printed documents that mention it. Others show some awareness of it in their writings but do not attempt to trace its origins. And still others who, from the titles of their works, might be expected to mention it do not. Miss Rose Graham did attempt to identify it in her edition of the register of Archbishop Winchelsey when she printed a document that mentions it, but she was not quite correct.[4] Nor can the English privilege be identified as the 'constitution of two days' published in the Fourth Lateran Council of 1215,[5] which provided that no one could

---

[2] Cant. Cath. MS Christ Church Letters, vol. ii, no. 320 (cf. 321), app. C; copied, reading 'Anglicane ecclesie indultum' for 'Anglicis esse indultum' in CUL MS Ee.v.31, f. 52. In the passage quoted, the italics are mine. Other similar examples: prior and convent of Canterbury, 1300 (CUL MS Ee.v.31, f. 83, reading 'Anglicis'); archbishop of Canterbury, 1300 (Reg. Winchelsey, 590, reading 'Anglicis'); abbot and convent of Gloucester, 1298 (Lunt, *Papal Revenues* i, 172, reading 'Anglicis'); bishop, prior, and convent of Durham, 1288 (Fraser, *Records of Antony Bek* (Surtees Soc. vol. 162), 13, reading 'Anglicis'); prior and convent of Durham, 1283 (Brentano, *York Metropolitan Jurisdiction*, 220-5, reading 'Anglicanis'); bishop of Exeter, 1274 (Reg. Bronescombe, 237, reading 'prelatis aut clericis de Anglia.').

[3] Professor E. B. Graves has very generously sent me a great many references concerning the use of the English privilege in royal writs of prohibition from some work that he did some time ago, although most of my own research about it in the pages that follow had already been completed independently. I am grateful to him for several helpful suggestions, although the conclusions that I have reached are my own.

[4] Reg. Winchelsey, 590; below, p. 145 n. 11.

[5] CIC, Decretal. Greg. IX, lib. I, tit. iii, cap. 28 (Friedberg, vol. ii, col. 31 = c. 37 of Fourth Lateran Council); Schroeder, *Disciplinary Decrees*, 272 (transl.), 574 (Latin text); *Conciliorum Oecumenicorum Decreta*, ed. Alberigo, 251-2. Cf. Lunt, *Papal Revenues* ii, 593 (index) and Sayers, *Papal Judges Delegate*, 60-5, for examples of the use of this constitution. Traditionally the archbishop of Canterbury and papal judges delegate and conservators of papal privileges could cite persons in spite of the constitution of two days or of a similar 'constitution of one day' of Boniface VIII, the decree *Statutum quod* (Churchill, *Canterbury Administration* i, 479, 502; RR f. 227v; Lunt, *Papal Revenues* i, 172; Sayers, *Papal Judges Delegate*, 64). Similar individual indults usually 'of two days' were also rather frequently issued in favour of particular persons or religious houses, such as a bull of Innocent IV granted to the abbot of Bury St. Edmunds in 1248 'ne ultra duas dietas a monasterio per litteras apostolicas abbas trahi non (MS *sic*) possit' (Lambeth MS 644, no. 7; Sayers, *Original Papal Documents in the Lambeth Palace Library*, p. 20, no. 44; cf. Sayers, *Papal Judges Delegate*, 63-5).

be cited by apostolic letters to judgement in a tribunal of the church
beyond a two days' journey outside his own diocese unless both parties
agreed or express mention was made of this indult. That the English
privilege and this constitution, *Nonnulli*, were separate items is indicated
by the fact that this constitution was often enumerated along with other
recourses in canon and civil law, including the English privilege, in the
lists of protections that English curial proctors were empowered to
renounce on behalf of their clients. This juxtaposition we have already
seen, for example, in the Canterbury procuration of 1293.[6]

The English privilege stems from an indult of Gregory IX to Henry III
dated 20 July 1231, and its text is entered in the papal register as follows:

> Illustri regi Anglie. Si iustum iuste non fiat debitus ordo iusticie non
> servatur qui non potest sine iuris iniuria pretermitti. Sane tua nobis devocio
> supplicavit ut cum non sit tutum Anglicis quod ad terram inimicorum
> suorum ubi non possunt ius suum prosequi ad iudicium protrahantur,
> magnatibus et baronibus regni tui ne per litteras apostolicas extra illud
> trahantur in causam dignaremur misericorditer indulgere. Nos autem pro
> eo quod apostolice sedis existis filius specialis graciam quam cum Deo
> possumus tibi exhibere volentes, serenitatis tue precibus inclinati[7] auctori-
> tate presencium indulgemus *ut magnates et barones predicti, vocati ad
> iudicium per huiusmodi litteras extra regnum Anglie citra mare, cum illuc
> ire nequeunt absque periculo corporum, vel terram inimicorum eos transire
> contingit, accedere minime teneantur.* Nulli ergo etc. nostre concessionis
> infringere. Si quis autem etc. Dat' Reate .xiii. kalendas Augusti, pontificatus
> nostri anno quinto.

At the same time the pope, perhaps anticipating the renunciations that
proctors might be empowered to make, warned the king that he would
not honour the privilege in any case where the defendant had bound
himself so as to be summoned outside the realm in spite of it.[8] The English

---

[6] Above, pp. 142-3. Other examples: the pope himself specified the constitution of two
days as distinct from the English privilege in 1264 (Wilkins i, 760; Potthast, no. 18839;
Rymer I:i, 438-9; BL MS Cott. Cleopatra E.i, f. 198), and again in 1284 (Reg. Martin IV, nos.
447-8). Proctors for Archbishop Winchelsey were empowered to renounce not only the
English privilege but also the constitutions of one and of two days (Reg. Winchelsey, 590).
See also Brentano, *York Metropolitan Jurisdiction*, 225.

[7] MS *inclinitati*.

[8] The privilege itself is transcribed here from Vatican Archives, Reg. Vat. 15, ff. 111v-
112; italics mine. Both the privilege and the warning are calendared in Reg. Greg. IX, nos.
690, 691, and CPL i, 128, none of which entries repeats the actual words of the pope's bull.
The warning is also found by itself in Rymer I:i, 201 (transcribed), PRO SC7/15/19, and
PRO List and Index XLIX, p. 228. Neither the privilege nor the warning appears to be in
Potthast. I have not found the privilege itself (no. 690) transcribed in print anywhere.

privilege and the pope's warning that accompanied it, both granted upon petition of the crown, were not the only indults granted at that time by Gregory IX at the English king's request, for on the very same day – 20 July – he issued no less than five other documents upon petition of Henry III,[9] two of which were to the effect that royal officials should be immune from sentence of excommunication while in the king's service and one of which was a faculty that the king might select bishops of his choice as his personal advisors. This is not the place to enter upon a full discussion of the causes and events surrounding the issue of the English privilege. It should be noted, however, that one matter precipitating it may have been the refusal of Richard le Poore, bishop of Durham, to pay a certain sum of money (owed by his predecessor) to two Roman citizens, which led to a mandate of Gregory IX that he must pay dated 23 January 1230/1231. Thus pre-dating the privilege by a few months, this mandate entered the canon law as the decretal *Dilecti filii* and occasioned much comment from subsequent glossators.[10]

Later, on 4 May 1235, Gregory IX granted a special form of the same privilege to the archbishop of Canterbury, Edmund of Abingdon, upon the archbishop's request, and this privilege was confirmed by Innocent IV to the Canterbury archbishop Boniface of Savoy in 1246.[11] It is this last

---

[9] CPL. i, 128; Reg. Greg. IX, nos. 688-92, 694; Rymer I:i, 200-1; Denton, *English Royal Free Chapels*, 21, 157-8 (transcription of one bull, 20 July, not in Gregory's register). Still more indults of a similar sort were granted at other times.

[10] Transcribed in Reg. Greg. IX, no. 538, dated 23 Jan. 1230-1 = CIC, Decretal. Greg. IX, lib. II, tit. ii, cap. 17 (Friedberg, vol. ii, cols. 254-5, dated only '1227-34'); Potthast, no. 9584; CPL. i, 124; Vatican Archives, Reg. Vat. 15, f. 49. For a summary of canonists' opinions on *Dilecti filii* compiled during the earlier fourteenth century, see Johannes Andreae, *In Quinque Decretalium Libros Novella Commentaria*, introd. S. Kuttner, ii, 27-8. *Dilecti* had an evolution and history of its own under the canonical heading 'de foro competenti', and much work remains to be done on the relation of *Dilecti* to the English privilege itself.

[11] Lambeth MS 1212, pp. 254, 271 (ff. 131, 137v), both with incipit *Super laboribus et expensis*. Neither this form of the privilege nor its confirmation appears to be in Reg. Greg. IX or Reg. Innocent IV or Potthast or CPL. Miss Graham (Reg. Winchelsey, 590) printed an instrument of Abp. Winchelsey, dated 1300, empowering his curial proctors to renounce the 'privilegium Anglicis indultum' and in a footnote she stated 'This appears to be a reference to a bull of Innocent IV dated September 23rd, 1246, cf. MS Lambeth 1212, p. 271'. This page reference in the Lambeth MS, however, is the confirmation by Innocent IV of the special form of the privilege granted to the archbishop by Gregory IX in 1235, and it contains the phrase 'ad instar felicis recordacionis Gregorii pape predecessoris nostri'. The 1235 bull of Gregory IX is in fact entered on p. 254 of the same MS, not cited by Miss Graham, and the wording of both bulls is substantially the same except for the omission in the original bull of the phrase just quoted. The confirmation by Innocent IV on p. 271 of the Lambeth MS is dated '.xii. kal' Oct.', which is 20 September rather than 'September 23rd' as Miss Graham considered.

bull that Miss Graham mistakenly identified as the original privilege. This
'ecclesiastical' variant of the privilege, granted to the Canterbury see in
1235, was invoked by Archbishop Pecham in 1284 and again in 1285
when he objected to being summoned to France before foreign judges
delegate to answer charges of the abbot of Fécamp resulting from
Pecham's excommunication of a monk of Fécamp in Chichester diocese
during a metropolitical visitation there.[12] Pope Martin IV committed the
Fécamp case to the official of the bishop of Amiens notwithstanding the
privilege.[13] A number of other references to the 'ecclesiastical' variant of
the privilege also survive, claiming variously that it had been granted to
the English church, to the prelates or clergy of England, or to the see of
Canterbury.[14]

We return to the main form of the privilege, granted in 1231, and to the
uses that were made of it. Traces of the English privilege, in slightly
varying words, can be found in royal documents throughout the century
after 1231. Later references usually state that the privilege was granted to
'Anglicis' rather than to 'magnatibus et baronibus regni nostri'. The
earliest actual use of the privilege that I have found comes from the year
1233. One Peter Mulet, a merchant of Douai licensed by the crown to do
business in England, had caused certain nobles of the realm to be cited
before papal judges delegate beyond the seas and because the nobles had
not appeared they had been pronounced excommunicate by the judges.
The king proceeded to ask the bishops of England not to proceed with the
sentence of excommunication, citing, among other reasons, the 'privilegium nobis a domino papa indultum'.[15] The crown again used the
privilege in 1234, this time in the case of Hubert de Burgh, begging the
pope not to summon him to judgement in Rome contrary to this indult.
To this Gregory IX replied that he did not believe he had granted such

[12] *Reg. Ep. Pecham* iii, p. 821: 'Non obstantibus privilegiis apostolicis sedi nostrae ab
olim indultis, ut trahi extra Angliam per literas apostolicas non possimus'; cf. p. 886.
Pecham's resistance was apparently effective: Douie, *Pecham*, 163.

[13] Reg. Martin IV, nos. 447-8, 20 Jan. 1283/1284; CPL i, 471-2. It is not possible to tell
from the pope's letter whether Pecham had in fact invoked both the original privilege and
its ecclesiastical variant, or whether there was some uncertainty in the pope's mind as to
where the issue lay: 'indulgentia qua dicto archiepiscopo specialiter vel illis de regno
prefato generaliter dicitur esse concessum, ut idem archiepiscopus, vel aliquis de regno
ipso, extra illud, vel citra mare Anglicanum, seu alia certa loca in causam trahi, vel ad
judicium evocari, ... per litteras apostolicas non facientes plenam et expressam de indulto
hujusmodi mentionem'.

[14] Above, . 2.

[15] Transcribed in *Close Rolls* 1231-4, 303-4, and in *Royal Letters, Henry III*, vol. i, p.
413; cf. CPR 1225-32, 247, 459, 464.

letters without the tacit or express renunciation of the indult.[16] A few years later, in 1239, the king empowered his proctors at the curia to renounce this privilege in order to permit one particular case to be heard in the Roman court.[17] Further case histories are not necessary for the present discussion, but some generalizations can be made from the evidence. In Prynne's *Records* and on the close rolls and elsewhere, there are a great many examples to show that the crown in the thirteenth century often and perhaps even usually cited this 'privilege of England' as the precedent when it took steps to stop citations and litigation in the Roman curia.[18] And while some of the thirteenth-century references to the English privilege come from its being put into operation by the crown, still others come from its being overridden in particular cases by the apostolic see. As early as 1247 and in several subsequent cases, papal mandates cited or threatened to cite various Englishmen to justice at the Roman court 'notwithstanding the indulgence to Englishmen that they shall not be cited across the English sea'.[19] There are instances of the apostolic see expressly honouring the privilege,[20] and there are English complaints that papal agents were citing Englishmen in derogation of it.[21] It was certainly a factor of some considerable significance in Anglo-papal relations during much of the thirteenth century.

This significance is heightened when the privilege is set in a broader historical perspective.[22] Before 1231, it is true, the English crown had from time to time prohibited appeals to the Roman court, and indeed some restriction of appeals to Rome in one way or another can be traced back at least to the reign of William the Conqueror. Some appeals were

---

[16] Rymer I:i, 211; cf. DNB, 1908 re-issue, vol. iii, p. 320.

[17] Prynne, *Records* ii, 561; *Close Rolls* 1237-42, 235; Rymer I:i, 239.

[18] Prynne, *Records* ii, 561, 628, 718, 941-2, 980-1, 995; ibid. iii, 227; *Close Rolls* 1231-4, 303-4; ibid. 1237-42, 235; ibid. 1242-7, 255-6; ibid. 1247-51, 109; ibid. 1256-9, 301, 309; ibid. 1259-61, 466; CCR 1272-9, 555; CPR 1232-47, 443; *Placitorum Abb.*, 152; *Rot. Parl.* i, 50. I am preparing a separate study of the privilege that will treat these and other cases in detail.

[19] CPL i, 239-40, 254, 380, 400-1, 493, 495-6; Reg. Innocent IV, nos. 3495, 4450; BL MS Cott. Cleopatra E.i, f. 198; Rymer I:i, 438-9; Wilkins i, 760.

[20] Reg. Innocent IV, no. 879; Rymer I:i, 211.

[21] P&C i, 392-6; *Annales Monastici ... de Dunstaplia*, 169-70 ('quod Anglici extra regnum trahuntur, et inter inimicos conveniuntur, contra jus scriptum et regis privilegia').

[22] My comments in this paragraph depend upon the following: Brooke, *The English Church and the Papacy*, 167, 203, 212; Davis, *England under the Normans and Angevins*, 145-6, 208, 213, 243; Phillimore, *The Ecclesiastical Law* ii, 967-8; Richardson and Sayles, *Governance*, 297-302; Saltman, *Theobald*, 154-9; Mayr-Harting, JEH xvi (1965), 39-53; Cheney, *From Becket to Langton*, 88-92; Weaver and Poole, *H. W. C. Davis Memoir*, 97-143.

permitted, of course, but others were prohibited, and the crown seems to have had its own working rules (which varied) as to which ones it would allow to proceed to Rome. Chapters four and eight of the Constitutions of Clarendon, 1164, had laid down that neither ecclesiastical persons nor appeals might go outside the realm without royal assent, but this had been modified in 1172 by the settlement of Avranches which provided that appeals might go to Rome so long as the appellants swore that they intended no infringement of royal rights. The theoretical basis, therefore, upon which appeals to Rome might be prohibited before 1231 was not very precise, and it is understandable why prohibitions before 1231 might be worded only with rather vague phrases about ancient custom and the royal dignity and the availability of justice within the English realm. The privilege of England, however, provided a new basis for such prohibitions, for now the crown under Henry III and Edward I could declare that its prohibitions rested upon the very word of the pope himself.[23]

Yet in the late thirteenth, or at least by the early fourteenth, century the history of the English privilege begins to trail off. An impression gained from reading the sources of the early fourteenth century is one of comparative silence about it. Whereas in 1244 a typical royal writ of prohibition to Rome might begin

> Cum a sede apostolica nobis specialiter sit indultum, ne quis de regno nostro in foro ecclesiastico extra regnum nostrum per litteras apostolicas trahatur in causam...[24]

a similar writ of the early fourteenth century would more often begin:

> Cum secundum consuetudinem in regno nostro optentam et hactenus approbatam, nullus de regno nostro trahi debeat in causam extra idem regnum...[25]

And this latter form continues to be quite typical for many years to come. It seems that there was a gradual eclipse of the privilege occurring over a transition period of several years during the later thirteenth and early fourteenth centuries, and as yet it is not possible to specify any particular date or dates as clearly determinative. I name first the latest citations of the privilege I have found by medieval English kings. Edward I in 1279

---

[23] For a similar assertion of the crown about the same time to the effect that it also possessed a general papal indult permitting its clerks to be nonresident in their benefices, see below, pp. 164-7.

[24] Prynne, *Records* ii, 628.

[25] PRO C47/18/4/2 (probably 1306). Cf. PRO E159/84, m. 57; Rymer II:i, 388, 406.

reminded Nicholas III of the privilege and asked him to correct abuses against its enforcement.[26] In a case of appeal to the Roman court in 1290 the king declared that the privilege should not be infringed.[27] A papal bull containing this privilege in a form issued by Innocent IV was known and handled by royal officers in 1315 and 1323.[28] And in 1308 Clement V specifically stated that he was acting upon the king's request when he extended the privilege to apply to the inhabitants of the Channel Islands of Guernsey, Jersey, Sark, and Alderney, all of the diocese of Coutances but which the pope described as known to be held by Edward II within Normandy.[29] We have already seen that Cardinal Gaillard de la Mothe regarded the privilege as legally significant in 1325. The latest curial procurations that I have found to mention it date from 1300, but there may well be others of subsequent dates. Exactly when the crown changed the form of its prohibition writs, and what the new forms were, is also uncertain. Some evidence suggests that the *Cum secundum consuetudinem* writs first issued in 1306,[30] and if so one of them was a prohibition against citing Walter Reynolds outside the realm in any dispute over his royal appointment to the provostship of Beverley,[31] but still other evidence suggests that *Cum secundum consuetudinem* may have issued as early as 1284, when the king made no mention of the privilege in prohibiting a certain case to Rome.[32]

[26] Prynne, *Records* iii, 227; CCR 1272-9, 555; Rymer I:ii, 565-6.

[27] *Rot. Parl.* i, 50.

[28] *The Red Book of the Exchequer*, ed. Hall, iii, 1042-6: 'Bulla Innocentii Papae iiiite, ne aliquis trahatur in placitum extra regnum contra privilegium domino Regi indultum'. This was one of twenty-four bulls of various popes found by John Sandale as chancellor among the memoranda of John Francis, a deceased king's clerk who had been a keeper of the great seal in 1310, which were delivered to the king's treasury of the exchequer in 1315 and calendared by Walter Stapledon in 1323 (*Ancient Kalendars*, ed. Palgrave, vol. i, p. 11, no. 20). I have been unable to trace this particular bull; it may have been in response to English complaints made in 1246 (P&C i, 392-6), or (less likely) it may simply be a reference to some papal letter mentioning the privilege such as Reg. Innocent IV, no. 879 or 3495. This bull may have been among the papal bulls and privileges, numbering perhaps forty, that were copied by certain chancery clerks in 1305 (Tout, *Chapters* ii, p. 70, nn. 1 and 2; CCR 1302-7, 300-1; Prynne, *Records* iii, 1074).

[29] CPL. ii, 45; Reg. Clem. V, no. 3165: 'apostolica indulgentia gaudeant, per quam Anglicis est concessum, quod citra mare Anglicanum in causam trahi vel ad iudicium evocari non possunt per litteras apostolicas non facientes plenam et expressam de indulto huiusmodi mentionem'. For background, see CCR 1302-7, 327.

[30] *Chapter Act Book of Beverley* i, 130, 135 (6 April and 2 May 1306); PRO C47/18/4/2.

[31] Below, Appendix 12, no. 5.

[32] Rymer I:ii, 651; CCR 1279-88, 347-8. The king did invoke the privilege in a prohibition writ of 19 June 1283 (Reg. Swinfield, 13-14).

The subsequent history of royal writs prohibiting cases to the Roman court but not mentioning the English privilege is too vast a subject of research for this current undertaking,[33] although later in this book attention will be given to a number of still other sorts of prohibition writs found in Reynolds' register. For the present, however, we are concerned only with sources that mention the English privilege, and with an explanation of its eclipse. To attempt some further investigation of this, I have made an analysis of a control group of twenty-five manuscript registers of writs from the thirteenth and fourteenth centuries, mostly in the British Library, all of which contain sample writs prohibiting cases to the Roman court. The tentative nature of the probabilities that may be drawn from such material must be acknowledged, although a greater degree of certainty is now afforded by the proposed approximation of dates for such registers that has been published by de Haas and Hall.[34] Nine of these 25 registers contain prohibition writs of the *Cum a sede apostolica nobis specialiter sit indultum* form, i.e. citing the English privilege,[35] and the other sixteen instead contain writs of the *Cum secundum consuetudinem* form.[36] Using the schedule proposed by de Haas and Hall, it would appear that seven of the nine containing the English privilege can be dated to the period from 1275 to 1307,[37] whereas twelve of the sixteen that contain the *Cum secundum consuetudinem* form fall in the later classification of 'fourteenth century'.[38] Two of the nine are placed

---

[33] A thorough study of the close rolls and the records of the king's bench in the later thirteenth and early fourteenth centuries would be necessary. Further, see Graves, 'The Legal Significance of the Statute of *Praemunire* of 1353', esp. pp. 57-64. For printed examples of the related writ *Ad iura nostra regia, ne depereant,* dating at least as early as 1307, see Rymer I:ii, 1011, and II:i, 77, 142-3, 240, 257, 452, 467, 764, 788, 990-1; Reg. Hethe, 297-8; Reg. Halton ii, 11-12. I am indebted to Prof. Graves for many of these references.

[34] *Early Registers of Writs,* p. xxiii. Further discussion of such registers is also given in this work.

[35] BL MSS Cott. Titus D.xxiii, f. 31; Harl. 1608, f. 26; Harl. 1690, f. 74v; Harl. 4351, ff. 22-22v; Harl. 5213, ff. 16v-17; Add. 11557, ff. 18-18v; 20059, f. 37v; 22174, f. 107; Lambeth MS 166, f. 128.

[36] BL MSS Harl. 858, f. 132; Harl. 869, f. 122; Harl. 927, f. 24; Harl. 947, f. 199v; Harl. 961, ff. 28v-29; Harl. 3942, f. 22; Lansdowne 476, ff. 130v-131; Lansdowne 652, f. 255; Royal 11.A.ix, ff. 36-36v; Add. 5761, f. 16v; 22162, f. 40v; 25142, f. 93v; 25237, ff. 58v-59v; 29499, ff. 38v-39; 34901, f. 56v; Lambeth MS 567, f. 26.

[37] BL MSS Harl. 1608, f. 26; Harl. 1690, f. 74v; Harl. 4351, ff. 22-22v; Harl. 5213, ff. 16v-17; Add. 11557 ff. 18-18v; 22174, f. 107; Lambeth MS 166, f. 128.

[38] BL MSS Harl. 927, f. 24; Harl. 947, f. 199v; Harl. 961, ff. 28v-29; Harl. 3942, f. 22; Lansdowne 476, ff. 130v-131; Royal 11.A.ix, ff. 36-36v; Add. 22162, f. 40v; 25142, f. 93v; 25237, ff. 58v-59v; 29499, ff. 38v-39; 34901, f. 56v; Lambeth MS 567, f. 26.

by de Haas and Hall in the later period,[39] however, and four of the sixteen are classified in the earlier period.[40] Thus far it can be said in a general way, then, that an examination of these registers with regard to their approximate dates confirms – with some exceptions – what has already been suggested from the other evidence: the greater prominence of the English privilege in royal writs of the thirteenth century and its comparative eclipse somewhat before or at least by the beginning of the reign of Edward II. There is even one explicit instance where reference to the privilege has been deleted. In a register of the earlier group, which has been dated about 1305, the words referring to the English privilege ('a sede apostolica sit indultum' and 'indulgencie memorate') have been struck out and a sign manual placed in the margin.[41]

Still other indications emerge from a scrutiny of these registers. All of the group of nine as well as six of the sixteen contain an additional writ, not invoking the English privilege, which is intended to prohibit pleas of English prelates in the Roman court concerning their fees which they hold of the crown, as the king is ready to render justice in his own court in such matters.[42] This additional writ does not mention the English privilege, even though nine of the registers that contain this additional writ are the same nine whose standard writ of prohibition to Rome does

[39] BL MSS Cott. Titus D.xxiii, f. 31; Add. 20059, f. 37v.

[40] BL MSS Harl. 858, f. 132; Harl. 869, f. 122; Lansdowne 652, f. 255; Add. 5761, f. 16v.

[41] BL MS Add. 11557, ff. 18-18v; for the date cf. *Early Registers of Writs*, ed. de Haas and Hall, p. cxv n. 10. This may not, of course, be contemporary with the date of the register. For another such example of deletion in the same manuscript see below, pp. 165-66; cf. also *Early Registers of Writs*, p. 25, and Logan, *Excommunication and the Secular Arm*, p. 124 and n. 29.

[42] The group of nine is named above in note 35. Of this group, Add. MS 20059 does not in fact contain this additional writ, but I have continued to include it within this group because it exhibits all the other characteristics of the group that are discussed here. The additional six are BL MSS Harl. 858, f. 132; Harl. 869, f. 122; Harl. 3942, f. 22v; Lansdowne 652, f. 255; Add. 5761, f. 16v; Lambeth MS 567, f. 26. The following words are typical for this writ: 'Rex tali episcopo, salutem. Cum secundum consuetudinem temporibus progenitorum nostrorum regum Anglie et nostro approbatam et optentam cogniciones causarum de libertatibus et aliis rebus ad feoda prelatorum regni nostri spectantibus pertineant ad dignitatem nostram ac talis episcopus iam trahat vos in causam in curia Romana super libertatibus et aliis rebus ad feoda prelatorum spectantibus ut audivimus in nostri preiudicium manifestum, vobis sub debito fidelitatis qua nobis tenemini necnon super terris et tenementis que de nobis tenetis districte inhibemus ne ecclesiasticum examen super libertatibus vel aliis rebus ad feoda vestra spectantibus subire presumatis, presertim cum parati sumus super premissis prefato episcopo plenam et celerem iusticiam in curia nostra secundum leges et consuetudines regni nostri exhibere ne dictum examen super huiusmodi aliquatenus subire poteritis sine iuris nostri offensa et lesione dignitatis regie ad cuius conservacionem sicut alii prelati de regno nostro iuramento estis astricti'.

contain the privilege. These nine containing the English privilege and these further six that do not may be said to constitute a group of fifteen together by virtue of the additional writ that they contain for prelates. Eleven of these fifteen are assigned by de Haas and Hall to the earlier, 1275-1307 period,[43] and it may be suggested that the other four are very close to them because of their similarities on this point. We should also observe that the standard writ of prohibition to the Roman court contained in all of these fifteen, which as we have seen is of the *Cum nobis a sede apostolica* form in the nine and of the *Cum secundum consuetudinem* form in the six, offers the following explanation for the prohibition: 'Maxime cum ipse paratus sit infra idem regnum in omnibus stare iuri'. Thus it would appear that whenever the crown was citing the English privilege in its writs of prohibition to the Roman court, and at least for a while after it had stopped and had begun to cite only the ancient custom of the realm, the most important explanation it chose to give was that the person in question was ready to answer at law within the English realm. The crown was not yet claiming normal cognizance of such cases for its own courts, and the implication is that such cases could be and frequently were being heard by ecclesiastical judges within England, even though the crown was already asserting the competence of its courts in the additional writ for English prelates concerning their lay fees.

The ten remaining registers of the twenty-five I have examined, all of which are placed by de Haas and Hall later in the general 'fourteenth-century' category, presumably after 1307, and which are thus probably later than the other registers we have been discussing, give some indication of the line of development.[44] They all contain standard prohibition writs of the *Cum secundum consuetudinem* form and not the English privilege. Yet, after the *Cum secundum consuetudinem* introduction, the standard prohibition writs in all these registers contain a significant insertion. The additional phrase is italicized in the example that follows: 'Cum secundum consuetudinem in regno nostro optentam et hactenus approbatam nullus de eodem regno *super hiis quorum cognicio ad nos pertinet* trahi debeat in causam extra idem regnum....' In every one of these ten registers this prohibition writ is followed by one or two

---

[43] BL. MSS Harl. 858, 869, 1608, 1690, 4351, 5213; Lansdowne 652; Add. 5761, 11557, 22174; Lambeth MS 166.

[44] BL. MSS Harl. 927, f. 24; Harl. 947, f. 199v; Harl. 961, ff. 28v-29; Lansdowne 476, ff. 130v-131; Royal 11.A.ix, ff. 36-36v; Add. 22162, f. 40v; 25142, f. 93v; 25237, ff. 58v-59v; 29499, ff. 38v-39; 34901, f. 56v.

attachments to the sheriff containing the same phrase about cognition pertaining to the crown.[45]

The introduction of this last phrase, I believe, indicates the line of development for our period.[46] Even a cautious interpretation of this evidence allows us to suggest that, perhaps in the later years of Edward I and at least certainly by the beginning of the reign of Edward II, the crown had apparently begun to expand its jurisdiction here and to assert the competence of its own courts over against those of the church whether within the realm or at Rome. No longer is it simply a matter of prohibition because justice is available within the realm, but now because cognition of the matter in question pertains to the royal courts. The privilege of England, however, did not support this assertion as well as arguments could that were based upon the royal prerogative and ancient custom, and a more vigorous policy seems to have been gradually formulated. At a time that can not yet be precisely dated, then, the basis of royal prohibition to Rome was changed. Appeals to Rome were no longer said, as in 1233, to be merely 'contra formam privilegii nostri',[47] but now rather, as in 1307, to be 'in enervationem juris nostri regii et exhaeredationem nostram et enormem laesionem dignitatis et coronae nostrae'.[48]

This gradual eclipse of the English privilege in the assertions of royal documents, we may note, corresponds with a parallel eclipse of its mention in the documents of the papacy. It is almost as if there has been a mutual, tacit agreement to phase it out. Perhaps Clement V, more probably John XXII, no longer wished to remind the crown or the Canterbury archbishop that it had granted such a privilege to the English. This privilege, if recalled, could not help but stand in the way when the papal grievances of 1309 and 1317 complained that royal officials were inhibiting apostolic citations of Englishmen outside the realm.[49] And the

---

[45] A register from the Bodleian Library (MS Rawlinson C292) dated to 1318-1320 and printed by de Haas and Hall (*Early Registers of Writs*, pp. 141-2, nos. 140-2) also exhibits this same sequence of writs. It is interesting to note the double reason given in this register's sample prohibition (no. 140): 'Maxime cum prefatus ... paratus sit infra idem regnum in omnibus *vel in hiis quorum cognicio ad nos pertinet* stare iuri' (italics mine).

[46] The earliest actual writs containing the 'super hiis quorum cognicio ad nos pertinet' insertion that I have encountered in use come from 1309 and 1310 (Reg. Halton i, 325-6; PRO E159/84, m. 57), although I have not made a very thorough search and there may well be earlier ones. Later examples proliferate; cf. Rymer II:i, 416. In some cases the reading is 'super aliquibus' instead of 'super hiis'.

[47] *Royal Letters, Henry III*, vol. i, p. 414.

[48] Rymer II:i, 20, 22, 24, 96, 130, 214-15; cf. *Liber Epistolaris* of Richard de Bury, no. 27.

[49] Below, Appendix 7.

English crown, as we have suggested, no longer wished to emphasize to all and sundry that the very basis upon which it had been prohibiting appeals to Rome rested at least in part upon a privilege granted by the pope himself. The assertion of the royal dignity was expanding apace with the extending jurisdiction of the royal courts over those of the church. The transformation of the privilege of England into the ancient custom of the realm was one more way in which that vague and clouded but vast and powerful current known as the *praerogativa regis* came to gather such momentum in the later years of Edward I.[50]

After nearly three hundred more years, remarkably, the English privilege surfaced again when it was brought to light by King Henry VIII in the fall of 1530.[51] Citing the 'consuetudo et privilegium regni, ne Angli extra Angliam litigare cogantur',[52] which he alleged had been granted by the apostolic see itself and confirmed by several popes, Henry urged that because of it (among other reasons) the appeal of Catherine of Aragon should not be heard at Rome but rather that the archbishop of Canterbury should give final sentence as primate and legate in England. Doubts were of course cast upon this at Rome, but the king managed to construct a rather impressive case, buttressing the privilege of England with other legislation from sources as diverse as Nicaea and Clarendon. Professor Scarisbrick, estimating its significance on the eve of the Reformation, has considered that Henry thereby 'enunciated a new theory of English monarchy'. This 'claim to a national privilege and some kind of national autonomy', Scarisbrick even asserts, became one of the mainstays of Henricianism.[53]

---

[50] For the development of the royal prerogative at this time, see Deeley, EHR xliii (1928), 513 seq.; Flahiff, *Mediaeval Studies* vi (1944), 285-8; Highfield, 'The Relations' i, 286 seq.; Powicke, *Thirteenth Century*, 324-33; Fraser, *Antony Bek*, 137; Smith, *Episcopal Appointments*, 64-5; *Statutes of the Realm* i, 225-7. It may be noted that Maitland (EHR vi (1891), 367-72) dated the classical statement known as the *Praerogativa Regis* from about the end of the thirteenth century.

[51] Scarisbrick, *Henry VIII*, 260-7; *Reg. Ep. Pecham* iii, p. 821 n. 1. We may be permitted to speculate, although there is no evidence, that it may have been one of Henry's agents who, searching the register of Reynolds for such information, wrote the words 'privilegium Angliae' that are penned in a post-medieval hand on f. 145v.

[52] Henry VIII, writing to his ambassadors at Rome, 7 Oct. 1530: *State Papers, Henry the Eighth*, vol. vii, part v (1527-37), pp. 261-2 (no. 283). This same letter also mentions the papal canon 'ne quis ultra duas dietas extra diocesim in litem trahatur', thus proving that Henry VIII knew the English privilege as something distinct from *Nonnulli* of the IV Lateran. It was probably this mention of the 'constitution of two days' by Henry that led Prof. Scarisbrick (p. 265) to imply (incorrectly, I believe) that the English privilege, which was not granted until 1231, had been 'confirmed' by Pope Innocent III.

[53] Scarisbrick, *Henry VIII*, 261, 267.

9

Royal Control of Episcopal Temporalities

Just as the crown by the time of Edward II was prepared to take a strong and – if necessary – independent line on the question of litigation in the Roman court, abiding by the customs of the past only when they suited present needs, so also in the control of ecclesiastical temporalities the crown was prepared to resist any attempt by the papacy to encroach upon the area which it regarded as its own domain. The investiture controversy was now largely a thing of the past, but the crown continually found it necessary to remind the church of Rome and the church in England that temporalities of bishoprics and abbeys were granted at its own pleasure and not at the pope's command.[1] The crown at this time could and did for various reasons seize the temporalities of bishoprics from their incumbents, it normally administered temporalities during episcopal vacancies,[2] and it also might for some reason withhold restoration of temporalities after a vacant see had been filled.[3]   Edward I in the later thirteenth century had successfully defeated the marcher lords' claims to the temporalities and even presentation rights of vacant Welsh sees, and this question would give little trouble in our own period.[4] Another storm over temporalities had come at the very end of Edward I's life. The old king had assumed that the administration of Canterbury temporalities during the suspension of Archbishop Winchelsey that began in 1306 was the crown's privilege, but Clement V made a strong protest and there was a conflict of patronage in which the papal administrators refused to admit a royal presentee to a rich benefice and favoured a papal

---

[1] Cf. Churchill, *Canterbury Administration* i, 242-3.
[2] Howell, *Regalian Right*; Henriques, 'Articles of Grievances', 46 seq.; Smith, *Episcopal Appointments*, 57.
[3] The king's rights in France seem to have been more restricted during vacancies (Lemarignier, Gaudemet, and Mollat, *Institutions ecclésiastiques*, 244, 250-1, 416, 420).
[4] Williams, *The Welsh Church*, 47-54. I owe this reference to Dr. R. R. Davies.

provisor instead. Complaints were raised against the papal policy in the parliament of Carlisle, but largely as a result of the diplomacy of Cardinal Peter of Spain Edward I restored the temporalities to the papal administrators and there the situation rested.[5] Such a settlement, however, could serve a dangerous precedent, for the next step might be a papal claim to administer temporalities during the normal vacancies of English sees.

Seizure of temporalities from incumbents for various reasons was one way of impressing the royal claims upon the English hierarchy. The story of Edward II's seizure of the temporalities of the see of Coventry and Lichfield in 1307-1308 has already been told by Miss Beardwood,[6] and in 1309 Archbishop Greenfield of York excused himself to the pope for failure to execute a papal mandate on the grounds that he feared forfeiture of temporalities as had befallen his predecessors Romeyn and Corbridge.[7] An entire history of the crown's attitude toward temporalities can not be written here, but the experience of Archbishop Reynolds with Edward II on the question of temporalities will help to fill in the picture. Although Reynolds had supported Edward II's seizure of the temporalities of Lincoln in 1321-1324 and of Hereford in 1324-1325 by his willingness to institute clerks there upon royal presentation – a policy which brought him the rebuke of John XXII,[8] yet Reynolds – together with the other bishops of the province – firmly opposed the crown's concurrent attack upon Bishop Orleton of Hereford in the February parliament of 1323/ 1324.[9] There is interesting evidence, also, of Reynolds himself fully collating to at least one vacancy in the Hereford diocese while the temporalities were supposedly still in the king's hands.[10] It has been suggested that the crown's promise in Edward III's first parliament of 1327 not to seize the temporalities of bishoprics in this way was perhaps made at the instigation of Orleton whose temporalities had just finally been restored,[11] but in 1333 the same king withheld the temporalities for

[5] Reg. Winchelsey, pp. xxv-xxvi; below, Appendix 3, no. 41.

[6] *The Trial of Walter Langton*, 11-13; Wilkins ii, 301-2; Rymer II:i, 39, 58.

[7] Reg. Greenfield iv, 209-11.

[8] Le Neve, *Lincoln*, 1; Le Neve, *Hereford*, 1; CPL ii, 471; Deeley, EHR xliii (1928), 510; Smith, *Episcopal Appointments*, 86-94.

[9] Rymer II:i, 549-50; *Rot. Parl.* ii, 427-9; Reg. Orleton Hereford, p. xxvii seq.; Sayles, *Select Cases in the Court of King's Bench under Edward II*, pp. 143-6; Usher, TRHS, 5th series, vol. xxii (1972), 39-41.

[10] RR f. 258v.

[11] Reg. Orieton Hereford, pp. xxvi-xxvii; *Statutes of the Realm* i, 255.

several months from Orleton himself after he had recently been translated to Winchester.[12]

Archbishop Reynolds was at least twice threatened by Edward II in full parliament with forfeiture of temporalities – once at the October parliament of 1320 when the king prohibited him from obeying a papal mandate,[13] and once in the June parliament of 1325 after Reynolds had complained about the king's nomination of Archbishop William Melton as treasurer.[14] The suggestion of a threat to seize episcopal temporalities for non-obedience, however, seems often to have been a standard form for the conclusion of royal commands to bishops at this time, and so we find numerous letters from Edward II even to Reynolds that conclude with clauses like the following:

> Scientes pro certo, quod si secus feceritis, ad vos et temporalia que de nobis tenetis, tanquam contemptorem et violatorem iuris nostri regii et corone nostre iuxta leges et consuetudines regni nostri graviter non inmerito capiemus;[15]

or:

> Et ideo vobis firmiter iniungendo mandamus quod istud mandatum nostrum taliter exequamini ne ad vos tanquam ad mandatorum nostrorum contemptorem manifestum per capcionem baronie vestre in manum nostram capere debeamus.[16]

The king's claim to ultimate control over ecclesiastical temporalities, however, was continually threatened head-on by the papacy's claim that episcopal provisors were granted not only the spiritualities but also the temporalities of their sees at the pleasure of the supreme pontiff.[17] It was necessary for the crown effectively to counter this claim if the basis of its own claim was to remain secure. This the crown managed to do, in a very direct way, by forcing episcopal provisors to take an oath swearing that they would receive their temporalities at the king's pleasure and not by the pope's grant. The origin of these oaths, centred in Edward I's opposition to the papal provision of Robert Kilwardby to Canterbury in 1272, has been set forth in *Councils and Synods II*, edited by Professors Powicke and

---

[12] Le Neve, *Mon. So. Prov.*, 46; Murimuth, *Con. Chron.*, 70.

[13] RR f. 98v; Wilkins ii, 499.

[14] Cant. Cath. MS Eastry Cor. i, 1, 2; Wilkins ii, 525; HMC Rep. Var. Coll., i, 270-1.

[15] RR f. 307v. For analysis of the value of the see of Canterbury, cf. Du Boulay, *The Lordship of Canterbury*, esp. pp. 16-51, 240-6, 312-16.

[16] RR f. 312. Other examples: RR ff. 297v, 300, 300v, 301, 302v, 303v, 304v, 305, 307v.

[17] For the earlier history of this papal claim, both in canon law and in continental practice, see Benson, *The Bishop-Elect*, 335-72.

Cheney, which also shows the application of similar oaths at the provisions of John Salmon to Norwich (1299) and William Gainsborough to Worcester (1303).[18] The temporalities of Canterbury were not released to Kilwardby until he had taken the oath. Recalling the provision of Nicholas of Ely to Winchester in 1268, the crown at the same time made a general statement of protest against the papal claim lest it should serve as an example for future times.

Powicke and Cheney point out that, as in the provision of Gainsborough, the crown's objection was to the phrase 'curam et administrationem ipsius tibi in spiritualibus et temporalibus committentes', which by the early fourteenth century had become a regular phrase in bulls of episcopal provision. It is interesting to note, however, that the papacy's claim to grant both spiritualities and temporalities was often preceded by a clever parallel phrase in which the provisor was described as a man possessed of 'spiritualium prudencia et temporalium providencia', or as being 'in spiritualibus providum et temporalibus circumspectum' or some such words. This double phraseology, which reinforced the papal claim, can be found in a number of the provisory bulls of Clement v and John xxii.[19] And so, as these phrases continued to be inserted in the bulls, the crown continued to enforce the swearing of oaths that renounced the words of the papal claim.

One file in the Public Record Office contains notarial instruments of fifty such oaths dating from 1312 to 1477,[20] but we must not be misled by it into thinking that these are the only ones, that this file is the only place where they were kept, or that these dates represent the earliest or latest ones that survive. A memorandum on the public instrument recording the king's protest and the provisor's oath when Rigaud d'Assier was provided to Winchester in 1320 informs us that three such instruments were made – one for chancery, another for the wardrobe, and a third for the treasury in the custody of the 'camerarii',[21] and traces of these oaths are to be found in a number of places. Some instruments survive attached to papal bulls in the SC7 category at the Public Record Office, often (but not always) the swearing of such an oath is mentioned on the calendars of

---

[18] P&C ii, 802-4, 1226-7; Sommer-Seckendorff, *Robert Kilwardby*, 72-3. Orford of Ely also took such an oath on the same day as Gainsborough (CPR 1301-7, 11).

[19] E.g., RR ff. 2v-3; PRO SC7/44/11, 15, 22; PRO SC 7/56/5, 11, 17, 19, 20. Edward II himself, however, also used a similar description when commending Walter Reynolds to the pope for the see of Worcester: 'quemque in spiritualibus novimus et temporalibus circumspectum' (Rymer II:i, 15).

[20] PRO C47/15/1.

[21] Reg. Asserio, 567-9.

patent rolls when the delivery of temporalities is recorded, and occasionally other references indicate that such oaths were taken. A typical specimen of these oaths is the one taken by Walter Jorz for the see of Armagh in 1307:

> Ego frater Walterus per sanctissimum patrem dominum Clementem divina providentia papam quintum in archiepiscopum Armachan' praefectus, illi particulae litterarum apostolicarum de mea promotione vobis illustri principi domino Edwardo Dei gratia regi Angliae et domino Hiberniae directarum in qua michi ipse pater praefatus temporalium ad meum archiepiscopatum spectantium curam et administrationem committit et omnibus aliis ipsarum litterarum ac tenori quatenus praejudicant vel praejudicare poterunt regio juri vestro coronae vel regiae dignitati vestrae, palam renuncio et expresse, ipsaque temporalia praedicta non virtute litterarum apostolicarum sed ex vestra regia gratia, cui me submitto totaliter in hac parte, me fateor recepturum.[22]

A typical notarial instrument, such as that recording Walter Reynolds' oath on 3 January 1313/1314 and attached to the bull translating him to Canterbury, asserts that he:

> omnibus in dictis litteris apostolicis contentis per quae juri regio seu dignitati aut coronae suae regiae derogari vel praejudicari poterit quovismodo et specialiter illis verbis per quae administratio temporalium dictae ecclesiae Cantuariensis sibi per dictum dominum papam committitur prout in eisdem litteris apostolicis continetur, pure sponte simpliciter et absolute renunciavit, asserens et protestans se nolle nec debere hujusmodi temporalia admittere nisi de mera gratia et liberatione domini regis supradicti.[23]

Of the approximately twenty-three English and Welsh bishops provided during the pontificates of Clement V and John XXII, the present writer has found evidence that definitely eight – and possibly three more – took these oaths renouncing the clause in their bulls of provision that purported to grant them the temporalities of their sees.[24] Still other

---

[22] Rymer II:i, 7; PRO SC7/44/22.

[23] Rymer II:i, 239; PRO SC7/44/11. On the same day Reynolds was granted the temporalities of the see (CPR 1313-17, 77).

[24] DEFINITE: REYNOLDS, CANTERBURY, 1314 (PRO SC7/44/11; Rymer II:i, 239); MAIDSTONE, WORCESTER, 1314 (CPR 1313-17, 84); BEAUMONT, DURHAM, 1317 (PRO SC7/56/5; CPR 1313-17, 644; Rymer II:i, 328; Smith, *Episcopal Appointments*, 25); D'ASSIER, WINCHESTER, 1320 (Reg. Asserio, 567-9; BL MS Cott. Cleopatra E.i, ff. 265-6 (top foliation); Smith, *Episcopal Appointments*, 35; PRO E135/17/19, E159/93/83; Rymer II:i, 422; CPR 1317-21, 438, 441); ECLESCLIFF, LLANDAFF, 1324 (CPR 1324-7, 11; *Rot. Parl.* ii, 21; Smith, *Episcopal Appointments*, 38-9; Williams, *The Welsh Church*, 74); STRATFORD, WINCHES-

provisors may have done so. Quite a few abbots and Irish bishops and archbishops were required to swear these oaths,[25] and bulls of provision were searched diligently for the offensive words.[26] Even Walter Reynolds, when he was translated from Worcester to Canterbury by papal provision at royal request, was required to take such an oath. Two different bulls providing Reynolds survive in his register, both addressed to Reynolds and both dated on the same day, one of which omits altogether the offensive phrase granting the temporalities. It is tempting to wonder if the former was intended for certain readers and the latter for other eyes; the former, which omits the crucial phrase, does not survive at all in the printed edition of Clement's register.[27]

TER, 1324 (PRO SC7/56/17; CPR 1321-4, 432; Smith, *Episcopal Appointments*, 41; Rymer II:i, 557; Fryde, BIHR xliv (1971), 155); ROS, CARLISLE, 1325 (CPR 1324-27, 132); MONTACUTE, WORCESTER, 1334 (CPR 1330-4, 526).

POSSIBLE: MELTON, YORK, 1317 (CPR 1317-21, 33, 58; Rymer II:i, 344; below, Appendix 6, no. 32); HETHE, ROCHESTER, 1319 (there is disagreement as to whether Hethe was actually provided or not; below, Appendix 6, no. 38; Powicke and Fryde, *Handbook*, 248; he apparently did take an oath of renunciation when he received, as was the custom with Rochester, his temporalities from Canterbury; Reg. Hethe, p. xiii); BURGHERSH, LINCOLN, 1320 (no evidence of the oath in CPR 1317-21, 494, which records mandate for delivery of temporalities, but his bull of provision [PRO SC7/56/11] is endorsed 'Bulla magistri Henrici de Burghersh super prefeccione ipsius in episcopatum Lincoln' et est preiudicialis, etc.').

[25] The following lists are not exhaustive:

ABBOTS: HUGH DE EVERSDON, ABBOT OF ST. ALBANS, 1310 (CPR 1307-13, 194, 221); RICHARD DE DRAGHTON, ABBOT OF BURY ST. EDMUNDS, 1313 (PRO C47/15/1/2, SC7/44/8; CPR 1307-13, 556, 593; CCW, 390); BONUS, ABBOT OF TAVISTOCK, 1328 (PRO C47/15/1/5; BL MS Cott. Cleopatra E.ii, f. 7v; CFR 1327-37, 89-90; CPL ii, 265; Finberg, *Tavistock Abbey*, p. 235 n. 7); RICHARD DE WALLINGFORD, ABBOT OF ST. ALBANS, 1328 (BL MS Cott. Cleopatra E.ii, f. 4v; CPR 1327-30, 184; CPL ii, 269; Pantin, *The English Church*, 57; Emden, *Oxford* iii, 1967).

IRISH PRELATES: RICHARD DE HAVERINGS, DUBLIN, 1307 (CPR 1307-13, 6); WALTER JORZ, ARMAGH, 1307 (PRO SC7/44/22; BL MS Cott. Cleopatra E.i, f. 252 (top foliation); CPR 1307-13, 4; Rymer II:i, 7; Mac Inerny, *Irish Dominicans* i, 516-29); MALACHY MACAODHA, ELPHIN, 1310 (CCW, 334); JOHN DE LECHE, DUBLIN, 1311 (CPR 1307-13, 378; Rymer II:i, 140); ROLAND JORZ, ARMAGH, 1312 (PRO C47/15/1/1, SC7/44/15; CPR 1307-13, 492, 525); MALACHY MACAODHA, TUAM, 1313 (BL MS Cott. Cleopatra E.i, ff. 257v, 287X verso (top foliation); CPR 1307-13, 562); WILLIAM FITZJOHN, CASHEL, 1317-18 (*Liber Epistolaris* of Richard de Bury, no. 342); STEPHEN SEGRAVE, ARMAGH, 1323 (PRO C47/15/1/3; Rymer II:i, 529; CPR 1321-4, 332); ROBERT PETIT, ANNADOWN, 1326 (CPR 1324-7, 278); WILLIAM OF ST. PAUL, MEATH, 1327 (PRO C47/15/1/4); RALPH OF KILMESSAN, DOWN, 1329 (CPR 1327-30, 381; Rymer II:ii, 760).

[26] CCW, 336.

[27] The former, which omits the phrase granting the temporalities, is *Praeclara tuarum dona virtutum* (RR f. 1). The latter, containing the phrase that grants the temporalities ('curamque et administracionem ipsius eidem electo in spiritualibus et temporalibus committendo') as well as a phrase that describes Reynolds as a man possessed of

In almost every case where an oath was required, the crown did not restore the temporalities until the oath was taken.[28] A number of important prelates and lay magnates were often present when the oaths were taken, and at times the notarial instruments record that the oaths were made in the presence of the king's council.[29] In a very few cases it appears that the crown demanded a fine of the provisor when it required the oath,[30] and the younger Despenser seems to have been influential in the levy of these fines,[31] but the evidence does not suggest that a fine was a normal part of the process and in fact several of the fines were later pardoned. One of those who took the oath, Richard de Draghton, who was confirmed by the pope as an abbot in 1313, protested that the clause in the bull granting the temporalities was not of his own will and that he had in fact attempted to get his bull in a different form.[32]

'spiritualium prudencia et temporalium providencia' and also containing other matter about the quashing of Cobham's election, is *Supernae dispositionis arbitrio* (Reg. Clem. v, no. 9713; CPL. ii, 115; RR ff. 2v-3; Reg. Gandavo, 477-8). Both bulls are dated 1 Oct. 1313 and both are printed in Wilkins ii, 430-1.

[28] A few exceptions have been noted: DRAGHTON, BURY ST. EDMUNDS, temporalities 17 May 1313 (CPR 1307-13, 593), oath 18 June 1313 (PRO C47/15/1/2); MELTON, YORK, temporalities 8 Oct. 1317 (Powicke and Fryde, *Handbook*, 264), his oath to the crown, which possibly renounced anything prejudicial in the bull of provision, was apparently later (Smith, *Episcopal Appointments*, 31); SEGRAVE, ARMAGH, temporalities 31 July 1323 (CPR 1321-4, 332, which does say that he has taken the oath), oath 2 Aug. 1323 (PRO C47/15/1/3); STRATFORD, WINCHESTER, temporalities 28 June 1324 (CPR 1321-4, 432, which does say that he has taken the oath), oath 30 June 1324 (PRO SC7/56/17).

[29] Roland Jorz, 1312 (PRO C47/15/1/1); MacAodha, 1313 (CPR 1307-13, 562); Draghton, 1313 (PRO C47/15/1/2); also Gainsborough, Worcester, 1303 (CPR 1301-7, 110).

[30] WALTER JORZ, ARMAGH, 1307, fined £1000 but possibly pardoned (BL. MS Cott. Cleopatra E.i, f. 252 (top foliation), CPR 1307-13, 4); HETHE, ROCHESTER, 1319, £10 to the king (Reg. Hethe, p. xiii; Wharton, *Anglia Sacra* i, 360-1); ECLESCLIFF, LLANDAFF, 1324, fined 1000 marks but pardoned (Williams, *The Welsh Church*, 74; *Rot. Parl.* ii, 21); BONUS, TAVISTOCK, 1328, fined 500 marks but pardoned in 1330 (CFR 1327-37, 89-90; Finberg, *Tavistock Abbey*, p. 235 n. 7; Lunt, *Financial Relations* i, 109; CCR 1330-3, 14). GAINSBOROUGH, WORCESTER, was fined 1000 marks when he took his oath in 1303, but this was pardoned in 1306 (CPR 1301-7, 110, 421; CFR 1272-1307, 449). HEMENHALE, WORCESTER, was fined 1000 marks when he took his oath in 1337 (Haines, *Administration*, 82).

[31] Reg. Hethe, p. xiii; Wharton, *Anglia Sacra* i, 360-1; Smith, *Episcopal Appointments*, 39; Davies, *Baronial Opposition*, 481; *Statutes of the Realm* i, 184; *Rot. Parl.* ii, 21; Bridlington, *Gesta Edwardi*, 69.

[32] PRO C47/15/1/2: 'Constanter asserens clausulam de temporalibus per ipsius procuracionem non fuisse appositam in litteris apostolicis supradictis, et quod in alia forma litteras apostolicas non potuit reportasse domino in facto huiusmodi dirigendas, licet quantum potuit super hoc insistebat'.

Thus it was that the crown safeguarded its claim to ultimate authority over episcopal temporalities, and these oaths may well have been the strongest resistance in England that the crown offered to papal claims in the early fourteenth century. By these oaths the crown's theoretical position was secure, no matter how much it chose to play with the pope about which man should have which see.

Miss Howell has shown that in the last half of the thirteenth century the crown had fairly well established its assertions that the temporalities of a vacant see included the episcopal patronage rights of that see, and that when the see became vacant these rights became part of the royal prerogative and as such were really lay patronage.[33] Studies by Hartridge have demonstrated that a large proportion of the royal presentations by Edward I were made in virtue of the temporalities of vacant sees and abbeys being in the king's hands.[34] Miss Deeley has pointed out that the date upon which the patronage rights of a see passed to a new bishop was not the date of his provision or consecration but that upon which the crown delivered him the temporalities,[35] and until the crown granted them no bishop could collate parish churches in his gift or attempt to confer the prebends in his cathedral. The early fourteenth century, moreover, witnessed the retroactive extension of the *droit de régale* – the doctrine that time does not run against the king – whereby the crown might claim to exercise patronage rights years after a vacant see or abbey was filled,[36] and the crown's exercise of patronage in this way was one of

[33] Howell, *The King's Government and Episcopal Vacancies*, 375-430, 477, 481. By the early fourteenth century these rights were held to extend over all benefices vacated during the incumbency of the previous bishop but not filled before his death (*Yearbooks of Edward II*, Selden Soc. vol. 45, pp. xxvi, 79-80).

[34] *Cambridge Historical Journal* ii (1927), 171.

[35] EHR xliii (1928), 508. The same was true in France; Lemarignier, Gaudemet, and Mollat, *Institutions ecclésiastiques*, 249.

[36] Davies, *History*, n.s. vol. xxxviii (1953), 118-20; Deeley, EHR xliii (1928), 514 seq.; P&C ii, 956-7, 1273-4; Pantin, *The English Church*, 80; Smith, *Episcopal Appointments*, 64 seq. The initiative of royal clerks in causing the crown to extend its patronage rights in this way has been emphasized by Howell, *The King's Government and Episcopal Vacancies*, 396-8, 406, and Deeley, EHR xliii (1928), 522 seq. Cf. BL MS Cott. Cleopatra E.i, ff. 284-286v (top foliation) for complaints against this practice. The French king at this time also claimed that time did not run against himself (Lemarignier, Gaudemet, and Mollat, *Institutions ecclésiastiques*, 421). In England an important qualification of the doctrine that time does not run against the king, upheld in court in 1314, was that the doctrine did not apply when the king was acting merely as the assignee of another's right; time could not run against the king only when he was acting in his own right by virtue of the crown (*Yearbooks of Edward II*, Selden Soc. vol. 37, pp. xlvi-xlviii, 166-79). There is some evidence for retroactive extension of the *droit de régale* in the late thirteenth century (Gray, EHR lxvii (1952), p. 494 n. 6), but there is also other evidence to suggest that as late

the primary complaints that John xxii made to his cardinal nuncios in England during the first year of his pontificate.[37] Therefore the crown's claim to grant the temporalities of its own free pleasure was an important assertion, well worth an oath; and it is perhaps no wonder that these oaths, originating in the later thirteenth century and probably reaching their maturity of development under Edward ii, are found not only throughout the Middle Ages but even in the reign of Queen Mary, who required them of provisors in spite of her personal sentiments.[38]

---

as 1323-1324 it was held that in certain circumstances time could run against the king (*Yearbooks of Edward ii*, Selden Soc. vol. 37, p. xlviii. I am unable to locate in *Statutes of the Realm* the citation mentioned without any source reference on this page of this *Yearbook* as 'chapter viii of Statute I of 17 Edward ii').

[37] Below, Appendix 7. It is interesting to note that this complaint is one of the few clauses in John's letter that had no antecedents in Clement's letter of 1309.

[38] Loades, jeh xvi (1965), 66. For Henry viii's objections to these oaths, see Hall, *Henry viii*, ed. Whibley, ii, 210-11.

10

Nonresidence for King's Clerks

If episcopal sees and great abbeys were the prizes of ecclesiastical patronage, whose temporalities the crown was concerned to keep within its own perimeters, it is no less true that the routine of royal administration depended significantly upon the full-time service of a considerable number of the non-episcopal clergy who were paid by means of the incomes from their benefices. Reynolds himself had learned this fact of life early in his career when, in 1306, he had been admitted as provost of Beverley by the chapter there out of respect for the crown and only after protest that the provost ought to be resident. Nearly all his other benefices before consecration, moreover, were held with papal dispensations for plurality.[1]

But whether a royal clerk obtained his benefice by papal provision or by royal presentation, or in any other way, the canon law generally expected him to reside in it unless it was a cathedral or collegiate prebend or other appointment clearly not having cure of souls. The crown therefore found it necessary to take measures to ensure that those of its clerks who were paid by means of benefices that did have cure of souls could nevertheless continue their work in person at the chancery or exchequer or wherever. It could not rely simply upon papal dispensations for nonresidence in individual cases.[2]

One of the five manuscripts of the royal response to a clerical complaint in 1280 that such clerks were not being held to the obligation of residence asserted 'quod rex habet privilegium pape quod sui clerici non cogantur ad residentiam dum steterint in obsequio suo', although Professors Powicke and Cheney are of the opinion that no such general privilege

---

[1] Below, Appendix 12, esp. no. 5.

[2] See generally Haines, *Administration of Worcester*, 204-9; Douie, *Archbishop Pecham*, 103-4; Smith, *Episcopal Appointments*, 111; Sayles, *Select Cases in the Court of King's Bench under Edward I* (Selden Soc. vol. 55), vol. i, p. lxxxvii, n. 11.

from the pope is known.[3] Nicholas IV in 1289 did grant the English king two indults that allowed for nonresidence of thirty royal clerks, but this was a limited privilege for a limited number and the crown apparently continued to claim for some time that it possessed from the pope a general privilege of nonresidence for its clerks. The crown's assertion about this papal indult, in fact, was not unlike its assertions about the English privilege that we have already discussed,[4] and a similar writ of non-residence existed that has also found its way into some of the registers of writs. My investigation of five such registers in the British Library,[5] all of which have been approximately dated in the recent work by de Haas and Hall to the period from 1275 to 1307,[6] shows in every case the crown making this claim in the writs to secure nonresidence for its clerks: 'Cum nobis a sede apostolica specialiter sit indultum ne clerici nostri nostris immorantur obsequiis...'. The corresponding writs in twelve other, later registers from the British Library that I have examined,[7] all of which are placed by de Haas and Hall in the general classification of 'fourteenth century', all begin with a different clause such as the following: 'Cum clerici nostri ad faciendam in suis beneficiis residenciam personalem dum nostris immorantur obsequiis compelli aut alias super eisdem molestari vel inquietari non debeant, nosque et progenitores nostri reges Anglie huiusmodi libertate seu privilegio pro clericis nostris a tempore cuius non extat memoria semper hactenus usi sumus...'. In one register of the former group, which has been dated about 1305, the words referring to the papal

---

[3] P&C ii, 879-80. Five such papal privileges in royal possession were calendared by Walter Stapledon in 1323, one of which (from Innocent IV to Henry III) does appear to be of a general rather than limited and particular character, although I have been unable to trace it further (*Ancient Kalendars*, ed. Palgrave, vol. i, p. 11, nos. 18, 19; p. 13, nos. 35, 36; esp. p. 13, no. 39; and cf. p. 32, no. 159).

[4] Above, pp. 146 seq.

[5] BL MSS Harl. 1608, f. 24; Lansdowne 652, f. 255v; Add. 5761, f. 17; 11557, f. 17v; 22174, f. 106v. Another such register is Lambeth MS 166, f. 127v.

[6] *Early Registers of Writs*, p. xxiii. Still another register of this type, although assigned by de Haas and Hall to a later (fourteenth-century) date, is Huntington MS EL 6107, f. 28.

[7] BL MSS Cott. Titus D.xxiii, f. 33; Harl. 927, f. 23v; Harl. 947, f. 199; Harl. 961, ff. 12-12v; Lansdowne 476, f. 130; Royal 11.A.ix, f. 36; Add. 20059, f. 38; 22162, ff. 40, 44; 25142, f. 93v; 25237, f. 59; 29499, f. 38v; 34901, f. 55v. Another such is Lambeth MS 567, f. 29. Still another register that matches this group, which has been dated to 1318-1320 and is printed by de Haas and Hall (pp. lxi, 108 seq.) is Bodleian MS Rawlinson C292, and its corresponding writ (p. 141, no. 138) can also be placed in this latter group. A further example of this latter form of the writ is to be found in an early fourteenth-century MS of English origin that may in part be a formulary reflecting the interests of a king's clerk of the time of Edward II: Cambridge, Corpus Christi College MS 450, p. 127.

indult have been struck out, and a sign manual has been placed in the margin.[8]

It would appear, then, that an evolution occurred here similar to the transformation of the English privilege from papal indult to ancient custom. This privilege of nonresidence for royal clerks was firmly established by the late thirteenth century, and the crown by this time apparently found its claim of a papal indult either no longer accurate, or no longer necessary, or no longer convenient.[9] In spite of the rather abortive attempts by Archbishop Winchelsey to force king's clerks to reside, attempts often countered by royal orders to desist,[10] the security of nonresidence for them was written by the crown into the *Articuli cleri* of 1316 as being 'a tempore cuius contrarii memoria non existit'.[11] The king also used similar words in describing this tradition to Reynolds, who accepted it and even granted particular dispensations for king's clerks not to reside.[12]

Reynolds also endeavoured to secure privileges of nonresidence for his own clerks.[13] Indeed, it was possible for a variety of people other than the king to gain limited privileges of this sort for limited numbers of their clerks by papal indult,[14] and even papal officials beneficed in England

[8]   BL MS Add. 11557, f. 17v; for the date cf. *Early Registers of Writs*, ed. de Haas and Hall, p. cxv n. 10. This may not, of course, be contemporary with the date of the register. For another such example of deletion in the same manuscript see above, p. 151.

[9]   As late as 1313, the king was writing the pope to seek dispensation from residence for one of his clerks in particular, but this may have been thought especially necessary because the clerk in question was the king's 'medicus' (Rymer II:i, 215; cf. also Reg. Clem. v, no. 2854; CPL ii, 40).

[10]   Powicke, *Thirteenth Century*, 718; Reg. Winchelsey, pp. xxi-xxii; CCR 1302-7, 88, 193.

[11]   *Statutes of the Realm* i, 171-4 (clause 8 of this edition); Davies, *Baronial Opposition*, 204-5.

[12]   RR ff. 287v, 289, 306, 307. Such pro forma dispensations for nonresidence to follow in the king's service are also found in other contemporary episcopal registers, e.g., Reg. Asserio, 523; *Reg. Pal. Dunelm.* i, 455.

[13]   RR f. 124v. Abp. Stratford sought (PRO 31/9/17a, ff. 81-81v) and obtained (CPL ii, 412) an indult for nonresidence for a limited number of his clerks in 1334 shortly after his translation to Canterbury. The papal nuncios Cardinal Arnaud Nouvel and Cardinals Gaucelme and Luca held similar privileges for their clerks, and so did Bp. Salmon of Norwich (CPL ii, 54, 105, 129). In view of this evidence, nonresidence for episcopal clerks at this time may have depended more upon specific indults rather than upon custom; this modifies the view of Dr. Haines, *Administration of Worcester*, 91. Earlier, however, such a privilege for episcopal, or at least archiepiscopal clerks may well have depended only upon custom, so far as it existed at all (Cheney, *Hubert Walter*, 158-9).

[14]   Some examples are the following. QUEEN ISABELLA: Reg. John XXII, nos. 3140, 13348, 26150, 45369, 45371; CPL ii, 44, 97, 149, 213, 253, 295-6. PRINCE OF WALES: CPL ii, 6; *Letters of Edward, Prince of Wales*, p. xv; Burns, AHP ix (1971), no. 55. COUNTESS OF

who were on the working staff of the curia were at times granted papal licenses for nonresidence.[15] All these indults, however, even those for papal officials, were ad hoc and strictly limited, and they did not have about them the aura of custom and prerogative that the crown managed to establish for its own clerical servants. Unlike the case of the English privilege, the text of a general papal indult of nonresidence has not survived, but in other respects the evolution of these two privileges in royal usage is strikingly parallel. In both cases, the crown in the late thirteenth and early fourteenth centuries was busily transforming papal privilege into custom immemorial.

PEMBROKE: Reg. John XXII, no. 59024; CPL ii, 381. EARLS OF LANCASTER: PRO SC7/64/14; Reg. John XXII, nos. 3826, 28581; CPL ii, 149, 258; for fines levied upon clerks of Thomas of Lancaster for nonresidence in 1315 by Abp. Greenfield, see Maddicott, *Thomas of Lancaster*, 21. EARL OF LINCOLN: CPL ii, 7. EARL OF RICHMOND: CPL ii, 54.

[15] E.g., Reg. John XXII, nos. 24917, 50640; CPL ii, 250, 322. On papal dispensation for papal clerks, see, e.g., CPL ii, 40.

11

King and Popes

The measures taken by the English crown in the early fourteenth century to safeguard the royal prerogative in dealings with the apostolic see were undoubtedly influenced by the particular complex of legal and feudal relationships that bound Clement v and Edward ii: Clement v, a Gascon and therefore an English subject by birth, had been as archbishop of Bordeaux ultimately a subject of the French king by reason of the feudal status of Aquitaine, while at the same time he remained the principal ecclesiastical dignitary of the English king's continental fief. Edward ii, on the other hand, as duke of Aquitaine had been the archbishop's overlord, yet he became Pope Clement's vassal by reason of the donation of King John.

Clement's English associations were of long standing. Apparently both he, as Bertrand de Got, and his brother Guillaume Seguin de Got, had been clerks of Edward i,[1] and Clement had represented Edward in some capacity at the Whitsun *parlement* of Paris in 1285. Having sought a benefice from Edward, the future pope was granted by the summer or autumn of 1289 a substantial payment and annual pension from the crown in return for services rendered until a suitable benefice could be found. Later in 1294 he was sent as a papal nuncio to England to collect procurations from the English clergy.[2] Edward i described him on 6 April 1295 as 'clericus noster' destined for the Roman court on the king's business,[3] but he had already been provided to the see of Comminges at the end of the previous month. As early as November of 1305, a few

[1] For Bertrand, the future pope, as king's clerk see Denton, EHR lxxxiii (1968), 303-14; for Guillaume Seguin, see Kicklighter, *Mediaeval Studies* xxxiii (1976), 492-5.

[2] Langlois, *Revue historique* xl (1889), 50-1; Lizerand, *Clément v et Philippe iv le Bel*, 26; Rymer I:ii, 811; Lunt, *Financial Relations* i, 552-3; Guillemain, *La Cour pontificale*, 121.

[3] Rymer I:ii, 818.

months after his coronation, Clement had urged that Isabella should marry Edward of Carnarvon,[4] and on 7 February of the following year he granted permission for six of the prince's clerks to be nonresident while engaged in the prince's service.[5] Clement's sister Agnes was also on friendly terms with Edward II, for in 1309 she wrote him seeking preferment for someone and was granted a positive response.[6]

John XXII had become well acquainted with English church-state relations in 1311-1312 when Pope Clement entrusted to him, even before he was made a cardinal, the examination of complaints in the council of Vienne against the oppressions of the secular powers. It was from this earlier experience, in fact, that John as pope was to complain to Edward II, probably in late 1318 or early 1319, that 'the state of ecclesiastical dignity is in the realm of England more notably depressed, or rather its liberty crushed, than in all the other parts of the world'.[7] Dr. Pantin and others have described John XXII's paternal attitude toward Edward II and the now well-known *Pater Sancte* letter whereby the pope was to be able to distinguish the genuine requests of the young Edward III.[8]

The numerous strong ties between Clement and Edward II have often been discussed,[9] and with certain modifications this close relationship between pope and king continued throughout the reign of John XXII. What had been established during the pontificate of Clement V could continue under that of his successor at least partly because they were both dealing with the same English king for the major parts of their pontificates. A certain continuity of papal policy is also indicated by the close similarity between papal complaints about the English situation made by Clement V in 1309 and those in John XXII's bull of 1317,[10] and

---

[4] Doherty, BIHR xlviii (1975), 247.

[5] Burns, AHP ix (1971), no. 55.

[6] CCW, 284-5.

[7] John XXII, Secret Letters, no. 792; Guillemain, *La Cour pontificale*, 122. For the grievances presented by the English church there, see P&C ii, 1353-6.

[8] Pantin, *The English Church in the Fourteenth Century*, 77-8; Crump, EHR xxvi (1911), 331-2. No English connections of Pope John prior to the time he assumed the papal throne are noted in Weakland, AHP x (1972), 161-85.

[9] Guillemain, *La Cour pontificale*, 165-6; Langlois, *Revue historique* xl (1889), 48-54; Mollat, *The Popes at Avignon*, 257-62; Pantin, *The English Church*, 76-7; Renouard, *Annales du Midi* lxvii (1955), 119-41; Brown, *Studies in Medieval and Renaissance History* viii (1971), 67, 90, 97; cf. *Liber Epistolaris* of Richard de Bury, no. 210 (consolations of Clement to Edward II upon death of his father). For the especially favourable relations between Clement and Edward immediately following the former's coronation, see Denton, EHR lxxxiii (1968), 311-14.

[10] Below, Appendix 7. This continuity of policy may also be seen in the comparison of parallel passages of other bulls issued by the two popes (above, pp. 9-10).

Pope John's affection for Edward II is preserved in the legendary tale of the former's reception of the latter for fifteen days at the papal court some time subsequent to the king's deposition and supposed murder.[11]

Among historians in the present century who have ventured an opinion on the topic there seems to have been a shift in the evaluation of relations between the papacy and the English crown in the period under review. Tout in his *Political History* of 1905, revised 1920, said of the reign of Edward II that:

> As time went on the disorders of the government and the weakness of the king surrendered everything to the pope.[12]

In his *Edward II* (1914), Tout proceeded to say that the reign was not so much a time when there was a conflict of the two swords, but rather a time

> in which the loosely grasped secular sword was pushed aside by the more skilfully directed sword of the church.[13]

Hilda Johnstone, who in her (1936) revision of Tout's *Edward II* did correct his impression that John XXII was the pope who established provision as the unvarying means of episcopal appointment,[14] nevertheless could still write in the *Cambridge Medieval History* in 1932:

> As to ecclesiastical affairs, though it is true that in the later years of Edward II England became more and more a vineyard with a broken hedge, whose grapes could be plucked by every passer-by, her exploitation was not due to the King, but to general conditions in the Church after the establishment of the Avignon Papacy.[15]

More recent historians, however, writing under the full impact of Professor Lunt's studies in Anglo-papal finances, have tended to view the crown in this period in a somewhat stronger position vis-à-vis the papacy. Although it is still necessary to see the person of Edward II himself as comparatively weak and conciliatory, yet historians such as Pantin and McKisack have underlined the fact that clerical taxation in his reign was a

---

[11] Stubbs, *Chronicles*, vol. ii, pp. ciii-cviii; CPL ii, 499; Tout, *Collected Papers* iii, 178-9. This tale, purportedly written by the papal notary Manuele Fieschi to Edward III, is slightly less incredible in view of the possibility that Manuele was a kinsman of Edward II (below, Appendix 3, no. 11).

[12] *The History of England from the Accession of Henry III to the Death of Edward III*, 254.

[13] *Place of the Reign of Edward II*, 1914 ed., p. 229; 1936 ed., p. 206.

[14] *Edward II*, 1936 ed., p. 208 n. 3.

[15] CMH vii, p. 433, and cf. p. 427.

system in which the 'pope incurred the odium and the king got the money'.[16] In such a relationship the royal government was far from being the loser.

The studies of the present writer in fields other than finance confirm this same trend of interpretation. Although it is not possible to say that the crown achieved success in every field, we can certainly say that the crown at this time – it would be going too far to say the king personally – did have a definite policy in papal relations which met with a degree of success in many areas. This policy has already been discussed in the areas of provisions to major and minor benefices, nonresidence for king's clerks, influence in the papal audience of causes, English proctors and envoys at Avignon, cardinals' pensions and benefices, litigation in the Roman court, the English privilege, and royal control of episcopal temporalities. Two other indications of English influence and favouritism at the papal court are (1) the fact that the first solemn papal exequies for a king in which the pope participated officially were those performed by Clement v and his court at Poitiers in the summer of 1307 for the soul of Edward i, which services set the future pattern for other royal exequies in papal liturgy,[17] and (2) the pope's 'personal' loan of 160,000 florins from the papal treasury to Edward ii, which resulted in the 'tempus obligacionis' (from March of 1313/1314 to November of 1317) when the revenues of Gascony were administered by papal agents.[18] Renouard has set forth the crown's policy in the distribution of favours to the friends and relatives of Clement v, and the researches of the present writer serve to supplement his study with respect to the English benefices and pensions held by Clement's cardinal-'nepotes'[19] as well as to demonstrate that such a policy was continued by the crown with respect to the friends and relatives of John xxii.[20]

In all of the above ways we may say that the crown in the early fourteenth century very definitely pursued a policy in papal relations that

---

[16] Pantin, *The English Church*, 79; McKisack, *Fourteenth Century*, 273, 286-7.

[17] Below, Appendix 11, no. 10.

[18] Lunt, *Financial Relations* i, 417; Renouard, *Annales du Midi* lxvii (1955), 128 seq.; Tout, *Edward ii*, 195-9, 217-21; Brown, *Studies in Medieval and Renaissance History* viii (1971), 146-53; *Gascon Rolls*, ed. Renouard, nos. 1130-4; Phillips, *Aymer de Valence*, 71-2.

[19] *Annales du Midi* lxvii (1955), 119-41; below, Appendix 3, nos. 4, 10, 13, 16, 24, 29, 38.

[20] Lunt, 'Clerical tenths levied in England by papal authority during the reign of Edward ii', p. 170 n. 88; ccw, 479; cpr 1317-21, 52, 59; below, Appendix 3, nos. 9, 17, 33, 37, 42. 43.

can be seen in a certain continuity under the three Edwards from Clement
v through John XXII, and that in finance and in many other areas – the
quest for an English cardinal and the competition for the patronage
released by *Execrabilis* are exceptions – achieved no small measure of
success in safeguarding the royal prerogative. Even the question of
episcopal provisions was kept under control by the enforcement of the
oaths renouncing the papal claim to temporalities, and the way in which
the papal origins of the English privilege were conveniently forgotten by
the early fourteenth century has already been told.

The reasons why the crown was able to pursue such a policy in the
early fourteenth century are complex, but a few of them may be
suggested. The protests of the lords and commons, expressed notably in
the parliaments of Carlisle (1307) and Stamford (1309), were largely
financial in character, and Professor Lunt has shown that the crown did in
fact go a long way towards meeting their demands.[21] The protests against
provisions, which were expressed only in rather general terms in the
documents that survive from these parliaments,[22] did serve as precedents
for future anti-papal measures; yet it was perhaps only later in the
century – with the Hundred Years War well under way and with much
stronger elements of the commons in parliament than was true of the
reign of Edward II[23] – that the crown was more inclined to allow its
policy to be directed by parliamentary pressures. In the early part of the
century one gets the definite impression that these protests were not so
strong, and it would be unsafe to infer from them that papal provisions
were the cause of widespread resentment at this time. For the pontificates
of Clement v and John XXII it is not possible to say, then, as Dr. Highfield
has done for the years 1342-1378,[24] that each peak period of papal
provisions was followed by a violent reaction in England. It is probable
that the pontificate of John XXII, which marked the zenith of cardinals'
provisions in the Avignon period, also saw the minimum of resentment
against them by king or parliament. Anglo-papal relations in the early
Avignon period were probably determined more by expediency than by
principle, and so the crown at this time was able to achieve a working
arrangement with the papacy that satisfied Popes Clement and John and at
the same time offered sufficient safeguards to its own understanding of

---

[21] EHR xli (1926), 344-5; Lunt, *Financial Relations* i, 490; P&C ii, 1231-40.
[22] One version of the petition against Testa presented at Carlisle in 1307 omits the
complaint against provisions (Thompson, EHR xxxv (1920), 420).
[23] McKisack, *Fourteenth Century*, 104, 182; Highfield, 'The Relations' i, 28.
[24] Highfield, *History*, n.s. vol. xxxix (1954), 332.

what its prerogative was. It is perhaps noteworthy that there could be such a crown policy at all in a period that experienced so considerable political unrest.

Still one other group that undoubtedly contributed to the crown's policy at this time was the bishops; whereas in the France of Philip the Fair royal servants were apparently the source of much anticlericalism, in the England of Edward ɪɪ there was a sharp increase in the proportion of crown servants who were promoted to the episcopate.[25] Indeed, by no means all of them gave even intermittent support to the crown, but the English bishops were a body that could act together on occasions – as at the time of *Execrabilis*, when they felt a particular papal measure called for their common action.[26] In this complex pattern of relationships, moreover, it was Walter Reynolds who held the see of Canterbury for the greater part of the reign of Edward ɪɪ, and – as will be suggested in the next and final part of this book – he wielded no small influence in guiding both bishops and king along a policy that ensured fairly smooth relations between church and state. From England's external dealings with the papacy, therefore, we now turn to matters within the realm. Consideration will be given to Reynolds' administration of several ecclesiastical institutions in which the crown also exercised or claimed jurisdiction, as well as to Reynolds' own political and primatial roles.

[25] Pantin, *The English Church*, 11, 44-5; Edwards, ᴇʜʀ lix (1944); above, pp. 95-96.

[26] For other examples of episcopal collaboration in cooperation with the government, see Edwards, ᴇʜʀ lix (1944), 327, 331, 344-5, 347; below, Appendix 11.

Part III

Conflict and Cooperation
within the Realm

1

The Conflict between the Courts,
and Clerical Grievances

A. THE CONFLICT

We have already noted how the crown by the early fourteenth century had altered the wording of one type of its prohibition writs in order to extend the competence of its own courts over certain cases that might have gone to the court of Rome. Within England itself, however, there were many other conflicts of jurisdiction between the church and the state courts, and the crown had many other types of prohibition writs that it employed. Indeed, the contemporary boundary between the system of secular and ecclesiastical courts within England was determined primarily by writs of prohibition and of consultation. It was chiefly by the writ of prohibition that a case might be moved from the ecclesiastical jurisdiction to that of the state, and by a writ of consultation that the process might be reversed. The boundary between these jurisdictions formed the main subject for complaint in the numerous contemporary sets of clerical grievances.

Cardinal Flahiff,[1] expanding considerably upon the initial essay of Miss Adams,[2] has set forth in great detail the development of these writs up to the close of their formative period at the end of the thirteenth century. It is not proposed to recount all his studies or definitions here, but rather to extend his work to give some picture of these writs in the early fourteenth century within the broader context of the relations between the two systems of courts. In general, it will be shown that this picture follows the

---

[1] Flahiff, *Mediaeval Studies* iii (1941), 101-16; vi (1944), 261-313; vii (1945), 229-90. The present chapter is indebted to these admirable studies even more than the footnotes can indicate.

[2] Adams, *Minnesota Law Review* xx (1936), 272-93; EHR lii (1937), 1-22.

trends indicated by Flahiff for the late thirteenth century, and that the boundaries of the royal courts continued to advance at the expense of the church's territory.[3]

Our sources for writs of prohibition and consultation lie scattered in many places – the plea rolls, patent and close rolls, fine rolls, year books, rolls of parliament,[4] archiepiscopal and episcopal registers, and elsewhere – and to attempt a total analysis even for a very limited period would be the subject of a separate monograph in itself. Dr. Highfield found that very few writs of prohibition survive in the episcopal and archiepiscopal registers of the period 1348-1378, although he did come across a little cache of nine of them and of one writ of consultation in the register of Archbishop Islip.[5] Miss Churchill found a number of these writs in the registers of Archbishops Courtenay and Arundel.[6] Turning to the early years of the fourteenth century, we may note that the register of Archbishop Winchelsey contains practically none of them, and the registers of Archbishops Mepham and Stratford are lost.

In the register of Archbishop Reynolds, however, we are fortunate to have the survival of a reasonably large quire of royal writs, dating mostly over the years 1317-1327, in which no fewer than thirty-five writs of prohibition and eight of consultation are extant. The importance of this number of writs of prohibition and consultation is underscored by the fact that in the register of Bishop Martival of Salisbury (which among episcopal registers of the early fourteenth century so far published[7] contains by far the largest section of royal writs) there is a total of only forty-five writs of prohibition and one of consultation, and thirty-three of the forty-five are all of the same category.[8] An independent search[9] of some thirty volumes of printed episcopal registers of the fourteenth century, moreover, turned up a total of only five writs of consultation. The forty-three writs of both sorts in Reynolds' register, therefore, provide a valuable manuscript source and will enable us to reconstruct the

[3] For a general survey of the subject in the thirteenth and fourteenth centuries, see Jones, *Studies in Medieval and Renaissance History* vii (1970), 77-120; cf. also Douie, *Archbishop Pecham,* 113-22; and S. F. C. Milsom in *Novae Narrationes,* ed. Shanks (Selden Soc. vol. 80), pp. cxcviii-cci. For the situation in the fourteenth-century consistory court at York, see Donahue, *Michigan Law Review* 72 (1974), 656-78.

[4] Cf. *Rot. Parl.*, index vol., 722, 838.

[5] Highfield, 'The Relations' i, 292.

[6] *Canterbury Administration* i, 529-34.

[7] Locations of the major sources for royal writs in other contemporary printed episcopal registers are cited in Reg. Martival, vol. iii, p. vii, n. 2.

[8] Reg. Martival, vol. iii, p. vii. The thirty-three writs are all of the *ne admittatis* type.

[9] By G. D. G. Hall in *Early Registers of Writs,* ed. de Haas and Hall, p. cxii n. 3.

borderline between the two judicial administrations as it may have been seen by Edward II's primate of all England during the major part of his archiepiscopate. This picture will be supplemented by materials from elsewhere.

These thirty-five writs of prohibition, divided into the categories established by Flahiff, are as follows:

(1) lay fee – 2,
(2) advowson (indirect, concerning tithes) – 3,
(3) secular debts and chattels – 13,
(4) trespass – 5,
(5) interlocutory (of various sorts) – 12.

Cardinal Flahiff found that by the late thirteenth century the number of writs of prohibition *de laico feudo* was decreasing, and the evidence of Reynolds' register confirms this trend with respect to the early fourteenth century.[10] Another type of writ, not frequent in the thirteenth century according to Flahiff, was that prohibiting an action of defamation in court Christian as the result of an accusation made or evidence given in the royal courts. There are none of these in Reynolds' register, although very early in the reign of Edward III the commons petitioned against collusive actions of defamation in the church courts that tried to defeat decisions at common law, and the crown willed that prohibitions issue in such cases.[11]

The question of advowsons is more complex. In spite of Alexander III's assertion that advowson was a purely spiritual matter belonging properly to the jurisdiction of the church, the king's claim to exclusive jurisdiction over cases of advowson – emphasized in the very first chapter of the Constitutions of Clarendon, was generally conceded by contemporary English church courts.[12] W. E. L. Smith, therefore, may well be right in his implicit criticism of Miss Deeley when he says it would be misleading to regard this claim as the main issue in disputes between Edward II and the pope.[13] There is also some evidence from the papal registers to show

[10] RR ff. 297v, 302; cf. Davies, *Baronial Opposition*, 153, 585.

[11] Highfield, 'The Relations' i, 275; *Statutes of the Realm* i, 256; below, pp. 190-1.

[12] Gray, EHR lxvii (1952), 481-509; Mayr-Harting, JEH xvi (1965), 40; Richardson and Sayles, *Governance*, 314-17; Smith, *Episcopal Appointments*, 107-9; Cheney, *From Becket to Langton*, 109-10; Jones, *Studies in Medieval and Renaissance History* vii (1970), 105; Sayers, *Papal Judges Delegate*, 183-95. For the question whether English practice differed from continental on this point, see Smith, *Episcopal Appointments*, 51; Deeley, EHR xliii (1928), 526; Lemarignier, Gaudemet, and Mollat, *Institutions ecclésiastiques*, 271, 411, 423, 426-7, 435-6.

[13] Smith, *Episcopal Appointments*, 107-8; Deeley, EHR xliii (1928), 508; Pantin, *The English Church*, 66, 80, 86.

that the apostolic see on occasions gave explicit recognition to recoveries of advowsons by both king and lay patrons in the royal courts.[14] Many writers have outlined the process by which advowson cases were actually handled within the secular courts themselves,[15] and the complicated progress of a great many of these cases can be followed in the volumes of *Yearbooks of Edward II* edited for the Selden Society. The crown also had to defend its jurisdiction in advowson cases against other lay courts such as those of the marcher lords.[16] Disputes about possession of benefices which did not directly involve the question of advowson, however, could be and were heard in the church courts.[17]

Flahiff has shown that the number of prohibitions *de advocacione* decreased during the thirteenth century, probably because of the church's acquiescence, and there are no such writs in Reynolds' register. A more common prohibition of this sort, however, was the indirect type of writ known as an *indicavit*. This writ would halt proceedings in the ecclesiastical court until the question of patronage was first settled in the king's court. It had been decreed in *Circumspecte agatis* of 1286 that a question of tithes was really a question of patronage if the tithes amounted to more than one-fourth the value of the benefice,[18] and there are three writs in Reynolds' register prohibiting proceedings in courts Christian until decisions were made in the secular courts as to whether the tithes

[14] Reg. John xxii, nos. 7420, 8001, 8002, 10314; cpl. ii, 177, 182, 200; Reg. Sandale, 77, 78, 95, 98, 151-4.

[15] Adams, ehr lii (1937), 1-22; Churchill, *Canterbury Administration* i, 106; Douie, *Archbishop Pecham*, 309; Highfield, 'The Relations' i, 286-90, and ii, 438-47; Hill, *Oliver Sutton*, 10, 34; Jenkins, 'Lichfield Cathedral' i, 181-2; Smith, *Episcopal Appointments*, 52 seq. This process could include the writ of right of advowson and two possessory actions, the assize of *darrein presentment* and the writ of *quare impedit*, and their variants. When a plea of advowson was pending in the royal court, the crown would do all it could to prevent some third party – such as a papal provisor – from intruding and taking possession of the church in dispute; for example, the king might order the bishop of the diocese to sequestrate the fruits of the church until the plea was settled (pro C47/16/8, m. 14/23, 24; cpr 1313-17, 4, 340; cpl. ii, 178). In 1314 Reynolds himself, as chancellor, was ordered to decide an advowson dispute between Bartholomew Badlesmere and the king (pro SC1/45/182).

[16] *Cal. Anc. Cor. concerning Wales*, pp. 181-2; ccw, 308; attempt by Humphrey de Bohun, earl of Essex and Hereford, to bring a writ of *quare impedit* in the court of his own franchise. I owe this reference to Dr. R. R. Davies.

[17] E.g., rr f. 133; Cant. Cath. ms S.V. i, 116. In 1320 Reynolds was faced with an abuse related to this procedure that had grown up in the court of Canterbury. When a beneficial dispute was pending there the officers of that court had often sequestrated the fruits of the benefice in question and usurped them for their own purposes, and Reynolds took action to correct this (Reg. Orleton Hereford, 135; Wilkins ii, 497-8).

[18] Prior to *Circumspecte agatis*, the figure was one-sixth.

amounted to one-fourth the value of the benefices and thus affected the advowsons.[19] In such cases the crown often inquired of the local ordinary the true value of the benefice and the value of the tithes in question.[20]

Cases relating to debts and chattels were claimed by the secular jurisdiction unless they were derived from the exclusively religious areas of marriage or last will and testament.[21] Flahiff shows that royal prohibitions *de catallis et debitis* were on the increase in the later thirteenth century, Adams says that this type became common in the early fourteenth century, and in Reynolds' register they form the largest single group of prohibitions.[22] Two of these writs constitute a special case, in which the king in 1321 prohibited a plea of debts and chattels before Archbishop Reynolds arising from settlement of the estate of Bishop Sandale of Winchester (brought by Sandale's successor, d'Assier, against Sandale's executors). The plea was prohibited until the crown itself had been satisfied at the exchequer for all royal debts owed by Sandale on the day he died. The king's writ associated the crown's action with the royal prerogative: 'Ex dignitate nostra regia in hoc prerogamur, quod debita nostra a quibuscumque debitoribus nostris prius levari debent, priusquam creditoribus suis de debitis suis satisfiat'.[23]

Since the time of Henry II and Becket there had remained some question whether action could be taken against a king's officer who had arrested a criminous clerk, and the prohibition writ *de transgressione* was developed in the late thirteenth century to stop actions in court Christian against the king's ministers for arresting a clerk who broke the peace. Three of the five writs of this type in Reynolds' register concern a royal bailiff who was impleaded in the church courts by the prior of Christ Church Canterbury not because he had arrested any clerk but because he had levied certains sums for the exchequer upon some tenants of the prior. The crown issued prohibition writs of trespass upon complaints of the bailiff because 'iniustum est quod ballivi alicuius ad mandatum nostrum super hiis que per ipsos racione officii sui rite fiunt trahantur in

---

[19] RR ff. 297bis, 298, 309. The last of these examples is very near to being a straight prohibition *de advocacione*, but the evidence is not sufficient to classify it as such with certainty. For a limitation placed upon *indicavit* writs by the crown in 1306, see *Statutes of the Realm* i, 147.

[20] PRO C47/18/4/3, 4 m. 4, and 6 m. 6.

[21] For background see Sheehan, *The Will in Medieval England*, and Sayers, *Papal Judges Delegate*, 204-12.

[22] RR ff. 299v, 301, 301v, 302v, 305, 307, 307v, 308, 308v.

[23] RR ff. 299v, 301v. In 1310 the crown prohibited the papal collector William Testa from taking a plea of secular debts and chattels to the Roman court on the grounds that such pleas belonged to the 'forum seculare' and the royal dignity (PRO E159/84, m. 57).

placitum in curia Christianitatis'.[24] Flahiff has remarked that before the end of the thirteenth century there might be writs of prohibition against cases of trespass in court Christian where both parties were laymen, but the evidence of Reynolds' register points only to cases in which the original plaintiffs in court Christian were clerks and the defendants laymen.

There was also a general category of prohibitions, called 'interlocutory writs' by Flahiff, which aimed at stopping proceedings in the ecclesiastical court on a given matter without claiming any authority for, or transfer of jurisdiction to, the secular courts on the same matter. Some of these interlocutory writs were temporary, merely interrupting proceedings in court Christian until some collateral issue which might jeopardize royal authority had been settled in the secular court. The writs of *indicavit*, subsidiary to some actions of tithes, can probably be considered as interlocutory writs as well as writs associated with cases of advowson. Another example of a temporary interlocutory writ was the *ne admittatis*, although it was directed not at the church court but at the bishop himself and forbade him to induct a clerk in a church until the king's court had first determined who was the true patron; three of these writs addressed to Reynolds are preserved in his register.[25] In a case in 1327 where *ipso facto* excommunication was alleged against a person who had procured a writ of *ne admittatis*, the crown made the interesting protest that excommunication for this reason was 'in exhaeredationem regiae dignitatis nostrae, cum omnes de eodem regno, de ecclesiarum advocationibus contendentes, ad litteras hujusmodi impetrandas convolant, et eis utuntur pro conservatione juris sui'.[26]

Other types of interlocutory writs were permanent and asserted flatly that the ecclesiastical courts had no jurisdiction on a given matter. In Reynolds' register there is one example each of the two types of this writ mentioned by Flahiff — a prohibition against ordinary jurisdiction in a royal free chapel (Bosham),[27] and a prohibition against a citation to the

---

[24] RR f. 306v; cf. ff. 297bis, 308.

[25] RR ff. 300v, 301, 302, 304v. In two of these cases further writs of *ut admittatis* are recorded, informing Reynolds of the recovery of advowson in the king's court and commanding him to admit a clerk upon presentation of the true patron. There are thirty-three writs of *ne admittatis* in Reg. Martival, vol. iii, p. xv seq.

[26] Rymer II:ii, 714; below, Appendix 6, no. 50.

[27] RR f. 306. The exemption of royal free chapels from ordinary jurisdiction had ample papal support: PRO SC7/24/9; BL MS Cott. Cleopatra E.i, f. 259v (top foliation); Reg. John XXII, nos. 3225, 3357; CPL ii, 135, 150, 433; Rymer II:i, 322; *Rot. Parl.* i, 297; for the preceding century see Denton, *English Royal Free Chapels 1100-1300*. Reynolds once (by deputy) made a visitation of the hospital of royal foundation at Ospringe (Kent), but he did

Roman court.[28] There were, of course, many more contemporary prohibitions of the latter sort which have been discussed earlier together with English litigation in the Roman curia. Four other types of permanent interlocutory prohibitions are to be found in Reynolds' register: to defend a royal recovery of advowson (two instances),[29] to protect a royal presentation *sede vacante* (three),[30] to protect nonresidence of a king's clerk (one),[31] and to defend the crown's collation of tithes devolved to it by custody or escheat (one).[32]

Nine of the thirty-five prohibition writs in Reynolds' register incorporate a device of circumlocution the origin of which has been explained by Cardinal Flahiff. As a result of episcopal denunciations of lower clergy who were using writs of prohibition to take cases into the secular courts, the subterfuge developed in the reign of Edward I whereby the king himself would sue the writ to remove the case from the ecclesiastical court. The king would then appear as the plaintiff in the prohibition plea and he would sue *ex relatu plurium*, thus enabling the original defendant to remain anonymous. The nine writs in Reynolds' register show that this device could be used in most types of prohibition pleas: advowson (*indicavit*, concerning tithes) (two instances),[33] secular debts and chattels (five),[34] trespass (one),[35] and interlocutory – to protest exemption of royal free chapels (one).[36] In every one of these, as in the cases examined by Flahiff, the original defendant in court Christian was a clerk. One of the nine writs is an interesting double form, in which the *ex relatu plurium* form is preceded by an *indicavit* clause (*monstraverunt*) that plainly reveals the defendant in the ecclesiastical court who has brought the suit into the secular jurisdiction.[37] The continued use of *ex relatu plurium* writs by clergy gives further point to the suggestion of Flahiff, that the use of prohibition writs was not a clear division of state against church but rather a situation in which all orders of society made use of all existing legal devices for maximum benefit.[38]

---

so in his capacity as chancellor of the realm (Churchill, *Canterbury Administration* i, 149; RR ff. 34v, 45v).

[28] RR f. 300; cf. CCR 1318-23, 510.

[29] RR ff. 300, 301.

[30] RR ff. 303v, 307v.

[31] RR f. 307.

[32] RR f. 308v; cf. RR ff. 149v, 295v; PRO C85/8/43.

[33] RR ff. 297bis, 298.

[34] RR ff. 301, 305, 307, 307v, 308v.

[35] RR f. 308.

[36] RR f. 306.

[37] RR f. 297bis.

[38] *Mediaeval Studies* iii (1941), 115. For further use of prohibition writs by clerics and

It was not difficult to obtain a writ of prohibition in the first instance, and some redress was needed by which the ecclesiastical judges could consult the king's justices in doubtful cases and obtain reversal of the process. This need was supplied late in the thirteenth century by the writ of consultation, which declared that a given case in question was really about some spiritual matter, and ordered it to proceed in court Christian notwithstanding the original prohibition. Although this practice of consulting amounted to a *de facto* recognition of the secular courts' right to determine questions of doubtful competence, it did at least provide a compensating factor in a border area that was gradually becoming less spiritual and more temporal. The eight writs of consultation in Reynolds' register, preceded by the cases for which writs of prohibition were originally issued, are as follows:

Original prohibition	Consultation	Interval between prohibition and consultation
lay fee	tithes[39]	124 days
advowson (indirect, concerning tithes)	tithes[40]	31 days
advowson (indirect, concerning tithes)	tithes[41]	79 days
secular debts and chattels	tithes[42]	372 days
secular debts and chattels	perjury and irregularity[43]	12 days
trespass	violent hands on a clerk[44]	2 days
trespass	nonresidence and incontinency[45]	25 days
interlocutory – to defend royal collation of tithes devolved by custody or escheat	canonical correction[46]	8 days

a decision of the Roman *rota* in the later fourteenth century that the English crown had no jurisdiction when they did, see Ullmann, 'A Decision of the Rota Romana on the Benefit of Clergy in England', 464-78.

[39] RR ff. 297v, 298.
[40] RR ff. 297bis, 298.
[41] Ibid.
[42] RR f. 302v.
[43] RR ff. 308v, 309.
[44] RR f. 297bis.
[45] RR ff. 308, 308v.
[46] RR ff. 308v, 309; cf. RR ff. 149v, 295v, and PRO C85/8/43.

Although the majority of these cases returned to the church courts concern tithes, there are numerous items among the ecclesiastical documents of the exchequer and elsewhere in the Public Record Office which indicate that a good number of cases concerning tithes in some way were being considered in the secular forum.[47]

Cardinal Flahiff has remarked that the consultation might be issued in the king's name or in that of his justices; all eight of these were issued in the name of the king alone. Four of the original prohibitions for which the consultations survive above were of the *ex relatu plurium* form.[48] This fact, and the fact that the eight consultations themselves cover all major types of prohibitions, together suggest that by the early fourteenth century a royal prohibition did not necessarily mean the end of a case in an ecclesiastical court, even for a clerk who sought his justice from the king, and that there was a machinery for redress that was perhaps working better now than in the previous century. By the year 1333, in fact, the commonalty of the realm were protesting that writs of consultation were bring granted too easily.[49]

B. The Grievances

In the thirteenth century Grosseteste and Pecham had, in different ways, fought the state over the question of prohibitions,[50] and Winchelsey in 1309 brought the question into his disputes with Edward II.[51] Reynolds' register, however, leaves us with only one trace of opposition to these writs. In 1320 a royal prohibition commanded the archbishop, in spite of a papal mandate, not to entertain a plea of lay fee in a case concerning the transfer of goods from the dissolved order of the Templars to that of the Hospitallers. Reynolds proposed to send some sort of explanation to the pope, and sought a consultation writ from the king and council. The king refused, and threatened Reynolds with forfeiture of temporalities for non-obedience, but in the end Reynolds decided to follow the papal mandate.[52] If Reynolds acted independently of the crown at this point,

---

[47] E.g., PRO E135/4/21, 43; E135/6/21, 22, 24; E135/16/21, 22; E135/17/13, 22; and E135/24/38.

[48] RR ff. 297bis, 298, 308, 308v.

[49] Sayles, ed., *Select Cases in the Court of King's Bench under Edward I*, Selden Soc. vol. 58, pp. lxxiv-lxxv.

[50] Flahiff, *Mediaeval Studies* vi (1944), 303-4.

[51] Henriques, 'Articles of Grievances', 28; cf. P&C ii, 1269-74.

[52] RR f. 98v; Wilkins ii, 499; Reg. Hethe, 90-1; below, pp. 224-6. The alternatives of procedure for failure to obey a writ of prohibition are outlined by Flahiff, *Mediaeval Studies* vii (1945).

however, the general impression given by his register is one of fairly smooth cooperation in the many frontier cases between the two jurisdictions. Often the crown would demand archiepiscopal assistance in the mesne process by which clerks who had no lay fee were brought to answer for breaches of royal justice, and the returns that Reynolds made to the numerous writs of *venire faciatis*,[53] *fieri faciatis, scire faciatis*, attachment upon lay fee, and distraint by and sequestration of ecclesiastical benefice, all[54] indicate an attempt to work with, rather than against, a secular power that frequently sought the aid of the church's existing administrative system.

Yet, in spite of the absence of any strong protests against these writs from the archbishop himself, there are other documents in Reynolds' register which show that not all was harmony between church and state in England at this time. The numerous writs in his register aimed at collecting tenths owed by clerks and at summoning clerks to important assemblies are but scattered traces of the reasons for a widespread feeling of discontent especially among the lower, or non-episcopal, clergy at this time. Part of this feeling took expression in what may be called grievances of a political or financial nature, and protests were registered in the convocations of both Canterbury and York. Such complaints, mainly concerned with objections to clerical taxation by both pope and king as well as with the implications of the form and substance of royal summonses of clergy to convocation and parliament, have been discussed extensively by Professor Lunt, Bishop Kemp, and Dr. Denton.[55] Particularly strident protests to Reynolds were made by the lower clergy of Canterbury province in 1314-1316 and 1322-1323 over what they considered was the derogation of proper ecclesiastical liberty. But

[53] An interesting complaint, that the secular courts were maltreating bishops whose clerks failed to respond to episcopal monitions prompted by writs of *venire faciatis*, was raised by the English delegation at the council of Vienne, but there is no evidence of such maltreatment in Reynolds' register beyond the customary royal threats to seize his temporalities (P&C ii, 1353; above, p. 157).

[54] RR ff. 298v-312v, and cf. f. 157. See further Churchill, *Canterbury Administration* i, 520-1; Graves, 'The legal significance of the first statute of *Praemunire*', 62-8; Reg. Halton, p. xlii; Reg. Martival, vol. iii, pp. xii-xxxiv (valuable formulary); below, Appendix 3, nos. 10, 12, 17, 42 (replies to writs of *fieri faciatis* and *levari faciatis* upon the benefices of cardinals for payment of tenths).

[55] Lunt, *Financial Relations* i, 404-18; Kemp, *Counsel and Consent*, 92-9; Denton, 'Walter Reynolds and Ecclesiastical Politics 1313-1316'; cf. Pantin, *The English Church*, 127-8. There is documentary material, also, for more extensive treatment of the clerical assemblies of the southern province especially in 1316 and 1319. See, for example, the petitions of the religious and clergy to Reynolds and his suffragans in convocation at St. Paul's on 28 April 1316 in BL MS Cott. Faustina A.viii, ff. 175v-176.

Reynolds' style of leadership, in cooperation with the crown, pope, and even the episcopal hierarchy, was a change from the politics of defense and confrontation to which the clergy had become accustomed under Archbishop Winchelsey. 'It is not easy', says Kemp,[56] 'to distinguish what was readiness to use any excuse to avoid taxation, what was personal opposition to Reynolds, and what was defense of the principle of ecclesiastical independence'. Further assessment of Reynolds' style of leadership must be deferred until the last chapter after all its component factors have been introduced,[57] but here it can be noted that by the end of his archiepiscopate the objectionable phraseology had been removed from the royal summonses and also by that time 'the clergy had established that they would tax themselves only in an assembly summoned by the archbishop and meeting under his presidency, and not in Parliament which they regarded as a secular court which they could not be required to attend'.[58]

Another document in Reynolds' register, the *Articuli cleri* of 1316, points to another category of grievances, those of an administrative and jurisdictional nature, and here the picture is rather different but more complex. If writs of prohibition and consultation were the primary method by which the crown chose to define the administrative boundary and to expand its own frontier, it is no less true that the many series of clerical *gravamina* that begin early in the second third of the thirteenth century and extend into the later Middle Ages were perhaps the principal way in which the church attempted to resist the crown's definitions and extensions of jurisdiction. Miss Henriques made a tentative analysis of the grievances of 1309 and their precursors,[59] and since the time that she wrote authoritative texts of these series have become available in the edition of *Councils and Synods* II by Professors Powicke and Cheney. After 1309, two other series within the period under review must concern us here, those of 1316 and those of 1327. An assessment of their significance is important.

The *Articuli cleri* of 1316,[60] which soon attained a particular pre-

---

[56] Kemp, *Counsel and Consent*, 98.

[57] Below, pp. 263-5.

[58] Kemp, 'The archbishop in convocation', 27.

[59] Jones, *Speculum* xli (1966), 209-45, offers a convenient summary of grievances 1237-1399, which incorporates much information that can be found in Miss Henriques' thesis. For a survey of Irish clerical *gravamina* with particular reference to the Irish *Articuli cleri* of 1291, see Watt, 'English Law and the Irish Church', 157-60.

[60] Medieval manuscripts of the *Articuli cleri* include Cambridge, Fitzwilliam Museum MS McClean 142. f. 42v seq.; CUL MS Mm.v.19, ff. 67-70; Lambeth MS 538, ff. 167v-171v;

eminence in the whole series of clerical *gravamina*, pertain exclusively to the relations of church and state within England. The clerical complaints here about such matters as violent hands upon clerks, royal interference with ecclesiastical property, burdens placed by the crown upon religious houses, and denial of clerical privilege in the correction of criminous clerks, all find their parallels in the complaints which John XXII sent to his nuncios in England the following year and which Clement V had also sent in October of 1309. Still other grievances of a similar sort are found only in the *Articuli cleri*: royal interference with the process of excommunication, with the rights of sanctuary and abjuration, with the examination of clerks presented to benefices, and with the process of ecclesiastical elections. Yet what is most interesting about the articles of 1316, and generally about the whole series of *gravamina* related to them, is that they reveal no concern on the part of the English church over those matters where the apostolic see clearly saw its own rights being oppressed and trampled in England. Whereas the papal grievance-letters of 1309 and 1317 against the crown encompass a rather full range of both Anglo-papal and English internal church-state matters,[61] the English bishops chose to complain to the crown only of the latter – of points at issue within the realm. It was left to the popes alone to protest that the king, royal officials, and nobles of the realm were disturbing cardinals and other apostolic officials in their benefices, impeding papal financial collections, inhibiting papal provisions of benefices, inhibiting citations to the apostolic see, refusing caption of persons excommunicated by papal nuncios, and impeding papal judges delegate. The *Articuli cleri* deal only with the rights and liberties of the church in England.

Oxford, Magdalen College MS 185, ff. 11-12; PRO C49/4/17 (probably the actual document submitted to the parliament at Lincoln; for a related document see PRO SC8/40/1895); RR f. 76v seq.; Huntington MS HM 906, ff. 136v-142 ('Articuli novi pro cleris'); Kilkenny, Ireland, Church of Ireland Episcopal Palace, Red Book of Ossory, ff. 47v-49v; Makower, *Constitutional History*, 39-40, reports a copy of the *Articuli* in Reg. Melton (now in the Borthwick Institute, York), ff. 514-515. Transcriptions of the Latin text of the *Articuli* are printed in Wilkins ii, 460-2 (gives other MS references); *Statutes of the Realm* i, 171-4 (cf. PRO C74/1, mm. 33v, 34v); Chrimes and Brown, *Select Documents*, 19-23 (taken from the text in *Statutes of the Realm* but newly collated with the manuscript used); *Historical Papers*, ed. Raine, 253-60; and Lyndwood, *Provinciale*, pt. iii, 37-9. English translations are printed in *Statutes of the Realm* i, 171-4; and Gee and Hardy, *Documents*, 96-102. The *Articuli* are calendared (from still other MSS) in CPR 1313-17, 607 (from the MS patent roll); Reg. Martival ii, 207; HMC, *Wells* i, 429; and *Magnum Registrum Album* (of Lichfield cathedral), ed. Savage, 14.

[61] Below, Appendix 7. See also John XXII, Secret Letters, no. 792, dated probably late 1318 – early 1319.

This insularity, if the term may be permitted, of the English hierarchy's concerns, not only emerges from reading the articles of 1316 but also stands in continuity with the English church's complaints of 1309 that preceded and of 1327 that followed. The editors of *Councils and Synods II* speculate that the complaints which the English prelates expressed in their *gravamina* of December 1309 may have influenced some of the complaints that Clement v had included earlier in his letter of October 1309, but the English *gravamina* of 1309, like their successors in 1316, contain no complaints of an Anglo-papal nature. The most that can be said for the English hierarchy's papal concerns is that a deputation of the English bishops did present the pope's complaints to Edward II as soon as the Lent parliament of 1310 had opened.[62] Again, the complaints of the English delegation to the general council of Vienne in 1311-1312 apparently had only pertained to church-state relations within the realm.[63] And the *gravamina* of the English church presented in the Epiphany parliament of 1327, although not closely related to those of 1316, are likewise not concerned with Anglo-papal issues. It is therefore difficult to resist the conclusion, which the surviving evidence seems to demand, that the English hierarchy of the period under review were, as a whole, rather insular in their concerns.

Richardson and Sayles in their analysis[64] have shown that the bulk of the sixteen[65] petitions of the *Articuli cleri* of 1316 derive substantially from the *memoriale* of 1280 (partially reiterated in the 'addition' to *Circumspecte agatis* of 1286)[66] and from the *gravamina prius non proposita* of 1309. Only two clauses are new, the complaints that some secular judges force criminous clerks to abjure the realm and that some secular judges do not release to the church authorities clerks who have confessed their offenses. Richardson and Sayles can speak of Reynolds himself as the one 'to secure the concession of the *Articuli cleri*',[67] although it must be noted that Reynolds was absent[68] from the Lincoln Hilary Parliament of 1316 at which the earl of Hereford read out the

[62] P&C ii, 1285, and n. 2.

[63] P&C ii, 1350-6.

[64] EHR lii (1937), 230-4.

[65] In my citations of the *Articuli* on the following pages I shall generally refrain from citing particular clauses by number because the numbering of the clauses varies in different printed texts; the best and most convenient printed Latin text, that of Chrimes and Brown, assigns no numbers at all to the clauses.

[66] Graves, EHR xliii (1928), 1-20; Douie, *Archbishop Pecham*, 302-21; P&C ii, 874-85.

[67] EHR lii (1937), 234; for a different view see EHR lix (1944), 331.

[68] Kemp, *Counsel and Consent*, 95; Edwards, EHR lix (1944), 329; Reg. Martival ii, 80.

king's replies to the prelates' petitions[69] in the king's presence and on the king's behalf.[70] Undoubtedly the clerical grants from both provinces made in October and November of 1316 were highly influential in causing the king to issue the *Articuli cleri* under letters patent on 24 November.[71]

In spite of their insular nature, and even if they were obtained partly in return for financial concessions, there are certain indications, however, that the *Articuli cleri* achieved a certain measure of success for the ecclesiastical jurisdiction in the time of Reynolds' archiepiscopate. Five of the eight writs of consultation surviving in Reynolds' register specifically state that they have been issued because of the principles 'in articulis clero regni nostri per nos nuper concessis'.[72] Four of these five consultations were granted upon the basis of the very first clause of the *Articuli*, that the royal prohibition has no place in cases of tithes, oblations, obventions, and mortuaries when they are proposed under these names.[73] The other of the five was granted upon the clause (repeated, like the first clause, from the grievances of 1280 and 1286) stating that anyone guilty of laying violent hands upon a clerk must answer to the king's officers for the peace violated and to the ecclesiastical forum for the excommunication incurred. A similar writ of consultation, said to be issued because of the same clause of the same articles, survives in a register of writs dated 1318-1320.[74] Thus the clerical grievances of 1316 were probably responsible in some measure for the continuing growth of the practice of consultation in the reign of Edward ii.

Still another way in which the *Articuli cleri* may represent a certain measure of success for the courts of the church is that they recognize the ecclesiastical jurisdiction for correction of cases of defamation, whereas in the previous century there had been a question whether the church courts should be hearing such cases at all.[75] In Reynolds' register there are no

---

[69] It is possible that these petitions constituted the roll that Baldock on 4 Dec. 1316 took to the king on behalf of the prelates and clergy of Canterbury province, which roll the king decided to send to the archbishop of Canterbury (Reynolds), the chancellor (Sandale), and the treasurer (Walter Norwich) for counsel and final decision (ccw. 450-1; Davies, *Baronial Opposition*, 285).

[70] For the event see Davies, *Baronial Opposition*, 291, 408, 410.

[71] Stubbs, *Constitutional History* ii, 356; Kemp, *Counsel and Consent*, 95; Edwards, EHR lix (1944), 331.

[72] RR ff. 297bis, 298, 302v.

[73] For another consultation granted by Edward iii upon the same basis in 1330, see *Rot. Parl.* ii, 38.

[74] *Early Registers of Writs*, ed. de Haas and Hall, p. 142, no. 143 (Bodleian MS Rawlinson C292).

[75] According to Donahue, *Michigan Law Review* 72 (1974), 667; see also Helmholz, *American Journal of Legal History* 15 (1971), 255-68.

writs prohibiting actions of defamation,[76] and in the register of writs that has been dated 1318-1320 there is a consultation writ, apparently issued pursuant to the *Articuli*, granted for the reason 'since it is contained in the articles lately granted by us to the prelates and clergy of our realm that in cases of defamation in which the imposition of a corporal penance is sought, the prelates may freely administer correction notwithstanding our prohibition'.[77] Only if pecuniary, rather than corporal, penances were levied would the king's writ of prohibition run in such matters as defamation and the laying of violent hands upon clerks, and even in these matters the articles allowed for commutation to financial payments provided the initial penances levied were corporal.

It is interesting to note, in passing, an attempt by the crown in 1327 to disregard one of the principles of the *Articuli cleri* as a special favour to a cardinal. The very first article stipulated that if tithes were sold for a money payment they became secular and ceased to be a matter for the spiritual courts. Yet the crown in the first year of Edward III specifically permitted Cardinal Gaucelme de Jean to sue in court Christian for payments for tithes sold from his English benefices in consideration of his 'laudable services' to the king, the king's father, and all the realm, and notwithstanding any royal writs of prohibition procured by the cardinal's debtors. The magnates and 'proceres', however, were not content to let this pass, and in parliament in 1328 they willed that one of the cardinal's debtors could have prohibitions and attachments from the spiritual court to the secular forum notwithstanding the king's special concession, because the king's permission had been given 'contra communem legem ejusdem regni'.[78]

Another indication of the success of the *Articuli cleri* during the time of Reynolds and Edward II may lie in the fact that none of these articles was repeated in the *gravamina* of the first parliament of Edward III. Even if it may be argued that Reynolds had not given political leadership to the lower clergy by opposing papal and royal taxation and by defending the liberties which they had been led by some of his predecessors (especially Winchelsey) to suppose were theirs, yet it does seem that his archiepiscopate witnessed not only an increased availability of consultation writs but also, over clerical grievances of a jurisdictional nature, at least a compromise that was found acceptable to both sides for the time being.

[76] Above, p. 179.
[77] *Early Registers of Writs*, ed. de Haas and Hall, p. 143, no. 144 (Bodleian MS Rawlinson C292).
[78] Rymer II:ii, 699, 734, 744-5; CPR 1327-30, 64, 103, 299.

Reynolds himself is known to have expressed a concern for the redress of clerical petitions on at least two occasions,[79] and his work with the other prelates in countering the worst effects of *Execrabilis* (which could have placed severe restrictions upon prominent members of the lower clergy) has already been noted.

In the Epiphany parliament of 1327 the prelates and clergy presented a further set of thirteen grievances.[80] Although most of these clauses may be located more or less in pre-1316 series of *gravamina*,[81] there are in fact traces of only two of the 1316 grievances and these are no more than faint suggestions. Yet, like the series of 1316, those of 1327 also are insular in nature and not concerned with problems of Anglo-papal relations.

The *gravamina* of 1327 do show that certain other problems, old problems, have come to the fore again. Among these are petitions related to *ex relatu plurium* and *indicavit* writs,[82] the former complaints tracing back to the series in 1280, 1295, and 1300-1301, and the latter to 1285, 1295, 1300-1301, and 1309. Another complaint,[83] stemming from the *ex relatu plurium* device and formerly raised in the series of 1300-1301, is that the anonymity of such writs precludes the legal existence of anyone who will pay the cost and damages even if the prohibition is proven false and the case returned to the church court. Chapter twelve of the Ordinances of 1311 had stipulated that damages should be awarded in cases where prohibitions were procured falsely,[84] and in at least one actual case of this sort Reynolds tried to remedy the situation by ordering the expenses to be paid by the plaintiff (the original defendant in the ecclesiastical court) who had unsuccessfully sued the prohibition *ex relatu plurium* in the state court.[85] Another clause in the 1327 schedule

---

[79] (1) In 1319: Lambeth MS 1213, f. 103v. (2) Probably 1326: PRO SC1/49/92; cf. Kemp, *Counsel and Consent*, 97, and Sayles, EHR liv (1939), 491.

[80] Printed by Richardson and Sayles, *Rot. Parl. Ang. hac. Ined.*, 106-10.

[81] My own analysis suggests the following sources: for c. 1 of 1327 see c. 1 of 1280 (P&C ii, 874), c. 5 of 1295 (P&C ii, 1139), c. 7 of 1300-1301 (P&C ii, 1209-10). For c. 2 of 1327 see c. 8 of 1300-1301 (P&C ii, 1210). For c. 3 of 1327 see c. 8 of 1285 (P&C ii, 967), c. 17 of 1295 (P&C ii, 1140-1), c. 9 of 1300-1301 (P&C ii, 1210-11), c. 7 of 1309 (P&C ii, 1272-3). For c. 4 of 1327 see c. 11 of 1300-1301 (P&C ii, 1211). For c. 5 of 1327 see c. 16 of 1300-1301 (P&C ii, 1212). For c. 6 of 1327 see c. 14 and c. 15 of 1300-1301 (P&C ii, 1212). For c. 7 of 1327 see c. 18 of 1300-1301 (P&C ii, 1213). For c. 8 of 1327 see c. 29 of 1295 (P&C ii, 1143). For c. 9 of 1327 see c. 4 of 1309 (P&C ii, 1272) and c. 10 of 1300-1301 (P&C ii, 1211). For c. 10 of 1327 see c. 17 of 1300-1301 (P&C ii, 1213). For c. 11 of 1327 see c. 12 of 1309 (P&C ii, 1273). These examples are not exhaustive, nor are they all exact duplications.

[82] C. 1, c. 3.

[83] C. 2.

[84] *Statutes of the Realm* i, 160; *Rot. Parl.* i, 282.

[85] RR f. 297bis; cf. Flahiff, *Mediaeval Studies* iii (1941), 112.

complained that secular courts were conducting inquiries about the vacancies of benefices, properly an ecclesiastical matter, but there are numerous cases in the *Yearbooks of Edward II* which show the royal courts specifically refusing to hear such questions and stating that cognizance of plenarty belongs to the ecclesiastical forum.[86] Still other complaints in 1327 treated the problem of ecclesiastical discipline, and these will be discussed below.

The particular significance of the 1316 *Articuli cleri* seems to be four-fold. (1) Their content suggests, in the area of the church's relations with the crown, that the English hierarchy were more concerned about protecting exclusively their own rights within the realm than about standing up for any privileges that the popes were claiming, even though the papal complaints of 1309 and 1317 embraced many of the concerns that the English bishops were pressing. (2) In the areas of tithes, violent hands upon clerks, and defamation cases, the *Articuli* seem to have achieved some greater measure of security for the church's jurisdiction, and they may be said at the least to represent a compromise that the crown was willing to cite as acceptable. Reynolds may well have been influential in effecting this, although the clergy of his province continued to withold their support from him because of political and financial grievances. (3) The set of the *Articuli* of 1316 achieved unusual importance among the various sets of clerical grievances both by its appearance as letters patent and by its entry on the statute roll. (4) Before the middle of the fourteenth century this entire set of sixteen *Articuli* was regarded collectively as a writ of prohibition in itself, so that no further specific prohibitions were deemed necessary on the points that it covered. Justice Thorpe in 1349 argued that an attachment *post prohibicionem* could be had on any of its clauses with no prior specific prohibition writ.[87] In the following century, William Lyndwood included part of the royal replies to the *Articuli* in his *Provinciale*.[88]

Nevertheless, the importance of the *Articuli cleri* must not be over-estimated. In view of the fact that the petitions of 1327 are largely

[86] *Yearbooks of Edward II*, Selden Soc. vol. 33, p. 170 seq.; vol. 43, pp. 95-8; vol. 54, pp. 94-7; vol. 61, pp. 231-3; vol. 63, p. 124. Examples could be multiplied. If the party with regard to whom plenarty was alleged had died, the cognizance might be taken by the king's court.

[87] Adams, *Minnesota Law Review* xx (1936), p. 281 n. 37. A writ of consultation, however, could still be issued in 1385 that cited a particular point in the *Articuli cleri* (Donahue, *Michigan Law Review* 72 (1974), p. 666 n. 99).

[88] Cheney, *The Jurist* xxi (1961), 411; reprinted in Cheney, *Medieval Texts and Studies*, 163.

derivative from those of 1309 and several earlier series, it would seem unwise to conclude with Miss Henriques that the grievances of 1309 were 'finally answered and disposed of' in 1316[89] or with Professor Powicke (who states that he consulted her thesis)[90] that the *Articuli cleri* 'ended the first stage in the long movement started by Grosseteste eighty years before, and defined the issue between Church and state in the century to come'. There were two or perhaps three further sets of petitions similar to the *Articuli* and the *gravamina* of 1327 that were current in the 1340s under Archbishop Stratford,[91] after which the grievances became less lengthy and detailed but more formalized and more closely linked with grants of taxation.[92]

---

[89] Henriques, 'Articles of Grievances', 1, 33.

[90] *Thirteenth Century*, 484.

[91] Jones, *Speculum* xli (1966), 227-31; Wilkins ii, 655-6.

[92] Highfield, 'The Relations' i, 200, 259-61.

2

The Crown and Ecclesiastical Discipline

A. Excommunication and Caption

Persons who secured writs of prohibition impeding justice properly belonging to the ecclesiastical forum were frequently the subjects of general excommunications, such as in 1279, 1281, and 1311,[1] even though excommunication for this reason was the one sentence of excommunication that the state courts refused to recognize.[2] Excommunication was the major weapon that the church could use against those who ignored the decisions and demands of her courts, and the crown's attitude to ecclesiastical discipline was frequently a topic of complaint in the series of clerical grievances. Yet it will be shown here that frequently excommunication was also levied both by the English church and by the papacy to support the crown against its criminal and political enemies.

There are two major sources for the study of excommunication and the secular arm in this period, episcopal registers and the letters of signification and reconciliation in the Public Record Office file C85, although additional material may be found in the PRO ancient correspondence, close rolls, and elsewhere. An estimated 7600 letters remain in the PRO C85 classification for the period from 1250 to the Reformation, and indeed the practice continued well into the seventeenth century, although it is significant that just over 1000 of these letters date from the years 1305-1334.[3] Even a greater bulk – the maximum – appears

---

[1] Flahiff, *Mediaeval Studies* vii (1945), 243-5; Johnstone, 'Archbishop Pecham and the council of Lambeth of 1281', 174-8; Powicke, *Thirteenth Century*, 476; P&C ii, 849, 906; Wilkins ii, 414. For application in a specific case in 1327, see Rymer II:ii, 714.

[2] Flahiff, *Mediaeval Studies* vii (1945), 245-6; Henriques, 'Articles of Grievances', 114; *Yearbooks of Edward II*, Selden Soc. vol. 20, pp. 134-5 (attachment upon a writ of prohibition, 1310, and decision that the defendant must answer even though the plaintiff's excommunication was proved, because the excommunication was levied at the suit of the defendant).

[3] For analysis, see below, Appendix 8, table A.

to come from the late thirteenth century, in which period Miss Henriques estimated these documents to average roughly 150 per year.[4]

R. C. Fowler in 1914 stated that very few significations were ever copied into the episcopal registers,[5] but this is not entirely true for the early fourteenth century. The present writer has made the following comparison between such letters in the register of Archbishop Reynolds and the similar letters in the C85 classification of the PRO. In the Record Office there are seventy-one letters of signification (sixty-four) and reconciliation (seven) in the file for Canterbury that date from the time of Reynolds' archiepiscopate and were issued by him. Of the sixty-four significations twenty-five are also recorded in Reynolds' register and thirty-nine are not. Of the reconciliations, four are recorded in Reynolds' register and three are not. In the register itself, on the other hand, there is a grand total of sixty-three letters of signification (forty-seven) and reconciliation (sixteen), of which twenty-two significations and twelve reconciliations are not to be found among the documents surviving in the PRO classification. Thus, apart from the middle ground of twenty-nine documents (twenty-five significations and four reconciliations) found in both the PRO and Reynolds' register, there are a further forty-two PRO documents not found in the register and a further thirty-four letters in the register not to be found in the PRO. In other words, nearly one-third of all the letters of signification and reconciliation issued under Archbishop Reynolds and extant either in his register or in PRO C85 are only to be found in his register. There is, then, a total of such evidence in Reynolds' register that is nearly as great as the total for his archiepiscopate in the PRO, and the amount of overlapping material is less than one-third.

While only some six significations can be traced from the index of the printed edition of Archbishop Winchelsey's register,[6] yet some thirty-two letters are said to survive in the register of Archbishop Pecham [7] and fifty-three in the register of Bishop Sutton of Lincoln.[8] Clearly, then, some episcopal registers constitute an important source of additional evidence, even as regards letters of signification and reconciliation in which the individual parties are named. Moreover, the PRO files tell us nothing of the

---

[4] Henriques, 'Articles of Grievances', 106; cf. Logan, *Excommunication and the Secular Arm in Medieval England*, 24, 68.

[5] TRHS, 3rd series, vol. viii (1914), 113; Logan, *Excommunication and the Secular Arm*, 66-8, 84.

[6] Reg. Winchelsey, 306, 345, 428, 432, 760, 1335-6; the last is a case that comes not from the actual register but is printed from a document in Canterbury Cathedral.

[7] Henriques, 'Articles of Grievances', 106.

[8] Rolls and Reg. Sutton, vol. iii, p. xliii.

great category of excommunications *ipso facto* nor of the political dynamics involved in such cases. For the C85 material in the Public Record Office, the exhaustive survey of F. D. Logan published in 1968, *Excommunication and the Secular Arm in Medieval England*, has superseded previous studies and reliably traces the main lines of development for the entire period from 1250 to 1534. It does not, however, rely upon the register of Reynolds for the early fourteenth century. Our purpose in the pages that follow, then, while not challenging Logan's general conclusions, will be to present a deeper analysis for a more limited period, making reference to his own work when appropriate but concentrating more upon the political uses to which excommunication was put by both crown and popes at this time.[9]

In sketching the general outlines of the history of excommunication, its pre-Christian origins, its comparative rarity in England before the Conquest, and its increasing frequency in the twelfth and thirteenth centuries,[10] Professor Rosalind Hill has suggested the probability of a gap that developed between the theory and practice in the later Middle Ages. In theory the consequences of major[11] excommunication were severe in the extreme, but in practice it may not have been much more than a slight inconvenience. There is considerable evidence that recourse to litigation in both secular[12] and ecclesiastical[13] courts was denied to excommunica-

---

[9] I am grateful to Fr. Logan for comments upon certain points in the pages that follow, and for sharing portions of his own work with me in page-proof.

[10] Hill, *History*, n.s. vol. xlii (1957), 1-11; see also Logan, *Excommunication*, p. 13 n. 3.

[11] The present writer has found no reference to the sentence of minor excommunication among manuscripts of the early fourteenth century. All statements in the present work, therefore, concern the sentence of major, or greater, excommunication. For minor excommunication, see Schroeder, *Disciplinary Decrees*, 198-9; and Vernay, *Le 'Liber de excommunicacione' du Cardinal Bérenger Frédol*, pp. xxiii, xxix.

[12] Adams, *Minnesota Law Review* xx (1936), 289; Flahiff, *Mediaeval Studies* vii (1945), 243-6, 263-4. The crown did not, however, recognize the excommunication of persons excommunicated for suing writs of prohibition against the ecclesiastical courts (above, p. 195 n. 2). If an excommunicate person who had been refused suit in the courts could later produce a letter of absolution, his case might be reopened (Sayles, *Select Cases in the Court of King's Bench under Edward III*, pp. 72-3). In the 1313-1314 Eyre of Kent it was held by Justices Staunton and Spigurnel that an excommunication pronounced by a deceased archbishop could not be pleaded as valid in the law courts (Bolland, Maitland, and Harcourt, *The Eyre of Kent*, Selden Soc. vol. 27, pp. 185-6; Logan, *Excommunication*, 26-7). They did not, however, necessarily mean that an excommunication lapsed with the death of the ordinary. There are instances of Archbishops Reynolds and Mepham signifying excommunications to the crown that had been pronounced by their predecessors, of the Canterbury prior in 1313 formally absolving someone excommunicated by Winchelsey, and of the archbishop's audience court in 1327 lifting an excommunication that had been pronounced by the late Archbishop Reynolds (PRO C85/

ted persons, but Dr. Salter even doubted whether any spiritual penalties were necessarily attached to excommunication in the fourteenth century.[14] The excessive and indiscriminate use of excommunication was certainly a point raised by the bishop of Angers at the council of Vienne.[15]

All of this may be, as Professor Hill suggests, because the church's policy was too thorough, because it used excommunication too freely. If the ordinance of the council at London and Lambeth in 1309 was being properly enforced, every Englishman of the southern province at mass on the four major feasts of every year would hear the ways in which he might incur the sentence of major excommunication *ipso facto*,[16] and Archbishop Greenfield enumerated some thirty grounds of excommunication in an appendix to his statutes for the York consistory court in 1311.[17] Nor were these occasions the first or the last times that the grounds for *ipso facto* excommunication were ordered to be published in England.[18] The early fourteenth century also saw the appearance of probably the first writer of a manual for English parish clergy that made use of both local legislation and general church law, William of Pagula, who in part one of his *Oculus Sacerdotis* (circa 1326-1328) enumerated

---

8/6, C85/9/4; RR f. 109v; Cant. Cath. MS Reg. Q, f. 101; Cant. Cath. MS Cart. Ant. A36 (II), p. 24). The last of these instances provides interesting evidence that an excommunicated person himself could be sued in a secular court. Here the excommunicate promised a monetary settlement out of the king's court in return for withdrawal of the suit against him by the plaintiff and the lifting of the excommunication by the ecclesiastical authorities.

[13] Rymer II:ii, 714; cf. Emden, *Oxford* iii, 1764; Rockinger, *Briefsteller und Formelbücher*, 656-7 (formulary of John of Bologna, dedicated to Archbishop Pecham).

[14] *Snappe's Formulary*, 22.

[15] Adam, *La Vie paroissiale*, 179-82, 188; Hefele, *Histoire des conciles*, vol. vi, part 2, p. 648; Lemarignier, Gaudemet, and Mollat, *Institutions ecclésiastiques*, 388.

[16] P&C ii, 1274-7.

[17] Wilkins ii, 413-15; P&C ii, 1319.

[18] Such a list was even published in the earliest surviving set of English diocesan statutes (dated 1213/1214: P&C i, 33; and cf. P&C ii, 1420 (index) for further instances). For other publications of such *sentencie generales*, see Boyle, TRHS, 5th series, vol. v (1955), p. 88 n. 1; Haines, *Administration*, 186-7; Highfield, 'The Relations' i, 312-14; Reg. Bourgchier, p. xxxii; Rolls and Reg. Sutton, vol. iii, p. xlvi; Vernay, *Le 'Liber de excommunicacione'*, p. xvii; Wilkins ii, 678-80. Professor Du Boulay indicates that Archbishop Bourgchier, faced with ever increasing numbers of *ipso facto* excommunications and ever decreasing effectiveness of the system in the mid-fifteenth century, decided to alter some excommunication censures from the status of *ipso facto* to that of *sentencia ferenda*, whereby the sentence would take effect only after canonical warning and sentence by the ecclesiastical judge (Reg. Bourgchier, pp. xxxiii-xxxiv). For the distinction between excommunication *sentencia ferenda* and excommunication *sentencia lata*, see Logan, *Excommunication*, 14-15.

some 140 ways of incurring greater excommunication.[19] Pagula's count also corresponds roughly with the figures of Cardinal Bérenger Frédol the elder, who circa 1294-1305 listed 101 *ipso facto* ways in his *Tractatus de excommunicatione et de interdicto*, and later after the publication of the Clementines wrote another tract listing thirty-one additional grounds.[20]

Excommunications *in genere*, those applied to certain classes of offenders who could not be identified by name, were extremely frequent by the early fourteenth century. Even though they were only binding *in foro interno*,[21] such excommunications were regularly used to support the discipline of the church, and the penalty of major excommunication was often threatened for failure to obey papal or archiepiscopal mandates.[22] For our purposes, however, the important point to note is that many of the excommunications *in genere* served to reinforce the power of the secular courts against lay criminals. Excommunications of the king's enemies in English synodal legislation went back at least to 1222,[23] and

[19] Boyle, TRHS, 5th series, vol. v (1955), 87, 89; Pantin, *The English Church*, 194-202. Parts of Pagula's list have affinities with Greenfield's list of 1311 (above, p. 198 n. 17). Boyle, TRHS, 5th series, vol. v (1955), p. 88 n. 1, mentions a number of excommunication lists current in the thirteenth century. An important addition to the few facts known about Pagula's life is the date and circumstances of his ordination to the priesthood, recorded on RR f. 11v. He was ordained priest by Archbishop Reynolds in Canterbury Cathedral on 1 June 1314 as vicar of Winkfield and under letters dimissory of the bishop of Salisbury. This was not mentioned by Boyle, TRHS, 5th series, vol. v (1955), 98-100, or Pantin, *The English Church*, 194-202, or Emden, *Oxford* iii, 1436-7; now, however, see Boyle, *Mediaeval Studies* xxxii (1970), 330.

[20] P. Viollet in *Hist. litt.* xxxiv, 145-52; Guillemain, *La Cour pontificale*, 220. The cardinal's treatise has been edited, with useful introduction, by E. Vernay. For the cardinal's decision in an English excommunication case at the Roman court, see below, Appendix 6, no. 34.

[21] Gray, *Studies in Church History* iii (1966), p. 56 n. 4.

[22] For examples see RR ff. 37 seq., 47v, 54, 67v, 69v, 98v, 222v, 230v, 231v (bis); PRO C47/16/8, m. 14/24, C47/19/3/3; P&C ii, 1349, 1393. When the pope made such a threat it was common for the bull to conclude with a 'non obstantibus' clause specifying that the excommunication would be incurred notwithstanding any previous papal exemptions from excommunication granted to the same person. E.g., RR ff. 211v, 215, 220v, 221, 222, 223, 223v seq., 227, 227v, 230, 230v. Excommunication could also be incurred for assault upon papal nuncios: e.g., Reg. Martival ii, 216-18. A contemporary example of the pettiness of matters that had become subjected to the church's only weapon is the excommunication by Bishop Orleton of Hereford, about the time of his quarrel with Edward II in 1323, of all persons whom the king had permitted to enter the bishop's woods for the purpose of capturing wild beasts there (Sayles, *Select Cases in the Court of King's Bench under Edward II*, p. cvii). Another example is the excommunication by Bishop Sutton of Lincoln of all those who failed to return a book borrowed from a certain person (Hill, *Studies in Church History* viii (1972), 135). See also Reg. Martival ii, 68-70, 84, 87, 157.

[23] P&C i, 106-7; Powicke, *Thirteenth Century*, 421.

fifty of the ways specified by William of Pagula were *ipso facto* excommunications that had become attached to breaches of Magna Carta[24] and the Charter of the Forest. Archbishop Winchelsey published excommunications *in genere* against thieves and pirates.[25] mandates were sometimes issued for the excommunication of unknown people who had injured others in non-ecclesiastical matters,[26] and both Winchelsey and Reynolds proclaimed major excommunications against persons disturbing the king's peace in Wales and against the king's enemies especially in Scotland.[27] In May of 1312 the bishops of the southern province threatened excommunication *ipso facto* against any who might infringe the Ordinances.[28] In 1333 and 1334 the crown itself requested general excommunications against public malefactors, with proclamations in all cathedral and collegiate churches on Sundays and feast days, as an aid to the process of secular justice.[29] One final, most interesting, but quite unusual, instance of excommunication employed as a threat against the crown's enemies is the document known as the Boulogne agreement of 31 January 1307/1308, by which nine leading lay magnates under their own seals proceeded to give Antony Bek bishop of Durham power to excommunicate any one of them who broke their agreement to preserve the royal honour and the rights of the crown.[30]

The papal attitude to excommunication also supported the crown. Edward I in 1297 had been able to cite a bull of Clement IV pronouncing *ipso facto* excommunication upon all who disturbed the peace of the realm,[31] and in 1317 and 1322 John XXII commanded Reynolds to publish excommunications against the enemies of king and realm.[32] In 1326

---

[24] For further such examples, see P&C ii, 1428-9 (index, Magna Carta); Reg. Winchelsey, 268-72, 409; Wilkins ii, 414; Maddicott, *Thomas of Lancaster*, 136. On the use of excommunication as a political weapon in the thirteenth century against supposed enemies of church and state, and in support of the Great Charter, see Gray, *Historical Studies* vi (1968), 23-38.

[25] P&C ii, 1373-4; Reg. Winchelsey, 41; cf. Wilkins ii, 414 (Greenfield's excommunication list, 1311).

[26] This is particularly evident in Lincoln and York dioceses (Hill, *History*, n.s. vol. xlii (1957), 10). Professor Hill explains this problem in detail in Rolls and Reg. Sutton, vol. iii, pp. xlvii-xlviii.

[27] Reg. Winchelsey, 1-5, 268-72; RR ff. 14v, 35v, 116v. For instances of Archbishop Melton absolving persons who had incurred excommunication by dealing with the Scots in 1319 and 1321, see *Historical Papers*, ed. Raine, 291-2, 309-10.

[28] P&C ii, 1369-71.

[29] Wilkins ii, 562; Rymer II:ii, 860, 880.

[30] Phillips, *Aymer de Valence*, 26-9, 316-17 (text); Maddicott, *Thomas of Lancaster*, 73.

[31] Fraser, *Antony Bek*, 70; Powicke, *Thirteenth Century*, 681; P&C ii, 726, 735.

[32] RR f. 215; CPL ii, 139, 443, 448; Reg. John XXII, no. 3349; PRO SC7/25/16; Reg.

Edward II ordered one of these bulls to be republished by Reynolds after Queen Isabella had landed from France.[33] Papal nuncios to England often had faculties to pronounce or revoke sentences of excommunication,[34] and such faculties were used by Cardinals Gaucelme and Luca under papal direction to support the crown in its difficulties with Robert Bruce.[35] The pope could, of course, pronounce excommunication directly from the apostolic see,[36] just as some cases of excommunication were reserved to him for absolution.[37] Excommunication could also be levied by auditors of causes of the apostolic palace in cases assigned to them.[38] Edward II negotiated directly with the apostolic see for the absolutions of Gaston I count of Foix,[39] Piers Gaveston,[40] and Bishop Walter Langton.[41] Edward II was granted a special faculty from John XXII in 1319 that allowed him to approach and treat with excommunicate persons.[42] The pope might also grant special privileges to members of the royal family – such as indults to Queen Isabella that her confessors could absolve excommunicate members of her household and that her person and her chapels might be exempt from excommunication.[43] Similar indults granting exemption from excommunication without the express order of the apostolic see were held by the king himself and this privilege also extended to the royal chapels.[44] Another series of papal privileges protected clerks serving in the

---

Greenfield v, 286-7; Reg. Orleton Hereford, 235-7; Rymer II:i, 320, 353, 484; Reg. Martival ii, 204, 407.

[33] RR ff. 215, 313; *Ann. Paul.*, 315; Stubbs, *Constitutional History* ii, 377. The date of the bull was not read publicly.

[34] Reg. Clem. v, nos. 2251, 8786, 8794, 8798, 8806, 8811, 8812; Reg. John XXII, nos. 5170, 43139; CPL ii, 31, 104-6, 129, 131, 289; Reg. Greenfield ii, 28, 178-9; RWR, 58, 71; *Chartulary of Sallay*, ed. McNulty, i, 45-6.

[35] RR f. 222; Reg. John XXII, nos. 5233, 5155, 10674-5, 10801, 11621; CPL ii, 127-8, 191-2, 199; Wilkins ii, 471-84; HMC Fifth Rep., app., 432; Cant. Cath. MS Cart. Ant. M378; Stubbs, *Chronicles* ii, 53; *Chron. Lanercost*, 224-5.

[36] E.g., CPL ii, 88; cf. CPL ii, 100; Reg. Winchelsey, 1074, 1208; Fraser, *Antony Bek*, 162-3.

[37] E.g., RR ff. 37 seq., 215; Reg. John XXII, nos. 21372, 44664, 45667; CPL ii, 243, 295, 297, 433. Cf. Haines, *Administration*, 178.

[38] Below, Appendix 6, no. 39.

[39] *Gascon Rolls*, ed. Renouard, nos. 75, 78, pp. 38-9; Rymer II:i, 30.

[40] Taylor, 'The Career of Peter of Gaveston' (London M.A. thesis), 165, 210, 265, 272, 306, 321, 340-2; Rymer II:i, 50. Gaveston died, however, excommunicate by Winchelsey.

[41] Rymer II:i, 167.

[42] Rymer II:i, 391.

[43] CPL ii, 47, 55, 113.

[44] For Edward I and Prince Edward see Rymer I:ii, 979; for Edward II see Rymer II:i, 74.

royal free chapels from the normal dangers of excommunication,[45] and this privilege had its counterpart in the ancient custom (asserted at Clarendon in 1164 and affirmed by papal indult in 1231) that no minister of the crown could be excommunicated without royal permission.[46]

Both the papacy and the church in England, therefore, often supported the crown at this time by proclaiming excommunications *in genere*. In addition, there were also countless instances of excommunications both *in genere* and *nominatim* in cases of a more purely spiritual nature. The contemporary ecclesiastical procedure has been outlined well by Professor Hill and Dr. Haines in regard to such cases.[47] A number of these were often settled within the *forum ecclesiasticum*, the offender repenting and receiving absolution within forty days before the ordinary signified the crown for his caption. This procedure may be seen working at this time in the registers of Archbishops Winchelsey[48] and Reynolds,[49] in the *sede vacante* records of Christ Church Canterbury,[50] and in the act-book that survives from Archbishop Stratford's court of audience.[51]

Let us look at some of the cases that Reynolds handled within the ecclesiastical forum itself. In 1322 Reynolds granted absolution to one Agnes atte Stigle of Elham (Kent) from major excommunication that she had incurred by not performing the penance the archbishop had formerly assigned to her on account of her sins committed with one Stephen atte Berne. For her new penance she was to offer one set of mass vestments worth above twenty shillings on the high altar of her parish church.[52] In

[45] BL MS Cott. Cleopatra E.i, f. 259v (top foliation); PRO SC7/24/9; Reg. John XXII, no. 3357; CPL ii, 135, 433; Rymer I:ii, 979, and II:i, 322.

[46] Stubbs, *Select Charters*, 165; P&C i, 283; Rymer I:i, 200; Reg. Greg. IX, no. 688; Makower, *Constitutional History*, 15, 243-4. Justices, sheriffs, and bailiffs were included within this privilege (Flahiff, *Mediaeval Studies* vii (1945), 245). For the situation in France, see Lemarignier, Gaudemet, and Mollat, *Institutions ecclésiastiques*, 296. An interesting complaint in the *Gravamina prius non proposita* of 1309 (P&C ii, 1272) and in the *Articuli cleri* of 1316 was that some of the king's tenants were claiming exemption from writs of caption, but the king claimed that the writ had not been and would never be denied in such cases and I have found no evidence of this practice in RR or in PRO C85; cf. Logan, *Excommunication*, 61-2.

[47] Rolls and Reg. Sutton, vol. iii, pp. xliii-xlix; Haines, *Administration*, 186-9. The procedure in contemporary France is given in Adam, *La Vie paroissiale*, 179 seq.

[48] Reg. Winchelsey, 76-7, 1325 (penances specified in each case); Churchill, *Canterbury Administration* i, 80, 82, 120.

[49] E.g., RR ff. 126 (cf. ff. 297bis, 298), 198.

[50] Cant. Cath. MS Reg. Q, ff. 101, 117v; CUL MS Ee.v.31, f. 136.

[51] Woodruff, *Arch. Cant.* xl (1928), 55, 60, 62; cf. Donahue and Gordus, *Bulletin of Medieval Canon Law*, n.s. vol. ii (1972), 46.

[52] RR f. 128v.

several *nominatim* instances of perjury at Christ Church Canterbury in 1324 and 1327, an offense against which Reynolds had pronounced excommunication *in genere* in 1320, the archbishop committed power of absolution to the Canterbury prior.[53] Another case, more complicated, arose out of a dispute over tithes in which writs of prohibition and consultation were involved,[54] and the knight John Malmeyns of Hoo (Kent) later died in a state of excommunication. His wife Matilda alleged that he had repented before death, and even though Reynolds had written the secular arm for John's caption,[55] the archbishop decided to grant postmortem absolution to John and ecclesiastical burial to his body.[56] Such procedure was rare, but within the bounds of canonical sanctions.[57] Reynolds once rebuked the official of the Canterbury archdeacon for pronouncing major excommunication unjustly upon a clerk William de Hykyndenn who had refused to perform the public corporal penance assigned to him for fornication with one Alice Gybbis. Reynolds ruled that the penance was excessive and unsuitable to the clerical status, and he ordered it to be mitigated within eight days.[58] One of the most common grounds of all for excommunication, finally, was the offense of laying violent hands upon a clerk.[59] Under the *Articuli cleri* of 1316 this offense was subject to a double penalty – before the crown for the peace violated and before the church for the ecclesiastical penance. Reynolds at times pronounced excommunications *in genere* against unknown persons guilty of this offence in specific instances,[60] and he also held a faculty from Clement v – granted at his own request – that enabled him to dispense up to 300 persons excommunicated for this reason even in cases reserved to the apostolic see. His register records fourteen absolutions (eight clerks and six laymen) under this faculty.[61]

---

[53] RR ff. 98 seq., 133v, 149v, 309.

[54] RR ff. 308v, 309.

[55] PRO C85/8/43; RR f. 295v.

[56] RR f. 149v, printed in Wilkins ii, 531-2.

[57] Haines, *Administration*, 191; Vernay, *Le 'Liber de excommunicacione'*, pp. lxxii-lxxiii. For other contemporary examples see Reg. Winchelsey, 402 (year 1301); *Historical Papers*, ed. Raine, 315 (year 1322); Woodruff, *Arch. Cant.* xl (1928), 60 (year 1342). Piers Gaveston was finally buried two years after his death, but there seems to be no evidence of his absolution (Taylor, 'The Career of Peter of Gaveston', 340-2).

[58] RR f. 199v.

[59] For the canons, see Haines, *Administration*, 178; Rolls and Reg. Sutton, vol. iii, p. xliv.

[60] RR ff. 36v, 109.

[61] RR ff. 50v-51, and cf. f. 56v (possibly a form letter).

There were, therefore, numerous instances of excommunication and absolution within the *forum ecclesiasticum* itself handled without any reference to the secular arm, but it would seem nevertheless true that the real compulsion behind the eventual reconciliation of most excommunicates of all sorts was the threat of the secular power. From as early as the fourth century ecclesiastical synods had claimed that the secular power should assist the church against such persons, and by the twelfth century some form of secular action was in use in most parts of western Europe.[62] Just as the church was willing to issue sentences of excommunication against the enemies of the crown, so the state in England was accustomed to render powerful assistance in the coercion of obdurate excommunicates. This working agreement was accomplished through a process whereby a person who remained excommunicate for forty days became an enemy of the state as well. The church in England had invoked the state's aid against such persons as early as Norman times.[63] Miss Henriques has indicated that by the middle of the twelfth century the principle had become fixed in England that excommunicates should be coerced by the royal power after a period of forty days, and by the end of that century it had been established that this coercion would be by imprisonment.[64] Father Logan has traced the general lines of this development in England.[65] After an excommunicate had remained delinquent for forty days or more, the bishop or other ordinary having ecclesiastical jurisdiction over the excommunicate would, at the instance of the ecclesiastical judge or an opposing party, invoke the secular arm by a 'letter of caption' addressed to the king with the explanation 'cum ecclesia Dei non habeat quid facere valeat ulterius in hac parte'.[66] The crown of its own grace might then issue a writ in chancery known as *significavit* or *de excommunicato capiendo* to the appropriate sheriff or sheriffs requesting the arrest and imprisonment of the offender until he made amends.[67] Anyone who maliciously impeded or refused to execute this royal writ was himself excommunicate *ipso facto*.[68]

The king's writ *de excommunicato capiendo*, which seems always to

---

[62] According to Logan, *Excommunication*, 16.

[63] P&C i, p. 107 n. 1 (year 1076).

[64] Henriques, 'Articles of Grievances', 102.

[65] *Excommunication*, 17-24, 72-6.

[66] E.g., RR f. 8v; PRO C85/8/11.

[67] A contemporary example of such a writ is PRO C47/18/6/11; very few survive.

[68] P&C ii, 849 (year 1279), 907 (year 1281); Logan, *Excommunication*, 102-3; Wilkins ii, 414 (year 1311).

have been granted automatically, or *de cursu*,[69] initiated the charac-
teristically and almost exclusively English feature of the process. In
France the state might, albeit reluctantly, assist the process as far as the
imposition of a fine or confiscation of goods. In the German part of the
empire, in Italy, and in Denmark, the ban was levied after a year and a
day. However, the actual caption of excommunicates by the secular
power (capture by judicial process) seems to have been an English method
of procedure that was not generally available in other countries.[70] Clement
v, writing of this practice in 1309, described it as a 'pious, laudable, and
religious custom',[71] and the letters of caption in the PRO addressed to the
crown from the various ordinary authorities convey this same impression
of an English practice that differed from the usage elsewhere:

> iuxta consuetudinem regni vestri (Canterbury, Hereford, Lincoln, and
> others);
> secundum preobtentam meritoriam et piam consuetudinem regni vestri,
> ut quem divinus timor a malo non revocat vestre maiestatis potestas
> coherceat temporalis (Durham);
> secundum preobtentam meritoriam et piam consuetudinem regni vestri,
> ut quod minus valet mitis mater ecclesia in hac parte vestre maiestatis
> potencia suppleatur (York).

The English delegation at the council of Vienne, likewise, explained the
procedure for caption as being 'de consuetudine regni Anglie approbata'.[72]

This characteristic feature of the English process, then, had taken
definite shape by the end of the twelfth century, and the letters of caption
surviving in the PRO C85 category of significations begin about the year
1220. In an appendix, I have tabulated all documents in this category at
the PRO from the years 1305-1334,[73] and they reveal some 852 cases of
excommunication and some eighty-eight letters of reconciliation. York
has the largest number of cases surviving at the PRO in this period (247
letters of caption), followed by Lincoln (123) and Canterbury (120).
Salisbury records only eleven cases of excommunication for our period,
whereas Exeter shows some seventy-nine excommunication cases and

---

[69] Logan, *Excommunication*, 86-91; in the thirteenth century it could even be issued in
opposition to a writ of prohibition already issued by chancery.

[70] Haines, *Administration*, p. 190 n. 3; Henriques, 'Articles of Grievances', 106; Adam,
La Vie paroissiale, 194-5; Lemarignier, Gaudemet, and Mollat, *Institutions ecclésiastiques*,
297-8; Logan, *Excommunication*, 16-17, 86-7, 109.

[71] Reg. Winchelsey, 1033; below, p. 207.

[72] P&C ii, 1356.

[73] Below, Appendix 8, table A.

thus ranks just behind Canterbury in the greatest numbers. None survives from the Welsh dioceses in this period, although we know from other sources that Archbishop Reynolds did not hesitate to excommunicate sinful Welshmen both *in genere* and *nominatim*.[74] Care must be taken, of course, when making any interpretation of the PRO figures in view of the highly incomplete nature of the records that survive there, and if the evidence were added from all the contemporary episcopal registers, as we have shown in the case of Reynolds, a rather different (though even still incomplete) picture might well emerge.

A detailed analysis of these 120 Canterbury excommunication cases from 1305-1334 reveals that the actual number of persons specified in these letters of caption was 261, and this fact – as well as the presence in Reynolds' register and others of numerous cases not in the PRO C85 class – must be remembered when making any estimate of total numbers of persons for whom caption was requested. Each surviving case, or letter of caption, will on the average represent two or three individual excommunicates.[75]

The authorities who could and did signify the crown of contumacious excommunicates within their jurisdictions during the early fourteenth century include all diocesan bishops,[76] the exempt abbots of St. Albans[77] and Bury St. Edmunds,[78] the dean of St. Martin's-le-Grand, and the archdeacon of Richmond. A bishop's vicar-general could signify when his superior was 'in remotis agente' or 'extra suam diocesim', and there is even one instance of such a signification from the vicar-general of the archdeacon of Richmond.[79] The keepers of spirituality *sede vacante*, at least at Canterbury and York, could signify,[80] and there are also

---

[74] RR ff. 116v, 294; PRO C85/8/34, 57. For the situation in the Welsh marches and the counties palatine of Chester and Durham, where the king's writ did not generally run at this time, see Logan, *Excommunication*, 112-15.

[75] Such an approximation is borne out by Logan's finding (p. 68) that, for the period in which I have found 852 cases surviving in the PRO, the same chancery records show a total of 1746 persons excommunicated.

[76] A bishop could apparently begin to signify when he was elect and confirmed (PRO C85/75/1: Exeter diocese; cf. Logan, *Excommunication*, 26).

[77] Cf. CCW, 395.

[78] Cf. CCW, 526.

[79] PRO C85/214/29.

[80] *Canterbury*: PRO C85/7/63, 64; Cant. Cath. MS Reg. Q. f. 98v. A challenge to the authority of the Canterbury priory *sede vacante* in this matter was made by seventeen rectors and vicars as a result of their excommunication just prior to the accession of Winchelsey (CUL MS Ee.v.31, ff. 65v-66v, 94-97v; Cant. Cath. MS Cart. Ant. A189c; Cant. Cath. MS S.V. i, 35, 78, 108; Reg. Winchelsey, 1310-13). See also Logan, *Excommunication*, 26-7.

York: PRO C85/177/64, 65, 66, 68, 69; C85/180/2-59.

Canterbury excommunications signified by the papal nuncio William Testa in his capacity as administrator of spirituality of Canterbury during the suspension of Winchelsey.[81] Significations are extant from a number of other abbots, deans, and archdeacons prior to the period under review,[82] and Dr. Salter has shown how the chancellor of Oxford University obtained the privilege of signification within the years 1335-1337.[83] I have been able to find no evidence that Archbishop Reynolds issued significations for excommunicates in Lincoln and Hereford dioceses during the period in the 1320s when he inducted royal presentees there while the temporalities of these sees were in the king's hands.[84]

The crown and its ministers, according to the complaints of Clement v in 1309 and John xxii in 1317,[85] refused to accept significations from papal nuncios or judges delegate, even though such papal officials had the power to excommunicate, and the canonists themselves differed with each other as to whether judges delegate had the power to invoke secular aid.[86] There are no cases of significations from papal officials in the PRO files of the early fourteenth century or in Reynolds' register, and it is interesting to note that Pope John, using words for this complaint almost identical with those of Clement, chose to omit Clement's phrase describing the English system of caption as 'pia et laudabilis ac religiosa consuetudo'. It may be that the shrewd lawyer-pope, while willing to renew in 1317 the form of his predecessor's complaint, nevertheless suspected that it would come to nothing and therefore decided not to be too fulsome in his praise for the system. It may be, too, that the crown's policy had tightened by the early fourteenth century, for Logan found that in the previous century several bishops were willing to signify upon request of papal judges delegate,[87] although no such evidence survives from the period under our consideration here.

Many of the letters of caption do not reveal the status of the excommunicates, but it is evident that a very sizeable portion of them were in fact closely identified with the church. Out of the total of 852 surviving cases from this period in the PRO, 164 were cases involving clergy and/or

---

[81] PRO C85/7/16, 18.
[82] PRO C85/210, 214; Logan, *Excommunication*, 33-6, 176-9.
[83] *Snappe's Formulary*, 23-4.
[84] For the inductions, see Smith, *Episcopal Appointments*, 86 seq.
[85] Reg. Winchelsey, 1033; above, p. 205; below, Appendix 7.
[86] Logan, *Excommunication*, 30-2.
[87] Ibid., 32.

religious.[88] Among the important persons excommunicated and signified in this period were the abbots of Boxley, Rufford, and Sawley, the priors of Bodmin, Brecon, Horkesley, and Tonbridge, the provost of Spalding, and the master of St. John's Hospital in Northampton.[89] Often large groups of excommunicates would be named – such as thirty monks of Rufford with their abbot,[90] or thirty-four Welshmen in 1318.[91] The names of many excommunicates, including some important political excommunicates such as Gaston I count of Foix, Piers Gaveston, the outlaw Gilbert Middleton, and Robert Bruce,[92] are not found in these files. An important ecclesiastical group for whom no signification exists is the chapter of Hereford Cathedral, excommunicated by a papal auditor in 1318.[93]

An interesting layman excommunicated was one Adam son of Eve,[94] and others were Katherine daughter of William the Clerk[95] and Alan son of the Rector of Whissonsett.[96] The wide variety of names in the files suggests a good cross-section of medieval society.[97] The identifications are often recorded, too, of the parties at whose instance the excommunications were levied, and these show clergy far more often than laity as the initiators of the excommunication process.

The letters of caption from the archbishopric of Canterbury in our period are unusually informative in recording the origins or grounds of

---

[88] Below, Appendix 8, table A. For excommunications, not in this period, of clergy for failure to pay clerical subsidies, see Logan, *Excommunication*, 53-61.

[89] PRO C85/155/1, C85/179/42, C85/178/3, C85/75/22, C85/7/57, C85/119/20, C85/143/36, C85/103/22, C85/7/12; RR f. 293v.

[90] PRO C85/179/42, 56.

[91] PRO C85/8/34.

[92] On the excommunication of Bruce, see Hill, *Studies in Church History* viii (1972), 135-8.

[93] Below, Appendix 6, no. 39.

[94] PRO C85/194/50.

[95] PRO C85/143/37.

[96] (Norf.) PRO C85/8/14.

[97] A selection of interesting names from the records of those excommunicated in the period under consideration is as follows: Maunser dictus Archer, John Aurifaber, Richard Bellewacher, John le Botiler, Roger Carectarius, Henry Carpentarius, John le Cok, John le Copursmyth, Reginald le Cupere, William Faber, Thomas Forestarius, Peter le Fourbeur, John Garcius, Gernon le Grater, Alexander le Harpour, John Marescallus, Robert Molendinarius, Stephen ad Molendinum, William Page, William Palefridarius, Benedict Pelliparius, Hugo Pictor, Geoffrey Piscator, Adam Portarius, William le Porter, Thomas le Salter, Christina le Schyppester, Adam Serviens, John le Skeppere, John dictus le Smermongere, John le Spicer, Nicholas de Stabulo, Clement Sutor, William le Taillour, Thomas le Taverner, Walter Tydenfaber, Richard dictus le Vyneter. Still other names include Barbitonsor, Candelmaker, Carinfex, Cissor, Cutter, Ligator Librorum, and Tonsor.

the excommunications. People from many dioceses came under the authority of the provincial court of Canterbury, and whereas the secular courts could compel by distraint and other processes, this court had the power of enforcement by the excommunication of those contumacious of its commands. In such instances the official of the court would proceed to notify the archbishop of the step taken, and the archbishop after forty days might signify the crown.[98] Of the total of eighty-six known significations issued by Archbishop Reynolds (twenty-five both in PRO and his register, thirty-nine additional in PRO, twenty-two additional in register), forty-six are designated as cases arising from the jurisdiction of the court of Canterbury. Most of these forty-six had devolved upon the court in one way or another, and two cases are specifically stated to be the result of tuitorial appeals.[99] Another case had devolved to the archbishop's 'audience'.[100]

Nine more cases arose out of the archbishop's metropolitical visitations: three of these were inherited from the visitations of Winchelsey,[101] and the six others came from Reynolds' metropolitical visitations in Ely and Lincoln dioceses.[102] Another case arose from the custody of spirituality of the London diocese *sede vacante*.[103] Eight cases involved the administration of goods of defunct persons, in which the executors of testaments were excommunicated. Other types of cases included tithes (four instances), matrimonial (three), suits over titles to benefices (three), defamation (two), impeding sequestration of the fruits of a church (two), contempt (one), and violent hands upon a priest (one). Interesting individual cases included the refusal of a dean to relinquish the seal of the deanery to his successor,[104] an attack with a sword in church during mass,[105] and refusal of a husband to provide marital affection in sustenance and clothing for his wife.[106] In another important case

---

[98] Churchill, *Canterbury Administration* i, 464-7; Flahiff, *Mediaeval Studies* vii (1945), 243-5; cf. PRO C47/18/6/11.

[99] (1) PRO C85/8/56. (2) PRO C85/8/3; RR f. 60v; Reg. Grandavo, 185-6, 324-5, 413-14, 546-8, 667, 766, 776. For another such case, *temp.* Winchelsey, see PRO C85/7/28.

[100] RR f. 293v.

[101] Visitation of London diocese: RR f. 293v; PRO C85/8/6. Visitation of Norwich diocese: PRO C85/8/30.

[102] Ely: PRO C85/8/20, 21, 33; RR ff. 90v, 92, 294. Lincoln: PRO C85/8/39, 48; RR ff. 293, 293v.

[103] PRO C85/8/42. cf. Churchill, *Canterbury Administration* i, 170-2.

[104] PRO C85/8/73; RR f. 296.

[105] PRO C85/8/65, 66.

[106] PRO C85/8/58.

Reynolds used excommunication and signification to support the decision of the king's court in a dispute over a benefice.[107]

Although there is no case of Reynolds signifying the crown of anyone excommunicated for heresy, the archbishop certainly encountered heresy in his metropolitical visitation of Lincoln diocese.[108] He excommunicated one woman for the heresy of denial of the incarnation ('incarnacionem domini non credens, abscondit faciem suam ad elevacionem corporis Christi in missa ut illam non videat'), but she repented and was absolved before letters of caption were issued. In another case in Lincoln diocese, of a man who had remained excommunicate for over a year and a half and who had evaded the crown's attempts to capture him, Reynolds pronounced the man unfaithful ('infidelis') and gravely suspect of heresy – a procedure that was suggested by canon law.[109] There is also an instance in the early fourteenth century of letters of caption for a man and his sister excommunicated for suspicion of heresy – in the Coventry and Lichfield diocese in 1316.[110] The king's officers were undoubtedly interested in such instances, because a case in Gascony probably in the reign of Edward I had suggested that the lands of convicted heretics should escheat to the crown.[111] In 1322 Edward II himself instructed his envoys to suggest to the pope that Robert Bruce and his men were suspect of heretical pravity because they did not respect the censures of the church.[112] Such suggestions, therefore, were not without their political value.

[107] RR f. 294.

[108] RR f. 71 seq., cf. f. 293.

[109] RR f. 71; Haines, *Administration*, p. 190 n. 4; Lemarignier, Gaudemet, and Mollat, *Institutions ecclésiastiques*, 388-9; Vernay, *Le 'Liber de excommunicacione'*, p. XXXV; Adam, *La Vie paroissiale*, 194.

[110] PRO C85/56/31 ('in causa seu negocio heretice pravitatis de qua vehementer sunt suspecti'). Another contemporary instance of suspicion of heresy is in Reg. Greenfield ii, 198-200 (mandate to excommunicate parishioners of St. Mary's, Pontefract, who have withheld offerings from the church 'non absque fermentum heretice pravitatis'). Richardson, EHR li (1936), 1-4, cites a number of cases of heresy prior to the mid-fourteenth century, which provide evidence that suspected heretics were liable to arrest by the lay power and that convicted heretics were liable to imprisonment and forfeiture. It could be dangerous to declare someone suspect of heresy, however, unless there was good evidence, for the imputation of heresy could result in an action of defamation (Helmholz, *American Journal of Legal History* 15 (1971), 258). For other early English cases of heresy, see Logan, *Excommunication*, p. 69 n. 138, and CPL ii, 453.

[111] *Gascon Rolls*, ed. Renouard, no. 676, p. 190; cf. no. 728, p. 204, and cf. app. p. 579, no. xxxix.

[112] PRO C47/27/12/3, 4; Sayles, *Select Cases in the Court of King's Bench under Edward II*, p. 125.

The process to bring a delinquent excommunicate to repentance was not an easy one, once he had made the decision to resist beyond the forty-day limit and to incur the possibility of imprisonment. At times a second or even third signification would have to be sent to chancery, and for one particular man no less than five letters of caption were issued.[113] Presumably some hardened criminals were never captured, and others returned before their letters of caption could be implemented. When and if the imprisoned excommunicate expressed penitence, made satisfaction, and merited absolution in the sight of the church, the ordinary would send a letter *de excommunicato deliberando* for his release.[114] A total of only nineteen such letters of reconciliation survive that were issued by Reynolds, most of them in his register, and as the original significations are extant for most of these we are enabled to say something about the time-gaps between the original significations and the dates by which the church was satisfied that the captioned excommunicates had repented. Fourteen pairs of dates provide this evidence: the shortest interval is fifty-eight days, the longest is 554, and the average interval between signification and reconciliation is 235 days.[115] The interval before repentance, however, was not necessarily a long one if the excommunication was not signified to the crown. A woman remained excommunicate for no more than eight days before her absolution in a case before the prior of Christ Church during the Canterbury vacancy of 1313.[116]

A number of factors might affect the speed of the process of reconciliation. One was an appeal to Rome, and three such appeals in excommunication cases have been set forth in an appendix to this book.[117] Pending an appeal the crown would suspend its writ of caption to the sheriff, 'nolentes quod eisdem ... per breve nostrum via precludatur quominus dicte appellacionis sue negocium prosequi possint in forma iuris maxime cum huiusmodi breve nostrum de gracia nostra procedat et appellancium status integer esse debeat'.[118] Appeal would be an obvious

---

[113] John 'dictus Bozoun' (PRO C85/7/17: C85/8/11, 13, 16, 17).

[114] For the procedure, and the distinction between absolution from sin and absolution from excommunication, see Logan, *Excommunication*, 137-49.

[115] The fourteen intervals of days are: 58, 61, 89, 109, 136, 143, 154, 195, 259, 261, 315, 471, 489, 554. For computation of intervals over the entire period from 1250 to 1534, see Logan, *Excommunication*, 155.

[116] CUL MS Ee.v.31, f. 136.

[117] Below, Appendix 6, nos. 30, 34, 46. Other appeals in such cases, prior to 1305, may be found in CCW, 157, 180, 227.

[118] RR f. 68; Edward II to sheriff of Northants. For another example see CCR 1302-7, 254-5.

way to avoid caption, at least temporarily, and there is evidence to suggest the existence of some sort of chancery process to determine when caption should be suspended and appeals allowed to continue or move to the Roman court.[119] As chancellor Archbishop Reynolds in 1314 had to deal with such a situation at the king's request after the abbot of Rufford begged the king to stay a writ of caption against him pending his appeal to Rome over his excommunication by the official of York.[120] In another case in 1320-1322 Reynolds himself requested the crown to desist from caption pending an appeal to Rome, but the crown had already been informed of the appeal and had taken action some months before Reynolds' letter.[121] A tuitorial appeal might also stay the process of caption.[122]

Another factor that might affect the reconciliation process was a writ *de caucione admittenda* in which the king, stating that the imprisoned excommunicate had declared his willingness to obey the mandates of the church, asked the bishop or other ordinary authority to command his release *caucione recepta* and threatened to take action if this was not done.[123] The writ for admitting caution was one way of effecting release, and the 'caution' generally consisted of an oath to obey the mandates of the church together with a payment or pledge to pay for court costs and damages if any. After receipt of such a royal mandate, Archbishop Reynolds might commission his official of the court of Canterbury to

---

[119] Douie, *Archbishop Pecham*, 307; Henriques, 'Articles of Grievances', 116-19; Logan, *Excommunication*, 120-36. For complaints against false appeals in 1309, see P&C ii, 1272. A probable instance of fraudulent appeal to avoid caption can be traced in CCR 1307-13, 350; PRO C47/18/4/31, C47/18/6/10, C47/20/4/5, C85/178/3; Gurney and Clay, *Fasti Parochiales* iv, 41-5; and *Chartulary of Sallay*, ed. McNulty, i, 44-53. For the procedure in such cases, and the question whether or not an excommunicate could have recourse to such legal action in an ecclesiastical court, see Logan, *Excommunication*, 116-20.

[120] Wilkinson, *Studies in the Constitutional History of the Thirteenth and Fourteenth Centuries*, 213; PRO C85/179/42; CCW, 401.

[121] Below, Appendix 6, no. 46. When the evidence from Reynolds' register is combined with the evidence from PRO C85, this case is seen to comprise not one but both forms of the appeal procedure set forth by Logan, *Excommunication*, 120-3.

[122] Sayles, *Select Cases in the Court of King's Bench under Edward III*, pp. 51-2.

[123] Some contemporary examples of such writs: RR f. 305v (to Reynolds); *Magnum Registrum Album*, ed. Savage, no. 1 (to Reynolds); Cant. Cath. MS Reg. Q, f. 97v (to prior of Christ Church as keeper of spirituality *sede vacante*, 1313); PRO C85/105/19 (to bishop of Winchester, mistakenly filed under Lincoln); PRO C85/133/33, 44 (to bishop of Norwich); PRO C85/182/45 (to archbishop of York). For this procedure in canon law, see Vernay, *Le 'Liber de excommunicacione'*, pp. lxx-lxxi, and Logan, *Excommunication*, 140-3, 150-4.

facilitate the release and give absolution,[124] or he might reply that he could do nothing because the party excommunicate had not in fact offered satisfaction.[125] The process of release from prison *caucione oblata* was a right recognized as early as Bracton,[126] and it – like the original process of signification – was described as 'secundum regni vestri consuetudinem'.[127]

The system of excommunication, caption, and reconciliation was not without its difficulties, and a fair number of the clerical grievances of the thirteenth and fourteenth centuries were related to it. Miss Henriques and Father Logan have already traced the history of some of these complaints,[128] and others have been mentioned here in passing,[129] but a few additional comments seem appropriate to the situation in the first third of the fourteenth century. Writs *de caucione admittenda* were a topic of the *Articuli cleri* of 1316, but the complaint then was that the crown was setting a time limit by which the excommunicate offering satisfaction had to be released, and there is no evidence of such a limit being set in the cases that the present writer has studied.

Two of the *gravamina* of 1327, echoing the grievance voiced by the English delegation at the council of Vienne, complained that captioned excommunicates were being released by the sheriffs before reconciliation or satisfaction.[130] The studies of Father Logan suggest that this practice, known in the earlier thirteenth century, had ceased well before our period,[131] and the repetition of these complaints now may have been something of a routine formality. No trace of this practice, apart from suspensions for appeal to the Roman court, has been found by the present writer in the C85 files of the Public Record Office or in the registers of Winchelsey and Reynolds. On the contrary, the few surviving records of releases after satisfaction all stress that fact that, even though the crown was convinced of the prisoner's repentance, the release of the man depended upon a letter from the ordinary himself.[132]

---

[124] RR f. 60v.

[125] PRO C47/18/6/12, mm. 17, 18; C85/8/54.

[126] Churchill, *Canterbury Administration* i, 522-3. For the process of release, see Logan, *Excommunication*, 145-9.

[127] PRO C85/8/66; Reg. Martival ii, 348.

[128] Henriques, 'Articles of Grievances', 107-20; Logan, *Excommunication*, 102-4, 134.

[129] Especially above, p. 202 n. 46, and p. 203.

[130] P&C ii, 1356; Richardson and Sayles, *Rot. Parl. Ang. hac. Ined.*, pp. 108-9, nos. 7 and 9; Douie, *Archbishop Pecham*, 306-7.

[131] Logan, *Excommunication*, 148-9, 153-4.

[132] The standard form of letters *de caucione admittenda* from the king to the ordinaries concluded: 'Therefore we command that, having received the said caution, you command

Another point connected with the same grievances of 1327 is the reply of the king's council that henceforth the ordinaries must specify in their letters of caption the reasons for the original excommunications. There is no evidence to illustrate any such change of practice in the PRO files from 1327-1334, although it is said that such practice had become more common by the middle of the fourteenth century.[133] There is at least some ground to doubt that the 1327 decision really intended that every signification state the reason, since the grievance itself concerned only cases where a man, excommunicated for failure to make a payment required by an ecclesiastical judge, later offered a *caucio* to obtain his release from prison without ever satisfying the party to which he owed the original payment. The gist of the reply by the king's council was that in such cases, which would henceforth be known by the statement of reasons in the signification, the writ *de caucione admittenda* would not run.[134]

B. Right of Sanctuary

Just as the secular arm was disciplined to enforce the church's judgment of excommunication, so also in the right of sanctuary the discipline of the church could be extended over those, most frequently robbers and homicides, who might be guilty in the eyes of the law. Generally, the right of sanctuary[135] meant the immunity of consecrated churches, and in some cases the churchyards and certain portions of religious houses,[136] from secular jurisdiction. Generally the sanctuaries in

---

that he be released from prison' (RR ff. 60v, 305v; Cant. Cath. MS Reg. Q, f. 97v; PRO C47/18/6/12, m. 17).

[133] Highfield, 'The Relations' i, 318.

[134] In the 1313-1314 Eyre of Kent it was held that the reason must be specified in any document put forth in the king's courts as proof of excommunication, but such documents were not necessarily letters of caption (Bolland, Maitland, and Harcourt, *The Eyre of Kent*, Selden Soc. vol. 29, pp. xxxi-xxxii, 161-7).

[135] Further see Cox, *The Sanctuaries and Sanctuary Seekers of Medieval England*; Trenholme, *The Right of Sanctuary*; Thornely, *Journal of the British Archaeological Association*, n.s. vol. xxxviii (1933), 293-315; Bellamy, *Crime and Public Order*, 106-14; Haines, *Administration*, 191-2; Hunnisett, *The Medieval Coroner*, 37-54; Hurnard, *The King's Pardon*, 383, 392 (index: abjuration, sanctuary); P&C i, p. 534 n. 2; ii, p. 763 n. 2; Wilkins ii, 414. For the French situation, see Lemarignier, Gaudemet, and Mollat, *Institutions ecclésiastiques*, 288-9.

[136] Not all portions of an abbey or priory, for example, and in many cases probably only the church itself, were considered within the privilege of sanctuary (Cam, *The Eyre of London*, Selden Soc. vol. 86, pp. 126-7, 196-8). In 1317 the crown extended sanctuary to the close of the canons and vicars of Salisbury (CCW, 471).

medieval England were of two types: (1) certain privileged minsters and abbeys, which by charter or in some other way possessed certain rights of immunity that extended for a specified distance around the church and could be enjoyed for life; (2) every consecrated church with its graveyard, which could provide sanctuary for a period of forty days. At the end of this time, if the felon refused either to surrender or to abjure the realm, he could still not be forcibly removed but he was no longer to be provided with food or drink.

During any time within the period of forty days a felon in sanctuary could exercise his right to abjure the realm in a ceremony before the coroner. This procedure, which has been set forth by R. F. Hunnisett, included confession of guilt and an oath of abjuration in which the criminal swore on the Gospels to leave the realm and never return without the king's express permission.[137] He was to go by the king's highway, carrying a wooden cross in his hand and not staying at any one place more than one night, to the nearest port of abjuration as assigned by the coroner. If he abjured the realm in this way, and stayed on the king's highway, as the crown promised in the *Articuli cleri* of 1316, he could leave the kingdom in the king's peace. Since only the kingdom of England was abjured, he could go to Ireland or Scotland. More frequently, however, the felon probably just escaped along the way, as no escort was provided. His goods and chattels, however, were forfeit to the crown.[138]

The penalty for breach of the privilege of sanctuary was excommunication *ipso facto*, although there were times – as at the parish church of New Windsor (Berks.) in Salisbury diocese where a fugitive's enemies in 1317 were preventing him from receiving food[139] – when the sentence of excommunication might be pronounced against specified violators in a particular case. Such a violation, we may note, was in contradiction of the crown's promise in the *Articuli cleri* of the previous year that fugitives in churches might freely have their necessaries brought to them for their living.[140] Vigilant watch over such fugitives was to be maintained, for the

---

[137] Hunnisett, *The Medieval Coroner*, 41-52. The abjuration procedure was also available to criminous clerks (P&C ii, p. 1146 n. 1), but the crown in the *Articuli cleri* of 1316 promised that clergy seeking sanctuary would not be compelled to abjure. For an example of the crown's pardon from abjuration in 1309, see CCW, 286.

[138] E.g., Cal. Memoranda Rolls 1326-7, no. 1999. It was within the competence of itinerant justices, and of course of the king himself, to annul an abjuration (Hurnard, *The King's Pardon*, 143).

[139] Reg. Martival ii, 179-82.

[140] Complaints were again made by the clergy against such violations in 1327 (Richardson and Sayles, *Rot. Parl. Ang. hac. Ined.*, p. 108). One customary exception to this general principle was that suspected felons who took sanctuary but refused to

easy escape of felons from sanctuary was a cause for the justices' censure in the London eyre of 1321 to the effect that the custom of London had been tolerating such a usage contrary to the common law. In this case, complaints that in London no watch was being kept over the churches where suspected felons had taken sanctuary and that neither the citizens nor the sheriffs were being held responsible for escapes therefrom eventuated in the issue of letters patent that henceforth in London watch was to be kept over fugitives as was done in the rest of England.[141]

Archbishop Reynolds threatened violators of sanctuary,[142] and at times he demanded that the crown restore persons who had been forcibly dragged away from the church's protection and imprisoned by the secular authorities.[143] In such cases a royal writ of chancery addressed to the justices of gaol delivery might require that the fugitive be returned to sanctuary. And, on the other hand, the church possessed and occasionally used the power to terminate its protection in individual cases, after which the sanctuary-seeker would then have to face the rigour of the state's justice.

One particular case where the church's protection was refused was that of a criminal seeking sanctuary inside the same church in which the same criminal had allegedly committed an act of homicide. In February of 1320/1321 the case came before the justices of the London eyre of a woman named Isabel of Bury, who was said to have chattered so noisily in the church of All Hallows on the Wall, near Bishopsgate, that the clerk of that church, Gilbert Lyter, told her to leave, whereupon Isabel drew a knife and stabbed Gilbert to death. Isabel promptly claimed sanctuary in that very church, but after a few days a ruling was obtained from the authorities of the bishop of London (and possibly from Archbishop Reynolds himself) that a certain decretal of the canon law provided in such cases for the slayer to be brought to court since the church did not protect those who had committed crimes within the precincts of its own church buildings. Isabel was subsequently imprisoned, tried, and hanged.[144]

---

acknowledge their felony were to be deprived of food (Cam, *The Eyre of London*, Selden Soc. vol. 85, p. 60).

[141] Cam, *The Eyre of London*, pp. xx, xxx, cxvii, 59-63. In the common law, a township could be amerced for an escape from sanctuary (Hunnisett, *The Medieval Coroner*, 43).

[142] RR f. 67v.

[143] PRO SC1/34/164; HMC Fourth Rep., app., 381; *Liber Epistolaris* of Richard de Bury, no. 145; cf. *Ann. Paul.*, 363-4.

[144] *Chroniques de London*, ed. Aungier, 42; Cam, *The Eyre of London*, pp. xxxiv, cxxii, 73-5; for 'juxta quoddam decretale', see ibid., 74; for Reynolds, see ibid., 75.

C. Purgation of Criminous Clerks

That there were in fact two systems of justice in medieval England – two standards of law – was a truth that must have been apparent to most people, and among informed laity the sterner law of the state was known to have very little punitive jurisdiction over the members of the clergy. Perhaps the only time that the church actively encouraged the placing of secular hands upon the priests of Christ was in the caption of excommunicates – we have seen that 164 of the 852 significations surviving in the PRO from this period were cases involving clerks or religious. By and large, however, the discipline of criminous clerks was kept within the competence of the ecclesiastical judges. The principal feature of this system of ecclesiastical justice, moreover, was the process of purgation, whereby a sworn declaration of innocence was made by an accused clerk in the presence of the ecclesiastical judge and a jury of clerks and was then supported by the oaths of (usually twelve) compurgators. The general history of ecclesiastical justice subsequent to the age of Henry ii and Becket, as well as the church's procedure for securing such clerks from the secular authorities and admitting their purgations, has been told many times, recently with interesting illustrations from the contemporary records of the Worcester diocese.[145] Nevertheless, some additional points are worthy of mention from the experience of Edward ii's primate as well as from the statements of purgation that are intermingled among the C85 files of excommunications in the Public Record Office.

Walter Reynolds must have had the whole question of benefit of clergy called vividly to his attention as early as November of 1304, while he was still treasurer or keeper for the prince of Wales, for in that year one Adam called 'le Corur' whom he had appointed as keeper of the goods of the prince's wardrobe in Canterbury had killed a carter named Alexander of Westwell within the grounds of Christ Church Priory and had taken

---

[145] For Worcester see Haines, *Administration*, 181-6. On the whole subject see further Gabel, *Benefit of Clergy*; and Bolland, Maitland, and Harcourt, *The Eyre of Kent*, Selden Soc. vol. 24, pp. lxxiii-lxxvii; Cheney, EHR li (1936), 215-36; Churchill, *Canterbury Administration* i, 524-8, 566; Duggan, BIHR xxxv (1962), 1-28; Henriques, 'Articles of Grievances', 71-92; Highfield, 'The Relations' i, 280-5, 304-7; Reg. Halton, pp. xxxiv-xxxv, xl-xli; Richardson and Sayles, *Governance*, 306, 310-12; Bellamy, *Crime and Public Order*, 151-5; Pugh, *Imprisonment in Medieval England*, 48-51, 134-7; Hurnard, *The King's Pardon for Homicide*, 375-80; Jones, *Studies in Medieval and Renaissance History* vii (1970), 178-92. On the purgation of Bishop Walter Langton at Rome in 1303, see Beardwood, *The Trial of Walter Langton*, 8.

refuge in the room where the wardrobe goods were stored. The seneschal of the prior's liberty, reluctant to seize Adam there, informed the prince and his council (of which Reynolds was a member) in London, and another keeper was appointed and permission given for the seneschal to seize and imprison Adam. A coroner's inquest held the following week showed that Adam had killed Alexander. In September of 1305, when the prisoner was finally brought for trial before Roger le Brabazon and his associates at Canterbury, Adam pleaded clergy and was released to the custody of the ordinary at Maidstone. The whole incident must have been one of the *causes célèbres* in the contemporary history of Christ Church Priory, for it is recorded in great detail in at least three Canterbury registers of the period.[146] These manuscripts all stop, however, at the point when Adam was delivered to ecclesiastical custody, and there is no further word of the man in the register of Archbishop Winchelsey. But in Reynolds' register, for the summer of 1315, there is the record of a commission to proceed in the purgation of a criminous clerk of the very same name.[147] It would be tempting to conclude that the new archbishop decided to use his influence to secure the benefits of the church's liberty for the man who had been his own deputy in 1304, but the lapse of nearly ten years since the initial plea of clergy makes this rather unlikely.[148]

Shortly after Reynolds went from Worcester to Canterbury, moreover, he was confronted with a schedule of nine cases of men who had been indicted and convicted[149] for various crimes in the recent Eyre of Kent, had all pleaded clergy, and had been delivered to the Canterbury prior while the see was still vacant. The men were subsequently turned over to

[146] BL MS Cott. Galba E.iv, f. 21; Cambridge, Trinity College MS O.9.26, f. 120; Cant. Cath. MS Reg. K, f. 143; HMC Ninth Rep., I, app., 77.

[147] RR f. 64v.

[148] Periods of two and four years, however, were not unknown in the fourteenth century (Pugh, *Imprisonment*, 49).

[149] In the practice of this period it seems there was always a jury inquest in the secular court before the man was released *pro convicto* to the church authorities. Cf. Gabel, *Benefit of Clergy*, 37-40. The usual reason given for these inquests in the gaol delivery rolls is 'Et ut sciatur qualis eis liberari debeat, inquiratur rei veritas per patriam' (e.g., PRO J.I. 1/383, m. 92). However, another reason may have been the right of the state to retain the convicted clerk's chattels, in the event that he would fail his purgation. The gaol delivery rolls frequently record the value of a convicted clerk's chattels in the hands of the sheriff. In some instances men who had pleaded clergy were found innocent by the inquest of the jury in the secular court, in which cases they were released and not handed over to the ecclesiastical representatives (e.g. PRO J.I. 1/383, mm. 92, 99). The plea of clergy might be made before or after the trial in the secular court (Pugh, *Imprisonment*; 48).

Reynolds, and in seven cases out of the nine the men successfully purged themselves and were set free.[150]

It is difficult to ascertain just how frequent the practice of purgation of criminous clerks was at this time, but some indication may be given from the sixty-three requests in the PRO C85 files from English ordinaries over the years 1305-1334 to the crown for the return of goods and chattels to clerks who had made successful purgations.[151] Only two of these certificates of purgation are from Archbishop Reynolds, and it is interesting to find that these same two cases are the only two such certificates entered in the pages of his Lambeth register.[152] On the other hand, the register also contains the records of preliminary and intermediate stages of nine other purgation cases of which no records survive in the PRO C85 files.[153] This suggests that in some of these cases the purgations may not have been successful,[154] although these clerks may have had no possessions seized by the crown or the certificates of their purgations may not have survived.

There are no specific cases in Reynolds' register of clerks who failed to purge themselves,[155] although there is one case where the primate gave an advance order for a clerk to be returned to the archiepiscopal prison at Maidstone if he did not succeed,[156] and there is another case in which Reynolds proceeded to the correction of a clerk for false purgation.[157] At times pressure was put upon an ordinary to assure the success of the purgation.[158] Also, on occasion, the church might examine a man who

---

[150] Cant. Cath. MS Reg. K, ff. 182-182v; Cant. Cath. MS S.V. iii, 55; HMC Ninth Rep., I, app., 77; CPR 1317-21, 110; PRO J.I. 1/383, mm. 92, 92v, 93, 94v, 95, 95v, 97v. None of these nine men is mentioned in the indexes of the printed records of this eyre (Selden Soc. vols. 24, 27, 29), although several other cases are listed (see vol. 24, p. 215, index).

[151] Below, Appendix 8, table A.

[152] PRO C85/8/8, RR f. 55; PRO C85/8/23, RR f. 90v.

[153] RR ff. 54, 54v, 64v, 105, 118, 133, 139, 152, 152v, 153v, 154, 285v. (In the last of these cases, the rector of Tarring (Sussex) wished to purge himself of a charge of concubinage.) Some cases from a slightly later period are edited by Woodruff in *Arch. Cant.* xl (1928), 59, 61.

[154] Cf. Gabel, *Benefit of Clergy*, 113; Haines, *Administration*, p. 185 n. 5.

[155] An archiepiscopal register from York in the late thirteenth century shows sixteen failures at purgation in twenty-nine cases, but such a high percentage of failure has been described as exceptional (Bellamy, *Crime and Public Order*, 154).

[156] RR f. 153v. For Reynolds' payments of alms in support of both clerks and laymen in his prison at Maidstone in 1316-1318, see Pugh, *Imprisonment*, 320-1, 366-7. For the archbishop's prison at Maidstone, see Du Boulay, *Lordship of Canterbury*, 310-11.

[157] RR f. 309.

[158] RR f. 118: Reynolds to Bp. Dalderby of Lincoln, 1316, on behalf of Walter Russel, clerk. For another instance see Cant. Cath. MS Reg. L, ff. 12, 16, and *Lit. Cant.* nos. 396, 418: 'ut predicti Iohannis purgacio, iuxta iuris exigenciam, favorabiliter iudicatur'.

had pleaded clergy and then declare that he was not a clerk and that there was no wish to claim him.[159] The penalty for failure at purgation was degradation from holy orders, together with a penance that might involve imprisonment as far as life, and a contemporary form for degradation does survive in the memorandum book of Prior Eastry.[160] At least five cases of degradation are known from the period under consideration, all from York under Archbishop Greenfield.[161]

Not all offenses were clergyable,[162] but we can name many that were because the offenses of the clergy who purged themselves are always given in the certificates addressed to the king. Some cases involved more than one charge, so that a total of eighty-one offenses are recorded for the sixty-three contemporary PRO cases. No less than thirty-five of these offenses were of robbery in some form ('roberia', 'furtum', 'latrocinium', 'asportacio bonorum', 'burgaria', 'depredacio').[163] Other offenses included homicide in some way (sixteen instances), reception of outlaws or felons (eleven), consent to death (six), rape ('raptus') (three), arson (two), and single cases of housebreaking, war against the king,[164] poisoning, gaol-breaking,[165] and counterfeiting the king's money.[166] An interesting case in 1334 was the purgation of one John Peverel, clerk of Worcester diocese, of the offenses of 'falsacio', 'controfaccio', and 'fabricacio' of the seals of Edward II and Edward III and of Queen Isabella. The purgation certificate was sent to the crown in September of 1334 under authority of the abbot

---

[159] Sayles, *Select Cases in the Court of King's Bench under Edward III*, p. 58.

[160] BL MS Cott. Galba E.iv, ff. 29-29v; cf. Haines, *Administration*, p. 186 n. 5.

[161] Reg. Greenfield i, no. 571; ii, no. 946; cf. Hurnard, *The King's Pardon*, 167.

[162] Pugh, *Imprisonment*, 50; Bellamy, *Crime and Public Order*, 151.

[163] A very helpful classification and explanation of these and other terms used for offences is given in Putnam, *Kent Keepers of the Peace*, pp. xxii-xxix.

[164] PRO C85/181/29. This was one of a total of six charges of which Nicholas de Lund, clerk, purged himself in 1318 under authority of Archbishop Melton of York: 'de eo quod guerram contra vos maliciose levavit, ac eciam super criminibus incendii, furti, roberie, receptamenti felonum ac auxilii, et assensus mortis'. For the king's mandate for return of goods after purgation, see CCR 1318-23, 44, 81.

[165] PRO C85/163/7. This certificate appears to say that gaol-breaking was the offense which the clerk denied he had done: 'super fraccione gaole ville Gloucestr' irretitus'.

[166] PRO C85/103/53. M. Ralph of Kent purged himself of this charge under authority of the bishop of Lincoln in 1319; for royal mandate for return of his goods after purgation, cf. CCR 1318-23, 89. This is possibly the same as the case of an unknown man accused of counterfeiting the king's money who pleaded clergy in 1319, as reported in *Yearbooks of Edward II*, Selden Soc. vol. 81, p. 122. For other cases of counterfeiting, see Gabel, *Benefit of Clergy*, 58-9; Sayles, *Select Cases in the Court of King's Bench under Edward II*, pp. 102-4.

of Westminster, although the letter includes no request for the return of John's goods.[167]

On the matter of criminous clerks there is no direct evidence of any clash between secular and ecclesiastical authorities in Reynolds' register, and Professor Tout in his introduction to Bishop Halton's register concluded that church and state worked together in perfect good will on this point in the Carlisle diocese at that time.[168] The clerical *gravamina*, however, tell a slightly different story. Among the English complaints at Vienne in 1311-1312, in the *Articuli cleri* of 1316, and in the grievances of 1327, there were complaints that clerks were being judged by laity and that ordinaries were even being fined if criminous clerks escaped from the church's prisons.[169]

One important charge that can be seen in the records is the complaint, raised in 1327 but made earlier in 1300-1301, that the royal justices were refusing to recognize commissions of gaol delivery from ordinaries unless the names of the justices were specified.[170] The clergy complained that the names might often change without their knowing, and in the reply of 1327 it was finally agreed that henceforth the names need not be stated in commissions. Reynolds can be seen stating the names in two commissions of gaol delivery prior to the 1327 grievances,[171] and in another commission after the date of that agreement he did not specify them.[172]

Abuses and complaints, no doubt, were always present in the system of ecclesiastical discipline, but from this outline three main conclusions may

[167] PRO C85/210/8; cf. CCR 1333-7, 503. Another case of a clerk degraded for falsification of the king's seal, in January of 1276/1277, is found in BL MS Cott. Galba E.iv, ff. 29-29v. This clerk, Richard of Exeter, priest of London diocese, was degraded from office and benefice in the presence of the archbishop of Canterbury and nine other bishops in St. Paul's London. For other contemporary cases of falsification, see Gabel, *Benefit of Clergy*, 58-9; Sayles, *Select Cases in the Court of King's Bench under Edward II*, pp. 56 seq., 158-61; CCR 1302-7, 234; CPR 1307-13, 20; *Ann. Paul.*, 272-3; Rymer II:i, 200-1; *Letters of Edward, Prince of Wales*, p. xx.

[168] Reg. Halton, pp. xl-xli.

[169] These protests are reflected among the papal complaints against the crown in 1309 and 1317 and suggest a general papal policy to support English allegations that jurisdiction was being usurped from the ecclesiastical forum (Reg. Winchelsey, 1031 seq.; below, Appendix 7). For Vienne see P&C ii, 1285, 1353-6.

[170] Richardson and Sayles, *Rot. Parl. Ang. hac. Ined.*, 107-8; cf. P&C ii, 1212.

[171] RR ff. 128, 129.

[172] RR f. 154v. This commission deputes the 'dean of Christianity of Canterbury', an officer not noted in the index of Miss Churchill's *Canterbury Administration* and mentioned at only this one place in RR. For the deans of Christianity of York, cf. below, Appendix 11, no. 47, and Robinson, *Beneficed Clergy*, 36-8, 42; for this official in Worcester diocese, cf. Cal. Reg. Bransford, p. xxii, and *Magnum Registrum Album*, ed. Savage, no. 477, p. 233. See also Tout's comments in Reg. Halton, p. xxxiv-xxxv.

be drawn: in excommunications the church had to rely upon secular
caption in order to enforce her own weapon of discipline, in purgation
cases the royal seizure of goods and chattels gained the crown a certain
indirect control over criminous clerks, and in both fields the administration of ecclesiastical discipline depended – probably increasingly – upon
the operation of the secular power. The right of sanctuary was one area in
which the crown's discipline did not enter, but the surviving evidence
does not suggest that abuses of it at this time were widespread or even that
the use of it was seriously impeding royal justice.

3

The Crown and the Religious Orders

A. The Caption of Rebellious Monks

Comparable with the process of signification and caption was the procedure by which abbots and priors, abbesses and prioresses, and other heads of religious houses might notify the crown of apostate members and request the secular aid to arrest them and return them to their proper houses for correction. This was a specific process that must be considered in addition to the crown's occasional mandates for the arrest of unnamed Dominicans and Franciscans who had left their religion.[1] The discipline of rebellious religious, in these ways, also depended upon the state's assistance.

Some fifty-eight specific requests of this sort survive in the files of the Public Record Office for the years 1305-1334, and they come from most of the major religious orders – Benedictines, Cluniacs and Carthusians, Cistercians, Augustinians, Premonstratensians, Sempringham, Friars Preachers and Minors, and Carmelites.[2] Most of these rebellious religious were reported as doing no more than wander about the country in lay attire, while some few had stolen various goods and chattels from their houses as well. It seems doubtful whether apostate monks and friars were automatically excommunicated,[3] and the procedure for caption provided a convenient – probably the only – way of securing their return in an age

---

[1] Rymer II:ii, 831, 870.

[2] PRO C81/1786/3, 18, 32, 33, 38, 44; C81/1787/1, 7, 15, 16; C81/1788/19, 32, 40, 47; C81/1789/43-6, 48; C81/1790/1, 3, 8, 9, 12; C81/1791/8, 11; C81/1792/15; C81/1793/11, 12, 14-18; C81/1794/6, 7, 12, 20; C81/1795/1, 2; C81/1796/10, 15. For Robert of Thanet, apostate monk of Christ Church Canterbury at the Roman Court, see below, Appendix 6, no. 37.

[3] Yet there was certainly a case of a nun excommunicated for apostasy in 1312 (*Yearbooks of Edward II*, Selden Soc. vol. 33, pp. xxxv, 211-14).

when there was no lawful means of escape from the obligations of religious vows.[4]

B. The Templars

There was one order of religious whose members were all turned out of their houses by the combined efforts of church and state in the period under review — the Templars, who were finally dissolved by papal authority at the council of Vienne. This is not the place to enter upon a full history of their dissolution,[5] but certain observations can be made here as regards Archbishop Reynolds' handling of the question in the time of Edward II. Reynolds was one of the witnesses in 1313 to the large notarial instrument reciting the formal request of the Hospitallers that Edward II transfer to them the Templars' former possessions in accordance with the grant of Clement V 'per modum provisionis apostolice seu ordinacionis'.[6] Yet, even though the crown acknowledged receipt of this instrument, it certainly did not comply with the request, and many interested parties continued to press their own claims.[7] The king himself set the example by treating the New Temple in London as if it had reverted to the crown, but such men as Pembroke, Lancaster, and the elder and younger Despensers also got shares of the takings.[8] The king had given the New Temple in London to Pembroke in December of 1312, and Pembroke under force had quitclaimed all his rights in it to Lancaster in September of 1314, but he regained it on 23 March 1321/1322 after the beheading of Lancaster.[9]

---

[4] Knowles, *The Religious Orders* i, 83-4.

[5] Further see P&C ii, 1444 (index); Perkins, AHR xv (1910), 252-63; Parker, *The Knights Templars*.

[6] PRO E30/1368; E41/193; E135/1/25; E159/87, m. 89d; SC7/12/12; SC7/64/20; cf. Perkins, AHR xv (1910), 259.

[7] Perhaps such reactions in England were not entirely out of order in view of the facts that the papacy itself soon managed to acquire the Templars' former possessions in Cahors and Avignon from the Hospitallers (Reg. John xxii, nos. 14347, 43561; Guillemain, *La Cour pontificale*, 500), and that in France and Spain a number of the Templars' former parish churches had been conferred upon a variety of persons by direct apostolic provision (Reg. Clem. v, no. 9879 seq.). Edward II in 1312 asked the pope to grant a certain Templar property in France to his valet Oliver of Bordeaux (Rymer II:i, 157). An interesting suit over one former Templars' church (Bustleham, Berks.) between the Hospitallers and someone who claimed he had been provided to it by Pope John is recorded in Reg. Martival iv, 78-86.

[8] Davies, *Baronial Opposition*, 88, 91, 110; McKisack, *Fourteenth Century*, 28-30, 67, 76; Parker, *The Knights Templars*, 102; Perkins, AHR xv (1910), 259; Williamson, *The History of the Temple, London*, 75-8.

[9] Phillips, *Aymer de Valence*, 52, 81, 227.

And in still other cases the crown intervened to divert the transfer of Templar properties from the Hospitallers to other religious, such as the Carmelites.[10]

The papal grant to the Hospitallers was unpopular in England, and it was widely held that by dissolution the Templars' possessions should have reverted to the several lords of the fees and that feudal superiors could claim titles by escheat. In various legal suits the prior of the Hospitallers, attempting to present to benefices formerly held by the Templars, encountered the claim that such advowsons had now become lay fees.[11] A claim of this very sort provided Reynolds with one of the major crises of his archiepiscopate when, in the parliament of October 1320, he was served a royal prohibition not to entertain such a plea from the Hospitallers because it was said to be of lay fee. Reynolds, failing to obtain a royal consultation, finally decided to follow the papal mandate for transfer of the Templars' goods and thus to risk the king's threat of forfeiture of temporalities.[12]

The king, Reynolds, and any other important people who might be favourably disposed, were continually exhorted by the apostolic see to facilitate and hasten the transfer of Templar possessions to the Hospitallers,[13] and it is clear that the papacy hoped for their support. On 16 November 1320, however, the English episcopal hierarchy collectively begged the pope to be excused from this duty, pleading that the crown had threatened seizure of temporalities if they failed to obey its prohibition writs that designated the Templar possessions as lay fees.[14] The king had explicitly forbidden Reynolds and the bishops to send such a letter to the pope; but Reynolds in the October parliament had determined to proceed with the transfer, he informed the bishops of Lincoln and Rochester and probably others on 26 November that he was doing so,[15] and on the same day he commissioned his commissary Robert de Malling to act upon the pope's bull under pain of excommunication. Malling replied, twenty-one days after the date of Reynolds' commission, that he had made public notice to this effect in Canterbury cathedral, but that a certain Lombard,

[10] *Liber Epistolaris* of Richard de Bury, nos. 300, 345.
[11] *Yearbooks of Edward II*, Selden Soc. vol. 54, pp. 129-34; cf. vol. 41, pp. xix-xxii, 73-9.
[12] Above, p. 185.
[13] RR ff. 228, 228v, 230, 230v; Reg. John XXII, nos. 5179, 10900, 10901, 13674; CPL ii, 131-2, 198-9, 424, 446, 449, 492; Reg. Sandale, 115-18; Reg. Hethe, 85-9; Reg. Martival ii, 307-9; Reg. Gandavo, 534-8.
[14] Reg. Hethe, 76-9.
[15] RR f. 98v; Reg. Hethe, 90-1.

keeper of the manor of Temple Ewell (near Dover) now said to be in the hands of the earl of Lancaster, had been present in the cathedral and had subsequently obtained a copy of the mandate and as a result various abuses and threats of torture and even death were made against him. The commissary, pleading in 'precibus lacrimosis' that he was a humble and simple person and entirely incapable of coping with the matter, declined to proceed further and begged to be excused. Reynolds then, explaining that he would handle the situation himself were he not needed personally for the king's business, proceeded to commission the abbot of St. Augustine's Canterbury, again under pain of excommunication, to act upon the mandate in place of the commissary.[16]

Reynolds' register, unfortunately, does not tell us anything further about this affair, and it is doubtful whether the king took any action against Reynolds for his obedience to the pope. In another incident arising from the same October parliament of 1320, however, we know that Reynolds certainly supported the Hospitallers in their attempt to obtain the presentation of the former Templar prebend of Blewbury in Salisbury cathedral. Bishop Martival had obtained an inhibition from the court of Canterbury to stop the Hospitallers from presenting, but Reynolds proceeded to quash it.[17] This action by Reynolds is understandable in the light of his decision to follow the papal mandate.

It was not until 1324 that parliament in the statute *De terris Templariorum* finally decreed that notwithstanding the rights of the king and the lords of the fees by inheritance, gift, purchase, or any other means, the property of the dissolved order should go to the Knights of the Hospital of St. John of Jerusalem, to the end that, pursuant to the intentions of the original donors, it might still be put to similar Christian uses.[18] This statute made no mention of the papal grant to the Hospitallers. Nor did it put an end to the difficulties of the transfer,[19] but we learn nothing further from Reynolds' register of his own activities after this date.

Apart from the Hospitallers' struggle to obtain the Templar lands, tenements, rents, fees, and advowsons, Reynolds faced one other important question from the same source. The people who had held

---

[16] RR f. 231v.

[17] Below, Appendix 6, no. 50.

[18] *Statutes of the Realm* i, 194-6.

[19] Perkins, AHR XV (1910), 260-3; Parker, *The Knights Templars*, 103-4, suggests that it was not until 1338 that the Hospitallers obtained at least nominal possession of the greater part of the Templar estates.

Templar corrodies and pensions had been allowed to establish their claims at the exchequer,[20] but the former Templars themselves – some 135 in number[21] – presented more of a problem. Reynolds in 1314 rebuked the Hospitallers' prior for failure to provide life necessities for them in accord with apostolic mandate and the decision of a Canterbury provincial convocation.[22] The pope in 1318 complained to Reynolds that certain former Templars were dressing and acting as laymen, even though the council of Vienne had by no means released them from their vows as religious. John XXII commanded that they must put away their wives, and that all former Templars must be located in religious houses – not over two in any house except in houses of the Hospitallers. Stipends were to be withdrawn from those who refused to be removed, and the aid of the secular arm was to be called if necessary. Reynolds, acting upon this, called certain of the former Templars before him and proceeded to arrange for their transfer to other houses.[23]

From the little we know, therefore, it seems that Reynolds tried to do as commanded on the question of the Templars, even disregarding the royal prohibition when he felt that the papal bull had to be obeyed. His decisions in the October parliament of 1320 and in the month following were probably decisive in turning the tide to the Hospitallers' favour.

C. Royal Requests for Favours

The crown undoubtedly took a large profit from its administration of the Templars' estates, as indeed it was a part of the royal policy at this time to reap the maximum benefits from its associations with all the orders of religious. If the crown was willing to aid the religious by the caption of rebellious monks and in other ways, it certainly demanded in return a high price by its continual requests for pensions, benefices, and corrodies

---

[20] Parker, *The Knights Templars*, p. 100 n. 106; Williamson, *The History of the Temple, London*, 73-5. These claims from the early years of Edward II may be studied in Cole, *Documents*, 139-230. One interesting case is in BL MS Cott. Vespasian E.xxii, f. 115: the abbot of Peterborough claimed that William de la More, former master of the Templars in England, had borrowed 100 marks from him and given him certain silver vases as security which had later been seized by the king's representatives at the time of the dissolution. The abbot in 1314 (?) took steps to establish his claim at the exchequer.

[21] Knowles and Hadcock, *Medieval Religious Houses*, 290; the list of houses follows.

[22] RR f. 46v.

[23] RR f. 227; Reg. John XXII, nos. 3191-2, 8753. Bishop Dalderby of Lincoln, likewise, in 1319 at the pope's request made arrangements for several former Templars to be received in other houses (LAO MS Reg. Dalderby III, ff. 425-430v), as did Bishop Gravesend in the same year (Reg. London, 213).

for its servants and for gifts, loans, and hospitality for itself. The most solid foundation for these requests was the royal prerogative right to name one clerk to be promoted to an appropriate benefice, or to be given a pension until such a vacancy occurred, by new bishops, abbots, abbesses, or other religious superiors upon their promotion, consecration, or blessing. This custom went back at least to the reign of Henry III,[24] and in the monasteries it was strongest in the houses of royal foundation or patronage – which by the early fourteenth century numbered over 100.[25] Nearly fifty such royal requests to religious houses upon the appointments of their new superiors have been found in the calendars of close rolls for Edward II's reign,[26] and there are numerous other instances of its exercise by the king in the first third of the fourteenth century.[27] The king might also transfer this right of nomination to other members of the royal family, and even place distraint upon those who disobeyed.[28] This right had its parallels in the 'option' of the archbishop of Canterbury[29] and in the 'droit de joyeux avènement' of the kings of France.[30] Prior Eastry remarked of it, when Archbishop Mepham upon his promotion to Canterbury in 1328 was faced with such a claim for one of the royal clerks: 'Magis de facto quam de iure hactenus est optentum.... Ista gratitudo quasi extorta in usum processit et iam consuetudinem ut dicitur introduxit.'[31]

Christ Church Priory at Canterbury, one of the most important monasteries in the kingdom and a house exceedingly proud and jealous of its

---

[24] Wood, *English Monasteries and their Patrons*, 113.

[25] Wood, ibid., 6, shows that out of 425 monastic houses (monks, regular canons, and nuns, but excluding cathedral priories) whose patrons have been found for a considerable part of the thirteenth century, 106 were of royal patronage, including most of the greatest. Hill, *The King's Messengers*, 74, points out that in a general way all founders and benefactors of religious houses were entitled to similar claims, although of them the king had 'the largest and least well-defined rights'. The ancient privileges of the crown in monastic houses were reasserted strongly at the parliament of Carlisle, 1307 (*Statutes of the Realm* i, 150-2).

[26] Tillotson, *Journal of Religious History* 8 (1974), 129. See, for example, CCR 1313-18, 190, 210, 305, 308, 312.

[27] *Cal. Anc. Cor. concerning Wales*, pp. 175, 178; CCW, 393, passim; CCR 1313-18, 439; Fraser, *Antony Bek*, 28; Haines, *Administration*, p. 95 n. 2; HMC Fourth Rep., app., 389, 393; *Rot. Parl.*, index vol., 681 ('pension'); Wilkins ii, 571; *Liber Epistolaris* of Richard de Bury, nos. 343, 346, 350-3.

[28] *Liber Epistolaris* of Richard de Bury, no. 352.

[29] Above, pp. 65-66.

[30] Lemarignier, Gaudemèt, and Mollat, *Institutions ecclésiastiques*, 244, 415; Caillet, *La papauté d'Avignon et l'église de France*, 400.

[31] Cant. Cath. MS Reg. L. f. 163; *Lit. Cant.* no. 266; HMC Ninth Rep., I, app., 97.

own rights and privileges,[32] was a favourite place for the crown to request pensions (grants of money) and corrodies (grants of board and sometimes lodging) for royal clerks and servants. Evidence to show the pattern and extent of such requests during this period at Canterbury is set forth in an appendix to this book.[33] Especially noticeable is the tendency on the part of the crown to assume the right to nominate a successor as it learned of the death of each previous royal corrodian. And in addition to these demands, the crown asked the monks of Christ Church for loans of money,[34] for presentations of royal clerks to benefices in the priory's gift,[35] and for carts and horses for defence of the realm.[36] The crown also tendered requests for receipt of its nominees in the school attached to the priory's new almonry chapel, founded in 1320 for the purpose of prayer for the royal family and others.[37] There was, in addition, a strong tradition that called for hospitality[38] and gifts[39] to the crown and royal household whenever they were at Canterbury, and such visits occurred almost annually. The priory was even asked to relinquish a particle of the bones of St. Thomas Becket to enhance Queen Isabella's collection of relics.[40] All this was a burden to bear, especially when multiplied by similar requests from other principals – including various cardinals[41] as well as Archbishop Reynolds.[42] The Canterbury priory did, however, manage in this

[32] Contemporary documents from the priory often include phrases like the following from the time of Prior Eastry: 'Sancta Cant(uariensis) ecclesia que pre ceteris occidentalibus ecclesiis quam pluribus libertatibus et consuetudinibus laudabilibus ab olim fuerat et adhuc est multipliciter insignita' (CUL MS Ee.v.31, ff. 158, passim). Cf. Lit. Cant. no. 694 (dated 1340): 'Ecclesia nostra Cantuariensis omnium ecclesiarum occidentalium est et esse solebat mater et domina'. For similar but more limited statements by Richard I and Abp. Stephen Langton, cf. Cheney, From Becket to Langton, p. 101 and n. 3.

[33] Below, Appendix 9; cf. Smith, Canterbury Cathedral Priory, 51.

[34] CUL MS Ee.v.31, ff. 130v, 263v; Cant. Cath. MS Reg. L, ff. 132, 169v; Lit. Cant. nos. 64, 277; HMC Ninth Rep., I, app., 93, 98.

[35] Cant. Cath. MS Reg. L, f. 189v; Lit. Cant. no. 46.

[36] CUL MS Ee.v.31, f. 176v; Cant. Cath. MS Reg. L, ff. 31, 31v; Lit. Cant. nos. 519-23; HMC Ninth Rep., I, app., 81.

[37] CUL MS Ee.v.31, f. 211v; Cant. Cath. MS Reg. L, f. 16v; Lit. Cant. no. 424; BL MS Cott. Galba E.iv, ff. 87 seq., 95.

[38] Cant. Cath. MS Reg. L, ff. 129, 144; Lit. Cant. nos. 168, 171; HMC Ninth Rep., I, app., 92-3, 95.

[39] Below, Appendix 10.

[40] RR f. 64. The queen made the request of Archbishop Reynolds in June of 1315, and he advised Prior Eastry to discuss the matter with her upon her approaching visit to Canterbury and to accede to her wishes.

[41] Cardinals Walter Winterbourne (CUL MS Ee.v.31, f. 101v), Raymond Guilhem de Farges, and Bernard de Garves (CUL MS Ee.v.31, f. 117).

[42] CUL MS Ee.v.31, f. 226v; Cant. Cath. MS Reg. L, f. 135v; Lit. Cant. nos. 80-2.

period to preserve its exemption from royal seizure of temporalities during prioral vacancies,[43] although the abbeys ranking as baronies held by tenants-in-chief were subject either to seizure during vacancies or to an annual payment.[44]

Even before his coronation, the future Edward II in 1304-1305 had sent a total of ninety-four letters to abbots and priors asking for benefices, pensions, or corrodies for his clerks,[45] and every important religious house of the kingdom must — like the cathedral priory at Canterbury — have felt the weight of these or similar requests at some time. The same king in two months of the year 1316 sent a further twenty-three royal servants to various religious houses with requests for their retirement and maintenance,[46] and a total of fifty-one such requests was sent to the Worcester cathedral priory alone between the years 1308-1327.[47] Evidence gathered only from the close rolls shows that there were at least 420 requests for corrodies from more than 200 houses during Edward II's reign, the peak years of their enrollment being 1316, 1317, and 1318.[48] Resistance was, of course, offered in various ways, some houses asking to be excused because they were not of royal foundation and others urging they should be burdened with no more than one corrodian at a time. Such excuses, however, availed little if anything in face of the royal prerogative, and if the king's first request was denied the letters might be reissued from chancery in a more urgent form.

As early as 1285 the state had made the assize of *Novel disseisin* available to persons claiming monastic corrodies,[49] and in the early fourteenth century such persons were bringing suit against abbots and prioresses in the king's courts[50] and the prior of Ely was even attached for failure to grant a corrody.[51] The practice of rewarding royal servants and providing for their sickness and old age by means of monastic corrodies and pensions has been described as especially characteristic of the reign of

[43] BI. MS Cott. Galba E.iv. f. 109v; Cant. Cath. MS Reg. L. f. 169v; *Lit. Cant.* nos. 279, 280; HMC Ninth Rep., I, app., 98.

[44] Knowles, *The Religious Orders* i, 278-9; ii, 248.

[45] Pantin, *The English Church*, 34.

[46] CCR 1313-18, 435-7.

[47] Cal. Reg. Bransford, p. ix.

[48] Tillotson, *Journal of Religious History* 8 (1974), 132.

[49] Douie, *Archbishop Pecham*, 311.

[50] *Yearbooks of Edward II*, Selden Soc. vol. 17, pp. 4-5; vol. 19, pp. 125-6; vol. 36, pp. 80-4. See also Cam, *The Eyre of London*, Selden Soc. vol. 86, p. 205: *novel disseisin* concerning a corrody and rent from the warden of the hospital of St. Katherine outside London, 1321.

[51] BI. MS Add. 41612, f. 41.

Edward II and the first half of that of Edward III, before and after which period the more customary methods were direct pension from the crown, grant of county alms, or assignment of other offices, houses, or lands.[52] Sometimes, also, corrodies or pensions to royal servants still in active service may have been granted instead of increased wages.[53] The notary and royal clerk Henry of Canterbury, for example, held pensions from both Canterbury and Peterborough long before the year 1345 in which he retired and was granted life maintenance in the priory at Norwich.[54]

In 1323 there is evidence from Canterbury, Peterborough, and Ely of a general inquiry by the crown to learn how many persons were receiving pensions and corrodies in these houses at royal request.[55] The replies state the names, their relationship to the crown, and the value and type of favour they were receiving. Some of the recipients, like Henry of Canterbury, had been sponsored by Edward II when he was prince of Wales. The replies also indicate a marked reluctance to make any additional grants, and the fact of this reluctance is confirmed by the file of contemporary replies to royal requests for corrodies in the PRO, in which documents the all but unanimous response is negative.[56]

Although the mounting number of royal requests for all these favours has been defended as well as denounced by later writers,[57] the practice in some contemporary ecclesiastical records was certainly being regarded and described as an abuse. Archbishop Reynolds in his visitation injunctions to the prioress and convent of Davington (Kent) specified that they were to grant no more corrodies without his special permission.[58] The crown's requests for these favours were the subject of complaints by the popes in 1309 and 1317,[59] both by religious and by secular clergy in 1309 and 1316 as well as earlier,[60] and later by William of Pagula in his

---

[52] Hill, *The King's Messengers*, 73-81.

[53] Ibid., 75.

[54] Below, Appendix 9, no. 1; BL MS Cott. Vespasian E.xxi, f. 72v; Cuttino, EHR lvii (1942), 308.

[55] Canterbury: CUL MS Ee.v.31, f. 233. Peterborough: BL MS Cott. Vespasian E.xxi, f. 72v. Ely: BL MS Add. 41612, ff. 62-3.

[56] PRO C47/17/7-12. Another group of negative responses from the time of Edward II is included within the file of BL Cott. Charter II.26, e.g., nos. 29 and 43.

[57] Hill, *The King's Messengers*, 74; Smith, *Canterbury Cathedral Priory*, 51.

[58] RR f. 273.

[59] Reg. Winchelsey, 1035; below, Appendix 7.

[60] P&C ii, 1138-9, 1216-17, 1271-2; *Statutes of the Realm* i, 153, 155 (1309, statute *De prisis iniustis*, and restriction upon purveyance at parliament of Stamford). RR ff. 76v seq., 77v; CPR 1313-17, 608; HMC Ninth Rep., I, app., 353; Wilkins ii, 459 (1316, *Articuli cleri*, and the royal letter patent). Cf. Wilson and Jones, *Corrodies at Worcester*, p. 10; Cal. Reg. Bransford, p. viii.

Epistola of early 1331 and his *Speculum regis* of 1332.[61] The unsatisfactory nature of the king's replies to these grievances is further reflected
in the crown's vague promise in the first year of Edward III that as regards
pensions, corrodies, and benefices the king 'will no more such things
desire but where he ought',[62] and in the crown's declaration in 1336 that
previous grants of corrodies, pensions, and sustenances at Christ Church
Canterbury upon royal request would not serve to the prejudice of that
house in the future 'saving always the king's right'.[63] Yet the crown
continued to expand the scope of its requests, no longer content with
demands only upon houses of royal foundation or patronage, but
extending its claims to all without exception, and refusals to grant such
requests continue in the PRO C47 file throughout the century.

D. THE DOMINICANS

If it was Abbot Thokey and the Benedictine monks of Gloucester who
claimed and buried the supposed body of Edward II,[64] it was nevertheless
the Dominicans who had tried to rescue him from Berkeley Castle and
who kept in circulation the rumours that he was still alive.[65] The
Dominicans were in the ascendant in this period, and Professor David
Knowles concluded that 'never, perhaps, did they stand higher in favour
at court than under Edward II'.[66] It was this king who founded the new
Dominican house at King's Langley, lavishly furnished and endowed for a
memorial of Piers Gaveston and as a place where fervent prayer on behalf
of the crown would be offered.[67] As prince of Wales Edward II had given
the Dominicans high place in his court and had selected them for his
confessors.[68] As king he continued to show a marked (but not exclusive)

---

[61] Boyle, TRHS, 5th series, vol. v (1955), 104; Pantin, *The English Church*, 196; *Vita
Edwardi Secundi*, pp. xvii, 75; Boyle, *Mediaeval Studies* xxxii (1970), 329-36.

[62] *Statutes of the Realm* i, 256.

[63] CPR 1334-8, 253; Cant. Cath. MS Reg. A, f. 89; Cant. Cath. MS Cart. Ant. C88; *Lit.
Cant.* no. 592; cf. Cant. Cath. MS Christ Church Letters i, 89.

[64] Knowles, *The Religious Orders* ii, 35.

[65] Clarke, 'Some Secular Activities', 190-213; Knowles, *The Religious Orders* i, 169-
70; McKisack, *Fourteenth Century*, 94; Murimuth, *Con. Chron.*, 255-6; Tanquerey, EHR
xxxi (1916), 122-3; Tout, *Collected Papers* iii, 145-90.

[66] *The Religious Orders* i, 169.

[67] Cf. Palmer, *The Reliquary* xix (1878), 37-43; *Liber Epistolaris* of Richard de Bury,
no. 34; CCW, 281, 381; CPR 1307-13, 397, 453.

[68] *Letters of Edward, Prince of Wales*, ed. Johnstone, pp. xv, 1, 94, 139; PRO E101/
363/18, ff. 3, 3v.

preference for Dominican confessors,[69] even though some members of the royal family in the early fourteenth century were partial to Carmelites or Franciscans. It was the Dominicans who, of all the orders at this time, were the most frequent nominees as suffragans and as bishops of the Welsh and Irish sees,[70] a development which the king encouraged. Edward II supported the Dominicans at the Roman court in their dispute over teaching rights at Oxford University[71] as well as in other matters.[72] The calendar of memoranda rolls for 1326-1327[73] shows that the king at this time was making alms payments of fifty marks a year to the friars preachers at Oxford as well as twenty-five to those at Cambridge, and it records no payments of royal alms to any other religious order. Mention has already been made of the importance of the English Dominican cardinals in the king's eyes.[74]

Certainly Edward II and possibly his father sought the masses and intercessory prayers of the Dominicans more frequently than those of any other order.[75] Edward II frequently coupled his requests for Dominican prayers with grants of alms at the meetings of their provincial chapters, the payments being arranged by his Dominican confessor.[76] The acts of no less than six Dominican general chapters surviving from the period under consideration reveal the friars responding to these requests by commending masses and other prayers for the English crown.[77] And at one such chapter, Maestricht in 1330, imprisonment was even threatened for any Dominican of the English province venturing to say anything that might in any way disturb the English king, the queen mother, or the realm![78] Even in Gascony, the surviving acts of six provincial chapters during our

[69] Clarke, 'Some Secular Activities', 43, 240-6; Knowles, *The Religious Orders* i, 167-8.

[70] Knowles, *The Religious Orders* ii, 369-70.

[71] Below, Appendix 6, no. 26.

[72] For example, *Liber Epistolaris* of Richard de Bury, nos. 171, 188-9.

[73] Nos. 1638, 1639, 2157.

[74] Above, p. 125 seq.

[75] Below, Appendix 11.

[76] PRO E101/373/15, f. 41; E101/375/8, f. 4; examples could be multiplied.

[77] Below, Appendix 11, nos. 15, 19, 48, 80, 86, 87.

[78] 'Cum ex verbis incaute prolatis frequenter scandala oriantur, sicut magistra rerum experiencia nostris temporibus manifestat, volumus et ordinamus, quod quicumque frater provincie Anglie, infra ipsam provinciam vel extra existens, verba quecumque quocumque pallio vel colore dicere ausus fuerit, ex quibus verbis serenissimus dominus rex Anglie vel domina regina mater sua et regnum ipsum Anglie posset merito perturbari, postquam legitime constiterit, carcerali custodie mancipetur' (Reichert, *Acta Capitulorum Generalium* ii, 196).

period show the Dominicans there granting masses and prayers for the English king and his family.[79]

On the continent, the Dominicans were the royal confessors in France;[80] and just as they were influential there in the distribution of crown patronage, evidence points to a parallel function of Edward II's Dominican confessor in arranging for corrodies for crown servants.[81] Clement V selected the Dominican convent at Avignon for residence in the years before the apostolic see appropriated the episcopal palace there,[82] and it was in the church of the friars preachers at Avignon that Archbishop Mepham was consecrated by Cardinal Pierre des Prés in 1328.[83] John XXII, whose election as pope took place in the Dominican house at Lyons,[84] manifested some favouritism for the friars preachers[85] and was especially fond of the English Dominican literary scholar and theologian Nicholas Trevet. In 1318 Pope John instructed the papal tax collector in England to make Trevet a gift of money to help meet his expenses in composing a literary work that he had commissioned, and in 1324 he sent to England for a copy of Trevet's commentary on the psalter.[86] The year 1323 saw the canonization of Thomas Aquinas,[87] and all the professors of theology in the school opened at the papal court later in the century were – with one exception – Dominicans.[88]

Archbishop Reynolds, too, often expressed partiality to the Dominican order,[89] and they undoubtedly ranked second only to the Canterbury Benedictines of his cathedral in his affections. Reynolds frequently in touching language asked the prayers and intercessions of the Dominican provincial chapters for himself and for the king and realm,[90] and the

---

[79] Douais, Les Frères Prêcheurs en Gascogne i, 123, 146, 159, 184, 200.

[80] Lemarignier, Gaudemet, and Mollat, Institutions ecclésiastiques, 427-8.

[81] Clarke, 'Some Secular Activities', 33; CCR 1313-18, 435-7.

[82] Guillemain, La Cour pontificale, 76.

[83] Cant. Cath. MS Reg. Q, f. 127v.

[84] Flores Hist. iii, 175.

[85] Cf. Hillenbrand, 'Kurie und Generalkapitel des Predigerordens unter Johannes XXII', 499-515.

[86] Knowles, The Religious Orders i, 234, 246, 251; Smalley, English Friars and Antiquity, 60; CPL ii, 461; Emden, Oxford iii, 1902-3.

[87] Reg. John XXII, no. 17801; 18 July 1323.

[88] Guillemain, La Cour pontificale, 384.

[89] RR ff. 33, 54v.

[90] RR ff. 70, 121v 125v, 234v, 278. E.g. f. 234v, Reynolds to prior provincial OP and all other friars gathered in provincial chapter at Cambridge (not dated): 'Et quoniam ad ordinem vestrum vestrique ordinis personas quasi a primis nostris cunabulis inmense affeccionis fervorem concepimus et sicuti potuimus continuavimus vos et vestros studendo venerari, quocirca vobis qui educti de seculi laqueis liberi sursum tenditis ad

Dominican general chapter of Montpellier in 1316 may even have commended each priest to say one mass on behalf of Reynolds.[91] Reynolds stayed and conducted business ('occupaciones') at times in a certain room of the Dominicans' London convent, and he sought the aid of the master of the entire order at the Roman court.[92] While bishop of Worcester Reynolds had been a conservator of the friars preachers in England,[93] and as archbishop he frequently took his Dominican confessor, friar Laurence of Sandwich, prior of their house at Canterbury, along on his travels.[94]

E. ALIENS

One class of religious that came up against the crown during the period under review was the aliens. Objections voiced in the Lent parliament of 1305 and earlier to payments made by dependent English houses of such orders as Cistercians, Premonstratensians, and Cluniacs to their foreign abbots soon found statutory sanction in the statute of Carlisle, 1307.[95] This statute forbade any religious of the king's jurisdiction to pay tax, rent, or tallage of any kind outside the kingdom. It also forbade foreign superiors to make such levies upon any house within the realm, although their rights to visit their English dependencies were specifically safeguarded.

One effect of the statute upon the English houses was a restriction upon attendance at general chapters and visitations to mother houses on the continent. In 1308, for example, seven English Cistercian abbots were detained by royal order for having crossed the sea without the king's license to attend the general chapter at Cîteaux.[96] These restrictions, and

---

celestia, qui terrena egressi habitacula mansionem celicam elegistis, qui elevatis oculis solum celum cernitis, pura mente Deum limpide contemplamini, ipsius Dei familiares et domestici estis constituti statum domini nostri regis et regni sui nostrumque et ecclesie nostre recommendamus humili ex affectu mente supplicantes devota ut pro ipsius et nobis indignis apud divinam clemenciam assiduis oracionibus insistatis ut ad laudem et honorem nominis sui firmam pacem et tranquillitatem regi et regno tribuat Anglicano'. Cf. RR f. 70. I have discovered no close parallel wording among the king's requests for prayers to the Dominican order; below, Appendix 11.

[91] Below, Appendix 11, no. 33.

[92] RR f. 119v; Berengar of Landorra.

[93] VCH *Worcester* ii, 168.

[94] RR ff. 113, 234v, 278.

[95] P&C ii, 1232; *Rot. Parl.* i, 217-18; *Statutes of the Realm* i, 150-2. For background see Desmond, 'The Statute of Carlisle and the Cistercians 1298-1369', 138-62.

[96] Desmond, 'The Statute of Carlisle and the Cistercians', 150.

the crown's determination to enforce them, may have met some opposition from the Premonstratensians,[97] but there is evidence that among the English Cistercians – already heavily burdened with taxation of all sorts – they were generally welcomed.[98] Protests were made at various times by the abbots of Cîteaux, Prémontré, and Cluny. The issue was not settled at Carlisle,[99] and the papacy under John XXII expressed limited support on behalf of the foreign parent houses to the king.[100] Clement V as early as 1307 had asked Edward II to allow the English Cistercian abbots to attend meetings of the general chapter at Cîteaux,[101] and even before Carlisle Clement in 1306 had boldly placed every absentee from the general chapter under *ipso facto* excommunication.[102] The king in practice seems to have permitted attendance so long as they had his license and carried no more money with them than that needed for expenses,[103] and in 1323 he even asked the Cistercian general chapter for prayers for himself and the realm.[104] At times, however, it was necessary for Edward II to reaffirm parts of the Carlisle statute, especially in 1313 when he learned that the Premonstratensians had been clearly violating it,[105] and again in 1316.[106]

Stemming from the same causes, the pressing financial needs of the central government and the fear of spying and treason aggravated by the threat of French invasion, there was also a succession of seizures of alien priories and of other alien property at this time. In such seizures it is necessary for us to consider alien secular clergy together with the alien regulars, because the crown often directed its proceedings against both groups. The confiscation that began in 1295 established the main lines of procedure to be followed later,[107] and the next major seizure came in 1324-1326 in the wake of the war of Saint-Sardos and the intrigues of Queen Isabella in France. Even Isabella's estates were now sequestrated

---

[97] Knowles, *The Religious Orders* ii, 142.
[98] Madden, *Catholic Historical Review* xlix (1963), 361-4; King, *Cîteaux and her Elder Daughters*, 50.
[99] For later developments, see King, *Cîteaux*, 54.
[100] CPL ii, 424, 450.
[101] Rymer II:i, 22.
[102] Desmond, 'The Statute of Carlisle', 153.
[103] Rymer II:i, 78, 173, 224; Desmond, 'The Statute of Carlisle', 151-3.
[104] Below, Appendix 11, no. 62.
[105] Rymer II:i, 234, 293, 604, 618, 619.
[106] Desmond, 'The Statute of Carlisle', 152.
[107] For this procedure see Matthew, *The Norman Monasteries and their English Possessions*, 82-3; Morgan, *History*, n.s. vol. xxvi (1941), 205; P&C ii, p. 1218 n. 1; Robinson, *Beneficed Clergy*, 32.

on this pretext,[108] and her physician M. Theobald of Troyes was confined to Peterborough Abbey with his valet and servant at the king's expense.[109] Several aliens, however, including Cardinals Gaucelme de Jean and Raymond de Roux, as well as the papal collector in England Hugh of Angoulême and his assistants, were granted special exemptions.[110] Cistercian abbots were prohibited from attending general chapter in the late fall of 1325, but Edward II did permit Cistercians from abroad to enter and carry out visitations within the realm.[111]

In England, the crown's order for the seizure of alien secular clergy in 1324-1325 specified that all such persons 'living near the sea or navigable waters leading to the sea', except men of Flanders and Brabant, were to be removed by the diocesans to more remote places where they could live without suspicion. Replies to this command were varied. The bishop of Chichester, John Langton, replied that he was unable to do this because his diocese lay near the coast of the sea and because he was unable to find any goods by which such clergy could be sustained and their benefices attended.[112] In 1326 again, in reply to a new command for removal of alien religious near the coast because of the French king's arrest of all Englishmen within his realm, the same bishop replied that he had found ten alien religious but was unable to move them because he had no other house within his diocese except near the sea. He also reported that the alien priors had agreed to find security for their good conduct and to make annual payments at the exchequer in return for custody of their houses, as the king's writ had provided and as had been permitted shortly after the 1295 seizure.[113] It is interesting to note that Langton did not count the prior of Lewes in the group of alien priors and specifically stated that he was English.

Other bishops found it easier to obey the royal commands. Droxford of Bath and Wells in 1325 reported seven alien secular clergy in his diocese, four of whom were nonresident. Their goods were sequestrated and placed in the hands of native Englishmen. Included in this group of benefices were the prebend of Cleeve held by the abbot of Bec, and the benefice of Merriott (Som.) held by Filippo son of Andreas Sapiti, both of

---

[108] McKisack, *Fourteenth Century*, 81; *Ann. Paul.*, 307.
[109] BL MS Cott. Vespasian E.xxi, f. 74v. King's writ specifies 'eciam si sint de hospicio nostro vel consortis nostre'.
[110] Rymer II:i, 578, 580; Lunt, *Financial Relations* i, 578.
[111] Desmond, 'The Statute of Carlisle', 154.
[112] PRO C47/18/1, m. 3.
[113] PRO C47/18/1, m. 6; cf. *Ann. Paul.*, 313.

whom were reported as nonresident. Concerning the alien religious, however, Droxford replied that one Henry Guldet', a knight and layman, had already seized all their goods at the king's command.[114] In Salisbury diocese Bishop Martival reported in 1326 that three alien priors had agreed to make annual payments at the exchequer, and that two alien monks had been removed from their cells near the coast to the house of Sherborne.[115] The exchequer itself kept a *Rotulus memorandorum de statu religiosorum alienigenarum* at this time, and reaped a considerable income from custody of the property of these houses.[116]

Archbishop Reynolds, too, felt the pressures of the war of Saint-Sardos in 1324 when the king called upon him to receive the oaths of persons charged with defence of the realm in Kent, to render counsel and advice to them, and to provide horses and even armed men, both on horse and on foot, for the same cause.[117] Reynolds in 1325 was commanded to proceed against alien secular clergy, but replied that he had made diligent scrutiny of the entire city and diocese of Canterbury and had found no alien seculars beneficed there.[118] In this report, however, he was apparently ignoring Guy de la Valle, a Norman kinsman of the king who had been given the rectory of Maidstone at the request of Queen Isabella in 1311.[119] For in July of 1326 the king prohibited Reynolds from hearing a suit in court Christian for 300 marks owed to Guy by the farmers of his benefice, the king having commanded the farmers not to pay Guy because he was an alien of the power of the French king.[120] Edward II had shown marked favouritism to Guy in earlier years, and this reversal of affection may have been due to Guy's close relationship with Queen Isabella. Nevertheless, Maidstone, valued in the 1291 taxation at £106.13s.4d. and thus one of

[114] PRO C47/18/1, m. 4/26, 27.

[115] PRO C47/18/1, m. 7.

[116] Cal. Memoranda Rolls 1326-7, nos. 577, 814, 823, 947, 1980, 1985-6, 2003, 2049, 2051, 2069-76, 2249, 2255. There was also, at least for Cornwall, a 'custos prioratuum et domorum alienigenarum' about whom very little is known (Reg. Stapledon, 430).

[117] RR ff. 309v-310v. For the extent to which the archbishop may have been liable for knight service to the crown at this time, see Du Boulay, *Lordship of Canterbury*, 78, 87, and Chew, *English Ecclesiastical Tenants-in-Chief*, 59-60.

[118] RR f. 311.

[119] Rymer II:i, 130; CCW, 347, 353, 383; above, pp. 57-58. Guy had to contend for this church both against a papal provisor and against a nominee of Archbishop Winchelsey (CPL ii, 70, 74-5; *Reg. Pal. Dunelm.* i, 223-42; Reg. Gandavo, 395-7; Reg. Woodlock, 552-3, 560; Emden, *Oxford* ii, 1204-5; Emden, *Cambridge*, 292; CCR 1307-13, 317-18; Rymer II:i, 207; PRO C85/7/46), but he was recognized by the apostolic see as rector at least by March of 1320 (CPL ii, 200; Reg. John XXII, no. 11183 and cf. 19650-1).

[120] RR f. 312v, and cf. f. 197.

the richest benefices in Canterbury diocese,[121] continued to be held in subsequent years by nonresident aliens. It was provided to Theobald de la Valle upon Guy's consecration as bishop of Le Mans in 1326,[122] and was reserved and then provided upon Theobald's death in 1329 to Cardinal Annibaldo Gaetani da Ceccano.[123] Shortly after Theobald's provision to Maidstone in 1326, Archbishop Reynolds commissioned one of his clerks to exercise spiritual jurisdiction within the benefice,[124] and a visitation of Maidstone in January of 1327/1328 made by the Canterbury priory authorities during the vacancy after the death of Reynolds reported that 'the rector is nonresident and does no good in the parish'. Numerous defects were noted.[125] Maidstone, therefore, provides a striking example of a benefice in which the interests of royal kinsmen, cardinals, and aliens all coincided to produce and sustain over a long period of years a situation that was certainly less than ideal.

The attempt to determine precisely who or what was 'alien' could also give rise to some interesting questions. Burwell (Lincs.), for example, a priory of La Sauve-Majeure in Gascony, had been seized in 1295 because La Sauve was then in French hands, but in 1324 it was not confiscated.[126] The crown's policy at Burwell was undoubtedly influenced by the fact that La Sauve was of English royal foundation and celebrated two masses daily for the English king and his ancestors.[127] The Cluniac priory of Castle Acre (Norf.) was seized apparently because the prior was Burgundian; order was then given for its release because the Earl Warenne and others testified that the prior and priory were not of the power of the king of France and were unaccustomed to make any payments to anyone of that king's power; then the latter command was rescinded because the priory was found to be subject to the priory of Lewes, which was of the French king's power, its prior being appointed by the Lewes prior.[128] The parish church of Lydd in Canterbury diocese

---

[121] *Taxatio Eccl.*, 3.

[122] Reg. John xxii, no. 24828; cpl. ii, 250; Barraclough, *Studi e Testi*, vol. 165 (1952), 122; cf. rr f. 196.

[123] Below, Appendix 3, no. 5.

[124] rr f. 262v.

[125] Woodruff, *Arch. Cant.* xxxiii (1918), 86-7. Woodruff (p. 71) is mistaken in his assumption that the cardinal was rector at this time.

[126] Trabut-Cussac, *Bulletin philologique et historique*, 1957, pp. 150-1. In both 1315 and 1323 the English crown certainly considered this priory within its Gascon sphere of influence (Brown, *Studies in Medieval and Renaissance History* viii (1971), 161).

[127] *Gascon Rolls*, ed. Renouard, p. 579, no. xxxiii.

[128] pro C47/18/1, m. 5; see, however, Cal. Memoranda Rolls 1326-7, no. 548.

was given special protection in 1324 because it was held by an Italian religious house and thus was not under French control.[129] Royal protections were also issued regularly throughout this period for certain Italian attorneys, such as Leo de Roma and Ursus de Adria, collecting alms in England under papal indult on behalf of the Hospital of the Holy Spirit in Sassia in Rome, attached to the church of St. Mary which was known as 'the church of the English', and for the warden of the church of All Saints, Writtle (Essex), which with its small hospital was dependent upon the hospital in Rome, as these persons were all known not to be in the power of the king of France.[130]

Further history and classification of the alien priories in England has been set forth elsewhere,[131] but it must be noted that there were also a number of secular benefices controlled by aliens in various ways. Some cathedral prebends were regularly held by French abbots: the prebend of Wilmington in Chichester cathedral was held by the abbots of Grestain (Eure),[132] that of Cleeve in Bath and Wells was leased by the abbots of Bec (Eure) to the abbots of Cleeve,[133] that of Loders in Salisbury was held by the abbots of Ste-Marie Montébourg (Manche),[134] that of Ogbourne in Salisbury by the abbots of Bec,[135] and that of Upavon in Salisbury by the

---

[129] CPR 1324-7, 56; RR ff. 102v, 200, 289v.

[130] The name 'Sassia', thought to be related to the word 'Saxon', had been the name for the 'English quarter' in Rome from Saxon times. The foundation of the hospital there, attached to the church of St. Mary 'quae vocatur Schola Saxonum', dated from the pontificate of Innocent III, and it was Innocent who placed it under the management of the confraternity of S. Spirito. The endowment of this hospital with the revenues of the church of Writtle was the work of King John. The 'English Hospice' at Rome, a different institution and under the patronage of the Holy Trinity and St. Thomas of Canterbury, was not founded until circa 1362. For the royal protections see CPR 1301-7, 101; ibid. 1317-21, 74; ibid. 1321-4, 11; ibid. 1324-7, 36; ibid. 1327-30, 339; ibid. 1330-4, 146, 317, 369; ibid. 1334-8, 2, 479; Cal. Charter Rolls 1300-26, 242; ibid. 1327-41, 97. More generally see New, *Alien Priories*, 1; Sayers, *Papal Judges Delegate*, 191; P&C ii, 1236; Burns, AHP ix (1971), no. 36; Lawrence, *English Church and the Papacy*, 52; Knowles and Hadcock, *Medieval Religious Houses*, 337, 406; Lunt, *Financial Relations* i, 12-14, 346, 512, 514; Levison, *England and the Continent*, 36 seq.; Croke, *Dublin Review* cxxiii (1898), 94-106, 305-17; Parks, *English Traveler to Italy* i, 32-6, 215; Brentano, *Rome before Avignon*, 19-23; and Moore, *Saxon Pilgrims to Rome and the Schola Saxonum*, 122-5.

[131] See Knowles, *The Religious Orders* ii, 157-66, and Matthew, *The Norman Monasteries*, and references cited therein.

[132] Le Neve, *Chichester*, 49.

[133] Le Neve, *Bath and Wells*, 22.

[134] Le Neve, *Salisbury*, 64.

[135] Ibid., 76. During the wars with France, its prior was allowed to hold his property in return for a heavy annual farm, for which the assessment in 1324 was £520 (Knowles and Hadcock, *Medieval Religious Houses*, 90).

abbots of Ste-Wandrille (Seine Inf.).[136] The archbishop of Rouen held a number of lands, tenements, and advowsons in England, some of which were confiscated probably in 1325 or 1326.[137] Several parish churches were also in the patronage of French abbots for various reasons. Archbishop Reynolds encountered at least six such benefices in the course of his administrative duties,[138] and in 1315 he singled out churches appropriated to aliens as a category for investigation during his visitation of Ely diocese.[139] However, some alien clergy were of very positive value in English benefices, such as the sons of Andreas Sapiti and other foreign clerks resident at the papal curia,[140] and such as the foreign bishops *in partibus* who shouldered a great load of routine episcopal duties for Reynolds and other members of the English hierarchy.[141] Moreover, it was not impossible that Englishmen might likewise hold benefices of some sort in France, and this was in fact the case with Reynolds who held the prebend of Quincy in Lyons cathedral.[142] This prebend had been granted in 1175 to the Canterbury archbishops in honour of St. Thomas, and in 1315 Reynolds took steps to ask the French king to appoint a guardian for the prebend and its manor. His register tells us nothing of any difficulties with the French authorities over Quincy, and in March of 1326/1327 he made fresh arrangements for a proctor there who would render annual payments to him from its farm.[143]

We may conclude that the seizure of alien priories and of the goods or benefices of alien secular clergy in the last two or three years of Edward II's reign was not by any means thorough, and that the crown itself at times changed its attitude in particular cases and certainly did permit some benefices to remain in the hands of nonresident aliens. Aside from financial profit, probably the king's most important gain from the custody of the alien priories was a windfall of patronage, and W. E. L. Smith has counted in the patent rolls of the last two years of the reign over sixty royal presentations to benefices normally in the gift of alien religious

---

[136] Ibid., 93.

[137] Rymer II:i, 43, 189; II:ii, 687-8, 726, 806.

[138] RR ff. 22, 102v, 119, 200, 257v, 289v.

[139] RR f. 53.

[140] Cf. Reg. Halton, pp. xxxv-xxxvi; above, pp. 112-13.

[141] Cf. Haines, *Administration*, 173. For Bishop Hugh of Byblos, suffragan to Antony Bek, see Fraser, *Antony Bek*, 60, 114, 163-6, 194. For Bishop Peter of Corbavia, suffragan to Reynolds, see RR ff. 102, 126, 126v, 131, 135v, 146v, 147, 149, 150, 151, 152v, 153v, 154, 158v, 159, 184v.

[142] Quinciacum, Quincieux: canton Neuville-sur-Saône, arr. Lyon, dep. Rhône.

[143] RR ff. 123v, 197; HMC Fifth Rep., 448-9; Douie, *Archbishop Pecham*, 52.

houses.[144] There is some little evidence that the papacy occasionally intervened in support of the alien parent houses, either by granting continental possessions in recompense for English losses or by asking the king himself to make satisfaction.[145] The next major seizure of alien property coincided with the outbreak of hostilities in 1337,[146] and in the same year the king, fearing a new papal tax, issued a prohibition against the Benedictine constitutions of 1336.[147] Further confiscations and further restrictions upon payments outside the realm continued in the fourteenth century whenever the war broke out afresh, and some houses purchased their freedom from royal control while others secured charters of denization and became fully English.[148] Theoretical justification for the crown's seizures of the properties of alien ecclesiastics was offered circa 1339 in William of Ockham's tract, *An rex Angliae pro succursu guerrae possit recipere bona ecclesiarum*, which advanced the view that even the possessions of the church could be confiscated by the crown when needed for public defence.[149]

[144] *Episcopal Appointments*, 94-9.
[145] Reg. Clem. v, nos. 7695, 8695; CPl. ii, 94, 103, 488.
[146] For an enquiry in 1334, see Wilkins ii, 574-5.
[147] Knowles, *The Religious Orders* ii, 3-4.
[148] Knowles, *The Religious Orders* ii, 159 seq.; King, *Cîteaux*, 54.
[149] Knowles, *The Religious Orders* ii, 66, 97.

Archbishop Walter Reynolds and Edward II

Throughout this book an attempt has been made to set forth Reynolds' activities and attitudes, when they can be known, on the major issues between church and state. Within the realm, it would seem that his primacy witnessed (1) an increase in availability of writs of consultation – at least partly from the influence of the *Articuli cleri*, (2) the frequent use of excommunication by both pope and primate in support of the crown, and (3) the probably increasing dependence of ecclesiastical discipline upon secular assistance in the fields of excommunication, criminous clerks, and rebellious monks. No discussion of the areas of conflict and cooperation between church and state, however, would be complete without some attempt to evaluate the man that Edward II chose to be primate of all England. Like so many medieval figures, Reynolds himself remains shadowy. The material does not exist for a really adequate biography, yet some attempt must be made – in conclusion – to throw more light upon the man himself. The sources that mention him are mostly official and impersonal in character, yet there are important points in his archiepiscopate where the impersonal office and the individual person do merge.

Reynolds' reputation has suffered severely at the hands of the author of the portion of the *Flores Historiarum* attributed to the Benedictine monk Robert of Reading, even though some contemporary chroniclers were neutral in their attitude to Reynolds and one of them, Trokelowe, spoke hopefully of him. In the *Flores*, at the narrative of his appointment to Canterbury, Reynolds gets his worst drubbing:

> vir siquidem laicus et in tantum illiteratus ut nomen proprium declinare penitus ignorabat, qui et ipse vir Belial et lubricus, regens tunc temporis indigne cathedram episcopalem sanctorum Oswaldi et Wlstani apud Wygorniam, atque ad archipraesulatum nequiter aspirans, ut tam crebram electionem de tanto viro factam per viam dampnatae symoniae penitus enarraret, et ad finalem expeditionem illicitae promotionis suae sic noviter

excogitatae papalem animum altis muneribus inclinaret. In his quoque vetitis operibus affuit ambitio praedicto; regalis intentio cum suggestionibus fautorum et effusa summatim insaturabili Papae multitudine auri et argenti copiosi predictam electionem, in Christi contemptum et ecclesiae Cantuariensis praejudicium manifestum ac in sui dampnationem perpetuam, injuste quassavit. Nec sic os infernalis avaritiae poterat exsaturari, donec, terra Gwasconiae sibi per regem ad tempus in vadimonium exposita, munus consecrationis una cum pallio per comitem Campaniae in suis rescriptis Christi sponsae et suis fidelibus inimico Papa transmisit. Quibus cum archipraesulatus infula pompose receptis, utebatur eis ut bos armaturis, depraedationibus ecclesiarum et oppressionibus religiosorum, luxuriae foeditatibus immoderatis indulgens, gaudens officio sui pronubi[1] magistri Willelmi de Berchestone,[2] cui causa lenocinii archidiaconatum Gloucestriae dudum contulerat, ut opera nequitiae liberius exerceret in

---

[1] *Flor. Hist.* iii, 155-6 and the original BL MS Cott. Cleopatra A.xvi, f. 95v both read *pronubet.*

[2] William de Birston is frequently described in contemporary records as 'magister' but he is not listed in Emden, *Oxford*, or *Cambridge*. Birston's associations with Reynolds certainly went back as far as Reynolds' appointment to the provostship of Beverley in 1306, when Birston served as his proctor and personal representative in the chapter there (below, Appendix 12, no. 5). Birston also worked under Reynolds in the household of the prince of Wales, and is mentioned as a clerk in the book that survives from the time when Reynolds was treasurer or keeper of the prince's wardrobe in 1306-1307 (BL MS Add. 22923, f. 12). He is again mentioned as being in the service of Reynolds in 1307-1308 when the latter was treasurer of Edward II (BL MS Add. 35093, f. 3). Birston became an important assistant of Reynolds in the see of Worcester, serving as his commissary-general and auditor in all cases coming before the bishop by reason of his ordinary authority (RWR, 44-5, 49; Haines, *Administration*, 131, 337). He accompanied Reynolds to the Roman court in 1309 (CPR 1307-13, 103), and also served as his proctor there at the time of Reynolds' translation to Canterbury (RWR, 68; RR ff. 1, 1v, 2; Reg. Clem. V, appendixes vol. i, p. 254, no. R). In 1317 he conveyed a gift of precious altar cloths from Reynolds to John XXII (RR f. 215v), and on the same mission he held power – together with Adam Murimuth – to grant moderate annual pensions in Reynolds' name to cardinals and others in the curia as seemed expedient to them (RR f. 88). He also facilitated royal payments of cardinals' pensions at this time (PRO E101/375/8, f. 2v; Soc. Ant. MS 120, ff. 23v, 24v, 25, 52v; Murimuth, *Con. Chron.*, 26), and in the same year Pope John made him a papal chaplain (CPL ii, 141). Back in England, Birston had accompanied Reynolds on his first visitation of Christ Church Canterbury in Feb. of 1313/1314 (Cant. Cath. MS Reg. Q, f. 92), and he is described as Reynolds' chancellor on 12 May 1314 (RR f. 48). Reynolds while bishop of Worcester had collated him to the archdeaconry of Gloucester (RWR, 148-9; Le Neve, *Mon. So. Prov.*, 60. The reference in Le Neve as f. 3b should be to Reynolds' Worcester register, not his Lambeth one.) Soon after translation to Canterbury Reynolds used his apostolic provisory faculty to secure for Birston a canonry and prebend of Lincoln (RR ff. 48, 123v, 125v; Le Neve, *Lincoln*, 48). Birston also held a plurality of other benefices (Haines, *Administration*, p. 38 n. 4). He died probably in Nov. of 1317 (Le Neve, *Mon. So. Prov.*, 60). Although Birston was obviously in long and close association with Reynolds, I have come upon nothing that would tend to substantiate the insinuations of Reading as regard their relationship.

praemissis. Praebuit itaque praemissus violator sacerdotii publice per provinciam perniciosum exemplum, docens in suis actibus doctrinam Balaam, populum edere et fornicare, soluto pudicitiae fraeno.[3]

Certain other chroniclers – Bridlington, Meaux, and the *Vita Edwardi Secundi*[4] – look with disfavour upon the arrangement between Edward II and Clement V to reserve Canterbury and quash Thomas Cobham's election to it in favour of Reynolds, and they recount their suspicions of a prior financial agreement between king and pope – suspicions for which no positive confirmation has been found.[5] Murimuth, however, who probably knew the workings of the papal court best of all the con-

---

[3] *Flores Hist.* iii, 155-6. For questions about the attribution to Reading see Tout, EHR xxxi (1916), 450-64.

[4] Bridlington, *Gesta Edwardi*, 45; *Chron. Melsa* ii, 329; *Vita Edwardi Secundi*, 45-7.

[5] I believe that Miss Edwards (EHR lix (1944), p. 326 n. 1) agreed too readily that Richardson's statement, 'the allegation by the chroniclers that Clement's acceptance was conditional on payment is undoubtedly true', is proved by the secret letter of Clement V that Richardson printed in EHR lvi (1941), 97-103. The letter may suggest that Clement had Cobham in mind for the primacy (contra see Denton, *Journal of Medieval History* i (1975), 323), but it proves nothing about a condition of payment. There is no evidence that Reynolds himself used the words 'non modica et intolerabilis pecunia' which Richardson quotes from a letter of Edward II printed in Rymer II:i, 257. Nor does this royal letter in Rymer prove 'beyond doubt' that there had been any specific agreement before Reynolds' translation; it simply alleges that such a sum is being demanded of Reynolds 'praetextu translationis'. This sum could well have been Reynolds' common service tax (Lunt, *Financial Relations* i, 467-8, 480 (cf. n. 5), 679; RR ff. 84, 114), although there are other possibilities for its identification (Lunt, *Financial Relations* i, 474-5, 488; RR ff. 62v, 84, 114v; Reg. Clem. v, nos. 4014-15; CPL ii, 52). Simon Mepham, Reynolds' successor, may well have had to spend as much money at the Roman court to obtain Canterbury as the sums paid by Reynolds or Edward II (CPL ii, 119, 121, 272; Reg. Clem. v, appendixes vol. i, p. 254, no. R; Reg. Clem. v, nos. 10062, 10075, 10159; Reg. John XXII, no. 41688; Göller, *Einnahmen* i, 671, 683; Hoberg, *Taxae pro communibus servitiis*, 28). The obligation of common service for Reynolds' appointment to the see of Canterbury is listed on 18 Dec. 1313 by Hoberg as being 7500 gold florins and a further 2500 'ex causa devotionis quam gerit ad ecclesiam Romanam'. The nature of this latter obligation is unclear, but it may have had its foundation in Reynolds' appointment (dated 17 Nov. 1313, well after he had been named to the see) of M. William de Birston as his proctor in the Roman curia for the purpose of promising to pay the pope 'illam summam florenorum que dicto procuratori nostro videbitur concedenda seu eciam promittenda quam ex causa mere liberalitatis et subvencionis gratuite sibi ex nunc offerimus et donamus' (RR f. 2). That this was an extraordinary payment is certainly possible, although the payments recorded by Hoberg (p. 28) for Canterbury in 1328 and 1334 each total 10,000 florins also. Moreover, such an obligation recorded in December, 1313, more than two months after the date when Clement provided Reynolds to Canterbury (1 Oct.), does not constitute 'proof' that Clement's 'acceptance' of Reynolds was 'conditional' on payment. Lunt (*Financial Relations* i, p. 480 n. 5) speculates that the 2500 florins may have been Reynolds' payment of private or secret service, and such payments of this amount or more were not uncommon at this time (ibid., 479-82).

temporary chroniclers,[6] is neutral in his estimate of Reynolds — neither denigrating his character nor repeating any story about a financial agreement,[7] and in this respect he leads another 'neutral' group of writers that includes the *Annales Londonienses*, the *Annales Paulini*, Birchington, the Continuation of Trevet, Higden, Knighton, and the Peterborough Chronicle.[8] Yet it is the chronicler Trokelowe, whose words are followed closely by Walsingham's *Historia Anglicana*,[9] who in the present writer's opinion comes nearest the mark in his analysis of Reynolds' provision to Canterbury. This is his description of the pope's action:

> Et quia Ecclesia Anglicana continuis tribulationibus vexabatur, idem Summus Pontifex de viro, per quem dictae tribulationes melius sedari possent, Ecclesiae viduatae providere sollicite cogitabat. Habito igitur super hiis tractatu prolixo, et diversorum consilio requisito, tandem in Dominum W(alterum), Wigorniensem Episcopum, Domini Regis Angliae Cancellarium, oculos dirigebat; acute praeponderans, quantam gratiam coram Domino Rege prae ceteris inveniebat, quam mature in suo officio erga omnes se habebat, quantaque discretione rancorem, inter Regem et suos proceres motum, temperabat; sperans talem virum Ecclesiae et regno multum posse proficere, qui inter saeculi tot varietates, absque alicujus offensione novit incedere, honorem Cantuariensis ecclesiae, una cum pallio, gratis sibi conferebat, praedicto Thomae spem promotionis honorificae promittendo.[10]

This theme, of Reynolds as a possible agent for the peace of the English church and king and realm, will be taken up again. But for the moment we must note that this theme was the very substance of Pope Clement's advice to Reynolds in one of his provisory bulls[11] and that it can be found in John xxii's correspondence to Reynolds time and again.[12] Reynolds

[6] Cf. Emden, *Oxford* ii, 1329-30.

[7] *Con. Chron.*, 19.

[8] For *Ann. Lond.*, *Ann. Paul.*, Higden, and Knighton, see Smith, *Episcopal Appointments*, 18-20. For Birchington see Wharton, *Anglia Sacra* i, 18; and for serious doubts about the authorship ascribed to Birchington by Wharton see *Chronica Johannis de Reading et Anonymi Cantuariensis*, ed. Tait, 63-75. For the others see *Nicolai Triveti Annalium Continuatio*, ed. Hall, 10, and *Chronicon Angliae Petriburgense*, ed. Giles, 160.

[9] Vol. i, p. 136.

[10] Trokelowe, *Chronica et Annales*, 82.

[11] The words are these: 'sic curam et administracionem illius sollicite geras et fideliter prosequaris, sicque karissimi in Christo filii nostri Edwardi regis Anglie illustris ac regni sui quietem et pacem studeas procurare, quod digne retribucionis premium consequaris a Domino, ac nostram et apostolice sedis benediccionem et graciam uberius merearis'. From the bull *Praeclara tuarum dona virtutum*, RR f. 1; above, p. 160 n. 27.

[12] One quotation must suffice: 'Age itaque, frater, constanter atque viriliter, et iuxta officii tui debitum ministerium tuum imple, et cum omni que datur instancia operare

himself seems to have incorporated it often in his various requests for prayers and in his other writings.[13]

Nevertheless, by and large historians and other writers of more recent times have chosen to portray Reynolds more in the school of the *Flores Historiarum* than in the style of Trokelowe. A sampling reveals the following descriptions:

Woolnoth and Hastings, *Graphical Illustrations of the Metropolitan Cathedral Church of Canterbury* (1816): 'his weakness of mind rendered him incapable of holding (the see of Canterbury) with dignity.... By temporising with all parties, he lost the esteem and reverence of all'.[14]

Foss, in *The Judges of England* (1851) began his remarks by citing Reynolds as 'an early instance in English history of the advance of an individual from the lower ranks of life to the highest ecclesiastical honours', but Foss went on to observe that 'On the queen's invasion of the kingdom, he basely deserted his patron and master' and Foss concluded that 'Any credit which he may have deserved for his liberality, or for his mildness, prudence, and capacity for business, must be overshadowed by the time-serving and abject weakness of his character'.[15]

Hasted, 1861 editions of *History of Canterbury* and *History of Kent*: 'under cover of a mild and courteous disposition, (Reynolds) sheltered a mean and abject spirit, which became notorious in his want of courage, constancy and fidelity, at the time when the king, his great benefactor, fell under distress, when he showed himself not only defective in duty, but was guilty of the greatest perfidy to him'.[16]

Hook, *Lives of the Archbishops of Canterbury*, 1865: 'Of all the Primates who have occupied the see of Canterbury, few have been less qualified to discharge the duties devolving upon a Metropolitan, than Walter

---

quecumque cedere videris ad Dei laudem et gloriam et dicti .. regis ac regni Anglie tranquillitatem et pacem, pro tuis et ecclesie tue opportunitatibus recursum ad nos fiducialiter habiturus' (RR f. 218v; Vatican Archives, Reg. Vat. 110, f. 119 [top foliation]). Other examples of the same theme in John XXII's bulls can be found in Reynolds' register: RR ff. 195, 213, 215v, 216, 218, 218v, 237v, 241v; CPL ii, 416, 428, 430-1, 439, 462, 468; John XXII, Secret Letters, nos. 792, 2201, 2427; Reg. Martival ii, 426-8, 471-2; below, Appendix 11, nos. 39, 44, 77.

[13] Above, p. 234. Below, Appendix 11, nos. 25, 28, 32, 35, 41, 52, 55, 58, 60, 65, 68, 70, 71, 73; RR f. 237v; Edwards, EHR lix (1944), 326 (cf. n. 2), 340-1; Salter, Pantin, and Richardson, *Formularies* i, no. 36.

[14] P. 158.

[15] Vol. iii, pp. 288-91.

[16] *Canterbury* ii, 379; *Kent* xii, 379.

Reynolds. He was not equal to the situation, whether we have regard to his talents, his learning, his piety, or his virtues'.[17]

Stubbs, *Constitutional History of England*, 1875: 'a mere creature of court favour'.[18] In his collection of *Chronicles of the Reigns of Edward I and Edward II*, 1883, Stubbs went on to speak of 'the weak and ungenerous primate at Canterbury'.[19]

Capes, *The English Church in the Fourteenth and Fifteenth Centuries*, 1900: (after a long string of quotations from the *Flores Historiarum*) 'certainly there are few signs of dignity or wisdom in (Reynolds') guidance of the Church in those dark days of trial'.[20]

Ramsay, *The Genesis of Lancaster*, 1913: 'a courtier and time-server; one who knew how to make friends of the Mammon of Unrighteousness'. Ramsay's following remark, no doubt in its context intended to be derogatory, is nonetheless probably true: 'His influence at the Papal Court was almost equal to his influence with Edward'.[21]

The judgment of Conway Davies (*The Baronial Opposition to Edward II*, 1918) was carefully guarded: 'Without accepting the chronicler's description of Reynolds as an illiterate man without dignity or learning, it can be well conceded that in piety as well as intellectual attainments he was inferior to Cobham and his appointment was stated to be due to the bribes of the king'.[22]

Miss Maude Clarke, *Medieval Representation and Consent*, 1936, who has more favourable words to say about his leadership of the prelates, nevertheless labels him 'the time-server Reynolds'.[23]

Miss May McKisack, *The Fourteenth Century*, 1959, is slightly more cautious: 'perhaps ... wholly unfitted for the office'.[24]

And more recently W. R. Jones, writing on clerical grievances in *Speculum*, 1966: a 'self-seeking curialist' from whom 'little of a courageous nature was to be expected'.[25]

Even T. F. Tout, whose essay on Reynolds' life in the *Dictionary of National Biography* (1896 and 1909 editions) remains the most com-

[17] Vol. iii, p. 455.
[18] Vol. ii: 1875 ed., p. 335; no change in 1929 reprint of fourth ed., p. 351.
[19] RS no. 76, vol. ii, p. xci.
[20] P. 51.
[21] Vol. i, p. 53.
[22] P. 332.
[23] P. 132.
[24] P. 296; cf. p. 93.
[25] Vol. xli, pp. 224-5.

prehensive sketch in print,[26] appears to make his judgments under the influence of Robert of Reading. Reynolds 'seems to have been one of those evil-living, secular-minded clerks whom Edward I did not scruple to use in his rougher business, and did not hesitate to add to the household of Edward, his young son'. Tout continues, citing only the *Flores Historiarum* as source, 'Reynolds was also accused of dissolute and indecorous life'. Again, citing only the *Flores*, he says that Reynolds' life 'continued to be a cause of scandal'. And finally, 'Intellectually and morally Reynolds was, of all the medieval archbishops of Canterbury, least deserving of respect'.[27] Also in his *Place of the Reign of Edward II* (1914 and 1936 editions) Tout speaks of 'the unworthy and incompetent Reynolds'.[28]

Yet the portion of the *Flores* attributed to Reading, as well as being rabidly Lancastrian in sentiment, is notoriously hostile to the king, the pope, the Dominicans, and Gaveston – all persons who were high in Reynolds' favour, and perhaps Reading's description of Reynolds is only to be expected in a chronicle of such biases.[29] The most balanced modern treatment of Reynolds, in my opinion, is to be found in Miss Edwards' account of 'The political importance of the English bishops during the reign of Edward II' published in the *English Historical Review* of 1944.[30] She accepts the traditional views of Reynolds' personal limitations, his seeming indecision and inability to lead, but she also makes a tentative estimate of another side of his character: 'his chief political object was apparently to work in peaceful co-operation with the ruling power in the state, whoever that might be'. Although she does not claim ancient precedent for her view, Miss Edwards here may be seen as following in modern language and with modern historical criteria the opinion of Trokelowe, and it is this line of interpretation that the present writer would like to press as a more accurate assessment of Edward II's primate.

[26] A very useful biographical outline of additional facts about Reynolds culled from many printed sources was presented by Miss Edwards in 1938 as an appendix to her London M.A. thesis, 'The Personnel and Political Activities of the English Episcopate during the Reign of Edward II', pp. 412-13.

[27] Tout, DNB, 1896 ed., vol. xlviii, and no significant change in 1909 re-issue, vol. xvi. My quotations are from the latter, pp. 963 (for the first three quotations), and 966.

[28] In the 1914 ed., p. 79; no change in 1936 revision, p. 71.

[29] For Reading on the justice of Lancaster's cause, see Maddicott, *Thomas of Lancaster*, 330.

[30] Vol. lix, p. 314; cf. pp. 340-1. My own assessment of Reynolds does not, however, agree with hers on every point, especially on the question of Reynolds' ability or inability to lead.

First, however, it is necessary to consider in detail one aspect of Reynolds' personality that has been almost totally neglected by modern authors. Was this primate of all England seriously defective in learning? Even if literacy in medieval usage meant strictly a knowledge of Latin,[31] was Reynolds illiterate? This opinion is incorporated in the three chronicles most hostile to Reynolds: the *Flores Historiarum*, 'vir siquidem laicus et in tantum illiteratus ut nomen proprium declinare penitus ignorabat'; the *Vita Edwardi Secundi*, 'simplex clericus et minus competenter litteratus'; and the chronicle of Lanercost, 'homo quasi illiteratus, et, secundum judicium humanum, tam ratione vitae quam scientiae omni gradu dignitatis indignus'.[32] It has been taken over and perpetuated in more recent times, as we have seen, by such historians as Hook and Tout.

What are we to make of this notion? Miss Edwards in her work on 'Bishops and learning in the reign of Edward II', which does not discuss Reynolds in any great detail, has concluded in a general way that the chronicle evidence usually tends to suggest a standard of learning somewhat lower than that known from other sources,[33] and I suggest that the same is true for Reynolds. The notion of Reynolds' supposed illiteracy must be discarded in the absence of proof and in the light of cumulative indications to the contrary. Even though Reynolds does not seem to have attended any university,[34] and even though we can agree with Miss Hilda Johnstone in rejecting the seventeenth-century invention that Reynolds was Prince Edward's tutor,[35] even though we readily admit that Reynolds was no scholar, yet there is considerable evidence not only to suggest that Reynolds was literate himself but also to prove that he was in a modest way a patron and promoter of academic learning.

[31] Johnstone, *Edward of Carnarvon*, 13.

[32] *Flores* iii, 155; *Vita*, 45; Lanercost, p. 222 in the Latin edition, ed. J. Stevenson, Edinburgh, 1839, and pp. 202-3 in the English translation by H. E. Maxwell, Glasgow, 1913.

[33] CQR cxxxviii (1944), 57-86. For discussions of the literacy of medieval English rulers see David, 'The Claim of King Henry I to be called learned', 45-56, and Galbraith, *Proceedings of the British Academy* xxi (1935), 201-38. For a summary of scholarly opinions on the probability that Edward II himself composed a rhymed Latin lament during the time of his captivity, see Galbraith, *Proceedings*, p: 231 n. 6, and Aspin, *Anglo-Norman Political Songs*, 93-6. On the literacy of Edward II, see Johnstone, *Edward of Carnarvon*, 18-21.

[34] He is not in Dr. Emden's registers for Oxford or Cambridge.

[35] Johnstone, *Edward of Carnarvon*, 20-1; cf. Reg. Orleton Hereford, 4. The notion was still held by Foss, writing in 1851 (*The Judges of England* iii, 288).

Let us first consider Reynolds as patron and promoter of learning. While bishop of Worcester his record in granting licenses for study was unusually good in comparison with other bishops who were supposedly more learned.[36] And there are indications that, during his years as archbishop, Reynolds took an active interest in the universities although he was not himself a graduate. In correspondence with the chancellor and masters of Cambridge, he expressed a positive concern for their university in connection with his commissaries' visitation of Ely diocese.[37] There is no evidence, however, for the assertion of Bateson that Reynolds was once chancellor of Cambridge.[38]

At Oxford, Reynolds by reason of his position as archbishop was the patron of Merton College, and there is evidence that he took this duty seriously. He once inhibited the bishop of Lincoln from visiting Merton,[39] and it was apparently Reynolds who initiated the process for appropriating the church of Wolford (Warwickshire) to Merton.[40] In 1326 we find Reynolds enquiring into the health and administrative competence of the warden M. John of Wantage.[41] At Reynolds' request the warden and scholars of Merton promised a scholarship among the founder's kin to one William called 'Perschore' of Windsor, a 'consanguineus' of Reynolds.[42]

In his relations with Oxford University as a whole, Reynolds was personally active in adjudication of the dispute between the University and the friars preachers,[43] in the collection of at least two levies for the

---

[36] Haines, *Administration*, p. 206 n. 8. Haines here observes that Miss Edwards' statement in CQR cxxxviii (1944), 79, that Reynolds issued 156 licenses, is mistaken, a mistake that is also repeated in Pantin, *The English Church*, p. 39 n. 2. The origin of this mistake can be seen from inspection of her London M.A. thesis, 'The Personnel and Political Activities of the English Episcopate during the Reign of Edward II', 477, where her original computation gave the figure of 156 as the total years of absence rather than the total of licences granted.

[37] RR ff. 121v-122.

[38] Bateson, *Cambridge Gild Records*, xviii and 24; cf. VCH *Cambs.* iii, 331, and Tanner, *Historical Register of the University of Cambridge*, 15-16.

[39] RR ff. 56, 122.

[40] This is the implication of the evidence in *Liber Ecclesiae Wigorniensis*, ed. Bloom, pp. ix, 39, 40, and RR f. 121v. For the part of Thomas Cobham in this matter, see Haines, *Administration*, 240, 247, and Reg. Cobham, 130, 135-6.

[41] RR f. 194. In this letter to Reynolds the master and scholars of Merton describe their house as 'domus vestra et nostra'.

[42] Cant. Cath. MS Reg. L, ff. 157, 160v; *Lit. Cant.* nos. 248, 255; HMC Ninth Rep., I, app., 97; Emden, *Oxford* iii, 1466. Selection for such a scholarship might imply (1) relation by kinship to the founder, Walter de Merton; (2) provenance from the diocese of Winchester; or (3) status as a poor orphan (Squibb, *Founders' Kin*, 6-7).

[43] Below, Appendix 6, no. 26.

University throughout the southern province – one as a general financial subsidy [44] and one to pay the stipend for the converted Jew John of Bristol to teach Hebrew there in obedience to the decree *Inter sollicitudines* of the council of Vienne,[45] and in the protection of a certain scholar of the University who had been attacked by the violent hands of laymen.[46] The University had already sought Reynolds' advice while he was still bishop of Worcester concerning some business of Balliol College, which Dr. Salter surmises was the building of its chapel.[47] In his words as archbishop Reynolds described the University as a place 'which gives polish to the uncultivated and strength to those who are weak', as a place 'which like a field of fertility brings forth rich fruits, in which the kernels of knowledge are brought together and men rich in a variety of virtues are produced', and as a place 'that produces flowers and fruits both rich and beautiful, from which an incessant fragrance of renowned fame distils the realm of England with honour'.[48]

As a result of a visitation of his cathedral priory early during his archiepiscopate, Reynolds urged that three or four of the Canterbury monks be sent to study at a university,[49] and later he encouraged the Canterbury priory to provide its own claustral lecturer with a proper

[44] Reg. London, 214-15; Reg. Martival ii, 235-7, 245-7; Cant. Cath. MS Eastry Cor. i, 21; *Lit. Cant.* no. 120; HMC Eighth Rep., 354.

[45] RR ff. 98v seq., 101; Wilkins ii, 499; Reg. Martival ii, 341-3; Roth, *Oxoniensia* xv (1950), p. 63 and n. 1; Roth, *History of the Jews in England*, 145. This canon of Vienne, which decreed that the cost of such instruction at Oxford should be borne by the English king, may be found in *Conciliorum Oecumenicorum Decreta*, ed. Alberigo, 379-80; Schroeder, *Disciplinary Decrees*, 395-7 (English) and 615-16 (Latin); and CIC, Clem., lib. V, tit. i, cap. i (Friedberg, vol. ii, col. 1179).

[46] M. Robert de Bridlington: RR f. 109, not noted in Emden, *Oxford* i, 265, under either clerk of the name.

[47] *Liber Epistolaris* of Richard de Bury, no. 438; Salter, *Balliol College Deeds*, no. 607, pp. 335-6.

[48] The first two texts are dated probably 1319-1320: 'que rudes erudit et debiles efficit virtuosos', and 'que velud fertilitatis ager fructus profert uberes, in quo grana sciencie colliguntur, virique producuntur virtutum varietate fecundi' (Salter, Pantin, and Richardson, *Formularies* i, nos. 36, 41, pp. 47-8, 54-5; *Liber Epistolaris* of Richard de Bury, no. 390). The third is dated 8 August 1319: 'que flores et fructus fecundos et decoros producit, ex quibus fame celebris regnum Anglie odor distillat indesinens cum honore' (Reg. London, 214-15; Reg. Martival ii, 235). In this and most other quotations from Reynolds, as from many other medieval figures of note, the question must be left open whether his words were really his own or were composed or copied from some other source by one of his assistants.

[49] RR f. 70; Wilkins ii, 455-6: 'ita quod tam nobilis ecclesia non cogatur pro lectore aliena suffragia mendicare', – probably a reference to the succession of Franciscans who had lectured at Canterbury.

study and to assign him a stipend and an assistant.[50] This last letter is especially worth quoting for the picture it gives of Reynolds' views on learning:

> Among all the responsibilities weighing upon our shoulders, we take it as the highest responsibility that the care for those persons reading in holy writ be stimulated and the fervour of their study be augmented, so that, from this, rich fruits may come forth for God's church in due time. And because we all without distinction of age desire to gain knowledge by reason of nature herself, as the most eloquent Julian testifies when he says 'Even if I had one foot in the grave I would still seek to learn more', so each of us ought quite reasonably to venerate our lectors and doctors by whom we are taught. For such persons like the stars of heaven are not extinguished by the density of the night, thus cleaving to the firmament of holy scripture, and they permit no persons instructed by them to be darkened by the false and frivolous fantasies of heretics. And in this way the faith shines un-contaminated, Christian observances flourish, and the enemies of the cross of Christ are put to confusion.[51]

Beyond this role of Reynolds as patron and promoter of learning, there are still other indications that he personally was not illiterate. In his years at Canterbury, Reynolds was able to use a clever phrase at times,[52] he is known to have preached on various occasions,[53] he could quote from the Bible in his letters,[54] and he was capable of expounding at least some

---

[50] Cant. Cath. MS Cart. Ant. C1294b; *Lit. Cant.* no. 49; HMC Fifth Rep., app., 447; Pantin, *The English Church*, 118; cf. Cambridge, Trinity College MS R.5.41, f. 119.

[51] Printed in Reg. Hethe, 341: 'Inter cunctas solicitudines nostris humeris in-cumbentes, summa solicitudine captamus ut in sacra pagina legencium excitetur cura et studendi fervor amplietur; ut ex hoc fructus uberes in dei ecclesia proveniant tempore oportuno. Et quoniam omnes absque delectu etatis naturaliter scire desideramus, testante eloquentissimo Juliano, qui dicit, "Etsi pedem haberem in tumulo, adhuc addiscere vellem", singuli nostros lectores et doctores per quos instruimur, racionaliter debemus venerari. Hii enim sicuti stelle celi noctis densitate non extinguntur, sic inherentes sancte scripture firmamento, per ipsosque imbuendos nullis hereticorum ymaginacionibus cavellosis et falsis permittunt obfuscari; sicque fides incontaminata splendet, Christiano-rum ritus pululat, et crucis Christi inimici exterminantur confusi'. Dated 1324; the late Professor F. Wormald suggested to me that 'the most eloquent Julian' may be Julian of Toledo or Julian of Le Mans. For some parallel wording, see Daniel 12.3.

[52] One example, RR f. 273: 'Legere et non intelligere sit necligere ... lecta necligantur non intellecta'. For a quotation similar to the first half of this one, see Cal. Reg. Bransford, 27, 511; I owe this reference to Dr. R. M. Haines.

[53] RR ff. 125, 198v; Cambridge, Trinity College MS R.5.41, f. 124v; Wharton, *Anglia Sacra* i, 367; *Chron. Lanercost*, 255; Clarke, *Medieval Representation and Consent*, 179, 184.

[54] RR ff. 66v, 115v, 272; Wilkins ii, 453; Reg. Martival ii, 139, 464.

elementary points in dogmatic, moral, and ascetical theology.[55] At his own request he secured a faculty from Clement v to grant indulgences of 100 days to all penitent and confessed who were present when he celebrated mass or preached.[56] John xxII once thanked him for translating papal letters for Edward II from Latin into French,[57] and Reynolds once caused his visitation injunctions for Davington priory (osb, Kent) to be set out in French so that the nuns there could understand them.[58]

Still more evidence comes from my own study of Reynolds' household and familial associates. Not only did he promote studies at his cathedral and in the universities but he also surrounded himself with an impressive number of men of academic qualifications. During his archiepiscopate, out of a total of seventy-nine clerks that I have identified in his archiepiscopal register as being members of his household or service in some sense, no less than thirty-eight were called *magistri* and of these there were six doctors of civil law, one doctor of canon law, one of both laws, and one of medicine, as well as at least two others of academic distinction.[59] Simon Moene, D.M., physician to Reynolds and his household from 1317 onwards, had been a regent master of Oxford as early as 1312.[60] There are, moreover, indications that Reynolds was willing to consult doctors of theology and canon law about points on which he felt the need for advice.[61] And Geoffrey Poterel, the monk from Canterbury whom Reynolds retained in his household, had studied at Paris.[62]

Of great interest, finally, in establishing Reynolds' literary inclinations is the record of his own private library. This survives in the Public Record Office among the accounts of the keepers of temporalities after his death,

---

[55] RR ff. 66v, 106, 106v, 108v, 272v; below, Appendix 11, nos. 68, 71; Wilkins ii, 445-6, 453; Cant. Cath. MS Eastry Cor. vii, 6.

[56] RR f. 212; Wilkins ii, 435; CPL. ii, 121; Reg. Clem. v, no. 10151.

[57] RR f. 218; Wilkins ii, 470; CPL. ii, 430-1; Vatican Archives, Reg. Vat. 110, f. 119 (top foliation): 'reducendis seu transferendis de Latino in Gallicum'.

[58] RR f. 273. On the use of French by bishops in their dealings with nuns in the fourteenth century, cf. Legge, *Anglo-Norman in the Cloisters*, 48-9.

[59] D.C.L.: M. John de Badesley, M. Thomas de Chartham, M. Adam Murimuth, M. Benedict de Paston, M. Robert de Redeswell, M. John de Ros; D.Cn.L.: M. Adam Orleton; D.Cn.&C.L.: M. William de Knapton; D.M.: M. Simon Moene. The other two were M. William de Duffield and M. Robert de Norton. For these see Emden, *Cambridge*, 340, and Emden, *Oxford* i, 601; ii, 1287, 1329-30, 1375, 1402-4; iii, 1433-4, 1590-1, 2209. Badesley and Chartham are not listed by Emden, but they are consistently designated by academic doctoral titles in Reynolds' Lambeth register.

[60] RR f. 19; Talbot and Hammond, *Medical Practitioners of Medieval England*, 323-4; Emden, *Oxford* ii, 1287.

[61] Cant. Cath. MS Eastry Cor. i, 57; v, 29.

[62] Cant. Cath. MS Misc. Accts. i, ff. 258v, 265.

and thus forms one more inventory to be added to the eighteen collections of books that Miss Edwards found owned by the bishops of Edward II's reign.[63] While this inventory bears out the facts that he was not a theologian or a canon lawyer, it also establishes that a number of books were in his possession which only a man of some education and letters could use:

Unum librum de cronica Martini, unum libellum de gestis Alexandri, unum librum Ysidori minoris, unam bibleam in tribus voluminibus, unum libellum de Anticlaudiano, unum librum de geometria, unum ordinale, unum libellum de gestis Hibernie, unum libellum de significacione misse, unum libellum de vita Christiana ad sororem suam viduam, unum quaternum de vita beati Thome martiris, unum quaternum de gestis Troianorum, duos libellos de gestis Brutann', unum rotulum de Genesi depictum, unum quaternum de descripcione candelabri, unum hanaperium cum quinque ramis de corall', quosdam munimenta et rotulos, diversas bullas et alia munimenta, diversas cartas de libertatibus archiepiscopatus Cantuar' et alios quaternos de diversis tractatibus auctorum, duos libellos unum rubeum et alium nigrum unum de gestis Britann' et alium de vita clericorum, rotulos et alia munimenta diversa, duo paria cultellorum de iaspide, unum parvum cultellum et unum baculum pastorale modici vel nullius valoris, et unum librum predicacionum et unum quaternum similiter de predicacionibus.[64]

[63] Edwards, CQR cxxxviii (1944), 69-71.

[64] Transcribed here from PRO SC6/1128/7; it is repeated, with only minor variations, in SC6/1128/8 and E372/173/44. In the first and last of these three MSS, values are assigned to the books, the highest being eight pounds for the Bible in three volumes. All books were apparently sold to Archbishop Mepham in 1328, and I have been unable to locate any of them surviving today. The 'cronica Martini' may well be the Chronicle of Martinus (Strepus) Polonus, abp. of Gniezno (Manitius, *Geschichte der lateinischen Literatur des Mittelalters*, vol. iii, pp. 408-11). For Alexander see Cary, *The Medieval Alexander*. The 'Anticlaudianus' was a long allegorical metric poem by Alan of Lille (died c. 1202-1203) on the effort of man to recover the original perfection of his nature; at least 32 MSS of it are known in England (Manitius, *Geschichte* iii, 797 seq.; Talbot, *Traditio* viii (1952), 403-4; Green, *Annuale Medievale* viii (1967), 3-16; Alain de Lille. *Anticlaudianus: Texte critique*, ed. Bossuat; and Alan of Lille. *Anticlaudianus*, transl. Sheridan). The 'gesta Hibernie' may be by Giraldus Cambrensis. The 'De vita Christiana ad sororem suam viduam' was a spurious work of St. Augustine (Migne, *Patrologiae, Series Latina*, vol. xl, col. 1031 seq., esp. cap. 15). For the Brut legend, see Taylor, EHR lxxii (1957), 423-37. The 'rotulus de Genesi depictus' would be quite unusual. For the 'descripcio candelabri' see Moore, *The Works of Peter of Poitiers*, 97-117, 188-96. The branches of coral may indicate a mild interest in sorcery of some sort. The 'gesta Britann' may be one of the MSS of Geoffrey of Monmouth, *History of the Britons*, now in Lambeth Palace (Sayers, BIHR xxxix (1966), 101). Archbishop Hubert Walter had also possessed two knives of jasper and of horn (Cheney, *Hubert Walter*, 176) which he left to his cathedral church of Canterbury

One can not help wondering, of course, how far Reynolds was acquainted with the inside as well as the outside of these books, and how far his own character and conduct were formed by their contents. What, for example, did he make of the deeds of Alexander or of the histories of the Trojans and Britons? Can we safely infer from the absence of theological works in this inventory that Reynolds read no theology at all, when, by contrast, the inventory of Winchelsey's books reveals a preponderance of heavy theological tomes but no histories of Alexander or the Trojans and Britons?[65] Surely Winchelsey must have read some history, and Reynolds probably read some theology. Nor can we conclude that Reynolds was unable to make use of canon law simply because no books on that subject are listed here. Especially in the years following the issue of the papal constitution *Execrabilis*, as we have seen,[66] he used canon law very cleverly. We may assume that Reynolds used his Bible and his books on preaching; he quoted from the Bible and he did preach. We also know from his testament or will that he bequeathed a Bible of three volumes (presumably the same one mentioned in the inventory as being sold to Mepham) to his cathedral priory at Canterbury.[67] Speculation about the influence of these books on his life could be endless, and the questions must be left open of how active Reynolds himself was in collecting them and of whether he personally read them: these questions remain open about the libraries of many persons. Yet it is certainly safe to conclude that this inventory when taken together with the other information at hand indicates a man of diverse opportunities for reading, a man able to draw upon the history of his own country and upon the examples of some of the figures in classical antiquity, a man who could read some Latin and French and who clearly saw value in the universities, and a man who possessed the literary equipment for a personal piety of his own.[68]

(Legg and Hope, *Inventories*, 50). I am indebted to the late Professor F. Wormald for assistance with some of these identifications.

[65] Emden, *Oxford* iii, 2059.

[66] Above, pp. 88-91.

[67] Cant. Cath. MS Cart. Ant. A14. None of Reynolds' other books are mentioned in his testament or will except his large and small breviaries and his two small missals.

[68] More can be said of Reynolds' piety: his membership in the guild of St. Mary at Cambridge (VCH *Cambs*. iii, 133; Camm, *Downside Review* xliii (1925), 9-14, shows the activities of this guild in the early fourteenth century; its primary purpose was prayer for the members, and Reynolds' name was entered upon its 'Bede Roll C'; Richard de Bury became a member of it a few years later; cf. Bateson, *Cambridge Gild Records*, 24); his discourses on prayer (below, Appendix 11, nos. 68, 71); his interest in the endowment of a chantry at Worcester cathedral (CPR 1307-13, 519); his relic of the true cross set within a

Like his earlier predecessor Becket, Reynolds too apparently felt no need for literary self-expression beyond the contents of his own official letters, and it was Becket, we may recall, who in 1163 had not dared preach because of his lack of skill in the Latin tongue.[69] Hubert Walter, too, had been criticized for poor latinity, one chronicler going so far as to pronounce him 'laicus et illiteratus'.[70] Miss Edwards and Dr. Pantin have convincingly rejected the supposed 'illiteracy' of some medieval bishops already,[71] and Beaumont of Durham, Burghersh of Lincoln, and Greenfield of York are among Reynolds' contemporaries who have already been cleared to some extent of such accusations. 'Illiteracy' is a charge that the historian today must not levy without hard evidence. This evidence is lacking in the case of Reynolds, cumulative indications point to the contrary, and I believe we must reject this charge of the chroniclers against him for these reasons.[72]

Another aspect of Reynolds' personality not unrelated to his interest in learning was his ability as an administrator, and here again it may be suggested that he was more competent than the traditional view would indicate. Tout himself doubts whether or not we can trust a chronicler who ignores Reynolds' early official career and Edward I's responsibility for his choice.[73] Even if our Walter was the son of a baker of Windsor named Reginald[74] – and the evidence to demonstrate his connection with Windsor is considerable[75] – it is unlikely that Edward I would have

---

cross of gold ornamented with precious stones, value estimated at £200 in money of the day (CUL MS Ee.v.31, f. 162v; Cant. Cath. MS Cart. Ant. C181); his legacies to the shrines of St. Thomas at Canterbury, Our Lady of Walsingham, and St. Edmund at Pontigny; his various breviaries and missals; his endowment of candles for the church of St. John Baptist in New Windsor (the last three are all in his will, Cant. Cath. MS Cart. Ant. A14). On the identity of his tomb in the south choir aisle at Canterbury, see Woodman, *Canterbury Cathedral Chronicle* 69 (1975), 14-23.

    [69] Poole, *Domesday Book to Magna Carta*, 197.
    [70] Cheney, *Hubert Walter*, 164, 181.
    [71] Edwards, CQR cxxxviii (1944), 57, 62-5, 85-6; Pantin, *The English Church in the Fourteenth Century*, 42-3.
    [72] For my own views of why the notion of Reynolds' illiteracy persisted, see *Studies in Church History* v (1969), 58-68.
    [73] *Edward II*, p. 71 n. 3.
    [74] 'Walterus, Reginaldi cujusdam pistoris Windesoriensis filius': Wharton, *Anglia Sacra* i, 532 (the *Continuatio* of Worcester); cf. Edwards, TRHS, 5th series, vol. ix (1959), 66.
    [75] Birchington (Wharton, *Anglia Sacra* i, 18) says he was 'of Windsor'. One Ralph of Windsor was Reynolds' clerk and 'commensalis' at Worcester (RWR, 66; Haines, *Administration*, 95-6) and is described as 'consanguineus' in RR f. 281 and Cant. Cath. MS Cart. Ant. A14. Reynolds bequeathed him a pair of jasper knives. We know that this same

presented Reynolds to important benefices[76] and allowed him to continue as head of the prince's household and manager of the prince's finances if he had been wholly incompetent. Whatever contemporaries may have thought of him, he neither suffered the fate of Gaveston nor, later, that of the Despensers. In Reynolds, moreover, for the first time since Hubert Walter in the time of King John, an archbishop of Canterbury, if only for a short while, also served as royal chancellor. His work as treasurer and chancellor of the realm and keeper of the great seal has been set forth by Tout,[77] who draws attention to the modifications in titles that the crisis of the Ordinances produced. Although Reynolds seldom acted personally in these offices (such personal control, at least of the chancery, was not the norm under Edward II), yet much of the machinery of state did move under his name and nominal supervision. As chancellor Reynolds also performed certain important ecclesiastical functions, nominating to benefices in the king's gift of less than twenty marks value,[78] visiting hospitals of royal foundation,[79] and exercising supervision as head of the Chapel Royal.[80] Reynolds no longer held official position in the government of the state after 20 April 1314, but Davies and Phillips show that he

---

Ralph was aged thirty-two when Reynolds died in 1327, and that at the age of fifteen he had received at Reynolds' request a dispensation from Clement V to hold churches in plurality (Reg. Clem. v, no. 10160; CPL. ii, 121; RWR, 151). An obit for the father and mother of one Ralph of Windsor is entered in 'Bede Roll C' of the Cambridge guild of St. Mary following that of Reynolds himself, the full text reading 'Pro anima domini Walteri Reynald quondam Cantuariensis archiepiscopi. Et animabus Willelmi patris domini Radulphi de Windeshore et Agnetis matris eius' (Bateson, *Cambridge Gild Records*, 24). Reynolds had another 'consanguineus', William called 'Perschore' of Windsor (above, p. 251; Emden, *Oxford* iii, 1466). One Nicholas Burnel of Windsor, acolyte, was presented to the church of Upper Helmsley (Yorks., N. Riding), in patronage of the master and brothers of St. Leonard's Hospital, York, in 1310 while Reynolds was its master (below, Appendix 12, no. 8; Reg. Greenfield iii, 57, no. 1261), and it was probably this same Nicholas who was ordained subdeacon by Reynolds as bishop of Worcester in 1311 (RWR, 124) and priest as archbishop of Canterbury in 1317 (RR f. 179v). Burnel figures prominently in Reynolds' Canterbury register as 'clericus familiaris' (RR ff. 19, 121v, 132v, 173v, 179v, 253). Reynolds' will tells us that Reynolds customarily sustained an endowment of candles for the church of St. John Baptist in New Windsor, and he bequeathed certain altar and mass vestments to the same church (Cant. Cath. MS Cart. Ant. A14). He also held several acres of land in Windsor forest of the king (CFR 1327-37, 165; CCR 1337-9, 364). There was a 'Reginald the Baker' among the witnesses to a Windsor document in 1332 (Dalton, *Manuscripts of St. George's Chapel, Windsor Castle*, 405).

[76] Below, Appendix 12.
[77] *Edward II*, 163, 285-8; *Chapters* ii, 215.
[78] Pantin, *The English Church*, 30; CCW, 395 seq., 401.
[79] Churchill, *Canterbury Administration* i, 149; RR ff. 34v, 45v.
[80] Rymer II:i, 193; *Placita Parliamentaria*, ed. Ryley, 535; CCR 1307-13, 586.

continued to exercise an extremely important unofficial role as one of the leaders of the king's council on into the year 1316.[81] He was a prominent figure on the commission appointed in the same year for reform of the royal household and the kingdom,[82] and during the next few months and years he frequently served as one of the principal intermediaries between the king and Thomas of Lancaster and the magnates.[83]

Recent interpretations of the reign of Edward II, moreover, have served to heighten the significance that must be accorded to the mediatorial role of Reynolds and the other prelates of Canterbury province, especially their initiative and diplomacy in the negotiations that surrounded the treaty of Leake in 1318. Phillips and Maddicott are agreed that there was no 'baronial opposition' to Edward II in the sense in which the term has been previously used to identify a particular group with a coherent plan or distinct set of policies,[84] and Phillips denies the existence of any 'middle party' at all[85] while Maddicott re-locates its origins several months later than has been previously supposed.[86] Thus, while Maddicott stresses the mediatorial importance of a middle party whose nucleus was 'Pembroke and the bishops',[87] Phillips proceeds to classify the king's capable and experienced councillors – who wanted a settlement with Lancaster – as one group, the king's favourites – whose position depended upon the king's passing infatuation and who did their best to destroy all hope of a settlement – as a second group, and an ecclesiastical group – consisting of

[81] Davies, *Baronial Opposition*, 331-6; Edwards, EHR lix (1944), 327; Phillips, *Aymer de Valence*, 84-5, 92, 96, 102, 106, 276; cf. Maddicott, *Thomas of Lancaster*, 166.

[82] Phillips, *Aymer de Valence*, 95-6, 143-4; Maddicott, *Thomas of Lancaster*, 182; Edwards, EHR lix (1944), 330.

[83] Phillips, *Aymer de Valence*, 123-4, 131, 156-8, 161, 164, 167-8, 170, 209, 217, 219. Reynolds' great seals of episcopal office, both from Worcester and from Canterbury, depict on either side of his effigy shields bearing the arms of England. This conjuncture of the symbols of 'church' and 'state' on Reynolds' seals is worthy of note, whether or not the study of ecclesiastical sigillography comes in time to vindicate the conjectures that his were the earliest episcopal seals to introduce the royal arms and that this may in some way have been related to the coincidence that his period as chancellor overlapped part of his time at Worcester and Canterbury. For discussion of these points, see Woodward, *Treatise on Ecclesiastical Heraldry*, 10, and Hope, *Proceedings of the Society of Antiquaries*, 2nd series, vol. 11 (1887), 280. Especially good specimens of this Canterbury seal are attached to BL Add. Charter 17353, Cant. Cath. MS Cart. Ant. C819, and LAO MS Dij/61/ii/20. For a picture of the first of these, see the frontispiece, plate A.

[84] Phillips, *Aymer de Valence*, viii, 21; Maddicott, *Thomas of Lancaster*, 325.

[85] *Aymer de Valence*, viii; for some reservations about Phillips' interpretation, see the review of his book by B. Wilkinson in *Speculum* xlix (1974), 752-3.

[86] *Thomas of Lancaster*, 195, 199, 208, 215.

[87] Ibid., 214-15, 221, 228.

the archbishop and prelates of Canterbury province, Archbishop Alexander de Bicknor of Dublin, and the papal envoys Cardinals Gaucelme and Luca – as a third.[88] The prelates, who were seen by their contemporaries as a neutral body that could be trusted by both sides, were well placed to mediate collectively between the king and Lancaster because they could not be suspected of seeking power for themselves as a group.[89] Phillips speaks of 'the province of Canterbury' as taking the lead in this matter in 1318,[90] and both he and Maddicott note that it was Reynolds and Bicknor who drew up the articles discussed in June of that year at Tutbury and elsewhere.[91] Phillips in his reassessment concludes that the 'really vital role' in the Leake talks played by the prelates of Canterbury province and the papal envoys

> has not hitherto been given the weight or the prominence which it deserves. Without this clerical intervention, which was made with the full knowledge and agreement of the King and his Council, it is unlikely that peace talks would have begun at all and almost certain that once begun they would not have succeeded to the extent they did.[92]

This observation seems well put, regardless of which way future debate may move concerning other aspects of the political and constitutional significance of Edward II's reign. The mediatorial stance taken by Reynolds in collaboration with the prelates of his province, especially in 1318 and again (with less success) in 1321,[93] contributed a considerable degree of stability that almost certainly would not have been achieved at that time (as I shall suggest below) if the English church had still been under the stormy leadership of a primate like Robert Winchelsey.

In ecclesiastical administration, it has been established convincingly by Professor Cheney that Reynolds did not originate the so-called provincial constitutions of 1322 attributed to him in Lyndwood and Wilkins[94] – an error that may well have occasioned Stubbs' comment that Reynolds sought to limit the ordination of unfit persons.[95] Yet there is a modicum of truth in Stubbs' assertion that Reynolds sought to limit pluralities, as we

---

[88] Phillips, *Aymer de Valence*, 147-8, 153.

[89] Ibid., 148, 174-5.

[90] Ibid., 161, 165, 174.

[91] Phillips, 165; Maddicott, 221-2.

[92] Phillips, 278.

[93] Ibid., 209, 278.

[94] EHR 1 (1935), 414-15; Cheney, *Medieval Texts and Studies*, 169-71; but also see P&C ii, 1387-8.

[95] *Constitutional History* (1929 ed.) ii, 438-9; also in Tout, DNB (1909 re-issue) xvi, 964.

have seen,[96] even though he himself had obtained several benefices in plurality before his provision to Worcester[97] and though the effects of *Execrabilis* were mitigated and manipulated by the English episcopate under his leadership.[98] At Canterbury perhaps his major administrative triumph was his clever application of the apostolic provisory faculty,[99] and material exists to show that he made extensive and systematic use of other faculties that he obtained from Clement v.[100] Although he undertook no personal visitation of his Worcester diocese,[101] yet there is evidence from his Canterbury administration that he made a number of diocesan and metropolitical visitations, at least some of which were in person.[102] As primate he kept a register for visitation, but it no longer survives.[103] Reynolds was present in his Worcester diocese for only eight months out of five years,[104] but after his translation to Canterbury he was frequently in residence at various manors of his diocese other than Lambeth.[105] At Worcester he at least made a start towards an extensive overhaul of manorial finances,[106] and as primate he carried out improvements at Lambeth, including works on the great front gate.[107] He took steps to augment the lands attached to his prebend of Quincy in Lyons cathedral.[108] It was probably he who brought to Canterbury from Worcester the developed notions of a sequestrator-general and an archi-episcopal council – administrative ideas which, however, in the long run may not have been prominent in his Canterbury administration. He also

[96] Above, pp. 72-73.

[97] Below, Appendix 12.

[98] Above, pp. 72 seq.

[99] Above, pp. 59 seq.

[100] For his dispensations, and his appointments of 'tabelliones' by apostolic authority, cf. Churchill, *Canterbury Administration* i, 507. For his prerogative nominations of women 'in monialem' see RR f. 49v and cf. Cant. Cath. MS Reg. G, f. 1v.

[101] Haines, *Administration*, 77-8.

[102] Churchill, *Canterbury Administration* i, 134-8, 307-14. There is some evidence of visitations other than those mentioned by Miss Churchill: Reg. Sandale, 13; Reg. Asserio, 394, 607-8; Cant. Cath. MS Cart. Ant. C412; *Chartulary of Winchester Cathedral*, ed. Goodman, no. 35; BL. MS Arundel 435, f. 305; LAO MSS Dij/62/1/12-14, and Dij/88/2/33-4; Salter, Pantin, and Richardson, *Formularies* i, no. 36, p. 47.

[103] Churchill, *Canterbury Administration* i, 314.

[104] Haines, *Administration*, 77. Of interest here is the king's safe conduct on 20 Oct. 1312 for royal servants with carts to carry Reynolds' books, rolls, and other goods from Worcester to London (CPR 1307-13, 504).

[105] Below, Appendix 13.

[106] Haines, *Administration*, 146.

[107] Lambeth MS Estate Document 545.

[108] RR f. 123v; above, p. 241.

encouraged the practice of commendations of churches in both his dioceses.[109] And he could be a stern prelate on occasions, assigning a penance of bread and water,[110] commanding a procession in bare feet,[111] rebuking his archdeacon's official for assigning an unsuitable penance.[112] The Worcester monks thought well enough of him to grant him confraternity when he was translated from their cathedral.[113] The pope, too, placed confidence in Reynolds' orgnizational abilities for the purpose of collecting various financial levies, especially Peter's Pence, the tribute, procurations of papal envoys, and various tenths levied by papal authority.[114] A full analysis of the strictly ecclesiastical side of Reynolds' career in his Lambeth register may reveal even more evidence of his administrative competence.

Thus far our discussion suggests that the assertions of the chroniclers hostile to Reynolds should be modified on some three important points: there is no definite proof of simony connected with his provision to Canterbury,[115] there is no positive evidence that he was illiterate and considerable to suggest that he was even a modest patron of academic learning, and there are indications that he was of at least average competence as an administrator. These points about his character bring us back to the theme of Trokelowe: a man who could moderate the tribulations of the English church and realm. While not seeking to exaggerate the stature of Reynolds or whitewash his character absolutely, let us now compare him with some of his contemporaries with a view to the possibility of further readjusting the perspective in which he must be seen. Can he, at least in some ways, be seen as a leader? Let us try to construct a picture of Reynolds which, although faithful to the evidence, is more in line with Trokelowe than with Robert of Reading. The tentative nature of this undertaking, however, must be emphasized.

When Reynolds went to Canterbury he made a definite break with the tradition of Winchelsey. Of some 111 men who from Reynolds' Lambeth register can be described as members of his household or clerks in his service in some way, only twelve can be traced to any close association

[109] Haines, *Administration*, 78, 116-20, 199; Churchill, *Canterbury Administration* i, 16, 61, 114.

[110] CUL MS Ee.v.31, f. 236.

[111] *Ann. Paul.*, 278.

[112] Above, p. 203.

[113] *Liber Albus of Worcester*, ed. Wilson, p. 40, no. 605. A similar grant was made to Thomas of Lancaster (p. 46).

[114] Lunt, *Financial Relations* i, 64-7, 71-2, 165-72, 379-410, 568-9, 622-3.

[115] Above, p. 245 n. 5.

with his predecessor in Winchelsey's register. Of the eleven doctoral graduates and men of academic distinction who advised Reynolds, only one can be found in the service of Winchelsey.[116] Whereas some previous primates, such as Pecham, must have placed high value upon the continuity of archiepiscopal administration,[117] in the case of Reynolds the major background of men in his service was his own administration at Worcester. Some of these men had even been with him in the household of the prince of Wales, and such associations find their undoubted parallel in the fact that almost the entire household staff of the prince himself was retained when the prince became king.[118] Mr. Conway Davies has emphasized the importance of Edward II's household for a proper understanding of the reign,[119] and the same may be said for the household of Walter Reynolds in understanding his career.

Reynolds also differed from Winchelsey in another way. He tried to work with the crown and seldom in direct opposition to it. This was, of course, to be expected from his own background in the royal service and his close personal relationship to the king. Whereas Winchelsey's independent and uncompromising convictions as leader of the church had often compelled him to oppose the head of state, Reynolds was a man of entirely different disposition. He, for example, had served as intermediary between Winchelsey and the king in 1310.[120] And whereas Winchelsey has been seen as giving a lead to the so-called baronial opposition and ordaining movement earlier in the reign, Reynolds was a leader of the mediating prelates, whom some historians have included within a 'middle party' in 1318.[121] It is probably true that Reynolds was incapable of thinking in the high terms of Winchelsey, but he did have a genuine desire to see the king and realm at peace and he used his influence to this end. The priory of Ely in 1315 explained why no resistance had been offered to Reynolds' commissaries after their visitation:

> sibi resistere ab ecclesia Elyensi nullus audebat, tam propter diutinam sedis apostolice vacacionem quia si quis appellasset non existente papa remedium non optinuisset, tam propter regiam potestatem quia archiepiscopus tunc

---

[116] M. John de Ros.

[117] Douie, *Archbishop Pecham*, 62.

[118] Tout, *Edward II*, 72.

[119] *Baronial Opposition*, 73. I am preparing a separate study of Reynolds' archiepiscopal household.

[120] Reg. Winchelsey, 1043.

[121] Above, pp. 259-60; Maddicott, *Thomas of Lancaster*, 117, 119, 124, 131; Edwards, EHR lix (1944), 314-25; Emden, *Oxford* iii, 2057-8.

> temporis erat consiliarius et ductor domini regis et si episcopus vel prior
> cum capitulo ei restitisset rex ad instanciam archiepiscopi libertates ecclesie
> et dominia temporalia causa ficta et simulata in manu eius cepisset vel eis[122]
> dampnum perpetrasset et sic ob maius malum evitandum minus malum
> permiserunt.[123]

Reynolds wrote letters to numerous ecclesiastical authorities backing royal nominations of persons as bishops, prebendaries, parish priests, abbesses, and nuns.[124] His policy of supporting the king's requests for clerical taxation may have contributed to his own unpopularity with a number of the chroniclers, but in view of the king's unpredictable attitudes – insisting that Reynolds cancel one convocation that had already been called,[125] sending messengers with financial demands to interrupt another[126] – it is hard to see what other course he could have followed. And in spite of strong protests from the non-episcopal clergy, who quite accurately saw that he was failing to lead them in the same way that Winchelsey had done,[127] he seems to have achieved at least moderate success in persuading the prelates themselves to favour such grants.[128]

Reynolds was capable of giving a lead to the English episcopal hierarchy on other occasions as well, both in support of the crown and also – in a tactful way – independently of it. Reynolds certainly had not the dominating personality of Winchelsey, but Miss Edwards may at some points have been too ready to accept the conventional view of Reynolds as unable and unwilling to lead.[129] Miss Maude Clarke, on the other hand, has spoken of 'Reynolds' party' among the bishops, consisting of prelates who followed their primate's lead on the question of taxation.[130] Reynolds' action in the aftermath of *Execrabilis* and his

---

[122] MS *eiis*.

[123] BL MS Add. 41612, ff. 34v-35; cf. Churchill, *Canterbury Administration* i, 309-10 n. 5.

[124] E.g., RR ff. 67, 117, 123, 125v, 165v.

[125] RR f. 308; CCR 1323-7, 153; CUL MS Ee.v.31; f. 232.

[126] BL MS Cott. Vespasian E.xxi, ff. 52v-53.

[127] Kemp, *Counsel and Consent*, 92-9; above, pp. 185-87; Denton, *Journal of Medieval History* i (1975), 317. His attitude towards the lower clergy in seeking to bring the ecclesiastical assemblies of his province into parliament, at least for the purpose of taxation, has nonetheless been seen as an opposition to 'entrenched views of clerical privilege' (Denton, 'Walter Reynolds and Ecclesiastical Politics 1313-1316', 261-2, 266, 271).

[128] Clarke, *Medieval Representation and Consent*, 334-5; Denton, 'Walter Reynolds and Ecclesiastical Politics 1313-1316', 258, 260, 266-7, 273-4.

[129] EHR lix (1944), 314, 326-7, 341, 347.

[130] *Medieval Representation and Consent*, 132-3, 334-5.

decision to follow the papal mandate about the Templars in spite of the king's threat have already been set forth, and his skilful use of the apostolic provisory faculty – to provide positions of revenue and prestige for many of his own staff and those in royal service – also gave an example which he encouraged other bishops to accept. The mediatorial role he took, together with his own suffragans, in the political affairs surrounding the treaty of Leake in 1318 has already been noted. If, as has been suggested, Reynolds' primacy witnessed a general policy of episcopal collaboration with the crown up to about the end of 1320, followed by a noticeable decline of cohesion and consistency,[131] then Reynolds' decision to follow the papal mandate about the Templars after the crisis in the October parliament of the same year may provide additional confirmation of a turning-point at that time.[132] And even though he had had an earlier dispute with Adam Orleton over the collection of the Hereford *sede vacante* income,[133] Reynolds in 1324 led the bishops in protecting Orleton when he was accused of treason.[134]

Our primate was also able to spread his influence beyond the members of his episcopal college in a way that has received little attention thus far – his frequent issue of provincial mandates for prayers on behalf of the crown. The frequency of such mandates was within his archiepiscopal discretion, and during his primacy he issued at least fourteen of them. 'Nos Anglici, qui catholice fidei devote tenemus unitatem', Reynolds began in one of his mandates, 'ad Christum, qui salvos facit sperantes in se, totalem erigere debemus mentis nostre intencionem...'.[135] These mandates for intercessions, sermons, fasting, processions, and almsgiving, usually coupled with indulgences of forty days, were ratified in numerous documents issued by the suffragans of his province[136] and were apparently intended to be effective in all cathedral, collegiate, monastic,

[131] Edwards, EHR lix (1944), 326-7.
[132] Above, pp. 225-26.
[133] Reg. Orleton Hereford, 23-5.
[134] Emden, *Oxford* ii, 1403; Reg. Orleton Hereford, pp. xxvi-xxvii; Trokelowe, *Chronica et Annales*, 141-2.
[135] Below, Appendix 11, no. 71; for his other mandates see nos. 25, 28, 32, 35, 41, 52, 55, 58, 60, 65, 68, 70, 73.
[136] E.g., Reg. Martival ii, 378, dated 1321: 'Venerabilis pater predictus (Reynolds) et septemdecim sue provincie Cant' suffraganei omnibus parochianis suis et eciam aliis vere contritis et confessis quorum diocesani indulgencias hujusmodi ratificaverunt qui pro salubri statu domini nostri regis quam in honore et bono conservet altissimus et eciam pro pace et tranquillitate regni sui oraverint pia mente quadraginta dies indulgencia concesserunt'. Cf. below, Appendix 11, no. 55.

and parochial churches. If they were, and there is some evidence in confirmation and none to the contrary, they must have been a notable factor in nourishing and uniting what support there was for the crown in Edward's reign.[137]

At the Canterbury cathedral priory, also, Reynolds marked a change from his predecessor. In view of the circumstances surrounding Reynolds' provision to the see by Clement v over the chapter's choice of Thomas Cobham, the ground was certainly laid for some hostility between the priory and the new primate. The Canterbury monks had not received official notice of the papal reservation of the see (dated 27 April 1313) until 7 July,[138] although the king had himself referred to the reservation in a letter to the pope written on the very day that he granted the monks the license to elect (23 May).[139] Then as if to add insult to injury, the actual

----

[137] No evidence exists to prove that Reynolds personally had any direct influence upon the designs of the seals that he used, but the design of the 'private round seal' of the Canterbury archbishops – of which the earliest description comes from his pontificate – is worthy of attention at this point. With the Trinity and two angels in the midst, its circumference depicts eighteen mitred bishops: the seventeen suffragans of Canterbury province gathered around their primate at top center, with his right hand in blessing and the primatial cross in his left. Inscriptions, perhaps the abbreviated names of their sees, or possibly words forming a single legend, are placed beneath the figure of each bishop. In the theology of the time, this would certainly have been recognized as an iconographic statement of the theoretical relationships of primacy and collegiality that were supposed to exist between the Canterbury archbishop and his suffragans. Whether Reynolds originated this representation we do not know, and how well the details of its design corresponded to realities of life may be a matter for conjecture, but it is certain that such a design could not help but speak of Reynolds' primatial leadership – at least in theory – to those who looked at it affixed upon the documents he sent them. The leading role that the prelates of the province collectively took, not only in prayer for the crown but also in political mediation (above, pp. 259-60) also gives the theory some substance. Contemporary descriptions of this seal by Reynolds, dating from 1320-1321 and 1327, are given in RR ff. 26v and 265v: 'sigillum nostrum privatum rotundum in custodia nostra remanens in cuius circumferencia octodecim episcoporum mitrata capita sunt insculpta'. For Reynolds' use of this seal, see RR ff. 26v, 66v, 67v, 118v, 265v, 283v; Lambeth MS 1212, p. 127; Cant. Cath. MS Reg. I, f. 343; Cant. Cath. MS Cart. Ant. A14 (Reynolds' will: 'ad maiorem cautelam clausum testamentum secreto meo sigillo rotundo feci consignari, ipso parvo sigillo apud me remanente'). For the theology of episcopal collegiality at this time, see Kemp, 'The Canterbury provincial chapter and the collegiality of bishops in the Middle Ages', and references cited therein. For discussions of this seal, see Churchill, *Canterbury Administration* i. 17; Fowler, *Archaeologia* lxxiv (1923-4), 111-12; and HMC Ninth Rep., I, app., 79. For its use, see also *Wykeham's Register* ii, 242. The earliest surviving example of this seal, depicted on the frontispiece, plate c, comes from 1376 in the archiepiscopate of Simon Sudbury.

[138] The only surviving copy of the bull of reservation, which is not entered in the papal registers, is found in Cant. Cath. MS Reg. Q, f. 89v (printed in Wilkins ii, 424-5); cf. CUL MS Ee.v.31, ff. 131v, 134; BL MS Add. 6159, f. 149v; Wilkins ii, 427-8.

[139] Richardson, EHR lvi (1941), 97-103.

bull providing Reynolds (dated 1 October) had somehow not reached the chapter until 8 January of the year following.[140] Also, the chapter's preference for Cobham had been grounded in part on personal and family ties, a background of status that Reynolds could not hope to match.[141] Clearly, then, the grounds were set for discord, and yet there was probably less friction between archbishop and monks during Reynolds' pontificate than under either Winchelsey before him or Mepham after him.

> Novit vestre discrecionis prudencia qualiter prelatus et subditi in Christo unum corpus existunt, ita quod ipse capud illi vero membra consistere dinoscuntur, unde sicut capud a ceteris membris decisum et ipsorum carens suffragio virtutis extat commodo destitutum, sic prelatus absque fulcimento et consilio subditorum nequaquam diu prospere subportatur...

wrote Reynolds as elect of Canterbury on 31 December 1313 in one of the earliest, if not the first, of his many letters to Prior Eastry. Reynolds in the same letter went on to express the hope

> quatinus spiritualis dileccionis fedus et vinculum unitatis inter nos contracta perpetuis temporibus illibata conservare ac indissolubili ligamine continuare velitis. Indecens enim est a capite membra discedere. Decet eciam et expedit patrem et filium se invicem mutua affeccione diligere, decet alterum alterius adversitati resistere, decet ipsos se utrumque exquisite consolacionis remedio confovere.[142]

And Reynolds kept up this spiritual bond with his Canterbury monks throughout his archiepiscopate. Just less than two months after the date of this letter he made his first visitation of the cathedral priory, confirming at that time the injunctions of Winchelsey.[143] In December of 1315 he issued visitation injunctions of his own – six in number.[144] He took a personal interest in appointments of monastic officers,[145] as well as in the correction of rebellious monks.[146] He often applied to the priory for loans,

---

[140] Cant. Cath. MS Reg. Q. f. 90v: 'Istam bullam recepit capitulum vi id. Ianuarii et non ante'.

[141] Below, pp. 272-73.

[142] Cant. Cath. MS Eastry Cor. vii, 6.

[143] RR ff. 33, 44; Cant. Cath. MS Eastry Cor. i, 59; HMC Rep. Var. Coll., i, 266; Cant. Cath. MS Reg. Q. f. 92 seq.

[144] RR f. 69v; Wilkins ii, 455-6.

[145] Cant. Cath. MS Eastry Cor., passim.

[146] For Robert of Thanet, see below, Appendix 6, no. 37; for Robert de Alyndone see Cant. Cath. MS Cart. Ant. C1294, all parts. References to both of these cases could be multiplied.

sometimes with success and sometimes not.[147] The priory for its part sought his aid to alleviate the burdens of royal taxation – 'Solet sponsus et pater sponsam suam et filios a molestis eventibus iugiter preservare', they wrote him on this matter in 1319.[148] The monks showered him with gifts,[149] and he bequeathed them several important legacies.[150] The year before his death Reynolds deeded them his archiepiscopal manor of Caldecote, after considerable discussion concerning its status as land held in chief of the king and as part of the archiepiscopal *mensa* under papal oath.[151]

Many letters on a variety of subjects were exchanged between the primate and the prior which still exist – some published[152] and some not – among the groups of Eastry Correspondence, *Cartae Antiquae*, Register L, and other documents at Canterbury, and they reveal a strikingly close relationship between Reynolds and Eastry. They demonstrate the considerable extent to which Eastry advised the primate, cautiously but realistically, even on important political affairs.[153] Whatever Reynolds may have thought – or known – of the fact that he had not been the original choice of either the pope or the Christ Church monks for the see of Canterbury, it can be concluded that his own relationships with the monks of his cathedral were remarkably happy and harmonious. The priory had had quarrels with Winchelsey over the system of nomination to monastic offices in the archbishop's gift, as well as over other matters, and the controversy over nominations broke out again under Mepham, whom the aging Eastry disliked considerably.[154] But no evidence of such discord has been found from the pontificate of Reynolds, and in this respect he may also be contrasted with Antony Bek 'in loco abbatis' at Durham. There the efforts of Bek to subdue his cathedral priory, which were vigorously resisted by the monks, finally triumphed in the papal decree *Debent superioribus* – a document whose interpretation (whether it

---

[147] E.g., Cant. Cath. MS Eastry Cor. i, 8; RR ff. 53v, 56v, 57, 102, 121.

[148] CUL MS Ee.v.31, ff. 208v, 210v.

[149] Lambeth MS 242, ff. 297-361v.

[150] Cant. Cath. MS Cart. Ant. A14.

[151] Modern Calcott (Kent), NE. of Canterbury. RR f. 196v; CUL MS Ee.v.31, ff. 249v, 253v, 261; Cant. Cath. MS Reg. K, ff. 253v-254; Reg. L, f. 146; Cant. Cath. MS Cart. Ant. C819, C820; Reg. John XXII, no. 26728; CPL ii, 254. There are numerous other references to the grant.

[152] HMC Ninth Rep., I, appendix; HMC Rep. Var. Coll.; *Literae Cantuarienses*.

[153] For use of this correspondence in constructing narrative of the last years of Edward II's reign, see Clarke, *Medieval Representation and Consent*, 177-8, 189.

[154] Reg. Winchelsey, 1314-15; Smith, *Canterbury Cathedral Priory*, 8, 35-6; Knowles, *The Religious Orders* i, 52, 255-6.

was intended to be local or general in application) puzzled even Prior Eastry.[155]

And if Reynolds brought an era of peaceful cooperation to the history of the relations between the primate and the principal cathedral of the realm, so also in the external relations of the English church with the apostolic see Reynolds' pontificate marked a change. The period of papal suspension is one of the most conspicuous episodes in Winchelsey's primacy.[156] Mepham, too, fell under papal suspension for refusing to admit the provisor Cardinal Annibaldo Gaetani da Ceccano to the benefice of Maidstone,[157] and Mepham died under excommunication for failure to obey the summons of the papal collector Concoreto.[158] Reynolds, however, managed to avoid such censures, and his most characteristic attitude to papal decrees may be seen in his adjudication of the dispute over the benefice of Harrow in 1317 after the case had been in the papal audience for five years. Reynolds gave definitive sentence in favour of M. William de Bosco on the grounds that he could be personally resident, but he awarded an annual pension from the proceeds of the benefice to the other claimant, Cardinal William Testa, because he recognized the necessity to provide financial support for the college of cardinals.[159] Here again Reynolds attempted to steer a middle course that would avoid discord and be just to all parties concerned.

On the question of papal provisions generally, we have seen that he did not resist provisors, but rather knew how to make the most of the system. Reynolds himself had been involved in suits at the curia over at least two of his benefices before his promotion to the episcopate,[160] he had launched a complicated appeal there once while bishop of Worcester,[161] he had personally led Edward II's first important mission there in 1309,[162] and his advice was considered important in drafting messages to the pope and cardinals.[163] He knew the Roman court, and he probably saw a close parallel between – on the one hand – the opportunity to use his provisory faculty on behalf of the clerks in his service, and – on the other – the necessity for his English suffragans to acquiesce in plurality of cardinals'

---

[155] Fraser, *Antony Bek*; Cant. Cath. MS Reg. L, ff. 115v, 171; *Lit. Cant.* nos. 166, 289.
[156] Below, Appendix 3, no. 41.
[157] Below, Appendix 3, no. 5.
[158] Below, Appendix 6, no. 63.
[159] Below, Appendix 6, no. 25.
[160] Below, Appendix 12, nos. 1, 2.
[161] Haines, *Administration*, 119-21.
[162] Above, pp. 115, 116 n. 10 (5), 120.
[163] E.g., CCW, 374, 452; above, p. 120.

benefices in order to finance the apostolic college. He could describe the see of Rome as 'mater omnium et magistra', but it is doubtful that such words at this time were anything more than a stock phrase in the use of his chancery.[164] Reynolds probably did not understand on any deep level the canon law, such as *Execrabilis* and *Si beneficia*, or the high theories of papal centralization implied in the provisions system, but he did know enough to consult with others and then put these canons to the best practical use in the opportunities that came before him.

The pope for his part, and especially John xxii, genuinely saw Reynolds as an agent capable of encouraging the king towards a peaceful settlement with his barons, Robert Bruce, Isabella, and the king of France.[165] And Reynolds took the papal exhortations seriously:

> id fideliter profiteor et promitto, perfruens brevi stilo ne vestram sanctitatem celestibus deditam mee scripture prolixitas inquietet, quod ipsum ... regem quem pretextu mandati vestri in locis iam quesivi remotis super premissis nunc oris alloquio nunc scripture ministerio prout potui et potero induxi efficaciter et induxero temporis oportunitate captata....[166]

The pope rebuked Reynolds at least once for failure to bring sufficient pressure upon the king,[167] and once again for performing the king's wishes in preference to papal desires,[168] but Reynolds was not a man to risk the alienation of the crown if he could help it. What has seemed to many writers as indecision on his part may really have been scrupulous deliberation, perhaps extenuated unnecessarily at times. This aspect of his personality was undoubtedly influenced by the uncertainty of the king's moods, as well as by the consistently cautious advice of Prior Eastry. Reynolds was capable of reaching a decision – as he did when confronted by *Execrabilis*, and when commanded he could move in a hurry – as when he told Pope John of his swift journey from Otford manor where he had been staying for Christmas one year up to London in order to obey a papal mandate on the 26th of December.[169] More often, though, Reynolds preferred to weigh carefully the effects that any proposal might have upon king and pope – such as we have seen in the situation produced by the papal mandate about the Templars' goods and in Reynolds' desire to grant

---

[164] In Feb. of 1318/1319: Reg. London, 204.
[165] Above, p. 246 and n. 12.
[166] RR f. 237v; Reynolds to John xxii, 1317.
[167] RR ff. 241v, 216; cf. below, Appendix 11, no. 39.
[168] By inducting certain clerks upon royal presentation: CPL ii, 471.
[169] RR f. 238v.

Caldecote to the monks of Canterbury. And when he did act he tried to achieve a harmony of interests – as is suggested by his grant of cardinals' pensions that paralleled the grants of Edward II, or by his name at the head of ten other bishops in a letter of 1324 asking the pope to intercede with the French king for peace between France and England.[170]

As to what Reynolds thought of Winchelsey we can not really be certain, but it seems probable that in his own way he admired him. He gave his support to the movement to canonize him,[171] cooperating with Thomas of Lancaster in gathering evidence for this purpose,[172] and he asked to be buried next to his tomb.[173] Of Winchelsey it has been remarked that he felt himself to be treading in the footsteps of Becket,[174] and the legend of that martyr was not far from Reynolds either. Reynolds' best set of high mass vestments in red and gold was embroidered with Becket's life, he bequeathed two magnificent pontifical rings to the martyr's shrine at Canterbury,[175] he owned a book about Becket,[176] and the martyrdom was depicted on Reynolds' small counterseal (as it had been on those of several of his predecessors) together with the legend 'Ad Christum pro me sit semper passio Thome'.[177] But the liberties of the church in England have to be interpreted for every age, and we may wonder if – given the character of Edward II and the political crises of his reign – another man of Winchelsey's uncompromising temperament, clerical claims, and baronial sympathies would have served as well.

Recent interpretations of Edward II's reign have emphasized that complexities of personal interests and motives were more prominent in those years than 'clear-cut constitutional issues consciously perceived in the history of the time'.[178] Reynolds was a man of that time, and like his contemporaries he seems to have thought and acted more in response to personal relationship than to great ecclesiastical principle. Must posterity, must later generations of historians, now applaud only the intractable primate whose high and independent convictions bring exciting clashes

---

[170] Reg. Martival ii, 452; Reg. Hethe i, 339-41.

[171] Cant. Cath. MS Reg. I, ff. 364, 418v; HMC Eighth Rep., I, app., 354; HMC Ninth Rep., I, app., 73; Wilkins ii, 536.

[172] Reg. Martival ii, 300-1, 318-19.

[173] Cant. Cath. MS Cart. Ant. A14.

[174] Edwards, EHR lix (1944), 313-14.

[175] Cant. Cath. MS Cart. Ant. A14.

[176] Above, p. 255.

[177] Good specimens of this counterseal are attached to BL Add. Charter 17353 and WAM 2442; for a picture of the former, see frontispiece, plate B.

[178] Phillips, Aymer de Valence, 288; cf. Maddicott, Thomas of Lancaster, vii.

between church and state, or can something be said also for the man who, conscientious but exceedingly cautious, tries as best he can to bring peace and unity to the situation in which he finds himself? Unlike Winchelsey or indeed Becket, Reynolds was disinclined – probably incapable – of transmuting the routine disputes that crossed his path into matters of high ecclesiastical principle. But must the ideal archbishop of Canterbury always be one who is a hero and protector to the lower clergy of his province, or – especially after the pontificate of Winchelsey – can not something be said for an archbishop (as Ramsay ironically remarked in *The Genesis of Lancaster*) whose 'influence at the Papal Court was almost equal to his influence with Edward'?[179]

We may further ask: if Edward's petitions had not been granted by Clement in 1313, what sort of primate would have ruled the see of Canterbury in the person of Thomas Cobham? Cobham was undoubtedly the intellectual superior of Reynolds[180] and he had many other personal qualities that would have made him an obvious choice. Yet he like Reynolds was a notable pluralist,[181] and there are aspects of his later episcopal career that suggest he was not unlike Reynolds in certain ways. There is little evidence that Cobham continued to harbour any resentment towards Reynolds after his initial shock at the loss of Canterbury, and later Cobham certainly joined with Reynolds in mediating between the king and Lancaster. In 1317 Reynolds had probably interceded with the king on Cobham's behalf for the see of Worcester,[182] and the two men seem to have had a certain amount of intimate correspondence.[183]

In his scholarship and in his independence of the crown Cobham was a man more in the stamp of Winchelsey than Reynolds was, yet Cobham's close personal and family relations with the Canterbury chapter over many years[184] as well as his business connections (he was retained regularly as one of their legal consultants) suggest that their election of him was not totally disinterested. As early as 1284 Cobham had been regarded a potential candidate for the episcopate by the Canterbury chapter when they granted him an annual pension of five marks as their clerk to promote their causes, a pension that continued to be paid with

[179] Above, p. 248.
[180] Emden, *Oxford* i, 450.
[181] Haines, *Administration*, 79; below, Appendix 12.
[182] Above, p. 95 n. 6.
[183] RR f. 114v.
[184] Cf. May, 'The Cobham Family in the Administration of England, 1200-1400', *Archaeologia Cantiana* lxxxii (1967), 1-31.

regularity until he was finally consecrated to Worcester in 1317.[185] It is interesting to find that the words the Canterbury chapter used in 1313 to describe him when announcing that they had elected him – *clericus secularis, magistratum habens, indigenus, de Cant(uariensis) provincia oriundus* – were the very same words they had just used to specify the sort of person their compromissors were to elect, words that were not used in the otherwise very similar forms for the elections of Winchelsey, Mepham, and Stratford.[186] The Canterbury election of Cobham, then, was also not without some prior arrangements, and had it succeeded it too might well have become a subject for the indignant commentary of certain chroniclers. Cobham would have undoubtedly felt some prior obligation to work amicably with the Canterbury chapter and readily accede to their wishes, and yet Reynolds – a comparative outsider with no such prior commitment – turned out to be their very good friend and protector.

Miss Edwards has remarked of Cobham's attitude to the king in the crisis at the end of the reign that he seems to have been as dismayed and undecided as Reynolds himself, and that he was no more heroic or useful at that time than the man who had been made primate in his stead.[187] Reynolds' own attitude at that time, his seeming indecision and apparent desertion of his royal patron, may not therefore be so reprehensible as some chroniclers and later historians have thought. Miss Edwards has also indicated that Reynolds did not finally decide to join the queen until it was clear that Edward II no longer had any chance of success, and there are signs – of which Reynolds may have been aware – that Pope John was likewise preparing to make a similar reversal of support.[188] When Reynolds finally did turn at that time, his very action must have given something of a lead, albeit delayed, whereby a transition could be made to the reality of the new government with less disturbance than otherwise.

Illiterate, stupid, simoniac, incompetent, indecisive; or a man who could moderate the tribulations of the English church and realm? Both these views preserve a modicum of truth about Reynolds, and the full story will never be known. The reassessment offered in this last chapter

---

[185] CUL. MS Ee.v.31, f. 19v: 'Si vero contingat prefatum magistrum Thomam ad episcopalem dignitatem evocari, cessante dicta pensione...' (18 March 1283/1284, transcribed by Sayles in *Law Quarterly Review* lvi (1940), 253-4. Payments are recorded passim in Cant. Cath MS Misc. Accts. i, ff. 142-271v, and ii, ff. 12-80v).

[186] For the election of 1313, cf. Cant. Cath. MS Reg. Q, ff. 73v-77v, 83, 84, 86v, 87; for the others cf. ff. 28, 128, 194 and Cant. Cath. MS Cart. Ant. A195 and S392.

[187] EHR lix (1944), 344.

[188] Ibid., 341.

does not demand a complete reversal of traditional views, but it does enter a plea for some considerable modification of conventional notions more along the lines of Trokelowe. This is what I believe we can say of Reynolds: practical, modest, somewhat withdrawn, certainly literate but not a scholar, a moderate patron of academic learning, of at least average competence as an administrator, helpful friend of the monks of Canterbury, a leader of the prelates mediating between the king and the magnates, a moderate leader also of the hierarchy in several ways but definitely unpopular with the lower clergy and a number of the chroniclers, attempting to steer a middle course between king and pope, clearly breaking with the tradition of Winchelsey, scrupulously deliberative even to the point of indecision at times. Indecision is perhaps the strongest charge we can lay to Reynolds, but indecision may not be a vice in a primate whose king is foolish and whose pope is clever.

The pattern of Anglo-papal and church-state relations throughout the first thirty years of the Avignon period is complex, and no useful purpose would be achieved by its oversimplification or hasty summary here. The real conclusions to a story of this sort have, for the most part, been told in the narrative. Nevertheless, perhaps two final observations will be permitted as regards the part that Reynolds did play: in affairs between England and the papacy he was the primate in a period marked by fairly smooth relations that were more satisfactory for English interests than has been generally recognized, and as regards internal matters his primacy saw the preservation and development of administrative forms and procedures that could protect the liberties of the church in a period of considerable domestic crisis.

The full outbreak of the Hundred Years War was not far away when John XXII died in 1334, after which the connections between England and the apostolic see at Avignon were not so close nor the relations so friendly. But in the period that has been under our review the degree of cooperation between these two powers – even if it was based more on expediency than on ultimate principles – was remarkably close, and we may venture to suggest that Walter Reynolds had more of a part in achieving this balance than has been previously acknowledged. Reynolds seems to have sensed, in his own modest way, that he was moving between two poles of authority – bound to the pope by the law of God and bound to the king perhaps no less by virtue of his own primacy than by his personal affection for Edward. Between these two poles stood the church of Canterbury, which Reynolds kept in the balance and administered as best he could.

Appendix 1

Tables of Provisions

The figures in all these tables refer only to direct provisions (not reservations) to English and Welsh benefices found in the printed Latin and English calendars of the papal registers.

For the principles followed in tabulating the provisions under Clement v and John xxii, see above, pp. 15-17, 23-26. In cases of essential difference between Bliss's English calendar and the Latin calendars, such as where the one reads 'reservation' and the other 'provision' or vice versa, the reading of the Latin calendars has been preferred.

In the Latin calendar of Clement v's register, the operative words generally taken to signify a provision are *confert, preficit, providet, accipit,* and *obtinet*. In John xxii's register, the words are *collat., collat. motu proprio, conf., confertur, conferuntur, conf. motu proprio, fit, preficitur, promovetur, provisio, prov.,* and *prov. motu proprio*.

Table A

Summary of Provisions to English Benefices by the Popes of Avignon

Pope	Pontifical Years	Provisions to English Benefices	
		Total	First Year Only
Clement v	1305-14	69 -3	26 -0
John xxii	1316-34	782 -20	121 -3
Benedict xii	1334-42	78 -3	24 -0
Clement vi	1342-52	1396-1610	441-631
Innocent vi	1352-62	683-933	153
Urban v	1362-70	773-1122	555
Gregory xi	1370-77(8)	990	

The principles followed in computing the figures for Clement v and John xxii are described above, pp. 15-17, 23-26. They are basically the same as those followed by the compilers (identified below) of the figures for Benedict xii and for the last four popes, with three exceptions: (1) The figures for the last four popes do not include provisions made to bishoprics, whereas the figures for the first three do. Those that do are followed by a superscript minus sign and the numbers of episcopal provisions that they include. (2) The figures for the first years of the last four popes run through 31 December of the year following the first year in which each pope began issuing provisions, whereas the figures for the first years of the first three popes are for their first pontifical years. (3) In the double figures given for Clement vi, Innocent vi, and Urban v, (a) the first figures represent the minimum numbers of provisions established by Dr. J. R. L. Highfield from the papal registers only, and (b) the second figures represent the maximum numbers established by Miss Candace Carstens from other sources as well as the papal registers (cf. above, p. 25 n. 34).

The source for the total of Benedict xii's provisions is B. Guillemain, *La politique bénéficiale du pape Benoit xii*, p. 79; for the figure of provisions during his first year the source is CPL ii, 515-29. The source for all figures of the last four popes (including the figures established by Miss Carstens) is the Oxford D.Phil. thesis of J. R. L. Highfield, 'The Relations between the Church and the English Crown 1349-1378', pp. 406-9, which is quoted here with his permission. For the first year of Clement vi, Highfield, 'Correspondence' in *History*, n.s. vol. xxxix (1954), 332, has also been used.

TABLE B

SUMMARY OF PROVISIONS BY CLEMENT V

(Elected 5 June 1305, crowned 14 Nov. 1305 [= beginning date of pontifical years], died 20 April 1314.)

Pontifical Years	Totals, which are	Dignities, canonries and prebends of cathedral and collegiate churches, which — — include:		Parish Churches	Bishoprics	Abbeys	Priories	Unspecified benefices in a named diocese, or in gift of a named patron	Further analysis of the 33 dignities, canonries, and prebends of cathedral and collegiate churches:	
			Archdeaconries	Precentorships						Designated [a]	Undesignated
1.	26	18			3				5	3	15
2.	2		1		2	1				0	0
3.	5	1	1	1				3		1	0
4.	7	3		1	2		1		2	2	1
5.	3	1	1		1					1	0
6.	13	5	2		8					2	3
7.	4	4				2	1		1	3	1
8.	9	1			4					0	1
9.	0									0	0
Totals	69	33	5	2	20	3	2	3	8	12	21

[a] A provision is 'designated' if the reasons for provision are given or/and a previous incumbent or particular prebend is specified.

Table C

Cathedral and Collegiate Provisions by Clement V

Pontifical Years:	1.	2.	3.	4.	5.	6.	7.	8.	9.	Totals
Cathedrals:										
Coventry & Lichfield	2				1	1		1		5
Exeter	1									1
Hereford	1					1				2
Lincoln	2			3			1			6
London, St. Paul's	1		1				1			3
Salisbury	4									4
York	3					1	1			5
Canterbury						1				1
Worcester							1			1
Cathedral totals:	14	0	1	3	1	4	4	1	0	28
Collegiate Churches:										
Beverley	1									1
Howden	1									1
Southwell	1					1				2
Wilton	1									1
Collegiate totals:	4	0	0	0	0	1	0	0	0	5
Grand totals	18	0	1	3	1	5	4	1	0	33

TABLE D

SUMMARY OF PROVISIONS BY JOHN XXII

(Elected 7 Aug. 1316, crowned 5 Sept. 1316 [= beginning date of pontifical years], died 4 Dec.

Pontifical Years	TOTALS, which are	Dignities, canonries, and prebends of cathedral and collegiate churches	Archdeaconries	Deaneries	Subdeaneries	Precentorships	Treasurerships	Parish Churches and Rectories[a]	Bishoprics	Abbeys	Priories	Unspecified benefice in gift of a named patron	Hospital	Designated[b]	Undesignated	Provisions recorded in the papal registers to benefices vacated
1.	121	109	1	1				1	9	3					12	97	
2.	56	20	2					1	35	1					8	12	34
3.	15	12	1						3						6	6	3
4.	37	26	1						9	2					3	23	8
5.	17	10	3						7						4	6	8
6.	15	12	1						2	1					4	8	2
7.	17	13	3						2	2					5	8	1
8.	20	19	1	1		1			1						9	10	
9.	16	13		1					1	2					4	9	
10.	18	16							2						3	13	
11.	26	20	1						3	2		1			8	12	
12.	60	53	3		1				2	2	2	1			18	35	1
13.	40	34		1					6						9	25	
14.	69	63	1					1	5	1					5	58	
15.	95	84	1						11						20	64	
16.	49	46	3						1			1	1		8	38	
17.	59	53	2	1					3			2		1	5	48	
18.	49	41	3	1					3	4	1				13	28	
19.	3	3													3	0	
Totals	782	647	27	6	1	1		3	105	20	3	5	1	1	147	500	57

[a] These figures include two moieties of parish churches, one perpetual portion of a parish church, and two perpetua

[b] A provision is 'designated' if the reasons for provision are given or/and if a previous incumbent or particular preb

[c] Edward II, Edward III, Isabella, and Philippa.

[d] For principles of tabulation, cf. above, pp. 16-17, 72 seq.

	Pontifical years																			Totals
	1.	2.	3.	4.	5.	6.	7.	8.	9.	10.	11.	12.	13.	14.	15.	16.	17.	18.	19.	
English and Welsh collegiate churches																				
Abergwili. Carms.																		2		7
Auckland. Dur.	2																	1	1	7
Beverley. Yorks.	1	2													6	1	3	1		23
Bosham. Sussex.	2		1					2								1	1		1	15
Bromyard. Heref.					1									1						2
Chester (St. John's). Ches.									1						2		1			5
Crediton. Devon.															1					5
Darlington. Dur.		1					1													2
Derby.																				
Gnosall. Staffs.	1																			
Hastings. Sussex.																				
Heytesbury. Wilts.	2		1							1				3	2	1	1			13
Howden. Yorks.	1																	1		2
Lanchester. Dur.														1						2
Ledbury. Heref.			1																	
Llanddewibrefi. Cards.		1										1								3
London (St. Martin's). Middx.	1										1					1				14
Norton. Dur.																	3			4
Penkridge. Staffs.	2				1						1			1		3	1			
Ripon. Yorks.	5	1													2					14
Romsey. Hants						1										1				4
St. Crantock. Corn.			1												1		1			
Shaftesbury. Dorset.															1					5
South Malling. Sussex.	1		1		2									3	3	2	6	1		3
Southwell. Notts.	7														3		2		1	32
Westbury-on-Trym. Glos.	1														1	1				3
Wherwell. Hants																		3	3	5
Wilton. Wilts.	1		1																	8
Winchester (St. Mary's). Hants															1		1		1	2
Wingham. Kent.	1																			7
Totals	38	7	2	10	1	2	2	4	2	4	16	4	1	7	18	19	9	20	10	177
Grand totals	109	20	12	26	10	12	13	19	13	16	20	53	34	63	84	46	53	41	3	647
Pontifical years:	1.	2.	3.	4.	5.	6.	7.	8.	9.	10.	11.	12.	13.	14.	15.	16.	17.	18.	19.	

N.B. I have assumed provisions of canonries simply designated 'London' to mean St. Paul's rather than St. Martin's.

Table E

Cathedral and Collegiate Provisions by John XXII

Provisions by Pope John xxii to dignities (including archdeaconries but not bishoprics), canonries, and prebends in English cathedral and collegiate churches, recorded in the calendars of papal registers.

Pontifical years:	1.	2.	3.	4.	5.	6.	7.	8.	9.	10.	11.	12.	13.	14.	15.	16.	17.	18.	19.	Totals
	7 Aug. 1316-5 Sept. 1317	5 Sept. 1317-18	1318-19	1319-20	1320-21	1321-22	1322-23	1323-24	1324-25	1325-26	1326-27	1327-28	1328-29	1329-30	1330-31	1331-32	1332-33	1333-34	5 Sept. 1344-4 Dec. 1334	
English secular cathedrals																				
Bath and Wells	7	1	0	0	0	1	1	2	1	0	3	5	2	7	12	3	2	2	0	49
Chichester	3	2	0	1	2	1	2	2	2	2	1	4	2	3	6	4	6	3	0	46
Coventry and Lichfield	8	1	1	1	0	1	1	1	2	1	1	2	3	3	5	4	2	1	0	37
Exeter	2	0	0	1	1	0	0	0	0	0	0	1	1	2	7	3	0	0	0	20
Hereford	3	1	0	0	0	0	1	1	1	1	1	2	1	3	3	5	1	2	0	25
Lincoln	17	3	4	5	0	3	1	1	2	0	0	4	4	7	7	6	3	5	0	73
London, St. Paul's	9	1	1	2	2	0	2	2	1	1	3	6	3	5	6	2	5	1	0	52
Salisbury	11	0	1	2	2	3	2	2	0	3	1	4	7	6	11	4	9	9	1	77
York	8	2	1	2	1	2	0	3	1	4	2	7	4	7	6	4	5	6	0	65
Totals	68	11	9	14	8	10	9	14	10	12	13	35	27	43	63	35	33	29	1	444
Welsh cathedrals																				
Bangor		1																		1
Llandaff	1	1									1			1						4
St. Asaph	1																			1
St. David's	1			2		1			1		2	1		1	2	1				12
Totals	3	2		2		1			1		3	1		2	2	1				18
English monastic cathedrals																				
Canterbury			1				1									1		2		5
Rochester																				2

	XECRABILIS[d]		
Mandates to assign. recorded in the papal registers. to benefices vacated by *Execrabilis*.	Total vacancies (incl. provisions and mandates to assign) resulting from *Execrabilis* recorded in the papal registers.		Provisions granted at Crown request[c]
			2
18	53		5
1	4		3
1	12		6
	8		2
	4		2
1	2		3
	1		5
			2
			4
			3
1	2		25
			16
			7
			31
			12
			31
			17
22	86		176

ïcarages.
d is specified.

Table F

Success of John XXII's Provisions at Lincoln and Salisbury

Analysis of the dignities, canonries, and prebends provided by John XXII at Lincoln and Salisbury as to the success or failure of the provisors in obtaining their provided benefices. For explanation of the method followed. cf. above. pp. 33-35.

Pontifical Years:	1.	2.	3.	4.	5.	6.	7.	8.	9.	10.	11.	12.	13.	14.	15.	16.	17.	18.	19.	Totals
Lincoln Numbers of Provisions	17	3	4	5	0	3	1	1	2	0	1	4	4	7	7	6	3	5	0	73
Yes	9	3	2	2		2					1	3	4	2	4	3	1	3		37
Yes ?	2					1									1	1				7
Affirmative totals	11	3	2	2		3		1			1	3	4	2	5	4	1	3		44
No	1			2												1				4
No probably	1		2				1						1	1						4
Not in Le Neve	4	2	1	1				1	2				4		1	1	2	2		21
Negative totals	6	2	3			3	1	1	2		1		5	2	2	2	2	2		29
Salisbury Numbers of Provisions	11	0	1	2	2	2	1	2	1	3	1	4	7	6	11	4	9	9	1	77
Yes	6	1	1	1	1	1	1	1		1	1	3	5	3	1	1	1	3		31
Yes ?							1	1											1	2
Affirmative totals	6	1	1	1	1	1	1	2	1	1	1	3	5	3	1	1	1	3	1	33
No														1	1					2
No probably														2						2
Not in Le Neve	5		1	1	1	1			1	2	1	2	2	3	9	3	8	5		40
Negative totals	5		1	1	1	1		1	1	2	1	2	3	10	3	8	6			44

TABLE G

COMPARISON OF NUMBERS OF PREBENDS AND PROVISIONS

Numbers of Provisions		Cathedral	Number of Prebends
1305-34	John xxii only		
81	77	Salisbury	52
79	73	Lincoln	55
70	65	York	36
55	52	London, St. Paul's	30
49	49	Bath & Wells	55
46	46	Chichester	29
42	37	Coventry & Lichfield	32
27	25	Hereford	28
21	20	Exeter	24

These English secular cathedrals are listed in descending order of the numbers of provisions made in each during the period. The numbers of prebends have been counted from the new volumes of Le Neve, and they include the total number of prebends apparently liable to provision in each cathedral in the period 1305-1334. They do not therefore include prebends founded at dates later than this period, but they do include prebends customarily held together with dignities as well as those held by abbots external to the cathedrals. These figures correspond generally, although not always exactly, with the numbers of prebends given by Miss Edwards in *English Secular Cathedrals*, p. 33.

Reliable information as to the numbers of prebends in the collegiate churches is not so readily obtainable, but known figures (from W. Greenaway, 'The papacy and the diocese of St. David's, 1305-1417' in CQR clxii (1961), 38-9) enable the above table to be extended as follows for the two collegiate churches in St. David's diocese:

Numbers of Provisions		Cathedral	Number of Prebends
1305-34	John xxii only		
7	7	Abergwili	22
1	1	Llanddewibrefi	13

Appendix 2

Gifts from the Crown to the Pope

1. EDWARD I TO CLEMENT V, OCT.-NOV. 1305.

Precious objects delivered by the keeper of the wardrobe (Droxford) to merchants of the Frescobaldi for conveyance to the Roman court to be presented by the royal envoys to the pope upon his coronation at Lyons, 14 Nov. 1305:

Chalice and paten, incense-boat, two pitchers, pair of basins, cup, ewer, dish, water-pitcher, and salt-cellar, all of gold; and one choir-cope embroidered with pearls, with buckle. Total value £1343.3s.5d.

(PRO E101/367/6; cf. *Flores Hist.* iii, 127)

2. EDWARD II TO JOHN XXII, 1316-1317.

Gifts to the pope 'upon his new creation': choir-cope embroidered with large white pearls, bought by the bishop of Ely from the executors of Catherine Lincoln, value £146.13s.4d; embroidered choir-cope bought from Rose de Bureford, value £66.13s.4d; gold ewer enamelled in clear enamel with matching gold basin, bought from Roger le Frowyk, London goldsmith, value £147.1s.8d; leather container bound in iron for holding the said ewer and basin, bought from Walter de Bardeneye, London basket-maker, value 12s.

Various precious objects obtained by merchants of the Bardi in London and Paris and delivered at Avignon to the royal envoys for presentation there to the pope as gifts from the king: gold buckle for choir-cope, set with divers gems, value £66.16s.8d; four basins, three ewers, one salt cellar, one cup, two cruets, and chalice with paten, all of gold and all enamelled in part with the arms of John XXII and Edward II, twelve gold salt-cellars, twelve gold spoons, twelve gold dishes, value £1177.3s.4d.

Gifts to the pope from Queen Isabella at same time, obtained by the Bardi and delivered to the queen's almoner John de Jargolio for presentation to the pope: incense-boat, ewer, gold buckle for choir-cope set with divers pearls and other precious stones, value £300.

(Soc. Ant. MS 120, ff. 53v, 54; cf. CPL ii, 417; Murimuth, *Con. Chron.* 26; Christie, *English Medieval Embroidery*, 36, 183-6).

3. EDWARD III TO JOHN XXII, 1333.

Gifts bought in Avignon and presented to the pope from the king during the mission of Richard de Bury: cup of gilded silver with stand and cover worked in divers gems, matching set of ewers, salt-cellar of crystal worked in pearls and divers other gems with foot and circumference of gilded silver and enamel. Total value £66.13s.4d.

(PRO E101/386/11: this entry is lightly crossed out in the MS)

A handsome gift comprising a large table service in pure gold, from Edward III to Benedict XII, 1336-1337, is recorded and described in PRO E101/311/25. (I owe this reference to Dr. E. B. Fryde and I thank Dr. M. G. A. Vale for assistance in reading it.)

Appendix 3

The Interests of the Cardinals in England

This list, compiled from many primary and secondary sources, is designed to illustrate the following English interests or connections of members of the college of cardinals who lived during the pontificates of Clement v and John xxii, 14 Nov. 1305 – 4 Dec. 1334: (1) cardinals who were papal nuncios to England, (2) pensions to cardinals granted by the English crown, bishops, and other sources, (3) gifts to cardinals from the English crown and other sources, and (4) English benefices that cardinals held or attempted to obtain during this period.

There are forty-three cardinals in this list; in addition, some twenty-seven other cardinals lived during this period for whom no information has been found to justify their inclusion here. Arrangement is alphabetical by cardinals' surnames. Benefices, including those obtained before promotion to the cardinalate, are listed in approximate chronological order.

In addition to the forms noted elsewhere in the List of Abbreviations, the following have also been employed in this appendix: card. b. = cardinal bishop, card. d. = cardinal deacon, card. p. = cardinal priest, disp. for plu. = dispensation for plurality, Eubel = C. Eubel, *Hierarchia Catholica Medii Aevi*, exch. = exchange, indult = indult for nonresidence, Baluze-Mollat = S. Baluzius, *Vitae Paparum Avenionensium*, ed. G. Mollat.

1. Pierre d'Arrablay

Created card. p. of S. Susanna by John xxii on 18-17 Dec. 1316 (Eubel i, 15), became card. b. of Porto before 5 Dec. 1325 (Rymer II:i, 616), died between 11 and 19 March 1330/1331 (Vatican Archives, O.S. 6, f. 102).

Pension:

Granted annual pension of £20 by Abp. Reynolds of Canterbury in 1321 or 1322 (RR f. 102).

2. ARNAUD D'AUX

Created card. b. of Albano by Clement v on 23 or 24 Dec. 1312 (Eubel i, 14), died 24 Aug. 1320 (Baluze-Mollat ii, 156, 162).

Retained as counsellor by Edward ii, 27 Jan. 1313/1314 (Rymer II:i, 241).

Nuncio:

Nuncio to England (with Card. Arnaud Nouvel), appointed 14 May 1312 – departed England after 7 July 1313 (Lunt, *Financial Relations* i, 562-4; P&C ii, 1377; CUL MS Ee.v.31, ff. 131v, 134; Cant. Cath. MS Reg. Q, f. 89; Phillips, *Aymer de Valence*, 41, 54-61; Burns, AHP ix (1971), no. 86). Report of the proceedings of their mission is edited by Roberts in Camden 3rd series, vol. 41.

Pensions:

Granted annual pension of 50 marks by Edward ii on 27 Jan. 1313/1314 (Rymer II:i, 241; CPR 1313-17, 83), still receiving 6 March 1317/1318 (Rymer II:i, 357), still 8 Aug. 1320 (Rymer II:i, 431).

Granted annual pension of 30 marks by Bp. Kellawe of Durham on 1 Nov. 1311 (*Reg. Pal. Dunelm*. i, 68; described as 40 marks in ibid. iv, 402-3, and in HMC, Fourth Rep., app., 391).

3. BERTRAND DE BORDES

Created card. p. of SS. Johannes et Paulus by Clement v on 18-19 Dec. 1310, died 12 Sept. 1311 (Eubel i, 14).

Named by Edward ii to his council in Aquitaine 14 March 1307/1308 (*Gascon Rolls*, ed. Renouard, pp. xxiv, 32, nos. 40, 42; Guillemain, *La Cour pontificale*, 483).

Pensions:

Granted annual pension of 30 marks by Edward ii on 4 March 1308/1309 (CPR 1307-13, 105; Rymer II:i, 69).

Granted annual pension of 40 marks by Bp. Woodlock of Winchester 15 Jan. 1310/1311 (Reg. Woodlock, 697).

4. ARNAUD DE CANTELOUP

'Nepos' of Clement v, created card. p. of S. Marcellus by Clement v on 15 Dec. 1305 (Eubel i, 14), died on or before 18 Dec. 1313 (Baluze-Mollat ii, p. 117 n. 1).

Benefice:

Deanery of London, by prov. probably 1304, occurs 1306 and 1307, litigation (Smith, *Episcopal Appointments*, 83-4), vacated at death (Le Neve, *St. Paul's London*, 4).

5. ANNIBALDO GAETANI DA CECCANO

Created card. p. of S. Laurencius in Lucina by John XXII on 18 Dec. 1327 (Eubel i, 16), became card. b. of Tusculum (Frascati) c. 15 Feb. 1332/1333, died in

July, possibly 17 July, 1350 (Dykmans, *Bulletin de l'Institut historique belge de Rome* xliii, 181, 278).

Retained as counsellor by Edward III, 30 Sept. 1334 (Rymer II:ii, 894).

Nuncio:

Nuncio to England (with Card. Pierre des Prés), appointed 30 June 1342 – terminated in 1343 (Lunt, *Financial Relations* ii, 636-8).

Pension:

Receiving annual pension of 50 marks from Edward III in 1333 (PRO E43/104; E101/386/11), still on 30 Sept. 1334 (Rymer II:ii, 894).

Benefices:

Parish church of Houghton-le-Spring (Dur.), vacant by prov. of Theobald de la Valle to parish church of Maidstone (Kent), prov. 25 March 1329 with disp. for plu. (Reg. John XXII, no. 44842; CPL ii, 287), litigation (CPL ii, 320, 491, 499; Reg. John XXII, no. 49894; Rymer II:ii, 801), vacated by resignation and prov. at the card's request to another, 22 July 1332 (Reg. John XXII, no. 57822; CPL ii, 357).

Parish church of Maidstone (Kent), vacant by death of Theobald de la Valle, mandate to assign 22 Sept. 1329 with disp. for plu. (Reg. John XXII, no. 46697; CPL ii, 299; Browne, *Maidstone*, 69-71), had been reserved to the card. 20 Sept. 1328 with disp. for plu. (Reg. John XXII, no. 42877; CPL ii, 282). Abp. Mepham was suspended from office for a time by John XXII for refusal to admit the card. as rector (Emden, *Oxford* ii, 1261; Stubbs, *Chronicles*, vol. i, pp. xciv, 347).

Canonry of Lincoln and prebend of Milton Manor, vacant by death of incumbent 'extra curiam Romanam', mandate to assign 8 Nov. 1329 (Reg. John XXII, nos. 46203, 47260; CPL ii, 310), had been reserved 3 Sept. 1329 (Reg. John XXII, no. 46202; CPL ii, 297), collated on strength of prov. 27 Feb. 1330/1331, vacated by exch. c. 10 Sept. 1331 for archdeaconry of Nottingham in York (Le Neve, *Lincoln*, 92).

Canonry of Bath and Wells and prebend of Henstridge, vacant by death of incumbent, prov. 29 Jan. 1330/1331 (Reg. John XXII, no. 52517; CPL ii, 339), vacated by exch. 26 Aug. 1331 for parish church of East Grinstead (Sussex) (Le Neve, *Bath and Wells*, 49).

Canonry of Chichester and prebend of Fittleworth, vacant at apostolic see by death of incumbent, prov. 16 June 1331, occurs 2 Oct. 1337, vacated at death (Le Neve, *Chichester*, 23).

Parish church of East Grinstead (Sussex), vacant by exch. at apostolic see of canonry of Bath and Wells and prebend of Henstridge, prov. 26 Aug. 1331 (Reg. John XXII, no. 54686; CPL ii, 328), still holding 7 July 1333 (Reg. John XXII, nos. 60712, 60715; CPL ii, 379, 384-5), vacated at death (CPL iii, 208-9).

Archdeaconry of Nottingham in York, vacant by exch. at apostolic see of canonry of Lincoln and prebend of Milton Manor, prov. 10 Sept. 1331 (Reg. John XXII, no. 54844; CPL ii, 359; Rymer II:ii, 838), indults (Reg. John XXII, nos. 54943, 64218; CPL ii, 367, 413), vacated by prov. to treasurership of York 1348 (Le Neve, *Nor. Prov.*, 24).

Archdeaconry of Buckingham in Lincoln, vacant by exch. at apostolic see of benefices outside England, prov. 7 July 1333 with disp. for plu. (Reg. John XXII, no. 60715; CPL. ii, 384-5), indults (Reg. John XXII, nos. 60792, 64217; CPL. ii, 379, 413), also granted commend of canonry of Lincoln with expectation of prebend on 7 July 1333 (Reg. John XXII, no. 60712; CPL. ii, 379), vacated at death (Le Neve, *Lincoln*, 15).

For English benefices held after 1334, see Chew, *Hemingby's Register*, 188, and Highfield, 'The Relations' ii, 349-50. For list of English benefices held c. 1335-48, see PRO C47/18/3, m. 1/7.

Card. in his will or testament dated 17 June 1348 bequeathed one complete vestment to each parish church and annexed prebend (not named) that he held in England, and the fruits received from his English benefices were to be divided in thirds between those churches themselves, the Roman church, and his testamentary executor (Avignon, Archives départementales, Archives de Vaucluse, H., Célestins de Gentilly, no. 6, m. 3; examined by photographic reproduction through the kindness of Prof. N. Zacour).

6. GIOVANNI COLONNA

Created card. d. of S. Angelus by John XXII on 18 Dec. 1327, died 3 July 1348 (Eubel i, 16).

Benefice:

Parish church of Downton (Wilts.), vacant by cons. at Avignon of Thomas Charlton to see of Hereford, prov. 17 June 1328 with disp. for plu. (Reg. John XXII, no. 41605; CPL. ii, 273).

7. PIETRO COLONNA

Created card. d. of S. Eustachius by Nicholas IV in May 1288, deposed 10 May 1297, restored without title 15 Dec. 1305 by Benedict XI, became card. d. of S. Angelus after 29 Oct. 1312 (Eubel i, 11), died between 8 Nov. 1325 and 8 Jan. 1325/1326 (Vatican Archives, O.S. 6, f. 51v; Baluze-Mollat ii, p. 137 n. 2).

Pension:

Granted annual pension of 50 marks by Edw. II on 4 March 1308/1309 (CPR 1307-13, 105; Rymer II:i, 69), still receiving in 1315 (PRO E101/375/8, f. 2v), still in 1319/1320 (PRO E372/170, m. 20v).

8. JEAN DE COMMINGES

Created card. p. of S. Vitalis by John XXII on 18 Dec. 1327, became card. b. of Porto in 1331 (Eubel i, 16; Baluze-Mollat ii, p. 255 n. 3), died between 29 Oct. 1348 and 9 Feb. 1348/1349 (*Clément VI ... Lettres closes, patentes et curiales se rapportant à la France*, nos. 3984, 4055).

Benefice:

Parish church of Blockley (Worcs.), vacant by cons. at apostolic see of incumbent to see outside England, granted 'in commendam' 10 Oct. 1332 (Reg. John XXII, no. 58540; CPL. ii, 370), occurs 18 June 1333 (Reg. John XXII, no. 60573;

CPL. ii, 382), vacated at death and appropriated to *mensa* of the bp. of Worcester (Haines, *Administration*, p. 23 n. 4; pp. 216-17, 250).

9. IMBERT DUPUIS

'Nepos' of John XXII, created card. p. of SS. XII Apostoli by John XXII on 18 Dec. 1327, died 26 May 1348 (Eubel i, 16).

Benefice:

Prebend of Broomesbury in St. Paul's London, claimed by prov. 24 Jan. 1327/1328, attempted to obtain stall by violence (Le Neve, *St. Paul's London*, 20; Stubbs, *Chronicles*, vol. i, pp. xci, 340).

10. RAYMOND GUILHEM DE FARGES

'Nepos' of Clement v, created card. d. of S. Maria Nova by Clement v on 18-19 Dec. 1310, died 5 Oct. 1346 (Eubel i, 14).

Pension:

Granted annual pension of 40 marks by Bp. Woodlock of Winchester 7 Aug. 1311 (Reg. Woodlock, 697).

Benefices:

Parish church of Leake (?Notts.), claimed on strength of prov. or reservation dated before 12 Aug. 1308 (Reg. Greenfield, vol. iv, pp. 48-51, no. 1769; vol. v, p. xvii; CPL. ii, 43), inducted 8 April 1310 (Reg. Greenfield, vol. iv, pp. 63-4, no. 1816), holding on 1 and 16 Nov. 1310 (Reg. Clement v, nos. 6147, 7484), still in 1329-1330 (Rymer II:ii, 776), still holding after 1335 (PRO C47/20/4/10), still holding in 1345 (Robertson, *Archaeologia Cantiana* xv (1883), 224).

Canonry of Lincoln and prebend of Ketton, by surrogation, installed 29 Aug. 1308, collated 13 Oct. 1310 (Le Neve, *Lincoln*, 70), disp. for plu. (CPL. ii, 82), litigation (RR ff. 66, 125v; Cole; *Associated Architectural Societies' Reports and Papers* xxxiv (1918), 234, 251; Smith, *Episcopal Appointments*, 72), displaced by royal nominee 1315 (Le Neve, *Lincoln*, 70).

Archdeaconry of Leicester in Lincoln, collated 13 Oct. 1310 on strength of prov., admitted 31 Oct. 1310, disp. for plu. (CPL. ii, 82), indult (CPL. ii, 107; Cole, 234, 251), vacated at death (Le Neve, *Lincoln*, 12).

Deanery of Salisbury (with annexed prebend of Heytesbury and annexed church of Sonning and dependent chapels), vacant by death of Card. Guillelmus Ruffat, mandate to admit following prov., 22 March 1310/1311. Nine exchequer writs of *levari faciatis* 1318-1328 upon ecclesiastical goods of dean of Salisbury for non-payment of tenths, to which Bp. Martival replied that the dean was a card. and had been pardoned by the king (Reg. Martival iii, 48, 101, 105, 196-7, 199-200, 209-10, 215, 220, 233-4); relaxations of same (ibid., 180, 192, 203-4, 218). Salisbury chapter in 1331 asked the card. to secure reversion of election of the dean to them (Chew, *Hemingby's Register*, 11, 195-6), vacated at death and prov. to the card's. brother (ibid., 195-8; Le Neve, *Salisbury*, 3).

Archdeaconry of Salisbury, so called 28 May 1312 (CPL ii, 107; Le Neve, *Salisbury*, 11), no other evidence, not mentioned in list of his benefices after 1335 (PRO C47/20/4/10).

Parish church of Driffield (?county; Coventry and Lichfield dioc.), royal presentation 19 July 1325 (CPR 1324-7, 156), not mentioned in his list of benefices after 1335 (PRO C47/20/4/10).

Parish church of Hornsea (Yorks.) with chapel of Reston, vacant by exch. of benefice outside England, prov. 9 April 1331 (Reg. John xxii, no. 53295; CPL ii, 326), occurs after 1335 (PRO C47/20/4/10).

Summary of the card's. activities in England in Chew, *Hemingby's Register*, 195-8; cf. Highfield, 'The Relations' i, 73. List of English benefices held by him and his relatives and chaplains, PRO C47/18/3, m. 1/6; similar list, dating after 1335, PRO C47/20/4/10.

11. LUCA FIESCHI

Created card. d. of S. Maria in Via Lata by Boniface viii on 2 March 1299/1300, held title of SS. Cosmos and Damianus 'in commendam' from 15 Dec. 1305 to 24 Jan. 1310/1311 or to 1318, died 31 Jan. 1335/1336 (Eubel i, 13; Cristofori, *Storia dei Cardinali*, 238; short biog. in Jenkins, 'Lichfield Cathedral' ii, app. F)

Addressed as 'consanguineus' by Edw. i in 1302 (Prynne, *Records* ii, 315), by prince of Wales in 1305 (*Letters of Edward, Prince of Wales*, ed. Johnstone, 54), and by Edw. ii in 1313, 1320, 1324, and 1325 (CCW, 388, 511; PRO C70/4/3v, C70/5/3, C70/6/5). Cf. Rymer II:i, 274: Carlo Fieschi, 'consanguineus noster carissimus', retained as counsellor by Edw. ii, 6 Aug. 1315.

Nuncio:

Nuncio to England (with Card. Gaucelme de Jean), appointed 17 March 1316/1317, left Avignon for England 13 May 1317, mission terminated 25 Aug. 1318, returned to Avignon 5 Nov. 1318 (Barraclough, *Studi e Testi*, vol. 165 (1952), 121; Lunt, *Financial Relations* i, 167, 564; John xxii, Secret Letters, no. 424; Vatican Archives, O.S. 3, f. 1v).

Pensions:

Granted annual pension of 50 marks by Edw. i on 14 Oct. 1302 (Prynne, *Records* ii, 315; PRO C47/3/51/6; Devon, *Issues of the Exchequer*, 115-16).

Granted annual pension of 40 marks by Edw. ii on 4 March 1308/1309 (CPR 1307-13, 105; Rymer II:i, 69).

Granted annual pension of 50 marks by Edw. ii on 18 July 1310 (CPR 1307-13, 269), still receiving 50 marks in 1325-1326 (PRO E101/309/32), possibly still – from Edw. iii – in 1328 (PRO E372/177, m. 40).

Granted annual pension of £20 by Abp. Reynolds of Canterbury 8 Sept. 1318 (RR f. 87v).

Granted annual pension of 40 marks from prior and chapter of Winchester 1 Jan. 1304/1305 (CPL i, 616; PRO 31/9/17a, f. 11), possibly still receiving in 1318 (CPL ii, 171; Reg. John xxii, no. 7235).

Gift:

Gift (to the card. nuncios Gaucelme and Luca) of 100 marks from Abp. Reynolds of Canterbury, 1317 (RR f. 285).

Benefices:

Canonry of Coventry and Lichfield and prebend of Longdon, vacant by death of papal notary, prov. 11 Oct. 1297 (CPL i, 572), granted quittance of tenths and other quotas (Cal. Memoranda Rolls 1326-7, no. 354), vacated at death (PRO 31/9/17a, f. 86v; Jenkins, 'Lichfield Cathedral' ii, app. F; Le Neve, *Coventry and Lichfield*, 45).

Parish church of Terrington St. Clement (Norf.), vacant by death of papal notary, prov. 11 Oct. 1297 (CPL i, 572), litigation 8 April and 16 Aug. 1333 (Reg. John XXII, nos. 59956, 60994; CPL ii, 378, 383), vacated at death (PRO 31/9/17a, ff. 87v-88).

12. VIDAL DU FOUR, O.Min.

Created card. p. of S. Martinus in Montibus by Clement v on 23 or 24 Dec. 1312, became card. b. of Albano 9 Sept. 1320, died 16 Aug. 1327 (Eubel i, 15; Baluze-Mollat ii, p. 162 n. 2).

Gift:

Gift of £18.6s.8d. from Edw. III in 1327 (PRO E101/309/38; E372/175, m. 40).

Benefices:

Canonry of St. Paul's London and prebend of Ealdstreet with two attached manors, vacant by cons. at Avignon of Thomas Cobham to see of Worcester, prov. 23 July 1317 (Reg. John XXII, no. 4491; CPL ii, 155), litigation (Reg. John XXII, no. 6382; CPL ii, 169), vacated at death (Le Neve, *St. Paul's London*, 35).

Parish church of Boxley (Kent), vacant by cons. at Avignon of Thomas Cobham to see of Worcester, prov. 23 July 1317 (Reg. John XXII, no. 4492; CPL ii, 156), annates paid 1317-1319 (Lunt, *Accounts*, 10), put to farm by 1324 (Reg. Cobham, 169, 174), royal writ 11 April 1326 of *fieri faciatis* upon ecclesiastical goods of rector of Boxley for non-payment of tenth in 10 Edw. II, to which Abp. Reynolds replied that the rector was a card. and therefore exempt (RR f. 312v), vacated at death (CPL ii, 305).

Parish church of Rotherfield (Sussex), vacant by cons. at Avignon of Thomas Cobham to see of Worcester, prov. 23 July 1317 (Reg. John XXII, no. 4493; CPL ii, 156), annates paid 1317 (Lunt, *Accounts*, 1), litigation with royal nominee (Reg. John XXII, no. 6382; CPL ii, 169, 483; *Reg. Pal. Dunelm.*, vol. iv, pp. lix, lxiv; Smith, *Episcopal Appointments*, 81-2; Rymer II:i, 393-4; Reg. Cobham, 169; *Liber Epistolaris* of Richard de Bury, nos. 195, 214, 238, 243-4; CCW, 500, 505-6).

13. BÉRENGER FRÉDOL, the elder

'Nepos' of Clement v, created card. p. of SS. Nereus et Achilleus by

Clement v on 15 Dec. 1305, became card. b. of Tusculum (Frascati) after 10 Aug. 1309, died 11 June 1323 (Eubel i, 14).

Gift:
Gift of 150 marks from Edw. ii in 1319-1320 (PRO E372/170, m. 20v).

14. BÉRENGER FRÉDOL, the younger

Created card. p. of SS. Nereus et Achilleus by Clement v on 23 or 24 Dec. 1312, became card. b. of Porto on 22 Aug. 1317, died Nov. 1323 (Eubel i, 14; Vatican Archives, O.S. 3, f. 174).

Gift:
Gift of 5 marks from Edw. ii on Christmas eve, 1322 (PRO E101/309/27).

15. FRANCESCO GAETANI

Created card. d. of S. Maria in Cosmedin by Boniface viii on 17 Dec. 1295, died 16 May 1317 (Eubel i, 12).

Pension:
Granted annual pension of 50 marks by Edw. i on 14 Oct. 1302 (Prynne, *Records* ii, 315).

Benefices:
Canonry of York and prebend of Knaresborough, mandate to admit 12 April 1292, vacated at death (Le Neve, *Nor. Prov.*, 59).

Archdeaconry of Richmond in York with annexed church of Easingwold, occurs 27 Dec.1301, litigation (CPL. ii, 53, 93, 115; Reg. Clem. v, nos. 4043, 4085, 7478, 9648; Smith, *Episcopal Appointments*, 66; below, Appendix 6, nos. 16, 24), indult (CPL. i, 596), vacated at death (Le Neve, *Nor. Prov.*, 25; Brown, *Yorkshire Archaeological Society, Record Series*, lxi (1920), 137).

Parish church of Thornton (?county), occurs 26 Aug. 1316 (CPR 1313-17, 538).

16. RAYMOND DE GOT

'Nepos' of Clement v, created card. d. of S. Maria Nova by Clement v on 15 Dec. 1305, died 26 June 1310 (Eubel i, 14; short biog. in Jenkins, 'Lichfield Cathedral' ii, app. F).

Benefices:
Priory of ?Ovingham (Northumb.), prov. by Clement v before 27 Dec. 1305 (not in papal registers), possibly litigation (PRO SC7/10/30; Rymer I:ii, 978). MS and Rymer read 'Otthingam', Durham dioc.; Knowles and Hadcock, *Medieval Religious Houses*, 142, says that Ovingham was not established as a priory until 1378.

Parish church of Manchester (Lancs.), vacant by resignation of incumbent, prov. by Clement v on or before 27 Dec. 1305 (not in papal registers), possibly litigation (PRO SC7/10/30; Rymer I:ii, 978).

Deanery of Lincoln, by prov. 9 March 1305/1306 (not in papal registers), litigation with Jocelyn de Kirmington, documents of which include draft resignation of Jocelyn 'until such time as he shall recover it by aid of the secular arm' (LAO MS Dij/63/i), Edw. I asked pope to cancel prov. to card. and restore Kirmington, canonically elected, because of inconveniences that would result from the card's. nonresidence, 1306-1307 (*Liber Epistolaris* of Richard de Bury, no. 31), reversion of election of the dean granted to chapter of Lincoln at the card's. request 1307 or 1308 (Reg. Clem. v, nos. 2631, 6330; CPL. ii, 38, 78), for king's complaint about the card's. nonresidence see BL. MS Harl. 3720, f. 15v, vacated at death (Le Neve, *Lincoln*, 3).

Precentorship of Lichfield, by prov. 5 July 1307 (not in papal registers), vacated at death (Jenkins, 'Lichfield Cathedral' ii, app. F; Le Neve, *Coventry and Lichfield*, 7).

Deanery of York, admitted 31 July 1307, confirmed by abp. 11 Aug. 1307, reversion of election of the dean granted to chapter of York at the card's. request 1307 or 1308 (Reg. Clem. v, nos. 2630, 6329; CPL. ii, 38, 78), vacated at death (Le Neve, *Nor. Prov.*, 6; Cole, *Associated Architectural Societies' Reports and Papers* xxxiv (1918), 225-30).

Prebend of Wetwang in York, confirmation of admission 11 Aug. 1307, vacated at death (Le Neve, *Nor. Prov.*, 90).

Deanery of Chichester, occurs 1307 and 1308 (Le Neve, *Chichester*, 4; PRO C47/19/3/3).

Prebend of Nassington in Lincoln, installed 15 Nov. 1309 on strength of prov., confirmed by bp. 31 Nov. 1309, vacated at death (Le Neve, *Lincoln*, 94).

Priory of Ogbourne (Wilts.), OSB alien, in gift of St. Mary's Abbey, Bec, prov. to the card. by the pope at some time, followed by a protest from the monks (Reg. Clem. v, no. 7693; CPL. ii, 94; *Liber Epistolaris* of Richard de Bury, no. 217). Same as the prebend of Ogbourne in Salisbury cathedral, which was held by the abbots of Bec (Le Neve, *Salisbury*, 76; Knowles and Hadcock, *Medieval Religious Houses*, 90; Morgan, *The English Lands of the Abbey of Bec*, 31-2).

17. GAUCELME DE JEAN

'Nepos' of John XXII, created card. p. of SS. Marcellinus et Petrus by John XXII on 18-17 Dec. 1316, became card. b. of Albano after 16 Aug. 1327, died 3 Aug. 1348 (Eubel i, 15; short biog. in Jenkins, 'Lichfield Cathedral' ii, app. F. On the alternate spelling 'Gaucelinus' see Bresslau, *Handbuch der Ukrundenlehre*, vol. i, p. 256 n. 7).

Member of king's council in Aquitaine 15 Oct. 1313 (*Gascon Rolls*, ed. Renouard, pp. xxv, 306, nos. 1120-1, 1123-4; Guillemain, *La Cour pontificale*, 483). Appointed king's clerk and 'of the Council and Household' 15 Jan. 1313/1314 in consideration of his good service to the king in the court of Rome and elsewhere (CPR 1313-17, 79).

Nuncio:

Nuncio to England (with Card. Luca Fieschi), appointed 17 March 1316/1317, left Avignon for England 9 May 1317, mission terminated 25 Aug. 1318, returned to Avignon 5 Nov. 1318 (Barraclough, *Studi e Testi*, vol. 165 (1952),

121; Lunt, *Financial Relations* i, 167, 564; John xxii, Secret Letters, nos. 147, 424; Vatican Archives, O.S. 3, f. 1v).

Pensions:

Granted annual pension of £20 by Edw. ii on 15 Oct. 1313 as member of king's council in Aquitaine; renewed on 15 Jan. 1313/1314 (references above).

Granted annual pension of 50 marks by Edw. ii 1316-1317 (PRO C47/29/9/4; Soc. Ant. MS 120, f. 52v; CPR 1317-21, 50; Rymer II:i, 348), still receiving in 1318 (PRO C47/29/9/4), still in 1325-1326 (PRO E101/309/32), possibly still – from Edw. iii – in 1328 (PRO E372/177, m. 40), still receiving in 1333 (PRO E101/386/11; Rymer II:ii, 854).

Granted annual pension of £20 by Abp. Reynolds of Canterbury 10 Jan. 1316/1317 (RR f. 88).

Gifts:

Gift of 1000 marks from Edw. ii, granted at some time 1317-1318 while the card. was nuncio in England, to be paid from issues of the king's treasury in Aquitaine, later apparently commuted to the profits of a certain fishery there (PRO C47/29/9/4; Rymer II:i, 492).

Reference in 1332-1333 to earlier grant of £400 from Edw. ii to be paid from profits of the duchy of Aquitaine in recompense for damages sustained by the card. while he was nuncio in England (Rymer II:ii, 854). Original grant may have been for 1000 florins (John xxii, Secret Letters, no. 424).

Gift in 1318 of beautiful gothic psalter from Geoffrey of Crowland, abbot of Peterborough, now in Brussels Royal Library (Knowles, *The Religious Orders* i, 300; scholarly study by Sandler, *The Peterborough Psalter in Brussels*, esp. pp. 109-10).

Gift (to the card. nuncios Gaucelme and Luca) of 100 marks from Abp. Reynolds of Canterbury, 1317 (RR f. 285).

Benefices:

Canonry and treasurership of Coventry and Lichfield and prebend of Sawley, vacant by cons. at Canterbury of John Sandale to see of Winchester, had been reserved to the card., prov. 25 Feb. 1316/1317 with disp. for plu. (Reg. John xxii, no. 2931; CPL ii, 137), litigation, annates paid 1317 (Lunt, *Accounts*, 5), vacated at death (Jenkins, 'Lichfield Cathedral' i, 184; ii, app. F; Le Neve, *Coventry and Lichfield*, 11).

Parish church of Hollingbourne (Kent), vacant by cons. at Avignon of Thomas Cobham to see of Worcester, prov. 27 April 1317 with disp. for plu. (Reg. John xxii, no. 3614; CPL ii, 147), had been granted expectation of benefice in Canterbury dioc. 24 April 1317 (Reg. John xxii, no. 3571), occurs 26 May 1318 (CPR 1317-21, 152), annates paid 1317-1319 (Lunt, *Accounts*, 10), probably put to farm by his proctor Raymond Pelegrini in 1345, probably vacated at death and presented by crown *sede Cant. vac.* (Browne, *Hollingborne*, 45, 91-2).

Parish church of Hackney (Middx.), vacant by cons. at Avignon of Thomas Cobham to see of Worcester, prov. 27 April 1317 with disp. for plu. (Reg. John xxii, no. 3615; cpl ii, 147), annates paid 131/ (Lunt, *Accounts*, 2), litigation (Chew, *Hemingby's Register*, p. 14 n. 4; Deeley, ehr xliii (1928), 512), still holding in 1318 (cpr 1317-21, 152) and in 1328 and 1334 (Reg. London, 287, 303), vacated at death (Hennessy, *Novum Repertorium*, 177; cpl iii, 140).

Canonry of Lincoln and prebend of Louth, collated 12 Oct. 1317 on strength of prov., admitted 15 March 1317/1318, annates paid 1317-1319 (Lunt, *Accounts*, 21), vacated at death (Le Neve, *Lincoln*, 86).

Canonry of York and prebend of Driffield, vacant by cons. at Avignon of William Melton to see of York, royal grant on 8 Nov. 1317, prov. 5 Feb. 1317/1318 (Reg. John xxii, no. 6240; cpl ii, 168), had been granted expectation of benefice in York dioc. 24 April 1317 (Reg. John xxii, no. 3574), special exemption by Edw. iii from tenth due on this prebend in 1332 (Rymer II:ii, 845), vacated at death (Le Neve, *Nor. Prov.*, 44).

Parish church of Brigham (Cumb.), royal presentation 8 Nov. 1317 (cpr 1317-21, 44), annates possibly paid in 1317 (Lunt, *Accounts*, 9).

Archdeaconry of Northampton in Lincoln, claimed at curia 1317 by prov. in surrogation from Thomas Grandisson, but apparently never in effective possession (Le Neve, *Lincoln*, 10).

Parish church of Lyminge (Kent), possibly held in 1317 (Murimuth, *Con. Chron.*, 27-8), occurs 6 Nov. 1320 (cpr 1317-21, 517), possibly litigation (rr ff. 19, 23, 24v).

Parish church of Pagham (Sussex), possibly held in 1317 (Murimuth, *Con. Chron.*, 27-8), annates paid 1317-1319 (Lunt, *Accounts*, 11), occurs 26 May 1318 (cpr 1317-21, 152), possibly litigation (rr ff. 21v, 91), as rector made presentation to perpetual vicarage of Pagham 24 Oct. 1324 (rr f. 254), royal writ 11 April 1326 of *fieri faciatis* upon ecclesiastical goods of parson of Pagham for non-payment of tenth in 11 and 13 Edw. ii, to which Abp. Reynolds replied that the parson was a card. and therefore exempt (rr f. 312v), Raymond Pelegrini proctor-general of the card. in England made presentation for him to vicarage of a chapel dependent upon Pagham 26 Jan. 1333/1334 (Cant. Cath. ms Reg. G, f. xxxix, verso), possibly still held in 1345 and cure of souls exercised by a vicar (Fleming, *History of Pagham*, 77-9).

Parish church of Hemingborough (Yorks.), occurs 26 May 1318 and 10 Nov. 1336 (cpr 1317-21, 152; cpr 1334-8, 330); special exemption by Edw. iii from tenth due on this benefice in 1332 (Rymer II:ii, 845), vacated at death (cpl iii, 138).

Parish church of Stepney (Middx.), vacant by cons. of Stephen Segrave to see of Armagh, prov. 28 May 1325 with disp. for plu. (Reg. John xxii, no. 22439; cpl ii, 244; Murimuth, *Con. Chron.*, 27-8), still holding in 1330, 1334, 1336 (Reg. London, 257, 292, 310), vacated at death (cpl iii, 138).

Parish church of Northfleet (Kent), occurs 6 Nov. 1320 (cpr 1317-21, 517), possibly holding 1320-1324 (Hennessy, *Novum Repertorium*, p. xcii; Robertson, *Archaeologia Cantiana* xv (1883), 224-5). Six royal writs of *fieri faciatis* 1321-1322 upon ecclesiastical goods of M. John de Winchelsey in Canterbury dioc., to which Abp. Reynolds twice replied that Winchelsey ('rector' of Northfleet at this time according to Emden, *Oxford* iii, 2057) had sold the fruits of Northfleet church to Card. Gaucelme and put it to farm for three years to the same card. (RR ff. 299, 300v, 302, 303v, 304v, 305).

18. THOMAS JORZ, OP

Created card. p. of S. Sabina by Clement v on 15 Dec. 1305, died 13 Dec. 1310; 'the English cardinal'; confessor to Edw. I (Eubel i, 14; Emden, *Oxford* ii, 1023; Clarke, 'Some Secular Activities', 149-57, 251-8).

Pensions:

Granted annual pension of 100 marks by Edw. II on 4 March 1308/1309 (CPR 1307-13, 105; Rymer II:i, 69), payment made for one-half year on 1 Oct. 1309 (Rymer II:i, 94), pension paid until the card's. death (Clarke, 'Some Secular Activities', p. 156 n. 2).

Annual pension of 20 marks from Abp. Greenfield of York renewed on 1 Nov. 1306 (Reg. Greenfield, vol. iv, p. 233, no. 2140).

Gift:

Gift of 500 florins from Edw. I, Jan. 1305/1306 (Langlois, *Revue historique* lxxxvii (1905), 70).

Benefice:

Canonry of Salisbury and prebend of Grantham Australis, granted to him 'in commendam' 26 May 1309 by Card. Guillelmus Ruffat who became dean; pope on 13 March 1307/1308 granted reversion of collation to true patron upon death or resignation of Card. Jorz (Reg. Clem. v, no. 3558; CPL ii, 48); vacated at death (Emden, *Oxford* ii, 1023; Le Neve, *Salisbury*, 53).

19. JEAN LEMOINE

Created card. p. of SS. Marcellinus et Petrus by Celestine v on 18 Sept. 1294, died 22 Aug. 1313 (Eubel i, 12).

Pensions:

Receiving annual pension of £30 from Edw. I 1305-1306 (PRO E101/369/11, f. 184v).

Granted annual pension of 20 marks by Abp. Winchelsey of Canterbury, 1300 (Reg. Winchelsey, 583).

20. GUGLIELMO LONGHI

Created card. d. of S. Nicholaus in Carcere Tulliano by Celestine v on 18 Sept. 1294, died on or before 9 Sept. 1319 (Eubel i, 12; Baluze-Mollat ii, p. 212 n. 3).

Pension:

Granted annual pension of 50 marks by Edw. I on 14 Oct. 1302 (Prynne, *Records* ii, 315; PRO C47/3/51/6; Devon, *Issues of the Exchequer*, 115-16), still in Feb. 1305/1306 (PRO E101/369/11, f. 184v).

21. Gentile da Montefiore, O.Min.

Created card. p. of S. Martinus in Montibus by Boniface viii on 2 March 1299/1300, granted title of S. Praxed's 'in commendam' by Clement v on 3 Nov. 1305, died 27 Oct. 1312 (Eubel i, 13; Baluze-Mollat ii, 41; iii, 124).

Pension:

Granted annual pension of 50 marks by Edw. i on 11 Jan. 1302/1303 (cpr 1301-7, 107; pro C47/3/51/6; Devon, *Issues of the Exchequer*, 115-16), still receiving in 1305-1306 (pro E101/369/11, f. 184v).

22. Bertrand de Montfavès

Created card. d. of S. Maria in Aquiro by John xxii on 18-17 Dec. 1316, died 1 Dec. 1342 (Eubel i, 15).

Nuncio:

Nuncio to England (with Card. Pedro Gomez), appointed 23 June 1337 – departed England 11 July 1338 (bl. ms Royal 12.D.xi, ff. 18, 21v, 25v, 26v; cpl. ii, 537-40; Lunt, *Financial Relations* i, 566; ibid. ii, 624-36).

Pensions:

Granted annual pension of 50 marks by Edw. ii on 25 March 1320 (cpr 1317-21, 433; Rymer II:i, 421; pro E372/170, m. 20v), still receiving in 1325-1326 (pro E101/309/32), still – from Edw. iii – in 1327-1328 (pro E30/1214; E101/309/37, 38; E372/175, mm. 46, 46v), possibly still – from Edw. iii – in 1328 (pro E372/177, m. 40), still receiving in 1333 (pro E30/1418, E101/386/11).

Granted annual pension of 100 florins by Bp. Orleton of Hereford 17 Jan. 1319/1320 (Reg. Orleton Hereford, 120).

Granted annual pension of 200 marks by prior and chapter of Durham some time between 1321-1340 (bl. ms Cott. Faustina A.vi, ff. 23, 23v).

Gift:

Gift of 5 marks from Edw. ii on Christmas eve, 1322 (pro E101/309/27).

Benefices:

Parish church of Wimbledon (Surrey), vacant by cons. at Canterbury of John Sandale to see of Winchester, granted 'in commendam' 25 Feb. 1316/1317 with disp. for plu. (Reg. John xxii, no. 2940; cpl. ii, 150), annates paid 1317 (Lunt, *Accounts*, 2), possibly litigation (rr ff. 17, 18v, 298v, 303), vacated at death (cpl. iii, 53).

Parish church of Wotton, (Glos.), vacant by cons. at Avignon of Adam Orleton to see of Hereford, prov. 26 May 1317 with disp. for plu. (Reg. John xxii, no. 3922; cpl. ii, 157).

Parish church of Brantingham (Yorks.), vacant by resignation of incumbent under force of *Execrabilis*, prov. 1 April 1320 with disp. for plu. (Reg. John xxii, no 11192; cpl. ii, 198), special exemption by Edw. iii from tenth due on this benefice in 1332 (Rymer II:ii, 845).

23. Pierre de Mortemart

Created card. p. of S. Stephanus in Coelio Monte by John xxii on 18 Dec.
1327, died 14 April 1335 (Eubel i, 16).

Pension:

Granted annual pension of 40 marks by Edw. iii on 4 March 1328/1329
(cpr 1327-30, 371; Rymer II:ii, 759), still receiving – 50 marks – in 1329 (pro
E101/127/12, 26, 27; I owe these references to Dr. E. B. Fryde), still in 1333 (pro
E30/1218, E101/386/11).

Benefices:

Priory of Montacute (Som.), osb Cluniac, vacant by death of litigant at the
apostolic see, prov. by surrogation 22 Aug. 1328 with disp. for plu. (Reg. John
xxii, no. 42240; cpl. ii, 277), litigation (Rymer II:ii, 807-8), not holding in 1331
(cpl. ii, 346).

Canonry of Salisbury and prebend of Blewbury, possibly litigation 22 Sept.
1328 (Rymer II:ii, 751-2; not in Le Neve, *Salisbury*, 37).

Treasurership of York, reserved to pope because of impending marriage of
incumbent, prov. 1 April 1330 with disp. for plu. (Reg. John xxii, no. 49044; cpl.
ii, 316), mandate to admit 1 July 1330, litigation (Reg. John xxii, nos. 54579,
59544, 62815; cpl. ii, 344, 379, 400, 501; Rymer II:ii, 803, 826, 849; Pantin, *The
English Church*, 80; Smith *Episcopal Appointments*, 62-3; below, Appendix 6, no.
10), vacated at death (Le Neve, *Nor. Prov.*, 13).

Archdeaconry of Northampton in Lincoln, vacant by death 'extra curiam'
of incumbent but had been reserved to pope 1 April 1329 while incumbent was
still living, prov. 19 Jan. 1330/1331 (Reg. John xxii, no. 52420; cpl. ii, 325),
collated 1 March 1330/1331, indults (Reg. John xxii, nos. 53292, 63119), vacated
at death (Le Neve, *Lincoln*, 10).

Prebend of Riccall in York, reserved 10 Feb. 1331/1332 because of
impending cons. of incumbent to see outside England (Reg. John xxii, no. 56414;
cpl. ii, 360), admitted 19 Aug. 1332, vacated at death (Le Neve, *Nor. Prov.*, 75).

Prebend of Thame in Lincoln, died holding it (Le Neve, *Lincoln*, 116).

24. Gaillard de la Mothe

'Nepos' of Clement v, created card. d. of S. Lucia in Silice by John xxii on
18-17 Dec. 1316, died 20 Dec. 1356 (Eubel i, 15).

Benefices:

Archdeaconry of Oxford in Lincoln, vacant by death of incumbent less than
two days' journey from Roman court, prov. 31 May 1312 with disp. for plu.
(Reg. Clem. v, no. 8703; cpl. ii, 104), indults (Reg. John xxii, nos. 3462, 14980,
20810, 47320, 58054; cpl. ii, 150, 303, 358), dispute concerning archidiaconal
jurisdiction over Oxford University (below, Appendix 6, no. 56), vacated at death
(Le Neve, *Lincoln*, 14).

Canonry of Lincoln and prebend of Milton Ecclesia, vacant by death of
incumbent less than two days' journey from Roman court, prov. 31 May 1312

with disp. for plu. (Reg. Clem. v, no. 8703; cpl ii, 104), litigation (Reg. John xxii, nos. 13993, 24937, 25341; cpl ii, 214-15, 250, 252; below, Appendix 6, no. 47), vacated at death (Le Neve, *Lincoln*, 91).

Precentorship of Chichester, occurs 31 May 1312 (Reg. Clem. v, no. 8703; cpl ii, 104; Le Neve, *Chichester*, 7).

Prebend of Ilton in Bath and Wells, possibly in 1320 (Le Neve, *Bath and Wells*, 54).

Prebend of Stoke in Lincoln, royal grant 8 Aug. 1322, apparently never in effective possession (Le Neve, *Lincoln*, 108; Smith, *Episcopal Appointments*, 87).

Prebend of Aylesbury (separated from prebend of Milton Ecclesia) in Lincoln, 1324, but possibly held as early as 1318 (lao ms Reg. Dalderby III, f. 381v), litigation (Smith, *Episcopal Appointments*, 103-5; Pantin, *The English Church*, p. 81 n. 2; below, Appendix 6, no. 47), vacant before 1329 (Le Neve, *Lincoln*, 25).

Parish church of Iffley (Oxon.), occurs 12 Oct. 1325 (ccr 1323-7, 415).

25. Arnaud Nouvel, O.Cist.

Created card. p. of S. Prisca by Clement v on 18-19 Dec. 1310, died 14 Aug. 1317 (Eubel i, 14).

Nuncio:

Nuncio to England (with Card. Arnaud d'Aux), appointed 14 May 1312 – departed England after 7 July 1313 (Lunt, *Financial Relations* i, 562-4, p&c ii, 1377; cul ms Ee.v.31, ff. 131v, 134; Cant. Cath. ms Reg. Q, f. 89; Phillips, *Aymer de Valence*, 41, 54-61; Burns, ahp ix (1971), no. 86). Report of the proceedings of their mission is edited by Roberts in Camden 3rd series, vol. 41.

26. Francesco Napoleone Orsini

Created card. d. of S. Lucia in Silice by Boniface viii on 17 Dec. 1295, died before 18 Jan. 1311/1312 (Eubel i, 12).

Pension:

Granted annual pension of 50 florins from Bp. Gainsborough of Worcester 26 Sept. 1303 (Reg. Gainsborough, 75). Possibly receiving annual pension of 100 marks from same 12 June 1304 (cpl i, 616).

Benefices:

Archdeaconry of Worcester, prov. before 1287, installed by proxy 8 Jan. 1288/1289, farmed to prior and convent of Worcester in 1290 (Haines, *Administration*, 32), vacated at death (Le Neve 1066-1300, *Monastic Cathedrals*, 106-7; Le Neve, *Mon. So. Prov.*, 62).

27. Giovanni Gaetani Orsini

Created card. d. of S. Theodorus by John xxii on 18-17 Dec. 1316, died 27 Aug. 1335 (Eubel i, 15; Baluze-Mollat ii, p. 232 n. 2; short biog. in Jenkins, 'Lichfield Cathedral' ii, app. F).

Benefices:

Canonry of York and prebend of Riccall, vacant by cons. at Boulogne of Henry Burghersh to see of Lincoln and reserved to the pope (Reg. John xxii, no. 16915), the card. had been prov. canonry of York with expectation of prebend 7 Sept. 1316 in confirmation of reservation made 12 Aug. 1316 before coronation of John xxii (Reg. John xxii, no. 713; cpl ii, 133), disp. for plu. 30 Dec. 1317 (Reg. John xxii, no. 6131; cpl. ii, 167), admitted to prebend of Riccall 3 Aug. 1320, vacated 1322-1323 upon promotion to prebend of Laughton (Le Neve, *Nor. Prov.*, 75).

Archdeaconry of Coventry, by exch. Aug. 1320, indult (Reg. John xxii, no. 21671; cpl. ii, 242), litigation (Reg. John xxii, no. 15466; cpl. ii, 221, 487), vacated at death (Jenkins, 'Lichfield Cathedral' ii, app. F; Le Neve, *Coventry and Lichfield*, 14).

Prebend of Laughton in York, admitted 29 Jan. 1322/1323 'after provision', vacated at death (Le Neve, *Nor. Prov.*, 64).

Parish church of Monkwearmouth (Dur.), vacant by cons. at Paris of William Airmyn to see of Norwich, prov. 23 Oct. 1325 with disp. for plu. (Reg. John xxii, no. 23622; cpl. ii, 247), vacated at death (cpl. ii, 524).

28. Napoleone Orsini

Created card. d. of S. Adrianus by Nicholas iv on 16 May 1288, died 23 March 1341/1342 (Eubel i, 11).

Pensions:

Possibly receiving annual pension of 50 marks from Edw. ii in 1307, as he had previously received from Edw. i (Rymer II:i, 7).

Receiving annual pension of 50 marks from Edw. ii 1316-1317 (Soc. Ant. ms 120, f. 52v), probably granted in same year (Rymer II:i, 348), still receiving in 1319-1320 (pro E372/170, m. 20v), still in 1325-1326 (pro E101/309/32), possibly still – from Edw. iii – in 1328 (pro E372/177, m. 40), still receiving in 1333 (pro E30/1217, E101/386/11).

Receiving annual pension of £10 for life from Bp. Dalderby of Lincoln 25 Feb. 1317/1318 (lao ms Reg. Dalderby III, f. 381v).

Gift:

Gift of 30 marks from bps. and clergy of Canterbury province, 1 April 1299 (Reg. Winchelsey, 552-3).

Benefices:

Canonry of Lincoln and prebend of Sutton-cum-Buckingham, occurs 7 March 1302/1303 and yearly in accounts until death, disp. to hold canonry and prebend of Lincoln in plurality before 19 Sept. 1305 (Reg. Clem. v, no. 4; Burns, ahp ix (1971), no. 49), papal disp. for nonresidence 1304-1306 (Edwards, *English Secular Cathedrals*, 328, 330), inquiry into damages of property 20 Nov. 1331 (Rymer II:ii, 829), special exemption by Edw. iii from tenth due on this prebend in 1333 (Rymer II:ii, 872), vacated at death (Le Neve, *Lincoln*, 113).

Prebend of South Cave in York, occurs 21 Sept. 1305 (Le Neve, *Nor. Prov.*, 41-2), disp. to hold canonry and prebend of York in plurality before 19 Sept. 1305 (Reg. Clem. v, no. 4; Burns, AHP ix (1971), no. 49), litigation, still holding in 1317 and 1332 (Smith, *Episcopal Appointments*, 66-7; Reg. Greenfield iv, 66-7), special exemption by Edw. III from tenth due on this prebend in 1333 (Rymer II:ii, 872), vacated at death (Le Neve, *Nor. Prov.*, 42).

29. ARNAUD DE PELLEGRUE

'Nepos' of Clement v, created card. d. of S. Maria in Porticu by Clement v on 15 Dec. 1305 (Eubel i, 14), died between 15 July and 25 Aug. 1332 (Vatican Archives, O.S. 6, f. 119).

Pensions:

Granted annual pension of 50 marks by Edw. II on 4 March 1308/1309 (CPR 1307-13, 105; Rymer II:i, 69).

Granted annual pension of 100 marks by Abp. Reynolds of Canterbury 6 Sept. 1316 (RR f. 87v).

Granted annual pension of 100 florins by Abp. Greenfield of York 6 April 1311 (Reg. Greenfield, vol. iv, p. 352, no. 2334).

Granted annual pension of 40 marks by Bp. Woodlock of Winchester 7 Aug. 1311 (Reg. Woodlock, 697).

Granted annual pension of 40 marks by Bp. Kellawe of Durham, n.d. (*Reg. Pal. Dunelm.* iv, 400-2; HMC Fourth Rep., app., 391).

Gift:

Gift of fees and other revenues in Aquitaine to annual value of £500 *tourn.* from Edw. II, 28 Nov. 1313 (Rymer II:i, 235).

30. TALLEYRAND DE PÉRIGORD

Created card. p. of S. Petrus ad Vincula by John XXII on 25-24 May 1331, became card. b. of Albano 4 Nov. 1348, died 17 Jan. 1363/1364 (Eubel i, 16).

Benefices:

Canonry of York and prebend of South Newbald, prov. 3 June 1317 with disp. for plu. (Reg. John XXII, no. 4012), admitted 3 Jan. 1324/1325 (Le Neve, *Nor. Prov.*, 71).

Archdeaconry of London, vacant by death of papal chaplain at apostolic see, prov. 12 Sept. 1320 with disp. for plu. (Reg. John XXII, no. 12343; CPL ii, 208), indult (Reg. John XXII, no. 12495; CPL ii, 210), litigation (Reg. John XXII, no. 13142; CPL ii, 211; Smith, *Episcopal Appointments*, 83), vacant by resignation by 16 April 1323, upon promotion to archdeaconry of Richmond (Le Neve, *St. Paul's London*, 8).

Canonry of St. Paul's London and prebend of Mapesbury, vacant by death of papal chaplain at apostolic see, prov. 12 Sept. 1320 with disp. for plu. (Reg. John XXII, no. 12344; CPL ii, 208), probably vacated before 1333 (Le Neve, *St. Paul's London*, 45-6).

Archdeaconry of Richmond in York, vacant by cons. at Hailes Abbey of Roger Northburgh to see of Coventry and Lichfield, prov. 15 July 1322 (Reg. John xxii, no. 15796; CPL ii, 218, 449; PRO SC7/24/15), admitted by proxy 2 Nov. 1322, litigation (John xxii, Secret Letters, nos. 2465-71, 2474; CPL ii, 470-1), bp. of Limoges 1324 but still holding until cons. 1328 to see of Auxerre (Le Neve, *Nor. Prov.*, 25).

Parish church of Newchurch (Kent), vacant by death of incumbent at apostolic see, prov. (possibly 'in commendam') 13 Oct. 1332 (Reg. John xxii, no. 58546; CPL ii, 379), resigned 25 Aug. 1347 (Zacour, *Talleyrand*, 75).

For list of all benefices, including English benefices held after 1334, see Zacour, *Talleyrand*, app. A, pp. 74-6.

31. RICCARDO PETRONI

Created card. d. of S. Eustachius by Boniface viii on 4 Dec. 1298, died 10 Feb. 1313/1314 (Eubel i, 13; for date of death, see Bignami-Odier, *Papers of the British School at Rome* xxiv (1956), p. 142 n. 2).

Pensions:

Granted annual pension of 20 marks by Abp. Greenfield of York 6 April 1311 (Reg. Greenfield, vol. iv, p. 352, no. 2334).

Granted annual pension of 20 marks by Abp. Winchelsey of Canterbury, 1300 (Reg. Winchelsey, 583).

Granted annual pension of 10 marks by prior and chapter of Christ Church Canterbury 26 March 1299 (CUL MS Ee.v.31, ff. 79, 79v; Cant. Cath. MS Eastry Cor., group viii). Payments first recorded in Cant. financial accounts for year 1300 (Cant. Cath. MS Misc. Accts. i, f. 228) and continue fairly regularly until 1307, after which no further payments are recorded (ibid. i, ff. 271v, 272v; ibid. ii, ff. 12, 14). The pension was then accumulated annually among 'debts owed to private friends' until 1313, when the debt had reached £40.13s.4d. (ibid. ii, f. 49). After 1313 this sum continued to be listed annually among debts outstanding until 1321, after which it was dropped and not mentioned again (ibid. ii, f. 116v).

32. RENAUD DE LA PORTE

Created card. p. of SS. Nereus et Achilleus by John xxii on 19 or 20 Dec. 1320, became card. b. of Ostia March 1321, obtained title of S. Praxed's 'in commendam' 1 Aug. 1321, died between 30 Aug. and 18 Sept. 1324 (Eubel i, 15; Vatican Archives, O.S. 6, f. 45v).

Benefice:

Parish church of Catton (Yorks., E. Riding), vacant by resignation of incumbent under force of *Execrabilis*, prov. 26 Feb. 1320/1321 with disp. for plu. (Reg. John xxii, no. 13033; CPL ii, 210). Catton in lay patronage and provision probably did not take effect (Robinson, *Beneficed Clergy*, 23-4).

33. BERTRAND DU POUJET

'Nepos' of John xxii, created card. p. of S. Marcellus by John xxii on 18-17

Dec. 1316, became card. b. of Ostia 18 Dec. 1327, died 3 Feb. 1351/1352 (Eubel i, 15).

Benefices:

Parish church of Tangmere (Sussex), possibly held it and vacated it by exch. with Card. Jacobus de Via 23 May 1317 (Reg. John XXII, no. 3858).

Canonry of Lincoln and prebend of Cropredy, vacant by death of Card. Jacobus de Via, prov. 2 July 1317 (Reg. John XXII, nos. 4236, 5370; CPL ii, 127, 156, 511), collated 27 Nov. 1317, vacated at death (Le Neve, *Lincoln*, 58).

Parish church of Ratcliffe-on-Soar (Notts.), vacant by cons. at Westminster of Lewis de Beaumont to see of Durham and reserved to pope, prov. 1 Nov. 1317 with disp. for plu. (Reg. John XXII, no. 5844), annates paid 1317 (Lunt, *Accounts*, 9), litigation (Reg. John XXII, nos. 8818, 10924-5, 18433, 18450, 43443; CPL ii, 183, 194, 234-5, 284, 471; Smith *Episcopal Appointments*, 85; below, Appendix 6, no. 48).

34. NICCOLÒ ALBERTINI DA PRATO, OP

Created card. b. of Ostia by Benedict XI on 18 Dec. 1303, died 1 April 1321 (Eubel i, 13).

Pensions:

Receiving annual pension of 50 marks from Edw. II 1316-1317 (Soc. Ant. MS 120, f. 52v), probably granted in same year (Rymer II:i, 348), still receiving in 1319-1320 (PRO E372/170, m. 20v; Rymer II:i, 403).

Granted annual pension of £20 or 40 marks (both sums are mentioned in MS) by Abp. Reynolds of Canterbury 20 Nov. 1316 (RR f. 87v).

Granted annual pension of 100 florins by Bp. Orleton of Hereford 17 Jan. 1319/1320 (Reg. Orleton Hereford, 120).

35. PIERRE DES PRÉS

Created card. p. of S. Pudenciana by John XXII on 19 or 20 Dec. 1320 (Eubel i, 15), became card. b. of Praeneste (Palestrina) as early as 10 May 1322 (Reg. John XXII, no. 15414; cf. John XXII, Secret Letters, no. 1692, note 1), died 16 May or 30 Sept. 1361 (Baluze-Mollat ii, p. 248 n. 2).

Nuncio:

Nuncio to England (with Card. Annibaldo Gaetani da Ceccano), appointed 30 June 1342 – terminated in 1343 (Lunt, *Financial Relations* ii, 636-8).

Benefices:

Archdeaconry of Rochester, vacant by resignation of incumbent under force of *Execrabilis*, prov. 9 Feb. 1320/1321 with disp. for plu. (Reg. John XXII, no. 12945; CPL ii, 210), indult (Reg. John XXII, no. 13532; CPL ii, 212), vacated by resignation Dec. 1322 – Jan. 1322/1323 after his promotion to archdeaconry of York or of West Riding (Le Neve, *Mon. So. Prov.*, 41).

Archdeaconry of York or of the West Riding, vacant by resignation of incumbent under force of *Execrabilis*, prov. 1 June or 1 July 1321 with disp. for plu. (Reg. John XXII, no. 13706; CPL ii, 213), admitted 14 Sept. 1321, indults (Reg.

John xxii, nos. 13734, 25201; cpl. ii, 213, 250), vacated at death (Le Neve, *Nor. Prov.*, 17).

Prebend of Wistow in York, reserved to him because of impending cons. of Roger Northburgh to see of Coventry and Lichfield 13 March 1321/1322 (Reg. John xxii, no. 15189), admitted 6 July 1322, vacated at death (Le Neve, *Nor. Prov.*, 93).

For English benefices held after 1349, see Highfield, 'The Relations' ii, 358.

36. Pelfort de Rabastens

Created card. p. of S. Anastasia by John xxii on 19 or 20 Dec. 1320, died 14 July 1324 (Eubel i, 16; Reg. John xxii, nos. 19927, 20305; cpl. ii, 239).

Benefice:

Parish church of Hornsea (Yorks.), vacant by cons. at Avignon of William Melton to see of York, prov. 5 Feb. 1320/1321 (Reg. John xxii, no. 12926; cpl. ii, 211), vacated at death (Reg. John xxii, no. 20305; cpl. ii, 239).

37. Raymond de Roux

Created card. d. of S. Maria in Cosmedin by John xxii on 19 or 20 Dec. 1320, died 31 Oct. 1325 (Eubel i, 16; Baluze-Mollat ii, p. 252 n. 1; cf. Vatican Archives, O.S. 6, f. 51v).

Benefices:

Parish church of Ufford (Northants.), vacant by resignation of incumbent under force of *Execrabilis*, prov. 22 Feb. 1320/1321 with disp. for plu. (Reg. John xxii, no. 12993; cpl. ii, 210), litigation, king begged him to desist in favour of royal nominee 12 May 1321 (pro C70/4/1; Rymer II:i, 449), apparently unsuccessful (Smith, *Episcopal Appointments*, 100-1).

Archdeaconry of Canterbury, vacant by death of papal chaplain, prov. 23 April 1323 (Reg. John xxii, no. 17222; cpl. ii, 229), indult (cpl. ii, 229), litigation (rr ff. 130v, 250, 254v, 307v; cpl. ii, 456, 459, 461; Cant. Cath. ms Reg. I, ff. 393-393v; hmc Ninth Rep., I, app., 72; pro SC7/56/14; Smith, *Episcopal Appointments*, 76-8), vacated at death (rr f. 144v; Le Neve, *Mon. So. Prov.*, 7).

38. Guillelmus Ruffat

'Nepos' of Clement v, created card. d. of SS. Cosmos et Damianus by Clement v on 15 Dec. 1305, became card. p. of S. Pudenciana 1 March 1305/1306, died 24 Jan. 1310/1311 (Eubel i, 14; Baluze-Mollat ii, p. 124 n. 2).

Pensions:

Granted annual pension of 40 marks by Edw. ii on 4 March 1308/1309 (cpr 1307-13, 105; Rymer II:i, 69).

Granted annual pension of 25 marks by Bp. Woodlock of Winchester 28 June 1308 (Reg. Woodlock, 680-1; pro C70/1/2, C70/2/1).

Benefices:

Prebend of Grantham Australis in Salisbury, vacant by death of incumbent, expecting 25 Aug. 1306, admitted by bp. 14 July 1307, vacated by promotion to deanery, papal faculty 28 April 1309 to appoint successor (CPL. ii, 58; Le Neve, *Salisbury*, 53).

Deanery of Salisbury, vacant by cons. of incumbent to see outside England, papal mandate to assign 9 March 1308/1309 (CPL. ii, 49), episcopal mandate to admit 23 April 1309, vacated at death (Le Neve, *Salisbury*, 3).

39. PETER OF SPAIN

Created card. b. of Sabina by Boniface VIII on 15 Dec. 1302, died 20 Dec. 1310 (Eubel i, 13).

Nuncio:

Nuncio to England, appointed and departed curia 28 Nov. 1306 – safe conduct for departure from England 14 Nov. 1307 (Lunt, *Financial Relations* i, 558-60; Johnstone, *Edward of Carnarvon*, 118-21; Rymer II:i, 15; CPL. ii, 31; Reg. Winchelsey, p. xxiv).

Pension:

Granted annual pension of 50 marks by Edw. I on 28 June 1307 (Rymer I:ii, 1017; CPR 1301-7, 530).

Gifts:

Gifts from Prince Edward to the card., delivered by the royal envoys at the Roman curia in 1303: gold cope purchased at the curia, value 130 marks (PRO C47/3/51/6; Devon, *Issues of the Exchequer*, 115-16); choir-cope embroidered with various work and white pearls, purchased in London from Lady Christiana of Enfield, value £60 (PRO E101/360/18, f. 23; Johnstone, *Edward of Carnarvon*, p. 118 n. 4; *Cal. Docs. relating to Scotland*, ii, 369).

Gift of gold cup and water-pitcher, pair of gilded silver basins, and two iron-grey palfreys from Edw. I, on 6 July 1307. Gift of another gold cup and water-pitcher, and pair of gilded silver basins enamelled with the arms of England, from Prince Edward, on same day (PRO E101/370/5).

Gift of two cloths of scarlet bought from a London merchant and sent with pelts of fur for the same cloths, and also jewels, from Edw. II upon the card's. departure from England 19 Nov. 1307, value £20 (PRO E101/373/15, f. 21v).

40. PIERRE TESSIER

Created card. p. of S. Stephanus in Coelio Monte by John XXII on 19 or 20 Dec. 1320, died 22 or 23 March 1324/1325 (Eubel i, 16; Baluze-Mollat ii, p. 249 n. 2).

Pension:

Granted annual pension of £20 by Abp. Reynolds of Canterbury 1 Jan. 1323/1324 (RR f. 88).

Benefice:

Parish church of Barrington (Cambs.), vacant by resignation of incumbent under force of *Execrabilis*, prov. 23 Feb. 1320/1321 with disp. for plu. (Reg. John XXII, no. 13008; CPL. ii, 210).

41. WILLIAM TESTA

Created card. p. of S. Cyriacus in Thermis by Clement v on 23 or 24 Dec. 1312, died between 3 and 25 Sept. 1326 (Eubel i, 14; Baluze-Mollat ii, p. 168 n. 3; Vatican Archives, O.S. 6, f. 57v).

Nuncio:

Papal nuncio and general papal collector in England, sent to England 25 Aug. 1305 – superseded 8 March 1312/1313 (Lunt, *Financial Relations* i, 621; Lunt, AHR xviii (1912), 57). Papal administrator of the see of Canterbury during suspension of Abp. Winchelsey, 20 April 1306 – 15 Feb. 1307/1308 (Reg. Winchelsey, pp. xxv-xxviii; P&C ii, 1229-31).

Pensions:

Receiving annual pension of 50 marks from Edw. II 1316-1317 (Soc. Ant. MS 120, f. 52v), probably granted in same year (Rymer II:i, 348), still receiving in 1325-1326 (PRO E101/309/32; E372/177, m. 40).

Granted annual pension of 40 marks by Abp. Reynolds of Canterbury 6 Sept. 1316 (RR f. 87v).

Receiving annual pension of 20 marks from Bp. Hethe of Rochester 15 Jan. 1320/1321 (Reg. Hethe, vol. i, pp. xviii-xix, 59, 102).

Benefices:

Parish church of East or West Ham (Essex; source reads 'Hames, London dioc.'), occurs 20 Oct. 1309 (CPL ii, 59; Reg. Clem. v, no. 4667).

Precentorship of Lincoln, vacant by cons. of incumbent to see outside England, prov. 20 Oct. 1309 with disp. for plu. (Reg. Clem. v, no. 4667; CPL ii, 59), episcopal mandate to admit 5 Feb. 1309/1310, appeared in person and was installed with permission for nonresidence 30 Aug. 1310 (Cole, *Associated Architectural Societies' Reports and Papers* xxxiv (1918), 230-2), vacated at death (Le Neve, *Lincoln*, 19).

Canonry of Lincoln and prebend of Langford Manor, vacant by cons. of incumbent to see outside England, prov. 20 Oct. 1309 with disp. for plu. (Reg. Clem. v, no. 4667; CPL ii, 59), collated 4 Feb. 1309/1310, appeared in person and was installed with permission for nonresidence 30 Aug. 1310 (Cole, 230-2), vacated by resignation by 16 Jan. 1312/1313 (Le Neve, *Lincoln*, 76).

Parish church of Harrow (Middx.), probably holding on 20 Oct. 1309 and 11 June 1312 (Reg. Clem. v, nos. 4667, 8075; CPL ii, 59, 96), litigation (Cant. Cath. MS Reg. Q, ff. 107, 113; CUL MS Ee.v.31, ff. 135, 138, 182; Reg. Clem. v, nos. 8075, 9206, 9456; CPL ii, 96, 113; Emden, *Oxford* i, 238-9; below, Appendix 6, no. 25), vacant by resignation 23 Oct. 1317 into hands of Abp. Reynolds who on 27 Oct. 1317 gave definitive sentence against the card. (CUL MS Ee.v.31, f. 182).

Archdeaconry of Ely, holding on 18 Dec. 1312 (Reg. Clem. v, no. 9206), indults (Reg. John XXII, nos. 9327, 25908; CPL ii, 118), pope granted reversion of collation to the bp. of Ely upon the card's. death or resignation 26 Sept. 1313 (Reg. Clem. v, no. 9781; CPL ii, 116), vacated at death (Le Neve, *Mon. So. Prov.*, 17).

Special faculty 22 April 1313 from the pope to retain all benefices after promotion to the cardinalate (Reg. Clem. v, no. 9210; CPL ii, 144).

Parish church of Spofforth (Yorks.), royal presentation 4 Nov. 1317 or 4 Jan. 1317/1318 (CPR 1317-21, 44, 68), annates paid 1317 (Lunt, *Accounts*, 9), occurs 12 Aug. 1320 (Reg. John XXII, no. 11903; CPL ii, 204).

Parish church of Shoreham (Kent), vacant by resignation of the card's. 'nepos' Vitalis de Testa under force of *Execrabilis*, prov. 22 Jan. 1317/1318 (Reg. John XXII, no. 6214; CPL ii, 169), annates paid 1317-1319 (Lunt, *Accounts*, 10). It had been collated to Vitalis some time between 20 April 1306 and 15 Feb. 1307/1308 by William Testa himself while he was administrator of Canterbury during suspension of Winchelsey (CPL ii, 69). The card's. proctor was admitted by Abp. Reynolds 10 July 1318 (RR f. 23v); vacated at death of Card. William Testa and prov. again to Vitalis (Reg. John XXII, no. 27599; CPL ii, 255).

Parish church of Kirton (Lincs.), vacant by resignation of incumbent under force of *Execrabilis*, prov. 12 Aug. 1320 with disp. for plu. (Reg. John XXII, no. 11903; CPL ii, 204, 406).

42. ARNALDUS DE VIA

'Nepos' of John XXII, created card. d. of S. Eustachius by John XXII on 20 June 1317, died 23 Nov. 1335 (Eubel i, 15; Baluze-Mollat ii, p. 235 n. 3).

Benefices:

Treasurership of Salisbury (with annexed prebend of Calne and annexed churches of Alderbury, Figheldean, and Pitton), vacant by death of Card. Jacobus de Via, prov. 1318 (not in papal registers). Nine exchequer writs of *levari faciatis* 1318-1329 upon ecclesiastical goods of the prebendary of Calne for non-payment of tenths, to which Bp. Martival replied that the prebendary was a card. and had been pardoned by the king (Reg. Martival iii, 48, 101, 105, 196-7, 199-200, 209-10, 215, 220, 233-4); relaxations of same (ibid. iii, 180, 192, 223); dispute over payments to his proctor Pietro Vaurelli in 1329 (Reg. Martival ii, 608-9); Salisbury chapter wrote the card. in 1331 pointing out the ill effects of nonresidence (Chew, *Hemingby's Register*, 80-4). Vacated at death (Le Neve, *Salisbury*, 19; Chew, *Hemingby's Register*, 11, 244-5).

Canonry and prebend of Howden, with annexed chapel or prebend of Thorpe, vacant by resignation of incumbent under force of *Execrabilis*, prov. 1 June 1318 with disp. for plu. (Reg. John XXII, no. 7338; York MS Reg. Melton, f. 3(9); Lunt, *Accounts*, 25).

43. JACOBUS DE VIA

'Nepos' of John XXII, created card. p. of SS. Johannes et Paulus by John XXII on 18-17 Dec. 1316, died 13 June 1317 (Eubel i, 15).

Gift:

Gift of basin, ewer, pitcher, chalice, and two cruets, all of gold, total value £53.6s., from Edw. II in 1317 (Soc. Ant. MS 120, f. 52v).

Benefices:

Treasurership of Salisbury, vacant by cons. at Westminster of Lewis de Beaumont to see of Durham, reserved or prov. to the card. by 10 April 1317 with disp. for plu. (Reg. John xxii, no. 5203; cpl. ii, 132; Burns, ahp ix (1971), no. 95), annates paid 1317 (Lunt, *Accounts*, 3), vacated at death (Le Neve, *Salisbury*, 19).

Canonry of Lincoln and prebend of Cropredy, vacant by cons. at Canterbury of John Sandale to see of Winchester, reserved or prov. to the card. by 10 April 1317 with disp. for plu. (Reg. John xxii, no. 5203; cpl. ii, 132), died before completion of process (Le Neve, *Lincoln*, 57).

Parish church of Tangmere (Sussex), possibly obtained by exch. with Card. Bertrand du Poujet 23 May 1317 (Reg. John xxii, no. 3858).

Appendix 4

Importance of the Cardinals to Edward II
as reflected in the Roman Rolls

This scale presents one possible indication of the relative importance or popularity of various members of the college of cardinals with Edward II. It is based solely upon the Roman Rolls in the Public Record Office (C70/ 2-6), which are probably the major surviving source of Edward II's letters to cardinals. When the king requested something of the pope or of a cardinal, he often sent numerous duplicate requests *mutatis mutandis* to other selected cardinals whom he considered well disposed, for various reasons, to further his own interests. The Roman Rolls record to which cardinals these requests, originals and duplicates, were sent.

Some other royal correspondence with cardinals remains in the PRO Ancient Correspondence (SC1) and Ancient Petititions (SC8) and in the Calendars of Patent and Close Rolls. Many additional letters were undoubtedly sent to cardinals under the privy seal, but most of these do not survive (Chaplais, EHR lxxiii (1955), 270-3).

The method here followed has been to compute the total number of letters to each cardinal recorded in the Roman Rolls, then to compute the total number of years and months which each cardinal lived during Edward II's reign, and from this information to determine the average number of letters per year sent to each cardinal by Edward II. The cardinals are here listed and numbered in order of the greatest yearly average numbers of letters sent to them by Edward II. It must be emphasized that these figures present only a relative evaluation, not a definitive ranking. I have Dr. E. B. Fryde to thank for suggesting the compilation of this scale.

Cardinal and title:	was sent:	making a yearly average of this many letters:
1. Bertrand de Bordes, of SS. Johannes et Paulus	11 letters in 9 mos.	14.67
2. Raymond de Got, of S. Maria Nova	26 letters in 3 yrs.	8.67
3. Jacobus de Via, of SS. Johannes et Paulus	4 letters in 6 mos.	8.00
4. William Testa, of S. Cyriacus in Thermis	107 letters in 13 yrs. & 9 mos.	7.78
5. Thomas Jorz, of S. Sabina	23 letters in 3 yrs. & 5 mos.	6.73
6. Arnaud d'Aux, of Albano	50 letters in 7 yrs. & 8 mos.	6.52
7. Gaucelme de Jean, of SS. Marcellinus et Petrus	63 letters in 11 yrs. & 1 mon.	5.68
8. Arnaud de Pellegrue, of S. Maria in Porticu	99 letters in 19 yrs. & 6 mos.	5.08
9. Luca Fieschi, of S. Maria in Via Lata	98 letters in 19 yrs. & 6 mos.	5.03
10. Arnaud Nouvel, of S. Prisca	32 letters in 6 yrs. & 8 mos.	4.80
11. Arnaud de Faugères, of Sabina	31 letters in 6 yrs. & 8 mos.	4.65
12. Simon d'Archiac, of S. Prisca	11 letters in 2 yrs. & 5 mos.	4.55
13. Bertrand de Montfavès, of S. Maria in Aquiro	45 letters in 11 yrs. & 1 mon.	4.06
14. Guillaume de Mandagout, of Praeneste	33 letters in 8 yrs. & 9 mos.	3.77
15. Arnaud de Canteloup, of S. Marcellus	24 letters in 6 yrs. & 5 mos.	3.74
16. Raymond de Roux, of S. Maria in Cosmedin	18 letters in 4 yrs. & 11 mos.	3.66
17. Guillelmus Ruffat, of S. Pudenciana	13 letters in 3 yrs. & 8 mos.	3.55
18. Michel du Bec, of S. Stephanus in Coelio Monte	20 letters in 5 yrs. & 8 mos.	3.53
19. Napoleone Orsini, of S. Adrianus	68 letters in 19 yrs. & 6 mos.	3.49
20. Raymond Guilhem de Farges, of S. Maria Nova	56 letters in 16 yrs. & 1 mon.	3.48
21. Guillaume de Peyre de Godin, of S. Cecilia, later of Sabina	49 letters in 14 yrs. & 1 mon.	3.48

22. Jacques Duèse, of Porto, later Pope John XXII	12 letters in 3 yrs. & 8 mos.	3.27
23. Peter of Spain, of Sabina	11 letters in 3 yrs. & 5 mos.	3.22
24. Vidal du Four, of S. Martinus in Montibus, later of Albano	45 letters in 14 yrs. & 1 mon.	3.20
25. Francesco Gaetani, of S. Maria in Cosmedin	30 letters in 9 yrs. & 10 mos.	3.05
26. Nicolas de Fréauville, of S. Eusebius	45 letters in 15 yrs. & 7 mos.	2.89
27. Guglielmo Longhi, of S. Nicholaus in Carcere Tulliano	34 letters in 11 yrs. & 9 mos.	2.89
28. Giacomo Colonna	32 letters in 11 yrs. & 1 mon.	2.89
29. Bernard de Garves, of S. Agatha in Suburra	46 letters in 16 yrs. & 1 mon.	2.86
30. Niccolò Albertini da Prato, of Ostia	38 letters in 14 yrs.	2.71
31. Bérenger Frédol, the elder, of SS. Nereus et Achilleus, later of Tusculum	42 letters in 15 yrs. & 11 mos.	2.64
32. Bérenger Frédol, the younger, of SS. Nereus et Achilleus, later of Porto	26 letters in 10 yrs. & 6 mos.	2.48
33. Pierre Tessier, of S. Stephanus in Coelio Monte	11 letters in 4 yrs. & 6 mos.	2.44
34. Pietro Colonna	46 letters in 19 yrs.	2.42
35. Arnaldus de Via, of S. Eustachius	23 letters in 9 yrs. & 7 mos.	2.40
36. Gaillard de la Mothe, of S. Lucia in Silice	26 letters in 11 yrs. & 1 mon.	2.35
37. Bertrand du Poujet, of S. Marcellus	24 letters in 11 yrs. & 1 mon.	2.17
38. Johannes de Murro, of Porto	11 letters in 5 yrs. & 6 mos.	2.00
39. Jean Lemoine, of SS. Marcellinus et Petrus	12 letters in 6 yrs. & 1 mon.	1.97
40. Giacomo Gaetani Stefaneschi, of S. Georgius ad Velum Aureum	36 letters in 19 yrs. & 6 mos.	1.85
41. Riccardo Petroni, of S. Eustachius	12 letters in 6 yrs. & 7 mos.	1.82
42. Pierre des Prés, of S. Pudenciana, later of Praeneste	11 letters in 6 yrs. & 1 mon.	1.81
43. Raymond de Saint-Sever, of S. Pudenciana	8 letters in 4 yrs. & 7 mos.	1.75
44. Pierre d'Arrablay, of S. Susanna	18 letters in 11 yrs. & 1 mon.	1.62

45. Pelfort de Rabastens, of S. Anastasia	5 letters in 3 yrs. & 9 mos.	1.33
46. Landolfo Brancaccio, of S. Angelus	7 letters in 5 yrs. & 4 mos.	1.31
47. Pierre de la Chapelle, of Praeneste	6 letters in 4 yrs. & 10 mos.	1.24
48. Bertrand de la Tour, of S. Vitalis, later of Tusculum	7 letters in 6 yrs. & 1 mon.	1.15
49. Leonardo Patrasso, of Albano	5 letters in 4 yrs. & 5 mos.	1.13
50. Francesco Napoleone Orsini, of S. Lucia in Silice	5 letters in 4 yrs. & 6 mos.	1.11
51. Renaud de la Porte, of SS. Nereus et Achilleus, later of Ostia	6 letters in 5 yrs. & 6 mos.	1.09
52. Etienne de Suisy, of S. Cyriacus in Thermis	4 letters in 4 yrs. & 5 mos.	0.91
53. Giovanni Gaetani Orsini, of S. Theodorus	9 letters in 11 yrs. & 1 mon.	0.81
54. Gentile da Montefiore, of S. Martinus in Montibus	4 letters in 5 yrs. & 4 mos.	0.75

A TOTAL OF 54 cardinals were sent a total of 1538 letters by Edward II 1307-1327 (19 yrs. & 6 mos.), making a yearly average of 78.87 letters to all cardinals recorded in the Roman Rolls. Most of the 1538 letters were duplicates, however, and the number of original letters to cardinals fully transcribed on the Roman Rolls for these years is approximately 288. A great many of these are printed in Rymer.

Appendix 5

Papal Officials Beneficed in England

This list is intended to show the extent and variety of the papal officials holding or claiming English benefices 1305-34, rather than to specify which benefices they held. Cardinals are not included here, except for William Testa, nor are cardinals' chaplains, except for those who also held papal offices. Papal officials also known to be king's clerks are marked by an asterisk (*). Earliest known dates for tenure of the papal offices are given when possible, and promotions to English or Welsh sees are noted. The references for all information as to English benefices held by the persons in this list are the indexes to the English and Latin calendars of the papal registers, as well as any other sources that may be cited here. Unbeneficed English religious who were papal chaplains during this period are not included.

1. M. John de Abbotsbury, called 'Ostiensis', scribe of the papal penitentiary (Emden, *Oxford* i, 2).

2. M. Robert de Adele, made papal chaplain by John xxII on 11 Jan. 1333/ 1334 (Reg. John xxII, no. 62431).

3. John de Aquablanca, papal chaplain and chaplain of Cardinal Guillelmus Ruffat of S. Pudenciana.

4. *M. John de Arundel, papal chaplain at time of death 1331 (Emden, *Oxford* i, 48).

5. *M. Rigaud d'Assier, D.C.L., papal chaplain by 4 Feb. 1316/1317, auditor of causes of the apostolic palace by 8 Dec. 1316, appointed papal nuncio to England 1 May 1317, general papal collector in England 1316-20-23, bishop of Winchester by provision 26 Nov. 1319 (Reg. Asserio, ix-xxxviii, 673-4; Edwards, 'The Personnel and Political Activities of the English Episcopate during the Reign of Edward II', 51-2, 95-7, 386-7, 400; Lunt, *Financial Relations*, 623; Lunt, *Accounts*, xxi-xxii).

6. M. Guillelmus de Balaeto, papal chaplain, appointed papal nuncio to England 8 March 1312/1313, general papal collector in England 1313-1317 (Lunt, *Financial Relations* i, 622-3).

7. M. Philip de Barton, papal chaplain by 1295 (Emden, *Oxford* i, 122).

8. *M. William Bateman, alias 'de Norwico', D.C.L., papal chaplain by 1330, auditor of causes of the apostolic palace (of the first grade) by 1332, papal nuncio to England 1340-1344, bishop of Norwich by provision 23 Jan. 1343/1344 (Emden, *Cambridge*, 44; Lunt, *Financial Relations* ii, 636, 638).

9. M. Anthony Bek, D.Th., made papal chaplain by John XXII, bishop of Norwich by provision 14 March 1336/1337 (Emden, *Oxford* i, 152-3).

10. M. James Berkeley, D.Th., papal chaplain by 1318, bishop of Exeter by election 5 Dec. 1326 (Emden, *Oxford* i, 174-5).

11. *M. William de Birston, made papal chaplain by John XXII on 12 March 1316/1317 (CPL ii, 141).

12. William de Bordis, papal chaplain, member of the king's council in Aquitaine under Edward I and Edward II (Guillemain, *La Cour pontificale*, 483).

13. M. William of Brescia, papal chaplain, papal physician (Guillemain, *Mélanges d'archéologie et d'histoire de l'École française de Rome*, lxiii (1951), pp. 146-7 n. 12, p. 155 n. 6).

14. *M. Richard de Bury, made papal chaplain and 'commensalis' by John XXII on 1 July 1331, bishop of Durham by provision 14 Oct. 1333 (Reg. John XXII, no. 54119; Emden, *Oxford* i, 323-6).

15. Nicola Capoche, made papal chaplain by John XXII on 15 Nov. 1327 (CPL ii, 485; CPR 1313-17, 340; PRO C47/16/8, m. 14/23, 24).

16. Bego de Cavomonte, papal chaplain, chaplain and 'familiaris' of Cardinal Raymond de Got of S. Maria Nova.

17. Tommaso da Ceccano, papal chaplain.

18. Odo Colonna, papal notary by 1310 (Jenkins, 'Lichfield Cathedral' ii, app. F).

19. Paulus de Comite, papal chaplain by 1316 (Jenkins, 'Lichfield Cathedral' i, 220; ii, app. F).

20. *M. Itherius de Concoreto, papal nuncio and general papal collector in England 1328 – c.1334 (Lunt, *Financial Relations* ii, 693-701; Lunt, *Accounts*, xxiii-xxviii; Robinson, *Beneficed Clergy*, 24).

21. Simon de Convenis, papal chaplain.

22. *John Droxford, made papal chaplain by Boniface VIII on 22 Sept. 1298, bishop of Bath and Wells by election 5 Feb. 1308/1309 (Brett-James, *Transactions of the London and Middlesex Archaeological Society*, n.s. vol. x (1951); CPL i, 577; Edwards, 'The Personnel and Political Activities', 30-1, 403-4; Cal. Reg. Droxford, p. xvii seq.; Jenkins, 'Lichfield Cathedral' ii, app. F).

23. John Eclescliff, OP, minor papal penitentiary from c. 1304-1305 until 1318, bishop of Llandaff by translation 20 June 1323 (Clarke, 'Some Secular

Activities', 144, 158; Edwards, 'Personnel and Political Activities', 95, 386; Williams, *The Welsh Church*, 74; Sayles, *Select Cases in the Court of King's Bench under Edward II*, pp. 125, 127).

24. M. Hugh de Engolisma (of Angoulême), papal 'panetarius' and member of the papal household by 1316, papal nuncio and general papal collector in England 1323-1328 (Guillemain, *La Cour pontificale*, 403; Lunt, *Financial Relations* i, 623-4).

25. M. Thomas Fastolf, D.C.L., appointed papal chaplain and auditor of causes of the apostolic palace by John XXII; clerk, chaplain, 'domesticus familie', and 'continuus commensalis' of Cardinal Giovanni Gaetani Orsini of S. Theodorus in May of 1326; bishop of St. David's by provision 22 Oct. 1352 (Emden, *Oxford* iii, 2174-5; Cerchiari, *Sacra Rota* ii, 26; Fliniaux, *Revue historique de droit français et étranger*, sér. iv, vol. iv (1925), 390-1; Greenaway, cQR clxi (1960), 443; Pantin, *The English Church*, p. 21 n. 3).

26. M. John of Ferrara, papal chaplain (Reg. Greenfield, vol. iv, p. 49, no. 1769; CPL ii, 49).

27. M. Manuele Fieschi, papal notary (Stubbs, *Chronicles*, vol. ii, pp. ciii-cviii; Reg. Martival iv, 67; York MS Reg. Melton, f. 529v (664v)).

28. Francesco Gaetani, the younger, papal chaplain.

29. Petrus de Galiciano, papal chaplain.

30. M. Hugh Geraldi, papal chaplain, 'referendarius' of Clement V, appointed auditor of causes of the apostolic palace by Clement V, papal nuncio and auditor in England, member of the king's council in Aquitaine under Edward I and Edward II (Cerchiari, *Sacra Rota* ii, 23; Guillemain, *La Cour pontificale*, 310-11, 483; Murimuth, *Con. Chron.*, 26-7; *Chron. Melsa* ii, 319; Burns, AHP ix (1971), no. 51).

31. M. John Grandisson, papal chaplain by 1322, bishop of Exeter by provision 12 Aug. 1327 (Emden, *Oxford* ii, 800-1).

32. *M. William Greenfield, D.C.L., papal chaplain by c. 1299, archbishop of York by election 4 Dec. 1304 (Emden, *Oxford* ii, 820-1).

33. M. John de Haverings, papal chaplain.

34. *M. Richard de Haverings, papal chaplain by 1305, vacated 1307, reappointed 21 Nov. 1310; archbishop of Dublin by election 30 March 1307, not consecrated, resigned 21 Nov. 1310 (Reg. Clem. V, no. 6402; Emden, *Oxford* iii, 2181-2).

35. Johannes Landulfi de Calumpnia, papal chaplain.

36. *Walter Langton, papal chaplain by Oct. 1295, bishop of Coventry and Lichfield by election 20 Feb. 1295/1296 (Beardwood, *Transactions of the American Philosophical Society*, n.s. vol. 54, part 3 (1964), pp. 8-9; Jenkins, 'Lichfield Cathedral' i, 36-9, 172-4; Thompson, *Associated Architectural Societies' Reports and Papers* xxxiii (1915-16), 57-9).

37. Henry 'de Lestre', member of the papal household.

38. *M. Thomas of Lugoure, D.C.L., papal chaplain by 1306 (Emden, *Oxford* ii, 1174-5, Burns, AHP ix (1971), no. 72).

39. Franciscus de Moliano, papal chaplain.

40. *M. Simon Montacute, made papal chaplain by John XXII on 14 Jan. 1329/ 1330, bishop of Worcester by provision 11 Dec. 1333, bishop of Ely by translation 14 March 1336/1337 (Reg. John XXII, no. 48112; CPL. ii, 315; Emden, *Oxford* ii, 1295-6).

41. *M. Adam Orleton, D.Cn.L., papal chaplain by 1311, appointed auditor of causes of the apostolic palace by John XXII, bishop of Hereford by provision 15 May 1317, bishop of Worcester by translation 25 Sept. 1327, bishop of Winchester by translation 1 Dec. 1333 (Emden, *Oxford* ii, 1402-4; Usher, TRHS, 5th series, vol. xxii (1972), 34; Cerchiari, *Sacra Rota* ii, 26).

42. M. Benedict de Paston, papal chaplain by 1326 (Emden, *Oxford* iii, 1433-4; Haines, *Administration*, 216).

43. *M. Raymond de Pinibus, papal chaplain and nuncio, chaplain and 'domesticus familiaris' of Cardinal Raymond de Got of S. Maria Nova (Rymer II:i, 85).

44. Berardus de Podio, papal chaplain.

45. M. William de Prato, papal chaplain, papal nuncio and collector in England 1306-1312 (Lunt, *Financial Relations* i, 621-2).

46. M. Geraldus de Pristinio, papal notary (Haines, *Administration*, p. 23 n. 4, p. 216).

47. M. Gualfredus de Regalibus, papal chaplain.

48. *M. John de Ros, D.C.L., papal chaplain and auditor of causes of the apostolic palace by 1317, clerk of Cardinal Thomas Jorz of S. Sabina probably by 1306, chaplain of another cardinal in 1320 and 1324, bishop of Carlisle by provision 13 Feb. 1324/1325 (Edwards, 'Personnel and Political Activities', 37-9, 97-8, 383-4, 386, 395, 413; Emden, *Oxford* iii, 1590-1; Yates, BIHR xlviii (1975), 16-21).

49. Peter of Savoy, papal chaplain, dean of St. Martin's-le-Grand, London, and dean of Salisbury, archbishop of Lyons from 1308-1332.

50. M. Pandulphus de Sabello, papal chaplain and notary (RR f. 84v; Smith, *Episcopal Appointments*, 68-9).

51. *M. Bonifazio dei Saluzzi, D.Cn.L., papal chaplain by Jan. 1296/1297 (Emden, *Oxford* iii, 1634).

52. *M. Giorgio dei Saluzzi, papal chaplain (Burns, AHP ix (1971), no. 94; CCW, 514).

53. M. Reginald de S. Albano, papal chaplain (Walsingham, *Gesta Abbatum* ii, 115).

54. M. Filippo Sapiti, papal chaplain (above, pp. 112-113).

55. Simone Sapiti, papal chaplain (above, p. 112; Jenkins, 'Lichfield Cathedral' ii, app. F).

56. M. John de Solers, papal chaplain by 1311 (Emden, *Oxford* iii, 1726).

57. *M. Walter Stapledon, D.Cn.&C.L., papal chaplain by 1306, bishop of Exeter by election 13 March 1307/1308 (Emden, *Oxford* iii, 1764-5).

58. *M. Robert Stratford, made papal chaplain by John XXII on 7 Feb. 1331/1332, bishop of Chichester by election 24 Aug. 1337 (Reg. John XXII, no. 56392; Emden, *Oxford* iii, 1799-1800).

59. M. Eustace de Swafeld, scribe of the pope.

60. M. William Testa, papal chaplain, papal nuncio and general papal collector in England 1305-1313, cardinal priest of S. Cyriacus in Thermis 23 or 24 Dec. 1312 (above, Appendix 3, no. 41; Lunt, *Financial Relations* i, 621).

61. Gerardus de Tyleto, papal chaplain.

62. M. Guido de Vichio, papal nuncio in England 1309.

Appendix 6

Some Examples of English Litigation at the Roman Court

This is not an exhaustive list of cases that went to the apostolic see in the early fourteenth century, nor is it intended to provide full documentation of those cases that are listed. Cases for which only the initial citation or initial appeal to the apostolic see could be found have not been included unless they seemed particularly interesting on other grounds. The information given here is primarily intended to show how the cases went to the Roman court and who dealt with them there (as far as this is known), although references to further information are also given. Some purely spiritual matters that were not technically litigation between two parties have been included to illustrate the wide variety of matters that did go to Avignon.

The order of presentation is as follows: (1) the benefice contested, or other matter of the case, listed in approximate chronological order, (2) approximate year-dates during which the case was, or may have been, subject to litigation or consideration in the court of Rome, (3) the parties involved, with the appellant's name listed first if possible, (4) notes, if any, and (5) references.

Within the above limits and for the period 1305-1334, this list includes most such cases to be found in the printed Latin and English calendars of the registers of Clement v and John xxii and in the manuscript register of Archbishop Reynolds, as well as some matter from other sources. Additional cases, especially ones involving penitential discipline, will be found in other episcopal registers and elsewhere. Further information about the cases listed here will also be found elsewhere – such as royal permissions for or prohibitions against litigation at the Roman court as recorded in the calendars of patent and close rolls. Beyond the cases listed here, many other disputes over benefices also probably went to the Roman see for which no record now survives.

N.B. In this appendix 'papal auditor' = papal chaplain and auditor of causes of the apostolic palace. All auditors of causes of the apostolic palace were honorary papal chaplains by the nature of their office, so this fact is not repeated after the name of each auditor (Guillemain, *La Cour pontificale*, 347). Also, A.S. = apostolic see.

1. *Parish church of Wimbledon (Surrey), 1294-1309.* M. John de Auxonne (Ausona, Ansone, Aniana, Axon) *vs.* Walter Reynolds. Reg. Winchelsey, 1101 seq.; Reg. Boniface VIII, no. 104; Reg. Clem. v, nos. 315, 335, 4014-15; CPL i, 558; CPL ii, 5, 6, 52; CPR 1292-1301, 128, 130, 354; Boase, *Boniface VIII*, 95.

2. *Priory of Durham and visitation rights therein, 1300-1308-1311.* Richard de Hoton, OSB *vs.* Henry de Luceby, OSB, and Bp. Antony Bek. Bek supported Luceby. Hoton died at the A.S. shortly after he was finally reinstated. Fraser, *Bek*, 153-70; Le Neve 1066-1300, *Monastic Cathedrals*, 36; Le Neve, *Nor. Prov.*, 109-10; Reg. Greenfield iv, 320.

3. *Election to see of London, 1304-1306.* M. Peter de Dene, D.Cn.&C.L. *vs.* M. Ralph Baldock. Dene appealed to pope against election of Baldock, who was then forced to go to Roman court. Dene withdrew his opposition under influence of Card. Walter Winterbourne, and Baldock was consecrated at Lyons (where A.S. then was) by Card. Peter of Spain on 30 Jan. 1305/1306. Reg. Winchelsey, pp. xxi-xxii, 671-3; Emden, *Oxford* iii, 2169; Le Neve, *St. Paul's London*, 1; Stubbs, *Registrum Sacrum Anglicanum*, 70.

4. *Right to collect first-fruits in Norwich diocese, 1304-1310.* Bp. John Salmon of Norwich *vs.* Abp. Winchelsey of Canterbury and the papal administrators of Canterbury during Winchelsey's suspension. Case was first heard by papal judges delegate in England, who decided in favour of Salmon, 1307. Appeal to A.S. was heard before M. Bernard Royardi, papal auditor. Reg. Winchelsey, pp. xxvi, 678, 1153-84; Wilkins ii, 404-6.

5. *Parish church of Reculver (Kent), 1306.* Walter de Maidstone *vs.* M. Simon de Faversham, D.Th. Faversham died while on way to A.S. to continue litigation. Reg. Clem. v, no. 2515; CPL ii, 36, Emden, *Oxford* ii, 672.

6. *Permission for consecration 'alibi' of Griffin ap Iorwerth to see of Bangor, 1306-1307.* Prior and chapter of Christ Church Canterbury *vs.* William Testa, papal administrator of see of Canterbury. At request of Prince Edward because of Iorwerth's feebleness of body, Testa had set the consecration to be at Leicester, rather than Canterbury, on 19 March 1306/1307 by Bp. Langton of Coventry and Lichfield or by any other bp. Iorwerth should choose if Langton could not be present. Citations to the suffragans were sent by the commissary of the bp. of London, the Canterbury monks gave their license for consecration *alibi*, and Iorwerth gave his 'caucio' to protect the rights of Canterbury. However, on the day set, there was deemed an insufficient number of bps. present at Leicester because of the parliament of Carlisle, so the consecration was postponed. Testa (who was himself present at Carlisle) then obtained permission from Abp. Greenfield of York for

Langton to consecrate Iorwerth within York province at Carlisle where the bps. were. Iorwerth was consecrated at Carlisle on 26 March 1307, but apparently by Card. Peter of Spain (Cant. Cath. MS Reg. A, f. 251; Reg. Greenfield, vol. v, p. 66 n. 1) rather than by Langton as is stated in Stubbs, *Registrum Sacrum Anglicanum*, 70. The Canterbury monks appealed to A.S. because Testa had made these arrangements without their permission. Among the contemporary profession copes in the inventory of the vestment room of Christ Church Canterbury none is listed from Iorwerth. Cant. Cath. MS Reg. A, ff. 75v-76, 251; Cant. Cath. MS Cart. Ant. C140, C1294; Cant. Cath. MS S.V. i, 178; Cant. Cath. MS Scrap Book A, p. 2; CUL MS Ee.v.31, f. 106v (printed in Wilkins ii, 287); BL MS Cott. Galba E.iv, ff. 113-14, *Lit. Cant.* no. 39; Reg. Greenfield v, 65-8; Reg. Woodlock, 169; LAO, MS Reg. Dalderby III, f. 112.

7. *Charges brought by the crown, 1306-1307.* Edward I *vs.* Abp. Winchelsey. Emden, *Oxford* iii, 2058; P&C ii, 1229-31.

8. *Election to see of Exeter, 1307-1308.* Richard de Plumstok *vs.* M. Walter Stapledon, D.Cn.L. Plumstok appealed to Rome against election of Stapledon, king petitioned pope on behalf of Stapledon, Plumstok withdrew appeal. Le Neve, *Exeter*, 1; Smith, *Episcopal Appointments*, 13.

9. *Canonry of York and prebend of Stillington, 1307-1316.* Francesco Gaetani the younger *vs.* John Bush *vs.* John de Hothum. Smith, *Episcopal Appointments*, 61-2, 124; Deeley, EHR xliii (1928), 506; Fraser, *Bek*, 194; Howell, 'The King's Government and Episcopal Vacancies', 425-6; Leadam and Baldwin, *Select Cases*, p. lx; Le Neve, *Nor. Prov.*, 78; Sayles, *Select Cases in the Court of King's Bench under Edward I*, Selden Soc. vol. 58, pp. 136-7, CPR 1301-7, 511.

10. *Treasurership of York, 1307-1350.* Francesco Gaetani the younger *vs.* Walter de Bedewynd; Card. Pierre de Mortemart of S. Stephanus in Coelio Monte *vs.* M. William de la Mare. There were several appeals to pope, and king issued numerous prohibitions. Case was heard at various times by Cards. Bérenger Frédol the elder of Tusculum, Bertrand de Montfavès of S. Maria in Aquiro, and Guillaume de Peyre de Godin, card. b. of Sabina. Francesco Gaetani the younger, a papal chaplain, proposed to marry and his benefices were reserved by the pope. Walter died *lite pendente*. Pope prov. treasurership to Card. Pierre. Reg. John XXII, no. 54579; CCW, 335, 337; CCR 1302-7, 532; Rymer I:ii, 1011; Deeley, EHR xliii (1928), 515-16; Leadam and Baldwin, *Select Cases*, pp. lvi-lxv, 18-27; Le Neve, *Nor. Prov.*, 13; Pantin, *The English Church*, 80; *Placita Parliamentaria*, ed. Ryley, 408; *Rot. Parl.* i, 374-5; Smith, *Episcopal Appointments*, 62-3. Prof. E. B. Graves informs me of the following sources of actions prohibiting appeals to Rome in this case: PRO, K.B. 27/236, rex m. 3; -/238 rex m. 15v; -/240 rex m. 9; -/242 rex m. 10v; -/244 rex m. 7v; -/246 rex m. 4v; -/248 rex m. 6v; -/250 rex m. 11v; -/262 rex m. 11; -/265 rex m. 6v; -/264 rex m. 3v, 21v; -/265 rex m. 22; -/266 rex m. 7v.

11. *Canonry of St. Paul's London and prebend of Mapesbury, 1308.* M. John de Bedford *vs.* M. Peter de Dene, D.Cn.&C.L. Decision of Roman court in Dene's favour, but prov. to Bego de Cavomonte upon Bedford's death in 1308. Le Neve, *St. Paul's London*, 45.

12. *Archdeaconry of London, 1308-1311.* M. John de Bedford *vs.* M. Peter de Dene; Bego de Cavomonte *vs.* M. Reginald de Sancto Albano. Suit with Dene at A.S. was unsettled at Bedford's death, 1308. Archdeaconry was then prov. to Cavomonte, who secured successful decision at Roman court against Dene, 1309. Then the suit turned between Cavomonte and Sancto Albano, and was to be heard before Card. Arnaud de Canteloup of S. Marcellus. However, at request of both parties, pope commissioned Card. Raymond Guilhem de Farges of S. Maria Nova to hear it. Sancto Albano died in 1311, and Cavomonte continued as archdeacon. Reg. Clem. v, nos. 2331, 5321; CPL. ii, 32; Le Neve, *St. Paul's London*, 7.

13. *Canonry of Salisbury and prebend of Horton, 1309.* Pontius de Varesio *vs.* M. Richard de Abingdon. Varesio took case to A.S., but switched his claim to prebend of Grantham Australis and then resigned the latter. Le Neve, *Salisbury*, 53, 60-1.

14. *Unspecified action against the pope by Bp. Walter Langton of Coventry and Lichfield, 1309.* Langton was cited to A.S. in Feb. 1308/1309, appeared before Bp. (later Card.) Arnaud d'Aux of Poitiers who established his innocence, and was absolved in Aug. of same year. Reg. Clem. v, nos. 3699, 4351; CPL. ii, 49, 58; Reg. Winchelsey, 1049-50; Beardwood, *The Trial of Walter Langton*, 14.

15. *Testamentary settlement, 1309.* M. Thomas de Chartham *vs.* Abp. Winchelsey of Canterbury. Chartham was executor of the testament of his uncle Thomas de Chartham who had been rector of Reculver (Kent). Winchelsey objected to the settlement and Chartham appealed to A.S. Winchelsey wrote to the pope and certain cardinals and others at the curia to use their influence in the case, especially before M. Bernard Royardi, papal auditor. Reg. Winchelsey, 1048-9, 1052-61.

16. *Archdeaconry of Richmond in York, 1309-1310.* Card. Francesco Gaetani of S. Maria in Cosmedin *vs.* John Sandale. The card. had been cited to appear before the commissaries of the abp. of York; then Sandale was cited to appear at the A.S. within three months; royal inhibition against summoning Sandale outside the realm. Reg. Clem. v, nos. 4043, 4085; CPL. ii, 53, 139; Rymer II:i, 96; Le Neve, *Nor. Prov.*, 25; Deeley, EHR xliii (1928), 516; CCW, 296-7; Smith, *Episcopal Appointments*, 66; *Liber Epistolaris* of Richard de Bury, no. 27; above, Appendix 3, no. 15.

17. *Chancellorship of Salisbury, 1309-1313.* Pontius de Varesio and Tydo de Varesio *vs.* William de Bosco (Boys), D.Th. The bp. of Salisbury, supporting Bosco, appealed to court of Canterbury. Pontius, claiming chancellorship by prov., appealed to A.S. Pope appointed M. Hugh Geraldi, papal auditor, to

hear the case. Pontius died *lite pendente*; surrogation to Tydo. Bosco died 1313. Reg. Clem. v, nos. 91, 7443-4; CPL ii, 2, 92; Le Neve, *Salisbury*, 17.

18. *Testamentary jurisdiction, estate of Hugh Bardolf, 1309-c.1320.* Bp. Dalderby of Lincoln *vs.* Abps. Winchelsey and Reynolds of Canterbury. Tuitorial appeal, court of Canterbury to the A.S. Winchelsey was cited to the curia by M. Giovanni Stephanelli, papal auditor, and he appointed a proctor to represent him there. *Libellus* of Dalderby was presented by his proctor at the curia before M. Bernard Royardi, papal auditor. Dispute was settled by compromise *temp.* Reynolds. Reg. Winchelsey, pp. xxix-xxx, 1131-53; RR ff. 67, 87; *Yearbooks of Edward II*, Selden Soc. vol. 65, pp. 134-44; *Rot. Parl.* i, 298; Reg. Gandavo, 334-5, 433-4; RWR, 11; Churchill, *Canterbury Administration* i, 383-4; Jacob, 'The Archbishop's Testamentary Jurisdiction', 38-41.

19. *Title to a church and a chapel, 1310.* Preceptor and brethren of Hospital of St. Thomas of Acon (London) *vs.* rector and convent of Ashridge (Herts., formerly Bucks.; Knowles and Hadcock, *Medieval Religious Houses*, 203), Bonhommes. Pope appointed Card. Guglielmo Longhi of S. Nicholaus in Carcere Tulliano to hear the case. CPL ii, 73.

20. *Canonry of York and prebend of Riccall, 1311.* Tommaso da Ceccano *vs.* M. John Fraunceys. Ceccano, papal chaplain, had been prov. Royal grant to Fraunceys, who caused Ceccano to be cited before abp. of York. Ceccano appealed to Rome, and pope committed the case to M. Gaucelme de Jean, papal auditor (later card.). Abp. of York was ordered to cite parties to appear at A.S., which he did. Fraunceys died in possession of the prebend, 1314. CPL ii, 83; Reg. Greenfield v, 171-2; Le Neve, *Nor. Prov.*, 75.

21. *Parish church of Whickham (Dur.), 1311.* M. Robert Baldock, B.C.L. *vs.* M. Richard de Leycestria. Case went to A.S. from court of York. Several appeals. Case was heard at various times by M. Sycardus de Vauro, M. Hugh Geraldi, M. Hermanus de Fontibus, and M. Guglielmo Accursi, papal auditors. Accursi apparently decided in favour of Richard. Further appeal. Pope committed case for final decision to Card. Pietro Colonna. Baldock and Bp. Antony Bek of Durham were excommunicated in process of appeal, but were absolved by Card. Pietro. Baldock apparently won the suit in the end, and is called rector of Whickham in 1314. Reg. Greenfield v, 105-8 (procurations and *libelli*); Emden, *Oxford* i, 97.

22. *Defect of orders, 1311-1312.* William de Halstok', Canterbury dioc., ordained as deacon and priest without prior ordination to the subdiaconate. Received absolution at A.S. from Card. Bérenger Frédol the elder of Tusculum, major papal penitentiary. The card. then returned the case to Abp. Winchelsey to impose penance, which he did. Reg. Winchelsey, 1249-53.

23. *Treasurership of Lichfield, 1312.* Thomas de Neville *vs.* John Sandale. Litigation before papal judges delegate, and appeal to Roman curia. Neville

was excommunicated by Abp. Winchelsey. PRO C85/7/55, E135/18/18;
Cant. Cath. MS Reg. Q, f. 113v; Le Neve, *Coventry and Lichfield*, 11.

24. *Visitation rights in archdeaconry of Richmond in York, 1312-1313.* Card.
Francesco Gaetani of S. Maria in Cosmedin, archdeacon *vs.* Abp. Greenfield
of York. Greenfield was cited to A.S., and pope appointed M. Sanson de
Calvomonte and M. Gregory of Piacenza, papal auditors, successively, to
hear the case. Reg. Clem. v, nos. 7478, 9648; CPL ii, 93, 115; below, no. 55.

25. *Parish church of Harrow (Middx.), 1312-1317.* M. William de Bosco (Boys),
D.Th. *vs.* Card. William Testa of S. Cyriacus in Thermis. Sentence was given
in favour of Testa by M. Hugh Geraldi, papal auditor, possibly in England, in
1312, and Bosco appealed to A.S. Case went to Roman curia before the
auditors of causes of the apostolic palace. Claims of both parties were later
submitted to Abp. Reynolds of Canterbury, who was the patron. Reynolds in
1317 gave definitive sentence in favour of Bosco, who was resident in
England, on the grounds that the said church needed the personal residence
of the rector for its care in both spirituals and temporals. Testa, whom
Reynolds described as 'a great pillar ... who for the convenience of the
universal church has to remain in the college of cardinals at continually
heavy expense', was awarded an annual life pension from the proceeds of
Harrow. CUL MS Ee.v.31, f. 182; Reg. Clem. v, no. 8075; CPL ii, 96; Emden,
Oxford i, 239; *Yearbooks of Edward II*, Selden Soc. vol. 39, pp. xxxviii-xli, 64
seq.; above, Appendix 3, no. 41.

26. *University teaching rights, 1312-1321.* Dominican friars *vs.* chancellor and
masters of Oxford University. OP appealed to A.S. against OU in 1312, and
case was heard by Card. Riccardo Petroni of S. Eustachius. King at different
times interceded with pope and cards. in favour of OP. Pope committed the
case to three judges delegate in England, Bps. Baldock of London, Reynolds
of Worcester, and Monmouth of Llandaff. Both parties in 1313 agreed that
the case should not be settled by judges delegate but *per compromissum*, each
party choosing two representatives. These four gave decision mainly in
favour of OU in 1314, shortly before death of Clement v. After accession of
John XXII in 1316, OP again appealed to A.S., and pope committed the case to
Cards. Guillaume de Mandagout of Praeneste, Giacomo Gaetani Stefaneschi
of S. Georgius ad Velum Aureum, and Raymond de Saint-Sever of S.
Pudenciana. Pope next granted power to Cards. Gaucelme and Luca, papal
nuncios, to make further settlement in England with some concessions to OP.
Then case was heard several times before Abp. Reynolds. In 1320 pope
appointed Reynolds and Bps. Stapledon of Exeter and d'Assier of Winchester
to effect a final agreement, which was reached in 1321 in favour of OU. Salter,
Pantin, and Richardson, *Formularies* i, 3-79; Burrows, *OHS Collectanea,
Second Series*, 193-273; RR f. 85v; Reg. John XXII, nos. 5787, 5834; RWR, 73;
Rymer II:i, 178, 198, 305; Emden, *Oxford* ii, 1181; P&C ii, 1357; Stubbs,
Chronicles, vol. i, p. lxi; Rashdall, *Universities* iii, 72-4.

27. *Deanery of York, 1313-1318.* Giorgio dei Saluzzi *vs.* M. Robert Pickering, D.C.L. Le Neve, *Nor. Prov.*, 6.

28. *Abbey of Bardney (Lincs.), OSB, 1314-1315.* Abbot Robert de Wayneflete was deprived at suggestion of Bp. Dalderby of Lincoln, and king seized abbey as if vacant, because of dilapidations. Appeal and process in Roman court, abbey was restored to Wayneflete at pope's request. Case was opened again in parliament upon complaint by certain monks of Bardney that Wayneflete was responsible for further dilapidations, and another inquest was ordered. *Rot. Parl.* i, 323, 328; CCW, 222-3, 270, 312; cf. Rymer II:i, 41, 296.

29. *Deprivation of deanery of York, canonry of York and prebend of Masham, and parish church of Womersley (Yorks.), 1314-1320.* Giorgio dei Saluzzi *vs.* Abps. Greenfield and Melton of York and others. Saluzzi, papal chaplain, held these benefices by prov. from Clement v. Greenfield opposed and was cited to A.S. in 1314. Case apparently rested during vacancy of see of Rome, then John XXII cited Melton and others concerned to appear before M. Arnaldo Scaraboti, papal auditor. In 1320 king wrote to M. Raymond Subirani, papal auditor, asking him to be gracious to Saluzzi, the king's nephew and clerk. Reg. John XXII, no. 6138; CPL ii, 168; CCW, 514; Smith, *Episcopal Appointments*, 80-1; Le Neve, *Nor. Prov.*, 66.

30. *Excommunication, 1315-1318.* Appeal to A.S. by Ralph de Drayton, rector of Lowick (Northants.), John de Wolaston, and William de Kendale, from sentence of excommunication given by Abp. Reynolds in court of Canterbury. King suspended his writ for caption pending their appeal, the case having gone as far as possible during vacancy of A.S. after death of Clement v. Drayton had apparently been excommunicated in a suit against Adam de Northampton, clerk of Lincoln dioc., over the title to his benefice. Case was probably heard at A.S. after accession of John XXII, Drayton being represented by his proctor Nicholas de Lodelawe. In 1318 Reynolds again signified Drayton's excommunication to the crown. RR f. 68; Cant. Cath. MS Cart. Ant. L403; PRO C85/8/32; *Placita Parliamentaria*, ed. Ryley, 411; CCW, 443.

31. *Appropriation of church of Kennington (Kent), 1316-1317.* Abp. Reynolds of Canterbury *vs.* abbot and convent of St. Augustine Canterbury, OSB. Reynolds appointed Adam Murimuth as his proctor in curia for this matter. RR f. 118; *William Thorne's Chronicle*, 396, 422-3, 534-6.

32. *Election to archbishopric of York, 1316-1317.* Six canons of York and possibly others *vs.* William Melton, elect of York. Case was to be heard at A.S. by Card. Arnaud d'Aux of Albano. PRO SC7/25/18; Reg. John XXII, no. 5652; CCW, 444; Rymer II:i, 305-7; CPL ii, 414, 440; Smith, *Episcopal Appointments*, 28-31; Le Neve, *Nor. Prov.*, 1.

33. *Archdeaconry of Northampton in Lincoln, 1317.* Thomas de Grandisson *vs.* M. Gilbert Middleton. Grandisson was in litigation at Roman court when he died there, and pope prov. it to Card. Gaucelme de Jean of SS. Marcellinus et

Petrus by surrogation. Reg. John xxii, no. 4611; cpi. ii, 140, 154; Le Neve, *Lincoln*, 10.

34. *Excommunication, 1317.* Robert de Cerne, osa, canon and former prior of the New Hospital of St. Mary without Bishopsgate (London). Case went to A.S. before Card. Bérenger Frédol the elder of Tusculum, major papal penitentiary, who found that Cerne had acted 'non in contemptum clavium sed per simplicitatem et iuris ignoranciam'. The card. returned the case to Abp. Reynolds to pronounce absolution and impose penance, which he did. rr f. 51; Reg. London, 36, 54-5.

35. *Canonry of Lincoln and prebend of Cropredy, 1317.* Johannes de Vicecomite *vs.* Bp. Dalderby of Lincoln. Benefice was vacant by cons. of a bp., and had been reserved to Card. Jacobus de Via of SS. Johannes et Paulus, who died before obtaining it. Pope then prov. it to Card. Bertrand du Poujet of S. Marcellus, notwithstanding the appeal of Vicecomite which was pending at the A.S. The card. was successful. Reg. John xxii, nos. 4236, 5187, 5370; cpi. ii, 127, 156; Le Neve, *Lincoln*, 57-8.

36. *Canonry of York and prebend of Masham, 1317.* John de Grandisson *vs.* Giorgio dei Saluzzi. Grandisson had been deprived by Abp. Greenfield of York, and Saluzzi provided, before 17 Jan. 1313/1314 (cpi. ii, 122, 168). Litigation not noted in Le Neve, *Nor. Prov.*, 66. Process of the case, heard probably 13-15 March 1316/1317 in presence of Card. Bertrand de Montfavès, survives in Vatican Archives, Instrumenta Miscellanea 601, calendared in Burns, ahp ix (1971), no. 94. According to the taxation of 1291, this prebend was the wealthiest in England, assessed at 250 marks per year (Edwards, *English Secular Cathedrals*, 39).

37. *Theft, apostasy, forgery, and lies, 1317-1318.* Prior and chapter of Christ Church Canterbury *vs.* Robert of Thanet, osb. Thanet, an apostate monk from Christ Church Canterbury, was thought to be inventing scandal against Abp. Reynolds and making appeals against Christ Church Canterbury at the Roman curia. The Canterbury monks arranged various procurations, letters, and other actions against him. rr ff. 69, 123v; Cant. Cath. ms Eastry Cor. i, 29; Lambeth ms 242, ff. 311v, 322, 324, 325, 330; cul. ms Ee.v.31, ff. 161, 176, 177, 177v, 178v, 180-181v, 188v, 190v-191v, 193v.

38. *See of Rochester, 1317-1319.* Johannes de Puteolis *vs.* Hamo Hethe, osb. King supported Hethe, queen supported Puteolis. Both appealed to Roman court. Upon advice of Card. William Testa the case was remitted to the papal nuncios in England (Cards. Gaucelme de Jean and Luca Fieschi), but was later referred back to curia. Pope again committed the case to Cards. Gaucelme and Luca upon their return to the curia, and they turned it over to the auditors Pierre de Nogaret and Seffridus de Vesano. Hethe was summoned to the curia in person, and he went there. Case was heard several times in curia, apparently by sixteen auditors and by various cardinals. Puteolis died. Final decision favoured Hethe, who was consecrated 1319 at

Avignon by Card. Niccolò Albertini da Prato of Ostia. Reg. Hethe, pp. x-xii; Le Neve, *Mon. So. Prov.*, 37; Smith, *Episcopal Appointments*, 31-3; Stubbs, *Registrum Sacrum Anglicanum*, 72.

39. *Payment of 'greater commons' in Hereford cathedral to a canon nonresident as papal auditor, 1317-1324.* M. John de Ros, D.C.L. *vs.* dean and chapter of Hereford. Ros as auditor of causes of the apostolic palace claimed he should continue to receive payments of 'greater commons' as a canon of Hereford while nonresident because he was in papal service. Chapter was excommunicated for refusal to pay him by order of another papal auditor, Buxolus Parmensis, in 1318. By arbitration of Card. William Testa in 1319 Ros renounced any rights to 'greater commons' and chapter agreed to pay 'petty commons'. Ros however renewed his claim in 1322; chapter was again censured and appealed again to the pope. Proctors of the chapter were at one point refused admission to the apostolic palace In final settlement of 1324 Ros again renounced his claim to 'greater commons' but was promised backpayment of all 'petty commons' by the chapter. Yates, BIHR xlviii (1975), 16-21; cf. Edwards, *English Secular Cathedrals*, 43, 52.

40. *Deprivation of parish churches of Campsall, Almondbury, and Penistone (all Yorks.), 1318.* M. Bonifazio dei Saluzzi *vs.* Abps. Greenfield and Melton of York and others. Greenfield was cited to A.S. in 1314 for depriving Saluzzi, papal chaplain. Melton was cited for doing same in 1318, and case was to be heard before M. Arnaldo Scaraboti, papal auditor. Reg. John XXII, no. 6139; CPL ii, 122, 168; Thompson and Clay, *Fasti Parochiales* i, 57-9; ii, 23-5.

41. *Canonry of Lincoln and prebend of Leighton Buzzard, 1318-1325.* M. Johannes de Podio Barzaco *vs.* William Airmyn and M. William de Weston, D.C.L. Abp. Reynolds was delegated by pope in 1321 to cite Airmyn to A.S., and he in turn appointed others to do it. King inhibited Airmyn from answering any citation outside the realm. John Stratford, royal envoy to the curia, handled the matter at Avignon in 1322-1323. Weston took over Airmyn's claim in 1324. Pope named Card. Pierre d'Arrablay of S. Susanna to hear the case in 1325, and the card. commanded Reynolds to cite Weston. RR ff. 126v, 145, 300; PRO E135/24/37; CCR 1318-23, 510; Deeley, EHR xliii (1928), 519-22; Sayles, *Select Cases in the Court of King's Bench under Edward II*, pp. 126, 128; Smith, *Episcopal Appointments*, 75-6, 125-6; Le Neve, *Lincoln*, 79. Prof. E. B. Graves informs me of the following sources of actions prohibiting appeals to Rome in this case: PRO K.B. 27/247, rex m. 11v; -/248, rex m. 7v; -/250, rex m. 2; -/251, rex m. 5v; C70/4, m. 2v; E135/6/23; C47/47/1/2.

42. *Archdeaconry of Salop in Hereford, 1319-1320.* M. William son of Thomas le Mercer of Rosse *vs.* ?. Appeal was 'made before' M. Stefano Hugoneti, papal auditor. Reg. John XXII, nos. 7431, 7436, 10938; CPL ii, 173, 182, 197; Le Neve, *Hereford*, 7.

43. *Dependent status of Dover Priory, 1319-1320*. Christ Church Canterbury *vs.* Dover Priory. Plea of Christ Church Canterbury was pending in the Roman court, then judges delegate were appointed. Haines, *Dover Priory*, 97; Lambeth MS 242, f. 325; HMC Eighth Rep., I, app., 354; Cant. Cath. MS Reg. I, ff. 369-369v; RR f. 99v; *Rot. Parl.* i, 326-7; CCW, 421-2.

44. *See of Lincoln, 1320*. M. Anthony Bek, D.Th. *vs.* M. Henry Burghersh. Bek was elected, king supported Burghersh. Bek went personally to Roman court but his election was quashed by the pope, who provided Burghersh. *The Book of John de Schalby*, transl. Srawley, 18; Bridlington, *Gesta Edwardi*, 60; *Vita Edwardi Secundi*, 105; Emden, *Oxford* i, 153; Le Neve, *Lincoln*, 1; Smith, *Episcopal Appointments*, 35-6.

45. *Tithes, 1320*. Abbot and convent of St. Augustine Canterbury, OSB *vs.* parishioners of the churches of Faversham and Preston (Kent). Both churches were appropriated to the abbey, the parishioners refused to pay certain tithes, and the abbey appealed to A.S. The pope delegated the case to the prior of St. Gregory Canterbury, OSA, and the proctor of Christ Church Canterbury at the A.S. contradicted the papal commission in the audience of contradicted letters to ensure that the monks of Christ Church would not be cited in the case as parishioners of Faversham or Preston. The proctor of St. Augustine agreed. Cant. Cath. MS Cart. Ant. C1297, C1298.

46. *Excommunication, 1320-1321*. John de Dorsete, vicar of All Saints, Catherington (Hants), excommunicated by authority of the court of Canterbury in 1320. Abp. Reynolds wrote king for caption. Then in 1321 Reynolds wrote king again, at request of vice-chancellor of the A.S., Card. Pierre Tessier of S. Stephanus in Coelio Monte, asking him to desist from caption while the case was pending in the Roman court, but the crown had already learned of Dorsete's appeal and taken action for his release. Dorsete died as vicar in 1322. RR ff. 293, 293v; PRO C85/8/45, 51 (transcribed in Logan, *Excommunication*, 201); Reg. Asserio, 514; CCR 1318-23, 377, 512.

47. *Separation of prebend of Aylesbury from prebend of Milton Ecclesia in Lincoln, 1320-1327*. Card. Gaillard de la Mothe of S. Lucia in Silice *vs.* Robert Baldock, D.C.L. John Stratford, royal envoy to Avignon, handled the matter at the curia in 1322-1323. Baldock was excommunicated. Case ended in compromise. Deeley, EHR xliii (1928), 521-2; Graves, 'The legal significance of the first statute of *Praemunire*', 63-4, 66; Le Neve, *Lincoln*, 91; Pantin, *The English Church*, p. 81 n. 2; Sayles, *Select Cases in the Court of King's Bench under Edward II*, pp. 126, 128; Smith, *Episcopal Appointments*, 103-5; above, Appendix 3, no. 24. Prof. E. B. Graves informs me of the following sources of actions prohibiting appeals to Rome in this case: PRO K.B. 27/249, rex m. 1; -/250, rex m. 18; -/251, rex m. 6v; -/254, rex m. 21; -/256, rex m. 15; -/258, rex m. 21; -/260, rex m. 24; -/262, rex m. 27v; -/264, rex m. 17v; C47/16/7/3.

48. *Parish church of Ratcliffe-on-Soar (Notts.), 1320-1328.* Card. Bertrand du Poujet of S. Marcellus *vs.* Geoffrey de Chintriaco, Cluniac prior of Lenton (Notts.), and Walter de Alisonde. Church was prov. to Card. Bertrand, Chintriaco was named papal executor, Alisonde occupied it by lay power, king issued prohibition against executing the provision. Chintriaco and Alisonde were cited to A.S., and Card. Pierre d'Arrablay of S. Susanna was appointed to hear the case. Chintriaco, forbidden by king to go overseas, was excommunicated for non-appearance at the curia, but was later absolved. Reg. John xxii, nos. 10924-5, 18433, 18450, 43443; cpl. ii, 194, 234-5, 284, 471; Smith, *Episcopal Appointments,* 84-5; above, Appendix 3, no. 33.

49. *Misappropriation of goods of Abingdon Abbey (Berks., osb), 1321-1322.* Prior and convent of Abingdon *vs.* Abbot John de Sutton. Case first heard by Card. Nicolas de Fréauville, op, of S. Eusebius, then by Card. Pierre Tessier of S. Stephanus in Coelio Monte, then in public consistory before the pope. Abbot Sutton found guilty of misappropriation of goods assigned to prior and convent to the sum of £1000, as well as of taking their muniments and imprisoning the prior and some of the monks. John xxii suspended Sutton from administration of both temporalities and spiritualities. Reg. Martival ii, 348-54, 385-6 (includes full schedule of charges against the abbot).

50. *Canonry of Salisbury and prebend of Blewbury, 1321-1326.* M. Thomas de Charlton, D.C.L. *vs.* M. Henry de Clif. Dispute over advowson in king's court, case went to Rome from tuitorial appeal in the court of arches. Pope committed the case to M. Johannes de Arpadella, papal auditor. Then both pope and Arpadella committed the case to Oliverus de Cerzeto, papal auditor, who gave definitive sentence 1326 in favour of Clif. rr f. 70v; Reg. Martival i. 37-54, 79-80, 175-223 (extensive records of process in the papal audience); ibid. iv, 50; Reg. Hethe, 85-9; Rymer II:ii, 714, 732, 751-2; Le Neve, *Salisbury,* 37.

51. *Canonry of Southwell and prebend of Rampton, 1321-1327.* Georgius de Solerio of Ivrea *vs.* William de Bevercote. Pope committed the case at the A.S. to M. Guigo de Sancto Germano, papal auditor. pro C49/5/13; rr f. 60; Reg. John xxii, no. 15907; Deeley, ehr xliii (1928), p. 517 n. 5; Mollat, *Revue d'histoire ecclésiastique* xxxii (1936), 883; Smith, *Episcopal Appointments,* 70-2. Prof. E. B. Graves informs me of the following sources of actions prohibiting appeals to Rome in this case: pro K.B. 27/244, rex m. 9; -/245, rex m. 10-10v; -/246, rex m. 5, 11, 32; -/247, rex m. 5, 9v; -/248, rex m. 13; -/249, rex m. 1, 8v; -/250, rex m. 6v, 13; -/252, rex m. 3v; -/253, rex m. 13; -/254, rex m. 7, 26v, 30v; -/255, rex m. 6, 9v; -/256, rex m. 24, 25; -/258, rex m. 25v; -/259, rex m. 11; -/261, rex m. 9v; -/264, rex m. 17v, 24.

52. *Sequestration of prebend of Banbury in Lincoln, 1322.* Georgius de Solerio of Ivrea, prebendary *vs.* Bp. Burghersh of Lincoln. Burghersh sequestrated the prebend upon royal command after Solerio had tried to make his appeal over a prebend of Southwell (above, no. 51) to the A.S. contrary to royal

prohibition. Solerio then appealed to A.S. for restitution of Banbury, and pope committed the case to M. Guigo de Sancto Germano, papal auditor. PRO SC7/56/12; Reg. John XXII, nos. 15907, 15910; CPL. ii, 223, 449; Le Neve, *Lincoln*, 31.

53. *Archdeaconry of Lincoln, 1323-1330*. Archambaud de Périgord *vs.* M. Hugh de Camera, D.C.L. Both resigned their claims into the hands of the pope. Litigation at curia, and decision in favour of Hugh. Reg. John XXII, nos. 17798, 48663-4; CPL. ii, 231, 339; Le Neve, *Lincoln*, 6; Emden, *Oxford* iii, 2158.

54. *Heretical doctrine, 1324-1328*. M. William of Ockham, OFM, cited to Roman curia, examined, and excommunicated. Emden, *Oxford* ii, 1384-7.

55. *Visitation rights in archdeaconry of Richmond in York, 1325*. Talleyrand de Périgord, archdeacon (later card.) *vs.* Abp. Melton of York. John XXII, Secret Letters, no. 2468; CPL. ii, 470; above, Appendix 3, no. 30; above, this Appendix, no. 24.

56. *Archidiaconal jurisdiction over members of Oxford University, c. 1325-1345*. Card. Gaillard de la Mothe of S. Lucia in Silice, archdeacon *vs.* Oxford University. Case was to be heard in Roman curia by Card. Bertrand de Montfavès of S. Maria in Aquiro, who commanded Abp. Reynolds to cite the chancellor and masters. Edw. II interceded on behalf of OU with pope and cards. OU finally obtained archidiaconal jurisdiction over its members in corrective and testamentary matters, provided they did not hold an Oxford benefice. RR f. 145v; Cant. Cath. MS Cart. Ant. A36 (I), f. 1; Rymer II:i, 620; Rymer II:ii, 763; Pantin, *The English Church*, p. 81 n. 3; above, Appendix 3, no. 24; Fletcher, *OHS Collectanea, First Series*, 16-20; Reg. Martival ii, 582-9.

57. *Priory of Montacute (Som.), OSB Cluniac, 1326-1327*. Robert Busse *vs.* Gicard de Jou. Busse was prov. by the pope. Jou, a monk of Cluny, was appointed by the abbot of Cluny. Jou was cited to the A.S., Busse died during litigation at the curia, and pope then prov. the priory to Card. Pierre de Mortemart of S. Stephanus in Coelio Monte. Edw. III supported Jou against the card. Reg. John XXII, nos. 26620, 28147, 29767; CPL. ii, 257, 278; Rymer II:ii, 807-8; above, Appendix 3, no. 23.

58. *Parish church of Turvey (Beds.), 1327*. Richard de Solberi, B.C.L. *vs.* ?. Reg. John XXII, no. 30571; CPL. ii, 266.

59. *Visitation rights in Norwich diocese, 1327-1330*. Prior and chapter of Norwich *vs.* Abp. Reynolds of Canterbury and M. John de Badesley (official of Norwich *sede vacante*). Norwich appealed to A.S. and Reynolds and Badesley were cited. Pope named M. Jesselin de Cassagnes, D.Cn.&C.L., papal auditor, to hear the case, and the *libelli* of both parties were exhibited before him. Reynolds sought the support of prior and chapter of Christ Church Canterbury for the negotiations at the curia; this was initially refused but later granted. Dispute was settled by composition under Abp. Mepham,

1330. RR ff. 193, 199, 276-278v; CUL MS Ee.v.31, ff. 259v, 262v; HMC Ninth
Rep., I, app., 96, 98; Cant. Cath. MS Reg. L, ff. 153v, 168, 173v; *Lit. Cant.*
nos. 159, 227, 309; Churchill, *Canterbury Administration* i, 194-6; ii, 61; CCR
1323-7, 534, 558.

60. *Canonry of Bath and Wells and prebend of Yatton, 1327-1334.* M. Thomas
Trilleck *vs.* M. Robert Stratford *vs.* M. Alan de Coningesburgh, D.C.L.
Emden, *Oxford* iii, 1907; Le Neve, *Bath and Wells*, 80; Smith, *Episcopal
Appointments*, 78-9; Reg. Orleton Hereford, p. xli n. 3.

61. *Alienation of tithes and other goods, 1328.* Abbot and convent of St. Albans,
OSB *vs.* abbot of Ramsey, OSB. Upon appeal from St. Albans, the pope
commanded Ramsey to make restoration of certain tithes and other goods.
The proctor of Christ Church Canterbury contradicted the papal order in the
audience of contradicted letters to ensure that the papal command would in
no way extend to the monks of Christ Church Canterbury. The proctor of St.
Albans agreed. Cant. Cath. MS Cart. Ant. C1299.

62. *Canonry of Ripon and prebend of Nunwick, 1329.* M. Thomas of Savoy *vs.* M.
Robert de Bridlington. Appeal to A.S., pope commissioned M. Peter of
Piacenza, papal auditor, to hear the case. Reg. John XXII, no. 47259; CPL ii,
310; Fowler, *Memorials of the Church of SS. Peter and Wilfrid, Ripon* ii, 192-
3; Mollat, *Revue d'histoire ecclésiastique* xxxii (1936), 883.

63. *Visitation rights and other matters, 1329-1333.* Abbot and convent of St.
Augustine Canterbury, OSB *vs.* Abp. Mepham of Canterbury. In a visitation of
his city and diocese, Mepham summoned the abbey to appear before him and
the auditors of his court. The abbey appealed to the Roman curia. Mepham
was summoned by the papal nuncio Itherius de Concoreto, but refused to
reply. Case was heard both at the Roman court and in England. Mepham in
1330 was suspended from office and excommunicated by Concoreto. Acting
as judge delegate, Concoreto gave judgment in favour of the abbey. Mepham
died excommunicate in 1333. Later Concoreto's judgment was set aside by
compromise between abbot and convent and Mepham's successor Abp.
Stratford. Cant. Cath. MS Reg. L, ff. 31, 174v, 185, 186; *Lit. Cant.* nos. 317,
483, 484, 505; HMC Ninth Rep., I, app., 99; PRO 31/9/17a, f. 84v; Emden,
Oxford ii, 1261; Haines, *Dover Priory*, 103; *William Thorne's Chronicle*, 440-
61, 481, 486; Lunt, *Accounts*, xxv-xxvi; Pantin, 'The letters of John Mason',
195-201.

64. *Appropriation of church of Warmington (Northants.), 1330.* M. Gilbert
Middleton *vs.* abbot and convent of Peterborough, OSB. Case went to A.S. but
was settled by composition. BL MS Cott. Vespasian E.xxi, f. 67v.

65. *Canonry of Bath and Wells and prebend of Wiveliscombe, 1330-1332.* Gerard
de Sudbury *vs.* Robert de Hillum. Both parties appealed to curia. Auditors of
causes of the apostolic palace ordered Hillum to be removed. Reg. John XXII,
no. 60707; CPL ii, 374; Le Neve, *Bath and Wells*, 77.

66. *Canonry of Abergwili and prebend of Llanarthney, 1331.* M. Robert de Tautone *vs.* ?. Reg. John XXII, no. 53934; CPL ii, 331.

67. *See of Salisbury, c. 1331, 1333.* Robert Wyvil *vs.* M. Nicholas de Lodelawe. Appeal was made to pope about the appointment of Wyvil. Lodelawe, resident at the Roman curia, was described as a centre of intrigue against Wyvil. Royal influence at A.S. in favour of Wyvil was managed by the king's proctor Andreas Sapiti. PRO 31/9/17a, f. 20v; Chew, *Hemingby's Register*, 213, 256; Le Neve, *Salisbury*, 1.

68. *Apostasy, 1331-1333.* M. Peter de Dene, OSB, D.Cn.&C.L. *vs.* abbot of St. Augustine Canterbury, OSB. Dene escaped from the abbey, was arrested and imprisoned by the abbot, and appealed to Rome. Pope ordered restoration. HMC Ninth Rep., I, app., 81; Emden, *Oxford* iii, 2169; *William Thorne's Chronicle*, 465-81.

69. *Jurisdiction of the dean of Lincoln, 1332.* M. Anthony Bek, D.Th., dean, *vs.* chapter of Lincoln. Bek appealed to A.S. and went there personally. Edw. III wrote John XXII asking him to command Bek to return home because personal residence of the dean was very important and because the dispute by its very nature ought not to be treated in the Roman curia. King outlined the duties of the dean and pointed out that when Bek was a canon of Lincoln, before he became dean, he had stood on the chapter's side over this very same question. But Bek won favour with the pope, who made him a papal chaplain and granted him indult for three years' nonresidence while at the papal court. BL MS Harl. 3720, ff. 13v-16; Emden, *Oxford* i, 153.

70. *Parish church of Buckland (near Dover, Kent), c. 1332.* John de Nottingham, rector *vs.* ?. Decision was given in Nottingham's favour in the Roman curia, and English executors were appointed to reinstate him. Cant. Cath. MS Reg. L, f. 24; *Lit. Cant.* nos. 474-6.

71. *Intrusion into subdeanery of Salisbury, 1333.* Chapter of Salisbury *vs.* William de Ayston and William de Codeford. Chapter claimed that Ayston had intruded and that Codeford, acting as commissary of the official of the court of Canterbury, had unjustly placed chapter of Salisbury under interdict, suspension, and excommunication. Chapter appointed its proctors against this in the Roman curia. Chew, *Hemingby's Register*, 99; Le Neve, *Salisbury*, 5.

72. *Canonry of Wilton and prebend of Chalke, 1333.* Robert de Trumpflete *vs.* John de Wodeforde. Sentence was given in favour of Robert, John appealed to pope, Robert died, and pope prov. the benefice to another person by surrogation. Reg. John XXII, no. 61954; CPL ii, 398.

73. *Matrimonial appeal, 1333-1334.* John de Grey, 'miles' *vs.* William la Zouch Mortimer, lord of Ashby la Zouch. Each claimed Eleanor, widow of Hugh Despenser, the younger, to be his wife. At least four appeals to pope were made, decision changed several times. Hearings were usually before delegates

in England, although case was handled at Avignon by Andreas Sapiti as king's proctor. PRO 31/9/17a, f. 69; Reg. John XXII, no. 60372; CPL ii, 394.

74. *Archdeaconry of Wiltshire in Salisbury, 1333-1334*. M. John de Whitchurch *vs*. M. Ralph de Querendon. Whitchurch had papal prov. to the archdeaconry. Querendon caused papal sentences against himself to be torn up publicly, and committed other outrages against Whitchurch's proctor and a notary public. Whitchurch appealed to curia, Querendon was cited. Querendon was given license from Salisbury chapter to go to Avignon on business about his benefices, and he also made arrangements for a loan. Chew, *Hemingby's Register*, 220-1; Reg. John XXII, no. 61090; CPL ii, 383-4.

75. *Canonry of Bath and Wells and prebend of Combe Duodecima, c. 1333-1334*. Robert de Taunton *vs*. M. Alan de Coningesburgh, D.C.L. Royal petition in favour of Taunton was handled in Roman curia by king's proctor Andreas Sapiti. Case went before M. Giles of Benevento, papal auditor. PRO 31/9/17a, ff. 21, 25, 33v-35v; Le Neve, *Bath and Wells*, 34.

76. *Provision to perpetual vicarage of Sourton (Devon.), 1334*. John Howel *vs*. Bp. Grandisson of Exeter. Pope prov. it to Howel, but Grandisson refused to execute papal letters. Howel appealed to A.S., and then died at A.S. *lite pendente*. Pope prov. it to another by surrogation. Reg. John XXII, no. 62788; CPL ii, 401.

Appendix 7

The Mandate of Pope John xxii
to his Cardinal Nuncios in England, 1317

Transcribed from Lambeth Palace MS Reg. Reynolds, ff. 216-218, with some emendations from Vatican Archives, Reg. Aven. (RA) 2, ff. 231-233, and Reg. Vat. (RV) 63, ff. 394-395. The Lambeth MS is badly faded in places. Principles of transcription are those set forth in the Notes on Style at the beginning of this book. Two dots in the transcription here indicate gemipunctus in the Lambeth MS; no gemipunctus occurs in RA or RV.

This bull, *Magna vestre discrecionis industria*, is calendared briefly in Reg. John xxii, nos. 5180-1 and in CPL ii, 132. In the Latin calendar it is mistakenly dated '.xvii. kal. Aprilis'. I have been unable to locate this bull in the Marini transcripts from the papal registers (BL MS Add. 15366) or in the seventeenth-century Vatican codex of documents relating to the mission of Cardinals Gaucelme and Luca in England (Vatican Library MS Barb. Lat. 2366). For a closely related bull of a more exhortatory sort addressed to the king himself, see Reg. John xxii, no. 5219, and CPL ii, 129.

The significance of this bull is the fact that John xxii in the first year of his pontificate decided in March of 1316/1317 to send instructions to his cardinal nuncios in England that were closely parallel to the complaints about English church-state relationships already set forth by Clement v in his bull *Supra montem excelsum* of 28 October 1309. For discussion of this significance, see above, pp. 10-11, 129, 138, 153, 187-89, 193, 205, 207, 221, 231.

Clement v's bull of 1309 is printed in Reg. Winchelsey, 1031 seq. and in Rymer II:i, 97-8, but not in Reg. Clem. v, and it is discussed in P&C ii, 1285. Some parallel passages are also found in the complaints of the English delegates at the council of Vienne 1311-1312, printed in P&C ii, 1353-6. To facilitate easy comparison of the present bull with that of Clement v, I have arbitrarily divided the text into three paragraphs, the first and last of which have only a few phrases similar to Clement's bull.

The long central paragraph, however, beginning in its first sentence at the word *citaciones*, follows very closely (with some exceptions) the middle portion of Clement's bull beginning with the same word *citaciones* in the printed edition of Reg. Winchelsey, 1032, ninth line from the bottom, and in Rymer II:i, 97, in the third paragraph from the bottom of the left column (*Et nichilominus...*).

I am indebted to Dr. P. T. V. M. Chaplais and Fr. L. E. Boyle, OP, for many helpful suggestions in preparing this transcription.

Bulla directa dominis cardinalibus, compulsoria contra . . officiales regios super gravaminibus, sed quo ad regem exhortatoria.

Iohannes episcopus servus servorum Dei dilectis filiis Gaucelmo tituli Sanctorum Marcellini et Petri presbitero et Luce Sancte Marie in Via Lata diacono cardinalibus apostolice sedis nunciis salutem et apostolicam bene-diccionem.[1] Magna vestre discrecionis industria quam in altis et arduis frequencius experimur nostros excitat cogitatus ut vobis in quibus secure quiescimus que sunt eciam grandis ponderis committamus. Ad nostri siquidem [2] apostolatus auditum multorum insinuacio clamosa perduxit,[3] quod nonnulli officiales et ministri ac familiares carissimi in Christo filii nostri Edwardi[4] regis Anglie illustris, eorum finibus non contenti,[5] quibusdam ex fratribus nostris[6] sancte Romane ecclesie cardinalibus ac officialibus apostolice sedis et diversis aliis personis ecclesiasticis in beneficiis, dignitatibus et personatibus que in regno Anglie canonice obtinere[7] noscuntur, graves molestias inferunt et irrogant lesiones, et quampluribus ex eis dictis beneficiis per violenciam spoliatis, iidem . . officiales, ministri et familiares per falsi suggestionem, nonnulla ex eis sibi et alia diversis aliis personis per dictum [8] regem conferri contra iusticiam procurarunt, multaque ipsi et quamplures nobiles dicti regni bona diversarum ecclesiarum et personarum ecclesiasticarum detinent violen-ter, in personarum et ecclesiarum ipsarum dispendium occupata, et, quod

---

[1] All the text up to this point is found in RR only. RA and RV read *eisdem cardinalibus*.
[2] RR possibly *sequidem*.
[3] RA *produxit* changed to *perduxit*; RV possibly *produxit*.
[4] RA and RV *Eduardi*.
[5] RV *contempti*.
[6] RR *nostribus*.
[7] RR *pertinere*.
[8] RR *per dictum* repeated.

graviori mente perferimus, .. officiales seu ministri prefati quominus per collectores ad hoc deputatos denarius beati Petri in dicto regno Anglie colligatur,[9] et residua decimarum et procuracionum legatorum et nunciorum sedis predicte, legata indistincte relicta, bona clericorum decedencium ab intestato, pene pecuniarie[10] apposite in contractibus pro terre sancte subsidio exigantur, ac pecunia[11] ipsis terre sancte[12] et ecclesie Romane debita de Anglie et[13] Scocie regnis ac Hibernie et Wallie[14] partibus extrahatur per manus quorumlibet .. mercatorum, impedire minus iuste presumunt, et nonnulla bona bone memorie patriarche Ierosolomitani et episcopi Dunolmensis[15] que ad usum dicte terre sancte fuerant deputata contra iusticiam detinere; legata quoque per ipsum facta in ipsius terre sancte subsidium, ac voti redempcio ad quod idem patriarcha vivifice crucis assumpto signaculo usque ad certum numerum militum[16] se adhuc vivens astrinxerat fieri, ac[17] debita in quibus eidem Romane ecclesie tenebatur, exigi valeant aliquatenus non permittunt. Preterea sensibus nostris ex eo multe turbacionis causa consurgit, quod cum de dignitatibus et beneficiis ecclesiasticis in regnis et terris dicti regis auctoritate apostolica sufficientibus personis et dignis, sicut sedes ipsa divino et humano iure licite potest et consuevit temporibus retroactis, provideri contingit, certis eis super hoc iuxta morem quem sedes ipsa servare in talibus consuevit executoribus deputatis, nonnulli ex dictis .. officialibus et ministris qui cum malefecerint gloriantur licencie[18] laxatis habenis, quamvis nulla in talibus attributa potestas vel iurisdiccio sit, eisdem executoribus ipsis eodem dissimulante[19] rege temerarie inhibere presumunt, ne commisse ipsis huiusmodi ministerium execucionis exerceant aut processus aliquos faciant super illis seu factos publicent vel faciant publicari, in excommunicacionum sentencias, quas, ut plurimum, executores huiusmodi graciarum in quoslibet impedientes quominus dicte gracie debitum sorciantur effectum proferant[20] incidendo. Et nichilominus rex prefatus asserens prescripcionem sibi non currere, beneficium

---

[9] RA corrected; RV *colligetur*.

[10] RR *peccuniarie*.

[11] RR *peccunia*.

[12] RR omitted; RA interlineated.

[13] RA and RV *ac*.

[14] RA and RV *Ibernie et Vallie*.

[15] RV *Dunelm*.

[16] RA and RV *militum numerum*.

[17] RA and RV *et*.

[18] RR *licencicie*, *ci* expunged.

[19] RR *dissimilante*.

[20] RR *proferunt*.

quod archiepiscopali vel episcopali sede vacante apostolica vel ordinaria ipsum eodem rege tunc non conferente auctoritate confertur, eciam si is[21] cui huiusmodi beneficium collatum existit,[22] illud per plures annos possederit pacifice et quiete, alii confert,[23] ac si tunc archiepiscopatus vel episcopatus ipse vacaret; et si aliquando eadem auctoritate beneficium archiepiscopatu vel episcopatu non vacante alicui conferatur,[24] et antequam ille qui huiusmodi collacionem obtinet possessionem huiusmodi beneficii[25] sit adeptus, prelatus forte decedat, idem rex racione temporalitatis quam in manibus suis habet, confert beneficium antedictum.

Predicti autem officiales et ministri tantis gravaminibus non contenti, citaciones[26] cum super aliquibus negociis sive causis ad ecclesiasticum forum spectantibus in eisdem regnis et terris auctoritate dicte sedis eciam si contra ecclesiasticas personas emanant, concessis iudicibus vel executoribus super illis et subdelegatis[27] ab eis, ne ad citaciones procedant easdem aut illas[28] fieri quoquomodo permittant, vel aliquem extra dictum regnum earumdem[29] litterarum auctoritate conveniant, tabellionibus quoque ne super ipsis publica conficiant instrumenta, citatis eciam ne racione citacionum huiusmodi ad sedem accedant prefatam, vel citacionibus eisdem pareant vel intendant, sub personarum et bonorum penis gravissimis, contra statuta canonica que in suos[30] excommunicacionis sentenciam proferunt contemptores, inhibere presumpcione temeraria non formidant. Et insuper quia collectores fructuum beneficiorum ecclesiasticorum pro ecclesie Romane necessitatibus interdum in regnis et terris reservatorum predictis a colleccione ipsorum eisdem[31] commissa, iuxta prohibicionem per dictos .. officiales minus racionabiliter eis factam, nolunt prout nec debent eciam resilire, iidem officiales et ministri non considerantes quod supereminens apostolice sedis auctoritas honoratur et spernitur in ministris, ipsos carcerali faciunt custodie in nostrum[32]

---

[21] RA and RV *is* corrected from *eis*.
[22] RR *extitit*.
[23] RA and RV *conferre*; RR *? confere* corrected to *confert*.
[24] RV *non conferatur*.
[25] RR *gracie*.
[26] Close parallelism with bull of Clement v begins at this point.
[27] RV *subdellegatis*.
[28] RA and RV *illos*.
[29] RA and RV *eorumdem*.
[30] RA and RV *suas*.
[31] RA corrected from *eorumdem*.
[32] RA *nostrum* corrected from *nostro*; RV *nostro*.

et dicte[33] sedis opprobrium mancipari, nec a dicto carcere, quod non absque rubore referimus, nisi precio se redimant liberantur. Excommunicatos vero sedis auctoritate predicte ad requisicionem nunciorum ipsius seu iudicum a sede concessorum eadem iidem rex, officiales et . . ministri capi facere denegant, quamvis ipsi ad instanciam ordinariorum regni predicti eorum auctoritate excommunicacionis sentencia innodatos,[34] dummodo ipsos sentenciam huiusmodi per quadraginta dies sustinuisse constiterit, personaliter capi faciant et sub carcerali custodia detineri. Et nichilominus ne delegati sedis eiusdem aut ordinarii memorati seu quicumque ecclesiastici viri de causis ad ecclesiasticum forum mere spectantibus, prout pertinet ad eosdem, cognoscere possint, dicti . . officiales et ministri impediunt minus iuste, et ne de cognicione huiusmodi se aliquatenus intromittant, eis districcius interdicunt,[35] quos[36] si contra interdictum huiusmodi cui minime parere tenentur eos venire contingat, bona eorum indebite capi faciunt impediendo per hoc iurisdiccionem ecclesiasticam manifeste, quam deberent pro dicte sedis reverencia promptis studiis defensare. Predicti quoque ordinarii aliquam personam ecclesiasticam, quantumcumque grave delictum[37] commiserit, non audent ut de ipsa per eos fiat iusticie complementum, dictorum officialium et[38] ministrorum minis[39] perterriti[40] capere vel tenere. Insuper autem officiales et ministri prefati non considerantes quod laicis in clericos nulla est attributa potestas, clericos eciam[41] in sacerdocii ordine constitutos et alias personas ecclesiasticas tam religiosas quam seculares, eciam si pontificali preemineant[42] dignitate, absque nostra vel aliorum superiorum [suorum][43] licencia, in derogacionem ecclesiastice libertatis, ut iuxta patrie vulgare loquamur, amerciant in pena pecuniaria[44] vel condempnant iniuste pro eorum libito voluntatis, ipsosque per capcionem et detencionem personarum et bonorum suorum ex eorum officio et alias ad instanciam quorumcumque tam super criminalibus quam personalibus et

---

[33] RR corrected from ? sancte.
[34] RA and RV sentencias inodatos.
[35] RR corrected from interdicant.
[36] RA and RV quos; RR quod.
[37] RA corrected from debitum.
[38] RA and RV ac.
[39] RA corrected from minus.
[40] RR preteriti.
[41] RR autem.
[42] RA and RV premineant.
[43] RR omits.
[44] RR peccuniaria.

aliis quibuscumque accionibus invitos et eciam renitentes, eorum declinantes forum et clericale privilegium allegantes, coram se respondere compellunt. Ceterum cum per . . officiales et ministros predictos aliquos clericos eciam in sacerdocii ordine constitutos, pro quovis delicto[45] quamvis indebite capi contingit, ipsos coram[46] se nudis pedibus capite discooperto[47] in sola tunica vel camisia sicut homicidas, laicos et[48] latrones dampnandos ad mortem, in magnam Summi Regis iniuriam et offensam, ac dicte sedis et tocius ordinis[49] clericalis opprobrium,[50] quantumcumque se clericos asserant et tonsuram et habitum deferant clericales, aliasque sit certum eisdem quod clerici sint, omnino coram se faciunt[51] presentari, et[52] eis turpissima[53] morte dampnatis, illos, nisi per ipsorum ordinarios requirantur, mandant suspendi patibulis vel capitibus detruncari, licet cum per eosdem ordinarios requirantur, restituantur[54] eisdem ordinariis condempnati. Si vero in casu absolucionis existant, per officiales absolvuntur eosdem, et extunc non permittunt quod ipsi ordinarii se de ipsis clericis intromittant. In casu autem huiusmodi contra dictos clericos, duodecim laici admittuntur[55] in testes, qui, si dicant [eos][56] se credere illud super quo accusantur[57] commisisse delictum, testibus creditur indubitanter eisdem, et ex[58] hoc ad mortem ut premittitur condempnantur, propter que non est dubium talia committentes excommunicacionis sentenciam incurrere[59] ipso facto. Bona vero prelatorum et ecclesiarum regnorum et parcium predictorum, eorumque fructus, redditus et proventus, officiales et[60] ministri prefati alieque gentes regis eiusdem eis invitis recipiunt et distrahunt violenter, illis satisfaccione de ipsis aliqua non impensa. Et alias tam iidem . . officiales et ministri quam nobiles regnorum et parcium predictorum, quod ecclesie et monasteria regnorum et parcium eorumdem fundata fuerunt ab ipsis

[45] RA corrected from *debito*.
[46] RR *eciam*.
[47] RA and RV *discoperto*.
[48] RA and RV *vel*.
[49] RA and RV *orbis*.
[50] RR *obpprobrium*.
[51] RA *faciunt*; RV *faciant*; RR ? *faciant*.
[52] RV *ut*.
[53] RV *turpissimam*.
[54] RV *requirunt, restituatur*.
[55] RR *admittantur*.
[56] RR omits.
[57] RV ? *accusatur*.
[58] RA interlineated.
[59] RA corrected from *incurrisse*.
[60] RA and RV *ac*.

hactenus pretendentes, domos religiosorum et aliarum [61] personarum ecclesiasticarum eiusdem regni et parcium predictorum eundo sepius et eciam redeundo adeo gravant et opprimunt, sicque duras exacciones exigunt ab eisdem, quod vix possunt sufficere sibi ipsis ab eis, quandoque mediam et interdum quartam et aliam certam partem bonorum ipsorum per violenciam extorquendo. Quod si forte [62] ipsorum aliquis in hoc eis contradicere quoquomodo presumat, [63] eodem rege non curante a proteccione sue defensionis excluditur, et bona ipsius occupantibus conceduntur. Si autem custodia episcopatuum, monasteriorum, [64] prioratuum vel aliorum beneficiorum ecclesiasticorum racione vacacionis vel alias pertineat ad eosdem, domos, vivaria, stagna, [65] porcos et feras ipsorum, molendina quoque et alia bona ad ipsos spectancia adeo dampnose distrahunt, consumunt et destruunt, [66] quod non possunt per longi temporis spacium reparari, [67] nec adhuc dicti officiales, ministri, nobiles et gentes tantis contenti pressuris, easdem personas et ecclesias diversis gravaminibus opprimunt, lacescunt iniuriis, [68] beneficiis eccleciasticis et bonis [69] aliis, iuribus et iurisdiccionibus propriis spoliant violenter, et alias se infestos reddentes [70] eisdem multipliciter et molestos, violare dicto dissimulante rege conantur ecclesiasticam libertatem, propter que [71] dicti .. officiales, ministri, nobiles ac gentes et alii [72] prestantes [73] circa premissa consilium, auxilium [74] et [75] favorem, divinam offensam incurrunt, et penis noscuntur gravissimis subiacere.

[61] RV *aliorum*.

[62] RR *fore*.

[63] RA and RV *presumant*.

[64] RR *ministeriorum*.

[65] RR *stangna*.

[66] RA *distrahunt* replaced by *destruunt*.

[67] From this point in the text down through the word *prestantes* indicated by footnote 73 in the text, another version of the bull, reducing these charges against the king's ministers to a more general statement, is also recorded in RA and RV and calendared in Reg. John XXII, no. 5181. Clement v's similar bull, printed in Reg. Winchelsey on p. 1035, moves from *reparari* (indicated by the present note 67 in this text) directly to *propter que* (indicated by note 71 in this text), omitting all the charges that lie between these two points in any of the versions of John's bull.

[68] RA *iniuriis* clumsily written; hence RV *vivariis*.

[69] RV *bonibus*.

[70] RV *redentes*.

[71] RV *quod*. See also footnote 67.

[72] RA and RV *et gentes ac alii*.

[73] See note 67, above.

[74] RV *axilium*.

[75] RA possibly *et*; RV omits.

Et quamvis felicis recordacionis Clemens papa quintus predecessor
noster prefatum regem per diversas litteras suas rogandum ut audivimus
duxerit ac[76] eciam exhortandum quod ab huiusmodi gravaminibus pro
divini[77] nominis gloria dictos .. officiales, ministros ac familiares et
nobiles cohiberet, ipso tamen preces et exhortaciones[78] obaudiente
predictas, nullus ex[79] eis effectus extitit subsecutus. Cum igitur vos ad
eadem [80] Anglie et[81] Scocie regna et Ibernie ac[82] Wallie[83] partes pro
magnis et arduis negociis destinemus, discrecioni vestre per apostolica
scripta mandamus quatinus prefato regi diligenter exposito quod
singularis ad personam suam nos urget affeccio, et[84] singularis afficit
caritas, ut in precavendo sibi non solum a noxiis sed eciam ab hiis que
saluti sue derogant et excellencie regalis honori non congruunt, nil
persuasisse sufficiat sed persuasis semper extimemus addendum, sibique
per salubris suggestionem consilii solercius ostendentes, quod quanto
inclitum genus suum abolim plenius fovit et exaltavit ecclesias, et
personas ecclesiasticas manutenere ac illibatam servare studuit ecclesiasticam libertatem, tanto amplius in ipso notatur, si ecclesias vel ecclesiasticas
personas opprimi aut libertatem ecclesiasticam violare permittit, quodque
per hoc non leve pondus adicitur preeminencie[85] status sui, cum excessus
in sublimioribus tanto dampnabilior habeatur quanto facilius quantoque
periculosius derivatur in alios per exemplum. Et ideo minus ab ecclesia
debet minusque potest[86] urgente consciencia tollerari, eumdem [87] regem
quod officiales, ministros, familiares et nobiles ac gentes antedictos a
premissis per que Dominus offenditur ulcionum, sue saluti detrahitur,
honoris gloria maculatur, gravis nobis et dicte sedi paratur offensa, pro
divina et ipsius sedis ac nostra reverencia cessare faciat et penitus
abstinere, ac in statum debitum revocet quicquid contra integritatem
libertatis eiusdem in dictis regnis ac terris dinoscitur attemptatum,[88]
solerter inducere et efficaciter exhortari cum provida persuasionis

---

[76] RA and RV *et*.
[77] RV *divinis*.
[78] RA and RV *hortaciones*.
[79] RA and RV omit.
[80] RA corrected from *eandem*.
[81] RA and RV *ac*.
[82] RA and RV *et*.
[83] RV *Vallie*.
[84] RA and RV omit.
[85] RA and RV *preminencie*.
[86] RV *post*.
[87] RA and RV *eundem*.
[88] RR *acceptatum*.

instancia studeatis,[89] eosdem officiales, ministros, familiares, nobiles, subditos ac gentes ad id si necesse fuerit per censuram ecclesiasticam et alias penas et sentencias de quibus expedire videritis, super quibus plenam vobis et unicuique vestrum liberam potestatem presencium tenore concedimus, per vos vel alium seu alios appellacione postposita compescendo. Dat' Avinion'[90] .xvi. kalendas Aprilis, pontificatus nostri anno primo (= 17 March 1316/1317).

[89] The conclusion that follows this point, granting either or both of the cardinals power to compel the king's ministers by ecclesiastical censure if necessary, completes the 'bulla compulsoria' found in RR and given as an alternative in RA and RV. There is another conclusion, registered before this alternative in RA and RV but not found in RR, that makes the basic letter in effect a 'bulla exhortatoria' simply asking the cardinals to caution the king. Both these versions are listed in Reg. John XXII, no. 5180, and it would seem that both were known to the clerk of Reynolds' chancery who wrote the heading over the 'compulsory' version of the bull registered in RR (above, p. 334). It is possible, also, that more than one version of the similar bull of Clement V was issued (Reg. Winchelsey, 1039). Still a third form of John's bull, an alternative within the 'exhortatory' version, has already been noted above, p. 339 n. 67.

[90] RR *Avinon'*.

Appendix 8

Excommunications, Reconciliations, and Purgations

EXCOMMUNICATIONS, RECONCILIATIONS, AND PURGATIONS

These figures represent all cases from the years 1305-1334 surviving in the Public Record Office C85/7-214 of (a) significations of excommunication (letters of caption), (b) letters for release of reconciled excommunicates, and (c) certificates of purgations of criminous clerks. All the letters are addressed to the crown. It is to be noted that each letter, or case, may involve more than one person. The figures in parentheses are the numbers of letters in which clergy or religious are named.

Diocesan bishop or other agent issuing letter:	a Excommunications		b Reconciliations		c Purgations
Canterbury	120	(36)	15	(2)	8
Bath and Wells	16	(1)	0	(0)	3
Chichester	11	(1)	1	(0)	1
Coventry and Lichfield	61	(4)	5	(0)	2
Ely	7	(1)	0	(0)	1
Exeter	79	(14)	1	(0)	5
Hereford	26	(3)	0	(0)	1
Lincoln	123	(28)	24	(10)	11
London	40	(10)	6	(3)	4
Norwich	27	(10)	9	(6)	1
Rochester	13	(2)	0	(0)	1
Salisbury	11	(1)	0	(0)	6
Winchester	27	(6)	1	(0)	1
Worcester	15	(2)	1	(0)	7
York	247	(37)	24	(3)	7
Carlisle	2	(0)	0	(0)	1
Durham	6	(0)	0	(0)	1
Welsh dioceses	0	(0)	0	(0)	0
Westminster Abbey	0	(0)	0	(0)	2
St. Albans Abbey	6	(2)	0	(0)	0
Bury St. Edmunds	9	(5)	0	(0)	0
St. Martin's-le-Grand	3	(1)	1	(0)	0
Archdeacon of Richmond	3	(0)	0	(0)	0
TOTALS	852[a]	(164)	88	(24)	63

ª This figure represents the total number of cases of excommunications found in the PRO in the period under consideration. A case could, however, and frequently did, involve more than one person. Logan, *Excommunication and the Secular Arm*, 68, using the same PRO sources, has counted the total number of persons excommunicated in the same period as being 1746.

TABLE B

ANALYSIS OF CANTERBURY EXCOMMUNICATIONS BY YEARS

The 120 significations of excommunication recorded under Canterbury in Table A of this appendix are distributed among the following years (beginning 1 January):

1305	7	1315	5	1325	2
1306	4	1316	4	1326	3
1307	–	1317	5	1327	2
1308	5	1318	5	1328	–
1309	8	1319	2	1329	2
1310	4	1320	5	1330	–
1311	9	1321	5	1331	6
1312	6	1322	2	1332	1
1313	4	1323	–	1333	–
1314	11	1324	8	1334	1

Subtotal	116
Uncertain	4
Total	120

Appendix 9

Corrodies and Pensions for Royal Clerks
and Servants at Christ Church Canterbury

1. *Henry of Canterbury*, clerk of the prince of Wales and notary public. Annual pension of 5 marks granted by Christ Church Canterbury 20 Jan. 1302/1303, to be paid until he receives a benefice of greater value. Letters informing king, queen, and prince of same stated that grant was made at request of each of them. Pension designated as £5 on 15 April 1307 (?1305) (CUL MS Ee.v.31, ff. 91, 91v, 103). All pensions to Henry from religious houses (not named) confirmed by the king 12 Dec. 1315 with promise that on Henry's death all religious bound by such payments will be quit of them (CPR 1313-17, 375-6). Fact of annual pension of £5 reported to the king in 1323 (CUL MS Ee.v.31, f. 233). Pension in arrears 25 Feb. 1326/1327, when Henry was rebuked by the priory for demanding payment and reminded that the pension was not a debt but a gratuity (Cant. Cath. MS Reg. L, f. 148v; *Lit. Cant.* no. 204).

2. *John Drake*. Life corrody for him and one 'garcio' granted 22 Sept. 1305 at king's request: food and drink in the monastery, $3\frac{1}{2}$ marks for clothes and shoes, and £2 for hay and fodder and other necessities to sustain one horse as long as John is able to ride. Complaint to king that John is disturbing the priory as to his corrody, 20 Jan. 1308/1309. Corrody redefined 15 Jan. 1308/1309 as 3 loaves, 3 gallons of ale, kitchen service, all daily, as well as $3\frac{1}{2}$ marks annually for clothes and shoes, one room with bed, covering, and candles for life, and £2 annually for sustenance of one horse as long as John is able to ride. Redefined 30 May 1309 as $1\frac{1}{2}$ gallons of good ale and one gallon of wine and 2 services of the kitchen, all for John, $1\frac{1}{2}$ gallons of servant's ale and one service of the kitchen for the 'garcio', as well as 2 monastic loaves of bread and one secular loaf, and clothes and shoes and horse as before. Corrody commuted 3 March 1313/1314 at request of Edward II to annual life pension of 20 marks (CUL MS Ee.v.31, ff. 103, 109v, 110, 143v). Payments recorded 1313-1316 in Cant. Cath. MS Misc. Accts. ii, ff. 46, 53v, 62v, 71. See below, no. 9.

3. *Edmund de Bawkwell*, king's clerk. Annual pension of 50s., 'as was held by Peter de Vernon', granted 21 Sept. 1309 at request of Queen Isabella (CUL MS Ee.v.31, ff. 109, 112). Annual payments of 50s. recorded 1310-1324 in Cant. Cath. MS Misc. Accts. ii, ff. 24v, 31, 38v, 46, 53v, 62v, 71, 80v, 85, 89v, 93v, 98v, 101v, 105v, 109, 113, 121v, 130, 139. Fact of the pension reported to the king in 1323 (CUL MS Ee.v.31, f. 233).

4. *Thomas de Bannebires*, 'miles', 'cheval', servant of Edward I and Edward II. Request of king for corrody on 9 June 1310 (CCR 1307-13, 267) refused on 16 June 1310 (CUL MS Ee.v.31, f. 113).

5. *William le Hunte*. Request of Queen Isabella for corrody refused on 10 March 1310/1311 (CUL MS Ee.v.31, f. 114).

6. *Thomas de Cotynge*. Grant of livery for life 'such as was held by M. William le Venur, defunct', on 4 May 1315 at king's request (CUL MS Ee.v.31, f. 157; CCR 1313-18, 205). Fact of annual garrison of 10 marks reported to the king in 1323 (CUL MS Ee.v.31, f. 233).

7. *John Griffon*. Request of king for livery formerly held by Thomas de Cotynge refused on 25 May 1318 (Cant. Cath. MS Reg. L, f. 189v; *Lit. Cant.* no. 47). Same request repeated 12 June 1328, and again refused 28 June 1328 (PRO C47/7/44, 45).

8. *Thomas Holebod*, king's yeoman. Request of king for life maintenance 'such as was held by Thomas Cotynge, defunct', 25 June 1329 (CCR 1327-30, 552). Request apparently denied (CCR 1330-3, 308).

9. *Gawein le Corder*, valet of Queen Isabella. Annual life pension of 20 marks 'formerly held by John Drake, defunct', granted 28 March 1316 at request of king and queen. Fact of the pension reported to the king in 1323 (CUL MS Ee.v.31, ff. 164v, 233; CCR 1313-18, 329). Annual payments of 20 marks recorded 1316-1325 in Cant. Cath. MS Misc. Accts. ii, ff. 71, 80v, 89v, 98, 105v, 113, 121v, 130, 139, 147, 156v, 166v, 177v, 185, 192v, 203v, 213, 223v, 233, 242v. Gawein in service of Christ Church Canterbury in 1316 and 1333 (Lambeth MS 242, f. 312v; Cant. Cath. MS Reg. L, f. 35; *Lit. Cant.* nos. 516, 517; HMC Ninth Rep., I, app., 81). See above, no. 2, and below, no. 10.

10. *Peter Bernard*. Annual pension of 20 marks, 'formerly held by Gawein le Corder', granted 12 June 1326 at king's request. Explanation that Gawein forfeited his pension by adhering to the king's enemies. Request of Queen Isabella to sequestrate Peter's goods, to which request priory replied on 28 Oct. 1326 that none of his goods were within their power (CUL MS Ee.v.31, ff. 249, 253; Cant. Cath. MS Reg. L, ff. 146v, 147; *Lit. Cant.* nos. 181, 192; HMC Ninth Rep., I, app., 95).

11. *Walter Boneyre*, clerk. Proctor or attorney appointed 7 June 1309 to receive annual pension of £5, granted at king's request, for five years after Walter set out for the holy land. Provision that the priory would be held to no one if Walter should die before the end of five years (CUL MS Ee.v.31, f. 111v).

12. *Richard de Airmyn*, king's clerk. Refusal of king's request for pension 'formerly held by Walter Boneyre while he lived', June 1316. Request and refusal repeated 29 Dec. 1318. Annual pension of £5 granted 7 March 1319/1320. Fact of the pension reported to the king in 1323 (CUL MS Ee.v.31, ff. 168, 198, 212v, 233). Payments recorded 1320-1335 in Cant. Cath. MS Misc. Accts. ii, ff. 105v, 113, 121v, 130, 139, 147, 156v, 166v, 177v, 185, 192, 203v, 213, 223v, 233, 242v.

Appendix 10

Gifts to the Crown and Royal Household
from Christ Church Canterbury

Taken from the monastery's expense accounts, Lambeth MS 242. The years begin at Michaelmas.

1313-1314

For the 'familia' of the king and queen at Canterbury for enthronement of Archbishop Walter Reynolds (17 Feb. 1313/1314), £4.13s.6d. (f. 297).

For two silver basins and one gilded silver cup given to Edmund de Maule, seneschal of the king, £7.16s.4d. (f. 297).

For two basins and one gilded and worked cup given to Queen Isabella upon return from pilgrimage, £17.12s.4d. (f. 297).

For present sent to queen upon her return from France, 52s. (f. 297v).

1314-1315

For present to queen upon her arrival at Canterbury on feast of St. Barnabas, 64s. (f. 301v).

For present sent to king upon his return from Hastings, 54s. (f. 301v).

Given to 'familia' of king and queen at Canterbury on feast of St. Barnabas apostle, £9.16s.8d. (f. 301v).

1315-1316

For present to queen on Ascension day when she was at Canterbury, 49s. (f. 308v).

Given to 'familia' of the queen, 26s.4d. (f. 308v).

1316-1317

For present to queen at Canterbury on feast of St. Barnabas apostle, 54s. (f. 316v).

1317-1318

Given to 'familia' of the king on feast of Sts. Vitus and Modestus, 6s.8d. (f. 325).

For John de Nanntoyl, marshal of the queen, 10s. (f. 325).

1319-1320

Given to 'familia' of the king at Canterbury on feast of St. Gregory, £6.7s. (f. 337).

For John Sautren', valet of the queen, 6s.8d. (f. 337).

For presents sent to the queen when she came from parts across the sea on feast of St. James apostle, £4.12s.8d. (f. 337v).

Given to 'familia' of king and queen on the translation of St. Richard, 41s.8d. (f. 337v).

Given to Robert Manefeld and his companions, nuncios of the king and queen, 10s. (f. 342).

1320-1321

For present sent to queen on feast of nativity of the Blessed Virgin, 66s.10d. (f. 344).

For present sent to king at Sturry on feast of St. Barnabas, 62s.6d. (f. 344).

Given to 'familia' of queen at Canterbury on feast of nativity of the Blessed Virgin, £4.14s.4d., and also 20s. (f. 344v).

1321-1325

These folios are missing from MS.

1325-1326

For the king's archer, 40d. (f. 352).

For presents sent to the king, £4.11s.6d. (f. 352v).

1326-1327

Given to 'familia' of king and queen on feast of St. Gregory, £4.18s. (f. 361).

Appendix 11

Prayers for the Crown

1. *13 April 1305.* King (Edward I) asks ordinary authorities and religious superiors in England, Ireland, Scotland, and Gascony for masses and prayers for soul of Jeanne late queen of Philip IV of France, half-sister-in-law of Queen Margaret, and mother of the future Queen Isabella (Rymer I:ii, 971; CCR 1302-7, 326-7). Abp. Winchelsey on 29 April forwards the request (repeating king's writ) to prior and chapter of Christ Church Canterbury, and asks that they certify to him the number of masses offered (Cant. Cath. MS Eastry Cor. v, 9).

2. *26 May 1305.* King asks ordinary authorities and religious superiors in England for masses and prayers for soul of Blanche, late duchess of Austria, sister of Queen Margaret (Rymer I:ii, 972; CCR 1302-7, 335-6).

3. *8 April 1306.* King asks OP soon to meet in general chapter at Paris for prayers for himself, queen, their children, and realm (Rymer I:ii, 984; CCR 1302-7, 434).

4. *12 July 1306.* King asks OP soon to meet in provincial chapter at York for prayers for himself, queen, their children, and realm (Rymer I:ii, 990; CCR 1302-7, 453).

5. *1 Dec. 1306.* King asks OP soon to meet in general chapter at Strasbourg for prayers for himself, queen, children, and realm (Rymer I:ii, 1005; CCR 1302-7, 519).

6. *c. 1306.* Bp. Baldock of London grants indulgence of 40 days to all penitent and confessed who say Lord's prayer with salutation of Blessed Virgin for the prince of Wales and for peace of realm and church (Reg. London, 10-11, *sine anno*).

7. *4 Feb. 1306/1307.* King asks OFM soon to meet in general chapter at Toulouse for prayers for himself, queen, prince of Wales, their other children, and the people committed to them (Rymer I:ii, 1009; CCR 1302-7, 523).

8. *1 April and 6 May 1307.* King commands Bp. Baldock of London (chancellor) to ask ordinary authorities, religious superiors, and universities in England for exequies, masses, and prayers for soul of his daughter Joan, late countess of Gloucester (Rymer I:ii, 1013, 1016; CCW, 259).

9. *20 May 1307.* King asks OSA assembled in provincial chapter at Lincoln for

prayers for himself, queen, their children, and realm (Rymer I:ii, 1016; Roth, *English Austin Friars* ii, no. 161).

10. *Week of 22-8 July 1307.* Solemn exequies for soul of Edward I performed in papal court at Poitiers in presence of Clement V. Celebrant was Card. Niccolò Albertini da Prato, OP. Composed under supervision of Card. Giacomo Gaetani Stefaneschi, these were the first such curial exequies for a king in which the pope participated officially, and they set the pattern for future royal exequies in papal liturgy (Ullmann, JEH vi (1955), 26-36; Schimmelpfennig, *Zeremonienbücher*, 52, 84-5, 101, 186-8, 288-9, 420). Awareness of the exequies at Poitiers is reflected in two contemporary poems lamenting the death of Edward I (Aspin, *Anglo-Norman Political Songs*, 79-92. Abp. Winchelsey was in exile at papal court at time of Edward's death; ibid., 83, 89).

11. *2 Aug. 1307.* Queen Margaret announces death of Edward I and asks prayers of prior and convent of Worcester for him. She asks to be notified of action taken. On 9 Aug. prior and convent reply that they will sing 1500 masses, remember him daily in prayers, enter his name in their martyrology, and observe his anniversary as king and as a brother of the chapter (*Liber Albus of Worcester*, p. 24, nos. 388, 389).

12. *7 Aug. 1307.* Abp. Greenfield of York asks his official to cause exequies, customary office, and mass for soul of Edward I to be celebrated in every cathedral, collegiate, and parish church of the province on appropriate days this side of Michaelmas. Indulgence of 40 days to all contrite, penitent, and confessed of York diocese, and of dioceses whose bishops ratify this indulgence, who say Lord's prayer and salutation of Blessed Virgin for soul of Edward I (*Historical Papers*, ed. Raine, 183-4).

13. *28 Oct. 1307.* Funeral of Edward I in Westminster Abbey. Six masses said by five bishops and the papal envoy (Card. Peter of Spain), final mass celebrated by Bp. Bek of Durham (Fraser, *Bek*, 213; *Chron. Lanercost*, 183; *Flores Hist.* iii, 138, 330). On same day King Edward II asks ordinary authorities and religious superiors in England for prayers for peace and prosperity of the realm and of other lands subject to him. Reference to the burden that has come upon him as a result of his father's death (Rymer II:i, 9; CCR 1307-13, 43). Prior of Worcester *sede vac.* on 17 Nov. commands the archdeacon of Worcester to cause execution of this writ throughout the archdeaconry, daily and especially on Sundays and feasts (*Reg. Worc. Sede Vacante* ii, 127).

14. *30 Oct. 1307.* King asks ordinary authorities and religious superiors in England for masses and prayers for soul of Edward I (Rymer II:i, 10; CCR 1307-13, 43). Prior of Worcester *sede vac.* on 17 Nov. commands archdeacon of Worcester to cause execution of this writ throughout the archdeaconry (*Reg. Worc. Sede Vacante* ii, 127).

15. *1 April 1308.* Royal mandate for letters to ask OP soon to meet in general chapter at Padua for prayers and masses for soul of Edward I, and for prayers

that God may give Edward II grace to govern realm and people to God's honour and their profit. Request that the king be certified of what is done. The letters of request are to be delivered by English friars going to the general chapter (ccw, 270). Dominican general chapter at Padua 1308 commends, for Edward former king of England, each priest to say four masses, each clerical brother not a priest to say the seven penitential psalms with litany, each brother 'conversus' to say 100 Pater Nosters with as many Ave Marias (Reichert, *Acta Capitulorum Generalium* ii, 37).

16. *Sunday, 7 July 1308*. Mass for soul of Edward I celebrated in special service at Westminster on first anniversary of his death, with *placebo* and *dirige* on Saturday preceding. King on 1 July asks that chancellor (Baldock) attend, together with treasurer (Reynolds) and other bishops, and that the service be well ordered (ccw, 276).

17. *23 July 1308*. Pope grants indulgence of 20 days to all penitent who pray for Queen Isabella (Reg. Clem. v, no. 3019; CPL ii, 44).

18. *9 March 1308/1309*. Bp. Reynolds of Worcester grants indulgence of 40 days for prayers for the soul of Edward I (RWR, 6).

19. *1309*. Dominican general chapter meeting at Saragossa 1309 commends, for Edward late king of England, each priest to say three masses (Reichert, *Acta Capitulorum Generalium* ii, 44).

20. *5 March 1309/1310*. King asks OP soon to meet in general chapter at Piacenza for prayers for himself, queen, and realm (Rymer II:i, 104; CCR 1307-13, 249).

21. *3 Aug. 1310*. King asks OP soon to meet in provincial chapter at Derby for prayers for himself, queen, and realm (CCR 1307-13, 330).

22. *1311*. Bp. Kellawe of Durham grants indulgence of 40 days to all penitent and confessed who say Lord's prayer with salutation of Blessed Virgin for souls of certain and all faithful departed and for tranquillity of king and realm (*Reg. Pal. Dunelm.* i, 42).

23. *24 May 1312*. Abp. Winchelsey and his suffragans in Canterbury provincial council at London, after pronouncing general excommunication against persons disturbing peace and tranquillity of king and realm, grant indulgence of 240 days (20 days from each of 12 prelates) to all penitent who defend peace and tranquillity of king and realm or who say Lord's prayer three times with salutation of Blessed Virgin for this purpose. Mandate for processions before masses for peace in all cathedral and collegiate churches of the province on Wednesdays and Fridays and in all parish churches at least once a week. Winchelsey asks his suffragans to certify what they have done about this, and Bp. Gandavo of Salisbury on 27 May replies that he has commanded execution of the letter by his archdeacons and dean. Bp. Reynolds of Worcester also acts upon the letter. Abp. Greenfield of York on 4 Sept. enjoins similar processions, prayers, and masses for king, queen, realm, and peace between king and his earls and barons (P&C ii, 1373-5; RWR, 44; *Liber Albus of Worcester*, pp. xxiii and 36, no. 546).

24. *1312*. King requests various religious houses in England to say masses for soul of Piers Gaveston (PRO E101/375/8, ff. 3, 15; *Chron. Lanercost*, 203; Davies, *Baronial Opposition*, 85, 157). Christ Church Canterbury on 6 Aug. certify that they have granted 500 masses (160 of Holy Spirit, 160 of Blessed Virgin, 180 of Blessed Thomas the Martyr) for king and queen and for souls of Edward I, Eleanor mother of the present king, and Piers Gaveston, defunct. Grant of participation in all spiritual benefits (CUL MS Ee.v.31, f. 119; printed in Wilkins ii, 421). Payment by king to OP London for masses for soul of Gaveston, 1312 (PRO E101/375/8, f. 3).

25. *9 April 1314*. Abp. Reynolds at king's request, because of Scots wars, asks Bp. of London to command other suffragans of the province to proclaim sermons and masses for peace of church, king, and realm in every church and monastery twice a week with the office *Salus populi*. Also customary prayers for peace, king, and those on journey to be said every Friday with processions, bells, litany, sermons, and prayers. Reynolds grants indulgence of 40 days to all of Canterbury diocese, confessed and contrite, who fast, give alms, and pray for this purpose. Also reminder of *ipso facto* excommunication upon persons disturbing peace of king and realm; king's enemies are to be denounced in every cathedral, collegiate, and parish church on every Sunday and feast day with bells and extinguishing of candles. Reynolds asks that he be notified before 26 May of action taken (RR f. 35v (mistakenly dated 1313 in MS); printed in Wilkins ii, 439). Bp. Gandavo of Salisbury commands his archdeacons and dean to execute Reynolds' letter (Reg. Gandavo, 494-6).

26. *10 May 1314*. King asks OP soon to meet in general chapter at London for prayers for himself, queen, son Edward, and state of realm and of other lands subject to him. Reference to danger of the Scots (Rymer II:i, 247; CCR 1313-18, 101).

27. *29 May 1314*. Abp. Greenfield, because of Scots wars, asks dean and chapter of York, official of York, and Bp. Kellawe of Durham to cause special mention with customary prayers for peace in masses in cathedral, collegiate, and parish churches for the king, his army, and his allies, that God will protect them and grant triumph over their enemies. Indulgence of 40 days to all contrite, penitent, and confessed of York diocese, and of dioceses whose bishops ratify this indulgence, who pray for king and his army (*Historical Papers*, ed. Raine, 220-2). Bp. Kellawe on 5 June grants indulgence of 40 days and commands prior and chapter of Durham to announce this in processions on Sundays and feasts (ibid., 222-4).

28. *15 June 1314*. Abp. Reynolds at king's request, because of Scots wars, siege of Stirling Castle and battle of Bannockburn, asks prayers, alms, and fasts for king and his men, and asks suffragans of the province to offer 'enticing gifts of indulgences' ('allectiva indulgenciarum munera') for this purpose and to notify him of action taken (RR ff. 54v, 109). Christ Church Canterbury on 24 June certify that they will comply with Reynolds' request (CUL MS Ee.v.31,

f. 146; printed in Wilkins ii, 447). Bp. Gandavo on 5 July certifies that he has ordered his archdeacons and dean to publish indulgence of 40 days for this purpose (Reg. Gandavo, 507-9).

29. *9 Aug. 1314.* Bp. Kellawe grants indulgence of 40 days to all contrite, penitent, and confessed who say Lord's prayer with salutation of Blessed Virgin for souls of certain and all faithful departed and for tranquillity of king and realm (*Reg. Pal. Dunelm.* i, 591).

30. *15 Dec. 1314.* King asks ordinary authorities and religious superiors in England for masses and prayers for soul of Philip IV, late king of France (Rymer II:i, 258; CCR 1313-18, 204). Masses celebrated in all churches of London for this intention on Sunday, 22 Dec. (*Ann. Paul.,* 277). Abp. Greenfield on 9 Jan. 1314/1315 commands his official to ensure that such exequies are held throughout the diocese (Reg. Greenfield i, 156; royal mandate is here dated 20 Dec.).

31. *14 Jan. 1314/1315.* Abp. Greenfield, referring to excommunication of Robert Bruce and the Scots for their evil deeds, asks prior of OP York to exhort friars preachers of the diocese who are doctors of theology or licensed to preach, and especially the OP prior of Yarm, to preach against the Scots and the enemies of the church in Dominican churches and elsewhere, to denounce excommunicates in the vulgar tongue, and to exhort all faithful people to defend state and church. Preachers are also to proclaim indulgence of 40 days to all contrite, penitent, and confessed of York diocese, and of dioceses whose bishops ratify this indulgence, who assist ('manus apposuerint adjutrices') defence of church and realm against the Scots (*Historical Papers,* ed. Raine, 238-9).

32. *25 June 1315.* Abp. Reynolds asks bp. of London to command other suffragans of the province to announce processions, bells, litanies, masses, sermons, prayers, fasts, and alms for peace and tranquillity of king and realm. Indulgence of 40 days to all catholics suitably prepared in the way of salvation who join in processions and who say Lord's prayer and salutation of Blessed Virgin for this intention. Reynolds asks to be notified of action taken (RR f. 66v; printed in Wilkins ii, 453). Request from Reynolds in similar wording, dated 14 July (Cant. Cath. MS Reg. I, f. 342; HMC Eighth Rep., I, app., 352). Form letter for reiteration of request, in which Reynolds informs 'venerabili fratri' that he has heard that his diocese is not participating, in RR f. 115v (*sine anno*).

33. *24 April 1316.* King asks OP soon to meet in general chapter 'at Toulouse' for prayers for himself, queen, son Edward, and state of realm and of other lands subject to him (Rymer II:i, 288; CCR 1313-18, 328). Galbraith, *Constitution of the Dominican Order,* 254, lists no general chapter 1316 in Toulouse but in Montpellier, and Dominican general chapter meeting at Montpellier in 1316 commends each priest to say one mass for Abp. Reynolds of Canterbury, but no mention of crown! (Reichert, *Acta Capitulorum Generalium* ii, 95).

34. *12 May 1316*. Bp. Martival of Salisbury, at king's request, asks archdeacon of Berkshire to cause prayers and exequies to be celebrated in all churches of his archidiaconal jurisdiction for soul of Elizabeth, late countess of Hereford, Holland, and Essex, the king's sister. Indulgence of 40 days to all who participate in such prayers (Reg. Martival ii, 83).

35. *8 July 1316*. Abp. Reynolds asks bp. of London and other suffragans of the province to cause proclamations at masses on Sundays and feast days announcing weekly processions and litanies in every church and market on Wednesdays and Fridays for peace and tranquillity of church, king, and realm, for good weather, and for repulsion of rebellious enemies of the realm. Indulgence of 40 days to all confessed and contrite who are present. Reynolds asks to be notified before 6 October of action taken. Bp. of London on 15 July informs bp. of Salisbury of this request, and the latter on 27 August commands his four archdeacons and the dean of Salisbury to publish this indulgence and notify him of action taken (Reg. Martival ii, 139-41).

36. *24 Aug. 1316*. King asks OP soon to meet in provincial chapter at Sudbury for prayers and masses for himself, queen, son Edward, and especially son John of Eltham (Rymer II:i, 296; CCR 1313-18, 430).

37. *4 April 1317*. King asks OP soon to meet in general chapter at Pamplona for prayers and masses for himself, queen, son Edward, son John of Eltham, and realm (Rymer II:i, 324; CCR 1313-18, 462).

38. *10 April 1317*. Pope John XXII at royal request grants indulgence of 20 days to all penitent and confessed for each day that they pray for king and realm. Similar indulgence to all who pray for Queen Isabella (RR f. 214v; Reg. John XXII, nos. 3390-1; CPL ii, 138).

39. *1 Aug. 1317*. Pope, in letters to Abp. Reynolds, Bp. Hotham of Ely, and Bp. Sandale of Winchester, commands Reynolds and his suffragans to proclaim prayers, masses, and sermons, and to publish papal indulgence already conceded, for king and realm. Complaint about oppression of church and clergy by king and royal officers (CPL ii, 437; RR ff. 241v, 216 [these are the first and last parts of the same bull; the single quire of ff. 240-241v in RR is misplaced and belongs in position immediately prior to f. 216]; Lambeth MS 1213, ff. 104-104v; Reg. Martival ii, 426-8; Reg. Orleton Hereford, 47-9; Cant. Cath. MS Reg. I, f. 362; HMC Eighth Rep., I, app., 354; ?*Magnum Registrum Album*, ed. Savage, no. 685). The entry in CPL is dated 1-4 John XXII, and that in Reg. Orleton is dated 1320 (4 John XXII).

40. *18 Aug. 1317*. Bp. Beaumont of Durham, at request of king who is going into Scotland with his army, asks prior and chapter of Durham to command processions and masses on Fridays, Sundays, and feasts for God's protection and defence of the king and those going with him. Beaumont asks that he be notified before 29 Sept. of action taken (*Historical Papers*, ed. Raine, 264-5).

41. *4 Sept. 1317*. Abp. Reynolds, at king's request, asks masses, prayers, alms, and fasts that king may have victory in Scots wars. Indulgences of 40 days to

all priests of the diocese who celebrate masses for this intention, and of 30 days to all who pray, give alms, fast, or do other works of charity for this purpose. Reynolds asks that he be notified before 13 Oct. of action taken. Christ Church Canterbury on 5 Oct. certify that they have complied with his request (CUL MS Ee.v.31, f. 179; printed in Wilkins ii, 468). Similar request, dated 29 Aug., in Cant. Cath. MS Eastry Cor. i, 30; HMC Rep. Var. Coll., i, 267.

42. *3 Nov. 1317.* Bp. Sandale asks official of archdeacon of Winchester to cause proclamations of masses, prayers, alms and fasts for king and his men in defence of realm against enemies. Proclamation is to be made in sermons and masses throughout the archdeaconry. Indulgence of 40 days to all penitent, confessed, and contrite who pray or do other works of piety for peace of king and realm (Reg. Sandale, 52-3).

43. *13 April 1318.* Bp. Dalderby of Lincoln grants indulgence of 40 days to all who pray for the soul of the late Queen Margaret of England, whose body lies in the choir of the conventual church of the friars minor at London (LAO, MS Reg. Dalderby III, f. 386v).

44. *25 May 1318.* Pope asks Reynolds and his suffragans for prayers for peace of king and realm. Reference to mission of Cards. Gaucelme and Luca (RR f. 219v).

45. *27 Jan. 1318-1319.* King asks OFM soon to meet in general chapter at Marseilles for prayers (Rymer II:i, 385; CCR 1318-23, 122).

46. *20 July 1319.* King, going to war in Scotland, asks ordinary authorities in England for prayers (Rymer II:i, 402; CCR 1318-23, 206).

47. *4 Sept. 1319.* Abp. Melton of York cites ('praemunientes') abbot of St. Mary's York and dean of York to join him personally with their own processions on Friday, 7 Sept., at church of Holy Trinity Micklegate for procession through city to York Minster because of king's war against the Scots. Reference to Melton's former command for processions and prayers for this intention. Dean of Christianity of York is commanded to cite ('mandamus ... praemunias') clergy and people of city of York, both exempt and non-exempt, to be present (*Historical Papers*, ed. Raine, 292-3).

48. *7 April 1320.* King asks OP soon to meet in general chapter at Rouen for prayers and masses for himself, queen, and their children (Rymer II:i, 421; CCR 1318-23, 187). Dominican general chapter meeting at Rouen in 1320 commends, for the king of England, each priest to say three masses (Reichert, *Acta Capitulorum Generalium* ii, 126).

49. *28 Aug. 1320.* King asks OP soon to meet in provincial chapter at Stamford for prayers and masses for himself, queen, and their children (Rymer II:i, 433; CCR 1318-23, 326).

50. *7 March 1320/1321.* King asks OP soon to meet in general chapter at Florence for prayers (Rymer II:i, 444; CCR 1318-23, 363).

51. *17 July 1321.* Bp. Martival of Salisbury at uncertain date commands arch-

deacon of Dorset to cause solemn processions in bare feet, prayers, and Lord's prayer with salutation of the glorious virgin on 17 July in all churches for the king and peace of the church and realm. Indulgence of 40 days to all contrite and confessed who participate (Reg. Martival ii, 365-6).

52. *21 July 1321*. Abp. Reynolds asks his commissary to cause proclamations at masses on Sundays and feast days announcing weekly processions and litanies in every church and city of the diocese on Wednesdays and Fridays for peace and tranquillity of church and realm. Indulgence of 40 days to all prepared in the way of salvation who join in processions and pray for this intention. Reynolds asks that he be notified of action taken (RR f. 70v; printed in Wilkins ii, 507).

53. *26 July 1321*. King asks OP soon to meet in provincial chapter at Pontefract for prayers and masses for himself, queen, and their children (Rymer II:i, 453; CCR 1318-23, 477).

54. *20 Dec. 1321*. Abp. Melton asks bps. of Durham and Carlisle, dean and chapter of York, and official of York to command processions with the seven penitential psalms, litanies and prayers every Wednesday and Friday in all cathedral, collegiate, and parish churches both exempt and non-exempt, for the king, queen, and their children, for church and realm, and for peace between king and his earls and barons. Priests are to make special commemoration for this intention in every mass, with customary prayers for peace. Indulgence of 40 days to all contrite, penitent, and confessed of York diocese, and of dioceses whose bishops ratify this indulgence, who pray for this intention and who are present at the processions (*Historical Papers*, ed. Raine, 311-13).

55. *24 Dec. 1321*. Bp. Martival of Salisbury at request of Abp. Reynolds and Edw. II commands archdeacon of Dorset to cause prayers and processions for the king and the peace of the realm. Indulgence of 40 days has been conceded by Reynolds and the seventeen suffragans of his province to all contrite and confessed who participate and whose diocesans have ratified it, which Martival hereby does. The archdeacon is to notify the bishop of action taken (Reg. Martival ii, 377-8).

56. *15 Jan. 1321/1322*. King asks ordinary authorities in England to cause explanation to be made in all churches that he is advancing towards Wales only to punish offenders. Request for prayers and masses for this purpose (Rymer II:i, 471-2; *Parl. Writs* II:i, 272, and II:ii (2), 174-5; CCR 1318-23, 513-14). Bp. Martival of Salisbury on 8 Feb. commands execution of king's writ by his archdeacons and dean: in every church of the diocese daily except on double feasts and requiems, in the mass between the Lord's prayer and the *Libera nos* there is to be inserted a special form of service which includes psalms, *Kyrie*, *Pater noster*, *Ave Maria*, versicles and responses, and prayers. (It is printed in full in Reg. Martival iii, 87-8.) For these prayers the congregation is to kneel, those at the altar are to stand, and bells are to toll as

at the elevation of the Host. This special insertion is to continue 'until the author of peace has granted peace'. The indulgences conceded by Reynolds and his suffragans for this are to be published. Martival asks to be notified of action taken.

57. *3 March 1321/1322*. King asks OP soon to meet in general chapter at Vienna for prayers and masses for himself, queen, and their children (Rymer II:i, 477; CCR 1318-23, 525).

58. *7 March 1321/1322*. Abp. Reynolds, at king's request dated 1 March, asks Bps. Cobham of Worcester and Orleton of Hereford and other suffragans for prayers for success of king against Thomas of Lancaster, the Scots, and other rebels. King's writ (repeated) asks that his message be read in all cathedral and collegiate churches and other covenient places, and that Reynolds send copies to all his suffragans for publication (CCR 1318-23, 525). Reynolds' letter asks for solemn processions weekly on Wednesdays and Fridays, with indulgences as seem opportune, and that he be notified of action taken. Bp. Cobham grants indulgence of 40 days to all who say Lord's prayer and angelic salutation for this purpose, and orders his commissaries to publish the indulgence and Reynolds' letter throughout the diocese. Bp. Martival grants indulgence of 40 days to all of his diocese, contrite and confessed, who join in such processions and prayers for peace, and orders dean of Salisbury and the four archdeacons to publish the indulgence and Reynolds' letter; he then certifies Reynolds of what he has done (Bod. MS Kent Roll 6, dd; Reg. Cobham, 122; Reg. Orleton Hereford, 218-20; Reg. Martival ii, 378, 381-2).

59. *(? '6 Nons. June 1321-2')*. Bp. Droxford of Bath and Wells orders his official to publish indulgence of 40 days granted by Abp. Reynolds in recent provincial council of London to all who pray, fast, make pilgrimages, or join in processions for peace of realm. All priests are to celebrate at least one mass for peace (Cal. Reg. Droxford, 196; dated *sic*).

60. *13 June 1322*. Abp. Reynolds, in response to request of king preparing for defence against the Scots, commands Bps. Orleton and Martival to cause solemn processions and prayers for peace throughout their dioceses twice weekly on Wednesdays and Fridays. He asks to be notified of actions taken. Bp. Martival commands his four archdeacons to cause such processions and prayers to be made in their archdeaconries and to notify him of action taken; he himself then certifies Reynolds of what he has done (Reg. Orleton Hereford, 235-7; Reg. Martival ii, 407-8).

61. *26 Feb. 1322/1323*. King asks OP soon to meet in general chapter at Barcelona for prayers and masses for himself, queen, and their children (Rymer II:i, 508; CCR 1318-23, 699).

62. *7 April 1323*. King asks O.Cist. soon to meet in general chapter at Cîteaux for prayers for himself, queen, son Edward, their other children, and state of realm (Rymer II:i, 514; CCR 1318-23, 707).

63. *9 Aug. 1323.* King asks OP soon to meet in provincial chapter at Bristol to pray on behalf of himself, queen, their children, and realm (CCR 1323-7, 130).

64. *10 Aug. 1324.* King asks OP soon to meet in provincial chapter at Cambridge for prayers and masses for himself, queen, their children, and the realm and other lands subject to him (Rymer II:i, 566; CCR 1323-7, 307).

65. *13 Aug. 1324.* Abp. Reynolds asks Bp. Gravesend of London to command other suffragans of the province to cause proclamations in sermons at masses on Sundays and feasts announcing fasts, weeping, lamentations ('rending hearts not garments'), and processions with litanies on every Friday for peace of king and realm. Indulgence of 40 days to all prepared in the way of salvation who join in processions for this intention. Reynolds asks to be notified of action taken. Gravesend on 17 Aug. requests dean and chapter of St. Paul's to execute Reynolds' letter (RR f. 272; HMC Eighth Rep., I, app., 633). Gravesend publishes this mandate to Bp. Martival of Salisbury on 15 Aug. and on 30 Aug. Martival certifies that he has granted 40 days indulgence and published the mandate through his four archdeacons (Reg. Martival ii, 463-6).

66. *20 Aug. 1324.* Bp. Martival, in response to king's request for aid in defence of realm, asks his archdeacons and dean to cause proclamations announcing processions and prayers according to previous form for peace of king, inhabitants, and realm. Special form to be inserted daily between Lord's prayer and *Libera nos* in all masses except on double feasts and requiems, almost same as above, no. 56. Indulgences granted by Reynolds and his suffragans are to be published. Martival asks to be notified before 29 Sept. of action taken (Reg. Martival iii, 129-30).

67. *6 March 1324/1325.* King asks OP soon to meet in general chapter at Venice for prayers for himself, queen, and their children (Rymer II:i, 594; CCR 1323-7, 353).

68. *9 March 1324/1325.* Abp. Reynolds asks bp. of London to command other suffragans of the province to cause proclamations in sermons at masses on Sundays and feasts urging prayers for expedition of Queen Isabella to France to secure peace on the question of Aquitaine. Short discourse by Reynolds on value and importance of prayer: 'Oracio enim est instans presidium, adversario incendium, angelis solacium, et Deo gratum sacrificium'. Reynolds grants indulgence of 40 days to all prepared in the way of salvation who say Lord's prayer and salutation of Blessed Virgin for king, peace of realm, queen, and their children, and urges suffragans to do likewise (RR f. 272v; Cant. Cath. MS Lit. D.8, f. 86; Reg. Hethe, 343-5; Reg. Martival ii, 500-1).

69. *21 Aug. 1325.* King asks OP soon to meet in provincial chapter at Lincoln to pray for himself, queen, and their children (CCR 1323-7, 503).

70. *22 Sept. 1325.* Abp. Reynolds asks bp. of London to command other suffragans of the province to announce prayers, alms, and fasts for king,

queen, son Edward, other children, and peace of realm on occasion of mission of queen and son Edward to France about the business of Aquitaine. Reynolds grants indulgence of 40 days to all prepared in the way of salvation who say Lord's prayer and salutation of Blessed Virgin for this intention, and urges suffragans to publish additions to this indulgence (RR f. 140v; LAO, MS Reg. Burghersh V, f. 384v; printed in Wilkins ii, 498-9, where it is mistakenly dated 1320). Bp. Hethe of Rochester on 13 Oct. asks his prior and chapter and his archdeacon's official to publish additional indulgence of 40 days to be gained beyond that of Reynolds (Reg. Hethe, 356-9).

71. *1 Jan. 1325/1326.* Abp. Reynolds asks Bps. Hethe and Orleton and other suffragans for sermons, prayers, fasts, masses, and processions for peace between England and France. Short discourse by Reynolds on prayer: '... Unde nos Anglici, qui catholice fidei devote tenemus unitatem, ad Christum, qui salvos facit sperantes in se, totalem erigere debemus mentis nostre intencionem, ipsius in re tam dubia tamque periculosa consilium et auxilium casto corpore et puro corde flagitando'. Reynolds commands: (a) the customary psalms with the prayer for peace daily in 'missa parochiali' after the *Agnus Dei*, (b) one special mass for peace every Wednesday in the cathedral and all parish churches, and (c) procession of clergy and people around the church every Sunday and feast day at conclusion of the 'magna missa'. Indulgences to all prepared in the way of salvation: to those present at masses and processions, 40 days; to those who otherwise pray, fast, or do anything else for peace, 30 days. Reynolds urges suffragans to add indulgences as they think fitting, and asks that he be notified of action taken. Bp. Hethe requests his prior and chapter and his archdeacon or official to grant further indulgences of equal value and to inform him of action taken (Reg. Hethe, 363-6; Reg. Orleton Hereford, 340-1).

72. *12 April 1326.* King asks OP soon to meet in general chapter at Paris for prayers for himself and the realm (CCR 1323-7, 556).

73. *25 April 1326.* Abp. Reynolds, to dispel rumours that king has banned the queen and son Edward and that the papal nuncios will be threatened in England, asks bp. of London to command other suffragans of the province to cause sermons at masses on Sundays and feasts to dispel such falsehoods, and to proclaim prayers for king, peace of church and realm, and safe and speedy return of queen and son from France. Reynolds asks to be notified of action taken (RR f. 148v; printed in Wilkins ii, 529; Reg. Orleton Hereford, 359-61; different date in Reg. Martival ii, 537). Bp. Hethe of Rochester on 14 May orders his archdeacon's official to execute Reynolds' letters (Reg. Hethe, 371-4).

74. *12 Aug. 1326.* King asks ordinary authorities in England to inform all people of his desire for peace with France, and to cause sermons, masses, alms, and prayers for this purpose (Rymer II:i, 637; CCR 1323-7, 642-3).

75. *6 Sept. 1326.* King asks universities of Oxford and Cambridge, same as above, no. 74 (Rymer II:i, 640-1; CCR 1323-7, 644).

76. *6 Sept. 1326.* King asks OP soon to meet in provincial chapter at Oxford for prayers for himself and state of realm (Rymer II:i, 641; CCR 1323-7, 643).

77. *28 Sept. 1326.* Pope grants indulgence of 20 days, to be published by abps. of Canterbury and York and their suffragans and to be explained in the vulgar tongue by sermons and other ways, to all penitent and confessed who pray for peace between the kings of England and France. Same request is made to clergy of France. Special form of service is to be inserted in every mass after the Lord's Prayer, to consist of psalm 122, *Kyrie*, versicles with responses, and a prayer (Reg. Martival ii, 532-4; John XXII, Secret Letters, nos. 2996-3007).

78. *15 April 1327.* King (Edward III) asks OP soon to meet in general chapter at Perpignan for prayers for himself, his mother and her children, and state of realm (Rymer II:ii, 703; CCR 1327-30, 112).

79. *1 Sept. 1327.* Pope at king's request grants indulgence of 20 days to all penitent who pray for king (Reg. John XXII, no. 29627; CPL ii, 261). King on 17 Oct. commands Abp. Melton to publish this bull (repeated) in York province (*Historical Papers*, ed. Raine, 351-2).

80. *25 Feb. 1327/1328.* King asks OP soon to meet in general chapter at Toulouse to pray for himself, queen, her children, and the realm (CCR 1327-30, 367). Dominican general chapter meeting at Toulouse 1328 commends, for Edward king of England and his queen consort and his mother, each priest to say two masses; and for Edward the former king of England, each priest to say two masses (Reichert, *Acta Capitulorum Generalium* ii, 184-5).

81. *29 Feb. 1327/1328.* Royal licence to abbot and convent of Gloucester, where Edward II is buried, to appropriate three churches (named) of their advowson, notwithstanding statute of Mortmain, to aid the expense of masses and prayers for soul of Edward II (Rymer II:ii, 729, 742).

82. *23 Oct. 1328.* Abp. Melton asks official and dean and chapter of York to command vigil of the dead, mass, and prayers in all parish churches and elsewhere for soul of Edward II. Indulgence of 40 days to all contrite, penitent, and confessed of York diocese, and of dioceses whose bishops ratify this indulgence, who pray at least the Lord's prayer with salutation of the Blessed Virgin for this intention. All priests are to be urged to celebrate three masses this side of 25 Dec. for soul of Edward II and all faithful departed (*Historical Papers*, ed. Raine, 355-6).

83. *29 Nov. 1328.* Abp. Mepham asks processions, litanies, and prayers for peace of realm and for approaching provincial council (Wilkins ii, 548).

84. *16 Dec. 1328.* Abp. Mepham asks his commissary general to cause processions, sung litanies, and prayers for church, king, and realm throughout Canterbury diocese weekly on Wednesdays and Fridays. Indulgence of 40 days to all penitent, confessed, and prepared in the way of salvation 'or wishing to prepare themselves within eight days' who join in

these observances (Cant. Cath. MS Reg. I, ff. 428v-429; HMC Ninth Rep., I, app., 74).

85. *23 July 1329.* Abp. Mepham grants indulgence of 40 days to all penitent and confessed of Canterbury province who visit the church of Mepham (Kent, immediate jurisdiction) and say the Lord's prayer with angelic salutation for peaceful state of realm and for souls of Mepham's parents and for all faithful departed or benefactors of said church (*Canterbury Cathedral Chronicle* xvi (Oct. 1933), 7-8).

86. *1330.* Dominican general chapter meeting at Maestricht in 1330 commends, for the king of England and his queen consort and his queen mother and John his brother, each priest to say three masses, and for Edward former king of England each priest to say one mass (Reichert, *Acta Capitulorum Generalium* ii, 199-200).

87. *12 Feb. 1330/1331.* King asks OP soon to meet in general chapter at Vitoria for prayers for himself, Queen Philippa, son Edward, and state of realm (Rymer II:ii, 808; CCR 1330-3, 283). Dominican general chapter meeting at Vitoria 1331 commends, for the king of England and his queen consort and their children, each priest to say three masses (Reichert, *Acta Capitulorum Generalium* ii, 213).

88. *12 April 1331.* King asks OFM soon to meet in general chapter at Perpignan, and O.Carm. soon to meet in provincial chapter at Gloucester, same as above, no. 87 (Rymer II:ii, 808; CCR 1330-3, 283).

89. *18 March 1332/1333.* King asks OP soon to meet in general chapter at Dijon to pray for himself, the queen, their children, and peace and prosperity of the kingdom (CCR 1333-7, 97).

90. *23 April 1333.* King asks ordinary authorities in England for prayers for his success in Scotland (Rymer II:ii, 858).

91. *22 July 1333.* King informs ordinary authorities in England and Gascony of his victory over Scots at Halidon Hill, near Berwick, and asks that prayers of thanksgiving be offered (Rymer II:ii, 866; Bridlington, *Gesta Edwardi*, 116-18). Clergy and people of London join in solemn procession at St. Paul's, carrying relics and singing *Te Deum laudamus* (*Ann. Paul.*, 358-9).

92. *28 July 1333.* King to commemorate above victory (no. 91) repairs a nunnery near the place of battle and grants it £20 yearly from the revenues of Berwick for a mass to be said in thanksgiving on the anniversary of the battle (Rymer II:ii, 867).

93. *10 Feb. 1333/1334.* King asks OFM soon to meet in general chapter at Assisi for prayers for himself, queen, and their children (CCR 1333-7, 294).

94. *23 Oct. 1334.* King asks ordinary authorities in England for prayers for success of his expedition to Scotland (Rymer II:ii, 896-7; Wilkins ii, 576; Reg. Hethe, 326; the text in Wilkins is dated 3 Oct.).

Appendix 12

Benefices of Walter Reynolds before Consecration

In this appendix, R = Reynolds.

1. *Parish church of Wimbledon (Surrey)*, valued in 1291 taxation at £40 (*Taxatio Eccl.*, 208), in king's gift by reason of vacancy of archbishopric of Canterbury. Deeley, EHR xliii (1928), 500, may be mistaken in statement that Westminster Abbey was normal patron; see Churchill, *Canterbury Administration* i, 63. Royal presentation 23 Jan. 1294/1295, repeated on 8 Feb. (CPR 1292-1301, 128, 130). Litigation in Roman court with M. John de Auxonne (Ausona, Ansone, Aniana, Axon), papal nominee (above, Appendix 6, no. 1). Royal presentation to R renewed 16 June 1298 upon decision of court Christian that Wimbledon was vacant at time of king's earlier presentation (CPR 1292-1301, 354). R apparently in possession by 27 Sept. 1305 when he paid £4 on papal tenth as rector of Wimbledon (CPR 1301-7, 301). Auxonne still described as rector by pope on 16 Jan. 1305/1306 (Reg. Clem. v, no. 335; CPL ii, 6). R described as rector by pope on 7 Feb. of same year, when pope dispensed him for plurality (Reg. Clem. v, no. 315; CPL ii, 5; Burns, AHP ix (1971), no. 54). R present at Wimbledon on 10 and 11 Jan. 1308/1309 (RWR, 181). Dispute between R and Auxonne described by Abp. Winchelsey as still pending at apostolic see on 11 Feb. 1308/1309, when Winchelsey declared the benefice vacant by consecration of R to Worcester and promised it to M. Henry of Derby, Winchelsey's domestic clerk and auditor of causes. Winchelsey stated he was unable to present until dispute was settled at curia, but in meantime appointed Derby 'yconomus' (Reg. Winchelsey, 1101-2). Wimbledon described by pope on 21 May 1309 as vacant at apostolic see by consecration of R to Worcester, but pope granted R dispensation to hold it for two more years in plurality because of R's expenses and debts (Reg. Clem. v, nos. 4014-15; CPL ii, 52). R had apparently vacated Wimbledon by 19 Aug. 1310, when Winchelsey collated it to John Sandale (Reg. Sandale, 315-16; Reg. Winchelsey, 1191-2). R bequeathed two frontals of 'kamoca' and two ridells of 'sindo' to church of St. Mary of Wimbledon in his will (Cant. Cath. MS Cart. Ant. A14). Modern memorial brass of R is placed on wall above rector's stall in present Wimbledon parish church.

2. *Canonry of St. Paul's London and prebend of Weldland* (cf. *Taxatio Eccl.*, 19). Granted to R possibly by Boniface VIII at request of prince of Wales. Last

occupant of this prebend listed in Le Neve 1066-1300, *St. Paul's London*, 85, is M. John de Sancto Claro, deprived before Jan. 1303/1304. Litigation in Roman court with M. Reginald de Sancto Albano, papal chaplain, by 21 Nov. 1304, when prince asked Bp.-elect Baldock of London to assist R (*Letters of Edward, Prince of Wales*, ed. Johnstone, 3-4). R described as incumbent by pope on 7 Feb. 1305/1306, when licensed for plurality (Reg. Clem. v, no. 315; CPL ii, 5). Weldland described by pope on 21 May 1309 as vacant at apostolic see by consecration of R to Worcester, but pope granted R dispensation to hold it for two more years in plurality because of R's expenses and debts (Reg. Clem. v, nos. 4014-15; CPL ii, 52). R said to have vacated Weldland by 5 April 1308 by reason of consecration to Worcester, and was followed by Gilbert Middleton (CPR 1307-13, 63; Le Neve, *St. Paul's London*, 66).

3. *Parish church of Ingram (Northumb.)*, valued in 1291 taxation at £53.6s.8d. (*Taxatio Eccl.*, 317), apparently in lay patronage (Dodds, *History of Northumberland* xiv, 458). R described as incumbent by prince of Wales on 25 May and 18 Oct. 1305 when prince wrote letters to protect R's interests there (*Letters of Edward, Prince of Wales*, 9, 150). R said to be holding it on 7 Feb. 1305/1306 when dispensed by Clement v for plurality (Reg. Clem. v, no. 315; CPL ii, 5; Burns, AHP ix (1971), no. 54). Probably vacated at some time after consecration to Worcester (Dodds, *Northumberland* xiv, 460).

4. *Parish church of Horsmonden (Kent)*, valued in 1291 taxation at £16.13s.4d. (*Taxatio Eccl.*, 7). Said to be holding 7 Feb. 1305/1306 when dispensed by Clement v for plurality (Reg. Clem. v, no. 315; CPL ii, 5; Burns, AHP ix (1971), no. 54).

5. *Provost of St. John's Beverley* (cf. *Taxatio Eccl.*, 355, index), vacant by death of late provost and in king's gift by reason of late voidance of see of York. Royal grant 3 April 1306 to R as king's clerk, and mandates to admit (CPR 1301-7, 421). Prince of Wales on 26 Sept. 1305 had asked the then provost of Beverley to promote R to a benefice as soon as possible, and to grant him competent annual pension in the meantime (*Letters of Edward, Prince of Wales*, 127). M. William de Birston as proctor of R appeared before Beverley chapter on 13 April 1306 and presented letters of royal grant as well as mandate to admit from vicar-general to the abp. of York. Chapter protested that provost ought to be present in person, but admitted him out of respect for the crown. They stipulated that R should appear personally before 1 Aug. 1306 and then inducted R's proctor in corporal possession (*Chapter Act Book of Beverley*, ed. Leach, vol. i, pp. 119-25). Royal prohibition to Beverley chapter 2 May 1306 against summoning R to any court outside the realm (ibid., 135). Birston as proctor of R was present in chapter on 4 June 1306 (ibid., 136). Royal protection for R as provost on 25 Sept. 1307 (CPR 1307-13, 3, 11). Although R was provost, he seems not to have held a canonry at Beverley (VCH *Yorks*. iii, p. 354 n. 18). R had vacated it by 22 Oct. 1308, by reason of his consecration (on 13 Oct.) to Worcester, when Abp. Greenfield collated it to William Melton (*Chapter Act Book of Beverley* i, 226-8; Reg. Greenfield i, 199).

6. *Parish church of South Creake (Norf.)*, valued in 1291 taxation at £56.13s.4d. (*Taxatio Eccl.*, 89), in patronage of Castle Acre Priory (Bryant, *Churches of Norfolk: Hundred of Brothercross*, 173-5). Royal presentation 17 Oct. 1306 (CPR 1301-7, 465). Doubtful if R ever obtained possession.

7. *Parish church of Sawbridgeworth (Herts.)*, valued in 1291 taxation at £46.13s.4d. (*Taxatio Eccl.*, 18), in patronage of Westminster Abbey. Prince of Wales on 26 May 1305 asked abbot and convent of Westminster to promote R (treasurer or keeper of prince's wardrobe) to benefice in their gift, and to grant him competent annual pension in meantime (*Letters of Edward, Prince of Wales*, 10). Annual pension of ten marks granted by the abbey on 12 March 1305/1306, half to be paid by abbot and half by prior and convent (WAM 5713; mistakenly dated 1305 in Harvey, *Wenlok*, p. 33 n. 13). Instrument presenting R to Sawbridgeworth has not been found. Sawbridgeworth described by pope on 21 May 1309 as vacant at apostolic see by consecration of R to Worcester, but pope granted R dispensation to hold it for two more years in plurality because of R's expenses and debts (Reg. Clem. v, nos. 4014-15; CPL ii, 52). R, bp. of Worcester, at Sawbridgeworth on 22 July 1309 received his registers from his vicar-general after returning from his mission to the Roman court (RWR, 10-11, 181). R had definitely vacated it by 24 Jan. 1309/1310, when king presented Inglehard de Warle by reason of the voidance of the abbey (CPR 1307-13, 205). R released prior and convent of Westminster from obligation for their half of the pension on 30 Oct. 1313 (WAM 5713). R bequeathed alb, amice, stole, maniple, and surplice to church of Blessed Mary of Sawbridgeworth in his will (Cant. Cath. MS Cart. Ant. A14).

8. *Master or warden of St. Leonard's Hospital, York*, royal foundation, cf. *Taxatio Eccl.*, 309, 329. Custody granted to R by the king on 3 Dec. 1308 after resignation of Walter Langton, bp. of Coventry and Lichfield, grant repeated on 10 Dec. (CPR 1307-13, 94, 96). Papal confirmation of royal grant, at king's request, on 21 May 1309, with licence to hold it in plurality (Reg. Clem. v, nos. 4014-15; CPL ii, 52). R active in protecting its liberties and extending its territory in 1309, 1310, 1311, 1313 (CCW, 297; CPR 1307-13, 129, 255, 370; CCR 1313-18, 79). R secured papal appropriation of a parish church to the hospital, 21 May 1309 (Reg. Clem. v, no. 4010; CPL ii, 52). Presentation of Nicholas Burnel, later 'clericus familiaris' of R (RR f. 19), to church of Upper Helmsley (Yorks., N. Riding, deanery of Bulmer, archdeaconry of Cleveland), in patronage of master of St. Leonard's, on 23 Nov. 1310 by master and brothers of St. Leonard's while R was master (Reg. Greenfield iii, 57, no. 1261). King asked R as master to grant corrodies therein to royal servants, 1312 (CCR 1307-13, 453-4). Royal protection to R as master on 3 May 1313 (CPR 1307-13, 568). R had resigned it into hands of the king by 28 Jan. 1313/1314, when king again granted it to Walter Langton (CPR 1313-17, 80).

9. *Canonry and prebend of Bangor*, vacated by R, upon consecration to Worcester, before 13 Jan. 1308/1309 (Le Neve, *Welsh*, 11; PRO SC1/34/64).

10. *Parish church of Snitterley (modern Blakeney, Norf.)*, valued in 1291 taxation at £33.6s.8d. (*Taxatio Eccl.*, 81), apparently in lay patronage of John de Cockfield. R described as rector in 1307 (Bryant, *Norfolk Churches* (part ix): *Hundred of Holt*, 17; Blomefield, *Norfolk* ix, 361-5; neither author gives MS source). Described by pope on 21 May 1309 as vacated at apostolic see by consecration of R to Worcester, but same day pope granted R dispensation to hold it for two more years in plurality because of R's expenses and debts (Reg. Clem. v, nos. 4014-15; CPL. ii, 52). R bequeathed alb, amice, stole, maniple, and surplice to 'church of Blessed Mary of Snitterley' in his will (Cant. Cath. MS Cart. Ant. A14). Blakeney parish church and its high altar were dedicated to St. Nicholas, although the altar in the south aisle was dedicated to Our Lady (Linnell, *Blakeney Church*, 1). Church of the Carmelite friars at Blakeney, completed 1321, was dedicated to Blessed Virgin (VCH *Norf.* ii, 425).

For Abp. Reynolds as prebendary of Quincy in Lyons cathedral, see above, pp. 241, 261.

Appendix 13

Itinerary of Archbishop Walter Reynolds

Each place-date in this itinerary represents a specific indication in the source cited that Reynolds was present or dated or witnessed a document at the place named on the day given. Each place-name is identified by county upon its first occurrence in the itinerary. I have generally translated 'iuxta' in place-names as 'near' and 'extra' as 'outside'. The precedent of Miss Churchill's *Canterbury Administration* has been followed in assigning dates *sine anno* in Reynolds' register to the known years of entries immediately preceding or following them, if the context seems to warrant doing so. However, dates *sine anno* from other sources have generally been omitted from the itinerary altogether. Dates for the period between 1 January and 24 March have been rendered in this itinerary in the style of years beginning on 1 January, although elsewhere in this book double indications of year dates have been given for this period. The number of a folio in Reynolds' register is usually that upon which a given document or entry begins, even though the date itself may actually be on a subsequent folio if the document or entry continues to the other side. Dates have been included here from some entries that have been crossed out in Reynolds' register. The sources given here for each date, it may be noted, constitute an index to all surviving dated documents of Reynolds as archbishop.

Note on the Charter Rolls

Maitland in 1893 (EHR viii, 726-33) presented cogent arguments for his opinion that, at least for the thirteenth century, the persons named in the witness-lists of the charter rolls (PRO C53) were actually at the given place on the given day in the presence of the king. He added, however, that he should 'not speak of much later times' and he did not raise the question of evidence external to the charter rolls that might conflict with their testimony. Tout also, in his introduction to the register of Bp. Halton (1913), cautiously inferred from Halton's attestations on the charter rolls that the bishop was 'at Court not infrequently' between the years 1307 and 1309 (Reg. Halton, vol. i, p. xxix n. 1). Still more recently, the studies of Professor J. C. Russell on attestations of charters in the reign of John (*Speculum* xv (1940), 480-98) and of Miss Diana Greenway on chronology for the revision of Le Neve's *Fasti* from 1066 to 1300 (*Studies in Church History* xi (1975), 53-60) have tended to confirm the general reliability of witness clauses from the twelfth and thirteenth centuries, but less has been written on this subject for the century following. Maxwell-Lyte in 1926 did note, however, the unreliability of place-dates in some charter witness-lists from the early and mid-fourteenth century, and in general the unreliability of dating clauses for instruments issued under the great seal, adding that 'it is much easier to state the facts than to explain them' (*Historical Notes on the Great Seal*, 234-58, esp. 252).

From PRO C53/100-114 I have collected some 308 place-dates over the years 1314-1327 in which Archbishop Reynolds is recorded as a witness. The great bulk of these can be made to duplicate or reasonably augment his itinerary as it is indicated from the documents in his register and many other sources, especially when 'Westminster' is taken as corresponding to 'Lambeth' on the same day. However, this evidence from the charter rolls does introduce at least seventeen outstanding discrepancies that should be noted: Reynolds on the charter rolls is listed as witnessing two documents dated 6 Dec. 1314 at Langley (C53/101, m. 18 and 19), whereas the other evidence shows him at Canterbury on that day. On 12 Aug. 1315 he is described as witness to two documents dated at Thundersley (Essex) (C53/102, m. 18), whereas two other independent sources both date him at Lambeth on the same day. Another charter roll shows him witnessing from Clarendon as late as 7 March 1316/1317 (C53/103, m. 13), but the evidence from his register places him back at Lambeth well before then. He also appears in six witness-lists from Northampton on 4 July 1317 (C53/103, m. 1-5), but documents in his register and elsewhere suggest he was at Lambeth at that time. Still other improbabilities from the charter rolls are Sulby (Northants.) on 14 March 1315/1316, Andover (Hants) on 11 April 1317, and Odiham (Hants) on 28 May 1320. Apart from these discrepancies, however, for which at present no satisfactory explanation is possible, there are still nearly 300 place-dates for Reynolds in the C53 lists that are at least congruent with his itinerary as it is known from his register and other sources.

Two itineraries recently constructed for leading political figures of Edward II's reign have used the evidence of the charter rolls, adding notes of caution and acknowledging occasional discrepancies (Phillips, *Aymer de Valence*, 323 seq., and cf. p. 45 n. 1; Maddicott, *Thomas of Lancaster*,

341 seq., and cf. 254), and I have decided to do likewise for Reynolds. Following Maitland (726-7) and Maddicott (90-2, 96), I have also decided to indicate that the king was present on these dates at these places, although of course this is not certain. No itinerary of this sort, it need hardly be added, can actually prove that an important person was always present when and where his documents were dated or witnessed.

Symbols

K = Presence of king.
B = Consecration of a bishop.
C = Convocation or congregation of clergy, or provincial council.
O = Ordination.
P = Parliament.

1313

October

| 27 | 'Hospicium' of Reynolds across from Westminster near London. | RR ff. 1,1v. |

November

1	London (Middx.)	RR f. 1v.
17	"	RR f. 2.
25	Westminster (Middx.), in the king's green chamber.	PRO E30/1368.

December

| 31 | London | Cant. Cath. MS Eastry Cor. vii, 6. |

1314

January

2	K	London/Windsor (Berks.)	*Parl. Writs* II:i, 110, and II:ii (2), 72; CCR 1313-18, 86.
3	K	Windsor, in the chapel of the manor of the king's park. *Receipt of temporalities.*	PRO SC7/44/11.
4	K	Windsor/London, 'Hospicium' of Reynolds 'quod inhabitabat iuxta crucem lapideam versus' Westminster.	RR f. 3v; *Parl. Writs* II:i, 110, and II:ii (2), 72.
5		London	RR f. 4.
8		Lambeth (Surrey)	RR f. 4.
10		"	RR f. 4v.
11		"	RR ff. 4v, 5.

1314
January

12		Lambeth (Surrey)	RR ff. 5, 6v; *Parl. Writs* II:i, 110, and II:ii (2), 72; CCR 1313-18, 87.
13	K	Lambeth/Sheen (Surrey)	RR f. 5; *Parl. Writs* II:i, 110, and II:ii (2), 72; CCR 1313-18, 87.
15		Lambeth	RR f. 5v.
16		"	RR f. 5v.
17		"	RR f. 6.
18		"	RR f. 6; *Parl. Writs* II:i, 110, and II:ii (2), 72.
19		"	RR f. 6.
20		Lambeth, Westminster	*Parl. Writs* II:i, 110, and II:ii (2), 72. *Gascon Rolls*, no. 1133, p. 312.
23		Lambeth	RR f. 6v; *Parl. Writs* II:i, 110, and II:ii (2), 72.
24		"	*Parl. Writs* II:i, 111, and II:ii (2), 72.
25	K	Lambeth/Windsor	RR f. 6v; *Parl. Writs* II:i, 111, and II:ii (2), 72; CCR 1313-18, 88.
27		Lambeth	RR f. 6v.
30		"	RR f. 7.
31		"	RR f. 6v.

February

1		Westminster, exchequer	CCR 1313-18, 89.
2		Lambeth	RR f. 6v.
7		Otford (Kent)	RR f. 7v.
9		Charing (Kent)	RR f. 7v.
11		Chartham (Kent). *Receipt of pallium.*	RR ff. 7, 9; Cant. Cath. MS Reg. Q. f. 91.
12		Chartham	Cant. Cath. MS Reg. Q. f. 91.
13		"	RR ff. 4, 7, 9.
17	K	Canterbury (Kent). *Enthronement.*	RR f. 4; Cant. Cath. MS Reg. Q, f. 91; *Ann. Paul.*, 275; Walsingham, *Hist. Angl.* i, 137; BL MS Cott. Faustina A.viii, f. 175.
21		Canterbury	CUL MS Ee.v.31, f. 143; Cant. Cath. MS Reg. Q. f. 91v.
23		Chartham	Cant.Cath. MS Reg. Q. f. 92; PRO C85/8/1.
25		"	RR ff. 33, 33v, 44, 44v.
27		Canterbury/Chartham	Cant. Cath. MS Reg. Q. f. 92.
28		Chartham	Cant. Cath. MS Reg. Q. f. 92.

March

1		Chartham	RR f. 9.
2	O	Canterbury	RR f. 10v.

1314
March

3		Chartham	RR f. 111v.
4		Canterbury/Chartham	RR ff. 7, 9; Cant. Cath. MS Reg. Q, ff. 92, 92v.
5		Faversham Abbey (OSB, Kent)	Cant. Cath. MS Reg. Q, f. 92v.
10	K	Westminster	PRO C53/100, m. 7.
11		'La Place' near Lambeth,	RR ff. 7, 9.
	K	Westminster	PRO C53/100, m. 6.
12		'La Place' near Lambeth	RR f. 9.
15		"	RR f. 9.
16		'La Place' near Lambeth,	RR ff. 33, 44; Cant. Cath. MS Eastry Cor. i, 59.
	K	Westminster	PRO C53/100, m. 5.
18		'La Place' near Lambeth,	RR f. 9.
	K	Westminster	PRO C53/100, m. 6 and 7.
23	K	Westminster	PRO C53/100, m. 7.
26	K	"	PRO C53/100, m. 6.
27		'La Place' near Lambeth	RR ff. 34, 34v, 45, 45v, 46.
28	K	Westminster	PRO C53/100, m. 4.
29		'La Place' near Lambeth	RR f. 9.
31	K	St. Albans (Herts.)	CCR 1313-18, 96.

April

1	K	St. Albans	*Parl. Writs* II:i, 114, and II:ii (2), 74.
4		'La Place' near Lambeth,	RR ff. 9, 35, 36v, 38v, 46, 284; Reg. Gandavo, 500.
		Otford	Reg. Gandavo, 484.
5		Otford	*Parl. Writs* II:i, 114, and II:ii (2), 74; CCR 1313-18, 96.
6		London,	RR f. 7v.
		Croydon (Surrey)?	RR f. 282.
8		Otford	RR f. 36.
9		"	RR ff. 7v, 35v, 46, 46v; Reg. Gandavo, 496.
11		"	RR ff. 7v, 36v.
12		"	RR f. 9.
17		Charing	RR f. 8.
18		Chartham	RR f. 8.
19		Canterbury	RR f. 8.
20		Canterbury/Wingham (Kent)	RR f. 8; Cant. Cath. MS Reg. Q, f. 92v.
21		Canterbury	RR f. 8.
22		Wingham	RR f. 8.
23		Canterbury	RR ff. 8v, 104.

1314
April

24	Ospringe (Kent)	CUL MS Ee.v.31, f. 145v; Cant. Cath. MS Reg. I, f. 328v.
25	Teynham (Kent)	RR ff. 8v, 104; Cant. Cath. MS Cart. Ant. C1294h.
26	Teynham/Northfleet (Kent)	RR f. 8v; CUL MS Ee.v.31, f. 145; Cant. Cath. MS Eastry Cor. i, 26; Cant. Cath. MS Reg. I, f. 437.
27	Northfleet	RR f. 8v.
28	Bermondsey (Surrey)	RR f. 8v.
29	̇̇	RR f. 8v.
30	̇̇	RR f. 104v.

May

1	Bermondsey,	PRO C85/8/11; RR f. 8v.
	Gillingham (Kent)	RR f. 9v.
6	London	RR f. 8v.
7	Bermondsey	RR f. 47v; Reg. Gandavo, 505; Charles and Emanuel, *Cal. Hereford Muniments*, vol. ii, pp. 748-9, no. 3155.
9	̇̇	RR ff. 8v, 105.
10	London	RR f. 8v.
11	Croydon	RR f. 105.
12	̇̇	RR f. 48.
13	̇̇	Reg. Gandavo, 502.
16	Croydon/Lambeth	RR ff. 9v, 105.
17	Lambeth	RR f. 9v.
18	̇̇	RR f. 9v.
19	̇̇	RR ff. 9v, 12.
20	Westminster	Cant. Cath. MS Reg. I, f. 328v.
21	Lambeth	RR ff. 9v, 105.
22	̇̇	RR ff. 9v, 56.
23	Lambeth,	RR f. 9v.
	London	RR ff. 9v, 106.
24	Lambeth	RR ff. 9v, 105, 105v.
26	Lambeth,	RR f. 9v.
	London	RR f. 106v.
27	Lambeth	RR f. 108v.

June

1	O	Windsor	RR ff. 11v, 104v.
5		Sheen	RR f. 108.
6		̇̇	RR ff. 9v, 56v; Cant. Cath. MS Reg. I, f. 331.
9		Lambeth	RR ff. 54, 108.
10		̇̇	RR f. 108; CUL MS Ee.v.31, f. 146v.

1314
June

11	Lambeth	RR f. 48v.
12	"	RR f. 46v.
13	"	RR f. 108.
14	Mortlake (Surrey)	RR f. 109.
15	"	RR ff. 54v, 108v, 109; CUL MS Ee.v.31, f. 146v; Reg. Gandavo, 508.
16	"	RR ff. 46v, 109.
17	Lambeth	RR f. 59v.
18	Mortlake	RR f. 10.
21	"	RR f. 60.
22	"	RR f. 10.
23	"	RR f. 10.
25	Mortlake,	RR f. 109; PRO C85/8/2.
	Lambeth	RR f. 109v.
27	Mortlake	RR f. 55v.
28	"	RR ff. 10, 55; PRO C85/8/8.

July

6	Lambeth	RR f. 109v; PRO C85/8/6.
7	"	RR f. 107.
10	"	RR f. 109v; PRO C85/8/9.
11	"	RR ff. 10, 56, 109; PRO C85/8/10.
12	"	RR f. 10.
13	"	RR ff. 10, 12, 12v, 46v, 56v, 109v.
14	"	RR f. 10.
16	"	RR ff. 10, 56v.
17	"	RR ff. 10, 46v, 56v, 109v.
18	"	RR f. 10.
19	"	RR ff. 56, 109v.
20	"	RR f. 111.
21	"	RR f. 282; CUL MS Ee.v.31, f. 156v.
23	"	RR f. 10.
24	"	RR f. 111.
25	"	RR ff. 12, 57, 111.
26	"	PRO C85/8/7.
31	Royston (Herts.)	RR f. 12.

August

6		Peterborough (Northants.)	CUL MS Ee.v.31, f. 159.
11		Burgh (Lincs.)	RR f. 57v.
15	K	York (Yorks.)	PRO C53/101, m. 22.
22		Croxton (Lincs.)	RR f. 7.

1314
September

14		Acomb near York (Yorks.),	RR f. 12.
	K	York	PRO C53/101, m. 22.
15		Acomb near York	RR f. 111.
16		Acomb near York,	PRO C85/8/4.
	K	York	PRO C53/101, m. 21 and 22.
19		Acomb near York	RR f. 12.
20		Acomb near York,	RR f. 58.
	K	York	PRO C53/101, m. 21.
21	K	York	PRO C53/101, m. 22.
22		Acomb near York	RR f. 12.
25		"	RR f. 58v.
26		"	RR f. 47.
27		"	RR f. 111.
28		Acomb near York,	RR f. 12.
		York	RR f. 281.
29	K	York	PRO C53/101, m. 17.

October

1		Acomb near York,	RR f. 58v.
	K	York	PRO C53/101, m. 20.
3	K	York	PRO C53/101, m. 20.
5	K	"	PRO C53/101, m. 20.
6	K	"	PRO C53/101, m. 20.
7		Acomb near York	RR f. 59v.
9	K	York	PRO C53/101, m. 18.
11		Lincoln (Lincs.)	LAO MS Dij/61/ii/20.
15		Yaxley (Hunts.)	Cant. Cath. MS Christ Church Letters ii, 24.
16		"	RR f. 47.
17		Sawtry (Hunts.)	RR f. 12.
25		Lambeth	RR f. 281.
27		Otford	PRO C85/8/5.
28		"	RR f. 281.
30		"	RR f. 281.

November

4		Malling (Kent)	RR f. 281.
7		Otford	RR f. 281.
9		Lambeth	RR f. 12.
11		St. Albans	Cant. Cath. MS Cart. Ant. A193d; Reg. Gandavo, 511.
13		Dunstable (Beds.)	RR f. 281.
20	K	Northampton (Northants.)	PRO C53/101, m. 20.

1314
December

1		Bromley (Kent)	Cant. Cath. MS Reg. I, f. 333v; PRO C85/8/3; Reg. Gandavo, 545; Reg. Stapledon, 121.
4		Canterbury	RR f. 281v.
6		Canterbury,	RR f. 281.
	K	Langley (Herts.)?	PRO C53/101, m. 18 and 19.
9		Otford	RR f. 111.
14	O	Lambeth	RR f. 13.
19		"	PRO C85/8/14.

1315
January

3	K	Langley. *Funeral of Gaveston.*	Trokelowe, *Chronica et Annales*, 88.
12	B	Canterbury	RR f. 281v; Cant. Cath. MS Reg. A, f. 257.
13		"	RR f. 281v.
14		"	RR f. 12.
23		Lambeth	RR f. 60v.
24	K	Westminster	PRO C53/101, m. 10 and 15.
27		Lambeth	RR f. 281v.
28		"	RR f. 281v.
30	K	Westminster	PRO C53/101, m. 15.

February

2	K	Westminster	PRO C53/101, m. 16.
5		Lambeth	RR ff. 12v, 111v, 281v.
6		"	RR f. 281v.
7		"	RR ff. 12v, 52v.
10	K	Westminster	PRO C53/101, m. 9 and 16.
13		Lambeth	RR f. 14v.
15		"	Reg. Gandavo, 555.
19		"	RR ff. 47, 282.
20		Lambeth,	RR ff. 58v, 282; PRO C85/8/13.
	K	Westminster	PRO C53/101, m. 6.
21		Lambeth	RR ff. 60v, 282; Cant. Cath. MS Eastry Cor. i, 25.
22		"	RR f. 53.
23		"	RR f. 14v.
28		"	RR f. 60v.

March

1	K	Westminster	PRO C53/101, m. 6 and 7.
3	C	London, Carmelites	Reg. Stapledon, 122.
7		Lambeth	RR f. 61.

1315
March

8	K	Westminster	PRO C53/101, m. 6.
10		Lambeth	RR ff. 15, 52, 61v.
11		London, St. Paul's	RR f. 14v.
12	K	Westminster	PRO C53/101, m. 6 and 7.
13		Lambeth	RR ff. 52, 282.
14		Lambeth,	RR f. 52.
	K	Westminster	PRO C53/101, m. 6.
15		Lambeth	RR ff. 47, 53.
16		"	RR f. 53; Reg. Stapledon, 502.
17		"	RR ff. 53, 114; BL MS Add. 41612, f. 32; PRO C85/8/12.
20		"	RR f. 15.
27		Otford	RR f. 62.

April

2		Mayfield (Sussex)	RR f. 62v.
3		"	RR ff. 84, 107.
4		"	RR ff. 84, 121.
5		"	RR f. 114.
6		"	RR f. 53v.
7		Mayfield,	RR f. 282v.
		Tonbridge (Kent)	RR f. 283.
8		Mayfield	RR f. 15.
10		Otford	RR ff. 62v, 282v.
11		"	RR ff. 15, 282v.
13		Bromley,	RR f. 15.
		Lambeth	RR f. 283.
15		Lambeth	RR ff. 112, 283.
16		"	RR f. 62v; Cant. Cath. MS Eastry Cor. i, 12.
18	K	Westminster	PRO E101/68/2/10; Davies, *Baronial Opposition*, app. no. 46.
20		Lambeth,	RR ff. 15, 283.
	K	Westminster	*Ann. Paul.*, 279; PRO C53/101, m. 6.
21		Lambeth	RR ff. 53v, 112; PRO C85/8/18.
22		"	RR f. 283.
24		"	PRO C85/8/15.
25		"	RR ff. 63, 112, 283.
26		"	RR ff. 15, 15v.
27		"	RR f. 283.
29		"	RR f. 47.
30		"	RR f. 15v.

1315
May

1	K	Westminster	PRO C53/101, m. 5 and 8.
3		Lambeth,	PRO C85/8/17; Reg. Martival ii, 270.
	K	Westminster	PRO C53/101, m. 5.
4	K	Westminster	PRO C53/101, m. 3 and 4.
5		Lambeth	RR f. 112.
7	K	Westminster	Davies, *Baronial Opposition*, app. no. 120.
9		Lambeth,	RR f. 112v; CUL MS Ee.v.31, f. 161.
		Westminster	*Rot. Parl.* i, 301.
14		Lambeth	RR f. 63v.
15		"	PRO C84/18/19.
17	O	Croydon	RR f. 170.
18		Hollingbourne (Kent)	CUL MS Ee.v.31, f. 162.
20		Lambeth	RR f. 283; Cant. Cath. MS Christ Church Letters ii, 31.
22		"	RR f. 112.
23		"	Reg. Hethe, 25.
29		"	RR f. 112v; BL MS Add. 41612, f. 32v.
31		"	PRO C85/8/16.

June

1		Lambeth,	RR f. 64.
	K	Westminster	PRO C53/101, m. 4.
3		Lambeth,	RR f. 282.
	K	Westminster	PRO C53/101, m. 3.
5		Lambeth	RR f. 64.
6		"	RR ff. 64v, 112v.
7		"	RP f. 15v.
9		"	RR ff. 64v, 65.
11		Lambeth,	RR ff. 65, 65v.
	K	Canterbury	PRO C53/101, m. 3.
12		Lambeth	Reg. Greenfield i, 273.
14		"	RR ff. 15v, 65.
15		"	RR f. 65.
16		"	RR f. 65.
17		"	RR f. 65v; Reg. Greenfield i, 274.
18	K	Saltwood (Kent)	PRO C53/101, m. 2.
19		Lambeth	RR f. 64v.
25		"	RR f. 66v.
27		Mortlake	RR f. 15v.
29		Mortlake/Lambeth	RR ff. 66v, 67.
30		Lambeth	RR f. 67.

1315
July

2		Lambeth	RR f. 67.
3		Lambeth,	RR ff. 66v, 67.
	K	Westminster	PRO C53/101, m. 1.
4	K	Westminster	PRO C53/101, m. 2.
5		Lambeth	RR ff. 66, 67.
7		''	RR f. 15v.
9	K	Westminster	PRO C53/102, m. 19.
11		Lambeth	RR f. 15v.
12		Lambeth,	RR f. 67.
	K	Westminster	PRO C53/102, m. 19.
14		Lambeth	RR ff. 84v, 85, 117; Cant. Cath. MS Reg. I, f. 342.
15		''	RR f. 84v.
16		''	RR ff. 15v, 67v.
17		''	RR f. 90; PRO C84/18/21.
21		''	RR f. 15v.

August

1		Lambeth	RR f. 67v.
2		''	RR f. 16.
12		Lambeth,	Bod. MS Kent Charter 149; CUL MS Ee.v.31, f. 164v.
	K	Thundersley (Essex)?	PRO C53/102, m. 18.
13		Lambeth	RR f. 124.
14		''	RR f. 283v.
30	K	Lincoln	PRO C53/102, m. 17.

September

1	K	Lincoln	PRO C53/102, m. 15, 16, and 17.
6		Yaxley	RR f. 16.
20	O	Bromley	RR f. 171v.
28	B	Canterbury	RR f. 125v; Cant. Cath. MS Reg. A, f. 228v.
30		Canterbury/Boughton (Kent)	RR f. 16; Cant. Cath. MS Reg. I, f. 343.

October

4		Northfleet/Lesnes (Kent)	RR ff. 66, 123.
7		Lambeth	RR f. 16.
10		''	RR ff. 107v, 284.
21		''	RR f. 16.
25		''	RR ff. 16, 123v.
26		''	RR f. 16.
30		''	RR f. 123v.
31		''	Reg. Woodlock, 979.

1315
November

1		Lambeth	Reg. Martival iii, 5.
2		"	RR f. 107v.
6		"	RR ff. 123v, 124.
22		"	Reg. Woodlock, 654; Reg. Martival ii, 49.
23		"	RR f. 283v.
26		"	RR f. 16.

December

3		Lambeth	RR ff. 16, 283v.
6		Lesnes	Reg. Woodlock, 981-2; Reg. Martival ii, 58.
10		Gillingham	RR f. 283v.
16		Canterbury	RR f. 284.
17		"	RR f. 284.
18		Hollingbourne	RR f. 284; Cant. Cath. MS Reg. I, f. 343v.
20	O	Maidstone (Kent)	RR f. 172v.
23		Otford	RR f. 284.
24		"	Reg. Woodlock, 676.
29		"	RR f. 284.
30		"	Cant. Cath. MS Christ Church Letters ii, 28.

1316
January

4		Lambeth	RR f. 16v.
6		"	RR f. 85.
7		"	RR ff. 16v, 107v.
10		"	RR f. 16v.
13		"	RR f. 124v.
14		"	RR f. 284.
16		"	RR ff. 68v, 284.
17		"	RR ff. 113, 124v.
18		"	Cal. Reg. Droxford, 104.
20		"	RR f. 284.
23		"	RR f. 107v.
24		"	RR ff. 16v, 124.
25		"	RR f. 125.
26		"	RR f. 124v.

February

8		Lambeth	RR f. 107v.
10		"	RR ff. 116v, 284.

1316
February

16		Lambeth	RR f. 107v.
17		"	RR ff. 16v, 284.

March

3		Lambeth	RR f. 113.
4		"	RR f. 174.
5		"	CUL MS Ee.v.31, f. 167; Reg. Martival ii, 80.
14	K	Sulby (Northants.)?	PRO C53/102, m. 4 and 6.
19		Lambeth	Lambeth MS Cart. Misc. VI/66.
23		"	RR f. 73; Reg. Martival ii, 81-2.
26		"	RR f. 174.
28		"	RR f. 284v.

April

3		Lambeth	PRO C85/8/22.
7		Mortlake	RR f. 174.
16		Lambeth	RR f. 73.
20		Lambeth,	RR f. 72v.
	K	Westminster	PRO C53/102, m. 6.
21	K	Westminster	PRO C53/102, m. 5.
25		Westminster	*Rot. Parl.* i, 355.
28		Lambeth,	RR f. 284v.
	C	London, St. Paul's	BL MS Cott. Faustina A.viii, ff. 175v-176.

May

1	K	Westminster	PRO C53/102, m. 6.
3		Lambeth	CUL MS Ee.v.31, f. 187v.
6	K	Westminster	PRO C53/102, m. 6.
9		Lambeth	RR f. 70.
10	K	Westminster	PRO C53/102, m. 5.
12		Lambeth,	RR f. 284v.
	K	Westminster	PRO C53/102, m. 4 and 5.
14		Lambeth,	RR f. 38v.
	K	Westminster	PRO C53/102, m. 5.
16	K	Westminster	PRO C53/102, m. 4.
17		Lambeth,	RR f. 16v.
	K	Westminster	PRO C53/102, m. 5.
19		Lambeth	RR ff. 16v, 285.
20		Lesnes	RR f. 284v.
23		Otford	PRO C85/8/19.
25	K	Westminster	PRO C53/102, m. 3.
26		Otford	RR f. 16v.

1316
May

27	K	Westminster	PRO C53/102, m. 5.
28		Lambeth	RR f. 284v.
29		"	RR f. 174.

June

15	K	Westminster	PRO C53/102, m. 1.
17		Lambeth	RR f. 284v.
18		"	Cant. Cath. MS Reg. I, f. 346v.
20	K	Westminster	PRO C53/102, m. 3.
23		Lambeth	Cant. Cath. MS Reg. I, f. 347v.
26	K	Westminster	PRO C53/102, m. 3.
30		Lambeth	RR f. 70; Cant. Cath. MS Christ Church Letters ii, 32.

July

3		Bromley	PRO C85/8/20.
7		Lewisham (Kent)	Reg. Martival ii, 112.
8		"	Reg. Martival ii, 139-41.
10		Lambeth	Reg. Martival ii, 112.
11	K	Westminster	PRO C53/103, m. 22 and 23.
13	K	"	PRO C53/103, m. 24.
14		Lambeth,	RR f. 117.
	K	Westminster	PRO C53/103, m. 24.
15		Lambeth,	RR f. 17.
	K	Westminster	PRO C53/103, m. 24.
16		Lambeth	RR f. 17v.
17		"	RR f. 117.
18		Tottenham (Middx.),	Cant. Cath. MS Eastry Cor. i, 23.
	K	Westminster	PRO C53/103, m. 24.
19		Cheshunt (Herts.)	RR ff. 117v, 118v.
20		Thele near Ware (Herts.)	RR f. 117v.
23		St. Ives (Hunts.)	RR f. 279.
28		Sleaford (Lincs.)	RR f. 117v; Reg. Martival ii, 91.

August

1		Nettleham (Lincs.)	RR f. 279.
3		"	RR f. 16v.
4	K	Lincoln	PRO C53/103, m. 24.
5	K	"	PRO C53/103, m. 22.
6		Nettleham,	RR f. 90v.
	K	Lincoln	PRO C53/103, m. 22.
7	K	Lincoln	PRO C53/103, m. 22.
8		Nettleham	RR f. 279.
9		Navenby (Lincs.)	RR ff. 117v, 118.

1316
August

10	Navenby (Lincs.)	Reg. Martival ii, 142.
11	"	RR f. 279.
13	Peterborough	RR f. 118v.
21	Lambeth	RR f. 279v.
22	Eltham (Kent)	BL. MS Cott. Faustina A.viii, f. 175.
23	Lambeth	RR f. 118v.

September

2	Lambeth	Reg. Martival ii, 146.
6	Teynham	RR ff. 87v, 237, 279v.
8	London,	RR f. 285.
	Lambeth	RR f. 90v; PRO C85/8/23.
11	Lambeth	RR f. 118v; Cant. Cath. MS Eastry Cor. v, 44.
13	"	RR f. 17.
17	"	RR f. 49v.
18	"	RR f. 174v.
19	"	RR ff. 17, 85v.
20	"	RR f. 279v.
21	"	RR f. 17.
22	"	RR f. 90v; PRO C84/18/52; Reg. Martival ii, 145.
24	"	RR f. 18.
26	"	RR f. 17v.
27	"	RR f. 17.

October

2		Canterbury	RR f. 17.
3	B	"	RR ff. 119, 279v; Cant. Cath. MS Reg. A, f. 247.
5		Chartham,	RR f. 17.
		Charing	RR f. 17.
8		Otford	RR f. 17.
11		Lambeth	RR f. 17.
12		"	RR f. 17v.
13		"	PRO C84/19/2.
14		"	RR f. 17v.
16		"	RR ff. 17v, 18, 279v.
17		"	RR f. 90v.
20		"	RR f. 18.
21		"	RR f. 18.
24		"	CUL. MS Ee.v.31, f. 170.
31	B	Canterbury	Reg. Sandale, 3, 125, 159; Cant. Cath. MS Reg. A, f. 222.

1316
November

2	Canterbury	RR f. 91.
3	"	RR ff. 174, 279v.
5	"	RR f. 174.
6	Chartham	RR f. 18.
10	Canterbury	RR f. 18.
13	"	RR ff. 87, 174.
16	Canterbury,	RR f. 91; PRO E164/27, f. 186.
	Charing	RR f. 86v.
17	Wrotham (Kent)	RR f. 18.
19	Otford	RR f. 280.
20	"	RR f. 87v.
26	Lambeth	PRO C85/8/21.
28	"	RR f. 280.
30	"	RR f. 87v.

December

2	Lambeth	PRO E164/27, f. 185v.
3	"	Lambeth MS 1213, f. 102.
4	"	RR f. 280.
6	"	RR f. 174.
8	"	RR f. 18v.
11	"	RR f. 18v.
13	"	RR f. 119.
14	"	RR ff. 18v, 119; Lambeth MS 1213, f. 103; PRO E164/27, f. 187v.
15	"	RR f. 18v.
16	"	RR f. 18v; CUL MS Ee.v.31, f. 174.
17	"	RR ff. 19, 91.
18	"	RR f. 19.
19	"	RR f. 280.
22	Otford	RR f. 119v.
23	"	RR ff. 76, 238v, 280.
26	Otford/London	RR f. 238v.
27	London	RR f. 238v.
29	"	RR f. 238v.

1317
January

1	Lambeth	RR f. 238v.
4	"	CUL MS Ee.v.31, f. 175.
6	Otford	RR f. 19.
10	"	RR f. 88.

1317
January

19		Lambeth	Reg. Martival i, 72.
21		"	RR f. 119v; Lambeth MS 1213, f. 102v.
26		"	Cant. Cath. MS Eastry Cor. vii, 8.
30		"	Cant. Cath. MS Eastry Cor. i, 37.

February

6		Winchester (Hants)	RR f. 19.
9	K	Clarendon (Wilts.)	PRO C53/103, m. 12 and 15.
14	K	"	PRO C53/103, m. 14.
15	K	"	PRO C53/103, m. 12; BL Harl. Charter 84.C.14; WAM 4528.
16	K	"	PRO C53/103, m. 12.
17		Salisbury (Wilts.),	RR f. 88.
	K	Clarendon	PRO C53/103, m. 12.
19	K	Clarendon	PRO C53/103, m. 10.
24	K	"	PRO C53/103, m. 12 and 13.
28		Lambeth	RR f. 19; CCW, 464.

March

1		Lambeth	RR f. 237v.
3		"	RR f. 19.
4		"	RR f. 19.
7	K	Clarendon?	PRO C53/103, m. 13.
8		Lambeth	RR ff. 19, 135v; CUL MS Ee.v.31, f. 175v.
11		"	RR f. 118.
12		Bromley	RR f. 19.
20		Lambeth	RR f. 19v.
25		"	RR f. 19v.
26		"	RR f. 90v; PRO C84/19/10.
27		"	RR ff. 88, 88v.
28		"	Cant. Cath. MS Eastry Cor. i, 55.
31		Otford	RR f. 19v.

April

1		Otford	RR f. 19v.
8		"	RR f. 88.
11	K	Andover (Hants)?	PRO C53/103, m. 10, 12, and 13.
13		Lambeth	RR f. 88v.
15		"	RR ff. 19v, 23.
16		"	PRO C85/8/28.
20		Lambeth,	RR f. 19v; Reg. Martival ii, 203.
	K	Westminster	PRO C53/103, m. 11.
28		Lambeth	RR ff. 88v, 239, 241.
29		"	RR f. 19v.

1317
May

2		Lambeth	RR ff. 20, 89.
5		"	RR ff. 20, 239.
14		Canterbury	RR f. 20.
15	B	Canterbury	RR f. 20; Cant. Cath. MS Reg. A, f. 217.
17	K	Westminster	PRO C53/103, m. 10.
24		Lambeth,	Reg. Greenfield v, 286.
	K	Westminster	PRO C53/103, m. 13.
25	K	Westminster	PRO C53/103, m. 13.
28	O	Lambeth	RR f. 175v.
30		Lambeth,	RR ff. 20, 20v, 91.
	K	Westminster	PRO C53/103, m. 80.

June

1		Lambeth	RR f. 20v.
4	K	Westminster	PRO C53/103, m. 9 and 10.
5		Lambeth	RR f. 20v; Reg. Orleton Hereford, 26.
6		"	RR f. 20v.
8		"	PRO C85/8/26.
10		Lambeth,	Cant. Cath. MS Eastry Cor. v, 27.
	K	Westminster	PRO C53/103, m. 7.
13		Lambeth	RR f. 20v; Cant. Cath. MS Eastry Cor. i, 65.
15	K	Westminster	PRO C53/103, m. 9.
16	K	"	PRO C53/103, m. 6.
17		Lambeth	RR f. 20v.
20		"	Reg. Orleton Hereford, 4.
26		"	RR f. 21.
29		"	RR f. 21.

July

2		Lambeth	RR f. 21; Reg. Orleton Hereford, 1.
3		"	RR f. 21.
4	K	Northampton?	PRO C53/103, m. 1, 2, 3, 4, and 5; *Chartulary of Winchester*, ed. Goodman, nos. 451, 454.
8		Lambeth	RR ff. 21v, 280.
11		Cheshunt	PRO C85/8/29.
20	K	Nottingham (Notts.)	PRO C53/104, m. 16.
22		Holme near Nottingham	RR f. 280.
24	K	Nottingham	PRO C53/104, m. 16.
27	K	"	PRO C53/104, m. 16.
28	K	"	PRO C53/104, m. 16.
30	K	"	PRO C53/104, m. 15.

1317
August

2	K	Nottingham	PRO C53/104, m. 14 and 15.
5		Peterborough	RR f. 21v.
6		Huntingdon (Hunts.)	Reg. Orleton Hereford, 15.
7	K	Nottingham	PRO C53/104, m. 14.
11		Lambeth	PRO C85/8/24.
13		"	RR f. 91.
14		"	RR f. 280.
22		Chartham	RR f. 280.
29		Aldington (Kent)?,	Cant. Cath. MS Eastry Cor. i, 30.
		Lambeth	Cant. Cath. MS Cart. Ant. C181.

September

2		Wingham	Reg. Orleton Hereford, 23.
4		Allington (Kent)?,	CUL MS Ee.v.31, f. 179v.
		Canterbury	RR f. 285.
13		Lambeth	Reg. Orleton Hereford, 25.
17		"	PRO C85/8/25.

October

4		Lambeth,	RR f. 21; Reg. Orleton Hereford, 35.
		Croydon,	RR f. 21.
7		Lambeth	RR f. 285.
9		"	RR f. 285.
10		"	Lambeth MS Cart. Misc. XI/46.
14		"	Reg. Martival ii, 208-9.
17		"	CUL MS Ee.v.31, f. 181v; Cant. Cath. MS Eastry Cor. i, 29.
19		"	RR f. 21v.
23		"	RR f. 21v; CUL MS Ee.v.31, f. 183v.
25		Lambeth,	RR f. 91v.
	K	Westminster	PRO C53/104, m. 11.
27		Lambeth	CUL MS Ee.v.31, f. 184.
28	K	Westminster	PRO C53/104, m. 10.
29		Lambeth	RR f. 21v.

November

2	K	Westminster	PRO C53/104, m. 11.
3		Lambeth	RR ff. 280, 285.
6		"	RR f. 285.
7		"	RR f. 285v.
8	K	Westminster	PRO C53/104, m. 11; Sharpe, Cal. London Letter-Books, vol. E, p. 98.
18		Lambeth	RR f. 21v.
20	K	Westminster	PRO C53/104, m. 10.
21		Lambeth	RR f. 21v.

1317
November

22		Lambeth	RR f. 21v; PRO C85/8/27.
29		"	RR f. 22.

December

5		Mortlake	RR f. 22.
7		Lambeth,	RR f. 22.
	K	Windsor	PRO C53/104, m. 10.
8		Lambeth,	RR f. 22.
	K	Windsor	PRO C53/104, m. 10.
16		Lambeth	RR f. 285v.
17	O	"	RR f. 178.
18		London, Carmelites	RR f. 22v.
22		Otford	RR ff. 22v, 91v.
23		"	RR f. 239.
24		"	RR f. 285v.
29		"	RR f. 22v.

1318
January

7	K	Westminster	PRO C53/104, m. 9.
8	K	"	PRO C53/104, m. 9.
15		Malling	CUL MS Ee.v.31, f. 188v.
18		"	RR f. 22v.
22	K	Windsor	PRO C53/104, m. 6.
30		Lambeth,	RR ff. 22v, 92; Reg. Hethe, 9.
	K	Westminster	PRO C53/104, m. 8.

February

1		Lambeth	RR f. 22v.
2		Lambeth,	*Cartulary of Worcester*, ed. Darlington, no. 499.
	K	Windsor	PRO C53/104, m. 9.
6		Otford	RR f. 285v.
7	K	Westminster	PRO C53/104, m. 7 and 8.
10	K	Windsor	PRO C53/104, m. 8.
13		Otford	RR f. 22v.
16		Croydon	RR f. 23.
18	K	Sheen	PRO C53/104, m. 8.
21	K	Windsor	PRO C53/104, m. 5.
22		Lambeth	Lambeth MS 171, f. 131.
23	K	Kennington (Surrey)	PRO C53/104, m. 5.
24		Lambeth	CUL MS Ee.v.31, f. 194v.
28		Lambeth,	RR f. 23.
	K	Westminster	PRO C53/104, m. 8.

1318
March

1	K	Westminster	PRO C53/104, m. 8.
2		Lambeth	RR f. 23.
3	K	Westminster	PRO C53/104, m. 5 and 8.
4		Lambeth	RR f. 88.
5		Lambeth,	RR f. 23; Reg. Stapledon, 515.
	K	Westminster	PRO C53/104, m. 5.
6	K	Westminster	PRO C53/104, m. 5.
18		Lambeth,	RR f. 113; Cant. Cath. MS Reg. G, f. 19v.
	K	Westminster	PRO C53/104, m. 5.
20	K	Westminster	CCR 1313-18, 607; PRO C53/104, m. 5.
26		Lambeth	RR f. 23.
27		"	RR f. 23.
30	K	Thundersley	PRO C53/104, m. 6.

April

1		Northampton	PRO C85/8/32.
9		Leicester (Leics.)	BL Add. Charter 41381; HMC Tenth Rep., IV, app., 416; *Liber Pensionum Wigorn.*, p. 24, no. 87.
12	P	"	Bridlington, *Gesta Edwardi*, 54.
26		Otford	RR f. 23.

May

6		Charing	RR f. 23.
8		Otford	RR ff. 113, 133v.
10	K	Windsor	PRO C53/104, m. 4.
11		Otford	PRO C85/8/31.
15		Lambeth	RR f. 113v.
16	K	Westminster	PRO C53/104, m. 6.
19		Lambeth	RR f. 23v.
20	K	Westminster	PRO C53/104, m. 2.
21	K	"	PRO C53/104, m. 3.
22		Lambeth,	Cant. Cath. MS Eastry Cor. i, 51.
	K	Westminster	PRO C53/104, m. 6.
25	K	Westminster	PRO C53/104, m. 3 and 6.
26	K	"	PRO C53/104, m. 7.
28	K	"	PRO C53/104, m. 7.
30		London	Reg. London, 184; Reg. Sandale, 93.

June

2		Lambeth,	RR f. 23v.
	K	Westminster	PRO C49/4/27; PRO C53/104, m. 7; Phillips, *Aymer deValence*, 161, 320-1.
3	K	"	PRO C53/104, m. 3.

1318
June

5	K	Westminster	PRO C53/104, m. 3.
9		Lambeth,	Cant. Cath. MS Eastry Cor. i, 13.
	K	Westminster, in the king's green chamber	*Parl. Writs* II:i, 208, and II:ii (2), 123; Reg. Sandale, 366; CCR 1313-18, 619.
10	K	Westminster	PRO C53/104, m. 1 and 3.
11		Lambeth	PRO C85/8/34.
12		Lambeth,	RR f. 23v.
	K	Westminster	PRO C53/104, m. 3.
17	O	Maidstone	RR f. 180.
18		"	RR f. 23v.
25	K	Woodstock (Oxon.)	PRO C53/104, m. 1.
26		Lambeth	RR ff. 92, 294; PRO C85/8/33.
29		"	RR f. 24.

July

6	K	Northampton	PRO C53/104, m. 1.
8	K	"	PRO C53/105, m. 18.
10		"	RR f. 23v.
11		"	Cant. Cath. MS Christ Church Letters ii, 36.
17	K	"	Cant. Cath. MS Christ Church Letters ii, 21; PRO C53/105, m. 18; *Cal. Shrewsbury Library* i, charter no. 59.
18		"	Cant. Cath. MS Christ Church Letters ii, 21.
19	K	"	PRO C53/105, m. 18.
20	K	"	PRO C53/105, m. 17 and 18.
21		Biddlesden (Bucks.)	Cant. Cath. MS Eastry Cor. i, 41.
26	K	Woodstock	PRO C53/105, m. 18.
27		Biddlesden	PRO C85/8/30.
28	K	Northampton	PRO C53/105, m. 18.
30	K	"	PRO C53/105, m. 18.

August

6		Leicester	RR f. 23v.
8		Leicester,	Cant. Cath. MS Eastry Cor. v, 50.
	K	Leake (Notts.)	Reg. Sandale, 277; PRO C53/105, m. 18.
9	K	Leake	*Parl. Writs* II:i, 215, and II:ii (1), 184; PRO C53/105, m. 18.
10	K	"	PRO C53/105, m. 17.
11		Leicester	RR f. 23v.
16		Harrow (Middx.)	Amundesham, *Annales* i, 200-1.

1318
August

| 27 | | Charing | RR f. 23v. |
| 31 | | Lyminge (Kent) | Lambeth MS Cart. Misc. XI/46. |

September

1		Wingham	RR f. 23v.
2		Canterbury	Cant. Cath. MS Reg. I, f. 356.
3		"	RR f. 89.
4		Teynham	RR f. 23v.
5		Gillingham	CUL MS Ee.v.31, f. 195v.
8		Lambeth	RR f. 87v.
9		"	RR ff. 23v, 280v, 285v.
13		"	CUL MS Ee.v.31, f. 197.
22		"	RR f. 24.
24		London, St. Paul's	*Ann. Paul.*, 283-4.
28		Otford	RR f. 24.

October

1		Maidstone	Cant. Cath. MS Eastry Cor. i, 39.
12		Lambeth	RR f. 24.
14		"	RR f. 280v.
16		"	RR f. 285v.
19		"	RR f. 24v; Cant. Cath. MS Christ Church Letters ii, 33.
20		"	RR f. 24.
31		Peterborough	RR f. 24v.

November

| 3 | | Peterborough | PRO C84/19/43; *Ann. Paul.*, 284. |
| 24 | | Lambeth | RR f. 285v. |

December

| 10 | | Dover (Kent) | Cant. Cath. MS Eastry Cor. vii, 9. |
| 23 | O | Maidstone | RR f. 181v; Reg. Hethe, 57. |

1319
January

14	B	Canterbury	RR f. 24v; *Ann. Paul.*, 284; Cant. Cath. MS Reg. A, f. 217.
18		Maidstone	RR f. 24v.
31		Lambeth	Reg. Hethe, 9.

February

16		Lambeth	CUL MS Ee.v.31, f. 199; Reg. Orleton Hereford, 107.
21		"	*Chartulary of Winchester*, ed. Goodman, no. 56.
22		"	WAM 5019.
25		"	Reg. London, 205.

1319
March

3	Maidstone	RR f. 24v.
7	"	RR f. 24v.
11	Wingham	CUL MS Ee.v.31, f. 200v.
21	Canterbury	Cant. Cath. MS Reg. Q, f. 119.
28	"	RR f. 24v.

April

8	Croydon	CUL MS Ee.v.31, f. 207.
9	Maidstone	CUL MS Ee.v.31, f. 201.
11	"	RR f. 24v.
19	Lambeth	RR f. 24v.
27	"	PRO C85/8/35.

May

1	Lambeth	PRO SC10/6/282.
25	Otford	RR f. 25.
26	Lambeth	CUL MS Ee.v.31, f. 206v.

June

2	Charing	RR f. 25.
11	Saltwood (Kent)	Reg. Hethe, 398.
24	Maidstone	Lambeth MS 1213, f. 105v.
29	Lambeth	RR f. 25; Reg. Hethe, 398.
30	"	RR f. 25.

July

2	Charing	RR f. 25.
3	Maidstone	Cant. Cath. MS Eastry Cor. vii, 7.
12	Charing	Cant. Cath. MS Eastry Cor. i, 24.
13	"	RR f. 25.
22	Canterbury	PRO SC1/35/166 and 167.

August

3	Lambeth	PRO C85/8/36.
4	"	CUL MS Ee.v.31, f. 209.
8	Lambeth,	Cant. Cath. MS Reg. I, f. 364; Reg. Cobham, 40; Reg. Martival ii, 235; Reg. London, 215.
	London	Cant. Cath. MS Reg. I, f. 363; Reg. Martival ii, 241.
22	Aldington	LAO MS Reg. Dalderby III, f. 423v.
23	Saltwood	CUL MS Ee.v.31, f. 210.

September

21	Lambeth	Cant. Cath. MS Christ Church Letters ii, 39.
22	"	Lambeth MS 1213, f. 105v.
24	London	RR f. 226v.

1319
October

5	Sempringham (Lincs.)	RR f. 25.
9	Lincoln	RR f. 110v; Reg. Hethe, 104; LAO MSS Dij/62/i/14 and Dij/88/2/33-4.
13	Torksey (Lincs.)	RR f. 89.
31	Grimsby (Lincs.)	BL Harl. Charter 43.G.29.

November

13	Barlings (Lincs.)	RR f. 89; Cant. Cath. MS Reg. I, f. 364.
14	"	Cant. Cath. MS Reg. I, f. 364.
21	Bracebridge (Lincs.)	*Magnum Registrum Album*, ed. Savage, no. 585.

December

21	Deeping (Lincs.)	RR f. 226v.

1320
January

1	Peterborough	RR f. 89v.
6	Ramsey (Hunts.)	RR f. 286; LAO MSS Dij/62/i/12-13 and Dij/88/1/16.
7	Huntingdon	RR f. 89v.
8	Huntingdon,	RR f. 25v.
	Huntingdon Priory	LAO MS Reg. Dalderby III, f. 432.
13	St. Neots (Hunts.)	RR f. 89.
17	Newnham near Bedford (Beds.)	RR ff. 89v, 126.
19	"	*Cart. Mon. de Ramesia* ii, 182-3.
29	Canons Ashby (Northants.)	RR f. 25.

February

4	Biddlesden	WAM 2442.
12	Notley (Bucks.)	Bod. MS Oseney Charter 41.
14	"	RR f. 25v.
17	Missenden (Bucks.)	PRO C85/8/37.
21	Wroxton (Oxon.)	Cant. Cath. MS Reg. I, f. 366v.
23	Chacombe (Northants.)	RR f. 126.

March

5	Launde (Leics.)	RR f. 25v.
9	Uffington (Lincs.)	RR f. 25v.
11	"	HMC *Wells* i, 190-1.
21	Mt. St. James outside Northampton (Northants.)	RR f. 25v.
28	"	Reg. Cobham, 82.

1320
April

6		Ashridge (Herts.)	RR f. 126.
13		Westminster, in the king's green chamber	*Parl. Writs* II:i, 241, and II:ii (1), 218.
16		Mortlake	RR f. 25v.
17		''	RR f. 25v.
21		Lambeth	PRO C85/8/38.
22		''	PRO C85/8/42.
27	K	Westminster	PRO C53/106, m. 1.
29		Lambeth	PRO C85/8/40.

May

16		Lambeth,	CUL MS Ee.v.31, f. 215.
		Maidstone	PRO C85/8/41.
26		Maidstone	RR f. 96.
28		Lambeth,	Reg. Martival ii, 300-1.
	K	Odiham (Hants)?	PRO C53/106, m. 1.
29		Otford	PRO C47/19/3/29, m. 2.

June

4	K	Westminster, in the king's green chamber	PRO E159/93/92; *Parl. Writs* II:i, 243, and II:ii (2), 146; CCR 1318-23, 237.
5		London	CCR 1318-23, 238.
6		Lambeth	Cant. Cath. MS Christ Church Letters ii, 29.
9	K	Westminster	PRO C53/106, m. 1.
16		Lambeth	RR f. 26.
21		Otford	RR f. 96v.
29		''	RR f. 26.

July

1		Otford	RR f. 293; PRO C85/8/39.
2		''	RR f. 293.
19		Lambeth	CUL MS Ee.v.31, f. 216; Cant. Cath. MS Cart. Ant. C412.
22		''	RR f. 97; Cant. Cath. MS S.V. ii, 5.
30		''	Reg. Orleton Hereford, 135.
31		''	Charles and Emanuel, *Cal. Hereford Muniments*, vol. ii, p. 813, no. 1372.

September

28		Wrotham,	RR ff. 97v, 286v.
		Otford	LAO MS Reg. Burghersh V, f. 260.

October

2		Lambeth	RR f. 26v.
6	KP	Westminster	*Parl. Writs* II:i, 251, and II:ii (1), 220; *Rot. Parl.* i, 365.
7	K	''	PRO C53/107, m. 8.

1320
October

8		Lambeth	RR f. 26.
13	P	Westminster	RR f. 70v.
15		Lambeth	RR f. 26.
20	K	Westminster	CCR 1318-23, 333; PRO C53/107, m. 8.
22		Lambeth	RR f. 26.
26		"	RR f. 286.
27	K	Westminster	PRO C53/107, m. 8.
28	K	"	PRO C53/107, m. 7 and 8.
30		Lambeth	RR f. 26.
31		Canterbury	Reg. Orleton Hereford, 311.

November

1		Lambeth	Reg. Hethe, 89.
4	K	Westminster	PRO C53/107, m. 8.
6		Lambeth	*Liber Albus of Worcester*, p. 70, no. 893.
9		London	Reg. Martival ii, 318-19.
10	K	Westminster	PRO C53/107, m. 7.
12	K	"	PRO C53/107, m. 6 and 7.
13		Lambeth	RR f. 26.
15		"	RR f. 26.
16		London,	Reg. Hethe, 79.
	K	Westminster	PRO C53/107, m. 6.
17	K	Westminster	PRO C53/107, m. 7.
18		Lambeth	Charles and Emanuel, *Cal. Hereford Muniments*, vol. ii, p. 816, no. 1444.
20		Lambeth,	BL Add. Charter 17353; CUL MS Ee.v.31, f. 219v.
	K	Westminster	PRO C53/107, m. 5 and 6.
22	K	Westminster	PRO C53/107, m. 5.
26		Croydon	RR ff. 98v, 231v, 293; Reg. Hethe, 90.

December

11		Croydon	RR ff. 26v, 293.
15		Otford	CUL MS Ee.v.31, ff. 216v, 217.
18		Wrotham	Reg. Martival ii, 311.
20	O	Maidstone	RR f. 182v.
22		Otford	RR f. 27.
24		"	RR f. 27.
30		"	RR f. 231v.

1321
January

3	Otford	RR f. 27.
4	Canterbury	CPR 1324-7, 177.

1321
January

12		Otford	RR f. 100v; Cant. Cath. MS Eastry Cor. i, 42.
16		Croydon	RR f. 99v.
17		"	RR f. 286.
20		Mortlake	Cant. Cath. MS Eastry Cor. v, 43.

February

2		Croydon	RR f. 293.
11		Lambeth	RR f. 293; PRO C85/8/45.
12		"	RR f. 293.
15		"	RR f. 286.
17		"	RR f. 293; PRO C85/8/47.
18	K	Westminster	PRO C53/107, m. 4.
23		Lambeth,	RR f. 100v.
	K	Westminster	PRO C53/107, m. 4.
24		Lambeth,	RR ff. 27, 100v, 101v.
	K	Westminster	PRO C53/107, m. 2.
26		Lambeth	RR f. 293v; PRO C85/8/48.

March

1	K	Westminster	PRO C53/107, m. 4.
2		Lambeth	RR f. 26v.
3		Croydon	RR f. 101.
14		Otford	RR f. 293; PRO C85/8/46.
17		"	RR f. 27.
21		"	RR f. 27; Reg. Martival i, 198.
25		Maidstone	RR f. 27v.
31		Northfleet	RR f. 89v.

April

4		Canterbury	CUL MS Ee.v.31, f. 221.
7		Lyminge	RR f. 27v.
8		"	RR f. 27v.
16 (?)		Charing	RR f. 286v.
22		"	RR f. 102v.
25		"	RR ff. 102, 126.
26		"	RR ff. 102, 286v.
27		"	Cant. Cath. MS Cart. Ant. C1294b.

May

2		Mortlake	RR f. 27v.
10	K	Westminster	PRO C53/107, m. 2.
13		Lambeth	RR f. 27v.
15		"	Reg. Orleton Hereford, 196.
16		"	RR f. 27v.

1321
May

17		Lambeth	RR ff. 102, 126, 293v.
18	K	Westminster	PRO C53/107, m. 2.
19		Lambeth	RR f. 27v.
20		Lambeth,	RR ff. 102, 286v.
	K	Westminster	PRO C53/107, m. 2.
22		Lambeth,	RR f. 293v; PRO C85/8/49.
	K	Westminster	PRO C53/107, m. 1.
23	K	Westminster	PRO C53/107, m. 1.
24	K	''	PRO C53/107, m. 2.
25		Lambeth	LAO MS Reg. Burghersh V, f. 286; CUL MS Ee.v.31, f. 222v.
28		''	RR ff. 27v, 28.
29		''	RR f. 28.

June

3		Biddlesden	Cant. Cath. MS Eastry Cor. i, 8.
19		Reading (Berks.)	Reg. Martival ii, 348-9.
24		Gillingham	RR f. 28.
25		''	RR f. 28.
26 (?)		''	RR f. 126v.
27		Lambeth	RR f. 28.

July

3		Maidstone	RR f. 28.
5		Wrotham	RR f. 28.
12		Lambeth,	RR f. 28v.
	K	Westminster	PRO C53/108, m. 9 and 11.
15	K	Westminster	PRO C53/108, m. 8.
20		Lambeth	RR f. 28v.
21		''	RR ff. 28v, 70v.
22		''	RR f. 126v.
23		''	RR ff. 28v, 87v, 293v; PRO C85/8/50.
26		''	RR f. 28v.
29		''	RR f. 28v.
30		''	RR f. 28v.
31		''	RR f. 293v.

August

4		Lambeth	RR f. 126
	K	Westminster	PRO C53/108, m. 8.
5		Lambeth	RR f. 71v.
6		''	RR f. 126v.
8	K	Westminster	PRO C53/108, m. 8; *Cartulary of Cirencester*, ed. Ross, i, 97.
9		Lambeth	RR f. 28v.
11		''	RR f. 71.

1321
August

17	K	Westminster	PRO C53/108, m. 8.
20		Lambeth,	RR f. 71v.
	K	Westminster	PRO C53/108, m. 8.
22		Lambeth	RR f. 71.
28		Croydon	RR f. 28v.

September

7		Otford	RR f. 126v.
8		``	RR f. 107v.
13		``	RR f. 107v.
14		Lambeth	Reg. Orleton Hereford, 208.
19	K	Harwich (Essex)	PRO C53/108, m. 8.
26		Croydon	RR f. 126v.
28		Lambeth	RR f. 29.
30	K	Tower of London	PRO C53/108, m. 8.

October

15		Otford,	RR f. 126v; Reg. London, 230.
		Croydon	RR f. 29.
17		Lambeth	RR f. 29.
19		``	RR f. 29.
27		``	RR f. 29.

November

13		Lambeth	RR ff. 29, 127.
14		``	CUL MS Ee.v.31, f. 224; Reg. Martival ii, 372; Reg. Cobham, 112; Reg. Orleton Hereford, 206-8.
22		``	RR ff. 29, 127.
23		``	RR f. 127v.
25		``	RR f. 127v.
26		``	RR f. 300v.
28		``	RR f. 29.
29		``	RR f. 29.

December

1		London	RR f. 29v.
	C	London, St. Paul's	*Ann. Paul.*, 300.
3		Lambeth	Reg. Cobham, 117.
4		``	RR f. 293v.
7		``	RR f. 128.
11		``	RR ff. 29v, 127v.
13		``	Reg. Martival ii, 376.
15		``	RR ff. 29v, 128.
16		London	PRO SC1/55/56.
27		Charing	RR f. 128.

1322

January

1		Charing	RR f. 29v.
3		Canterbury	RR f. 29v; Cant. Cath. MS Reg. I, f. 397v; Cant. Cath. MS S.V. iii, 40.
5		''	RR f. 128.
7		''	RR f. 29v.
15		Northfleet	RR f. 30.
24		Lambeth	RR f. 128.
25		''	RR f. 128.
27		''	RR f. 303.
29		''	RR f. 128.

February

1		Lambeth	RR ff. 30, 293v; PRO C85/8/51.
14		''	RR ff. 30, 128v.
17		''	RR f. 128v.

March

6	O	Newington near Lambeth (Surrey)	RR f. 183v.
7		London, St. Paul's,	*Ann. Paul.*, 302.
		Lambeth	Bod. MS Kent Roll 6, dd; Reg. Cobham, 122; Reg. Orleton Hereford, 220; Reg. Martival ii, 378.
9		''	RR f. 293v.
11		''	RR f. 30.
18		''	RR f. 128v.
22		''	RR f. 128v.
24		''	RR ff. 30, 293v.
26		''	RR f. 102v.
28		''	RR f. 128v.
30		''	Reg. Martival ii, 388-9.

April

2		Lambeth	RR f. 128v.
5		''	RR f. 129.
7		''	RR f. 30.
12		Mortlake	RR f. 129.
14		''	RR f. 129.
17		Lambeth	RR f. 129.
20		''	RR f. 129.

May

8		York	RR f. 30.
10	K	York	PRO C53/108, m. 4.
12		Acomb near York	BL MS Cott. Vespasian E.xxi, f. 49v; Reg. Asserio, 490; Reg. Martival ii, 394-5.

1322
May

15	K	York	PRO C53/108, m. 4.
18		Acomb near York	RR f. 129v.
24		Stow Park (Lincs.)	RR f. 129v.
28		Bourne Abbey (OSA, Lincs.)	RR f. 30.
31		Peterborough	RR f. 129v.

June

3		Puckeridge (Herts.)	RR f. 30.
13		Lambeth	Reg. Orleton Hereford, 237; Reg. Martival ii, 407.
16		Mortlake	RR ff. 30, 294.
20		London, St. Paul's	*Ann. Paul.*, 304.
21		Mortlake	Reg. Hethe, !12.
30		"	RR f. 30v.

July

7		Mortlake	RR f. 30v.
10		Lambeth	RR f. 286v.
13		"	RR f. 294.
17		Mortlake	RR f. 102.
20		"	RR f. 30v.
23		"	RR ff. 30v, 287.
25		"	RR f. 287.

August

3		Mortlake	RR ff. 30v, 294.
4		"	RR f. 31.
7		"	RR ff. 113v, 286v.
11		"	RR f. 31.
30		Wingham	*Liber Albus of Worcester*, p. 73, no. 952.

September

6		Canterbury	RR f. 31.
7		Chartham	RR f. 113v.
18	O	Canterbury	RR f. 184.
19		"	RR f. 31.
21		"	RR f. 305v.
23		Canterbury, Charing	RR f. 31. Cant. Cath. MS Reg. Q, f. 119v.

October

2		Otford	RR f. 31.
9		Croydon	RR f. 31.
12		Lambeth	RR f. 31v.

1322
October
17   Mortlake   RR ff. 31v, 287.
22   Lambeth   RR f. 287.
23   "   RR f. 31v.
25   "   RR f. 31v; Reg. London, 232.

November
1   Otford   RR f. 31v.
6   Charing   RR f. 287v.
7   Charing,   RR f. 287; Cant. Cath. MS Reg. Q, f. 120.
            Chartham   Cant. Cath. MS Reg. Q, f. 120.
9   Wrotham   RR f. 92.
12   Lambeth   RR f. 287v.
14   "   RR f. 287v.
15   "   RR f. 287v.
16   "   RR f. 31v.
18   "   RR f. 287v.
21   Cheshunt,   RR f. 32.
            Ware (Herts.)   RR f. 287v.
23   Caxton (Cambs.)   RR f. 32.
28   Lincoln   RR f. 287v.
30   Kirton (Lincs.)? RR f. 32.

December
2   Lincoln   BL MS Cott. Vespasian E.xxi, f. 50v;
                              Liber Albus of Worcester, p. 74, no.
                              955; Reg. Martival ii, 421-3.

1323
January
15   Lincoln   RR f. 289.
22   "   BL MS Cott. Vespasian E.xxi, f. 53.
27   Yaxley   RR f. 289.

February
5   Lambeth   RR f. 289.
8   "   RR f. 32v.
10   "   RR f. 32v.
11   "   RR ff. 32v, 289.
12   "   RR f. 32v.

March
15   Lambeth   RR f. 129v.
16   "   RR f. 32v.
19   "   RR ff. 32v, 289.
20   "   RR f. 138; CUL MS Ee.v.31, f. 229v.
22   Otford   RR f. 164.
23   "   RR f. 129v.

1323
April

3	K	Westminster	PRO C53/109, m. 4.
11		Mortlake	RR f. 130.
14		Lambeth	RR f. 130.
16		Lambeth,	RR f. 130.
	K	Tower of London	PRO C53/109, m. 2.
18		Lambeth	RR f. 250.
19		"	RR f. 250.
23		"	RR f. 289v.
25		"	RR f. 250.
26		Mortlake	RR f. 130v.
29		"	RR f. 250; Cant. Cath. MS Eastry Cor. i, 7.

May

15	Bishop's Waltham (Hants)	RR ff. 250, 250v.
23	Hyde Abbey outside Winchester (OSB, Hants)	RR f. 250v.
24	"	RR f. 250v.

June

23	Lambeth	*Chartulary of Winchester*, ed. Goodman, no. 135.
25	Mottisfont (Hants)	RR f. 130v.
27	Otford	Reg. Asserio, 608; *Chartulary of Winchester*, ed. Goodman, no. 35.
28	"	RR f. 250v.

July

2		Otford	RR f. 250v.
3		Otford,	RR f. 250v.
	K	Westminster	PRO C53/109, m. 4.
4		Otford	RR f. 250v.
7		"	RR f. 250v.
13		Leeds (Kent)	RR f. 131v.
27		Saltwood	Cant. Cath. MS Eastry Cor. i, 27.

August

2	Charing	RR f. 130v.
4	"	CUL MS Ee.v.31, f. 232.
8	Otford	Reg. Orleton Hereford, 261.
30	"	RR f. 131.

September

6	Otford	RR f. 251.
22	Mortlake	RR f. 131.
23	"	RR f.131.

1323
September
25 　　Mortlake 　　　　　RR ff. 250, 251.
28 　　　　" 　　　　　　RR f. 131.

October
4 　　Puckeridge 　　　　RR f. 251.
9 　　Langtoft (Lincs.) 　RR f. 251.

November
12 　K 　Nottingham 　　BL Harl. Charter 51.H.2; PRO C53/110,
　　　　　　　　　　　　　　m. 9.
16 　K 　　　" 　　　　PRO C53/110, m. 10.
18 　K 　　　" 　　　　PRO C53/110, m. 9.
29 　　Mortlake 　　　　　RR f. 251.

December
7 　　Lambeth 　　　　　RR f. 289v; Reg. Orleton Hereford, 270;
　　　　　　　　　　　　　Reg. Martival ii, 433.
13 　　　" 　　　　　　RR f. 289v.
17 　　Mortlake 　　　　　RR f. 131v.
19 　　Croydon 　　　　　RR f. 289v.
26 　　Otford 　　　　　　RR f. 251.
28 　　Mortlake 　　　　　PRO E164/27, f. 189.
30 　　Otford 　　　　　　RR f. 249v.

1324
January
1 　　Otford 　　　　　　RR ff. 88, 251v.
4 　　　" 　　　　　　　PRO E164/27, f. 193.
5 　　　" 　　　　　　　Cant. Cath. MS Eastry Cor. i, 58.
6 　　　" 　　　　　　　RR f. 251v.
8 　　　" 　　　　　　　RR ff. 251v, 308; Reg. Orleton Here-
　　　　　　　　　　　　　ford, 271.
10 　　Lambeth 　　　　　RR f. 308; Reg. Orleton Hereford, 271.
12 　　Mortlake 　　　　　RR f. 235v; Reg. Orleton Hereford, 273-
　　　　　　　　　　　　　5; Reg. Martival ii, 435.
13 　　　" 　　　　　　RR f. 251v.
17 　　Lambeth 　　　　　CUL MS Ee.v.31, f. 234v.
21 　　　" 　　　　　　RR f. 294v.
22 　　　" 　　　　　　PRO C85/8/44.
24 　　Otford 　　　　　　RR f. 80v; CUL MS Ee.v.31, f. 234.
26 　　　" 　　　　　　RR f. 251v.
28 　　Leeds, 　　　　　　RR f. 251v.
　　　Charing 　　　　　　RR f. 80v; CUL MS Ee.v.31, f. 234.

February
2 　　Charing 　　　　　　RR f. 251v.
8 　　Canterbury 　　　　RR f. 251v.

1324
February

9		Canterbury	Reg. Hethe, 154.
12		''	RR f. 251v.
13		''	RR f. 103; PRO E164/27, f. 195v.
14		''	RR f. 252.
16		''	RR ff. 252, 294v; PRO C85/8/54.
17		Canterbury,	RR f. 252.
		Charing	RR f. 131v.
19		Maidstone	RR f. 252.
22		Otford	RR f. 289v.
26		Lambeth	RR ff. 252, 294v.
29		''	LAO MS Dij/16/i/14.

March

1		Lambeth	RR f. 289.
2		''	RR f. 289v.
3	K	Westminster	PRO C53/110, m. 5.
4		Lambeth,	RR f. 252.
	K	Westminster	PRO C53/110, m. 7.
8		Lambeth	RR f. 290.
10	K	Westminster	PRO C53/110, m. 7.
12	K	''	PRO C53/110, m. 7.
13		Lambeth	RR f. 294v; PRO C85/8/53.
15		''	RR f. 290.
16		''	RR f. 252.
17		''	RR f. 290.
23		''	RR f. 252.
24	K	Westminster	PRO C53/110, m. 6.
25	K	''	PRO C53/110, m. 5, 6, and 7.
27		Lambeth	RR ff. 132, 294v; PRO C85/8/62, 64.
29	K	Westminster	PRO C53/110, m. 6.

April

1	K	Westminster	PRO C53/110, m. 5 and 6.
2		Croydon	RR f. 252v.
3		''	RR f. 252v.
5		''	RR f. 132.
8		Otford	RR f. 132.
10		''	Cant. Cath. MS Eastry Cor. v, 46.
13		''	RR f. 252v.
23		Lambeth	RR f. 253.
29		Mortlake	RR f. 252v.
30		''	PRO C85/8/61.

1324
May

5		Lambeth	RR f. 252v.
6		"	RR f. 252v; Reg. Martival ii, 451-2.
7	K	Westminster	PRO C53/110, m. 5.
8	K	"	PRO C53/110, m. 3.
10		Lambeth,	Reg. Martival iv, 100.
	K	Westminster	PRO C53/110, m. 3 and 4.
12		Lambeth	RR f. 290.
13		"	RR f. 253.
14		"	RR f. 295; PRO C85/8/63.
18		"	PRO C47/18/6/12, m. 18.
20		Lambeth,	RR f. 131v; Reg. London, 236.
	K	Westminster	PRO C53/110, m. 3.
21		Lambeth	RR f. 290.
23		"	RR f. 132v; Cant. Cath. MS Eastry Cor. i, 28.
29		Westminster	Reg. Martival ii, 452.

June

1	K	Westminster	Reg. Hethe, 341; PRO C53/110, m. 2.
7		Lambeth	RR f. 133.
8		"	RR f. 290.
10	K	Westminster	PRO C53/110, m. 1.
15		Mortlake	RR f. 253.
16		"	Reg. Hethe, 133.
22		"	RR f. 253.
23		"	RR f. 132v.
25		"	RR f. 253.
26		"	RR f. 253.
27		"	RR f. 253v.
28	K	Tonbridge (Kent)	PRO C53/110, m. 2.
29		Mortlake,	RR f. 133.
	K	Tonbridge	PRO C53/110, m. 1.

July

1		Lambeth	RR f. 295.
11		Mortlake	RR f. 133; *Historical Papers*, ed. Raine, 326-8.
13		"	RR f. 295; PRO C85/8/56.
26		Saltwood	RR f. 253v.
29		Otford	RR f. 253v.

August

4	K	Guildford (Surrey)	PRO C53/111, m. 11.
6	K	"	PRO C53/111, m. 11.

1324
August

8		Mortlake	RR f. 253v.
13		Otford	HMC Eighth Rep., I, app., 633; Reg. Martival ii, 463-5.
15		"	RR f. 133.
22	K	Otford/Bromley	PRO E101/380/12.
24		Maidstone	RR f. 254.
26	O	"	RR f. 185v.
29		"	PRO C85/8/60.
30		"	RR ff. 290, 295.
31		Mayfield	RR f. 133.

September

10		Slindon (Sussex)	Reg. Hethe, 341.
11		Lavant (Sussex)	RR f. 290v.
16		"	RR f. 254.
20		Slindon	RR f. 290v.
25		Southwick (Sussex)	RR f. 290v.

October

4		Mayfield	Cant. Cath. MS Eastry Cor. i, 19.
12		Saltwood	RR f. 133v.
13		Canterbury	RR f. 290v.
15		"	RR f. 254.
24		Lambeth	RR f. 254.
27		"	RR ff. 164v, 295v; PRO C85/8/59.
30		"	Reg. Hethe, 149.
31	K	Mortlake	PRO E101/380/12.

November

1		Lambeth	RR f. 133v.
3		"	PRO C85/8/55.
5		"	PRO C85/8/57.
6		"	RR f. 254.
10		"	RR f. 295; PRO SC1/34/164.
11	K	Westminster	HMC *Wells* i, 493; PRO C53/111, m. 5, 7, and 9.
18		Lambeth	Reg. Martival ii, 468.
19		"	CUL MS Ee.v.31, ff. 252-252v; Reg. Martival ii, 470.
20		"	Cant. Cath. MS Reg. I, f. 402v.
25		"	RR f. 254v.
26		"	RR f. 134.
27		"	RR f. 254v.
28		Mortlake	RR f. 254v.

1324
December

1		Mortlake	RR f. 134; Cant. Cath. MS Reg. A, f. 222v.
11		Faversham (Kent)	RR f. 254v.
13		''	RR f. 134.
15		Otford	PRO C85/8/65.
17		''	PRO C85/8/58.

1325
January

| 14 | | Otford | RR ff. 254v, 272v. |
| 20 | | '' | RR f. 254v. |

February

2	K	Mortlake	PRO E101/380/12.
5		Lambeth	RR f. 295v.
11		''	RR ff. 165, 295v; PRO C85/8/66.
12	K	Westminster	PRO C53/111, m. 4.
13		Lambeth	RR ff. 165, 255.
14		Lambeth,	RR f. 165v.
	K	Westminster	PRO C53/111, m. 3.
15		Lambeth	RR ff. 165v, 255.
16		''	RR ff. 134v, 255.
17		''	RR f. 166.
22		''	RR ff. 166, 295v; PRO C85/8/67.
23		''	RR f. 291.
24		''	RR f. 255.
26		''	RR f. 134v.
28		''	RR f. 255.

March

4		Lambeth	RR f. 255.
5		Northfleet	RR f. 135.
8		Canterbury	RR f. 135.
9		Dover	RR ff. 165, 291; Cant. Cath. MS Lit. D.8, f. 86; Reg. Martival ii, 500; Reg. Hethe, 344.
10		Wingham	RR f. 135.
17		''	RR f. 135.
19		''	RR f. 166.
25		''	RR f. 135v; CUL MS Ee.v.31, f. 241v.

April

3		Charing	RR ff. 166v, 255.
9		Lambeth	RR f. 275v.
17		''	RR f. 291.
21		''	RR f. 291.

1325
April

23		Mortlake	RR f. 135v.
29		Winchester	RR f. 255.

May

1		Hursley (Hants)	RR f. 255v.
2		Wolvesey (Hants)	Reg. Martival ii, 470-1.
4		Alton (Hants)	RR f. 166.
10		Lambeth	Reg. Martival ii, 473-4.
14		Mortlake	RR f. 135v.
21		''	RR ff. 136, 137v.
23		Lambeth	RR f. 256.
27		Otford	RR f. 295v; Reg. Hethe, 348.
29		''	RR f. 249v.

June

2		Otford	RR f. 256.
3		''	RR f. 167.
7		''	RR f. 166v.
11		''	RR f. 256.
18		Lambeth	RR f. 167.
19		Lambeth,	RR f. 275; CUL MS Ee.v.31, f. 243; Cant. Cath. MS Eastry Cor. i, 1.
		Mortlake	RR f. 295v.
22		Mortlake	RR f. 136.
26	K	Westminster	PRO C53/111, m. 2.
29		Lambeth	RR f. 274v.

July

1	K	Westminster	PRO C53/111, m. 2.
2		Lambeth	RR f. 137.
3		''	RR f. 136v.
4		Lambeth,	RR ff. 256, 275v, 291; Reg. Hethe, 355.
	K	Westminster	PRO C53/111, m. 2.
5		Lambeth,	Cant. Cath. MS Eastry Cor. i, 2.
	K	Westminster	PRO C53/111, m. 2.
6		Lambeth	RR f. 291.
8		''	RR ff. 167, 276.
9		''	BL Harl. Charter 43.I.20.
10		''	RR f. 137.
11		''	RR ff. 275v, 276.
12		''	RR f. 276.
15		Chesterton (Cambs.)	RR f. 295v.
17		Newmarket (Suff.)	RR f. 137v.
19		Thetford (Norf.)	RR f. 137v.

1325
July

22		Norwich (Norf.)	RR f. 256v.
23		Thorpe near Norwich (Norf.)	RR ff. 137, 256v.
25		"	RR f. 256v.
26		"	RR f. 256v.
28		"	RR f. 276v.
29		"	RR f. 278v.
31		"	RR ff. 164v, 276v.

August

2		Wymondham (Norf.)	RR f. 277v.
6		Bury St. Edmunds (Suff.)	RR f. 137v.
8		Stoke by Clare (Suff.)	RR ff. 256v, 278v.
12		Lambeth	RR ff. 277v, 278.
14		"	RR ff. 278, 295v.
21	K	Wingham	PRO E101/381/16.
24		St. Radegund Abbey near Dover (O.Praem., Kent)	RR ff. 278, 278v.
26		Canterbury	Lambeth MS 1212, p. 127.

September

1		Saltwood	CUL MS Ee.v.31, f. 244; Lambeth MS 1212, p. 127.
3	K	Langdon Abbey near Dover (O. Praem., Kent)	RR f. 138.
4		"	RR f. 138.
7		St. Radegund Abbey near Dover	RR f. 256v.
8		"	RR f. 138.
10		"	RR ff. 138v, 256v.
13		Faversham Abbey (OSB, Kent)	RR ff. 291v, 295v.
14		Teynham	RR f. 139; Roth, *English Austin Friars* ii, no. 240.
17		Charing	RR f. 291v.
18		"	Cant. Cath. MS Christ Church Letters ii, 42.
22		"	RR f. 140v; Reg. Hethe, 357; LAO MS Reg. Burghersh V, f. 384v.
23		Charing,	RR f. 257.
	K	Maresfield (Sussex)	PRO C53/112, m. 9.
28		Otford	RR f. 295v.

October

| 2 | | Otford, | RR f. 141. |

1325
October

14		Lambeth,	RR f. 141v.
		Croydon	RR f. 296.
15		Croydon	RR ff. 140v, 142, 143v.
17		''	RR f. 142.
18		Lambeth	RR f. 142v.
25		Croydon	RR f. 142v.
26		''	RR f. 257.
27		''	RR f. 143.

November

2		Croydon	RR f. 150.
5		''	RR f. 257.
8		''	RR f. 143v.
22		Lambeth	*Cart. Mon. de Ramesia* ii, 194-5.
24		Lambeth,	RR f. 145.
	K	Westminster/Croydon	PRO E101/381/16.
25	K	Otford	PRO E101/381/16.
26		Lambeth	RR f. 257.
27	K	Charing	PRO E101/381/16.

December

4		Lambeth	RR f. 291v; HMC *Wells* i, 213-14.
5		''	RR f. 258; Reg. Hethe, 361.
6		''	RR f. 144.
9		''	RR f. 146v.
11		''	RR ff. 144, 291v; CUL MS Ee.v.31, f. 246.
19		''	RR f. 144v.
21	O	Newington near London (Surrey)	RR f. 185v.
23		Lambeth	RR f. 257.
27		Otford	RR f. 144v.
29		''	RR f. 258v.
30		''	RR f. 292.

1326
January

1		Otford	Reg. Hethe, 365; Reg. Orleton Hereford, 341.
2		''	PRO SC1/49/90-1-2.
7		''	RR f. 146v.
10		''	RR f. 164v; Cant. Cath. MS Reg. L, f. 128v.
12		Lambeth	RR f. 257v.
14		Croydon	RR f. 257v.
18		Otford	RR f. 145v.

1326
January

19		Otford	RR f. 291v.
23		"	RR f. 257v.
29		"	RR f. 258.
31		Wrotham	RR f. 258.

February

3		Maidstone	RR f. 291v.
12		Lambeth	RR f. 148.
15	O	Canterbury	RR f. 186.
17		"	RR ff. 200, 259; Reg. London, 237.
18		"	CUL. MS Ee.v.31, f. 259.
20		"	RR f. 146v.
24		Charing	RR f. 258v.
25		"	PRO C85/8/68.
26		"	RR f. 146v.

March

3		Charing	RR f. 147.
4		"	RR ff. 258v, 292.
12		"	RR f. 258v; Reg. Orleton Hereford, 374.
13		"	RR f. 147v.
14		"	RR f. 147v.
15		Otford	CPR 1327-30, 199.
19		Maidstone	RR f. 259.
25		Otford	RR f. 259v.
29		Maidstone	RR f. 292.

April

1		Otford	RR f. 259v.
2		"	RR f. 259v.
25		"	RR f. 148v; Reg. Hethe, 373; Reg. Orleton Hereford, 361.

May

7		Otford	RR f. 260.
9		"	RR f. 260.
10		"	RR f. 260.
13		"	RR f. 149.
14		"	RR f. 260.
17	O	"	RR ff. 187, 260.
20		"	RR f. 134.
24		Lambeth	RR f. 260v.
25	K	Croydon/Lambeth	Cant. Cath. MS Eastry Cor. i, 61.
26		Lambeth/Mortlake	Cant. Cath. MS Eastry Cor. i, 61.
29	K	Saltwood	PRO E101/381/16.

1326
May

30		Mortlake	RR f. 260v.

June

2		Mortlake	Cant. Cath. MS Eastry Cor. i, 61.
3		"	RR f. 292.
7	K	Saltwood	PRO E101/381/16.
9		Canterbury	RR f. 154v; Cambridge, Trinity College MS R.5.41, f. 120v.
13		"	RR ff. 193-4.
23		Otford	Reg. Martival ii, 528.
26		"	RR ff. 149, 292.
28		"	RR f. 260v.
30		"	RR f. 262v.

July

2		Otford	RR f. 262v.
8		"	RR f. 149.
9		"	PRO C85/8/70.
11		"	RR ff. 262v, 263.
15		"	CUL MS Ee.v.31, f. 253v.
16		Lambeth	RR f. 194.
19		Bishopsbourne (Kent)	PRO C85/8/69.
20		Lambeth,	RR f. 263; Reg. Orleton Hereford, 369.
	K	Westminster	PRO C53/113, m. 1.
21		Lambeth	RR f. 149.
22		Croydon	RR f. 263.
24		Otford	RR ff. 149, 263.
26		"	RR f. 263v.
27		"	RR f. 263.
28		"	Reg. Hethe, 377.

August

8	Charing	RR f. 263v.
9	"	RR ff. 263v, 292.
12	"	RR f. 263v.
16	Chartham	RR f. 195.
18	Wingham	RR f. 263v.
25	Chartham	RR ff. 273v, 292v.

September

10		Otford	RR ff. 149v, 263v.
12		Orsett (Essex)	RR f. 314.
29	K	London, Tower of London	RR f. 313.
30		London, St. Paul's	RR ff. 215, 313; *Ann. Paul.*, 315; Cambridge, Trinity College MS R.5.41, f. 121v.

1326
October

1		Lambeth	RR f. 264.
2		"	RR f. 313.
3	K	Westminster	PRO C53/113, m. 1.
4		Lambeth	RR f. 292v.
15		Lambeth/Croydon/Otford	Cant. Cath. MS Eastry Cor. i, 47; Cambridge, Trinity College MS R.5.41, f. 122.
16		Otford,	RR f. 264.
		Maidstone	Cant. Cath. MS Eastry Cor. i, 47; Cambridge, Trinity College MS R.5.41, f. 122.
17		Maidstone	RR f. 264.
18		"	RR ff. 156, 278v.
21		"	Cant. Cath. MS Eastry Cor. i, 47.
26		Canterbury	Cambridge, Trinity College MS R.5.41, f. 123.
28		"	RR f. 149v.

November

3	Canterbury	RR ff. 150, 264, 278v; CUL MS Ee.v.31, f. 254.
5	"	RR f. 150.
12	Charing	Cant. Cath. MS S.V. iii, 40.
15	"	RR f. 292v.
24	"	RR f. 292v.
27	"	RR f. 149.

December

1	Charing	RR f. 292v.
2	"	RR f. 195v.
3	"	RR ff. 150, 156, 292v.
5	Maidstone	CUL MS Ee.v.31, f. 254v.
6	"	RR f. 313v; CUL MS Ee.v.31, f. 260v.
8	"	RR f. 313v.
9	"	RR ff. 2, 292v.
11	Otford	RR f. 151; Reg. Martival ii, 530-1.
16	Croydon	RR ff. 151, 292v.
17	Mortlake	RR f. 151.
23	Lambeth	RR f. 152v.
29	Newington near Wallingford (Oxon.)	RR f. 200.

1327
January

8	Lambeth	RR ff. 151v, 152, 157.

1327
January

13		London, Guildhall,	*Ann. Paul.*, 322-3.
	P	Westminster	Clarke, *Medieval Representation and Consent*, 183.
24		Lambeth	RR f. 152.
25		,,	RR f. 152v.
27		,,	RR f. 200.
28		,,	RR f. 153v; LAO MS Dij/61/iv/26.
29		,,	RR f. 152v; Reg. Martival ii, 537.
31		,,	RR ff. 152v, 264v.

February

1	K	Westminster Abbey: *Coronation of Edward III.*	CCR 1327-30, 100; Rymer II:ii, 684; *Ann. Paul.*, 324.
3		Lambeth	RR f. 264v; CUL MS Ee.v.31, f. 256.
4	K	Westminster	PROC53/114, m. 46.
6		Lambeth	RR f. 200.
8		,,	RR ff. 153, 296.
9		,,	RR f. 200.
12		,,	RR f. 264v.
14	K	Westminster	PRO C53/114, m. 35.
15	K	,,	PRO C53/114, m. 46.
18		Lambeth	RR f. 200.
20	K	Westminster	PRO C53/114, m. 46.
21		Lambeth	RR f. 296.
22		,,	RR f. 200.
26	K	Westminster	PRO C53/114, m. 43 and 44.
27		Lambeth,	RR ff. 153v, 264.
	K	Westminster	PRO C53/114, m. 43.

March

1		Lambeth	RR f. 264v; CUL MS Ee.v.31, f. 258v.
2	K	Westminster	PRO C53/114, m. 44.
3	K	,,	PRO C53/114, m. 33 and 38.
4		Lambeth,	PRO C85/8/71.
		Charing	RR f. 292v.
6		Lambeth,	RR f. 265.
	K	Westminster	*Ann. Paul.*, 332; PRO C53/114, m. 35 and 45.
8	K	Westminster	PRO C53/114, m. 36, 38, 40, and 45.
10	K	,,	PRO C53/114, m. 34.
13		Croydon	RR f. 265.
14	K	Westminster	PRO C53/114, m. 35.
15		Otford	RR f. 196v; CUL MS Ee.v.31, f. 258.
16		,,	RR f. 153v.

1327
March

17		Otford,	RR f. 265.
		Lambeth	RR f. 200.
20		Lambeth,	RR f. 197.
		Charing	RR f. 265.
22	B	Canterbury	RR f. 149v; Cant. Cath. MS Reg. A, f. 244v.
23		"	RR f. 196v; Cant. Cath. MS Cart. Ant. C819, C820; Lambeth MS 1226, no. 10.
25		Wingham,	RR f. 149v.
	K	Westminster	PRO C53/114, m. 32.
28		Wingham,	RR f. 200.
	K	Westminster	PRO C53/114, m. 33.

April

1		Canterbury	RR ff. 153v, 265.
3		Charing	RR f. 265.
6		Maidstone	RR f. 164v.
10		Croydon	RR f. 265.
11		Harrow	RR f. 197.
19		Langtoft	RR f. 265.
21	K	Stamford (Lincs.)	PRO C53/114, m. 31.
22		Langtoft	RR f. 197.

May

2		Northfleet	RR f. 265.
13		Charing	RR f. 265.
15		"	RR f. 154.
18		"	RR f. 265v.
19		"	RR f. 154.
23		"	RR f. 296; PRO C85/8/73.
27		"	Cant. Cath. MS Reg. L, f. 150.
29		"	RR f. 200v.

June

7		Charing	RR f. 154v.
9		"	RR f. 200.
13		Maidstone	RR f. 149v.
15		Scotney (Kent)	RR ff. 154, 154v.

July

1		South Malling (Sussex)	RR f. 155.
3		"	RR f. 265v.
4		"	RR f. 155; Windsor Castle MS XI.G.54.
8		"	RR f. 265v.

1327
July

9	Mayfield	RR f. 167v.
20	"	RR f. 155v.
27	"	RR f. 158.

August

10	South Malling	RR f. 198v; Windsor Castle MS XI.G.54.
11	"	RR f. 296.
16	"	RR ff. 158v, 198v.
23	Slindon	RR f. 200.
25	"	RR f. 198v.
29	"	PRO SC1/35/121; Reg. Martival ii, 540-1; LAO MS Reg. Burghersh V, f. 407v.
30	"	RR f. 199.
31	"	RR f. 157v.

September

2	Slindon	RR f. 265v.
4	Mayfield	RR ff. 158v, 206.
7	Otford	RR ff. 167v, 199v.
8	"	RR ff. 167v, 199.
9	"	RR f. 167v.
10	Otford,	RR ff. 206, 206v, 265v.
	Northfleet	RR f. 159.
12	Orsett (Essex), manor of the bishop of London	PRO SC1/37/102.
13	"	RR f. 158v.
15	"	RR f. 200v.
16	"	RR f. 158v.
18	"	RR ff. 159, 266.
23	Otford	RR f. 206v.
28	"	RR ff. 200v, 207; LAO MS Reg. Burghersh V, f. 408.
29	"	RR f. 159; LAO MS Reg. Burghersh V, f. 408; Reg. Martival ii, 542.

October

3	Chartham	RR ff. 206v, 207; PRO C84/20/42.
8	"	RR f. 159.
9	Charing	RR f. 200v.
12	Maidstone	PRO SC8/237/11833.
21	Mortlake	RR f. 266.
26	"	RR f. 159.
27	"	RR f. 207v.
31	"	RR f. 266v.

1327
November

1	Mortlake	RR f. 200v.
2	"	RR f. 159v.
4	"	RR f. 267.
5	"	RR f. 266v; CUL MS Ee.v.31, f. 264.
6	"	RR f. 266v.
8	"	RR f. 266v.
10	"	RR f. 159v.
11	"	Cant. Cath. MS Cart. Ant. A14.
16	Mortlake. *Death*.	Cant. Cath. MS Reg. Q, f. 123.

Bibliography

1. Manuscript sources

Avignon, Archives Départementales
Archives de Vaucluse, H., Célestins de Gentilly, no. 6: Testament of Cardinal
Annibaldo Gaetani da Ceccano.

Cambridge, Cambridge University Library
MS Ee.v.31.
MS Mm.v.19.

Cambridge, Corpus Christ College
MS. 450.

Cambridge, Fitzwilliam Museum
MS McClean 142.

Cambridge, Trinity College
MS O.9.26.
MS R.5.41.

Canterbury, Canterbury Cathedral Library (Dean and Chapter)
Cartae Antiquae.
Christ Church Letters i, ii.
Eastry Correspondence i, ii, v, vii, viii.
Literary MS D.8.
Miscellaneous Accounts, i, ii.
Registers A. B. G. I. K. L. Q.
Scrap Book A.
Sede Vacante Scrapbooks i, ii, iii.

Kilkenny, Ireland, Church of Ireland Episcopal Palace
Red Book of Ossory.

Lincoln, Lincolnshire Archives Office (Dean and Chapter Muniments)
MSS Dij, Dvi (Accounts).
Register of Bishop John Dalderby, III.
Register of Bishop Henry Burghersh, V.

London, British Library (formerly British Museum)
Additional Charters 17353, 41381.
Additional MSS 5761, 6159, 11557, 15366, 17362, 20059, 22162, 22174,
22923, 25142, 25237, 29499, 34901, 35093, 41612.
Arundel MS 435.

Cotton Charter II.26.
Cotton MSS Cleopatra A.xvi, E.i (top foliation is always cited), E.ii.
Cotton MSS Faustina A.v, A.vi, A.viii.
Cotton MS Galba E.iv.
Cotton MS Nero C.viii.
Cotton MS Titus D.xxiii.
Cotton MSS Vespasian E.xxi, E.xxii.
Harleian Charters 43.G.29, 43.I.20, 51.H.2, 84.C.14.
Harleian MSS 858, 869, 927, 947, 961, 1608, 1690, 3720, 3942, 4351, 5213.
Lansdowne MSS 476, 652.
Royal MSS 11.A.ix, 12.D.xi.

London, Lambeth Palace Library
Cartae Miscellanae VI/66, XI/46.
Estate Document 545.
MSS 166, 242, 538, 1212, 1213, 1226.
Register of Archbishop Walter Reynolds.

London, Public Record Office
  Chancery

C47/3/51	Miscellanea.
C47/15-21	Miscellanea, Ecclesiastical Documents.
C47/27 and 29	Miscellanea, Diplomatic Documents.
C49/4 and 5	Parliamentary and Council Proceedings.
C53/100-114	Charter Rolls.
C70/1-7	Roman Rolls.
C81/1705 and 1706	Warrants for the Great Seal.
C81/1786-1796	Rebellious Monks.
C84/18-20	Ecclesiastical Petitions.
C85/7-214	Significations of Excommunication.

  Exchequer

E30/1214, 1217, 1218, 1368, 1418	T.R., Diplomatic Documents.
E36/274	T.R., Books.
E41/193	T.R., Ancient Deeds.
E43/104 and 528	T.R., Ancients Deeds (Wardrobe Debentures).
E101/68	K.R., Accounts Various (Indenture).
E101/126 and 127	K.R., Accounts Various (Foreign Merchants).
E101/309-311	K.R., Accounts Various (Nuncii).
E101/354-386	K.R., Accounts Various (Wardrobe and Household).
E135	K.R., Ecclesiastical Documents.
E159/82-93	K.R., Memoranda Rolls.
E164/27	K.R., Miscellaneous Books.
E352/125	Chancellor's Rolls (Pipe Office).

E372/170, 173, 175, 177   Pipe Rolls (Pipe Office).
E403   Issue Rolls.

Special Collections
  SC1   Ancient Correspondence.
  SC6   Ministers' Accounts.
  SC7   Papal Bulls.
  SC8   Ancient Petitions.
  SC10   Parliamentary Proxies.

  PRO 31/9/17a   Rome Archives, partial transcript of Andreas
                                      Sapiti's register.

  J.I. 1/383   Justices Itinerant.

London, St. Paul's Cathedral Library (Dean and Chapter)
  WD1 (Liber A).

London, Society of Antiquaries
  MS 120.

London, Westminster Abbey, Muniments
  2442, 4528, 5019, 5713.

Oxford, Bodleian Library
  MS Kent Charters 84, 149.
  MS Kent Roll 6.
  MS Oseney Charter 41.
  MS Tanner 197.

Oxford, Magdalen College
  MS 185.

San Marino, California, Henry E. Huntington Library
  HM 906.
  EL 6107.

Vatican City, Vatican Archives (Archivio Segreto Vaticano)
  Collectoriae 52, 184, 492A.
  Obligationes et Solutiones (O.S.) 3, 6.
  Reg. Aven. (R.A.) 2, 160.
  Reg. Vat. (R.V.) 15, 63, 109, 110A, 113, 114, 116.

Vatican City, Vatican Library (Biblioteca Apostolica Vaticana)
  MS Barb. Lat. 2126 (= MS Barb XXXI, 11). Register of Andreas Sapiti.
    Examined by microfilm and compared with partial transcript in PRO
    31/9/17a.
  MS Barb. Lat. 2366. Seventeenth-century transcription of bulls and other
    documents relating to mission of Cardinals Gaucelme and Luca,
    papal nuncios in England 1317-1318. Examined on Microfilm 870
    Positive from National Library of Ireland, Dublin, by kindness of
    authorities there.
  MS Vat. Lat. 1404.

Windsor, Windsor Castle
   MS XI.G.54.
York, Borthwick Institute
   Register of Archbishop William Melton.

2. PRINTED SOURCES

Alain de Lille. *Anticlaudianus: Texte critique avec une introduction et des tables.* Ed. R. Boussat. Paris, 1955.

——. *Anticlaudianus.* Transl. J. J. Sheridan. Toronto, 1973.

Amundesham, John. *Annales.* Ed. H. T. Riley. RS no. 28, v. Vol. i. London, 1870.

Ancient Kalendars and Inventories of the Treasury of H.M. Exchequer. Ed. F. Palgrave. 3 vols. London: Rec. Com., 1836.

Andreae, Johannes. *In Quinque Decretalium Libros Novella Commentaria.* 5 vols. in 4. Facsimile of 1581 ed. with introd. by S. Kuttner. Turin, 1963.

Annales Londonienses. In vol. i of *Chronicles of the Reigns of Edward I and Edward II,* ed. W. Stubbs. RS no. 76. London, 1882.

Annales Monastici. Ed. H. R. Luard. RS no. 36, vol. 3: *De Dunstaplia.* London, 1866.

Annales Paulini. In vol. i of *Chronicles of the Reigns of Edward I and Edward II,* ed. W. Stubbs. RS no. 76. London, 1882.

Aspin, Isabel S. T., ed. *Anglo-Norman Political Songs.* Oxford, 1953.

Baluzius, S. *Vitae Paparum Avenionensium.* Ed. G. Mollat. 4 vols. Paris, 1914-1927.

Barraclough, G., ed. *Public Notaries and the Papal Curia: A Calendar and a Study of the Formularium Notariorum Curie from the Early Years of the Fourteenth Century.* London, 1934.

Bateson, Mary, ed. *Cambridge Gild Records.* Cambridge Antiquarian Society, octavo series, no. xxxix. Cambridge, 1903.

Bolland, W. C., Maitland, F. W., and Harcourt, W.V., eds. *The Eyre of Kent 6 & 7 Edward II.* Selden Society vols. 24, 27, 29. London, 1910-1913.

The Book of John de Schalby, Canon of Lincoln (1299-1333), Concerning the Bishops of Lincoln and Their Acts. Transl. J. H. Srawley. Lincoln Minster pamphlets no. 2. Lincoln, 1949.

Bridlington, Canon of. *Gesta Edwardi de Carnarvan.* In vol. ii of *Chronicles of the Reigns of Edward I and Edward II.* Ed. W. Stubbs. RS no. 76. London, 1883.

Burrows, M., ed. *OHS Collectanea, Second Series.* Oxford Historical Society, vol. xvi. Oxford, 1890.

Calendar of Ancient Correspondence concerning Wales. Ed. J. G. Edwards. Univ. of Wales, Board of Celtic Studies, History and Law series, no. ii. Cardiff, 1935.

Calendar of Chancery Warrants. Vol. i, Privy Seals 1244-1326. London: HMSO, 1927.

Calendar of the Charter Rolls. Vols. i-iv. 1226-1341. London: HMSO, 1903-1912.

Calendar of the Close Rolls, 1272-1337. 12 vols. London: HMSO, 1892-1900.

Calendar of Documents Relating to Scotland. Ed. J. Bain. Vol. ii, 1272-1307. London: HMSO, 1884.

Calendar of Entries in the Papal Registers Relating to Great Britain and Ireland: Papal Letters. Vols. i-iii, 1198-1362. Eds. W. H. Bliss and C. Johnson. London: HMSO, 1894-1897.

Calendar of the Fine Rolls. Vols. i-iv, 1272-1337. London: HMSO, 1911-1913.

Calendar of Memoranda Rolls (Exchequer), Michaelmas 1326–Michaelmas 1327. Ed. R. E. Latham. London: HMSO, 1968.

Calendar of the Patent Rolls, 1232-1338. 16 vols. London: HMSO, 1891-1913.

Calendar of the Register of John de Drokensford, Bishop of Bath and Wells (A.D. 1309-1329). Ed. E. Hobhouse. Somerset Record Society, vol. i. 1887.

A Calendar of the Register of Wolstan de Bransford, Bishop of Worcester 1339-49. Ed. R. M. Haines. London, 1966.

Cam, Helen M., ed. *The Eyre of London, 14 Edward II, A.D. 1321.* Selden Society, vols. 85-6. London, 1968-1969.

Cartularium Monasterii de Rameseia. Eds. W. H. Hart and P. A. Lyons. RS no. 79. Vol. ii. London, 1886.

The Cartulary of Cirencester Abbey, Gloucestershire. Ed. C. D. Ross. 2 vols. London, 1964.

The Cartulary of Worcester Cathedral Priory. Ed. R. R. Darlington. Pipe Roll Society, Publications, n.s. vol. xxxviii. London, 1968.

Chaplais, P., ed. *The War of Saint-Sardos (1323-1325): Gascon Correspondence and Diplomatic Documents.* Camden 3rd series, vol. 87. London, 1954.

Chapter Act Book of the Collegiate Church of St. John of Beverley. Ed. A. F. Leach. Surtees Society, vols. 98, 108. Durham, 1898-1903.

The Chartulary of the Cistercian Abbey of St. Mary of Sallay in Craven. Ed. J. McNulty. One vol. in 2 parts. Yorkshire Archaeological Society, Record Series, lxxxvii and xc. Wakefield, 1933-1934.

Chartulary of Winchester Cathedral. Ed. A. W. Goodman. Winchester, 1927.

Chew, Helena M., ed. *Hemingby's Register.* Wiltshire Archaeological and Natural History Society, Records Branch, xviii. Devizes, 1963.

Chrimes, S. B., and Brown, A. L., eds. *Select Documents of English Constitutional History 1307-1485.* London, 1961.

Chronica Johannis de Reading et Anonymi Cantuariensis, 1346-1367. Ed. J. Tait. Publications of the Univ. of Manchester, Historical series, no. 20. Manchester, 1914.

Chronica Monasterii de Melsa. Ed. E. A. Bond. RS no. 43. 3 vols. London, 1866-1868.

The Chronicle of Lanercost. Transl. H. E. Maxwell. Glasgow, 1913.

The Chronicle of St. Mary's Abbey, York. Eds. H. H. E. Craster and M. E. Thornton. Surtees Society, vol. 148. Durham, 1934.

Chronicon Angliae Petriburgense. Ed. J. A. Giles. London, 1845.

Chroniques de London, depuis l'an 44 Hen. III; jusqu'à l'an 17 Edw. III. Ed. C. J. Aungier. Camden old series, vol. 28. London, 1844.

Clément VI (1342-1352): Lettres closes, patentes et curiales se rapportant à la France. Eds. E. Déprez, J. Glenisson, and G. Mollat. BEFAR, sér. 3. 4 vols. Paris, 1910-1961.

Close Rolls of the Reign of Henry III. Vols. i-xiv, 1227-1272. London: HMSO, 1902-1938.

Cole, H., ed. *Documents Illustrative of English History in the Thirteenth and Fourteenth Centuries.* London: Rec. Com., 1844.

Conciliorum Oecumenicorum Decreta. Ed. J. Alberigo, *et al.* 3rd ed. Bologna, 1973.

Corpus Iuris Canonici. Ed. E. A. Friedberg. 2 vols. Leipzig, 1879-1881.

Denifle, H., and Chatelain, E., eds. *Chartularium Universitatis Parisiensis.* 3 vols. Paris, 1889-1897.

Deputy Keeper of the Public Records. *Seventh Report.* London: HMSO, 1846.

Devon, F., ed. *Issues of the Exchequer, Henry III-Henry VI, from the Pell Records.* London: Rec. Com., 1837.

Early Registers of Writs. Eds. Elsa de Haas and G. D. G. Hall. Selden Society vol. 87. London, 1970.

Fayen, A., ed. *Lettres de Jean XXII (1316-1334).* Analecta Vaticano-Belgica, vols. ii and iii. Rome, 1908-1912.

Fletcher, C. R. L., ed. *OHS Collectanea, First Series.* Oxford Historical Society, vol. v. Oxford, 1885.

Flores Historiarum. Ed. H. R. Luard. RS no. 95. Vol. iii. London, 1890.

Fowler, J. T., ed. *Memorials of the Church of SS. Peter and Wilfrid, Ripon.* Surtees Society, vols. 74, 78, 81, 115. Durham, 1882-1908.

Fraser, Constance M., ed. *Records of Antony Bek.* Surtees Society, vol. 162. Durham, 1953.

Gascon Rolls Preserved in the Public Record Office 1307-1317. Ed. Y. Renouard. London: HMSO, 1962.

Gee, H., and Hardy, W. J., eds. *Documents Illustrative of English Church History.* London, 1896.

Harvey, Barbara F., ed. *Documents Illustrating the Rule of Walter de Wenlok, Abbot of Westminster, 1283-1307.* Camden 4th series, vol. 2. London, 1965.

Historical Manuscripts Commission. *Calendar of the Manuscripts of the Dean and Chapter of Wells.* Vol. i. London: HMSO, 1907.

——. *Fourth, Fifth, Eighth, Ninth, and Tenth Reports with Appendixes.* London: HMSO, 1874-1901.

——. *Report on Manuscripts in Various Collections.* vol. i. London: HMSO, 1901.

Historical Papers and Letters from the Northern Registers. Ed. J. Raine. RS no. 61. London, 1873.

Jean XXII: Lettres communes analysées d'après les registres dits d'Avignon et du Vatican. Ed. G. Mollat. BEFAR, sér. 3. 16 vols. Paris, 1904-1947.

Leadam, I. S., and Baldwin, J. F., eds. *Select Cases before the King's Council 1243-1482*. Selden Society vol. 35. Cambridge, Mass., 1918.

Letters of Edward, Prince of Wales. Ed. Hilda Johnstone. Roxburghe Club, Cambridge, 1931.

Lettres secrètes et curiales du pape Jean XXII, 1316-1334, relatives à la France. Eds. A. Coulon and S. Clémencet. BEFAR, sér. 3. 3 vols. in 4 parts. Paris, 1900-1972.

The Liber Albus of the Priory of Worcester. Ed. J. M. Wilson. Worc. Hist. Soc., 1919.

Liber Ecclesiae Wigorniensis. Ed. J. H. Bloom. Worc. Hist. Soc., 1912.

The Liber Epistolaris of Richard de Bury. Ed. N. Denholm-Young. Oxford, 1950.

Liber Pensionum Prioratus Wigorn. Ed. C. Price. Worc. Hist. Soc., 1925. ·

Literae Cantuarienses: The Letter Books of the Monastery of Christ Church, Canterbury. Ed. J. B. Sheppard. RS no. 85. 3 vols. London, 1887-1889.

Lunt, W. E., ed. *Accounts rendered by Papal Collectors in England 1317-1378*. With additions and revisions by E. B. Graves. Philadelphia, 1968.

Lyndwood, W. *Provinciale, seu Constitutiones Angliae*. Oxford, 1679.

Magnum Registrum Album. Ed. H. E. Savage. Wm. Salt Archaeol. Soc. Lichfield, 1926 (for 1924).

Murimuth, Adam. *Continuatio Chronicarum*. Ed. E. M. Thompson. RS no. 93. London, 1889.

Nicolai Triveti Annalium Continuatio. Ed. A. Hall. Oxford, 1722.

Novae Narrationes. Ed. Elsie Shanks. Selden Society vol. 80. London, 1963.

Ottenthal, E. von, ed. *Regulae Cancellariae Apostolicae. Die päpstlichen Kanzleiregeln von Johannes XXII. bis Nicholaus V*. Innsbrück, 1888.

Pantin, W. A., ed. *Documents Illustrating the Activities of the General and Provincial Chapters of the English Black Monks 1215-1540*. Camden 3rd series, vols. xlv, xlvii, and liv. London, 1931-1937.

——. 'The Letters of John Mason: A Fourteenth Century Formulary from St. Augustine's, Canterbury'. In *Essays in Medieval History Presented to Bertie Wilkinson*, eds. T. A. Sandquist and M. R. Powicke, pp. 192-219. Toronto, 1969.

The Parliamentary Writs and Writs of Military Summons .... Ed. F. Palgrave. 2 vols. in 4. London: Rec. Com., 1827-1834.

Placita Parliamentaria. Ed. W. Ryley. London, 1661.

Placitorum ... Abbreviatio. Eds. G. Rose and W. Illingworth. London: Rec. Com., 1811.

Powicke, F. M., and Cheney, C. R., eds. *Councils and Synods with Other Documents Relating to the English Church*, vol. ii, 1205-1313. 2 parts. Oxford, 1964.

Prynne, W. ... *An Exact Chronological Vindication* .... 3 vols. London, 1666-1668. [Commonly called Prynne's *Records*.]

Putnam, Bertha H., ed. *Kent Keepers of the Peace 1316-1317*. Kent Records vol. xiii. Ashford, 1933.

The Red Book of the Exchequer. Ed. H. Hall. rs no. 99. 3 vols. London, 1896.

Regestum Clementis Papae v. Ed. by Benedictines of Monte Cassino. 8 vols. Rome, 1885-1892. Tables and index, ed. R. Fawtier and G. Mollat. BEFAR, sér. 3. 2 vols. Paris, 1948-1957.

Register of Bishop Godfrey Giffard. Ed. J. W. W. Bund. 2 vols. Worc. Hist. Soc., 1902.

The Register of the Diocese of Worcester during the Vacancy of the See, usually called Registrum Sede Vacante, 1301-1485. Ed. J. W. W. Bund. Worc. Hist. Soc., 1893-1897.

The Register of Henry Chichele, Archbishop of Canterbury 1414-1443. Ed. E. F. Jacob. 4 vols. CYS, 1937-1947.

The Register of John de Grandisson, Bishop of Exeter, A.D. 1327-1369. Ed. F. C. Hingeston-Randolph. 3 vols. London, 1894-1899.

The Register of John de Halton, Bishop of Carlisle, A.D. 1292-1324. Transcr. W. N. Thompson, intro. by T. F. Tout. 2 vols. CYS, 1906-1913.

'The Register of Roger de Norbury, Bishop of Lichfield and Coventry from A.D. 1322 to A.D. 1358: an abstract of contents and remarks by Bishop Hobhouse'. In *Collections for a History of Staffordshire*, pp. 241-88. William Salt Archaeological Society, vol. i. Birmingham, 1880.

The Register of Thomas de Cobham, Bishop of Worcester, 1317-1327. Ed. E. H. Pearce. Worc. Hist. Soc., 1930.

The Register of Walter Reynolds, Bishop of Worcester, 1308-1313. Ed. R. A. Wilson. Dugdale Society and Worc. Hist. Soc., 1927.

The Register of Walter de Stapledon, Bishop of Exeter, A.D. 1307-1326. Ed. F. C. Hingeston-Randolph. London, 1892.

The Register of William de Geynesburgh, Bishop of Worcester, 1302-1307. Eds. J. W. W. Bund and R. A. Wilson. Worc. Hist. Soc., 1907-1929.

The Register of William Greenfield, Lord Archbishop of York, 1306-1315. Ed. A. H. Thompson. Surtees Society, vols. 145, 149, 151-3. Durham, 1928-1940.

The Registers of John de Sandale and Rigaud de Asserio, Bishops of Winchester (A.D. 1316-1323). Ed. F. J. Baigent. Hampshire Record Society. London, 1897.

The Registers of Roger Martival, Bishop of Salisbury 1315-1330. Eds. Kathleen Edwards, C. R. Elrington, and Susan Reynolds. 4 vols. CYS, 1959-1974.

The Registers of Walter Bronescombe (1257-80) and Peter Quivil (1280-91), Bishops of Exeter. Ed. F. C. Hingeston-Randolph. London, 1889.

Les Registres de Boniface VIII .... Eds. G. Digard, M. Faucon, A. Thomas, and R. Fawtier. BEFAR, sér. 2. 4 vols. Paris, 1884-1939.

Les Registres de Grégoire IX .... Ed. L. Auvray, *et al.* BEFAR, sér. 2. 4 vols. Paris, 1896-1955.

Les Registres d'Innocent IV .... Ed. E. Berger. BEFAR, sér. 2. 4 vols. Paris, 1884-1921.

Les Registres de Martin IV .... BEFAR, sér. 2. Paris, 1901-1935.

Registrum Ade de Orleton Episcopi Herefordensis. Ed. A. T. Bannister. Cantilupe Society and CYS, 1908.

Registrum Epistolarum Johannis Peckham, Archiepiscopi Cantuariensis. Ed. C. T. Martin. RS no. 77. 3 vols. London, 1882-1886.

Registrum Hamonis Hethe, Diocesis Roffensis. Ed. C. Johnson. 2 vols. CYS, 1914-1948.

Registrum Henrici Woodlock, Diocesis Wintoniensis, A.D. 1305-1316. Ed. A. W. Goodman. 2 vols. CYS, 1940-1941.

Registrum Palatinum Dunelmense: The Register of Richard de Kellawe, Lord Palatine and Bishop of Durham 1311-1316. Ed. T. D. Hardy. RS no. 62. 4 vols. London, 1873-1878.

Registrum Radulphi Baldock, Gilberti Segrave, Ricardi Newport, et Stephani Gravesend, Episcoporum Londoniensium, A.D. 1304-1338. Ed. R. C. Fowler. CYS, 1911.

Registrum Ricardi de Swinfield Episcopi Herefordensis, A.D. 1283-1317. Ed. W. W. Capes. Cantilupe Society and CYS, 1909.

Registrum Roberti Winchelsey, Cantuariensis Archiepiscopi, A.D. 1294-1313. Ed. Rose Graham. 2 vols. CYS, 1952-1956.

Registrum Simonis de Gandavo, Diocesis Sarisbiriensis, A.D. 1297-1315. Eds. C. T. Flower and M. C. B. Dawes. 2 vols. CYS, 1934.

Registrum Simonis Langham, Cantuariensis Archiepiscopi. Ed. A. C. Wood. CYS, 1956.

Registrum Thome Bourgchier, Cantuariensis Archiepiscopi A.D. 1454-1486. Ed. F. R. H. Du Boulay. CYS, 1948-1957.

Reichert, B. M., ed. *Acta Capitulorum Generalium Ordinis Praedicatorum*, vol. ii (1304-1378). Vol. iv of *Monumenta Ordinis Fratrum Praedicatorum Historica.* Rome, 1899.

Richardson, H. G., and Sayles, G. O., eds. *Rotuli Parliamentorum Anglie hactenus Inediti, MCCLXXIX-MCCCLXIII.* Camden 3rd series, vol. li. London, 1935.

Roberts, R. A., ed. 'Edward II, the Lords Ordainers, and Piers Gaveston's Jewels and Horses (1312-1313)'. In *Camden Miscellaney* vol. xv. Camden 3rd series, vol. 41. London, 1929.

Rockinger, L., ed. *Briefsteller und Formelbücher des eilften bis vierzehnten Jahrhunderts.* Quellen und Erörterungen zur bayerischen und deutschen Geschichte, ix. Munich, 1863.

The Rolls and Register of Bishop Oliver Sutton, 1280-1299. Ed. Rosalind M. T. Hill. Lincoln Record Society vols. 39, 43, 48, 52, 60, 64, 69. 1948-1975.

Rotuli Parliamentorum; ut et Petitiones et Placita in Parliamento. 6 vols. London: Rec. Com., 1783. Index, 1832.

Royal Letters, Henry III. Ed. W. W. Shirley. RS no. 27. 2 vols. London, 1862-1866.

Rymer, T., ed. *Foedera, Conventiones, Litterae* .... Reedited by A. Clarke, *et al.* 4 vols. in 7. London: Rec. Com., 1816-1869.

Salter, H. E., ed. *Balliol College Deeds.* Oxford Historical Society, vol. 64. Oxford, 1913.

——. *Snappe's Formulary and Other Records.* Oxford Historical Society, vol. 80. Oxford, 1924.

——, Pantin, W. A., and Richardson, H. G., eds. *Formularies Which Bear on the History of Oxford c. 1204-1420.* Oxford Historical Society, n.s. vols. 4 and 5. Oxford, 1942.

Sayles, G. O., ed. *Select Cases in the Court of King's Bench under Edward I.* Selden Society vols. 55, 57, 58. London, 1936-1939.

——. *Select Cases in the Court of King's Bench under Edward II.* Selden Society vol. 74. London, 1957.

——. *Select Cases in the Court of King's Bench under Edward III.* Selden Society vol. 76. London, 1958.

Schroeder, H. J., ed. *Disciplinary Decrees of the General Councils. Text, Translation, and Commentary.* St. Louis, 1937.

Sharpe, R. R., ed. *Calendar of Letter-Books preserved among the Archives of the City of London at the Guildhall.* 11 vols. London, 1899-1912.

State Papers during the Reign of Henry the Eighth. Vol. vii. London: Rec. Com., 1852.

Stubbs, W., ed. *Chronicles of the Reigns of Edward I and Edward II.* RS no. 76. 2 vols. London, 1882-1883.

——. *Select Charters and Other Illustrations of English Constitutional History.* 9th ed. Oxford, 1913.

Tangl, M. *Die päpstlichen Kanzlei-Ordnungen von 1200-1500.* Innsbruck, 1894.

Taxatio Ecclesiastica Angliae et Walliae Auctoritate P. Nicholai IV circa A.D. 1291. London: Rec. Com., 1802.

Treaty Rolls, Preserved in the Public Record Office. Ed. P. Chaplais. Vol. i, 1234-1325. London: HMSO, 1955.

Trokelowe, John. *Chronica et Annales.* Ed. H. T. Riley. RS no. 28, iii. London, 1865.

Vernay, E., ed. *Le 'Liber de excommunicacione' du Cardinal Bérenger Frédol.* Paris, 1912.

Vita Edwardi Secundi, by the so-called Monk of Malmesbury. Ed. and transl. N. Y. Denholm-Young. London, 1957.

Walsingham, Thomas. *Historia Anglicana.* Ed. H. T. Riley. RS no. 28, i. 2 vols. London, 1863-1864.

——. *Gesta Abbatum Monasterii Sancti Albani.* Ed. H. T. Riley. RS no. 28, iv. 3 vols. London, 1867-1869.

Wharton, H., ed. *Anglia Sacra.* 2 vols. London, 1691.

Wilkins, D., ed. *Concilia Magnae Britanniae et Hiberniae A.D. 446-1717.* 4 vols. London, 1737.

William Thorne's Chronicle of Saint Augustine's Abbey Canterbury. Transl. A. H. Davis, intro. by A. H. Thompson. Oxford, 1934.

Wilson, J. M., and Jones, Ethel C., eds. *Corrodies at Worcester in the 14th Century.* Worc. Hist. Soc., 1917.

Wykeham's Register. Ed. T. F. Kirby. Hampshire Record Society, 1896-1899.

Yearbooks of Edward II. Eds. F. W. Maitland, G. J. Turner, W. C. Bolland, P. Vinogradoff, L. Ehrlich, M. Dominica Legge, W. Holdsworth, J. P. Collas, and T. F. T. Plucknett. Selden Society vols. 17, 19, 20, 22, 26, 31, 33, 34, 36, 37, 38, 39, 41, 42, 43, 45, 52, 54, 61, 63, 65, 70, 81. London, 1903-.

3. Secondary Works

Adam, Paul. *La Vie paroissiale en France au XIVe siècle.* Vol. iii of *Histoire et sociologie de l'église,* eds. G. Le Bras and J. Gaudemet. Paris, 1964.

Adams, Norma. 'The writ of prohibition to court Christian'. *Minnesota Law Review* xx (1936), 272-93.

——. 'The judicial conflict over tithes.' EHR lii (1937), 1-22.

Albe, E. *Autour de Jean XXII. Hugues Géraud, évêque de Cahors.* Cahors, 1904.

Barraclough, G. *Papal Provisions.* Oxford, 1935.

——. 'The executors of papal provisions in the canonical theory of the thirteenth and fourteenth centuries.' In *Acta Congressus Iuridici Internationalis Romae 1934,* 3: 109-53. Rome, 1936.

——. 'Praxis beneficiorum.' *Zeitschrift der Savigny-Stiftung für Rechtsgeschichte* lviii (1938), (Kanonistische Abteilung 27), 94-134.

——. 'Minutes of papal letters (1316-17).' In *Miscellanea Archivistica Angelo Mercati,* pp. 109-27. Studi e Testi, vol. 165. Vatican City, 1952.

Bartolini, F. 'Suppliche pontificie dei secoli XIII e XIV.' *Bullettino dell'Istituto Storico Italiano per il Medio Evo e Archivio Muratoriano,* no. 67 (Rome, 1955), 1-187.

Baumgarten, P. M. *Von der apostolischen Kanzlei. Untersuchungen über die päpstlichen Tabellionen und die Vizekanzler der heiligen römischen Kirche im XIII, XIV, und XV. Jahrhundert.* Köln, 1908.

Beardwood, Alice. *The Trial of Walter Langton, Bishop of Lichfield 1307-1327.* Transactions of the American Philosophical Society, n.s. vol. 54, part 3. Philadelphia, 1964.

Behrens, B. 'Origins of the office of English resident ambassador in Rome.' EHR xlix (1934), 640-56.

Bellamy, J. *Crime and Public Order in England in the Later Middle Ages.* London, 1973.

Benson, R. L. *The Bishop-Elect: A Study in Medieval Ecclesiastical Office.* Princeton, 1968.

Bernard, J. 'Le népotisme de Clément v et ses complaisances pour la Gascogne.' *Annales du Midi* lxi (1948-1949), 369-411.

Bignami-Odier, Jeanne. 'Le testament du Cardinal Richard Petroni (25 Jan. 1314).' In *Papers of the British School at Rome,* vol. xxiv (n.s. vol. xi), pp. 142-57. London, 1956.

Blomefield, F. *An Essay towards a Topographical History of the County of Norfolk.* Continued by C. Parkin. 11 vols. London, 1805-1810.

Boase, T. S. R. *Boniface VIII.* London, 1933.

Boyle, L. E. 'The *Oculus Sacerdotis* and some other works of William of Pagula. TRHS, 5th series, vol. v (1955), 81-110.

——. 'William of Pagula and the *Speculum Regis Edward III*.' *Mediaeval Studies* xxxii (1970), 329-36.

——. *A Survey of the Vatican Archives and of its Medieval Holdings.* Toronto, 1972.

——. 'The Quodlibets of St. Thomas and Pastoral Care.' *The Thomist* xxxviii (1974), 232-56.

Bradshaw, H., and Wordsworth, C. *Statutes of Lincoln Cathedral.* 3 vols. Cambridge, 1892-1897.

Brentano, R. L. *York Metropolitan Jurisdiction and Papal Judges Delegate 1279-96.* Univ. of California Publications in History, vol. 58. Berkeley, 1959.

——. *Two Churches: England and Italy in the Thirteenth Century.* Princeton, 1968.

——. *Rome before Avignon.* New York, 1974.

Breslau, H. *Handbuch der Urkundenlehre.* Vol. i. 2nd ed. Leipzig, 1912.

Brett-James, N. G. 'John de Drokensford, bishop of Bath and Wells.' *Transactions of the London and Middlesex Archaeological Society*, n.s. vols. 10-11 (1951-1953).

Brooke, Z. N. *The English Church and the Papacy, from the Conquest to the Reign of John.* Cambridge, 1931.

Brown, Elizabeth A. R. 'Gascon Subsidies and the Finances of the English Dominions, 1315-1324.' In *Studies in Medieval and Renaissance History* viii, ed. H. L. Adelson, pp. 33-163. Lincoln, Nebr., 1971.

Brown, W. 'A list of benefices in the diocese of York vacant between 1316 and 1319.' *Yorkshire Archaeological Society, Record Series*, lxi (Miscellanea, vol. i), 136-48. Leeds, 1920.

Browne, John Cave. *The History of the Parish Church of All Saints', Maidstone.* Maidstone, 1889.

——. *The Story of Hollingborne, its church and its clergy.* Maidstone, 1890.

Bryant, T. H. *Norfolk Churches,* part ix: *The Hundred of Holt.* Norwich, 1902.

——. *The Churches of Norfolk: Hundred of Brothercross.* Norwich, 1914.

Burns, C. 'Sources of British and Irish History in the Instrumenta Miscellanea of the Vatican Archives.' *Archivum Historiae Pontificiae* ix (1971), 7-141.

Caillet, L. *La papauté d'Avignon et l'église de France: la politique bénéficiale du Pape Jean XXII en France (1316-1334).* Publications de l'Université de Rouen. Paris, 1975.

Calendar of the Deeds and Charters in the Shrewsbury Free Public Library, vol. i. HMC, National Register of Archives. London, 1960.

Cambridge Medieval History. Vol. vii. Cambridge, 1932.

Camm, B. 'The Mediaeval Gilds of Cambridge.' *Downside Review* xliii (1925), 9-20.

Capes, W. W. *The English Church in the Fourteenth and Fifteenth Centuries.* Vol. iii of *A History of the English Church*, eds. W. R. W. Stephens and W. Hunt. London, 1900.

Cary, George. *The Medieval Alexander.* Ed. D. J. A. Ross. Cambridge, 1956.

Cerchiari, E. *Capellani papae et apostolice sedis auditores causarum palatii apostolici seu Sacra Rota.* 4 vols. Rome, 1919-1921.

Chaplais, P. 'Privy seal drafts, rolls, and registers (Edward i – Edward iii).' EHR lxxiii (1958), 270-3.

Charles, B. G., and Emanuel, H. D., compilers. *A Calendar of the Earlier Hereford Cathedral Muniments.* 3 vols. 1955. Typescript, deposited in National Register of Archives, London, no. 6186.

Cheney, C. R. 'Legislation of the medieval English church.' EHR l (1935), 193-224, 385-417.

——. 'The punishment of felonous clerks.' EHR li (1936), 215-36.

——. *From Becket to Langton.* Manchester, 1956.

——. 'William Lyndwood's *Provinciale.'* *The Jurist* xxi (1961), 405-34.

——. *Handbook of Dates for Students of English History.* Royal Historical Society, Guides and handbooks, no. 4. London, 1961.

——. 'England and the Roman Curia under Innocent iii.' JEH xviii (1967), 173-86.

——. *Hubert Walter.* London, 1967.

——. *Medieval Texts and Studies.* Oxford, 1973.

Chew, Helena M. *The English Ecclesiastical Tenants-in-Chief and Knight Service, especially in the Thirteenth and Fourteenth Centuries.* London, 1932.

Christie, A. Grace I. *English Medieval Embroidery.* Oxford, 1938.

Churchill, Irene J. *Canterbury Administration.* 2 vols. London, 1933.

Clarke, Maude V. *Medieval Representation and Consent.* London, 1936.

Clarke, R. D. 'Some Secular Activities of the English Dominicans during the Reigns of Edward i, Edward ii, and Edward iii (1272-1377).' London University, M.A. thesis, 1930.

Cobban, A. B. 'Edward ii, Pope John xxii and the University of Cambridge.' BJRL xlvii (1964), 49-78.

Cole, R. E. G. 'Some papal provisions in the cathedral church of Lincoln, 1300-1320.' *Associated Architectural Societies' Reports and Papers* xxxiv (1918), 219-58.

Cook, G. H. *English Collegiate Churches in the Middle Ages.* London, 1959.

Cox, J. C. *The Sanctuaries and Sanctuary Seekers of Mediaeval England.* London, 1911.

Cristofori, F. *Storia dei Cardinali di Santa Romana Chiesa, dal secolo v all'anno del signore MDCCCLXXXVIII.* Rome, 1888.

Croke, W. J. D. 'The National Establishments of England in Mediaeval Rome.' *Dublin Review* cxxiii (1898), 94-106, 305-17.

Crump, C. G. 'The arrest of Roger Mortimer and Queen Isabel.' EHR xxvi (1911), 331-2.

Cuttino, G. P. 'Henry of Canterbury.' EHR lvii (1942), 298-311.

——. 'A memorandum book of Elias Joneston.' *Speculum* xvii (1942), 74-85.

——. 'King's clerks and the community of the realm.' *Speculum* xxix (1954), 395-409.

——. *English Diplomatic Administration 1259-1339.* 2nd ed. Oxford, 1971.

Dalton, J. N. *The Manuscripts of St. George's Chapel, Windsor Castle.* Windsor, 1957.

David, C. W. 'The Claim of King Henry I to be called learned.' In *Anniversary Essays in Medieval History by Students of Charles Homer Haskins,* ed. C. H. Taylor, pp. 45-56. Boston, 1929.

Davies, Cecily. 'The statute of Provisors of 1353.' *History,* n.s. vol. xxxviii (1953), 116-33.

Davies, J. C. *The Baronial Opposition to Edward II.* Cambridge, 1918.

Davis, H. W. C. 'The Canon Law in England.' *Zeitschrift der Savigny-Stiftung für Rechtsgeschichte* xxxiv (1913), (Kanonistische Abteilung iii), 344-62.

——. *England under the Normans and Angevins, 1066-1272.* Vol. ii of *A History of England,* ed. C. W. C. Oman. 13th ed. London, 1949.

Deeley, Ann. 'Papal provision and royal rights of patronage in the early fourteenth century.' EHR xliii (1928), 497-527.

Denholm-Young, N. 'Richard de Bury 1287-1345.' TRHS, 4th series, vol. xx (1937), 135-68.

Denton, J. H. 'The Career of Robert Winchelsey, Archbishop of Canterbury, 1294-1313.' Cambridge University, Ph.D. thesis, 1966.

——. 'Pope Clement V's early career as a royal clerk.' EHR lxxxiii (1968), 303-14.

——. *English Royal Free Chapels 1100-1300: A Constitutional Study.* Manchester, 1970.

——. 'Canterbury archiepiscopal appointments: the case of Walter Reynolds.' *Journal of Medieval History* i (1975), 317-27.

——. 'Walter Reynolds and Ecclesiastical Politics 1313-1316: A Postscript to *Councils & Synods, II.*' In *Church and Government in the Middle Ages: Essays presented to C. R. Cheney on his 70th Birthday,* eds. C. N. L. Brooke, D. E. Luscombe, G. H. Martin, and D. M. Owen, pp. 247-74. Cambridge, 1976.

Desmond, L. A. 'The Statute of Carlisle and the Cistercians 1298-1369.' In *Studies in Medieval Cistercian History presented to Jeremiah F. O'Sullivan,* pp. 138-62. Cistercian Studies Series, 13. Spencer, Mass., 1971.

Dictionary of National Biography. Eds. L. Stephen and S. Lee. 66 vols. 1885-1901. Reprinted in 22 vols., Oxford, 1921-1922.

Dictionary of Welsh Biography down to 1940. Pub. and ed. by the Honourable Society of Cymmrodorion. London, 1959.

Dodds, Madeleine H. *A History of Northumberland.* Vol. xiv. Newcastle-upon-Tyne, 1935.

Doherty, P. 'The date of the birth of Isabella Queen of England 1308-1358.' BIHR xlviii (1975), 246-8.

Donahue, C., Jr. 'Roman Canon Law in the Medieval English Church: Stubbs vs. Maitland Re-Examined after 75 Years in the Light of Some Records from the Church Courts.' *Michigan Law Review* 72 (1974), 647-716.

——, and Gordus, J. P. 'A Case from Archbishop Stratford's Audience Act Book and Some Comments on the Book and its Value.' *Bulletin of Medieval Canon Law*, n.s. vol. ii (1972), 45-59.

Douais, C. *Les Frères Prêcheurs en Gascogne au XIIIme et au XIVme siècle*. 2 vols. Paris, 1885.

Douie, Decima L. *Archbishop Pecham*. Oxford, 1952.

Driver, J. T. 'The papacy and the diocese of Hereford, 1307-77.' CQR cxlv (1947), 31-47.

Du Boulay, F. R. H. *The Lordship of Canterbury*. London, 1966.

Duggan, C. 'The Becket dispute and the criminous clerks.' BIHR xxxv (1962), 1-28.

Dykmans, M. 'Le Cardinal Annibal de Ceccano (vers 1282-1350): Étude biographique et testament du 17 juin 1348.' *Bulletin de l'Institut historique belge de Rome*, fasc. xliii (Rome, 1973), 145-344.

Edwards, Kathleen, 'The Personnel and Political Activities of the English Episcopate during the Reign of Edward II.' London University, M.A. thesis, 1938.

——. 'Bishops and learning in the reign of Edward II.' CQR cxxxviii (1944), 57-86.

——. 'The political importance of the English bishops during the reign of Edward II.' EHR lix (1944), 311-47.

——. 'The social origins and provenance of the English bishops during the reign of Edward II.' TRHS, 5th series, vol. ix (1959), 51-79.

——. *The English Secular Cathedrals in the Middle Ages: A Constitutional Study with Special Reference to the Fourteenth Century*. 2nd ed. Manchester, 1967.

Ehler, S. Z. 'On applying the modern term "state" to the Middle Ages.' In *Medieval Studies presented to Aubrey Gwynn, S.J.*, eds. J. A. Watt, J. B. Morrall, and F. X. Martin, pp. 492-501. Dublin, 1961.

Emden, A. B. *A Biographical Register of the University of Oxford to A.D. 1500*. 3 vols. Oxford, 1957-1959.

——. *A Biographical Register of the University of Cambridge to 1500*. Cambridge, 1963.

Eubel, C. *Hierarchia Catholica Medii Aevi*. Vol. i: 1198-1431. Münster, Westphalia, 1913.

Faucon, M. *La librairie des papes d'Avignon, 1316-1420*. BEFAR xliii and l. 2 vols. Paris, 1886-1887.

Finberg, H. P. R. *Tavistock Abbey*. Cambridge Studies in Medieval Life and Thought, n.s. vol. 2. Cambridge, 1951.

Flahiff, G. B. 'The use of prohibitions by clerics against ecclesiastical courts in England.' *Mediaeval Studies* iii (1941), 101-16.

——. 'The writ of prohibition to court Christian in the thirteenth century.' *Mediaeval Studies* vi (1944), 261-313, and vii (1945), 229-90.

Flanagan, U. 'Papal provisions in Ireland, 1305-78.' In *Historical Studies III* (Papers read before the Fourth Irish Conference of Historians), pp. 92-103. London, 1961.

Fleming, L. *History of Pagham in Sussex*. 3 vols. Ditchling, 1949-1951.

Fliniaux, A. 'Contribution à l'histoire des sources du droit canonique. Les anciennes collections des *decisiones Rotae.*' *Revue historique de droit français et étranger*, sér. iv, vol. iv (1925), 61-93, 382-410.

Foss, E. *The Judges of England.* 9 vols. London, 1848-64.

Fowler, R. C. 'Secular aid for excommunication.' TRHS, 3rd series, vol. viii (1914), 113-17.

——. 'Seals in the Public Record Office.' *Archaeologia* lxxiv (1923-1924), 103-16.

Fraser, Constance M. *A History of Antony Bek, Bishop of Durham 1283-1311.* Oxford, 1957.

Fryde, E. B. 'Loans to the English crown 1328-31.' EHR lxx (1955), 198-211.

Fryde, Natalie M. 'John Stratford, Bishop of Winchester, and the Crown, 1323-30.' BIHR xliv (1971), 153-61.

Gabel, Leona C. *Benefit of Clergy in England in the Later Middle Ages.* Smith College Studies in History, vol. xiv, nos. 1-4. Northampton, Mass., 1928-1929.

Gaignard, R. 'Le gouvernement pontifical au travail: l'exemple des dernières années du règne de Clément v, 1er août 1311 – 20 avril 1314.' *Annales du Midi* lxxii (1960), 169-214.

Galbraith, Georgina R. *The Constitution of the Dominican Order, 1216 to 1360.* Manchester, 1925.

Galbraith, V. H. 'The Tower as an Exchequer record office in the reign of Edward II.' In *Essays in Medieval History Presented to Thomas Frederick Tout*, eds. A. G. Little and F. M. Powicke, pp. 231-47. Manchester, 1925.

——. 'The Literacy of the Medieval English Kings.' *Proceedings of the British Academy* xxi (1935), 201-38.

Giblin, C. 'Vatican Library: MSS. *Barberini Latini* (A guide to the material of Irish interest on microfilm in the National Library, Dublin).' *Archivium Hibernicum* xviii (1955), 67-144.

Girard, J. *Évocation du vieil Avignon.* Paris, 1958.

Göller, E. 'Zur Geschichte der *Audiencia contradictorum.*' *Römische Quartalschrift für christliche Altertumskunde und für Kirchengeschichte* xvii (1903), 411-12; xviii (1904), 101-2.

——. *Die Einnahmen der apostolischen Kammer unter Johann XXII.* Görres-Gesellschaft, *Vatikanische Quellen zur Geschichte der päpstlichen Hof- und Finanzverwaltung*, vol. i, Paderborn, 1910.

Gottlob, T. *Der kirchliche Amtseid der Bischöfe.* Kanonistische Studien und Texte, 9. Bonn, 1936.

Grassi, J. L. 'William Airmyn and the bishopric of Norwich.' EHR lxx (1955), 550-61.

Graves, E. B. '*Circumspecte agatis.*' EHR xliii (1928), 1-20.

——. 'The legal significance of the first statute of *Praemunire.*' In *Anniversary Essays in Medieval History by Students of Charles Homer Haskins*, ed. C. H. Taylor, pp. 57-80. Boston, 1929.

Gray, J. W. 'The *ius praesentandi* in England from the Constitutions of Clarendon to Bracton.' EHR lxvii (1952), 481-509.

——. 'Canon Law in England: Some Reflections on the Stubbs-Maitland Controversy.' *Studies in Church History* iii (1966), 48-68.

——. 'The Church and Magna Charta in the Century after Runnymede.' *Historical Studies* vi (1968), 23-38.

Green, R. H. 'Alan of Lille's *Anticlaudianus*: Ascensus mentis in Deum.' *Annuale Medievale* viii (1967), 3-16.

Greenaway, W. 'The papacy and the diocese of St. David's, 1305-1417.' CQR clxi (1960), 436-48; clxii (1961), 33-49.

Greenway, Diana. 'Ecclesiastical Chronology: *Fasti* 1066-1300.' *Studies in Church History* xi (1975), 53-60.

Guillemain, B. 'Le personnel de la cour de Clément v.' *Mélanges d'archéologie et d'histoire de l'École française de Rome* lxiii (1951), 139-81.

——. 'Les chapelains d'honneur des papes d'Avignon.' *Mélanges d'archéologie et d'histoire de l'École française de Rome* lxiv (1952), 217-38.

——. *La politique bénéficiale du pape Benoît xii (1334-1342).* Bibliothèque de l'École des Hautes Études, Sciences historiques et philologiques, fasc. 299. Paris, 1952.

——. *La Cour pontificale d'Avignon (1309-1376): Étude d'une société.* BEFAR cci. Paris, 1962.

Gurney, Norah K. M., and Clay, C. *Fasti Parochiales*, vol. iv. Yorkshire Archaeological Society, Record Series, cxxxiii. Wakefield, 1971.

Haines, C. R. *Dover Priory.* Cambridge, 1930.

Haines, R. M. 'The Administration of the Diocese of Worcester "Sede Vacante" 1266-1350.' JEH xiii (1962), 156-71.

——. 'Wolstan de Bransford, Prior and Bishop of Worcester c. 1280-1349.' *University of Birmingham Historical Journal* viii (1962), 97-113.

——. *The Administration of the Diocese of Worcester in the First Half of the Fourteenth Century.* London, 1965.

Hall, E. *Henry viii.* Ed. C. Whibley. 2 vols. London, 1904.

Haller, J. *Papsttum und Kirchenreform.* Vol. i. Berlin, 1903.

Hardy, T. D. *Syllabus (in English) of ... 'Rymer's Foedera'.* RS no. 177. Vol. i. London, 1869.

Hartridge, R. A. R. 'Edward i's exercise of the right of presentation to benefices as shown by the patent rolls.' *Cambridge Historical Journal* ii (1927), 171-7.

Hartshorne, C. H. *The Itinerary of King Edward the Second.* [London?], 1861.

Hasted, E. *The History and Topographical Survey of the County of Kent.* 2nd ed. 12 vols. Canterbury, 1797-1801.

——. *The History of the Ancient and Metropolitical City of Canterbury.* 2nd ed. 2 vols. Canterbury, 1801.

Hefele, C. J. von. *Histoire des conciles d'après les documents originaux.* Transl. and amended by H. Leclercq. Vol. vi, part 2. Paris, 1915.

Helmholz, R. H. 'Canonical Defamation in Medieval England.' *American Journal of Legal History* 15 (1971), 255-68.

Hennessy, G. L. *Novum Repertorium Parochiale Londinense*. London, 1898.

Henriques, Ursula R. Q. 'Articles of Grievances of the English Clergy in the Thirteenth and Early Fourteenth Centuries with Special Reference to the Gravamina of 1309.' Oxford University, B.Litt. thesis, 1940.

Highfield, J. R. L. 'The Relations between the Church and the English Crown 1349-1378 – from the Death of Archbishop Stratford to the Outbreak of the Great Schism.' Oxford University, D.Phil. thesis, 1951.

——. 'Correspondence'. In *History*, n.s. vol. xxxix (1954), 331-2.

——. 'The English hierarchy in the reign of Edward III.' TRHS, 5th series, vol. vi (1956), 115-38.

Hill, Mary C. *The King's Messengers 1199-1377. A Contribution to the History of the Royal Household*. London, 1961.

Hill, Rosalind M. T. *Oliver Sutton*. Lincoln Minster Pamphlets no. 4, Lincoln, 1950.

——. 'The theory and practice of excommunication in medieval England.' *History*, n.s. vol. xlii (1957), 1-11.

——. 'Belief and practice as illustrated by John XXII's excommunication of Robert Bruce.' *Studies in Church History* viii (1972), 135-8.

Hillenbrand, E. 'Kurie und Generalkapitel des Predigerordens unter Johannes XXII.' In *Adel und Kirche: Gerd Tellenbach zum 65. Geburtstag dargebracht von Freunden und Schülern*, eds. J. Fleckenstein and K. Schmid, pp. 499-515. Freiburg i.B., 1968.

Hinschius, P. *System des katholischen Kirchenrechts*. Vol. iii. Berlin, 1883.

Histoire littéraire de la France. Vols. xxiv-xxxviii. Paris, 1862-1949.

Hoberg, H. *Taxae pro communibus servitiis ex libris obligationum ab anno 1295 usque ad annum 1455 confectis*. Studi e Testi, vol. 144. Vatican City, 1949.

Hogan, T. L. 'The Memorandum Book of Henry of Eastry, prior of Christ Church Canterbury.' London University, Ph.D. thesis, 1966.

Hook, W. F. *Lives of the Archbishops of Canterbury*. 12 vols. London, 1860-1876.

Hope, W. H. S. 'The Seals of English Bishops.' *Proceedings of the Society of Antiquaries of London*, 2nd series, vol. 11 (1887), 271-306.

Howell, Margaret E. 'The King's Government and Episcopal Vacancies in England, Eleventh to Fourteenth Century.' London University, Ph.D. thesis, 1955.

——. *Regalian Right in Medieval England*. Univ. of London Historical Studies, no. 9. London, 1962.

Hunnisett, R. F. *The Medieval Coroner*. Cambridge, 1961.

Hurnard, Naomi D. *The King's Pardon for Homicide before A.D. 1307*. Oxford, 1969.

Jacob, E. F. 'To and from the court of Rome in the early fifteenth century.' In *Studies in French Language and Medieval Literature. Presented to Professor M. K. Pope by Pupils, Colleagues, and Friends*, pp. 161-81. Publications of the Univ. of Manchester, no. 268. Manchester, 1939. Reprinted in *Essays in Later Medieval History* (New York, 1968), pp. 58-78.

——. 'Petitions for benefices from English universities during the Great Schism.' TRHS, 4th series, vol. xxvii (1945), 41-59.

——. 'The archbishop's testamentary jurisdiction.' In *Medieval Records of the Archbishops of Canterbury*, pp. 35-49. Lambeth Lectures, 1960. London, 1962.

Jenkins, Hester T. 'Lichfield Cathedral in the Fourteenth Century.' Oxford University, B.Litt. thesis, 1956.

Johnstone, Hilda, 'Archbishop Pecham and the council of Lambeth of 1281.' In *Essays in Medieval History Presented to Thomas Frederick Tout*, eds. A. G. Little and F. M. Powicke, pp. 171-88. Manchester, 1925.

——. *Edward of Carnarvon 1284-1307*. Publications of the Univ. of Manchester, Historical series, no. 83. Manchester, 1946.

Jones, W. R. 'Bishops, politics, and the two laws: the *Gravamina* of the English clergy, 1237-1399.' *Speculum* xli (1966), 209-45.

——. 'Relations of the Two Jurisdictions: Conflict and Cooperation in England during the Thirteenth and Fourteenth Centuries.' In *Studies in Medieval and Renaissance History* vii, ed. W. M. Bowsky, pp. 77-210. Lincoln, Nebr., 1970.

Kantorowicz, E. H. 'Inalienability.' *Speculum* xxix (1954), 488-502.

Kemp, E. W. *Counsel and Consent*. London, 1961.

——. 'The archbishop in convocation.' In *Medieval Records of the Archbishops of Canterbury*, pp. 21-34. Lambeth Lectures, 1960. London, 1962.

——. 'The Canterbury provincial chapter and the collegiality of bishops in the Middle Ages.' In *Études d'histoire du droit canonique dédiées à Gabriel Le Bras*, vol. i, pp. 185-94. Paris, 1965.

Kicklighter, J. A. 'An Unknown Brother of Pope Clement v.' *Mediaeval Studies* xxxviii (1976), 492-5.

King, A. A. *Citeaux and her Elder Daughters*. London, 1954.

Kingsford, C. L. 'John de Benstede and his missions for Edward I.' In *Essays in History Presented to Reginald Lane Poole*, ed. H. W. C. Davis, pp. 332-59. Oxford, 1927.

Kirsch, J. P. 'Andreas Sapiti, englischer Prokurator an der Kurie im 14. Jahrhundert.' *Historisches Jahrbuch* (Görres-Gesellschaft) xiv (1893), 582-601.

Knowles, D. *The Religious Orders in England*. Vols. i and ii, Cambridge, 1948-1955.

——, and Hadcock, R. N. *Medieval Religious Houses: England and Wales*. 2nd ed. London, 1971.

Kuttner, S. 'The date of the constitution *Saepe*, the Vatican manuscripts, and the Roman edition of the Clementines.' In *Mélanges Eugène Tisserant*, vol. iv, part 1, pp. 427-52. Studi e Testi, vol. 234. Vatican City, 1964.

Langlois, C.-V. 'Documents relatifs à Bertrand de Got.' *Revue historique* xl (1889), 48-54.

——. 'Le fonds de l'ancienne correspondence au Public Record Office de Londres.' *Journal des Savants*, n.s., 2nd year (1904), 380-93, 446-53.

——. 'Notices et documents relatifs à l'histoire du xiiie et du xive siècle.' *Revue historique* lxxxvii (1905), 55-79.

Larson, A. 'The payment of fourteenth-century English envoys.' EHR liv (1939), 403-14.

——. 'English embassies during the Hundred Years' War.' EHR lv (1940), 423-31.

Lawrence, C. H., ed. *The English Church and the Papacy in the Middle Ages.* London, 1965.

Leff, G. *Richard FitzRalph.* Manchester, 1964.

Legg, J. W., and Hope, W. H. S. *Inventories of Christchurch Canterbury.* Westminster, 1902.

Legge, Mary Dominica. *Anglo-Norman in the Cloisters.* Edinburgh, 1950.

Lemarignier, J.-F., Gaudemet, J., and Mollat, G. *Institutions ecclésiastiques.* Vol. iii of *Histoire des institutions françaises au moyen âge.* Paris, 1962.

Le Neve, J. *Fasti Ecclesiae Anglicanae 1066-1300.* New editions, compiled by Diana E. Greenway. 2 vols. London, 1968-1971.

——. *Fasti Ecclesiae Anglicanae 1300-1541.* New editions, compiled by Joyce M. Horn, B. Jones, and H. P. F. King. 12 vols. London, 1962-1967.

Levison, W. *England and the Continent in the Eighth Century.* Oxford, 1946.

Linnell, C. L. S. *Blakeney Church.* Letheringsett, 1954.

Lizerand, G. *Clément v et Philippe iv le Bel.* Paris, 1910.

Loades, D. M. 'The enforcement of reaction, 1553-1558.' JEH xvi (1965), 54-66.

Logan, F. D. *Excommunication and the Secular Arm in Medieval England.* Toronto, 1968.

Lunt, W. E., 'The first levy of papal annates.' AHR xviii (1912), 48-64.

——. 'William Testa and the parliament of Carlisle.' EHR xli (1926), 332-57.

——. 'Clerical tenths levied in England by papal authority during the reign of Edward ii.' In *Anniversary Essays in Medieval History by Students of Charles Homer Haskins*, ed. C. H. Taylor, pp. 157-82. Boston, 1929.

——. *Papal Revenues in the Middle Ages.* Columbia Univ. Records of Civilization: Sources and studies no. 19. 2 vols. New York, 1934.

——. *Financial Relations of the Papacy with England*; vol. i: *to 1327*; vol. ii: *1327-1534.* Medieval Academy of America, publications nos. 33 and 74. Cambridge, Mass., 1939-1962.

Lux, C. *Constitutionum Apostolicorum de Generali Beneficiorum Reservatione ... 1265-1378 ... Collectio et Interpretatio.* Breslau, 1904.

MacFarlane, L. 'The Vatican Archives.' *Archives* iv (1959), 29-44, 84-101.

MacInerny, M. H. *A History of the Irish Dominicans.* Vol. i. Dublin, 1916.

Madden, Sister James Eugene. 'Business monks, banker monks, bankrupt monks: the English Cistercians in the thirteenth century.' *Catholic Historical Review* xlix (1963), 341-64.

Maddicott, J. R. *Thomas of Lancaster 1307-1322.* Oxford, 1970.

Maitland, F. W. 'The *Praerogativa Regis.*' EHR vi (1891), 367-72.

——. 'History from the Charter Roll.' EHR viii (1893), 726-33.

——. *Roman Canon Law in the Church of England.* London, 1898.

——. 'Execrabilis in the common pleas.' In *The Collected Papers of Frederic William Maitland*, ed. H. A. L. Fisher, vol. 3, pp. 54-64. Cambridge, 1911.

Makower, F. *The Constitutional History and Constitution of the Church of England.* London, 1895.

Manitius, M. *Geschichte der lateinischen Literatur des Mittelalters.* Teil III. Handbuch der Altertums-Wissenschaft, neu herausgegeben von Walter Otto, Abt. 9, Teil 2, Band 3. München, 1931.

Matthew, D. J. A. *The Norman Monasteries and their English Possessions.* London, 1962.

Maxwell-Lyte, H. C. *Historical Notes on the Use of the Great Seal of England.* London: HMSO, 1926.

May, Teresa. 'The Cobham Family in the Administration of England, 1200-1400.' *Archaeologia Cantiana* lxxxii (1967), 1-31.

Mayr-Harting, H. 'Henry II and the papacy.' JEH xvi (1965), 39-53.

McKisack, May. *The Fourteenth Century 1307-1399.* Vol. v of *The Oxford History of England*, ed. G. Clark. Oxford, 1959.

Mirot, L., and Déprez, E. 'Les ambassades anglaises pendant la guerre de cent ans.' *Bibliothèque de l'École des Chartes* lix (1898), 550-77; lx (1899), 177-214.

Moé, E.-A. van. 'Suppliques originales adressées à Jean XXII, Clément VI, et Innocent VI.' *Bibliothèque de l'École des Chartes* xcii (1931), 253-76.

Mollat, G. *La collation des bénéfices ecclésiastiques sous les papes d'Avignon.* Paris, 1921. [It is also found as the introduction to vol. viii of *Jean XXII: Lettres communes*, ed. G. Mollat.]

——. 'Contribution à l'histoire de l'administration judiciaire de l'église romaine au XIVe siècle.' *Revue d'histoire ecclésiastique* xxxii (1936), 877-928.

——. 'Contribution à l'histoire du Sacré Collège de Clément V à Eugène IV.' *Revue d'histoire ecclésiastique* xlvi (1951), 22-112, 566-94.

——. *The Popes at Avignon, 1305-1378.* Transl. J. Love. London, 1963.

Moore, P. S. *The Works of Peter of Poitiers.* Notre Dame, Ind., 1936.

Moore, W. J. *The Saxon Pilgrims to Rome and the Schola Saxonum.* Fribourg, Switzerland, 1937.

Moorman, J. R. H. *Church Life in England in the Thirteenth Century.* Cambridge, 1955.

Morgan, Marjorie M. 'The suppression of the alien priories.' *History*, n.s. vol. xxvi (1941), 204-12.

——. *The English Lands of the Abbey of Bec.* London, 1946.

Müller, E. *Das Konzil von Vienne, 1311-1312. Seine Quellen und seine Geschichte.* No. 12 of *Vorreformationsgeschichtliche Forschungen*, ed. H. Finke. Münster, Westphalia, 1934.

New, C. W. *History of the Alien Priories in England to the Confiscation of Henry V.* Chicago, 1916.

Palmer, C. F. R. 'The Friars Preachers of King's Langley.' *The Reliquary* xix (1878), 37-43.

Pantin, W. A. *The English Church in the Fourteenth Century*. Cambridge, 1955.

Parker, T. W. *The Knights Templars in England*. Tucson, Ariz., 1963.

Parks, G. B. *The English Traveler to Italy*. Vol. i. Rome, 1954.

Pennington, K. 'The Canonists and Pluralism in the Thirteenth Century.' *Speculum* li (1976), 35-48.

Perkins, C. 'The wealth of the Knights Templars in England and the disposition of it after their dissolution.' AHR xv (1910), 252-63.

Phillimore, R. *The Ecclesiastical Law of the Church of England*. 2 vols. London, 1895.

Phillips, J. R. S. *Aymer de Valence, Earl of Pembroke 1307-1324*. Oxford, 1972.

Plucknett, T. F. T. '*Execrabilis* in the Common Pleas: further studies.' *Cambridge Law Journal* i (1921), 60-75.

Poole, A. L. *From Domesday Book to Magna Carta*. Oxford, 1951.

Potthast, A. *Regesta Pontificum Romanorum A.D. 1198-1304*. 2 vols. Berlin, 1874-1875.

Powicke, F. M. *King Henry III and the Lord Edward*. 2 vols. Oxford, 1947.

——. *The Thirteenth Century 1216-1307*. Vol. iv of *The Oxford History of England*, ed. G. Clark. Oxford, 1953.

——, and Fryde, E. B. *Handbook of British Chronology*. Royal Historical Society, Guides and handbooks, no. 2. 2nd ed. London, 1961.

Pugh, R. B. *Imprisonment in Medieval England*. Cambridge, 1968.

Queller, D. E. *The Office of Ambassador in the Middle Ages*. Princeton, 1967.

Ramsay, J. H. *The Genesis of Lancaster*. 2 vols. Oxford, 1913.

Rashdall, H. *The Universities of Europe in the Middle Ages*. New ed. by F. M. Powicke and A. B. Emden. 3 vols. London, 1936.

Renouard, Y. 'Édouard II et Clément V d'après les Rôles Gascons.' *Annales du Midi* lxvii (1955), 119-41.

Richardson, H. G. 'Heresy and the lay power under Richard II.' EHR li (1936), 1-28.

——. 'Clement V and the see of Canterbury.' EHR lvi (1941), 97-103.

——. 'The *Annales Paulini*.' *Speculum* xxiii (1948), 630-40.

——, and Sayles, G. O. 'The clergy in the Easter parliament, 1285.' EHR lii (1937), 220-34.

——, ——. 'The parliament of Carlisle, 1307 – Some new documents.' EHR liii (1938), 425-37.

——, ——. *The Governance of Medieval England from the Conquest to Magna Carta*. Edinburgh, 1963.

Robertson, W. A. S. 'The rectors of Clyffe at Hoo.' *Archaeologia Cantiana* xv (1883), 223-5.

Robinson, D. *Beneficed Clergy in Cleveland and the East Riding 1306-1340*. Borthwick Papers, no. 37. York, 1969.

Roth, C. 'Jews in Oxford after 1290.' *Oxoniensia* xv (1950 [Oxford, 1952]), 63-80.

——. *A History of the Jews in England.* Oxford, 1964.

Roth, F. *The English Austin Friars 1249-1538.* 2 vols. New York, 1961-1966.

Russell, J. C. 'Attestation of Charters in the Reign of John.' *Speculum* xv (1940), 480-98.

Saltman, A. *Theobald Archbishop of Canterbury.* London, 1956.

Sandler, Lucy F. *The Peterborough Psalter in Brussels and other Fenland Manuscripts.* London, 1974.

Sandquist, T. A. 'The Holy Oil of St. Thomas of Canterbury.' In *Essays in Medieval History presented to Bertie Wilkinson*, eds. T. A. Sandquist and M. R. Powicke, pp. 330-44. Toronto, 1969.

Sayers, Jane E. 'The medieval care and custody of the archbishop of Canterbury's archives.' BIHR xxxix (1966), 95-107.

——. 'Canterbury Proctors at the Court of *Audientia Litterarum Contradictarum.*' *Traditio* xxii (1966), 311-45.

——. *Original Papal Documents in the Lambeth Palace Library: a Catalogue.* BIHR Special Supplement no. 6. London, 1967.

——. *Papal Judges Delegate in the Province of Canterbury 1198-1254.* Oxford, 1971.

——. 'Proctors representing British Interests at the Papal Court 1198-1415.' In *Proceedings of the Third International Congress of Medieval Canon Law.* Monumenta Iuris Canonici, series C: Subsidia, vol. 4, ed. S. Kuttner, pp. 143-63. Vatican City, 1971.

Sayles, G. 'Medieval Judges as Legal Consultants.' *Law Quarterly Review* lvi (1940), 247-54.

Scarisbrick, J. J. *Henry VIII.* London, 1968.

Schimmelpfennig, B. *Die Zeremonienbücher der römischer Kurie im Mittelalter.* Tübingen, 1973.

Segrè, C. 'Un Inglese ad Avignon nel 1333.' *Nuova antologia*, 4th series, vol. xciii (1901), 612-22.

Sheehan, M. M. *The Will in Medieval England.* Studies and Texts, 6. Toronto, 1965.

Smalley, Beryl. *English Friars and Antiquity in the Early Fourteenth Century.* Oxford, 1960.

Smith, R. A. L. *Canterbury Cathedral Priory.* Cambridge, 1943.

Smith, W. E. L. *Episcopal Appointments and Patronage in the Reign of Edward II.* Chicago, 1938.

Sommer-Seckendorff, Eleonore M. F. *Studies in the Life of Robert Kilwardby, O.P.* Institutum Historicum FF. Praedicatorum Romae, Dissertationes historicae, fasc. 8. Rome, 1937.

Squibb, G. H. *Founders' Kin.* Oxford, 1972.

Stubbs, W. 'An account of the courts which have exercised ecclesiastical jurisdiction in England up to the year 1832.' In Royal Commission on Ecclesiastical Courts, *Report*, 'Historical Appendix I', pp. 21-51. Parliamentary Papers, vol. xxiv. London, 1883.

438   BIBLIOGRAPHY

——. *Registrum Sacrum Anglicanum.* 2nd ed. Oxford, 1897.

——. *The Constitutional History of England.* Vol. ii. 4th ed. Oxford, 1929.

Sutcliffe, Dorothy. 'The financial condition of the see of Canterbury 1279-1292.' *Speculum* x (1935), 53-68.

Talbot, C. H. 'A List of Cistercian manuscripts in Great Britain.' *Traditio* viii (1952), 402-18.

——, and Hammond, E. A. *The Medical Practitioners of Medieval England.* London, 1965.

Tanner, J. R. *Historical Register of the University of Cambridge.* Cambridge, 1917.

Tanquerey, F. J. 'The conspiracy of Thomas Dunheved, 1327.' EHR xxxi (1916), 119-24.

Taylor, Aileen A. 'The Career of Peter of Gaveston and His Place in History.' London University, M.A. thesis, 1939.

Taylor, J. 'The French "Brut" and the reign of Edward II.' EHR lxxii (1957), 423-37.

Thompson, A. H. 'Pluralism in the medieval church, with notes on pluralists in the diocese of Lincoln, 1366.' *Associated Architectural Societies' Reports and Papers* xxxiii (1915-1916), 35-73; xxxiv (1917-1918), 1-26; xxxv (1919-1920), 87-108, 199-204; xxxvi (1921-1922), 1-41.

——. 'Notes on colleges of secular canons in England.' *Archaeological Journal* lxxiv (1917), 139-239.

——, and Clay, C. T. *Fasti Parochiales.* One vol. in 2 parts. Yorkshire Archaeological Society, Record Series, lxxxv and cvii. Wakefield, 1933-1943.

Thompson, E. Margaret. 'The Petition of 1307 against Papal Collectors.' EHR xxxv (1920), 419-20.

Thorneley, Isobel D. 'Sanctuary in medieval London.' *Journal of the British Archaeological Association,* n.s. vol. xxxviii (1933), 293-315.

Tihon, C. 'Les expectatives *in forma pauperum* particulièrement au xive siècle.' *Bulletin de l'Institut historique belge de Rome,* fasc. v (Rome, 1925), 51-118.

Tillotson, J. H. 'Pensions, Corrodies, and Religious Houses: an Aspect of the Relations of Crown and Church in Early Fourteenth-Century England.' *Journal of Religious History* 8 (1974), 127-43.

Tout, T. F. 'The Westminster chronicle attributed to Robert of Reading.' EHR xxxi (1916), 450-64.

——. *The History of England from the Accession of Henry III to the Death of Edward III (1216-1377).* Vol. iii of *The Political History of England,* eds. William Hunt and R. L. Poole. London, 1920.

——. *Chapters in the Administrative History of Medieval England.* Publications of the Univ. of Manchester, Historical series, nos. 34, 35, 48, 49, 57, 64. 6 vols. Manchester, 1920-1933.

——. *Collected Papers.* Publications of the Univ. of Manchester, Historical series, no. 66. Vol. iii. Manchester, 1934.

——. *The Place of the Reign of Edward II in English History.* Publications of the

Univ. of Manchester, Historical series, no. 21. 2nd ed., revised by Hilda Johnstone. Manchester, 1936.

Trabut-Cussac, J.-P. 'Les possessions anglaises de l'abbaye de la Sauve-Majeure: le prieuré de Burwell (Lincolnshire) 1100 – c. 1439.' *Bulletin philologique et historique* (Paris, 1957), pp. 137-83.

Trenholme, N. M. *The Right of Sanctuary in England.* Univ. of Missouri Studies, vol. i, no. 5. Columbia, Missouri, 1903.

Ullmann, W. 'The curial exequies for Edward I and Edward III.' JEH vi (1955), 26-36.

——. 'Thomas Becket's Miraculous Oil.' *Journal of Theological Studies*, n.s. vol. viii (1957), 129-33.

——. 'A Decision of the Rota Romana on the Benefit of Clergy in England.' In *Collectanea Stephan Kuttner*, vol. iii, pp. 455-89. Studia Gratiana, vol. 13. Bologna, 1967.

Usher, G. A. 'The Career of a political bishop: Adam de Orleton (c. 1279-1345).' TRHS, 5th series, vol. xxii (1972), 33-47.

The Victoria History of the Counties of England. Several vols. London, 1900-.

Warren, W. L. 'Simon Sudbury, Bishop of London and Archbishop of Canterbury.' Oxford University, D.Phil. thesis, 1956.

Watt, D. E. R. 'Sources for Scottish history of the fourteenth century in the archives of the Vatican.' *Scottish Historical Review* xxxii (1953), 101-22.

——. 'University clerks and rolls of petitions for benefices.' *Speculum* xxxiv (1959), 213-29.

Watt, J. A. 'English Law and the Irish Church: the Reign of Edward I.' In *Medieval Studies presented to Aubrey Gwynn, S.J.*, eds. J. A. Watt, J. B. Morrall, and F. X. Martin, pp. 133-67. Dublin, 1961.

Waugh, W. T. 'Archbishop Pecham and pluralities.' EHR xxviii (1913), 625-35.

Weakland, J. E. 'Administrative and Fiscal Centralization under Pope John XXII, 1316-1334.' *Catholic Historical Review* liv (1968), 38-54, 285-310.

——. 'John XXII before his Pontificate, 1244-1316: Jacques Duèse and his Family.' *Archivum Historiae Pontificiae* x (1972), 161-85.

Weaver, J. R. H., and Poole, A. L., eds. *Henry William Carless Davis 1874-1928: A Memoir.* London, 1933.

Weske, Dorothy Bruce. *Convocation of the Clergy.* Church Historical Society, Publications, n.s. no. 23. London, 1937.

Wilkins, H. J. *Westbury College from 1194 to 1544 A.D.* Bristol, 1917.

Wilkinson, B. *The Chancery under Edward III.* Publications of the Univ. of Manchester, Historical series, no. 51. Manchester, 1929.

——. *Studies in the Constitutional History of the Thirteenth and Fourteenth Centuries.* Publications of the Univ. of Manchester, Historical series, no. 73. 2nd ed. Manchester, 1952.

Wilks, M. J. *The Problem of Sovereignty in the Later Middle Ages.* Cambridge Studies in Medieval Life and Thought, n.s. vol. 9. Cambridge, 1963.

Williams, G. *The Welsh Church from Conquest to Reformation.* Cardiff, 1962.

Williamson, J. B. *The History of the Temple, London*. London, 1924.

Wood, Susan M. *English Monasteries and their Patrons in the Thirteenth Century*. London, 1955.

Woodcock, B. L. *Medieval Ecclesiastical Courts in the Diocese of Canterbury*. London, 1952.

Woodman, F. 'Two Tombs in the South Quire Aisle.' *Canterbury Cathedral Chronicle* 69 (1975), 14-23.

Woodruff, C. E. 'Some early visitation rolls preserved at Canterbury-II.' *Archaeologia Cantiana* xxxiii (1918), 71-90.

——. 'Notes from a fourteenth-century act-book of the consistory court of Canterbury.' *Archaeologia Cantiana* xl (1928), 53-64.

Woodward, J. *A Treatise on Ecclesiastical Heraldry*. Edinburgh, 1894.

Woolnoth, W., and Hastings, T. *A Graphical Illustration of the Metropolitan Cathedral Church of Canterbury*. London, 1816.

Wright, J. R. 'The Supposed Illiteracy of Archbishop Walter Reynolds.' *Studies in Church History* v (1969), 58-68.

Yates, W. N. 'John of Ross and a Dispute over Commons, 1317-24.' BIHR xlviii (1975), 16-21.

Zacour, N. P. *Talleyrand: the Cardinal of Périgord, 1301-1364*. Transactions of the American Philosophical Society, n.s. vol. 50, part 7. Philadelphia, 1960.

Index

References to footnotes are indicated for single pages only. Inclusive references to two or more pages may, or may not, include references to footnotes on those pages. Thus, *p. 88n* indicates a footnote on that page, whereas *pp. 88-92*, which indicates at least one reference on every page between and including 88 and 92, may or may not include references to footnotes on one or more of these pages.